States' Responses to the Foreign Terrorist Fighters Phenomenon

Leiden Studies on the Frontiers of International Law

VOLUME 16

The titles published in this series are listed at *brill.com/lsfi*

States' Responses to the Foreign Terrorist Fighters Phenomenon

Shunning Responsibilities, Shifting Risks and the Limits of Public International Law

By

Ida Asscher

BRILL | NIJHOFF

Part of Chapter 3 has previously been published in I. Asscher, 'Shifting responsibilities and security threats by depriving foreign terrorist fighters of their nationality', *Journal of Conflict & Security Law,* Volume 29, Issue 2 (2024): 231–248.

ISSN 2212-4195
ISBN 978-90-04-77379-0
ISBN 978-90-04-77380-6 (PDF)
DOI https://doi.org/10.1163/9789004773806

Library of Congress Control Number: 2026949472

Brill Nijhoff and Koninklijke Brill BV are part of De Gruyter Brill.
www.degruyterbrill.com

Questions about General Product Safety Regulation: productsafety@degruyterbrill.com

Abbreviations

AANES	Autonomous Administration of North and East Syria
ACHPR	African Charter on Human and Peoples' Rights
ACHR	American Convention on Human Rights
AIVD	Dutch General Intelligence and Security Service
ARSIWA	Articles on the Responsibility of States for Internationally Wrongful Acts
CCAIL	German Code of Crimes against International Law
CRC Committee	Committee on the Rights of the Child
CRC	Convention on the Rights of the Child
CTC	Counter-Terrorism Committee
CTED	Counter-Terrorism Committee Executive Directorate
DARIO	Draft Articles on the Responsibility of International Organizations
ECHR	European Convention for the Protection of Human Rights and Fundamental Freedoms
ECN	European Convention on Nationality
ECtHR	European Court of Human Rights
EU	European Union
FTF	Foreign Terrorist Fighter
GCI	First Geneva Convention
GCII	Second Geneva Convention
GCIII	Third Geneva Convention
GCIV	Fourth Geneva Convention
GCTF	Global Counterterrorism Forum
IAC	International armed conflict
IACtHR	Inter-American Court of Human Rights
ICC Statute	Rome Statute of the International Criminal Court
ICCPR	International Covenant on Civil and Political Rights
ICCT	International Centre for Counter-Terrorism – The Hague
ICJ	International Court of Justice
ICRC	International Committee of the Red Cross
ICSR	International Centre for the Study Radicalisation
ICTR	International Criminal Tribunal for Rwanda
ICTY	International Criminal Tribunal for the Former Yugoslavia
IHL	International humanitarian law
ILC	International Law Commission
IS	Islamic State
NCTV	Dutch National Coordinator for Security and Counterterrorism

NIAC	Non-international armed conflict
OHCHR	Office of the United Nations High Commissioner for Human Rights
PCIJ	Permanent Court of International Justice
PKK	Kurdistan Workers' Party
PYD	Democratic Union Party
SDF	Syrian Democratic Forces
UDHR	Universal Declaration of Human Rights
UN	United Nations
UNAMI	United Nations Assistance Mission for Iraq
UNGA	United Nations General Assembly
UNICEF	United Nations Children's Fund
UNODC	United Nations Office on Drugs and Crime
UNSC	United Nations Security Council
VCCR	Vienna Convention on Consular Relations
VCDR	Vienna Convention on Diplomatic Relations
YPG	People's Defense Unit

CHAPTER 1

Introduction

1 The Foreign Fighters Phenomenon

Foreigners joining a party to an armed conflict abroad is not a new phenomenon. Well-known examples include the Frenchman Marquis de Lafayette, who fought in the American Revolutionary War in the 1770s; the British poet Lord Byron, who aided the Greek in their liberation struggle from the Ottoman Empire in the 1820s; the Italian revolutionary Giuseppe Garibaldi who fought in the Uruguayan Civil War in the 1840s; and the British writer George Orwell, who wrote a novel titled *Homage to Catalonia* about his experiences fighting alongside the Republicans during the Spanish Civil War in the 1930s. Historically, the term 'volunteers' applied to those individuals who joined a party engaged in an armed conflict abroad.[1] As Arielli notes, those who joined France in the First World War were referred to as *volontaires*, those who fought for Germany in the Second World War were called *Freiwilligen* and those foreign nationals who offered their service to the emerging state of Israel in the 1948 Arab–Israeli War were called *mitnadvim*.[2] Such foreign volunteers fought for many different causes. For example, to support national movements in their struggle for independence, such as during the wars of independence in Latin America in the early 19th century and the War of Italian Unification from 1859 to 1861.[3] Yet other volunteers fought for or against fascism or communism, such as during the Spanish Civil War and the Second World War.[4] Responses by Western states towards these early examples of foreign volunteer mobilizations were characterized by a 'laissez-faire attitude'.[5] Although by the time of the Spanish Civil War many states had enacted legislation prohibiting their nationals from serving abroad, the extent to which

---

1 M. Flores, 'Foreign Fighters Involvement in National and International Wars: A Historical Survey' in A. de Guttry, F. Capone and C. Paulussen (eds.), *Foreign Fighters under International Law and Beyond* (T.M.C. Asser Press 2016) 28.

2 N. Arielli, *From Byron to bin Laden: A History of Foreign War Volunteers* (Harvard University Press 2018) 5.

3 *Ibid.* 40–48.

4 *Ibid.* 48–57.

5 A. Rinaldi, *Ghosts of International Law: The Figure of the Foreign Fighter in a Cultural Perspective* (Cambridge University Press 2024) 164.

 | HTTPS://DOI.ORG/10.1163/9789004773806-002

these laws were actually applied depended to a large extent on national and foreign policy considerations.[6]

The Soviet invasion of Afghanistan from 1979 to 1989 was the start of an important turning point in the way in which foreign volunteers were perceived. During the 10 years of war between the Soviet Union and Afghanistan, volunteers came to Afghanistan to fight against the foreign occupying power, the Soviet Union. This was the first time foreigners traveled to join an armed conflict abroad as part of jihad, the struggle or fight against the enemies of Islam. The Soviet–Afghan War marked the start of the global jihadist movement, and such volunteers "laid down the ideological principles of jihadist travel, developed recruitment mechanisms, and cemented far-reaching jihadist networks".[7] After the Soviet–Afghan War, those individuals who were previously labeled 'volunteers', were increasingly referred to as 'foreign fighters'.[8] Some of those foreign fighters went on to other conflict zones that could qualify for jihad, such as Algeria, Bosnia and Tajikistan.[9] In 2001, Afghanistan became the theater of jihad again when the United States invaded the country, and in 2003, many foreign fighters traveled to Iraq to fight against the United States. A large number of those foreign fighters in Iraq were recruited by Al Qaeda, created during the Soviet–Afghan War, and other terrorist organizations. This increasingly blurred the lines between foreign fighters and terrorists. Increased violence linked to jihadism and concerns about terrorism, especially after the 9/11 attacks, led to a changed perception of foreign fighters and states' attitude towards the phenomenon.[10] The issue "was no longer whether foreign volunteers who fought in one conflict would go on to take part in other wars [...]. Instead, involvement in terrorism became the key concern."[11] This conflation of foreign fighters and terrorism only increased with the outbreak of the Syrian Civil War in 2011 and the subsequent large-scale mobilization of foreign fighters to Syria and Iraq.

---

6 D. Malet and J. Fritz, 'Historical Responses to Foreign Fighters and Returnees' in F. Capone, C. Paulussen and R. Mignot-Mahdavi (eds.), *Returning Foreign Fighters: Responses, Legal Challenges and Ways Forward* (T.M.C. Asser Press 2023) 41.

7 E. Pokalova, *Returning Islamist Foreign Fighters: Threats and Challenges to the West* (Palgrave Macmillan 2020) 12.

8 N. Arielli 2018 (n. 2) 5.

9 E. Pokalova 2020 (n. 7) 25–29.

10 D. Byman, *Road Warriors: Foreign Fighters in the Armies of Jihad* (Oxford University Press 2019) 18, 221.

11 N. Arielli 2018 (n. 2) 198.

2 Foreign Terrorist Fighters in Syria and Iraq

In 2004, after the United States' invasion of Iraq, Al Qaeda in Afghanistan was expanded by the creation of Al Qaeda in Iraq. In 2006, Al Qaeda in Iraq's leader established a new organization, the 'Islamic State in Iraq'. When the Syrian Civil War broke out in 2011, the Islamic State in Iraq used the opportunity to expand its operations from Iraq into Syria. The group became known as the 'Islamic State in Iraq and Syria' or the 'Islamic State of Iraq and the Levant', and was able to take over large parts of Syrian and Iraqi territory, including the cities of Raqqa and Mosul. In June 2014, the group established its caliphate and rebranded itself as the 'Islamic State' (IS). At its peak, IS controlled around 100,000 square kilometers of territory in Syria and Iraq, and had control over millions of inhabitants.[12] Even before the establishment of the IS caliphate in June 2014, a first wave of foreign fighters had traveled to the conflict zone. It is estimated that at the end of 2013, up to 11,000 foreign fighters from 74 states were fighting in Syria.[13] Those foreign fighters in the first wave were often able to return home relatively easily. This was different for the second wave of foreign fighters who traveled to Syria and Iraq after 2014 and the establishment of the IS caliphate. On 24 September 2014, the United Nations Security Council (UNSC or Security Council) adopted Resolution 2178, in which it required states to take far-reaching measures against so-called foreign terrorist fighters (FTFs).[14] Besides imposing broad obligations upon member states to, *inter alia*, prevent and criminalize the travel, recruitment, financing and facilitating of FTFs, the Security Council had defined the new term FTF, that was first coined in Security Council Resolution 2170 (2014).[15]

It is estimated that between around 44,000 and 52,000 individuals originating from 80 different states traveled to the conflict zone in Syria and Iraq and became affiliated with IS.[16] Although most FTFs became affiliated with IS, others joined other terrorist organizations such as Jabhat al Nusra, which

---

12 S. Jones, J. Dobbins and D. Byman et al., 'Rolling Back the Islamic State' RAND Corporation (2017) 84, 100.

13 A. Zelin, 'Up to 11,000 Foreign Fighters in Syria; Steep Rise among Western Europeans' The Washington Institute for Near East Policy (17 December 2013).

14 UNSC Res. 2178 (24 September 2014) UN Doc. S/RES/2178 (2014).

15 UNSC Res. 2170 (15 August 2014) UN Doc. S/RES/2170 (2014).

16 J. Cook and G. Vale, 'From Daesh to 'Diaspora' II: The Challenges Posed by Women and Minors after the Fall of the Caliphate' 12 CTC Sentinel (2019) 6: 31; J. Cook and G. Vale, 'From Daesh to 'Diaspora': Tracing the Women and Minors of Islamic State' International Centre for the Study Radicalisation (ICSR) Report (2018) 4, figure 1. The United Nations spoke of 40,000 FTFs originating from 110 different states. See, 'Greater Cooperation Needed to Tackle Danger Posed by Returning Foreign Fighters, Head of Counter-

later became known as Jabhat Fateh al-Sham and thereafter Hayat Tahrir al-Sham, and yet others joined groups fighting against IS such as the Free Syrian Army, which later became known as the Syrian National Army, and the Kurdish People's Defense Units (YPG). Yet other foreign nationals joined the Syrian Governmental forces. However, those individuals who participated in the armed conflict on behalf of state actors will not be the focus of this study. More specifically, this study will focus on those who became affiliated with IS.

Besides the rapid pace and unprecedented numbers in which FTFs traveled,[17] there are a number of other reasons why the mobilization of such individuals was unprecedented in nature. First, it was truly a global phenomenon, as FTFs came from all over the world.[18] Second, many FTFs traveled together with their family members, including children. There were more female departees than in previous conflicts. It is estimated that more than 6,700 women traveled to the conflict zone and became affiliated with IS.[19] In addition, it is estimated that around 6,500 children traveled to the conflict zone with their parents or were born in the region.[20] Jihad was thus more family-oriented in Syria and Iraq than in previous conflicts.[21] Third, and most important for the purpose of this research, the FTFs phenomenon in Syria and Iraq was unprecedented because of the far-reaching responses of states of nationality and states of habitual residence.

In their responses, states of nationality and habitual residence have emphasized the alleged threat these individuals pose upon return. For example, UK Foreign Secretary William Hague warned that FTFs "will seek to carry out attacks against Western interests in the region or in Western states now or in the future".[22] Russia's Foreign Minister Sergej Lavrov commented that for-

---

Terrorism Office Tells Security Council' SC/13097 (28 November 2017). Available at: <https://press.un.org/en/2017/sc13097.doc.htm> accessed 27 February 2025.

17 P. Gurski, *Western Foreign Fighters: The Threat to Homeland and International Security* (Rowman & Littlefield 2017) 67.

18 To give an indication, around 19,000 FTFs affiliated with IS came from the Middle East and North Africa, around 13,000 from European states and around 7,000 from Central and South-East Asia. These estimates are drawn from figures reported between April 2013 and June 2018. See, J. Cook and G. Vale 2018 (n. 16) 14, figure 3.

19 J. Cook and G. Vale 2019 (n. 16) 31, 35–38.

20 *Ibid.*

21 T. Renard, 'Europe and Its Returning Foreign Fighters: Overview of the Policy Response' in F. Capone, C. Paulussen and R. Mignot-Mahdavi 2023 (n. 6) 10.

22 D. Mcelroy, 'William Hague warns of threat to Britain from Syria fighters' (*The Telegraph*, 24 April 2013). Available at: <https://www.telegraph.co.uk/news/worldnews/middleeast/syria/10016310/William-Hague-warns-of-threat-to-Britain-from-Syria-fighters.html?ICID=continue_without_subscribing_reg_first> accessed 3 March 2025.

eign fighters from Russia and other former Soviet states, "will return and will do their black deeds in our country".[23] Likewise, United States' President Barack Obama warned that FTFs "were likely to return to their home countries to carry out attacks",[24] and France's Minister of Interior Manuel Valls called the threat that returning FTFs pose "a ticking time bomb".[25] FTFs have indeed been involved in terrorist attacks upon return. For example, the May 2014 attack against the Jewish Museum in Brussels was carried out by a returnee from Syria, and a number of those who carried out the November 2015 attacks in Paris had also returned from Syria where they fought with IS. Despite these examples, how big the terrorist threat posed by returnees really is, remains unclear and challenging to assess.[26]

When the IS caliphate lost its last territory in Syria after the fall of Baghouz in March 2019, thousands of IS fighters, including FTFs and their families, were captured and detained. While most captured male FTFs were brought to prisons run by the Syrian Democratic Forces (SDF) in Northeast Syria or to Iraqi prisons, many third-country women and children, believed to be affiliated with or part of IS, were brought to camps in Northeast Syria also operated by the SDF. The SDF is a coalition of, *inter alia*, Kurdish, Arabic and Christian fighters, but predominantly consists of Kurdish forces and in particular YPG fighters.[27] It was created in October 2015, with support from the United States,

---

23 S. Walker, 'Russian media turn attention to Syria as Ukraine conflict dies down' (*The Guardian*, 1 October 2015). Available at: <https://www.theguardian.com/world/2015/oct/01/russian-media-syria-ukraine> accessed 3 March 2025.

24 'Security Council Unanimously Adopts Resolution Condemning Violent Extremism, Underscoring Need to Prevent Travel, Support for Foreign Terrorist Fighters' SC/11 580 (24 September 2014). Available at: <https://press.un.org/en/2014/sc11580.doc.htm> accessed 3 March 2025.

25 E. Schmitt, 'Worries Mount as Syria Lures West's Muslims' (*The New York Times*, 27 July 2013). Available at: <https://www.nytimes.com/2013/07/28/world/middleeast/worries-mount-as-syria-lures-wests-muslims.html> accessed 3 March 2025.

26 Some experts have cautioned against exaggerating the threat that FTFs allegedly pose. See, for example, D. Byman and J. Shapiro, 'Be Afraid. Be A Little Afraid: The Threat of Terrorism from Western Foreign Fighters in Syria and Iraq' Foreign Policy at Brookings, Policy Paper No. 34 (November 2014); E. Bakker, C. Paulussen and E. Entenmann, 'Returning Jihadist Foreign Fighters: Challenges Pertaining to Threat Assessment and Governance of this Pan-European Problem' 25 Security and Human Rights (2014) 1: 16–19; D. Malet and R. Hayes, 'Foreign Fighter Returnees: An Indefinite Threat?' 32 Terrorism and Political Violence (2018) 8.

27 H. Allsopp and W. van Wilgenburg, *The Kurds of Northern Syria: Governance, Diversity and Conflicts* (Iraq Institute for Strategic Studies/Bloomsbury Publishing Plc 2019) 66, 67. The YPG is the military wing of the Democratic Union Party (PYD), a Kurdish political party in Northeast Syria.

to help defeat IS.[28] The SDF is the military branch of the Autonomous Administration of North and East Syria (AANES), which was responsible for the administration of the region in Northeast Syria under the SDF's control.[29] In defeating IS, the SDF was the West's closest ally and was financially and militarily supported by the United States as well as by other states that were part of the US-led coalition against IS.[30] Despite this support, neither the SDF's nor the AANES' autonomous role and authority in the region was formally recognized by those states.[31] After the territorial defeat of IS, the SDF continued to guard the camps and prisons in Northeast Syria, in which thousands of IS fighters, including FTFs and their family members, were and still are detained in deplorable and dangerous conditions.[32] Human Rights Watch estimated that as of 23 January 2023 almost 10,000 third-country nationals from around 60 states were still detained in two of the SDF-controlled camps in Northeast Syria, the al-Hol and al-Roj camps.[33] This number does not yet include those third-country nationals detained in other detention facilities in (Northeast) Syria and Iraq. Other FTFs and family members may have already returned, may have died on the battlefield or are still believed to be in the region, includ-

28 *Ibid.* 66, 67 and 186–193.

29 'Beyond the Frontlines: The Building of the Democratic System in North and East Syria' Rojava Information Center Report (2019) 20–30. Available at: <https://rojavainformationcenter.org/2019/12/report-beyond-the-frontlines/> accessed 4 March 2025.

30 M. Knights and W. van Wilgenburg, *Accidental Allies: The U.S.–Syrian Democratic Forces Partnership Against the Islamic State* (The Washington Institute for Near East Policy/Bloomsbury Publishing Plc 2021).

31 W. van Wilgenburg, 'Syrian Democratic Forces (Syria)' in 'Guns and Governance: How Europe should talk with non-state armed groups in the Middle East' European Council on Foreign Relations. Available at: <https://ecfr.eu/special/mena-armed-groups/syrian-democratic-forces-syria/> accessed 4 March 2025.

32 See for example, Human Rights Watch, 'Thousands of Foreigners Unlawfully Held in NE Syria' (23 March 2021). Available at: <https://www.hrw.org/news/2021/03/23/thousands-foreigners-unlawfully-held-ne-syria> accessed 5 March 2025; E. Lederer, 'UN official: 700 people died in Syrian camps for IS families' (*AP News*, 10 July 2020). Available at: <https://apnews.com/article/9732632ffe89f1acf64ff91cd60dd76a> accessed 5 March 2025; United Nations Children's Fund (UNICEF), 'Nearly 850 children at immediate risk as violence continues in northeast Syria' (23 January 2022). Available at: <https://www.unicef.org/mena/press-releases/nearly-850-children-immediate-risk-violence-continues-northeast-syria> accessed 5 March 2025.

33 Human Rights Watch, 'Revictimizing the Victims: Children Unlawfully Detained in Northeast Syria' (27 January 2023). Available at: <https://www.hrw.org/news/2023/01/27/revictimizing-victims-children-unlawfully-detained-northeast-syria> accessed 18 December 2024.

ing elsewhere in Syria, Iraq or in states like Türkiye, which captured many FTFs and family members on its side of the border.[34]

3 The Horizontal Dimension: Shunning Responsibilities and Shifting Risks

This research will focus on the way in which states of nationality and states of habitual residence have responded to the FTFs phenomenon in Syria and Iraq. Their responses have in earlier legal research primarily been scrutinized from a 'vertical perspective', meaning with a focus on the relationship between states of nationality as well as states of habitual residence and 'their' FTFs and family members. For example, with regard to the prevention of FTF travel and the issue of prosecution, existing research predominantly focuses on the criminalization or qualification of the individual's conduct within the state's domestic legislation and the impact that criminal as well as administrative measures have on the human rights of the individual concerned.[35] Moreover, the response of nationality deprivation has often been scrutinized from a human rights perspective and has been criticized in legal research for being difficult to justify under certain human rights principles.[36] Finally, the issue of repatriation in the context of FTFs in Syria and Iraq has mostly been dealt with by asking the question whether there exists an obligation or a right to be

34 See, for example, the following overview from the Dutch General Intelligence and Security Service (AIVD) of the numbers of Dutch FTFs and family members who are believed to have died or who are believed to be still in the region. AIVD, 'Uitreizigers en terugkeerders: Hoeveel Nederlanders zijn uitgereisd en bevinden zich nog in de regio?'. Available at: <https://www.aivd.nl/onderwerpen/terrorisme/uitreizigers-en-terugkeerders> accessed 5 March 2025.

35 See, for example, A. Conte, 'States' Prevention and Responses to the Phenomenon of Foreign Fighters against the Backdrop of International Human Rights Obligations' in A. de Guttry, F. Capone and C. Paulussen (eds.) 2016 (n. 1); T. Van Poecke and H. Cuyckens, 'The Qualification of the Activities of (returned) Foreign Fighters under National Criminal Law' in F. Capone, C. Paulussen and R. Mignot Mahdavi (eds.) 2023 (n. 6); B. Boutin, 'Administrative Measures against Foreign Fighters: In Search of Limits and Safeguards' ICCT Research Paper (December 2016).

36 See, for example, H. Duffy, '"Foreign Terrorist Fighters": A Human Rights Approach?' 29 Security and Human Rights (2018) 149–152; C. Paulussen, 'Stripping foreign fighters of their citizenship: International human rights and humanitarian law considerations' 103 International Review of the Red Cross (2021) 916–917; S. Jaghai and L. van Waas, 'Stripped of Citizenship, Stripped of Dignity? A Critical Exploration of Nationality Deprivation as a Counter-Terrorism Measure' in C. Paulussen and M. Scheinin (eds.), *Human Dignity and Human Security in Times of Terrorism* (T.M.C. Asser Press 2020).

repatriated under international (human rights) law.[37] These approaches thus emphasize the relationship between, on the one hand, states of nationality and habitual residence and, on the other hand, the individual concerned.

However, when one moves away from such a vertical perspective and looks at these responses from a horizontal, inter-state perspective instead, one can see that these responses may not only have an impact on the individual concerned but also on other states involved, such as states of other nationality, states of destination, states of transit and states where such individuals otherwise reside after departure. First, with regard to the prevention of travel, FTFs departing from their state of nationality or habitual residence can significantly harm other states, especially states of transit and states of destination; including by establishing networks within states whose territory they transit and by potentially increasing the intensity, duration and intractability of the conflict in states of destination. The acts or omissions of states of nationality and habitual residence in preventing their FTFs from traveling can, therefore, potentially pose harm to other states. Second, it can be argued that through the response of nationality deprivation, states essentially shun their responsibilities and export the problem to other states or actors like the SDF/AANES.[38] Furthermore, when the person poses a possible security threat, it is not only a responsibility over the person that is exported to other states but also a risk of terrorism as well as a burden to counter that risk. Third, with regard to states' refusal or reluctance to repatriate their FTFs and family members, it can be said that states basically evade the challenges and responsibilities that come with repatriation, and at the same time, shift the burden of dealing with their nationals, i.e., to detain and potentially prosecute them, to other states or the SDF/AANES. Fourth, with regard to the issue of prosecution, a number of states have proposed that the crimes should be prosecuted where they were committed, i.e., in Syria and Iraq. In Syria, such proposals would mean that FTFs would have to be prosecuted by the AANES, a non-state actor with a court system that is not recognized by other states. In Iraq, such proposals

---

37 See, for example, A. Spadaro, 'Repatriation of Family Members of Foreign Fighters: Individual Right or State Prerogative?' 70 International and Comparative Law Quarterly (2021) 1; D. McKeever, 'Repatriating Foreign Terrorist Fighters and Their Family Members: What International Law Requires, and What National Courts Will Do' 28 Journal of Conflict & Security Law (2022) 1; S. Bagheri and A. Bisset, 'International Legal Issues Arising from Repatriation of the Children of Islamic State' 27 Journal of Conflict & Security Law (2022) 3; C. Forcese, 'Homeward Bound? International Law and a State's Obligation to Repatriate Nationals Affiliated with Da'esh' 51 Israel Yearbook on Human Rights (2021).

38 I. Asscher, 'Shifting responsibilities and security threats by depriving foreign terrorist fighters of their nationality' 29 Journal of Conflict & Security Law (2024) 2: 236–238.

for prosecution in the region would mean that FTFs would have to be prosecuted in a state which imposes the death penalty and which is known for a lack of fair trial standards. Instead of bringing them back to prosecute them at home, states thus appear to shift the burden of prosecution to a non-state actor and a state imposing the death penalty. These responses may provide for the short-term benefit of keeping FTFs and their family members out of the country, but do not provide for an effective, long-term solution to the problem and the potential security threat that these individuals pose.

This research will examine the way in which states have responded to the FTFs phenomenon in Syria and Iraq from such a 'horizontal perspective', meaning with a focus on inter-state relations and the effects that such responses have on other states or, in the case of the SDF/AANES, a non-state actor involved. This horizontal dimension suggests first that, through such responses, states appear to have shunned their responsibilities. Shunning refers to the persistent avoidance or evasion of responsibilities, including in the form of legally binding obligations. In other words, it refers to efforts by states in trying to avoid becoming legally responsible to take action. Such responsibilities do not always have to be strict legal obligations, but could also refer to less strict or non-binding responsibilities based on international law and responsibilities of a moral or political nature. Admittedly, the concept of responsibilities is rather broad. However, which specific responsibilities the research refers to, will be clarified within each chapter. Second, states also appear to have shifted security risks as well as a burden to counter such risks to other states or the SDF in control of Northeast Syria. This can also be referred to as responses in which elements of 'buck-passing' are visible. The Oxford Dictionary of Politics and International Relations notes that 'buck-passing' in political terms is "the unwillingness or failure to accept responsibility" and that "States can [...] be guilty of passing the buck when they defer responsibility to deal with a local or regional conflict."[39] It is also explained that the term stems from poker, "when a player can defer their chance to deal the cards to the next player".[40]

For now, it is important to mention that the FTFs phenomenon in Syria and Iraq is not the only context in which such practices of shunning responsibilities and risk exportation are visible. Similar approaches can be identified within immigration and asylum policies, where states try to externalize immi-

39 A. Mumford, 'Buck-passing' in G. Brown, I. McLean and A. McMillan (eds.), *A Concise Oxford Dictionary of Politics and International Relations* (4th edn., Oxford University Press 2018).

40 *Ibid.*

gration and border controls in order to avoid obligations to protect vulnerable individuals.[41] For example, states of destination have concluded agreements with states of transit or departure to prevent asylum seekers from arriving at their borders. An illustration of such an agreement is the Malta Declaration between the European Union (EU) and Libya. In exchange for monetary compensation, Libya would take efforts in reducing the flow of asylum seekers leaving its territory and traveling to the frontiers of the EU.[42] Such externalization policies have been criticized because more powerful states are essentially calling upon other states to do their "dirty work".[43] In addition, such strategies "can result in placing important and unequal burdens" on other states with "lesser resources".[44] In that respect, states have also started to conclude agreements to transport asylum seekers to third states. For example, such agreements have been concluded between the United Kingdom and Rwanda,[45] between Italy and Albania,[46] and the Netherlands is currently exploring a plan to send rejected asylum seekers to Uganda.[47] With such exter-

---

41 I. Asscher 2024 (n. 38) 232.

42 European Council, 'Malta Declaration by the members of the European Council on the external aspects of migration: addressing the Central Mediterranean route' Press Release (3 February 2017). Available at: <https://www.consilium.europa.eu/en/press/press-releases/2017/02/03/malta-declaration/> accessed 6 March 2025.

43 K. Tennis, *Outsourcing Control: The Politics of International Migration Cooperation* (McGill-Queen's University Press 2020) 169.

44 E. del Nonno, L. Haquin Saenz and M. Kaygusuz Akbay, 'The Externalization of Asylum: A Process to Limit Asylum?' in A. Nikodinovska Krstevska, M. Gavouneli and M. Savić Bojanić, *Outsourcing and Cooperation with Third Countries: Deconstructing the Formal and the Informal in Migration and Asylum Policies* (Editoriale Scientifica S.r.l. 2022) 122.

45 'What is the UK's plan to send asylum seekers to Rwanda?' (*BBC News*, 13 June 2024). Available at <https://www.bbc.com/news/explainers-61782866> accessed 6 March 2025. In the case of *N.S.K. v. the United Kingdom* (App No. 28774/22), the European Court of Human Rights issued an order to block the first flight of asylum seekers being transferred to Rwanda. 'The European Court grants urgent interim measure in case concerning asylum seeker's imminent removal from the UK to Rwanda' Press Release (14 June 2022). Available at: <https://hudoc.echr.coe.int/eng-press#{%22itemid%22:[%22003-7359967-10054452%22]}> accessed 7 March 2025. Later the UK Supreme Court unanimously held that the Rwanda policy was unlawful. See, *R* (*on the application of AAA and others*) (*Respondents/Cross Appellants*) *v Secretary of State for the Home Department* (*Appellant/Cross Respondent*) [2023] (judgement) UKSC 42 (15 November 2023).

46 R. Shehu, 'Italy sends migrants to Albania in third try to start scheme' (*Deutsche Welle*, 31 January 2025). Available at: <https://www.dw.com/en/italy-sends-migrants-to-albania-in-third-try-to-start-scheme/a-71464347#:~:text=According%20to%20the%202023%20agreement,seekers%20were%20returned%20to%20Italy> accessed 7 March 2025.

47 S. Pronk, 'Kabinet wil mogelijkheid verkennen asielzoekers uit te zetten naar Oeganda' (*NRC*, 16 October 2024). Available at: <https://www.nrc.nl/nieuws/2024/10/16/kabinet-wil-mogelijkheid-asielzoekers-uit-te-zetten-naar-oeganda-verkennen-a4869608> accessed 6 March 2025.

nalization policies, states essentially shun their responsibility to take care of vulnerable individuals and leave third states that have less economic strength and fewer organizational capabilities, with the burden of dealing with the influx of asylum seekers and the protection obligations that come with them. Therefore, through such practices states likewise appear to shun their responsibilities and shift the burden to other states in a manner that may provide for a short-term solution or which entails short-term benefits but which may not be sustainable in the long run. It is thus important to note that such practices seem neither new nor specific to the FTFs phenomenon in Syria and Iraq, and are rather part of a greater pattern. Although this research only focuses on such responses within this specific context, it seems to be a broader issue and findings in this research may well be relevant beyond the more specific context of FTFs in Syria and Iraq.

4 Aim, Questions and Temporal Scope of This Research

It is clear from the previous sections that this research zeroes in on the way that states have responded to the FTFs phenomenon in Syria and Iraq, and that it aims to examine such responses from a horizontal, inter-state perspective. This study will further develop the preliminary argument that states appear to have shunned their responsibilities and shifted security risks by the way in which they have responded to the phenomenon. In particular, this research aims to untangle whether and to what extent such responses and their horizontal dimension are governed by public international law. In other words, this research will be guided by the question: to what extent does public international law limit the shunning of responsibilities and the shifting of security risks, as visible in states' responses to the phenomenon of foreign terrorist fighters and their family members in Syria and Iraq? In its final part, this chapter will further expand upon this question by providing clarity on who is a 'foreign terrorist fighter' and who is a 'family member'.

For the purpose of answering the central research question, this study aims to zero in on four (non-)responses by states as regards FTFs and their family members: (1) prevention of travel; (2) nationality deprivation; (3) refusal or reluctance to repatriate; and (4) prosecution or, rather, the push for prosecution by Iraq or the AANES in Northeast Syria. Through this selection, this study will admittedly leave out other important issues, for example, the rehabilitation and reintegration of FTFs and their family members after their return. However, the four responses were selected because they are arguably the most interesting ones to assess from a public international law point of view and from the perspective that this study adopts. In other words, it can be asserted that the shunning of responsibilities and the shifting of security risks become clearest in these four responses.

The broader aim of this research is not only to contribute to the academic literature on FTFs by adding a different perspective to assessing states' responses to the phenomenon. It also aims to inform and influence future state policy within and beyond the context of FTFs in Syria and Iraq.

With regard to its temporal scope, the research covers the period between March 2011, when the Syrian Civil War started, attracting the first wave of F(T)Fs, and the end of November 2024. By the time this research is published, inevitably much will have changed. Especially after the fall of the Assad regime in December 2024, followed by the new Syrian government taking control of Northeast Syria in January 2026, rapid developments were visible and a new reality on the ground in Syria emerged. Although this research focuses on the way in which states of nationality and habitual residence have responded to the phenomenon and the way in which they have dealt with their responsibilities within the time period mentioned, the legal analysis carried out in this research and any conclusions drawn may be of broader relevance and may not be confined to this particular time frame.

5 Structure of This Research

The structure of this research essentially follows how states' responses to the FTFs phenomenon in Syria and Iraq evolved over time. While states were at first mostly concerned with the prevention of FTF travel, this focus rapidly shifted to states being predominantly concerned with how to prevent their return and to debates about how to bring them to justice.[48] Accordingly, the research will start with the prevention of travel, then move on to the issues of nationality deprivation and states' refusal or hesitance to repatriate, and will end with the matter of prosecution.

Chapter 2 will focus on the prevention of travel. This chapter will first discuss the broader legal basis of an obligation to prevent travel for terrorist

48 B. van Ginkel, 'The International Legal and Policy Framework on Returning Foreign Fighters: Focus on the United Nations and the Global Counterterrorism Forum' in F. Capone, C. Paulussen and R. Mignot-Mahdavi (eds.) 2023 (n. 6) 75.

purposes under public international law. To that effect, this research will analyze the international law of neutrality, the non-intervention principle as well as the no-harm and precautionary principles. A focus on these underlying norms will bring the horizontal perspective of an obligation to prevent FTF travel, and states' actions and omissions in relation to other states, more to the foreground. Thereafter, the obligation to prevent travel in a number of Security Council resolutions, in particular Resolution 2178 (2014), will be examined. Finally, a number of criminal and administrative measures that states have taken in order to prevent the departure of their nationals will be analyzed.

In Chapter 3, the response of nationality deprivation will be dealt with. This chapter will start with an introductory part in which it will set out the historical context of the response of nationality deprivation and how this measure has increasingly been used as a counter-terrorism measure since the beginning of the 21st century. In addition, it will be discussed which states were particularly active in depriving their FTFs and family members of their nationality. Thereafter, in examining whether or to what extent public international law limits this practice when it results in the shunning of responsibilities and the shifting of security risks, this part of the research will first discuss this measure as a means to circumvent the obligation to (re)admit nationals and as a possible violation of the right to expel aliens. Second, the research will consider the potential role of the notion of predominant nationality and will, finally, discuss more general, over-arching obligations of prevention and cooperation, as well as principles of inter-state behavior.

Chapter 4 will zoom in on the reluctance or refusal of some states to repatriate their nationals from Iraqi prisons, detention facilities in Northeast Syria or other states where they may have ended up. This chapter will also start with an introductory part in which a number of potential legal bases for repatriation in public international law will be presented and in which it will be discussed which states were active in the repatriation of their nationals and which states can be considered as inactive in their repatriation efforts. After this introductory part, this chapter will, first, examine states' refusal to repatriate FTFs and their family members as a situation of *de facto* banishment. In that respect, the research will analyze why the ancient punishment of banishment eventually ceased to exist and the extent to which those reasons can likewise be applied to non-repatriation in the FTFs context in Syria and Iraq. Second, this chapter will assess states' reluctance or refusal to repatriate in light of their obligation to ensure respect for international humanitarian law

(IHL), including the obligation to ensure respect by non-state actors like the SDF. Thereafter, the research will delve into the question of state responsibility for the inhumane circumstances in which FTFs and family members are being detained in Northeast Syria and will explore whether there is a suitable construction for such responsibility for states that refuse to repatriate. In this context, repatriation will also be analyzed as a possible means to give effect to the obligation to make reparations for internationally wrongful acts.

In Chapter 5, the matter of prosecution will be addressed, and in particular certain states' push for the prosecution of FTFs in the region. Like the previous two chapters, this final chapter will start with an introductory part in which the prosecution of FTFs and their family members in a number of states of nationality's national courts will be set out. This part of the research will also explain a number of legal challenges faced by prosecutors on the national level. The second part of this chapter will assess states' inaction with regard to prosecution in light of their obligation to prosecute war crimes and terrorist offences. Thereafter, it will be explored whether public international law imposes limits to states of nationality referring to the primacy of territorial states' jurisdiction. This will mainly be done by discussing the potential role of the principle of subsidiarity. Finally, this chapter will assess states' push for prosecution in the region in light of their *non-refoulement* obligation.

In Chapter 6, the study will draw conclusions and answer the central research question as presented in the previous section.

6 Key Concepts: 'Foreign Terrorist Fighters' and 'Their Family Members'

In order to further explain and eventually answer the central research question, it is necessary to address the meaning of two key concepts used in this research. First, the term 'foreign terrorist fighters' and second, the term 'their family members'. Put differently, who qualifies as an FTF and who qualifies as an associated family member?

6.1 Foreign Terrorist Fighters

With the adoption of Resolutions 2170 (2014) and 2178 (2014), the Security Council coined and defined a new term to respond to those who traveled to Syria and Iraq to join different terrorist organizations. The Security Council labeled such individuals as 'foreign terrorist fighters' and defined them as "individuals who travel to a State other than their States of residence or nationality for the purpose of the perpetration, planning, or preparation of, or participation in, terrorist acts or the providing or receiving of terrorist training, including in connection with armed conflict".[49] The term FTF and the definition given to it by the Security Council raise a number of questions and issues, some of which will be highlighted in this sub-section.

As Capone notes, the aim of the Security Council "was not to outlaw *tout court* foreigners' participation in an armed conflict abroad, a practice which under international law is not forbidden in absolute terms, but to thwart their association with terrorist groups".[50] Put differently, the Security Council's definition of an FTF differentiates it from the broader notion of a foreign fighter, because the former is concerned with individuals who travel abroad with a 'terrorist purpose'. However, there is no universal agreement on the definition of terrorism and the Security Council did not provide any guidance on this point in this particular context.[51] The Security Council thus left it up to member states to determine the scope of the concept.[52] Because the Security Council required states to take far-reaching measures to prevent, suppress, criminalize and punish, *inter alia*, the (attempt to) travel, the financing, recruiting, organizing, transporting and the equipping of such FTFs,[53] without defining what 'terrorist', a 'terrorist act' or 'terrorist training' actually is, this raised questions as to whom exactly falls within this category. For example, Jeremy Corbyn, member of the UK Parliament for the Labour Party, noted that while it is clear that individuals who join IS "will be deemed to be a terrorist", what "if they fight for the free Syrian army [...] and they do things as despicable as they would in any other force, are they then deemed to be all right?".[54] What about when someone fights "with the Kurdish forces [...] against the forces of

49 UNSC Res. 2178 (2014) (n. 14) pre-ambular para. 8.

50 F. Capone, 'Countering "Foreign Terrorist Fighters": A Critical Appraisal of the Framework Established by the UN Security Council Resolutions' 25 Italian Yearbook of International Law (2016) 1: 230.

51 The Security Council did previously define terrorism in Resolution 1566 but did not refer to this Resolution or the definition of terrorism contained in it in Resolution 2178. See, UNSC Res. 1566 (8 October 2004) UN Doc. S/RES/1566 (2004) para. 3.

52 B. Saul, 'Terrorism in International and Transnational Criminal Law' Sydney Law School Legal Studies Research Paper No. 15/83 (September 2015) 15.

53 UNSC Res. 2178 (2014) (n. 14) paras. 4, 5, 6, 8.

54 UK Parliament, Hansard, 'Counter-Terrorism and Security Bill Volume 589: debated on Monday 15 December 2014'. Available at: <https://hansard.parliament.uk/Commons/2014-12-15/debates/14121545000001/Counter-TerrorismAndSecurityBill> accessed 24 March 2025; See also, A. Rinaldi 2024 (n. 5) 175, 176.

the Syrian Government and against ISIS", "how [do] we decide who is a good fighter and who is a terrorist; who is struggling for liberation and who is a terrorist".[55] Although the Security Council's definition of an FTF is not linked to which groups are formally listed as terrorist, for most states the decisive criterion seems to be whether the group the individual joins or intends to join is labeled as terrorist, regardless of whether he or she has prepared or committed specific terrorist offences.[56] Besides explicitly naming IS, Jabhat al Nusra and other groups associated with Al Qaeda as listed under the IS and Al Qaeda sanctions regime, the Security Council leaves it to the discretion of states to include other groups, depending on each state's understanding of which group qualifies as 'terrorist'.[57] Leaving it up to states to determine who fulfills the terrorist element within the definition of an FTF and, therefore, with regard to whom the far-reaching measures required by Resolution 2178 (2014) are implemented, entails a risk of abuse and the implementation of national laws which are too broad in scope and reach.[58] Moreover, presuming someone to be a terrorist based on whether the group he or she joins or intends to join is included on an already existing list, instead of the actual offences that he or she may have prepared or committed, entails a risk of politicization and selectiveness.[59]

Another element that causes uncertainty is the term 'foreign'. There is something misleading in labeling such individuals as 'foreign'. First, because although they participate in armed conflicts in other states, they pose a potential threat to their state of nationality or state of habitual residence. And second, because they radicalized in and traveled from their state of nationality or state of habitual residence, to whom they are not 'foreign'. The former Dutch Minister of Foreign Affairs, Bert Koenders, adequately captured this paradox by saying that "[t]he uncomfortable truth is that they are not foreign at all. They may be foreigners in the countries where they are going. But in reality [...] [t]hey are part of our societies. Perhaps the only thing that's foreign to us is

55 UK Parliament 2014 (n. 54).

56 S. Krähenmann, 'The Obligations under International Law of the Foreign Fighter's State of Nationality or Habitual Residence, State of Transit and State of Destination' in A. de Guttry, F. Capone and C. Paulussen (eds.) 2016 (n. 1) 239, 240. For example, the European Union (EU) has established its own sanctions list on which groups and individuals are listed who are subject to restrictive measures with a view to combating terrorism, pursuant to Council regulation 2580/2001. Groups on this list include, the Kurdistan Workers' Party (PKK), the military wing of Hizbollah, Hamas and the Fuerzas Armadas Revolucionarias de Colombia (FARC).

57 UNSC 2178 (2014) (n. 14) para. 10.

58 H. Duffy 2018 (n. 36) 134, 135.

59 *Ibid.* 135.

their mentality."[60] It is also unclear when exactly an individual is 'foreign', as there is uncertainty with regard to dual nationals or persons with strong connections to other states than those of habitual residence or nationality, such as members of the diaspora.[61] Resolution 2178 (2014) only highlights the situation of dual nationals traveling to their state of nationality but does not give any guidance on how dual nationals would fall within the given definition of a 'foreign terrorist fighter'.[62]

A third element that lacks legal certainty, is the term 'fighter'. Not all of those who traveled to Syria or Iraq actually fought. It has been established that individuals who traveled to the conflict zone in Syria and Iraq performed a variety of roles, some of which do not include fighting or otherwise participating in hostilities. This is especially the case with regard to women and children,[63] which will be further addressed in the next sub-section. Another reason why the term 'fighter' is problematic, is because it seems to extend 'terrorism' to acts committed during a situation of armed conflict, to which the rules of IHL apply.[64] This is confirmed by the Security Council's definition of such fighters, through the words "including in connection with armed conflict".[65] Applying counter-terrorism law to situations of armed conflict may lead to the criminalization of acts *not* prohibited by IHL, which may undermine the relevance and effectiveness of IHL.[66] More detailed reasons why this

60 Rijksoverheid, 'Toespraak van minister Koenders op het Global Counterterrorism Forum (GCTF) [Speech of Minister Koenders at the Global Counterterrorism Forum (GCTF)] (11 January 2016). Available at: <https://rijksoverheid.sitearchief.nl/#archive> accessed 22 April 2025.

61 H. Duffy and L. van den Herik, 'Terrorism and the Security Council' in R. Geiß and N. Melzer (eds.), *The Oxford Handbook on the International Law of Global Security* (Oxford University Press, 2021) 207; S. Krähenmann, 2016 (n. 56) 235, 236.

62 UNSC Res. 2178 (2014) (n. 14) pre-ambular para. 20.

63 See, for example, D. Margolin and J. Cook, 'The Agency and Roles of Foreign Women in ISIL' in S. Ashraph, C. Cheung Ka-man and J. Cook (eds.), *Holding ISIL Accountable: Prosecuting Crimes in Iraq and Syria* (ICCT Press 2024) 54–104.

64 S. Krähenmann 2016 (n. 56) 240.

65 UNSC Res. 2178 (2014) (n. 14) pre-ambular para. 8.

66 See on this issue, for example, B. Saul, 'From conflict to complementarity: Reconciling international counterterrorism law and international humanitarian law' 103 International Review of the Red Cross (2021) 916–917; H. Cuyckens and C. Paulussen, 'The Prosecution of Foreign Fighters in Western Europe: The Difficult Relationship Between Counter-Terrorism and International Humanitarian Law' 24 Journal of Conflict & Security Law (2019) 3; H. Cuyckens, 'Foreign fighters and the tension between counterterrorism and international humanitarian law: A case for cumulative prosecution where possible' 103 International Review of the Red Cross (2021) 916–917; J. Pejic, 'Armed Conflict and Terrorism: There is a (Big) Difference' in A. de Frías, K. Samuel and N. White (eds.), *Counter-Terrorism: International Law and Practice* (Oxford University Press 2012).

conflation between counter-terrorism law and IHL is problematic will be set out in Chapter 5 of this study.

There are a number of other terms that have been suggested to describe those individuals who traveled to Syria and Iraq to join different terrorist organizations. For example, Sexton suggests to label such individuals as 'radical travelers', which he defines as

> individuals who are motivated by ideology and a desire to play an active role in securing social, political or economic change to leave their country of residence, citizenship or nationality to travel to an area in which political violence is prevalent and join or align themselves with a party to that violence.[67]

This term and definition are broader than those provided for by the Security Council in the sense that the terrorist element is missing from both the term and its definition. Others called such individuals IS-affiliates. For example, Cook and Vale use this term to capture "all foreign nationals that were born into IS, or travelled to Syria and Iraq (whether willingly or coercively) who became associated with the group".[68] This definition is broader in the sense that, depending on the interpretation of 'affiliation' or 'association', it also includes women and children who may not fall within the Security Council's definition of an FTF. At the same time, it is narrower because it explicitly only applies to those who became affiliated with IS instead of terrorist organizations more broadly. Yet others use the broader term foreign fighters, which, like the term 'radical travelers', lacks the terrorism element. There is no internationally accepted definition of the term foreign fighter. Multiple definitions have been proposed. For example, Malet defines foreign fighters as "noncitizens of conflict states who join insurgencies during civil conflicts".[69] This definition thus excludes individuals who join a foreign state's armed forces. Krähenmann defines a foreign fighter as "an individual who leaves his or her country of origin or habitual residence to join a non-state armed group in an armed conflict abroad and who is primarily motivated by ideology, religion, and/or kinship".[70] Besides excluding individuals who join foreign states' armed

67 M. Sexton, 'What's in a Name? Proposing New Typologies for 'Foreign Fighters'' 162 The RUSI Journal (2017) 5: 37.

68 J. Cook and G. Vale 2018 (n. 16) 13.

69 D. Malet, *Foreign Fighters: Transnational Identity in Civic Conflicts* (Oxford University Press 2013) 9.

70 S. Krähenmann, 'Foreign Fighters under International Law' Geneva Academy of International Humanitarian Law and Human Rights, Academy Briefing No. 7 (October 2014) 6.

forces, this definition also places emphasis on the motivation of the individual concerned. Finally, the UN Working Group of Mercenaries, whose mandate also consists of foreign fighter related issues, defines the notion as "individuals who leave their country of origin or habitual residence and become involved in violence as part of an insurgency or non-state armed group in an armed conflict".[71] Thus, it not only excludes the motivational aspect and individuals joining states' armed forces but also adds the need for involvement in violence. There thus exist multiple, diverging definitions of a foreign fighter.

Despite its flaws as described above, this research will still use the term 'foreign terrorist fighter' and the definition given to it by the Security Council. This is not only because it is the most authoritative term, but also because it makes clear that this study focuses on those individuals who traveled to Syria and Iraq to join terrorist organizations, and in particular IS. Terms like 'radical travelers' and 'foreign fighters' lack this focus on terrorism. It is important to emphasize that this research acknowledges the lack of clarity surrounding the term FTF and the definition given to it by the Security Council. However, this research will not try to further specify the term and definition in order to create a clearer working definition of an FTF by, for example, trying to define terrorism, on which entire books have been written.[72] Rather, this research will address the problems associated with this term and definition adopted in a legally binding resolution by the Security Council and will, where necessary, highlight how these issues have trickled down to the national level.

Although the Security Council definition of an FTF only speaks of states of nationality and states of residence, this study will also use the term 'states of origin', which will be used to capture both states of nationality and states of habitual residence. Moreover, it is important to make a distinction between, on the one hand, those who fall within the definition of an FTF and, on the other hand, those women and children who may be affiliated with IS but who do not fall within the definition of an FTF. The term 'IS-affiliates' lacks this distinction as the wife of a male FTF, whose role may have been confined to the household, or a child of an FTF, can also be considered an IS-affiliate. In

---

71 UN General Assembly, Report of the Working Group on the use of mercenaries as a means of violating human rights and impeding the exercise of the right of peoples to self-determination on its mission to Belgium (8 July 2016) UN Doc. A/HRC/33/43/Add.2, para. 14.

72 See for example, B. Saul, *Defining Terrorism in International Law* (Oxford University Press 2006); K. Maniszewska, *Towards a New Definition of Terrorism: Challenges and Perspectives in a Shifting Paradigm* (Springer 2024); A. Richards, *Conceptualizing Terrorism* (Oxford University Press 2015).

order to make this distinction clear, this research will use 'and their family members', to which we will turn now.

6.2 Their Family Members

At first, women were often labeled as "jihadi brides", portraying them as "naïve victims".[73] However, with information about the role of women in the IS caliphate and the threat posed by returnees becoming increasingly clear, "the narrow-minded narrative of females as hopeless and passive individuals lured to the Middle East and forced to join ISIS against their will" started to change.[74] Women played a variety of roles in the IS caliphate. Although most women were confined to the household and their main role was to support their husbands and raise their children in line with IS ideology, women were also active in fundraising, recruitment, education and medical roles.[75] In addition, women fulfilled policing roles, such as in the female religious police, tasked with the enforcement of religious laws.[76] There is also evidence that, when circumstances required, women were active in combat and as suicide bombers.[77] In Resolution 2396,[78] adopted on 21 December 2017, the Security Council called upon states to distinguish FTFs from "other individuals, including their accompanying family members who may not have been engaged in foreign terrorist fighter-related offenses",[79] while also emphasizing that women "may have served in many different roles, including as supporters, facilitators, or perpetrators of terrorist acts".[80] While some women indeed qualify as FTFs, others rather qualify as family members. However, this does not necessarily mean that they did not commit any crimes at all.

---

73 T. Renard, T. Mehra and M. Herbach, 'Introduction' in T. Mehra, T. Renard and M. Herbach (eds.), *Female Jihadis Facing Justice: Comparing Approaches in Europe* (ICCT, 2024) 3.

74 F. Capone, 'The Status of Foreign Fighters' Family Members Under Counter-Terrorism Law and International Humanitarian Law: Overcoming the Victims/Perpetrators Dichotomy?' in F. Capone, C. Paulussen and R. Mignot-Mahdavi 2023 (n. 6) 53.

75 D. Margolin and J. Cook, 'The Agency and Roles of Foreign Women in ISIL' in S. Ashraph, C. Cheung Ka-man and J. Cook (eds.), *Holding ISIL Accountable: Prosecuting Crimes in Iraq and Syria* (ICCT Press 2024) 54–104.

76 *Ibid.* 78–80.

77 *Ibid.* 81–83; F. Capone 2023 (n. 74) 53, 54.

78 UNSC Res. 2396 (21 December 2017) UN Doc. S/RES/2396 (2017).

79 *Ibid.* para. 4.

80 *Ibid.* para. 31.

Children who were born in or were brought to the caliphate by their parents, or who traveled on their own, may have also committed crimes. The recruitment of children was an important part of IS's activities, as children "were seen as its present and future, a critical component to ensure its resilience and continuation while they also proved useful to project its global threat of terrorism".[81] Children have been recruited on a large scale, have been forced to take part in hostilities and forced to commit crimes. Boys have received military training as young as eight years old.[82] In general, children have been exposed to violence, jihadi indoctrination and have potentially been radicalized from a very young age. As will further be explained in Chapter 5 of this research, children recruited by armed forces and armed groups should primarily be treated as victims.[83] Although it is highly questionable whether children should be labeled FTFs, the Security Council's definition of an FTF does not contain an age limit. Therefore, when following this definition of an FTF, children who have committed FTF-related acts, also qualify as FTFs. Nevertheless, they should certainly be treated in a different manner than adult FTFs, i.e., primarily as victims and with a focus on the best interest of the child.[84] Other children, who may not have engaged in FTF-related acts, should not be labeled as FTFs, but rather qualify as family members.

What can be concluded is that the status of each individual needs to be determined on a case-by-case basis. By speaking of FTFs and 'their family members', the research tries to make clear that a distinction needs to be made between (1) those who fall within the definition of an FTF, (2) those adults who are affiliated with IS but who may not fall within the definition of an FTF and (3) children who are associated with FTFs but who may not have committed FTF-related acts. Adding the term 'and their family members' captures individuals, and in particular women, who may be affiliated with IS but

81 T. Hamming and A. Amarasingam, 'Cubs of the Caliphate' in S. Ashraph, C. Cheung Kaman and J. Cook (eds.) 2024 (n. 75) 31.

82 *Ibid.* 42.

83 See, for example, R. van Ark, D. Prabhat and F. Gordon, *Children's Rights, 'Foreign Fighters' and Counter-Terrorism: Children of Nowhere* (Edward Elgar 2024); C. Nyamutata, 'Young Terrorists or Child Soldiers? ISIS Children, International Law and Victimhood' 25 Journal of Conflict & Security Law (2020) 2; F. Capone, '"Worse' than Child Soldiers? A Critical Analysis of Foreign Children in the Ranks of ISIL' 17 International Criminal Law Review (2017) 1.

84 OSCE Office for Democratic Institutions and Human Rights, 'Guidelines for Addressing the Threats and Challenges of "Foreign Terrorist Fighters" within a Human Rights Framework' (12 September 2018) 68–73. Available at: <https://www.osce.org/odihr/393503> accessed 28 April 2025.

who do not fall under the definition of an FTF as well as children of FTFs who were born in or brought to the IS caliphate by their parents and who have not committed FTF-related acts. One final element that should be mentioned here is that, although some may have committed crimes and should in that regard be perceived as perpetrators, there will be family members, and in particular children, who should at the same time be perceived as victims. For example, victims of terrorism, of human trafficking and of online grooming.

CHAPTER 2

Prevention of Travel

1 Introduction

Following the outbreak of the Syrian Civil War in 2011, tens of thousands of foreigners from around the world traveled to Syria and Iraq to join IS or other terrorist groups. To give an indication, around 19,000 FTFs affiliated with IS came from the Middle East and North Africa, around 13,000 from European states and around 7,000 from Central and South-East Asia, making the FTFs phenomenon in Syria and Iraq a truly global phenomenon.[1] Much research has been conducted on the possible reasons why these individuals traveled to Syria and Iraq and the so-called 'push' and 'pull' factors.[2] Push factors commonly mentioned include socio-economic factors, such as unemployment or a lack of opportunities, mental health issues and criminal backgrounds. Often discussed pull factors include the jihadist ideology and religiosity, and the role of both social networks and online social networks. These great numbers of FTFs traveling to Syria and Iraq also direct attention to the issue of prevention of travel.

States of origin use their concern that FTFs may pose a terrorist threat upon return as an incentive to prevent the departure of potential FTFs together with their family members.[3] These states are concerned that they may pose an aggravated threat when they return from the conflict zone, as they may have gained battlefield experience, received combat training, were exposed to vio-

1 For an estimate of numbers of foreign fighters from other regions, see J. Cook and G. Vale, 'From Daesh to "Diaspora": Tracing the Women and Minors of Islamic State' ICSR Report (2018) 14. Estimates are drawn from figures reported between April 2013 and June 2018. In a subsequent article the authors updated this dataset with information released between July 2018 and July 2019. See, J. Cook and G. Vale, 'From Daesh to "Diaspora" II: The Challenges Posed by Women and Minors After the Fall of the Caliphate' 12 CTC Sentinel (2019) 6.

2 See, for an overview of relevant findings, L. Dawson, 'A Comparative Analysis of the Data on Western Foreign Fighters in Syria and Iraq: Who Went and Why?' ICCT (International Centre for Counter-Terrorism – The Hague) Research Paper (February 2021); See also D. Malet, *Foreign Fighters: Transnational Identity in Civic Conflicts* (Oxford University Press 2013).

3 S. Krähenmann, 'The Obligations under International Law of the Foreign Fighter's State of Nationality or Habitual Residence, State of Transit and State of Destination' in A. de Guttry, F. Capone and C. Paulussen (eds.), *Foreign Fighters under International Law and Beyond* (T.M.C. Asser Press 2016) 230.

 | HTTPS://DOI.ORG/10.1163/9789004773806-003

lence, have new contacts within international jihadist networks and potentially suffer from post-traumatic stress disorders.[4] For example, British intelligence warned in 2014 that "[t]he skills, contacts and status acquired overseas can make these individuals a much greater threat when they return to the UK, even if they have not been tasked directly to carry out an attack on their return".[5] Despite this alleged threat upon return, there are only few cases of FTFs staging terrorist attacks upon return. For example, the attack against the Jewish museum in Brussels in 2014 was carried out by Mehdi Nemmouche, who traveled to Belgium from Syria where he had fought with IS.[6] A number of those who carried out the Paris attacks in November 2015 fought in Syria, and traveled to France to carry out the attacks.[7] Finally, some of the attackers during the Brussels suicide bombings in 2016 had fought in Syria with IS and later traveled to Belgium.[8] Despite these few examples, it is uncertain how big the threat of returning FTFs really is.[9]

States of transit (i.e., states through which FTFs travel to reach the conflict zone) also have reasons to prevent the travel of FTFs. For example, because they might establish networks within states whose territory they transit.[10] These networks make states of transit also vulnerable for infiltration by future

---

4 B. van Ginkel and E. Entenmann (eds.), 'The Foreign Fighters Phenomenon in the European Union: Profiles, Threats & Polies' ICCT Research Paper (April 2016) 14; E. Bakker, C. Paulussen and E. Entenmann, 'Returning Jihadist Foreign Fighters: Challenges Pertaining to Threat Assessment and Governance of this Pan-European Problem' 25 Security and Human Rights (2015) 1: 18.

5 D. Byman, *Road Warriors: Foreign Fighters in the Armies of Jihad* (Oxford University Press 2019) 5.

6 K. Rawlinson, 'Brussels Jewish museum terror attack: French citizen convicted' (*The Guardian*, 7 March 2019). Available at: <https://www.theguardian.com/world/2019/mar/07/brussels-jewish-museum-terror-attack-french-citizen-convicted> accessed 28 Nove mber 2024.

7 'Paris attacks: Who were the attackers?' (*BBC News*, 27 April 2016). Available at: <https://www.bbc.co.uk/news/world-europe-34832512> accessed 28 November 2024.

8 'Brussels attacks: Suspect Osama Krayem charged over Paris' (*BBC News*, 20 April 2016). Available at: <https://www.bbc.co.uk/news/world-europe-36094380> accessed 28 Nov ember 2024.

9 Some experts have argued that governments have exaggerated the threat posed by returning foreign fighters and FTFs, and that history shows that not all foreign fighters and FTFs pose a security risk. See, for example, D. Byman and J. Shapiro, 'Be Afraid. Be A Little Afraid: The Threat of Terrorism from Western Foreign Fighters in Syria and Iraq' Foreign Policy at Brookings, Policy Paper No. 34 (November 2014); E. Bakker, C. Paulussen and E. Entenmann 2014 (n. 4) 1: 16–19; D. Malet and R. Hayes, 'Foreign Fighter Returnees: An Indefinite Threat?' 32 Terrorism and Political Violence (2018) 8.

10 S. Krähenmann 2016 (n. 3) 230, 231.

FTFs who could benefit from those established networks.[11] An illustrative example is that Syria was the most important state of transit of FTFs traveling to join Al Qaeda after the US invasion of Iraq in 2003.[12] When the Civil War broke out in Syria in 2011, FTFs were able to activate those networks and benefit from them to enter Syria.[13] Through these networks, it is also likely that they were able to bring in more fighters.[14] Pokalova notes that when the Syrian Civil War erupted in 2011, "the networks of smugglers, transportation, and safe houses that served the Iraq War shifted toward Syria".[15]

In addition, states of destination (i.e., states on whose territory the conflict takes place) might have an incentive to prevent FTFs from traveling to, and entering their territory, *inter alia*, because FTFs may increase the intensity, duration and intractability of the conflict on their territory.[16]

In the past, states have been accused of failing to prevent the travel of foreign fighters from or through their territories, and thereby passing the buck to other states. For example, during the US invasion of Iraq in 2003, Syria was accused of willingly ignoring and possibly abetting foreign fighters heading to Iraq, in order to destabilize its neighbor.[17] Likewise, Iran was been said to have tolerated jihadists to transit its country on their way to Afghanistan in the 1990s, where they joined various groups including Al Qaeda.[18] Although Iran's exact motives remain unclear, Byman notes that Iran wanted to maintain relations with the various groups operating in Afghanistan as well as to "help instigate problems among rivals like Saudi Arabia and Egypt".[19]

In the context of the Syrian Civil War, various states have likewise been accused of failing to prevent, or even encourage their nationals to travel to

---

11 *Ibid.*

12 *Ibid.*; J. Denselow, 'Iraq's Ho Chi Minh Trail: The Syrian-Iraqi Border Since 2003' 1 CTC Sentinel (May 2008) 6: 19–21.

13 S. Krähenmann 2016 (n. 3) 230, 231; A. Zelin, 'Foreign Fighters Trickle into the Syrian Rebellion' The Washington Institute for Near East Policy (11 June 2012) Policy Watch No. 1950.

14 S. Krähenmann 2016 (n. 3) 230, 231; A. Zelin 2012 (n. 13).

15 E. Pokalova, *Returning Islamist Foreign Fighters: Threats and Challenges to the West* (Palgrave Macmillan 2020) 54.

16 S. Krähenmann 2016 (n. 3) 230, 231; These risks have also been acknowledged by the UN Security Council in Resolution 2178. See, UNSC Res. 2178 (24 September 2014) UN Doc. S/RES/2178, pre-ambular paras. 10, 11.

17 J. Felter and B. Fishman, 'Becoming a Foreign Fighter: A Second Look at the Sinjar Records' in P. Bergen and others (eds.), *Bank Accounts, & Bleedout: Al-qa'ida's Road in and Out of Iraq* (Combatting Terrorism Center at West Point, Harmony Report 2006) 62; D. Byman 2019 (n. 5) 118; E. Pokalova 2020 (n. 15) 36.

18 D. Byman 2019 (n. 5) 65.

19 *Ibid.*

the conflict zone. For example, Türkiye has been accused of turning a blind eye to FTFs and family members traveling through its territory on their way to Syria.[20] In turn, as a response to the many FTFs originating from other states on its territory, Türkiye emphasized that 'source countries' should not let their FTFs leave their territories and should take more responsibility over their FTFs who ended up in Türkiye.[21] Reportedly, at the beginning of the uprising against the Assad regime, Saudi Arabia, Jordan, Tunisia, Libya and Egypt did not prevent their nationals from traveling to Syria as these individuals were considered "as part of their support for the campaign to overthrow the Assad regime and to confront Iran and Shi'ite Islam".[22] And while officially backing the Assad Regime, in order to get rid of its own Islamists from the north Caucasus, Russia has been said to have initially acquiesced in or even encouraged them to travel to Syria.[23] In Byman's words, Russia used Syria before 2014 as a "convenient dumping ground" for its own jihadists.[24] Put differently, Russia may have passed the buck of dealing with nationals perceived as dangerous or radicalized to another state. These examples raise the following questions. Are states of origin under an international legal obligation to prevent FTFs from

---

20 L. Sly, 'Turkey confronts policy missteps on Syria with rise of al-Qaeda across the border' (*Washington Post*, 16 November 2013). Available at: <https://www.washingtonpost.com/world/middle_east/turkey-confronts-policy-missteps-on-syria-with-rise-of-al-qaeda-across-the-border/2013/11/16/e6183f12-4e27-11e3-97f6-ed8e3053083b_story.html> accessed 15 May 2025; D. Byman 2019 (n. 5) 186.

21 Turkish Ministry of Foreign Affairs, 'Türkiye'nin DAEŞ ile mücadelesi ve Yabancı Terörist Savaşçılar (YTS) konusuna yaklaşımı [Turkey's fight against Daesh and its approach to Foreign Terrorist Fighters]'. Available at: <https://www.mfa.gov.tr/turkiye_nin-yabanci-terorist-savascilarla-mucadelesi.tr.mfa> accessed 14 January 2025; Turkish Ministry of Interior, '2011 Yılından Günümüze, 102 Farklı Uyruktan 9 Bin Yabancı Terörist Savaşçı Sınır Dışı Edildi [Since 2011, 9,000 foreign terrorist fighters of 102 different nationalities have been deported]' (2 August 2022). Available at: <https://www.icisleri.gov.tr/2011-yilindan-gunumuze-102-farkli-uyruktan-9-bin-yabanci-terorist-savasci-sinir-disi-edildi> accessed 14 January 2025.

22 The Meir Amit Intelligence and Terrorism Information Center, 'The Phenomenon of Foreign Fighters from the Arab World in the Syrian Civil War, Most of Them Fighting in the Ranks of Organizations Affiliated with Al-Qaeda and the Global Jihad' (May 2014). Available at: <https://www.terrorism-info.org.il/en/20646/> accessed 25 November 2024.

23 K. Hille, 'Russia and radicalisation: Homegrown problem' (*Financial Times*, 7 December 2015). Available at: <https://www.ft.com/content/77156ed2-9ab0-11e5-be4f-0abd1978acaa> accessed 25 November 2024; O. Belova-Dalton, 'Foreign (Terrorist) Fighters and their Families in Finland, Sweden, Latvia, Lithuania, (Northwestern) Russia and their Impact on Estonia' Estonian Academy of Security Sciences (2022) 37. Available at: <https://digiriiul.sisekaitse.ee/bitstream/handle/123456789/2850/Foreign%20terrorists2022.pdf?sequence=1&isAllowed=y> accessed 25 November 2024.

24 D. Byman 2019 (n. 5) 184.

traveling? And if so, what is the nature and legal basis of such an obligation under public international law?

This research focuses on the FTFs phenomenon in Syria and Iraq. There is no longer a major influx of FTFs into these countries since the fall of the caliphate in 2019. Still, these questions remain relevant, also for all future situations in which FTFs, and foreign fighters more broadly, travel to an armed conflict abroad. Furthermore, as Ruys pointed out, the Syrian Civil War indicated "that there is perhaps, to a certain extent, a legal vacuum in this context" and that it is still open for discussion "whether third States [...] are legally obliged to take steps to prevent persons under their jurisdiction from joining one of the warring parties in the conflict".[25] Earlier legal research primarily dealt with the discussion on the prevention of FTF travel by focusing on the criminalization of the individual's conduct within states' domestic legislative framework and possible human rights implications of states' approaches to prevent travel. Such a focus emphasizes, what this study has called, the 'vertical dimension': the relationship between the state of origin and its national or resident intending to travel. However, as explained above, FTFs departing from their state of origin can significantly harm other states, e.g., states of destination and states of transit. The acts or omissions of states of origin in preventing their FTFs from traveling can influence the potential harm posed to other states. By not taking sufficient steps to prevent departure, states essentially shun their responsibility over potentially dangerous individuals and shift the possible security risks that they pose to other states. There is thus also a clear 'horizontal dimension' or inter-state relationship present. This dimension is, however, often overlooked when discussing the issue of preventing FTF travel. In line with the overall approach of this research, and although issues such as criminalization of travel and human rights implications will be touched upon where necessary, the present chapter will primarily analyze the issue of prevention of travel from this inter-state perspective. The chapter will do so by focusing on the norms that provide the international legal basis for an obligation to prevent FTF travel: the international law of neutrality, the non-intervention principle and the no-harm principle.

The issue of FTF travel does not only include the departure from their states of origin, but also the transit through other states and the entry into their states of destination. However, as the research as a whole focuses on the obligations and responsibilities of states or origin, this chapter will also primarily focus on preventing the departure of FTFs from the territories of those states.

---

25 T. Ruys, 'Of Arms, Funding and "Non-Lethal Assistance" – Issues Surrounding Third State Intervention in the Syrian Civil War' 13 Chinese Journal of International Law (2014) 1: 49.

The chapter will draw illustrations from the practice of states from which FTFs traveled to Syria and Iraq. Emphasis will be placed on the practice of one state of origin in particular, namely the practice of Australia. As compared to other states of origin, a relatively low number of FTFs traveled from Australia to Syria and Iraq. Between April 2013 and June 2018 an estimated 214 FTFs and family members traveled from Australia to Syria and Iraq and became affiliated with IS.[26] Australia has taken far-reaching legal measures, especially in its criminal laws, to prevent individuals from traveling to another country with an intention to engage in hostile activities. In fact, Australia seems to be one of the only Western states which outlaws foreign fighting per se.[27] This raises an additional question regarding an obligation to prevent FTF travel: what are possible limits to the obligation to prevent the travel of FTFs?

First, this chapter will discuss the basis of an obligation to prevent travel for terrorist purposes under public international law. In order to do so, this research will analyze the law of neutrality, the non-intervention, no-harm and precautionary principles. Thereafter, this chapter will discuss a number of UN Security Council resolutions which address prevention of FTF travel and a number of legal measures that states have taken in order to prevent the departure of their nationals. Through this discussion, it will be established whether states of origin owe an international legal obligation to prevent the departure of FTFs to other affected states, and if such an obligation can be said to exist within international law, its nature will be analyzed through this discussion. Finally, a number of conclusions will be presented.

2 The Legal Basis of an Obligation to Prevent Travel

This section will discuss the basis within public international law for an obligation to prevent travel for terrorist purposes. It will be established whether an obligation to prevent the departure of FTFs to Syria and Iraq can be inferred from international law. First, the international law of neutrality will be discussed. This body of law contains certain rights and duties for neutral states. In the past, the issue of foreign volunteers, and states' obligations with regard to such individuals, was mainly addressed by the law of neutrality.[28]

26 See, J. Cook and G. Vale 2018 (n. 1) 18.

27 A. Hoffman and M. Furlan, 'Challenges Posed by Returning Foreign Fighters' Program on Extremism (March 2020) 12. Available at: <https://extremism.gwu.edu/challenges-posed-returning-foreign-fighters> accessed 25 November 2024.

28 I. Brownlie, 'Volunteers and the Law of War and Neutrality' 5 International & Comparative Law Quarterly (October 1956) 4: 570, 571.

Although this body of law only applies in international armed conflict (IAC), it should still be analyzed to understand the full legal framework of states' obligations to prevent individuals from crossing their borders. Second, the non-intervention and no-harm principles under general international law will be discussed. As Lloydd notes, if discussed at all, these principles under general international law are often only analyzed as "underlying background information" to the FTFs phenomenon, "rather than being considered of primary relevance".[29] A focus on these principles will bring the perspective of states of origin's responsibilities and their actions and omissions in relation to other states more to the foreground. This is mainly because the principles of non-intervention and no-harm, "refer primarily to harm or risk posed to a foreign State, and only secondarily to the risk to the parent State".[30] This chapter will analyze whether an obligation upon states of origin to prevent such travel can be deduced from these principles. Third, the precautionary principle will be analyzed within the counter-terrorism context. The analysis of this principle aims to show that measures to prevent FTFs from traveling fit within the logic of this principle and connection can be sought to it when assessing a duty to prevent prospective FTFs from departing a state's territory.

2.1 International Law of Neutrality

The international law of neutrality originated in the 19th and early 20th centuries and governs the rights and duties of neutral states, i.e., states not party to an armed conflict. This body of law has mainly developed through state practice but its essential parts have also been codified in two international conventions, the 1907 Hague Convention Respecting the Rights and Duties of Neutral Powers and Persons in Case of War on Land (Hague Convention V), and the 1907 Hague Convention of Neutral Powers in Naval War (Hague Convection XIII).[31] These two conventions, together with customary international law, embody the international law of neutrality. Under this body of law,

29 M. Lloydd, 'Framing Foreign Fighting: Exploring the Scope of Prevention and the Categorisation of Fighters in International Law' in C. Paulussen and M. Scheinin (eds.), *Human Dignity and Human Security in Times of Terrorism* (T.M.C Asser Press 2020) 223.

30 M. Lloydd, 'Retrieving Neutrality Law to Consider 'Other' Foreign Fighters under International Law' European Society of International Law Conference Paper Series, Conference Paper No. 8/2017 (ESIL Research Forum, Granada, 30–31 March 2017) 23.

31 Hague Convention Respecting the Rights and Duties of Neutral Powers and Persons in Case of War on Land (adopted 18 October 1907, entered into force 26 January 1910) 205 CTS 299; Hague Convention of Neutral Powers in Naval War (adopted 18 October 1907, entered into force 26 January 1910) 205 CTS 395.

neutral states have a right to remain apart from the IAC, i.e., an armed conflict between two or more sovereign states, and not be adversely affected by it.[32] There are three core obligations upon a neutral state in order to maintain its neutral status: (1) a neutral state is obliged to refrain from participation in an IAC; (2) a neutral state is prohibited from providing military assistance to either of the parties at war, which includes an obligation to prevent acts which violate its neutrality occurring on its own territory;[33] and (3) a neutral state has an obligation to treat belligerents equally.[34] Belligerents are for their part under an obligation to respect the inviolability of the territory of a neutral state and may, therefore, not use this territory in any way for their military operations.[35]

The international law of neutrality only applies to IAC. However, the wars on the territories of both Syria and Iraq between their respective governmental authorities, as well as between third state forces like those of the US-led coalition and Türkiye, and several armed groups such as IS, Hayat Tahrir al-Sham, the Syrian National Army and Kurdish militias, and between such groups, can be classified as non-international armed conflicts (NIACs).[36] In fact, multiple and overlapping NIACs have been or are occurring on the territories of Syria and Iraq. In contrast, the conflicts between Syria and the US-led coalition, Türkiye and Israel have been classified as IACs.[37] Yet, these IACs were not the conflicts FTFs joined. FTFs joined IS or other armed groups labeled as terrorist and fought on Syrian or/and Iraqi territory against other armed groups, the Syrian and/or Iraqi Governmental forces, or third state's forces. Even if there is still a place for the international law of neutrality in contemporary international law, which is questionable for a number of rea-

32 M. Bothe, 'Neutrality, Concept and General Rules' Max Planck Encyclopedia of Public International Law (MPEPIL) (October 2015) 2.

33 Hague Convention V, Article 5; Hague Convention XIII, Article 25.

34 Hague Convention V, Article 9; Hague Convention XIII, Article 9; P. Seger, 'The Law of Neutrality' in A. Clapham and P. Gaeta, The Oxford Handbook of International Law in Armed Conflict (Oxford University Press 2014) 249. The neutral state is, however, entitled to continue commercial relations with the belligerents.

35 Hague Convention V, Articles 1, 2 and 3.

36 Rulac Geneva Academy, 'Non-international armed conflicts in Syria' (last updated 10 August 2023). Available at: < https://www.rulac.org/browse/conflicts/non-international-armed-conflicts-in-syria> accessed 28 November 2024. Rulac Geneva Academy, 'Non-international armed conflicts in Iraq' (last updated 18 May 2023). Available at: <https://www.rulac.org/browse/conflicts/non-international-armed-conflicts-in-iraq> accessed 28 November 2024.

37 Rulac Geneva Academy, 'International armed conflicts in Syria' (last updated 7 December 2023). Available at: <https://www.rulac.org/browse/conflicts/international-armed-conflict-in-syria> accessed 28 November 2024.

sons set out below, this law does not apply to these NIACs and, therefore, does not apply to individuals who traveled to Syria and Iraq, as they joined armed (terrorist) groups active in a NIAC. However, it is still relevant and important to discuss this body of law. First, because the non-intervention and no-harm principles, which will be discussed in the following sub-sections, have roots in neutrality law. Second, because the issue of foreign volunteers leaving neutral territory, and states' obligations with regard to such individuals, was initially addressed by the international law of neutrality.[38]

Despite the obligation to prevent acts which violate its neutrality occurring on its own territory, such as the establishment of, or publicity for voluntary corps or recruiting agencies on its territory to assist the belligerents,[39] Article 6 of the Hague Convention V explicitly states that "[t]he responsibility of a neutral Power is not engaged by the fact of persons crossing the frontier separately to offer their services to one of the belligerents". Hence, the neutral state is not required to prevent its nationals from joining a party to an armed conflict on their own initiative, as long as they do so in an isolated manner and it does not amount to the organization of a hostile expedition, as in the latter case the neutral state is required to prevent the organization of such expeditions and the departure of such organized corps or bands which have been formed on its territory.[40] A decisive factor for the question of whether the responsibility of the neutral state is engaged seems to be whether there was an 'organization'. Therefore, the obligation to prevent travel under the international law of neutrality does not extend to individual volunteers departing a neutral state's territory to join an armed conflict abroad.[41] Elements that could be taken into account to prove the existence of an organization include, "their number, their attitude, their continuous marching past, or other circumstances".[42]

However, even before its codification in 1907, a significant number of states went further than what was required by the international law of neutrality at the time, and did exert legal control over their citizens' foreign military service

38 I. Brownlie 1956 (n. 28) 570, 571.

39 Hague Convention V, Articles 4, 5.

40 I. Brownlie 1956 (n. 28) 572, 573.

41 *Ibid.* 572; C. Forcese and A. Mamikon, 'Neutrality Law, Anti-Terrorism, and Foreign Fighters: Legal Solutions to the Recruitment of Canadians to Foreign Insurgencies' 48 University of British Columbia law review (2015) 2: 348.

42 J. Scott, Proceedings of the Hague Peace Conferences: Translation of the Official Texts (William S. Hein & Co, 2000) III, 33.

in any type of armed conflict, including in NIAC.[43] As Arielli notes, between 1794 and 1938, 49 states adopted laws to exert such control over the enlistment of their nationals abroad.[44] These early national laws were, therefore, not based on an international legal obligation to prevent individual volunteers from departing their territories but rather reflect political decisions.[45] For example, the US Neutrality Act of 1794 stated:

> If any person shall within the territory or jurisdiction of the United States begin or set on foot or provide or prepare the means for any military expedition or enterprise […] against the territory or dominions of any foreign prince or state of whom the United States was at peace that person would be guilty of a misdemeanor.[46]

In accordance with the British Foreign Enlistment Act of 1819, British subjects could not "without the permission of His Majesty enlist in the military services of any foreign prince, state, potentate, colony, province or part of any province or people, or of any person or persons exercising or assuming to exercise the powers of government in or over any foreign country".[47] However, the extent to which these laws were actually applied was to a large extent subject to national and foreign policy considerations. In other words, "[w]henever it was opportune to do so, governments turned a blind eye and in some cases even encouraged the foreign enlistment of their citizens".[48]

Some present-day scholars have called for a renewal of these earlier domestic neutrality laws to complement counter-terrorism laws, as a response to individuals traveling to Syria and Iraq to join one of the parties to the armed conflict.[49] For example, Forcese and Mamikon call for a 'back-to-the-future strategy' of renewing antiquated national neutrality laws, instead of using

43 Between 1794 and 1938, 49 states exerted such legal control over their citizens. See, J. Thomson, 'State Practices, International Norms, and the Decline of Mercenarism' 34 International Studies Quarterly (1990) 1: 34.

44 N. Arielli, *From Byron to Bin Laden: A History of Foreign War Volunteers* (Harvard University Press 2018) 122.

45 K. Heller, 'The Law of Neutrality Does Not Apply to the Conflict with Al-Qaeda, and It's a Good Thing Too: A Response to Chang' 47 Texas International Law Journal (2011) 115: 121.

46 M. Flores, 'Foreign Fighters Involvement in National and International Wars: A Historical Survey' in A. de Guttry, F. Capone and C. Paulussen (eds.) 2016 (n. 3) 30.

47 Cited in N. Arielli, G. Frei and I. Van Hulle, 'The Foreign Enlistment Act, International Law, and British Politics, 1819–2014' 38 The International History Review 4: 638 (Italics omitted).

48 N. Arielli (n. 44) 138.

49 C. Forcese and A. Mamikon 2015 (n. 41) 309.

counter-terrorism laws, in order to inhibit foreign fighter travel, as such laws would, among other benefits, ease prosecutorial burdens.[50] As will be elaborated upon in Section 4.1, Australia prohibits foreign fighting as such in its criminal law. Most other states do not criminalize foreign fighting in itself, unless there is, for example, evidence of intent to join a terrorist organization or commit (terrorist) crimes abroad. Australia, on the other hand, criminalizes entering a foreign country with an intention to engage in a hostile activities, unless serving in or with the armed forces of the government of a foreign country, under the offence of foreign incursion.[51] Therefore, some authors have argued that Australia's prohibition of foreign fighter travel constitutes a contemporary deployment of earlier national neutrality laws.[52]

There are a number of reasons why it has been argued that the relevance of the international law of neutrality is substantially diminished.[53] First, because the system of collective security provided for in the UN Charter prohibits the use of force, which also entails an obligation not to support an aggressor or to recognize the effects of military aggression.[54] Therefore, if there is a clear aggressor in an armed conflict, it is questionable whether the prohibition on the use of force, now a fundamental norm under public international law, leaves room for neutral stances towards acts of aggression.[55] Furthermore, the international law of neutrality contrasts with the system of collective security where the international community as a whole responds to threats to international peace and security through the UNSC.[56] Therefore, even if there is no clear aggressor, neutral stances towards parties engaged in an IAC

50 *Ibid.* 309, 358; See, also, J. Ip, 'Reconceptualising the Legal Response to Foreign Fighters' International & Comparative Law Quarterly 69 (January 2020) 1: 130–133.

51 See, Part 5.5, Section 119.1(1) of the Australian Criminal Code Act 1995 (Criminal Code).

52 C. Forcese and A. Mamikon 2015 (n. 41) 344; J. Ip 2020 (n. 50) 128–133.

53 P. Seger 2014 (n. 34) 251; J. Upcher, *Neutrality in Contemporary International Law* (Oxford University Press 2020) 1, 2.

54 United Nations Charter (signed 26 June 1945, entered into force 24 October 1945) 1 UNTS 16.

55 P. Seger 2014 (n. 34) 251, 261–263; J. Upcher 2020 (n. 53) 1, 19, 20; H. Lauterpacht, 'The Future of Neutrality, December 1941' in E. Lauterpacht (ed.), *International Law: Being the Collected Papers of Hersch Lauterpacht Vol. V* (Cambridge University Press 2004) 675–683. In contrast, the law of neutrality dates back to a time in which war was considered legitimate.

56 However, it has been suggested that there exists an exception to the laws of neutrality for measures of collective security adopted by the UNSC under Chapter VII of the UN Charter. See, P. Seger 2014 (n. 34) 262; D. Fleck, 'The Law of Neutrality' in D. Fleck (ed.), *The Handbook of International Humanitarian Law* (4th edn., Oxford University Press 2021) 606, 607; M. Bothe 2015 (n. 32) 4, 5; J. Upcher 2020 (n. 53) 161.

contrast with the collective security system in the UN Charter. Second, as no significant revision or amendment of the international law of neutrality as codified in the two Hague Conventions has taken place since their adoption more than a hundred years ago, the law contains lacunae with regard to modern warfare, such as missile and cyber warfare.[57] Third, because of an increase in NIACs involving non-state actors, such as terrorist groups. As mentioned above, the international law of neutrality only applies to IACs between two or more states,[58] and therefore, not to NIACs between government authorities and one or more organized armed groups or between such groups within a state.[59] Besides the international law of neutrality formally not being applicable, it also seems ill-suited to address or symmetrically apply to NIACs as it requires equal treatment of all parties to the conflict, which may not be possible with regard to a conflict between a state and one or more non-state armed groups in all respects and with regard to certain groups, like IS, even undesirable.

Still, third states are subject to different restrictions under international law with regard to NIACs, such as the armed conflicts in Syria and Iraq. These restrictions have certain roots in the international law of neutrality, including those emanating from the non-intervention principle,[60] at which we will look now.

2.2 Non-intervention Principle

States have frequently condemned the acts of other states as interfering in their internal affairs. For example, China accused the US President George W. Bush of interfering in China's internal affairs by attending a ceremony at which the Dalai Lama, the spiritual leader of Tibet, received the Congressional Medal of Honor.[61] Another example, in an armed conflict context, is Ukraine accusing the Russian Federation of intervening in their internal affairs by supporting pro-Russian separatists in the eastern Ukrainian regions of

57 P. Seger 2014 (n. 34) 252, 253.

58 The international law of neutrality also applied to situations in which the insurgents had been recognized as belligerents.

59 P. Seger 2014 (n. 34) 249; *The Prosecutor v Dusko Tadić* (Trial Chamber, Judgment) International Criminal Tribunal for the Former Yugoslavia (ICTY) IT-94-1-T (7 May 1997) para. 561.

60 M. Lloydd 2017 (n. 30) 5.

61 M. Jamnejad and M. Wood, 'The Principle of Non-intervention' 22 Leiden Journal of International Law (2009) 2: 346.

Donetsk and Luhansk.[62] Both the law of neutrality and the principle of non-intervention regulate and restrict third-state assistance for parties engaged in an armed conflict. However, as described in the previous sub-section, the law of neutrality only applies to IACs. The principle of non-intervention, on the other hand, complements neutrality law and prohibits third-state intervention during IAC, NIAC as well as in times of peace. As opposed to the international law of neutrality, the principle of non-intervention is not enshrined in a specific treaty devoted to it. However, the principle, as well as the underlying obligation, is part of customary international law and prohibits all states to intervene directly or indirectly in the internal or external affairs of other states.[63] The principle derives from the concepts of sovereignty and sovereign equality of states in international law.[64] In the *Nicaragua* Case, the International Court of Justice (ICJ) identified two conditions that have to be met in order to constitute a violation of the non-intervention obligation, by stating:

> A prohibited intervention must accordingly be one bearing on matters in which each State is permitted, by the principle of State sovereignty, to decide freely. One of these is the choice of a political, economic, social and cultural system, and the formulation of foreign policy. Intervention is wrongful when it uses methods of coercion in regard to such choices, which must remain free ones.[65]

In other words, there must be: (1) state action that constitutes coercive interference; and (2) in another state's *domaine réservé*.

According to the ICJ, the requirement of coercion constitutes the very essence of intervention.[66] Although the criterion of 'coercion' is not clearly defined, it does delimit the principle to some extent as "[o]nly acts of a certain magnitude are likely to qualify as 'coercive'".[67] This is because coercion involves a certain amount of pressure or compulsion on the side of the

62 L. Ferro and N. Verlinden, 'Neutrality During Armed Conflicts: A Coherent Approach to Third-State Support for Warring Parties' 17 Chinese Journal of International Law (2018) 1: 27–29.

63 *Case Concerning Military and Paramilitary Activities In and Against Nicaragua* (*Nicaragua v. United States of America*) (Merits) [1986] ICJ Rep. 14, paras. 202 and 205.

64 A. Ansong, 'The Concept of Sovereign Equality of States in International Law' II The Ghana Institute of Management and Public Administration Law Review (2016) 1: 22.

65 *Case Concerning Military and Paramilitary Activities In and Against Nicaragua* 1986 (n. 63) 205.

66 *Ibid.*

67 M. Jamnejad and M. Wood 2009 (n. 61) 348.

coercing state.[68] The degree of pressure or compulsion that is necessary for a coercive act to infringe the non-intervention obligation will, however, vary in each case.

The principle of non-intervention has also featured in a number of authoritative UN General Assembly (UNGA or General Assembly) resolutions. In the 1970 Declaration on Principles of International Law concerning Friendly Relations and Co-operation among states in accordance with the Charter of the United Nations (1970 Friendly Relations Declaration), adopted by the General Assembly in Resolution 2625 (XXV),[69] it is clarified that the principle of non-intervention does not only include armed intervention, but "all forms of interference or attempted threats against the personality of the State or against its political, economic and cultural elements".[70]

From the beginning of the Syrian Civil War, Syria has accused FTFs' states of origin, as well as states of transit, of unlawfully interfering in Syria's affairs by actively fostering terrorism on its territory.[71] As shown in the preceding sub-section, the international law of neutrality only imposes an obligation upon neutral states to prevent foreign volunteers from traveling to an IAC if the organization requirement is met. The question is whether the principle of non-intervention requires the same standard of behavior or whether it imposes more strict or lenient requirements upon states of origin to prevent FTF travel.

The ICJ determined that "if one State, with a view to the coercion of another State, supports and assists armed bands in that State whose purpose is to overthrow the government of that State, that amounts to an intervention by the one State in the internal affairs of the other".[72] Furthermore, the ICJ specified that the mere supply of funds will 'undoubtedly' constitute such support or assistance amounting to an act of intervention in the internal affairs of the

---

68 H. Moynihan, 'The Application of International Law to State Cyberattacks: Sovereignty and Non-intervention' Chatham House Research Paper (2 December 2019) 28.

69 UNGA Res. 2625 (XXV) (24 October 1970) UN Doc. A/Res/2625(XXV).

70 *Ibid.* para. 1.

71 See, for example, Letter dated 18 June 2014 from the Permanent Representative of the Syrian Arab Republic to the United Nations addressed to the Secretary-General (20 June 2014) UN Doc. S/2014/42; Statement of the representative of the Syrian Arab Republic during the discussions on the Report of the Secretary-General on the implementation of Security Council Resolution 2139 (26 June 2014) UN Doc. S/PV.7212, 4–6; Statement from the representative of the Syrian Arab Republic during a discussion on the situation in the Middle East (14 July 2014) Un Doc. S/PV.7216, 12–15.

72 *Case Concerning Military and Paramilitary Activities In and Against Nicaragua* 1986 (n. 63) para. 241.

other state.[73] The 1970 Friendly Relations Declaration, which is considered to be declaratory of customary international law,[74] provides that, as part of the principle of non-intervention, states may not *tolerate* "subversive, terrorist or armed activities directed towards the violent overthrow of the regime of another State, or interfere in civil strife in another State".[75] This non-toleration obligation goes beyond prohibiting support for or assistance of such terrorist or armed groups by making a failure to act against such groups illegal.[76] Roscini notes that, "[a]s a minimum, the obligation not to tolerate or acquiesce in subversive, terrorist, or armed activities directed towards the overthrow of a foreign government requires the state that is aware of such activities to inform the target state".[77] This non-toleration obligation can be said to impose a standard of due diligence upon states, requiring reasonable measures of prevention.[78] This standard of due diligence is further strengthened by the no-harm principle and will, therefore, be discussed in more depth in the following sub-section. The non-toleration rule, as part of the non-intervention principle, can be referred to as a basis for arguing that international law requires states of origin to exercise a standard of due diligence to prevent FTFs from departing their territories.

Toleration or complete inaction of states of origin in preventing FTFs from departing their territories might, to a certain degree, be considered as coercive. First, because it may foment or aggravate civil unrest, revolt or civil strife

---

73 *Ibid.* 228.

74 *Ibid.* 188; B. Saul, *Defining Terrorism in International Law* (Oxford University Press 2006) 196.

75 UNGA Res. 2625 (XXV) (1970) (n. 69) para. 1; Milanovic distinguishes two models of coercion: (1) coercion-as-extortion, under which "the coercing state issues a demand to the victim state, and threatens or implements certain harms if that demand is not met" and (2) coercion-as-control, which "conceptualizes coercion as an action by the coercing state that removes the victim state's ability to exercise control over its policy choices". According to Milanovic, the non-toleration obligation as formulated by the General Assembly is an example of coercion-as-control as it "deprives the victim state of the ability to control its internal affairs and exercise its sovereign authority over its entire territory". See, M. Milanovic, 'Revisiting Coercion as an Element of Prohibited Intervention in International Law' 117 American Journal of International Law (2023) 4: 605, 641 and 642.

76 M. Jamnejad and M. Wood 2009 (n. 61) 361.

77 M. Roscini, *International Law and the Principle of Non-Intervention: History, Theory, and Interactions with Other Principles* (Oxford University Press 2014) 191.

78 S. Krähenmann, 'Academy Briefing No. 7: Foreign Fighters under International Law' Geneva Academy of International Humanitarian Law and Human Rights (2014) 50; R. Pisillo-Mazzeschi, 'The Due Diligence Rule and the Nature of the International Responsibility of States' 35 German Yearbook of International Law (1992) 9: 34; M. Lloydd 2017 (n. 30) 3.

in states of destination.[79] Second, because FTFs may, to some extent, be capable of influencing the course of the hostilities.[80] Besides the propagandistic purpose for which foreign fighters are often recruited, it has been observed that foreign fighters, including FTFs, also bring weapons, connections, funds and tactics to the armed conflict, and increase the radicalization process in areas under effective control of armed (terrorist) groups.[81] In Resolution 2178 (2014), the Security Council expressed its concerns that FTFs increase the intensity, duration and intractability of conflicts.[82] A study from 2017 by Chu and Braithwaite, about the impact of foreign fighters on the outcomes of civil conflicts between 1946 and 2013, concluded that foreign fighters are associated with a decreased likelihood of government victory.[83] Malet also concludes that "insurgencies employing foreign fighters tend to be disproportionately successful" and that "both historic and contemporary foreign fighters have been responsible for greater levels of violence and for prolonging conflicts".[84] Although foreign fighters have certainly made a difference on the battlefield, Malet also notes that it is difficult to conclusively argue that the presence of foreign fighters tip the military balance because "it may simply be the case that the best-organized and most effective insurgencies were those that also had the capacity to recruit abroad".[85] Finally, Arielli concludes that as opposed to international armed conflicts between states, "[i]n conflicts characterized by guerrilla or irregular warfare, because of their fluid structures and relatively small size of insurgent forces, foreign volunteers have a greater potential to make an impact".[86] This is not to say that a lack of due diligence in preventing the travel of FTFs would meet the coercion requirement of the non-intervention principle. This is to say that such inaction by states as well as the consequences emanating from such inaction, can be assessed under this principle, and particularly the non-toleration obligation.

The assertion that the non-intervention principle forms a legal basis for an obligation upon states of origin to take steps to prevent the departure of FTFs

---

79 P. Kuning, 'Prohibition of intervention' MPEPIL (2008) para. 24.

80 T. Ruys 2014 (n. 25) 49, 50; See also *Institut de Droit International*, Resolution on the Principle of Non-Intervention and Civil Wars (1975) Article 2(d).

81 UNGA, Use of mercenaries as a means of violating human rights and impeding the exercise of the right of peoples to self-determination (19 August 2015) Un Doc. A/70/330. para. 43.

82 UNSC Res. 2178 (2014) (n. 16) pre-ambular para. 10.

83 T. Chu and A. Braithwaite, 'The impact of foreign fighters on civil conflict outcomes' 1 Research and Politics (2017) 7: 1–7.

84 D. Malet 2013 (n. 2) 52, 211.

85 *Ibid.* 52, 53.

86 N. Arielli 2018 (n. 44) 177.

is strengthened by states' obligations under the non-intervention principle with regard to mercenaries. Specific obligations under the principle of non-intervention are set out in more detail in the 1981 Declaration on the Inadmissibility of Intervention and Interference in the Internal Affairs of States.[87] This Declaration specifies the duty upon states "to prevent [...] the sending of such mercenaries into the territory of another state, and to deny facilities, including financing, for the equipping and transit of mercenaries".[88] Therefore, as part of the non-intervention principle, states are under an obligation to prevent the sending of mercenaries into the territory of another state as well as to deny their transit. What should be clarified is that FTFs cannot be classified under the term mercenaries and 'sending' constitutes more active behavior on the part of the state than letting individuals depart their territory.[89] However, this quite similar obligation with respect of mercenaries under the principle of non-intervention may strengthen the argument that the same principle speaks to states' behavior in preventing the departure of FTFs and also provides a legal basis to hold states accountable in this regard.

This sub-section shows that an obligation to prevent FTF travel may find its legal basis in the principle of non-intervention, and particularly in its non-toleration obligation. A number of scholars seem to agree with this contention. For example, Brownlie argued that "[i]n principle, omission to prevent such departure to fight against the legitimate government in a civil war [...] would engage the responsibility of a State for interference in the internal affairs of the

87 UNGA Res. 36/103 (9 December 1981) UN Doc. A/RES/36/103.

88 *Ibid.* Principle II(g). See, also, Articles 5 and 6 of the International Convention against the Recruitment, Use, Financing and Training of Mercenaries (adopted 4 December 1989, entered into force 20 October 2001) 2163 UNTS 75.

89 See, for a definition of mercenaries, Article 47(2) Additional Protocol I to the Geneva Conventions. Protocol additional to the Geneva Conventions of 12 August 1949, and relating to the protection of victims of international armed conflicts (Protocol I) (signed 8 June 1977, entered into force 7 December 1978) 1125 UNTS 3. It is difficult for a foreign fighter or FTF to fulfill the criteria of this definition. Mercenaries are often distinguished from foreign fighters and FTFs as the primary motive of a mercenary, which is also required by the referenced definition, is a monetary award, rather than ideological, religious or political motives. See, also, E. Sommario, 'The Status of Foreign Fighters under International Humanitarian Law' in A. de Guttry, F. Capone and C. Paulussen (eds.) 2016 (n. 3) 156–157. However, there are different opinions on this matter. For example, the General Assembly's Working Group on the Use of Mercenaries as a Means of Violating Human Rights and Impeding the Exercise of the Right of Peoples to Self-determination, deems foreign fighters, including FTFs, as mercenary-related activity. See UNGA, Report of the Working Group on the Use of Mercenaries as a Means of Violating Human Rights and Impeding the Exercise of the Right of Peoples to Self-determination (6 August 2018) UN Doc. A/73/303, para. 9.

State in which insurrection occurred".[90] Similarly, Krähenmann noted that "[g]iven the broad scope of the principle of non-intervention, including the duty of states to prevent harm emanating from their territory, it can be argued that states have an obligation to prevent the movement of foreign fighters".[91] In addition, in its 1975 Resolution on the principle of non-intervention in civil wars, the *Institut de Droit International* clarified that "[t]hird States shall use all means to prevent inhabitants of their territories, whether natives or aliens, [...] from crossing the border or from embarking from their territories with a view to fomenting or causing a civil war".[92] Finally, in the case *Alqudsi v the Commonwealth*, the Supreme Court of New South Wales explicitly made clear that the offence of foreign incursion, which criminalizes FTF travel and which will be discussed in more depth in section 4.1, and other related offences, were intended and designed to support the non-intervention principle and other principles under the UN Charter. Justice Adamson stated that "[b]y criminalising preparatory acts, s7 (1) (e) is, on its face, intended, and designed, to support the principle of the sovereignty and equality of States as well as the principle of non-intervention".[93]

2.3 No-Harm Principle

The obligation to prevent the departure of FTFs is further shaped by the no-harm principle. The no-harm principle entails an obligation upon states to prevent harm emanating from their territory, or otherwise under their jurisdiction or control, upon other states. This principle is articulated in Article 3 of the ILC Draft Articles on Prevention of Transboundary Harm from Hazardous Activities, which indicates that states "shall take all appropriate measures to prevent significant transboundary harm or at any event to minimize the risk thereof".[94] Furthermore, the ICJ has determined in the *Corfu Channel* Case that it is "every State's obligation not to allow knowingly its territory to be used for acts contrary to the rights of other States".[95] This obligation to prevent

90 I. Brownlie 1956 (n. 28) 573, 574.

91 S. Krähenmann 2014 (n. 78) 50.

92 *Institut de Droit International*, The Principle of Non-Intervention in Civil Wars, Session of Wiesbaden (14 August 1975). Available at: <https://www.idi-iil.org/en/sessions/wiesbaden-1975/?post_type=publication> accessed 25 November 2011.

93 *Alqudsi v Commonwealth of Australia* [2015] NSWSC 1222 (27 August 2015), para. 139.

94 ILC, 'Draft Articles on Prevention of Transboundary Harm from Hazardous Activities, which indicates that States ' in the Report of the International Law Commission on the work of its 53rd session (2001) UN Doc. A/RES/56/82, Article 3.

95 *The Corfu Channel Case* (Merits) [1949] ICJ Rep. 4, p. 22.

harm to another state, has been well established in international environmental law. It was reaffirmed in the 1972 Stockholm Declaration and the 1992 Rio Declaration,[96] and its customary nature was acknowledged by the ICJ in the *Nuclear Weapons* Advisory Opinion.[97] However, the obligation to prevent harm to other states applies generally in international law and has also been recognized with regard to counter-terrorism.[98]

Like the non-toleration obligation under the principle of non-intervention, states' obligation to prevent harm under the no-harm principle also imposes a standard of due diligence.[99] Although harm does not necessarily emanate from illegal activity, the Permanent Court of International Justice (PCIJ) confirmed in the *S.S. Lotus* Case that "[i]t is well settled that a State is bound to use due diligence to prevent the commission within its dominions of criminal acts against another nation or its people".[100] But what does this due diligence rule entail? Due diligence is a standard of conduct, which assesses whether states have employed their best efforts and did what was reasonably expected of them when responding to certain risks or threats of harm.[101] In other words, it is a degree of care that is expected of a good government.[102] Furthermore, due diligence is a flexible standard, which means that it is subject to, among others, a state's knowledge, capacity, magnitude of the risk, severity of the potential harm and other factual circumstances.[103] The standard of conduct required by a due diligence obligation varies depending on these factors. For example, the higher the risk and the graver the potential harm, the greater the

96 Report of the United Nations Conference on the Human Environment (Stockholm, 5–16 June 1972) UN Doc. A/CONF. 48/14/Rev.1, p. 5, principle 21; Report of the United Nations Conference on Environment and Development (Rio de Janeiro, 3–14 June 1992) UN Doc. A/CONF.151/26 (Vol. I), p. 1, principle 2.

97 *Legality of the Threat or Use of Nuclear Weapons* (Advisory Opinion) [1996] ICJ Rep. 226, para. 29.

98 V. Proulx, 'Babysitting Terrorists: Should States Be Strictly Liable for Failing to Prevent Transborder Attacks?' 23 Berkeley Journal of International Law (2005) 3: 659–660.

99 K. Trapp, *State Responsibility for International Terrorism* (Oxford University Press 2011) 64; R. Pisillo-Mazzeschi 1992 (n. 78) 34; ILC (2001) (n. 94) commentary to Article 3, para. 7.

100 *The Case of the S.S. Lotus* (*France v. Turkey*) (Judgement) [1927] PCIJ Rep Series A, No. 10, para. 269.

101 A. Coco, T. de Souza Diaz, 'Part I: Due Diligence and COVID-19: States' Duties to Prevent and Halt the Coronavirus Outbreak' EJIL:TALK! (24 March 2020).

102 J. Kulesza, *Due Diligence in International Law* (BRILL 2016) 2; ILC 2001 (n. 94) commentary to Article 3, para. 17.

103 V. Proulx 2005 (n. 98) 661–666; T. Becker, *Terrorism and the State: Rethinking the Rules of State Responsibility* (Hart Publishing 2006) 142.

effort that is required from states to prevent the harm from occurring.[104] However, states are not required to actually prevent the harm from taking place. Instead, they are required to take all reasonable and necessary measures to prevent the harm to their best capabilities.[105] This also means that the better, *inter alia*, logistical, financial, military or scientific capabilities a state has, the more is expected of its prevention efforts.[106] In other words, the due diligence obligation to prevent harm emanating from a state's own territory to another state is not one of result but rather one of conduct. Based on the foregoing, it can be concluded that the due diligence obligation to prevent FTF travel resulting from the no-harm principle does not require the same standard of conduct from every state. The intensity of the obligation may differentiate depending on a number of factors, including a state's capacity to act.

However, a state cannot evade the obligation to prevent harm by merely referring to a lack of capacity. It has been submitted that the due diligence standard actually imposes two distinct but coexisting duties upon states. On the one hand, it requires states to acquire and maintain, through reasonably available means, the necessary capacities, and on the other hand, the due diligence standard requires states to adequately use that capacity.[107] Trapp distinguishes three types of capacities which together form a state's total capacity to prevent: institutional capacity, which includes a legal regime; resources capacity, which includes in particular a state's financial, technical and human resources necessary to use its institutional capacity; and territorial capacity, in the sense of a state's capacity to exert control over its territory.[108]

Besides the capacity of states, the due diligence obligation to prevent is, furthermore, subject to a state's knowledge. This does, however, not mean that a state can evade responsibility by claiming that it did not have actual or demonstrable knowledge about specific activities on its territory, as responsibility is also engaged when a state *should have known* about those activities.[109] Essential is actual or constructive notice that should have alarmed a state of activities against which it is required to take preventative measures.[110] When a (potentially) harmful activity is one in a series of such activities instead of being an isolated and unexpected event, a presumption is raised

104 ILC 2001 (n. 94) commentary to Article 3, para. 18.
105 V. Proulx 2005 (n. 98) 661.
106 *Ibid.* 662.
107 T. Becker 2006 (n. 103) 144; R. Pisillo-Mazzeschi 1992 (n. 78) 26.
108 K. Trapp 2011 (n. 99) 70–75.
109 *Ibid.* 133; *The Corfu Channel Case* 1949 (n. 95) 22.
110 T. Becker 2006 (n. 103) 134, 135.

that the state knew or at least should have known about the harmful activity.[111] This presumption is further strengthened when the conduct has an open or infamous character.[112]

As mentioned before, the no-harm principle has also been acknowledged with respect to counter-terrorism. A duty of preventing terrorist threats and activities has also explicitly been included in the majority of specialized international treaties addressing specific acts of terrorism, such as in Article 18 of the International Convention for the Suppression of the Financing of Terrorism and Article 15 of the International Convention for the Suppression of Terrorist Bombings.[113] As part of the no-harm principle, states are also under a general obligation to prevent acts of international terrorism, as this constitutes a particular type of harm that might emanate from its territory.[114] This obligation, which is similarly subject to a standard of due diligence,[115] has been invoked with regard to states which were accused of harboring, or being unable to act against terrorist or armed groups operating or launching terrorist attacks in another state.[116] For example, the obligation was invoked with regard to the Palestinian Liberation Organization in Tunisia, Al-Qaeda in Afghanistan and Hezbollah in Lebanon.[117] This general obligation to diligently prevent acts of international terrorism constitutes another basis for arguing that international law obliges states of origin to a standard of due diligence, to prevent aspirational FTFs from traveling to another state to join a terrorist group engaged in an armed conflict with the government of that state.[118]

111 *Ibid.*

112 *Ibid.*

113 International Convention for the Suppression of the Financing of Terrorism (adopted 9 December 1999, entered into force 10 April 2002) 2178 UNTS 197; International Convention for the Suppression of Terrorist Bombings (adopted 15 December 1997, entered into force 23 May 2001) 2149 UNTS 256.

114 K. Trapp 2011 (n. 99) 64; J. Kulesza 2016 (n. 102) 286.

115 K. Trapp 2011 (n. 99) 64; T. Becker 2006 (n. 103) 141; J. Kulesza 2016 (n. 102) 281; H. Duffy, *The 'War on Terror' and the Framework of International Law* (Cambridge University Press 2015) 90, 91.

116 S. Krähenmann 2014 (n. 78) 50.

117 *Ibid.*; T. Ruys, 'Crossing the Thin Blue Line: An Inquiry into Israel's Recourse to Self-Defense against Hezbollah' 43 Stanford Journal of International Law (2007) 2: 285; K. Trapp, 'Back to Basics: Necessity, Proportionality, and the Right of Self-Defence Against Non-State Terrorist Actors' 56 International & Comparative Law Quarterly (2007) 1: 148, 149. Some states have argued that if a territorial state is harboring, or unable or unwilling to act against, such terrorist groups, this entitles other states to resort to the use of force out of self-defense against such non-state actors.

118 See, also, S. Krähenmann 2016 (n. 3) 233.

A number of elements of this obligation to diligently prevent FTF travel as part of the broader no-harm-principle, deserve some clarification.

First, the element of harm or a risk of harm potentially resulting from FTF travel. As explained in the previous sub-section, FTFs may instigate or exacerbate civil unrest, revolt or civil strife in states of destination, and may influence the outcome, intensity, duration and intractability of conflicts. Based on a study by Quinn and Shrader from 2005, Malet notes that "although transnational insurgents comprised less than 10 percent of the Iraqi resistance, they were responsible for more than 90 percent of suicide bombings and high-lethality attacks".[119] Therefore, it can be said that FTFs can inflict harm on states of destination and those neighboring the conflict zone.[120] In addition, FTF travel poses a serious threat of harm not only to states of destination and states neighboring zones of armed conflict but, as the Security Council acknowledged, also to states of transit and "all regions and Member States, even those far away from the conflict zones".[121] The impact of FTFs may extend beyond the conflict in Syria and Iraq, as some fighters may travel to other states after the conflict or to future armed conflicts.[122] For example, many foreign fighters who were involved in the Soviet invasion of Afghanistan, later moved to other conflict zones, including in the Middle East.[123] It can thus be said that FTFs traveling to Syria and Iraq are capable of inflicting harm or at least a threat of harm to states of destination, and potentially to even more states in the region and beyond.

Second, the knowledge element of the obligation to diligently prevent FTF travel. After the 9/11 attacks, it could be said that an environment of continuous international terrorist threats and activities together with extensive media exposure and resolutions by the Security Council have built an ongoing level of notice of, and therefore also knowledge of, the threat of international terrorism into the counter-terrorism system.[124] This makes it more difficult for states to claim that they did not have actual or constructive knowledge of the threat posed by international terrorism. On the one hand, the same conclusion on the reach of the knowledge element could potentially be drawn with

---

119 D. Malet 2013 (n. 2) 6.

120 UNSC Res. 2178 (2014) (n. 16) pre-ambular para. 10; See, also S. Krähenmann, 'Foreign-fighters, Terrorism and Counter-terrorism' in B. Saul (ed.), *Research Handbook on International Law and Terrorism* (2nd edition, Edward Elgar Publishing 2020) 240; UNGA 2015 (n. 81) para. 44.

121 UNSC Res. 2178 (2014) (n. 16) pre-ambular para. 10.

122 UNGA 2015 (n. 81) para. 45.

123 *Ibid.*

124 T. Becker 2006 (n. 103) 135; K. Trapp 2011 (n. 99) 66.

strict.[136] Many of these definitions are incompatible with each other and critiqued for various reasons.[137] One way to construe the precautionary principle is if and when a threat of serious or irreparable harm arises, a lack of certainty on the occurrence of the harm cannot apply as a reason not to take preventative measures.[138] The principle therefore extends beyond only taking preventative measures when it has sufficiently been established that the harm will actually occur or has already occurred. As Borgers and van Sliedregt stated, the central idea of the precautionary principle "is that one must remain a step ahead of danger and subsequently take preventive measures, even if it is not certain whether the feared risk/danger will actually materialise".[139]

The precautionary principle has especially gained traction within the field of environmental protection and public health. It received clear support in Principle 15 of the 1992 Rio Declaration, which states:

> In order to protect the environment, the precautionary approach shall be widely applied by States according to their capabilities. Where there are threats of serious or irreversible damage, lack of full scientific certainty shall not be used as a reason for postponing cost-effective measures to prevent environmental degradation.[140]

Some authors have even argued that within the field of environmental protection, the principle may have become part of customary international law.[141]

The precautionary principle also entered into debates within the field of terrorism, and has received increasing attention.[142] Preventative counter-terrorism measures fit within the logic of the precautionary principle.[143] There

---

136 *Ibid.* 18; See, in general, J. Morris, 'Defining the Precautionary Principle' in J. Morris (ed.), *Rethinking Risk and the Precautionary Principle* (Butterworth Heinemann 2000).

137 C. Sunstein 2005 (n. 135) 18–20; See, in general, J. Morris 2000 (n. 136).

138 M. Borgers and E. van Sliedregt, 'The Meaning of the Precautionary Principle for the Assessment of Criminal Measures in the Fight Against Terrorism' 2 Erasmus Law Review (2009) 2: 183; C. Sunstein 2005 (n. 135) 4; J. Stern and J. Wiener, 'Precaution Against Terrorism' 9 Journal of Risk Research (2006) 4: 394, 395.

139 M. Borgers and E. van Sliedregt 2009 (n. 138) 184.

140 1992 Rio Declaration (n. 96), Principle 15.

141 See, in general, O. McIntyre and T. Mosedale, 'The Precautionary Principle as a Norm of Customary International Law' 9 Journal of Environmental Law (1997) 2; A. Trouwborst, *Evolution and Status of the Precautionary Principle in International Law* (Kluwer Law International 2002) 33–55.

142 C. Sunstein 2005 (n. 135) 4; A. Trouwborst, 'Prevention, Precaution, Logic and Law: The Relationship Between the Precautionary Principle and the Preventative Principle in International Law and Associated Questions' 2 Erasmus Law Review (2009) 2: 113, 114.

143 J. Stern and J. Wiener 2006 (n. 138) 397, 398.

seems to be general agreement that the threat of terrorism is at least realistic, so there is a threat of serious harm caused by terrorism.[144] However, the probability of occurrence of a terrorist attack cannot be determined, let alone with full certainty.[145] Under the precautionary principle as described above, such a situation would certainly dictate preventative counter-terrorism measures, as such measures must be taken even if it is not certain whether the terrorist threat will actually materialize. The same can be said with regard to potential FTFs. There seems to be more or less consensus on the threat that FTFs can potentially pose, including to states of transit, states of destination and upon return to states of origin.[146] However, the probability of these individuals conducting a terrorist attack in either of these states or the extent to which they influence the conflict is uncertain. Again, a situation to which the precautionary principle speaks and which would dictate preventive measures.

As preventative counter-terrorism measures are often repressive in nature, applying the precautionary principle to prevent acts of terrorism might have (far-reaching) negative effects on, for example, individual's human rights and fundamental freedoms.[147] In the context of preventing the travel of FTFs one could think of restrictions on freedom of movement, the right to private and family life, and the right to liberty. This is also the reason why some authors are critical about the principle, as such a precautionary approach might produce harm which otherwise would not have occurred and hence, in the words of Sunstein, "the principle bans what it simultaneously mandates".[148] It is possible that a strict application of the precautionary principle to prevent terrorism, including in order to prevent potential FTFs from traveling, would have undesirable consequences from a human rights perspective and would pose an equal or even greater harm or risk thereof to the individual.[149] This discussion also relates to the question, posed in the introduction to the present chapter, what the limits are to a potential obligation upon states to prevent their

---

144 M. Borgers and E. van Sliedregt 2009 (n. 138) 187; As of December 2019 the Dutch National Coordinator for Security and Counterterrorism (NCTV) determined the terrorism threat level in the Netherlands to be 3 on a scale of 1 to 5, which means that the possibility of a terrorist attack is significant. See <https://www.nctv.nl/onderwerpen/dtn> accessed 18 March 2022.

145 M. Borgers and E. van Sliedregt 2009 (n. 138) 188.

146 S. Krähenmann 2016 (n. 3) 230, 231.

147 G. Lennon, 'Precautionary tales: Suspicionless counterterrorism stop and search' 15 Criminology & Criminal Justice (2015) 1: 46, 54–57.

148 C. Sunstein 2005 (n. 135) 14, 15, 29.

149 J. Stern and J. Wiener (n. 138) 398; M. Borgers, *De vlucht naar voren* (Boom Juridische uitgevers 2007) 17.

nationals and residents from traveling, when they are suspected of potentially becoming FTFs.

In sum, this sub-section certainly did not try to argue that the precautionary principle applies within the field of terrorism like it does within the field of environmental protection, or that this would necessarily be desirable. Nor does this sub-section argue that an obligation to prevent FTF travel can be read into the precautionary principle itself. It can be concluded that although measures to prevent FTFs from traveling fit within the logic of the principle, the application of this principle to preventing FTF travel may be undesirable from a human rights perspective. Nevertheless, the precautionary principle shapes the debate about harm, risks of harm and security, and therefore provides a viewpoint which might be considered, and to which connection can be sought, when assessing a duty to diligently prevent prospective FTFs from departing a state's territory.

The duty to prevent potential FTFs from traveling has been reaffirmed and further developed in a number of Security Council resolutions. Those resolutions will be discussed in the next part of this chapter.

3 The Obligation to Prevent Travel in United Nations Security Council Resolutions

This section will examine a number of Security Council resolutions relevant for the obligation to prevent FTF travel. In particular, Resolutions 1373 (2001), 2170 (2014) and 2178 (2014) will be examined. The latter two specifically address the phenomenon of FTFs traveling to Syria and Iraq. Through a discussion of those Resolutions, it will be shown that the Security Council reaffirmed and further shaped the obligation to prevent FTF travel. But before we turn to the Resolutions adopted by the Security Council, it is necessary to briefly touch upon the Security Council's role in countering terrorism.

3.1 The Security Council and Counter-terrorism

Initially, the international legal framework to counter-terrorism was dominated by specialized, often described as 'sectoral', treaties adopted as of the 1960s.[150] These treaties require states to criminalize specific acts or manifes-

150 H. Duffy and L. van den Herik, 'Terrorism and the Security Council' in R. Geiß and N. Melzer (eds.), *The Oxford Handbook on the International Law of Global Security*

tations of terrorism, such as the hijacking of planes,[151] hostage-taking or terrorist financing,[152] to establish jurisdiction over such specific offences, and to cooperate in the investigation and prosecution or extradition (*aut dedere aut judicare*) of individual suspects. However, after the 9/11 attacks, this predominant conventional approach to terrorism shifted and the Security Council took up a central role in countering terrorism on the international level. This role of the Security Council within the field of counter-terrorism consists of two components.

First, this role is substantiated through its sanctions regimes, including its 1267/1989/2253 IS and Al-Qaeda sanctions regime.[153] This regime requires states to take a number of restrictive measures with respect to IS, Al-Qaeda and other individuals, groups, undertakings and entities associated with them, as designated on the IS and Al-Qaeda sanctions list.[154] These measures include the imposition of a travel ban.[155] Notably, the responsibilities surrounding the implementation of such a travel ban rest on states of entry and transit, rather than on states of origin.[156] In Resolutions 2170 (2014) and 2178 (2014) the Security Council confirmed that FTFs and individuals associated with their recruit-

---

(Oxford University Press 2021) 193; B. Saul, 'Preface' in B. Saul (ed.), *Research Handbook on International Law and Terrorism* (2nd edition Edward Elgar Publishing 2020) p. xxiii.

151 Convention for the Suppression of Unlawful Seizure of Aircraft (adopted 16 December 1970, entered into force 14 October 1971) 806 UNTS 105.

152 International Convention Against the Taking of Hostages (adopted 17 December 1979, entered into force 3 June 1983) 1316 UNTS 205.

153 The 1267 UN sanctions regime was established by UNSC Resolution 1267 (1999) to impose sanctions on designated individuals and entities associated with the Taliban. UNSC Res. 1267 (15 October 1999) UN Doc. S/RES/1267 (1999). Later, the 1267 sanctions regime was expanded to cover the threat posed by Al-Qaeda. Thereafter, this sanctions regime was split into two separate regimes, one established pursuant to Resolution 1988 (2011) covering the Taliban (the 1988 sanctions regime) and the other pursuant to Resolution 1989 (2011) covering Al-Qaeda (the 1989 sanctions regime). UNSC Res. 1988 (17 June 2011) UN Doc. S/RES/1988 (2011) and UNSC Res. 1989 (17 June 2011) UN Doc. S/RES/1989 (2011). In 2015, the 1989 sanctions regime was expanded by Resolution 2253 to cover IS. UNSC Res. 2253 (17 December 2015) UN Doc. S/RES/2253 (2015). Therefore, this sanctions regime has been referred to as the 1267/1989/2253 ISIL (Da'esh) and Al-Qaeda sanctions regime.

154 The list of individuals, groups, undertakings and entities associated with IS and Al-Qaeda is available at: <https://www.un.org/securitycouncil/sanctions/1267/aq_sanctions_list> accessed 28 January 2022.

155 UNSC Res. 2610 (17 December 2021) UN Doc. S/RES/2610 (2021), para. 1.

156 IS and Al-Qaida Sanctions Committee, Travel ban: explanation of terms (approved on 24 February 2015). Available at: <https://www.un.org/securitycouncil/sites/www.un.org.securitycouncil/files/eot_travel_ban_english.pdf> accessed 2 February 2022.

to prevent the movement of terrorists or terrorist groups, in accordance with applicable international law, among others, by effective border controls and exchange of information.[169] Thereafter, the Security Council encourages states to dissuade FTFs from traveling to Syria and Iraq.[170] However, Resolution 2170 (2014) mostly reiterated obligations already enshrined in Resolution 1373 (2001). By contrast, Resolution 2178 (2014) did introduce a new set of binding obligations upon states.

Resolution 2178 was adopted on 24 September 2014, also by unanimous vote. In addition to adopting new obligations, the Security Council also gave a definition to the term 'foreign terrorist fighters', which was missing in Resolution 2170 (2014). This definition and some of the critiques that it has generated have been described in the introduction to this research. In Resolution 2178 (2014), the Security Council expressed its concern about those who (attempt to) travel to become FTFs and emphasized the global nature of the threat.[171] The Security Council recognized that in order to tackle this worldwide threat, states must address underlying factors and inhibit FTF travel. The Resolution reaffirms the obligation upon states of origin to prevent the departure of FTFs. First, by reaffirming the obligation to prevent the movement of terrorists.[172] Second, paragraph 4 of the Resolution acknowledges the obligation to prevent the departure of FTFs, containing the obligation to prevent FTFs from crossing states' borders. Besides merely imposing the obligation to prevent FTFs from crossing states' borders, the Security Council also provides that, as part of this obligation, states are required to "prevent and suppress the recruiting, organizing, transporting or equipping of [FTFs], and the financing of their travel and of their activities".[173] In order to do so, the Security Council requires states to criminalize travel for terrorist purposes in their national legislation. It requires states to have the necessary legislation in place to prosecute and penalize:

> "(a) their nationals who travel or attempt to travel to a State other than their States of residence or nationality, and other individuals who travel or attempt to travel from their territories to a State other than their States of residence or nationality, for the purpose of the perpetration, planning or preparation of, or participation in, terrorist acts, or the providing or receiving of terrorist training;

169 *Ibid.*
170 *Ibid.* para. 9.
171 UNSC Res. 2178 (2014) (n. 16) pre-ambular paras. 9, 10.
172 *Ibid.* para. 2.
173 *Ibid.* para. 5.

(b) the willful provision or collection, by any means, directly or indirectly, of funds by their nationals or in their territories with the intention that the funds should be used, or in the knowledge that they are to be used, in order to finance the travel of individuals who travel to a State other than their States of residence or nationality for the purpose of the perpetration, planning or preparation of, or participation in, terrorist acts or the providing or receiving of terrorist training; and,

(c) the willful organization, or other facilitation, including acts of recruitment, by their nationals or in their territories, of the travel of individuals who travel to a State other than their States of residence or nationality for the purpose of the perpetration, planning or preparation of, or participation in, terrorist acts or the providing or receiving of terrorist training".[174]

Therefore, Resolution 2178 (2014) not only reaffirms the obligation to prevent FTF travel but also requires states to *criminalize* travel, financing, organization and facilitation of travel.

It should be noted that the above-cited paragraph 6 has been described as 'the most alarming provision' of the Resolution.[175] The paragraph has been criticized for being too broad, as all preparatory acts are included, no matter how remote they are from an actual terrorist offence.[176] And although Resolution 2178 (2014), like Resolution 2170 (2014), requires member states to implement their obligations in consistency with international human rights law, international refugee law, and IHL,[177] paragraph 6 of the Resolution has been criticized for the impact it has on individual's rights and fundamental freedoms, such as freedom of movement, freedom of entry into a state and the right to return to one's own country.[178] This is exacerbated by the definitional deficits surrounding the concept of an FTF, as elaborated upon in the introduction to this study. Uncertainties surrounding the definition of an

174 *Ibid.* para. 6.

175 M. Scheinin, 'Back to post-9/11 panic? Security Council resolution on foreign terrorist fighters' Just Security (23 September 2014).

176 F. Capone, 'Countering "Foreign Terrorist Fighters": a Critical Appraisal of the Framework Established by the UN Security Council Resolutions' 25 The Italian Yearbook of International Law (2016) 1: 249.

177 UNSC Res. 2178 (2014) (n. 16) pre-ambular para. 7.

178 A. Conte, 'States' Prevention and Responses to the Phenomenon of Foreign Fighters against the Backdrop of International Human Rights Obligations' in A. de Guttry, F. Capone and C. Paulussen (eds.) 2016 (n. 3) 285, 286.

FTF, create uncertainties as to whose foreign travel is to be prevented and criminalized and whose foreign travel should rather be facilitated.

In addition, it is uncertain whose interests are to be protected by preventing and criminalizing travel. The interests of states of origin? States of destination? Or perhaps also the interests of transit states or states who are otherwise affected? Nevertheless, states have criminalized the act of traveling abroad for terrorist purposes in different ways in their national legislation. A number of the criminal measures taken by states of origin in order to comply with the above cited paragraph 6 of Resolution 2178 (2014) will be discussed in section 4.1.

As shown, the obligation to prevent FTF travel is one of due diligence. Hence, the obligation to criminalize, prosecute and penalize FTF travel and related activities, is only one part of a state's obligation to diligently prevent travel. The Security Council imposes several other obligations and recommendations upon states in order to prevent FTFs from traveling. Those pertain to border controls, controls on issuance of identity papers and travel documents, evidence based traveler risk assessments and screening procedures, exchange of operational information regarding actions or movements of terrorists or terrorist networks, cooperation in their efforts to address the threat posed by FTFs, listing on the IS and Al-Qaeda sanctions list, requiring airlines to provide advance passenger information and affording one another the greatest measure of assistance in connection with criminal investigations or proceedings.[179] Notably, in a subsequent resolution in response to the FTFs phenomenon in Syria and Iraq, Resolution 2396 (2017), the Security Council used binding language and thus imposed legally binding obligations upon states with regard to the use of advance passenger information systems, passenger name record data, watch lists of known and suspected terrorists, and systems to collect biometric data. In addition to the criminal measures taken by states, in order to adhere to the full scope of the obligation to prevent FTF travel, states have thus also taken a wide range of other types of measures. In section 4.2, the research will in particular delve into a number of administrative measures taken by states of origin.

What should finally be mentioned is that, although this research focuses upon states of origin, Resolution 2178 (2014) also explicitly contains an obligation to prevent the entry and transit of FTFs. Therefore, the Resolution does not only impose an obligation upon states of origin but also upon states of transit and states of destination.[180]

---

179 UNSC Res. 2178 (2014) (n. 16) paras. 2–4, 7, 9, 11, 12.

180 *Ibid.* paras. 8, 11.

Now that it has been established that the Security Council reaffirmed the obligation to diligently prevent FTF travel in a number of binding Resolutions, the next section will examine what legal measures states, and particularly Australia, have taken in order to comply with these Resolutions and the obligation to diligently prevent FTF travel contained in it.

4 The Implementation of the Obligation to Prevent Travel

States have taken a wide variety of measures in order to prevent and repress aspirational FTFs from departing their territory. This section will focus on the *legal* measures that states have taken, with a focus on those adopted by Australia. Furthermore, two types of legal measures will be concentrated upon, criminal measures and administrative measures, as those are interesting to look at from a legal perspective and most relevant for the present research. This section will certainly not discuss all legal measures that have been adopted by states in their effort to prevent FTFs from departing their territory. Rather, the section aims to give an idea of the various legal measures taken by zeroing in on a few of them.

4.1 Criminal Measures

The term 'criminal measures' refers to repressive measures taken on the basis of a state's national criminal laws. At the start of the phenomenon of FTFs traveling to Syria and Iraq, there was a lack of national criminal laws to prosecute those individuals and existing criminal laws were not sufficient to prevent FTF travel.[181] However, as a response to their nationals traveling to Syria and Iraq, states have introduced new offenses in their criminal laws. It is important to note from the outset that in this sub-section, criminalization of FTF travel will be discussed as a preventative measure and that the criminal prosecution of FTFs will be discussed later in Chapter 5 of this study.

As expressly required by Resolution 2178 (2014), states have criminalized FTF travel as part of their obligation to prevent such travel. However, they have done so in different ways. Some states have implemented autonomous crimes in their national laws, by explicitly criminalizing the act of travel for terrorist purposes. For example, Canada enacted a number of offences which criminalizes departing, or attempt to depart Canadian territory for the pur-

181 UNSC, 'Implementation of Security Council Resolution 2178 (2014) by States Affected by Foreign Terrorist Fighters' UN Doc S/2015/338, Annex, summary para. 4.

pose of participating in activity of a terrorist group,[182] facilitating terrorist activity,[183] committing an offence for a terrorist group,[184] or committing an offence that is terrorist activity.[185] Belgium has a similar provision in Article 140sexies of its Penal Code, criminalizing departure of Belgian territory for the purpose of committing or participating in a terrorist activity. Likewise, Germany amended Section 89a of its Criminal Code to criminalize leaving Germany for the purpose of committing a serious offence endangering the state or for the purpose of receiving terrorist training. Besides autonomous crimes, states have also used terrorist crimes to capture FTF travel, such as joining a terrorist organization and receiving training for terrorist purposes. For example in the Netherlands, provisions that are used to capture FTF travel include the prohibition to provide support to or to participate in a terrorist organization,[186] and assistance to (preparing) a terrorist crime.[187] Likewise, the US prosecuted aspirational FTFs, who were preparing to travel to the conflict zone, for the existing terrorist crime of attempting to provide material support to a listed terrorist organization.[188] Some states also used common crimes to deal with the FTF issue and prevent them from traveling. For example, the Netherlands used the crimes of preparing to commit an act of arson or an explosion as well as preparing to commit murder to prosecute aspiring FTFs.[189]

Like Canada, Belgium and Germany, Australia adopted an autonomous crime to criminalize FTF travel in its national laws. In Australia's national legislation, the crime that captures FTF travel can be found in Part 5.5, Section 119.1(1) of its Criminal Code, which was incorporated by the 2014 Foreign Fighters Amendment Act in order "to respond to the foreign fighter threat".[190]

---

182 Canadian Criminal Code R.S.C. 1985 c. C-46 (Canadian Criminal Code), Part II.1 (Terrorism), Section 83.181 (Leaving Canada to participate in activity of terrorist group).

183 *Ibid.* Section 83.191 (Leaving Canada to facilitate terrorist activity).

184 *Ibid.* Section 83.201 (Leaving Canada to commit offence for terrorist group).

185 *Ibid.* Section 83.202 (Leaving Canada to commit offence that is terrorist activity).

186 Dutch Criminal Code 1881, Article 140a.

187 *Ibid.* Article 134a.

188 US Department of Justice, Office of Public Affairs, California Man Sentenced to 12 Years in Prison for Attempting to Join ISIL (7 June 2016). Available at: <https://www.justice.gov/opa/pr/california-man-sentenced-12-years-prison-attempting-join-isil> accessed 26 November 2024.

189 District Court of Rotterdam, ECLI:NL:RBROT:2013:8266 (23 October 2013); District Court of Rotterdam, ECLI:NL:RBROT:2013:8265 (23 October 2013).

190 The Parliament of the Commonwealth of Australia, Counter-Terrorism Legislation Amendment (Foreign Fighters) Bill 2014, Replacement Explanatory Memorandum, para. 2. Available at: <https://www.aph.gov.au/Parliamentary_Business/Bills_Legislation/Bills_Search_Results/Result?bId=s976> accessed 11 April 2022.

This provision criminalizes, under the offence of foreign incursion and subject to a penalty of imprisonment for life, the entering of a foreign country with an intention to engage in hostile activities, unless serving in or with the armed forces of the government of a foreign country.[191] The Foreign Fighters Amendment Act, which amended more than 20 laws, removed the need to prove the intention to engage in hostile activities in a *particular* foreign country, by making it an offence to engage in such activities in *any* foreign country. Beside the offence of foreign incursion itself, preparations for incursions into foreign countries, as well as preparing another person, for instance through providing training, for the purpose of engaging in hostile activities, is also criminalized as per Section 119.4. Furthermore, not only is entering a foreign country with the intent to engage in a hostile activities illegal, the actual engagement in hostile activities is also illegal.[192] In all of these provisions, contained in Part 5.5 of the Criminal Code, the term 'engage in hostile activities' means the following:

> a person ***engages in a hostile activity*** in a foreign country if the person engages in conduct in that country with the intention of achieving one or more of the following objectives (whether or not such an objective is achieved): (a) the overthrow by force or violence of the government of that or any other foreign country (or of a part of that or any other foreign country); (b) the engagement, by that or any other person, in action that: (i) falls within subsection 100.1(2) but does not fall within subsection 100.1(3); and (ii) if engaged in in Australia, would constitute a serious offence; (c) intimidating the public or a section of the public of that or any other foreign country; (d) causing the death of, or bodily injury to, a person who is the head of state of that or any other foreign country, or holds, or performs any of the duties of, a public office of that or any other foreign country (or of a part of that or any other foreign country); (e) unlawfully destroying or damaging any real or personal property belonging to the government of that or any other foreign country (or of a part of that or any other foreign country).[193]

---

191 According to Section 119.1(1)(b) this is only the case "when the person enters the country, the person: (i) is an Australian citizen; or (ii) is a resident of Australia; or (iii) is a holder under the *Migration Act 1958* of a visa; or (iv) has voluntarily put himself or herself under the protection of Australia". Although the offence is subjected to a penalty of life imprisonment, most cases have led to a (much) lower sentence.

192 Australian Criminal Code Part 5.5, Section 119.1(2).

193 Australian Criminal Code Part 5.5, Section 117.1(1).

Conversely, when the individual enlists on the side of a foreign government with which the Commonwealth or the Australian Defense Force is not at war,[194] the act of enlisting is not illegal under Australian law.[195]

However, Australia's Autonomous Sanctions Act 2011 supplements the Criminal Code, criminalizing fighting for the Syrian Government. The Autonomous Sanctions Regulation 2011 imposes autonomous sanctions in relation to Syria "to reflect Australia's grave concern at the Syrian regime's deeply disturbing and unacceptable use of violence against its people".[196] As part of this Syrian sanctions regime it is prohibited to provide services to Syria which relate to a military activity.[197] According to the Attorney General's Department and the Department of Foreign Affairs and Trade, this prohibition is broad enough to capture fighting for the Syrian Government.[198] Therefore, traveling to Syria to fight on the side of the Syrian Government is unlawful under its unilateral sanctions law.[199] Australia's criminal law together with its unilateral sanctions law has the effect of criminalizing foreign fighting with insurgencies in Syria and Iraq as well as fighting for the Syrian Government. As Australia has criminalized foreign fighting as such, it goes beyond only criminalizing FTF travel. In other words, further than travel "for the purpose of the perpetration, planning, or preparation of, or participation in, terrorist acts or the providing or receiving of terrorist training, including in connection with armed conflict".[200] Therefore, this approach is considerably broad compared to other states' legal measures to prevent travel as illustrated above.

Australia's approach to criminalize FTF travel is even more expansive, since it has also incorporated a 'declared area offence'.[201] The declared area offence

---

194 The Australian Criminal Code Part 5.1, Section 80.1AA stipulates that enlisting with the armed forces of a foreign country with which the Commonwealth or the Australian Defense Force is at war is criminalized, under the crime of treason, and subjected to a sentence of imprisonment for life.

195 Australian Criminal Code Part 5.5, Section 119.1(4).

196 Australian Government, Department of Foreign Affairs and Trade, 'Syria sanctions regime'. Available at: <https://www.dfat.gov.au/international-relations/security/sanctions/sanctions-regimes/syria-sanctions-regime> accessed 4 April 2022.

197 Autonomous Sanctions Regulations 2011, Regulation 5.

198 Australian Government, Independent National Security Legislation Monitor, Annual Report 2014 (28 March 2014) 26, 27; C. Forcese and A. Mamikon 2015 (n. 41) 322.

199 Australian Federal Police, 'Fighting Terrorism Overseas' available at: <https://www.afp.gov.au/what-we-do/crime-types/fighting-terrorism/fighting-terrorism-overseas> accessed 5 April 2022.

200 UNSC Res. 2170 (2014) (n. 125) pre-ambular para 8; B. Saul, 'Australia and International Counter-Terrorism Law and Practice' Sydney Law School Legal Studies Research Paper No. 16/41 (16 May 2016) 15.

201 Australian Criminal Code Part 5.5 Section 119.2.

criminalizes the entering, or remaining, in a declared area, subjected to a sentence of imprisonment for 10 years.[202] Australia was the first state enacting such an offence. According to Section 119.3, the Foreign Affairs Minister may declare an area in a foreign country "if he or she is satisfied that a listed terrorist organisation is engaging in a hostile activity in that area of the foreign country".[203] Among other organizations, Al Qaeda, IS, Jabhat Fatah al-Sham (formerly listed as Jabhat al-Nusra) and the Kurdistan Workers' Party (PKK) are listed as terrorist organizations under the Criminal Code.[204] Currently, there are no declared areas in effect.[205] However, between 2 March 2015 and 19 December 2019, the Mosul district in the Ninewa province of Iraq was declared as an area where a listed terrorist organization, namely IS, was engaging in hostile activities. Between 4 December 2014 and 29 November 2017 the al-Raqqa province in Syria, IS's *de facto* capital from which it's operations were largely directed,[206] was declared as such an area.[207] Within these periods of time, Australian citizens or residents who entered or remained in these areas were subject to possible investigation, arrest and prosecution by Australian authorities.[208] Besides Australia, there are two other states which have similar area offences in their national legislations. Denmark enacted such an offence

---

202 Unless the person enters or remains in the declared area for a number of legitimate purposes contained in Section 119.2(3) and (4), such as providing aid of a humanitarian nature, making a news report of events in the area or making a *bona fide* visit to a family member.

203 Australian Criminal Code Part 5.5 Section 119.3(1).

204 Australian Government, Australian National Security, 'Listed Terrorist Organizations'. Available at: <https://www.nationalsecurity.gov.au/what-australia-is-doing/terrorist-organisations/listed-terrorist-organisations> accessed 30 March 2022.

205 Australian Government, Australian National Security, 'Current declared areas'. Available at: <https://www.nationalsecurity.gov.au/what-australia-is-doing/places-you-cant-go/current-declared-areas> accessed 30 March 2022.

206 Australian minister for Foreign Affairs, 'Declaration of Al-Raqqa Province in Syria', media release (4 December 2014). Available at: <https://www.foreignminister.gov.au/minister/julie-bishop/media-release/declaration-al-raqqa-province-syria> accessed 30 March 2022.

207 Australian minister for Foreign Affairs, 'Declaration of Al-Raqqa Province in Syria', media release (4 December 2014). Available at: <https://www.foreignminister.gov.au/minister/julie-bishop/media-release/declaration-al-raqqa-province-syria> accessed 30 March 2022.

208 Or those who are holders under the *Migration Act 1958* of a visa or who voluntarily put themselves under the protection of Australia, see Australian Criminal Code Act 1995, Section 119.2(1).

in 2016 and the UK in 2019.[209] In the Netherlands, a declared area offence has also been under discussion.[210]

This criminal measure goes beyond what is required by the obligation to prevent FTF travel under international law, because the offence does not only aim to prevent FTFs from traveling, but due to its broad formulation, it prevents all individuals from traveling to the declared area, irrespective of a terrorist intent and irrespective of the individual's intended or actual conduct in the area. Furthermore, the offence lies deeply in the pre-crime sphere as it is far removed from actual criminal conduct.[211] A positive consequence of this broad formulation is, however, that it removes many evidentiary challenges in investigations and prosecutions.[212] First, because it is not necessary to prove the intent of the suspect to engage in or support terrorist activity. Second, because it is not necessary to prove what exactly the person has done in the area he or she traveled to or stayed in. Despite this positive consequence from an evidentiary point of view, there is much criticism on the declared area offence. Such criticism includes concerns about the necessity and proportionality of the offence in relation to its limiting effect on the right to freedom of movement and other fundamental human rights, and concerns relating to the access to declared areas by certain actors, such as journalists and those who provide aid of a humanitarian nature.[213] Nevertheless, in 2024 the operation of the declared area provisions was extended for a further 3 years.[214]

---

209 See, with regard to the United Kingdom's Declared Area Offence, T. Gherbaoui, *Europe's Foreign Fighter Conundrum: Legal Responses, the Rule of Law, and Human Rights* (T.M.C. Asser Press 2025) 143–148.

210 Letter from the Dutch Ministry of Justice to the Senate, 'Wetsvoorstel strafbaarstelling verblijf in een door een terroristische organisatie gecontroleerd gebied (35 125)' 12 May 2021. Available at <https://www.rijksoverheid.nl/documenten/kamerstukken/2021/05/12/tk-wetsvoorstel-strafbaarstelling-verblijf-in-een-door-een-terroristische-organisatie-gecontroleerd-gebied-35-125> accessed 6 April 2022.

211 C. Paulussen and E. Gillard, 'Staying in an Area Controlled by a Terrorist Organisation: Crime or Operational Necessity?' ICCT Perspective (11 January 2021).

212 Letter from the Dutch Ministry of Justice to the Senate (2021) (n. 210); J. Ip 2020 (n. 50) 130, 131.

213 C. Paulussen and E. Gillard 2021 (n. 211); J. Ip 2020 (n. 50) 128–130; Australian Human Rights Commission, 'Independent National Security Legislation Monitor (INSLM) Statutory Deadline Review: Australian Human Rights Commission Submission to the Acting INSLM' (15 May 2017) 10–14; Australian Human Rights Commission, 'Review of the 'declared areas' provisions: Australian Human Rights Commission Supplementary Submission to the PJCIS' (3 November 2017), both available at: <https://www.aph.gov.au/Parliamentary_Business/Committees/Joint/Intelligence_and_Security/DeclaredAreasProvisions/Submissions> accessed 6 April 2022.

214 Australian Counter-Terrorism Legislation Amendment (Declared Areas) Bill 2024, adopted on 2 September 2024.

Furthermore, in a case before the European Court of Human Rights (ECtHR) against Denmark, the question arose whether the Danish declared area offence unlawfully interfered with the right to freedom of movement as laid down in Article 2 of Additional Protocol 4 to the European Convention for the Protection of Human Rights and Fundamental Freedoms (ECHR).[215] The Court concluded that there was no unlawful interference and emphasized that the restriction served the legitimate purpose "of ensuring that persons who were Danish nationals or habitually resident within the Danish State did not independently join any of the parties to the ongoing armed conflict and pose a threat to society upon their return to Denmark".[216] Thus, placing a focus on Danish national security and the potential threat upon return.

What can be concluded is that this declared area offence as well as some provisions criminalizing, or used to criminalize FTF travel reach far in the pre-crime sphere and some of them, including the declared area offence, have quite far-reaching consequences for the individual's human rights. In addition to the criminalization of travel in states' domestic legislation, in order to adhere to the full scope of the obligation to prevent FTF travel, states have also taken a wide range of administrative measures, to which we will turn now.

4.2 Administrative Measures

The term 'administrative measures' does not have an established meaning at the international level.[217] Nor can the term be equated with the domestic concept of administrative law, since the contours of that concept vary in different national legal systems.[218] Boutin, however, proposes the following definition of 'administrative measures' within the counter-terrorism context: "[r]estrictive measures aimed at preventing terrorism within the territory of a state, decided upon and ordered by the executive (or with its close involvement), and subject to limited judicial review".[219] Examples of administrative measures taken in order to prevent FTF travel include travel bans and other types of travel restrictions, freezing of assets, preventative detention, and the invalidation of passports and identity cards. Such administrative measures are subject to less guarantees than the aforementioned criminal law meas-

215 *Case of Mørck Jensen v. Denmark* [2023] (Judgement) ECtHR App. No. 60785/19 (18 January 2023); ECHR (signed 4 November 1950, entered into force 3 September 1953) ETS 5.
216 *Case of Mørck Jensen v. Denmark* (n. 215) para. 67.
217 B. Boutin, 'Administrative Measures against Foreign Fighters: In Search of Limits and Safeguards' ICCT Research Paper (December 2016) 4.
218 *Ibid.*
219 *Ibid.* 5.

ures, as they are not subject to the procedures and guarantees of criminal prosecution, such as fair trial guarantees, opportunities to challenge, judicial review, high standards of proof, and there is often limited or no information concerning the basis of the measures due to security reasons.[220] Administrative measures can potentially have far-reaching effects on the protection of not only a person's procedural human rights but also its substantive human rights, such as the right to freedom of movement, the right to liberty and security of person, and the right to private and family life. Initially, administrative measures had a primarily preventative function, as they were mainly aimed at protecting the public by disrupting terrorist activity.[221] However, administrative measures are increasingly used as a repressive tool or sanction instead of a preventive tool, when it is suspected that an individual is involved in terrorism (related) activities but there is a lack of evidence to bring criminal charges against the individual.[222]

Just like the variety of criminal measures, states have also adopted a myriad of administrative measures, a number of which will be highlighted in this subsection. In accordance with the obligation to prevent the movement of terrorists or terrorist groups by effective border controls and controls on the issuance of identity papers and travel documents, imposed by Security Council Resolution 2178 (2014),[223] a common administrative measure used by states is the imposition of travel bans through the invalidation of passports or identity cards. For example, France allows the Minister of Interior to ban a person from leaving French territory when there are serious reasons to believe that the person is (1) planning to travel abroad for the purpose of participating in terrorist activities; or (2) travel abroad to an area where terrorist groups operate and in conditions conducive to the person posing a threat to public security upon return to French territory.[224]

---

220 *Ibid.* 19–20; H. Duffy, "Foreign Terrorist Fighters": A Human Rights Approach?' 29 Security and Human Rights (2018) 148, 149; M. van Noorloos, 'Legal Regulation of Subversive Expressions in Relation to Terrorist Travel: The Dutch Situation Against the Backdrop of International Human Rights Law' in F. Capone, C. Paulussen and R. Mignot-Mahdavi (eds.), *Returning Foreign Fighters: Responses, Legal Challenges and Ways Forward* (T.M.C. Asser Press 2023) 259.

221 B. Boutin 2016 (n. 217) 19.

222 *Ibid.* 19–21; C. Paulussen, 'Stripping foreign fighters of their citizenship: International human rights and humanitarian law considerations' 103 International Review of the Red Cross (2021) No. 916–917: 607, 608.

223 UNSC Res. 2178 (n. 16) para. 2.

224 *LOI n° 2014–1353 du 13 novembre 2014 renforçant les dispositions relatives à la lutte contre le terrorisme* (French Strengthening Provisions on the Fight Against Terrorism Law), Article 1.

Australia resorted to a similar administrative measure. As a response to individuals traveling to the conflict in Syria and Iraq, Australia resorted to refusing, suspending and canceling passports and other travel documents in order to prevent such travel. Under the Australian Passports Act 2005, a travel document may be refused or canceled for a number of reasons.[225] For example, a passport or other travel document may be refused or canceled where there are reasonable grounds to believe that the person might prejudice the security of Australia or a foreign country; might endanger the health or physical safety of other persons (whether in Australia or a foreign country); its conduct might constitute an indictable offence; or where the passport or travel document should be refused or canceled to prevent the person from engaging in such conduct.[226] Until June 2021, around 250 Australian passports have been canceled or refused in relation to the conflict in Syria and Iraq.[227] In addition, on request of the Australian Security Intelligence Organisation, an Australian person's passport and all other travel documents the person possesses, may be suspended for 28 days if it is suspected that the person may leave Australia to engage in conduct that might prejudice the security of Australia or a foreign country.[228]

Other administrative measures adopted by states to prevent the departure of aspirational FTFs include control orders, preventative detention, custom detention, nationality deprivation and other types of restrictions on freedom of movement. Nationality revocation is, however, primarily used as a measure to prevent FTFs from returning to their states of origin rather than preventing their departure and will be elaborated upon in the next chapter of this study. The other mentioned administrative measures will be discussed respectively. First, the control order. Under Australian law, a control order may be imposed for a number of purposes.[229] The Foreign Fighters Amendment Act introduced two additional grounds on which a control order may be requested. One of those grounds is when such an order would substantially assist in preventing the provision, support for or the facilitation of a terrorist act.[230] A control order may consist of certain obligations, prohibitions and restrictions.

---

225 Those reasons are set out in Part 2, Division 2 of the Australian Passports Act 2005.

226 Australian Passports Act 2005, Division 2(B)(14)(1)(a) and (b).

227 Australian government, Independent National Security Legislation Monitor, Annual Report 2020–2021 (7 December 2021) 54; See also B. Saul 2016 (n. 200) 1.

228 Australian Passports Act 2005, Division 3(22A)(2). This power to suspend an Australia's passport was incorporated in the Australian Passports Act 2005 by the Foreign Fighters Amendment Act.

229 Those purposes are set out in Part 5.3, Section 104.2(2) of the Australian Criminal Code.

230 Australian Criminal Code Part 5.3, Section 104.2(2)(c).

For example, a prohibition or restriction on the person leaving Australia or a requirement that the person be subject to electronic monitoring, e.g., by having to wear a monitoring device at all times.[231]

Second, the administrative measure of custom detention. The Australian Customs Act was amended by the Foreign Fighters Amendment Act to allow customs officers to detain a person if the officer is satisfied on reasonable grounds that the person is, or is likely to be, involved in an activity that is a threat to national security or the security of a foreign country.[232]

Finally, the issuance of preventative detention orders. Under Australian law, such an order allows a person to be detained for a short period of time in order to, among others, prevent a terrorist act that is capable of being carried out, and could occur within the next 14 days.[233] According to Saul, this measure is unnecessary because when grounds exist for the imposition of preventative detention

> it will almost always be the case that there would be evidence and grounds to charge the person with one or more of the many existing preparatory terrorism offences, or to hold the person for extended pre-charge questioning in terrorism matters under existing powers to gather further evidence.[234]

Furthermore, the measure of preventative detention received criticism for not being in compliance with states' international human rights obligations, including the right to liberty and security of person. In 2015, the French Government requested an opinion of the *Conseil d'État* (the French Council of State) on possibly implementing a preventative detention measure. The *Conseil d'État* advised that such a measure "would constitute a flagrant violation of fundamental rights guaranteed by the Constitution and by international human rights law".[235] Although only relatively few measures were discussed, what can be concluded from this sub-section is that some of them go quite far in restricting the individual's substantive and procedural human rights.

---

231 *Ibid.* Section 104.5A(3)(d).

232 Customs Act 1901, Section 219ZJCA.

233 *Ibid.* Section 105.1(a).

234 B. Saul, Submission to the PJCIS, Inquiry into the Counter-Terrorism Legislation Amendment (Foreign Fighters) Bill 2014, para. 4. Available at: <https://www.aph.gov.au/Parliamentary_Business/Committees/Joint/Intelligence_and_Security/Counter-Terrorism_Legislation_Amendment_Foreign_Fighters_Bill_2014/Submissions> accessed 12 April 2022.

235 B. Boutin 2016 (n. 217) 15, 16; Conseil d'État, Avis sur la constitutionnalité et la compatibilité avec les engagements internationaux de la France de certaines mesures de prévention du risque de terrorisme' No. 390867 (17 December 2015).

5 Conclusions

The obligation to prevent FTF travel has its foundation in the non-intervention and no-harm principles under general international law, which for their part have roots in the international law of neutrality. Both these principles form the basis within international law for imposing an obligation upon states of origin to diligently prevent FTFs from departing their territories. Furthermore, and especially because of its legal basis in these two principles, the obligation to prevent FTF travel is subject to a standard of due diligence. This implicates that states of origin are required to take all reasonable and necessary measures to their best capabilities. The obligation being one of due diligence also means that the standard of conduct required is flexible and varies depending on a number of factors, including a state's capacity to counter-terrorism. A number of Security Council resolutions, and in particular Resolution 2178 (2014), confirm the obligation upon states to prevent FTF travel.

Some of the measures that states have taken in order to implement this obligation go far in restricting the individual's human rights and fundamental freedoms. A possible explanation for this can be found in the fact that the scope of Resolution 2178 (2014) and, therefore, the obligations enshrined in it, are not entirely clear. The Resolution gives each member state 'sweeping latitude' to interpret the obligations enshrined in the Resolution without any geographical or time limit, and leaves it up to each member state to interpret the breath and contours of the concepts of 'terrorism' and 'foreign terrorist fighter'.[236] For the most part, the Resolution leaves it up to member states to choose the means through which the travel of FTFs is to be thwarted. This broad margin of appreciation left to states and the absence of legislative clarity creates a risk of abuse and a risk of significant human rights restrictions through the implementation of the Resolution. In that respect, it can be said that states can indeed also go too far in preventing the departure of their nationals.

This human rights dimension aside, what can be concluded from this chapter is that a state's prevention obligation should be viewed in light of the principles in which it finds its legal basis, as a focus on these international legal principles and associated obligations brings the perspective of states of ori-

236 Global Center on Cooperative Security, Human Security Collective and the ICCT, 'Addressing the Foreign Terrorist Fighters Phenomenon from a European Union Perspective: UN Security Council Resolution 2178, Legal Issues, and Challenges and Opportunities for EU Foreign Security and Development Policy' Policy brief (December 2014) 2.

gin's responsibilities and their actions and omissions in relation to other states more to the foreground. States have responded differently to foreign fighters and FTFs leaving their territory, depending on the side of the foreign conflict those individuals intended to join and political considerations in that regard. It is important to take into account that a lack of effort in taking steps to prevent the travel of FTFs, can inflict significant harm upon other states. Not only states of destination but also states of transit as well as other potentially affected states. Nevertheless, the security interests of other states, as well as potential harm posed upon them and their populations, do not seem to be properly taken into account by states of origin. At least, not to the extent required by the norms of public international law which form the legal basis of the obligation to diligently prevent FTF travel. Contrary to the counter-terrorism paradigm, the non-intervention principle as well as the no-harm principle, primarily refer to harm posed to the foreign state. States of origin should be more aware of the inter-state dimension to their obligation to prevent FTF travel. They should realize that preventing FTFs from traveling is, as former Australian Senator Edwards said, 'an act of a responsible neighbour'.[237]

---

237 Senator Edwards, Senate Hansard, Counter-Terrorism Legislation Amendment (Foreign Fighters) Bill 2014 Second Reading Speech (28 October 2014). Available at: <https://www.aph.gov.au/Parliamentary_Business/Bills_Legislation/Bills_Search_Results/Result/Second_Reading_Speeches?BillId=s976&Page=2> accessed 15 May 2025.

CHAPTER 3

Nationality Deprivation

1 Introduction[1]

This chapter will focus on the measure of nationality deprivation.[2] States have resorted to this measure to prevent the return of FTFs and their accompanying family members or to exclude them from the society to which they, according to the authorities, have turned their backs. As will be argued in this chapter, nationality deprivation can be seen as a way to shun responsibilities and shift security risks to other states. States of nationality have arguably tried to get rid of nationals whom they had come to see as unwanted through the withdrawal of their nationality, and they did so to the detriment of other states. In particular, Western states like the United Kingdom, the Netherlands, Belgium, France, Australia and Denmark, were active in stripping FTFs and associated family members of their nationality.

As a justification to withdraw their nationality, states have referred to the protection of their national security and the potential terrorist threat that these FTFs and family members pose. In a media briefing on 15 February 2019, the British Secretary of State talked about Shamima Begum, a British national who was denationalized by the United Kingdom while detained in Northeast Syria, and said,

> [w]e must remember that those who left Britain to join Daesh were full of hate for our country. […] My message is clear – if you have supported terrorist organisations abroad I will not hesitate to prevent your return. […] We have a range of tough measures to stop people who pose a serious threat from return-

1 Part of this chapter has previously been published in I. Asscher, 'Shifting Responsibilities and Security Threats by Depriving Foreign Terrorist Fighters of Their Nationality' 29 Journal of Conflict & Security Law (2024) 2: 231–248.

2 Historically, the term citizenship referred more to the domestic aspects of the legal bond between the individual and the state and the term nationality referred more to the international aspects of this bond. This research will, however, not make such a distinction and will use the term nationality and citizenship interchangeably.

HTTPS://DOI.ORG/10.1163/9789004773806-004

> ing to the UK, including depriving them of their British citizenship or excluding them from the UK.[3]

When Australia announced that Neil Prakash, an Australian and Fijian dual national who traveled to Syria to fight for IS, would be stripped of his Australian nationality while detained in Türkiye, the Australian Home Affairs Minister said: "[t]he priority for us is to make sure that people like Neil Prakash don't come back to Australia. We don't want them here."[4] Likewise, in response to a new law on citizenship stripping, primarily designed to target Danish FTFs and family members, the Danish Prime Minister expressed that "[t]hese people have turned their backs on Denmark and used violence to combat our democracy and freedom. They are not wanted in Denmark."[5]

However, certainly not all states resorted to the measure of nationality deprivation. As will be shown in this chapter, some states, like the United States, Sweden, the Czech Republic, Tunisia and several states in Central Asia, did not strip their FTFs and associated family members of their nationality. Canada also provides an interesting example, as Canada first expanded its nationality deprivation powers on grounds of terrorism and national security in 2014, but reverted those changes in 2017 after the election of a new government.

Although the Security Council imposed broad obligations upon states to adopt measures against FTFs and their family members,[6] it never required or recommended states to resort to the measure of nationality deprivation to respond to the potential threat posed by those individuals. In fact, the Security Council has reaffirmed that nothing "shall oblige any State to deny entry or require the departure from its territories of its own nationals or permanent residents".[7] Matters of nationality and the withdrawal thereof largely fall within the sovereignty of each individual state. In other words, it is within the sovereignty of states to decide by their own legislation the rules governing

---

3 L. Bannnerman et al., 'Family of Isis bride Shamima Begum make plea for mercy' (*The Sunday Times*, 15 February 2019). Available at: <https://www.thetimes.com/article/family-of-isis-bride-shamima-begum-make-plea-for-mercy-gdz5qwvor> accessed 9 December 2024.

4 D. Wroe, 'Prakash citizenship revocation could jeopardise extradition chances, says Law Council' (*The Sydney Morning Herald*, 3 January 2019). Available at: <https://www.smh.com.au/politics/federal/prakash-citizenship-revocation-could-jeopardise-extradition-chances-says-law-council-20190103-p50ph6.html> accessed 9 December 2024.

5 'Denmark passes legislation to strip ISIL fighters of citizenship' (*Al Jazeera*, 24 October 2019). Available at: <https://www.aljazeera.com/news/2019/10/24/denmark-passes-legislation-to-strip-isil-fighters-of-citizenship> accessed 9 December 2024.

6 Among others in UNSC Resolution 2178 (24 September 2014) UN Doc. S/RES/2178 (2014) and UNSC Resolution 2170 (15 August 2014) UN Doc. S/RES/2170 (2014).

7 UNSC Resolution 2178 (2014) (n. 6) para. 8.

the conferral and loss of nationality.[8] Nevertheless, international law, including international human rights law, limits states' discretion in decisions concerning nationality deprivation. For example, states' discretion is limited by the obligation to avoid statelessness,[9] the prohibition of arbitrary deprivation of nationality and the prohibition of discrimination.[10] The revocation of nationality has been criticized for being difficult to justify under some of these human rights principles.[11] The practice has been extensively scrutinized from a human rights perspective. This is not surprising as, at first glance, there is only one category of 'victims' of this practice, which is the former national of the depriving state.[12] However, when one goes a step further and moves away from this vertical perspective and, instead, looks at the practice of nationality deprivation from a horizontal, inter-state perspective, one can see that nation-

8 *Nottebohm Case* (*Liechtenstein v. Guatemala*) (Second Phase) [1955] ICJ Rep. 4, p. 20.

9 See, for example, Convention on the Reduction of Statelessness (1961 Statelessness Convention) (signed 30 August 1961, entered into force 13 December 1975) 989 UNTS 175, Article 8; European Convention on Nationality (ECN) (adopted 6 November 1997, entered into force 1 March 2000) ETS No. 166, Articles 4(b) and 7(3); Protocol to the African Charter on Human and Peoples' Rights Relating to the Specific Aspects of the Right to a Nationality and the Eradication of Statelessness in Africa (signed 18 February 2024, not yet in force) adopted by Doc. Assembly/AU/Dec.885(XXXVII), Article 15(6).

10 See, for example, Universal Declaration of Human Rights (UDHR) (adopted 10 December 1948) UNGA Res 217 A(III), Articles 7 and 15(2); International Covenant on Civil and Political Rights (ICCPR) (adopted 16 December 1966, entered into force 23 March 1976) 999 UNTS 171, Article 26; Convention on the Right of the Child (CRC) (signed 20 November 1989, entered into force 2 September 1990) 1577 UNTS 3, Articles 2 and 8(1); ECN, Articles 4(c) and 5; American Convention on Human rights (ACHR) (signed 22 November 1969, entered into force 18 July 1978) 1144 UNTS 123, Articles 1 and 20(3).

11 See, for example, C. Paulussen, 'Stripping foreign fighters of their citizenship: International human rights and humanitarian law considerations' 103 International Review of the Red Cross (2021) No. 916–917; L. van Waas and S. Jaghai, 'All Citizens are Created Equal, but Some are More Equal than Others' 65 Netherlands International Law Review (2018); L. van Waas, 'Foreign Fighters and the Deprivation of Nationality: National Practices and International Law Implications' in A. de Guttry, F. Capone and C. Paulussen (eds.), *Foreign Fighters under International Law and Beyond* (T.M.C. Asser Press 2016); H. Duffy, '"Foreign Terrorist Fighters": A Human Rights Approach?' 29 Security and Human Rights (2018) 149–152. The measure of nationality deprivation has also been criticized for other reasons. For example, nationality deprivation would not be an effective measure to protect national security. See, for example, S. Jaghai and L. van Waas, 'Stripped of Citizenship, Stripped of Dignity? A Critical Exploration of Nationality Deprivation as a Counter-Terrorism Measure' in C. Paulussen and M. Scheinin (eds.), *Human Dignity and Human Security in Times of Terrorism* (T.M.C. Asser Press 2020) 174.

12 A. Sánchez Frías, 'From Dangerous Citizens to Foreign Criminals: Effects on Human Rights and State Sovereignty of Recent International and European Responses to the Terrorist Threat' Revista de Estudios Europeos (2020) 75: 120.

ality deprivation can also have a negative impact on other states.[13] As will be illustrated, the measure of nationality-stripping can lead to the shunning of responsibilities and the shifting of potential terrorist threats and a burden to engage in counter-terrorism to other states. First, when multiple states of nationality are involved, responsibilities are passed to one or more other states of nationality. In other words, the depriving state is no longer responsible to take back its former national, while the other state(s) of nationality becomes solely responsible to admit the person and somehow deal with the potentially dangerous individual. Second, when the individual is abroad and deprived of his or her nationality, responsibilities are not only passed to one or more other state(s) of nationality, but in the first instance, to the territorial state. That state is now responsible for an individual on its territory with potentially no other state willing to accept the person.

Spiro addressed this inter-state perspective arguing that international law limits state sovereignty in matters of nationality when those matters affect, or impinge upon the interests of other states. This may be when states are, "drawing their membership circles too broadly, especially when they laid claim to individuals over whom other states might establish better claims".[14] The underlying example of Spiro's argument is Russia's passportization policy.[15] The question prevalent in this chapter is the opposite, namely, whether international law also limits state sovereignty in nationality matters when states impinge upon the interests of other states by drawing their membership circles too narrowly; in other words, by depriving nationality. This question pursues the thinking of Burchardt and Gulati, who noted that withdrawal of nationality while the unwanted national is abroad might "affect the fundamental international law principle of noninterference: as the concerned individual is forced elsewhere, the receiving state's sovereignty is potentially violated".[16]

13 *Ibid.*

14 P. Spiro, 'A New International Law of Citizenship' 105 The American Journal of International Law (October 2011) 4: 697, 698.

15 Russia has adopted a policy of large scale conferral of its nationality to persons residing in other states, in particular in former-Soviet Union States, without those persons having to take residency in Russia. As a result, Russia has conferred its nationality to large groups of persons from the Donetsk and Luhansk regions in Ukraine and the Abkhazia and South Ossetia regions in Georgia.

16 D. Burchardt and R. Gulati, 'International Counter-terrorism Regulation and Citizenship-stripping Laws: Reinforcing Legal Exceptionalism' 23 Journal of Conflict & Security Law (2018) 2: 225.

In this sense, an interesting comparison can be made between nationality deprivation and banishment as a punishment. Both acts constitute forms of burden shifting, albeit one more direct than the other.[17] Banishment gradually disappeared as a punishment, among other reasons, because it was deemed to be at odds with the sovereign rights of other states, including the right to decide upon the admission and expulsion of aliens.[18] Thus, banishment caused a tension between the sovereignty of the state expelling its unwanted nationals and that of the state to which such unwanted nationals were expelled. This chapter will address a similar tension, a tension caused by nationality deprivation between the rights and interests of depriving states on the one hand and the rights and interests of states to which a burden is shifted, on the other hand.

Instead of focusing on international human rights law and the obligation to avoid statelessness, this chapter will focus upon this inter-state perspective to nationality deprivation by examining other norms and obligations under public international law. Although some human rights, including those with an *erga omnes* character, can also be considered as having an inter-state dimension, human rights law will not be the focus of this chapter. Leaving aside international human rights law, this chapter will try to examine to what extent public international law imposes limits on the practice of denationalizing FTFs and their family members when such a response results in the shunning of responsibilities and the shifting of security risks.

To address this question, this chapter will first examine the measure of nationality deprivation more broadly. The historical context of the measure will be set out and the more recent practice of using this measure to counter terrorism will be elaborated upon. Secondly, the chapter will zero in on nationality deprivation practices as a response to the FTFs phenomenon in Syria and Iraq, more specifically. The question will be addressed which states have been particularly active in this practice and which states have not. For those states that were active in resorting to this measure, it will also be examined on what grounds and under which conditions these states were able to revoke nationality. Moreover, through the discussion of multiple examples, it will be illustrated how this practice leads to the shunning of responsibilities and the shifting of security threats. After this introductory part, this chapter will, first, discuss the obligation to re-admit nationals and the right to expel

---

17 Voltaire criticized the punishment of banishment by stating that it is an equivalent to 'throwing into our neighbour's field the stones that incommode us in our own'. Voltaire, *A Philosophical Dictionary: Vol. 2* (William Dugdale 1843) 192.

18 M. Gibney, 'Banishment and the Pre-history of Legitimate Expulsion Power' 24 Citizenship Studies (2020) 3: 296.

aliens. It will be argued that nationality deprivation circumvents the obligation to (re)admit nationals and affects territorial states in the effective exercise of their right to expel aliens. Second, the potential role of the notion of predominant nationality and a special responsibility upon states of predominant nationality will be analyzed. Finally, this chapter will discuss some more general obligations under public international law, including the obligations to prevent and to cooperate in combating terrorism as well as general principles of inter-state behavior, particularly the general principle of good faith.

2 The Practice of Nationality Deprivation

The measure of nationality deprivation refers to a "unilateral act, by a State, of withdrawing a person's nationality and formally breaking the (legal) bond with that citizen".[19] After a person's nationality is stripped, the person concerned is no longer considered a national of the depriving state. Losing one's nationality does not necessarily mean losing legal residence. However, when the individual is deprived of his or her nationality while inside the depriving state, the deprivation decision is usually followed by a decision declaring the person's stay illegal and an order to leave the depriving state. When the individual is deprived while outside the depriving state, the deprivation decision is usually followed by a measure which prevents legal entry.[20] This section elaborates upon the measure of nationality deprivation, more generally. It will first be discussed in a historical context. It will be shown that nationality deprivation is not a new measure but has been used to respond to certain acts in the past. Second, this section discusses how, especially European states, have expanded the scope of this measure since 2000 and how they have increasingly used it as a national security or counter-terrorism measure.

2.1 Historical Context

Nationality deprivation is not a new measure, unique to the 21st-century counter-terrorism context. Physical expulsion through banishment, in some cases, accompanied by the revocation of citizenship status, was a common

19 S. Jaghai and L. van Waas 2020 (n. 11) 156.

20 See, M. Bolhuis and J. van Wijk, 'Citizenship Deprivation as a Counterterrorism Measure in Europe; Possible Follow-Up Scenarios, Human Rights Infringements and the Effect on Counterterrorism' 22 European Journal of Migration and Law (2020) 3: 351–363.

practice in Europe until the 1800s.[21] The practice of banishment was already used in ancient Greece, both as a fixed punishment for certain crimes, including unintentional homicide and attempted tyranny, and as a political practice called *ostracism*.[22] *Ostracism* was a practice according to which, subject to a democratic vote, it could be decided to send a citizen away for a limited period of 10 years without charges. However, the person in question retained citizenship status.[23] This was different from the practice of banishment in the Roman Empire, or at least from banishment in its most extreme form, which was called *deportatio*, where the individual did lose citizenship permanently.[24]

Influenced by Roman law, banishment was also a common practice by European states in the Middle Ages.[25] The measure was used to respond to "individuals allegedly guilty of serious crimes or those who had been disloyal or somehow breached their allegiance to the king".[26] Although banishment gradually disappeared as a punishment from the late 18th century,[27] states continued to resort to practices of excluding people from their society, including through the deprivation of nationality. Already in the 19th century, states resorted to this measure. An early example is its use in response to so-called 'zouaves' who traveled to Rome from 1861 to 1870 to defend Pope Pius IX and the Papal state. Within this period, thousands of Catholic individuals came from all over Europe and beyond to voluntarily join the Papal army and protect the Holy See against Italian nationalists who wanted a united Italian state.[28] These foreigners who traveled to Rome to volunteer in the Pope's legion came from a variety of states, including the Netherlands, Switzerland,

---

21 M. Gibney, 'Deprivation of Citizenship through a Political Lens: A political Scientist's Perspective' in Institute on Statelessness and Inclusion, The World's Stateless: Deprivation of Nationality (March 2020) 207. Available at: <https://files.institutesi.org/WORLD's_STATELESS_2020.pdf> accessed 14 March 2023.

22 Ostracism, Encyclopaedia Britannica (6 March 2023). Available at: <https://www.britannica.com/topic/ostracism> accessed 14 March 2023; M. Gibney 2020 (n. 18) 280, 281.

23 C. Prener, *Denationalisation and Its Discontents: Citizenship Revocation in the 21st Century: Legal, Political and Moral Implications* (Brill Nijhoff 2023) 11–13.

24 *Ibid.* 13.

25 M. Gibney 2020 (n. 18) 283.

26 C. Prener 2023 (n. 23) 13, 14.

27 M. Gibney 2020 (n. 18) 278.

28 However, the exact numbers of Zouaves who traveled to Rome differ. See, for example, S. Sarlin, 'Mercenaries or soldiers of the faith? The Pontifical Zouaves in the defense of the Roman Church (1860–1870)' 43 Millars: Espai i historia (2017) 2: 191; C. Coulombe, *The Pope's Legion The Multinational Fighting Force that Defended the Vatican* (Palgrave Macmillan, 2008) 11.

Belgium, France, Canada and the United Kingdom.[29] While it seems that some states, like France and the United Kingdom, only threatened with the withdrawal of their nationality for serving a foreign power,[30] the Netherlands did actually strip them of their nationality on such grounds, leaving them stateless.[31] The Netherlands could do so based on Article 9(2) of the Dutch Civil Code 1838, which provided that nationality may be withdrawn because of foreign military service when no permission for such service was given by the King. Conversely, other states seem to have received returning zouaves as heroes, like Belgium and Ireland (back then part of the United Kingdom).[32]

Another example is nationality deprivation in response to individuals traveling to Spain to fight in the Spanish Civil War from 1936 to 1939. The Spanish Civil War was fought between the Nationalists, headed by General Franco, and the Republicans, representing the governmental side. Although foreign volunteers fought for both sides, the International Brigades on the Republican side attracted most of those volunteers, originating from several states.[33] Some states, including the United States and the United Kingdom,[34] tolerated or took little action against their nationals volunteering in the International Brigades, despite having issued laws prohibiting the participation in military action abroad and publicly supporting a non-intervention policy.[35] Other states, like the Netherlands and Poland,[36] stripped them of their nationality. The Netherlands had replaced its nationality provisions in the Civil Code, and

---

29 C. Coulombe 2008 (n. 28) 11. With regard to the United Kingdom, especially many Irishmen joined the Papal Army. See, F. O'Driscoll, 'Confounding the Garibaldian Liars: The Letters of Albert Delahoyde, Irish Soldier of the Papal Battalion of St Patrick and Papal Zouave in Italy, 1860–1870' 6 Studi irlandesi. A Journal of Irish Studies (2016) 6: 51.

30 C. Coulombe 2008 (n. 28) 55; C. Harrison, 'Gender, Catholic Spirituality, and French Responses to the Roman Question' 79 The Journal of Modern History (2007) 2: 278; M. Simpson, 'Serving France in Rome: The *Zouaves Pontificaux* and the French Nation' 27 French History (2013) 1: 74, 75.

31 However, the Netherlands later posthumously reinstalled their nationality in 1947. See, C. Coulombe 2008 (n. 28) 101, 203.

32 *Ibid.* 203; F. O'Driscoll 2016 (n. 29) 52.

33 M. Flores, 'Foreign Fighters Involvement in National and International Wars: A Historical Survey' in A. de Guttry, F. Capone and C. Paulussen (eds.) 2016 (n. 11) 39–41.

34 A. Layeb, 'Mercenary Activity: United States Neutrality Laws and Enforcement' 10 New York Law School Journal of International and Comparative Law (1989) 3: 294, 295; See, in general, S. Mackenzie, 'The Foreign Enlistment Act and the Spanish Civil War, 1936–1939' 10 Twentieth Century British History (1999) 1.

35 M. Flores 2016 (n. 33) 40.

36 See, in general, S. Kruizinga, 'The First Resisters: Tracing Three Dutchmen from the Spanish Trenches to the Second World War, 1936–1945' 27 War in History (2020) 3; J. Pietrzak, 'Poles in the Spanish Civil War (1936–1939): During the Conflict and After' Cuadernos de Historia Contemporánea 43 (2021) 175, 176.

during this time, was able to deprive these individuals of their nationality based on Article 7(4) of the Dutch Citizenship and Residency Act 1892. This provision enabled nationality deprivation on grounds of foreign military or state service. Poland could strip its nationals of their nationality on the basis of the Act of 20 January 1920 on Polish Citizenship, Article 11(2) of which also provided that nationality could be revoked when someone took public office of a foreign country or joined a foreign country's military without permission.

A final example, outside the context of an armed conflict, is the United States' policy, which started in the beginning of the 20th century, to strip nationality of naturalized nationals who were considered political dissidents, such as communists, socialists and fascists.[37] The United States did so, on the basis of the 1906 Naturalization Act, Section 15 of which provided a ground for denaturalization because of fraud or illegally procured citizenship. 'Illegally procured' being interpreted to include, *inter alia*, a lack of good moral character.[38] In addition, the US Neutrality Act of 1794, which was mentioned in the previous chapter, prohibited the acceptance of commissions in foreign military forces as well as enlisting or recruiting others, subject to a penalty of loss of nationality.[39]

These examples illustrate that the measure of nationality deprivation has been used by states in the past, among others, to respond to disloyal behavior of the individual concerned. States formally broke the bond with their citizens to respond to what was seen as an already broken bond of allegiance to the state, caused by the individual's behavior.

A survey conducted by the ILC in 1953, on national legislation concerning grounds for deprivation of nationality, also shows that this measure has a longer history than its use in the 21st-century counter-terrorism context. It demonstrates that foreign military service was not the only common ground for the revocation of nationality.[40] As the survey shows, grounds for the deprivation of nationality existed in the national legislation of the majority of states at the time. For example, according to the ILC's survey, Brazil allowed for denationalization of naturalized nationals "guilty of activities against the

37 P. Weil, *The Sovereign Citizen: Denaturalization and the Origins of the American Republic* (University of Pennsylvania Press 2013) 56.

38 *Ibid.* 35.

39 D. Malet, *Foreign Fighters: Transnational Identity in Civic Conflicts* (Oxford University Press 2013) 35, 36.

40 ILC, 'Nationality, including Statelessness – National Legislation Concerning Grounds for Deprivation of Nationality – Memorandum Prepared by Mr. Ivan S. Kerno, Expert of the International Law Commission' UN Doc. A/CN.4/66 (6 April 1953).

national interest".[41] Bulgaria enabled nationality stripping on grounds of, *inter alia*, "service of other government without authorization" and "harming the prestige or interests of the nation".[42] Chile's national legislation allowed nationality stripping on the basis of "incidents having occurred which render the holder unworthy of citizenship".[43] According to the survey, New Zealand also provided a number of nationality deprivation grounds in its national legislation, including when a person is "guilty of an act or speech which is disloyal or disaffected towards His Majesty".[44] Finally, in the United States, there were multiple grounds of denationalization, such as desertion, treason and voting in a foreign election.[45]

What can be observed from the ILC's survey, and which was also evidenced by the earlier mentioned examples of nationality deprivation in the 19th and early 20th centuries, is that some of the nationality laws in which these early grounds for nationality deprivation were included date back a long time ago. The examples show that states had a wide variety of grounds on the basis of which nationality could be withdrawn. While some of these early grounds are now no longer in force, others, including those relating to foreign military service and states' national security interests, still exist today.[46] However, none of the states whose nationality laws were included in the ILC's 1953 survey allowed nationality deprivation on the ground of being a member of a terrorist organization or on other grounds explicitly mentioning terrorism. Throughout the 20th century, the practice of nationality stripping, which used to be an exclusive matter of state sovereignty, became more regulated by public international law.[47] Yet, this did not lead to a decrease of the prac-

---

41 *Ibid.* 8.

42 *Ibid.*

43 *Ibid.* 9.

44 *Ibid.* 13.

45 *Ibid.* 16. Fraud was interpreted as including, *inter alia*, becoming a member, within 5 years of naturalization, of an organization which would have barred the person from being naturalized. According to Sections 313 and 340 of the McCarran Act of 1952, such organizations referred to, *inter alia*, 'any organization that advocated or teaches, opposition to all organized government', the Communist Party of the United States, any other totalitarian party, or the Communist Political Association.

46 S. Jaghai and L. van Waas 2020 (n. 11) 157, 158.

47 A number of (human rights) treaties were adopted in the 20th century to prevent statelessness, including the Convention on Certain Questions Relating to the Conflict of Nationality Law (signed 13 April 1930, entered into force 1 July 1937) 179 UNTS 89 (1930 Hague Convention) and the 1961 Statelessness Convention (signed 30 August 1961, entered into force 13 December 1975) 989 UNTS 175. In addition, the right to a nationality and the prohibition on arbitrary and discriminatory deprivation of nationality was adopted in multiple human rights instruments, including in Article 15 of the 1948

tice. Instead, as will be shown in the next section, with the start of the 21st century, states began to expand their nationality deprivation powers, a trend especially visible in Europe.

2.2 Counter-terrorism Context

Since the beginning of the 21st century, deprivation of nationality has increasingly been used as a counter-terrorism measure, which fits into a broader trend of repressive counter-terrorism measures after 9/11. There has been a gradual increase, or one could say a trend, of states adopting or expanding nationality revocation powers. The Institute on Statelessness and Inclusion and the Global Citizenship Observatory found in their March 2022 report that between 2000 and 2022, a total of 37 states introduced or expanded grounds for nationality deprivation relating to national security.[48] This number does not include those states which already had those powers in force and which remained unchanged as such but possibly more heavily used. This is, for example, the case in France, where its use as a counter-terrorism measure was already introduced in 1996.

States increasingly adopt or expand national security grounds for denationalization, especially European states. Eighteen out of the 37 states that introduced or expanded national security grounds for the deprivation of nationality are European.[49] Those grounds implicitly or, in some instances,

---

UDHR; Article of the CRC; Article 26 of the ICCPR; League of Arab States, Arab Charter on Human Rights (signed 23 May 2004, entered into force 15 March 2008) 12 Int'l Hum. Rts. Rep. 893 (2005), Article 24; ACHR, Article 20(3).

48 In 2022, the Institute on Statelessness and Inclusion and the Global Citizenship Observatory published a report in which relevant legislative provisions in force between 1 January 2000 and 1 January 2022 of 190 states were analyzed and compared. This section builds, among other available sources, on the observations and data provided by this report. See, Institute on Statelessness and Inclusion and Global Citizenship Observatory, Instrumentalizing Citizenship in the Fight Against Terrorism (March 2022). Available at: <https://files.institutesi.org/Instrumentalising_Citizenship_Global_Trends_Report.pdf> accessed 22 March 2023.

The report looked at the introduction or expansion of nationality deprivation grounds for 'disloyalty'. On page 3, the report notes that 'disloyalty' means "involuntary loss of citizenship by a person due to behavior or offence that is based on a concept of disloyalty *or harm to the interests or security of the country* of which he/she is a citizen, including offences such as treason" (emphasis added). Furthermore, the report notes that in almost all cases of states introducing or expanding nationality deprivation powers since 2000, national security or terrorism grounds were cited.

49 Institute on Statelessness and Inclusion and Global Citizenship Observatory 2022 (n. 48) 26. Albania, Austria, Azerbaijan, Belarus, Belgium, Bosnia and Herzegovina, Denmark,

explicitly capture nationality stripping for terrorism-related acts. In over half of those 18 countries, terrorism was explicitly added as a ground on the basis of which nationality could be withdrawn.[50] For example, Romania amended Article 25(1) of its Citizenship Law, now allowing the denationalization of a naturalized national who "is known to have links with terrorist groups or has supported them, in any form, or has committed other acts that endanger national security".[51] Austria first amended its Citizenship Act in 2015, to include denationalization of "a citizen who actively and voluntarily participates in an organized armed group fighting abroad in situations of armed conflict".[52] In 2021, Austria's nationality deprivation powers were expanded again to include being convicted of a number of terrorist offences such as membership of a terrorist organization and travel for terrorist purposes.[53] Italy amended its nationality legislation in 2018 by allowing for the deprivation of nationality when a person has been convicted of a terrorist offence.[54] The United Kingdom's nationality legislation does not mention terrorism explicitly but has a very broad national security ground for nationality deprivation. The UK introduced amendments to the British Nationality Act 1981 in 2003, 2006 and 2014. In 2003, specific grounds for nationality deprivation were replaced by a general power to deprive a person of his or her nationality if the person had done anything "seriously prejudicial to the vital interest of the State".[55] With this amendment, the UK's nationality deprivation power was extended beyond naturalized nationals to include nationals by birth. In 2006, after the London bombings of July 2005, the ground for nationality deprivation, when the individual's behavior was contrary to the 'vital interests of the state', was changed to cases when the measure, i.e., not the person's behavior, is "conducive to the public good",[56] which is arguably a much lower standard. In 2014, the UK amended the Nationality Act again and included an exception to the

---

Estonia, Finland, Germany, Italy, Kazakhstan, Latvia, Liechtenstein, the Netherlands, Norway, Romania and the UK.

50 *Ibid.* 27.

51 Act No. 21/1991 on Romanian Citizenship, Article 25(1).

52 Austrian Citizenship Act, Article 33(2).

53 *Ibid.* Article 33(3).

54 Article 10-bis Italian Citizenship Act 1992, inserted by Article 14 Decree Law 113/2018 and Law 132/2018.

55 Nationality, Immigration and Asylum Act 2002, Section 4, amending the British Nationality Act 1981, Section 40.

56 Immigration, Asylum and Nationality Act 2006, Section 56, amending the British Nationality Act 1981, Section 40(2).

clause protecting against statelessness.[57] This amendment made it possible for naturalized persons to be stripped of their nationality if,

> the Secretary of State is satisfied that the deprivation is conducive to the public good because the person, while having that citizenship status, has conducted him or herself in a manner which is seriously prejudicial to the vital interests of the United Kingdom, any of the Islands, or any British overseas territory.

And "the Secretary of State has reasonable grounds for believing that the person is able, under the law of a country or territory outside the United Kingdom, to become a national of such a country or territory".[58] This amendment made it possible for naturalized nationals to be stripped of their British nationality even if they do not actually hold a second nationality at the time the deprivation decision is made.

The second largest region in which states introduced or expanded their nationality deprivation laws to include national security grounds is the Middle East and North Africa region. Eight states in this region amended their nationality laws.[59] For example, Bahrain expanded nationality deprivation grounds in its 1963 Nationality Act in 2014 and 2019, by including the possibility to revoke nationality of a Bahraini national who "causes harm to the interests of the Kingdom or act in a manner that contradicts the duty of loyalty to it"[60] or of a national who is convicted of a terrorist offence.[61] Another example is Algeria, which expanded its denationalization powers in 2005, albeit not mentioning terrorism explicitly. Algeria included nationality deprivation of naturalized nationals for crimes "affecting the fundamental interests" of the state.[62]

---

57 Immigration Act 2014, Section 66, amending the British Nationality Act 1981, Section 40. This amendment was a response to the failure to deprive Hilal al Jedda, an Iraqi born naturalized British citizen, of his nationality. See, *Secretary of State for the Home Department v Al-Jedda* (Judgement) [2013] UKSC 62 (9 October 2013).

58 British Nationality Act 1981, Section 40(4A).

59 Institute on Statelessness and Inclusion and Global Citizenship Observatory 2022 (n. 48) 27.

60 1963 Bahraini Nationality Act, Article 10(c).

61 *Ibid.* Article 10(d). See also Human Rights Watch, Bahrain: Citizenship Rights Stripped Away Authorities Take New Powers to Arbitrarily Revoke Nationality (21 August 2014). Available at: <https://www.hrw.org/news/2014/08/21/bahrain-citizenship-rights-stripped-away> accessed 20 March 2023; A. Almutawa and C. Walker, 'Citizenship as a Privilege and the Weakness of International Law: The Consequences for Citizenship Deprivation in Bahrain and the UK' 14 Journal of Human Rights Practice (2022) 3: 1042–1045.

62 1970 Code de la Nationalité, Article 22(1).

Thus, different nationality deprivation grounds were introduced or broadened since the early 2000s. Some are only applicable to naturalized nationals, like those in Romania and Algeria, while others are also applicable to individuals who acquired their nationality by birth, like those in Austria. Some grounds require a criminal conviction before nationality may be stripped, like those relating to terrorist offences in Italy and Austria, while other grounds do not require such a conviction, including the United Kingdom's national security ground. Furthermore, the majority of states implemented the measure as an administrative measure, meaning that it is decided upon by an organ of the executive, like a minister or the head of state, with only limited involvement of the judiciary in its application or review.[63] This is, for example, the case in the United Kingdom. Notably, when the power to withdraw nationality as an administrative measure is based on notions of 'terrorism' or used in response to the ill-defined concept of a 'foreign terrorist fighter', problems associated with broad or vague definitions of such notions "thus replicated beyond the criminal law in powers that are, moreover, enforceable on the basis of a lower standard of proof" and that are not subject to the procedures and guarantees of criminal prosecution.[64] A small number of states implemented such powers as a judicial measure, which means that the measure is decided upon by a judicial decision or court ruling.[65] Interestingly, in Romania, a dedicated committee was established to decide upon the withdrawal of nationality, the "Citizenship Commission".[66]

Although as shown above, "[n]ationality has been revived as a weapon against terror suspects",[67] exact numbers on how many individuals have actually been stripped of their nationality on national security and terrorism grounds are difficult to obtain. Often, there is no data available on whether, and if so, in how many cases, these powers have actually been used in practice. In some instances, it could also be the case that these powers have not been

63 B. Boutin, 'Administrative Measures against Foreign Fighters: In Search of Limits and Safeguards' ICCT Research Paper (December 2016) 5, 6; Institute on Statelessness and Inclusion and Global Citizenship Observatory 2022 (n. 48) 20.

64 D. McKeever, 'Old Rules to Fix New Problems: Counterterrorism, Refugees and Withdrawal of Nationality' 29 Journal of Conflict & Security Law (2024) 1: 114.

65 Institute on Statelessness and Inclusion and Global Citizenship Observatory 2022 (n. 48) 20. This is, for example, the case in Belgium, whose grounds for nationality deprivation grounds will be discussed in the next section.

66 Act No. 21/1991 on Romanian Citizenship, Article 14(1).

67 C. Walker, 'Exporting Human Security in the Cause of Counter-Terrorism' in C. Paulussen and M. Scheinin (eds.) 2020 (n. 11) 48. Only those suspects with a 'foreign origin'. In light of the obligation to avoid statelessness, states may only deprive nationality if the individual holds multiple nationality.

used in practice at all. However, when data is available and there is evidence that the measure has actually been used in practice, it seems that numbers remain low, generally between 10 and 20 cases per state or even less.[68] These numbers seem to indicate that, although there has been an increase in the introduction or expansion of grounds for denationalization in relation to national security and terrorism, the number of cases in which this measure has actually been used remains relatively low. There are, however, some exceptions to this observation, the UK and Bahrain. It seems that Bahrain denationalized 434 citizens between 2011 and 2022, either on the basis of a conviction for a terrorism offence or on the basis of Article 10(c) of its 1963 Nationality Act.[69] In addition, the UK stripped 212 nationals of their nationality between 2000 and 2022, on the basis of its national security ground contained in Section 40 of the British Nationality Act 1981.[70]

In contrast, there are also states, who in 2000, did not and still do not provide the opportunity for nationality revocation based on security-related grounds, like Argentina, Armenia, Bolivia, Burundi, Cambodia, the Czech Republic and Sweden.[71] There is also an, albeit smaller, counter-trend of states

---

68 See, for example, Institute on Statelessness and Inclusion and Global Citizenship Observatory 2022 (n. 48) 29 and M. Bolhuis and J. van Wijk 2020 (n. 20) 341–349 and table 2 on page 351.

69 However, this high number might also include, *inter alia*, human rights defenders, political dissidents and lawyers. See, Institute on Statelessness and Inclusion and Global Citizenship Observatory 2022 (n. 48) 19, 29; see also Salam for Democracy and Human Rights, Institute on Statelessness and Inclusion and the Hawiati MENA Statelessness Network, Arbitrary Revocation of Nationality in Bahrain: A Tool of Oppression (2021). Available at: <https://salam-dhr.org/arbitrary-revocation-of-nationality-in-bahrain-a-tool-of-oppression/> accessed 10 December 2024. Furthermore, Alsabeehg notes that "[o]f the nearly one thousand individuals who had their citizenship revoked since 2012, including the 439 who until the end of 2020 still are denaturalised, the overwhelming majority can be linked to Bahrain's protest movement that aims to achieve greater political rights for citizens". See, Z. Alsabeehg, 'Report on Citizenship Law: Bahrain' Global Citizenship Observatory (March 2021) 16. Available at: <https://cadmus.eui.eu/bitstream/handle/1814/70577/RSCAS_GLOBALCIT_2021_6.pdf?sequence=1&isAllowed=y> accessed 22 March 2023.

70 Institute on Statelessness and Inclusion and Global Citizenship Observatory 2022 (n. 48) 29. See also M. Bolhuis and J. van Wijk 2020 (n. 20) 348 and table 2 on page 351; C. Mckinney, How many people have been stripped of their British citizenship? (10 January 2022). Available at: <https://freemovement.org.uk/how-many-people-have-been-stripped-of-their-british-citizenship-home-office-deprivation/> accessed 20 March 2023.

71 Institute on Statelessness and Inclusion and Global Citizenship Observatory 2022 (n. 48) 23, figure 4.1. This figure provides a list of states without nationality deprivation for 'disloyalty'. However, as previously mentioned in footnote 48, the report notes that disloyalty includes grounds relating to behavior or offence that harm "the interests or security of the country".

repealing or narrowing the scope of their nationality deprivation powers since 2000, including Peru in 2001, Chile in 2005, Nepal in 2009, Kenya in 2010 and Canada in 2017.[72] Canada provides a particularly interesting example here as Canada first expanded its powers in 2014. This was done because it was deemed necessary to protect "the safety and security of Canadians and promot[e] Canadian interests and values".[73] The expansion allowed citizenship to be stripped, *inter alia*, when a person "was convicted of a terrorism offence [...] and sentenced to at least five years of imprisonment"[74] or when there were "reasonable grounds to believe that a person [...] served as a member of an armed force of a country or as a member of an organized armed group and that country or group was engaged in an armed conflict with Canada".[75] Procedural changes were also incorporated, restricting the authority of the Federal Court in nationality revocation decisions and expanding that of the Minister. However, many of the changes that were made to the Canadian Citizenship Act in 2014 were reverted in 2017, after the election of a new government.[76]

Nevertheless, the Institute on Statelessness and Inclusion and the Global Citizenship Observatory notice in their report that most states, which repealed or restricted their nationality deprivation laws, did so before 2011. As they indicate, the fact that not many nationality deprivation laws were repealed or restricted after 2011 may be linked to the start of the Syrian Civil War, the rise of IS and the beginning of the FTFs phenomenon in Syria and Iraq.[77] At the same time, most states which did introduce or expand their nationality deprivation powers on national security and terrorism-related grounds did so between 2016 and 2022. This may likewise be explained by the FTFs phenomenon in Syria and Iraq, and in particular, by the question of what to do with

72 Institute on Statelessness and Inclusion and Global Citizenship Observatory 2022 (n. 48) 25.

73 Government of Canada, Strengthening Canadian Citizenship Act: Protecting and promoting Canada's interests and values (6 February 2014). Available at: <https://www.canada.ca/en/news/archive/2014/02/strengthening-canadian-citizenship-act-protecting-promoting-canada-interests-values.html> accessed 22 March 2023.

74 Strengthening Canadian Citizenship Act (19 June 2014) S.C. 2014, c. 22, Section 10(2)(b).

75 *Ibid.* Section 10.1(2).

76 See also T. Boekestein, 'Deprivation of Nationality as a Counter-Terrorism Tool: A Comparative Analysis of Canadian and Dutch Legislation' 5 Transnational Human Rights Review (2018) 38–47.

77 Institute on Statelessness and Inclusion and Global Citizenship Observatory 2022 (n. 48) 25.

those unwanted nationals who have returned or still wish to return,[78] as states "fear an influx of returning [FTFs] who pose a threat to national security".[79]

3 Nationality Deprivation as a Measure Targeting FTFs and Their Family Members in Syria and Iraq

This section will address nationality deprivation as a response to the FTFs phenomenon in Syria and Iraq, more specifically. It will first be set out which states were particularly active in the practice of denationalizing their FTFs and/or family members, and which were not. For those states that did actively participate in this practice, and whose grounds for nationality deprivation were not yet discussed in the previous section, it will be analyzed on what basis and under which conditions they were able to do so. Thereafter, it will be explained how this practice has led to the shunning of responsibilities and the shifting of security risks. This will be done through the discussion of multiple examples, including the more infamous cases of Shamima Begum, Jack Letts and Suhayra Aden.

3.1 A Practice of Western (European) States

The description of a few grounds for nationality revocation in the previous section, indicate that some newly introduced grounds for the withdrawal of nationality were inspired by the FTFs phenomenon in Syria and Iraq. For example, Germany expanded its nationality revocation powers in 2019 by including a ground applicable to Germans "who actively participate in fighting by a terrorist organization abroad".[80] The explanatory note attached to the legislative proposal stated that this new ground was intended to target "fighters [who] are still in the remaining bastions or retreats of IS".[81] However, it seems that Germany has not yet deprived any of its FTFs or German family

78 *Ibid.* 27.

79 S. Jaghai and L. van Waas 2020 (n. 11) 154.

80 German Nationality Act of 22 July 1913, Section 28(1)(2).

81 J. Lepoutre, 'Citizenship Loss and Deprivation in the European Union (27 + 1)' EUI Working Paper RSCAS 2020/29 (2020) 11; Deutscher Bundestag, Entwurf eines Dritten Gesetzes zur Änderung des Staatsangehörigkeitsgesetzes, Report No. 19/9736 (29 April 2019) 7. Available at: <https://dserver.bundestag.de/btd/19/097/1909736.pdf> accessed 23 March 2023.

members of their nationality based on this ground.[82] Like the use of nationality revocation as a counter-terrorism measure, more generally, it is difficult to obtain exact data on the use of this measure in response to FTFs and their family members in Syria and Iraq, more specifically. The data that is available suggests that there are six states that have in particular been active in denationalizing their FTFs and accompanying family members.[83] Those states are Australia, Belgium, Denmark, the Netherlands, the United Kingdom and Saudi Arabia. Those states' practice and nationality deprivation legislation will be addressed respectively.

Compared to other states, Australia's nationality deprivation provisions are relatively precise. Terrorism-related grounds were first introduced in 2015 through an amendment of the Australian Citizenship Act 2007, to respond to "the threat that foreign terrorist fighters presented to Australia and its interests".[84] This 2015 amendment introduced two new grounds of nationality deprivation and the expansion of another ground. The first two (the now repealed Sections 33AA and 35) entailed the automatic loss of citizenship through the person's own (terrorist) conduct. The third (the now repealed Section 35A) entailed the deprivation of nationality through a ministerial decision when

82 This can also be explained by the fact that these changes to the German Nationality Act were adopted in 2019 and may not be applied retroactively. However, it should also be mentioned that Germany has a troubled past when it comes to nationality deprivation. Nazi Germany collectively stripped German Jews of their nationality, in accordance with the Reich Citizenship Law of 15 September 1935. See, for example, D. Fraser and F. Caestecker, 'Jews or Germans? Nationality Legislation and the Restoration of Liberal Democracy in Western Europe after the Holocaust' 31 Law and History Review (May 2013) 2.

83 The Foreign Terrorist Fighters Knowledge Hub, developed by the T.M.C. Asser Institute and the ICCT, provides relevant data on, *inter alia*, state responses to FTFs and their associated family members, including deprivation of nationality. Although it, for now, only focuses on states which are member of the GCTF, as well as Belgium, Lebanon and Tunisia, this section will draw from the information provided by the FTF Knowledge Hub as it constitutes one of the most comprehensive databases on the issue. Nevertheless, it should be mentioned again that with regard to some states there is no data available on the use of nationality deprivation, which can of course also indicate that they have not used this measure at all in response to their FTFs and family members. The Foreign Terrorist Fighters Knowledge Hub is available at: <https://www.foreignterroristfighters.info/> accessed 23 March 2023.

84 Australian Citizenship Amendment (Allegiance to Australia) Act 2015; The Parliament of the Commonwealth of Australia, House of Representatives, the Australian Citizenship Amendment (Citizenship Cessation) Bill 2019, Explanatory Memorandum (2019) 1. Available at: <https://www.aph.gov.au/Parliamentary_Business/Bills_Legislation/Bills_Search_Results/Result?bId=r6409> accessed 23 March 2023.

the person had been convicted for a (terrorist) offence and sentenced to imprisonment of at least 6 years.

In 2020, the Act was amended again by the Australian Citizenship Amendment (Citizenship Cessation) Act 2020 and contained, *inter alia*, the following two grounds for nationality deprivation. First, Section 36B provided the opportunity for nationality deprivation when "the Minister is satisfied" that the person, whether a naturalized national or a national by birth, has: (1) engaged in certain (terrorist) conduct, which includes "fighting for, or being in the service of, a declared terrorist organisation";[85] (2) "the conduct demonstrates that the person has repudiated their allegiance to Australia"[86] and (3) "it would be contrary to the public interest for the person to remain an Australian citizen".[87] A second relevant ground was contained in Section 36D, which provided the opportunity to withdraw nationality when a person is convicted of a (terrorist) offence and has been sentenced to imprisonment of at least 3 years.[88] As with the first ground, the Minister would have to be satisfied that "the person has repudiated their allegiance to Australia" and that remaining a citizen would be "contrary to the public interest".[89] Both grounds contained a clause that protects against statelessness, as nationality may not be withdrawn "if the Minister *is satisfied* that the person would […] become a person who is not a national or citizen of any country".[90] This clause, however, provided a slightly weaker protection against statelessness than the previous statelessness clauses did under the earlier Sections 33AA, 35 and 35A. These previous clauses determined that nationality may only be withdrawn if, as a matter of fact, the person concerned is a national of another state. Stripping nationality on these two grounds was an administrative measure as it was the Minister who decided.

However, in two separate judgements by the High Court of Australia, Sections 36B and 36D of the Australian Citizenship Act 2007 were held to be unconstitutional.[91] First, in June 2022, the High Court of Australia rendered a judgement in the case of *Alexander v Minister for Home Affairs* in which it held Section 36B of the Australian Citizenship Act 2007 to be unconstitutional

---

85 Australian Citizenship Amendment (Citizenship Cessation) Act 2020, Sections 36B(1)(a), 36B(5)(a)-(j) and 36C.
86 *Ibid.* Section 36B(1)(b).
87 *Ibid.* Section 36B(1)(c).
88 *Ibid.* Section 36D(1)(a) and (b) and, in particular, Section 36D(5)(f).
89 *Ibid.* Section 36D(1).
90 *Ibid.* Section 36B(2); Section 36D(2) (emphasis added).
91 *Alexander v Minister for Home Affairs* [2022] (Judgement) HCA 19 (8 June 2022); *Benbrika v Minister for Home Affairs & Anor* [2023] (Judgement) HCA 33 (1 November 2023).

and invalid, because its purpose was punitive. The case concerned the Australian-born Delil Alexander, a dual national of both Australia and Türkiye, who traveled to Syria in 2013 and 'likely' joined IS. While imprisoned in Syria, the Australian Minister for Home Affairs determined to deprive his Australian nationality on the basis of Section 36B(i) of the Australian Citizenship Act 2007 because he "had engaged in foreign incursions while outside Australia, which demonstrated a repudiation of his allegiance to Australia" and "it would be contrary to the public interest for Mr Alexander to remain an Australian citizen".[92] The Court did not test whether the conditions of Section 36B were met, but instead, it determined Section 36B as such to be unconstitutional because the purpose of nationality deprivation on this basis is sanction or punishment and the imposition of punishment is an exclusive judicial power and, therefore, not within the power of the Minister.[93] Likewise, in November 2023, the High Court of Australia rendered a judgement in the case of *Benbrika v Minister for Home Affairs & Anor* in which the Court held Section 36D to be unconstitutional and invalid, as it likewise imposed the "exclusively judicial function of punishing criminal guilt" on the Minister.[94]

As a result of these two judgements, the Australian Citizenship Act 2007 was amended again, this time by the Australian Citizenship Amendment (Citizenship Repudiation) Act 2023, adopted in December of that year. This Amendment Act allows a court to strip nationality instead of the Minister. More specifically, in accordance with the newly introduced Sections 36C and 36D, when a person has been convicted of a serious criminal offence, including terrorism offences and the offence of foreign incursion, and has been sentenced to at least 3 years in prison, the court may decide to withdraw the person's Australian nationality or the Minister may make an application to request the court to make such a decision. In deciding whether to withdraw nationality, the court must, *inter alia*, have regard to the fact that it may not make such a decision if it "is satisfied that the person would, if the court were to make the order, become a person who is not a national or citizen of any country",[95] and that "the person's conduct to which the conviction or convictions relate is so serious and significant that it demonstrates that the person has repudiated their allegiance to Australia".[96] Australia belongs to those states that effectively deprived their FTFs and associated family members of their

92 *Alexander v Minister for Home Affairs* 2022 (n. 91) para. 15.
93 *Ibid.* paras. 157, 158.
94 *Benbrika v Minister for Home Affairs & Anor* 2023 (n. 91) para. 49.
95 Australian Citizenship Act 2007 as amended by the Australian Citizenship Amendment (Citizenship Repudiation) Act 2023, Section 36C(2).
96 *Ibid.* Section 36C(4)(c).

nationality. It seems that Australia stripped 17 non-returned FTFs or associated family members of their nationality.[97]

Belgium amended its relevant nationality deprivation grounds in the Code of Belgian Nationality in 2012 and 2015. Before these amendments, nationality could be deprived on the grounds contained in Article 23 of the Code, including when a person seriously falls short of his or her duties as a Belgian national,[98] which could also capture terrorism-related acts.[99] In 2012, new grounds were introduced in Article 23/1, including an explicit terrorism-related ground.[100] However, this ground was only applicable if nationality was obtained less than 10 years before commission of the acts. In 2015, this terrorism ground was moved to a separated Article 23/2, its scope was expanded to include more terrorist offences and the requirement of possessing the Belgian nationality for at least 10 years was abandoned.[101] According to this Article, Belgian nationals who did not obtain their nationality from a parent or through birth can have their nationality stripped if convicted of certain specific terrorist offences and sentenced to prison for at least 5 years. The provision also contains a clause which provides that nationality may not be revoked if it leads to statelessness.[102] Furthermore, Belgium implemented the measure as a judicial measure. It must be requested by the public prosecutor and approved by a court.[103] The decision only becomes effective after the exhaustion of all remedies and when properly registered.[104] Belgium may also be considered as active in the practice of denationalizing their non-returned FTFs or associated family members, as it seems to have done so in one to 19 cases.[105]

---

97 The Foreign Terrorist Fighters Knowledge Hub (n. 83). The available data in the FTF Knowledge Hub does not make a distinction between FTFs and family members.

98 Code of Belgian Nationality 1984, Article 23(1)(2).

99 M. Bolhuis and J. van Wijk (2020) (n. 20) 341; P. Wautelet, 'Deprivation of citizenship for 'jihadists' Analysis of Belgian and French practice and policy in light of the principle of equal treatment' (11 January 2016). Available at: <https://papers.ssrn.com/sol3/papers.cfm?abstract_id=2713742> accessed 24 March 2023.

100 Article 20 of the Act of 4 December 2012 Amending the Code of Belgian Nationality in order to Make the Acquisition of Belgian Nationality Migration-Neutral, introducing Article 23/1 in the Code of Belgian Nationality 1984.

101 Article 6 and 7 of the Act of 20 July 2015 to Strengthen the Fight Against Terrorism, amending Article 23/1 and introducing Article 23/2 in the Code of Belgian Nationality 1984.

102 Code of the Belgian nationality, Article 23/2(2).

103 *Ibid.* Article 23/2(1).

104 *Ibid.* Article 23/2(3).

105 The Foreign Terrorist Fighters Knowledge Hub (n. 83).

Denmark uses nationality deprivation both as an administrative and as a judicial measure. On the one hand, Article 8B of the Act on Danish Nationality provides a ground for nationality deprivation by a court order when a Danish national is convicted of a crime and has "thereby demonstrated a conduct seriously prejudicial to the vital interests of the state".[106] On the other hand, the same provision also provides the possibility of depriving a Danish national's citizenship as an administrative measure, which was introduced in 2019 because,

> [t]here have been situations in which persons have left for e.g. Syria and Iraq to fight for a terrorist organisation and where the foreign fighters' continued stays abroad have meant that – due to current legislation – it was not possible to conduct criminal proceedings against them although they had been placed in remand in absentia in Denmark. In this connection, there has been a wish to be able to deprive such persons, who are Danish nationals, of their nationality while they are still abroad and thus also prevent them from being able to return to Denmark where they would pose a threat against Danish society.[107]

This amendment made it possible for the Minister for Immigration and Integration to decide upon the deprivation of nationality when a Danish national has "displayed conduct seriously prejudicial to the vital interests of Denmark", without the need for a criminal conviction.[108] Like Australia and Belgium, the provision contains a safeguard against statelessness. Article 8B(1), containing the ground for nationality deprivation as a judicial measure, mentions that such an order may not be given if this were to be against Denmark's international obligations, which is arguably a broader safeguard than just against statelessness. Article 8B(3), containing the ground for nationality deprivation

106 Act on Danish Nationality 1950, Article 8B(1) and (2). Translation retrieved from: Danish Ministry of Immigration and Integration, International Migration – Denmark Report to the OECD (November 2022) 60. Available at: <https://uim.dk/media/11385/international-migration-denmark-2022.pdf> accessed 24 March 2023.

107 Ministry of Foreign Affairs of Denmark, Response by the Government of the Kingdom of Denmark to communication of the Special Rapporteur on extrajudicial, summary or arbitrary executions, reference AL DNK 3/2019 (29 November 2019), Appendix A – Response by the Government of the Kingdom of Denmark to questions two and three from the United Nations Special Rapporteur on extrajudicial, summary or arbitrary executions on foreign fighters, 1. Available at: <https://spcommreports.ohchr.org/TMResultsBase/DownLoadFile?gId=35114> accessed 27 March 2023; Act on Danish Nationality 1950, Article 8B(3).

108 Act on Danish Nationality 1950, Article 8B(3); Translation retrieved from: Danish Ministry of Immigration and Integration 2022 (n. 106) 61.

as an administrative measure, mentions more specifically that the Minister may not withdraw nationality if this would render the person stateless.

In 2020, Denmark again introduced an amendment to the Act on Danish Nationality. This amendment entails that a child born to a Danish parent who had illegally entered or stayed in conflict zones will not acquire Danish nationality by birth, unless the child would end up stateless. The Danish Government explained that "[t]hese children are born to parents who have turned their back to Denmark and Danish values, and they cannot be expected to grow up under circumstances that will provide for their attachment to Denmark and Danish values".[109] Like Australia, these provisions apply to all nationals, whether naturalized or by birth. Denmark seems to have deprived 11 non-returned and 5 returned FTFs or family members of their nationality.[110]

The Netherlands' grounds for nationality deprivation can be found in Article 14 of the Dutch Nationality Act 1984. In 2010, the Netherlands adopted a new ground for denationalization in Article 14(2) of the Act, which made it possible for the Minister to deprive a Dutch national of his or her nationality when convicted of one or more certain (terrorist) offences. In 2017, another new ground was introduced in Article 14(4), which allows the Minister to deprive Dutch nationality in the interest of national security,

> of a person who reached the age of 18 and who is outside the Kingdom of the Netherlands, if his or her conduct shows that he or she has joined an organization that has been placed by the Minister [...] on a list of organizations participating in a national or international armed conflict and posing a threat to national security.[111]

This list includes, among others, IS and organizations associated with it.[112] This new ground "aims to eliminate the threat of terrorist activities in the Netherlands or any of the other countries of the Kingdom, which threat ema-

109 E. Ersbøll, 'Birthright citizenship and children born in a conflict zone' European Network on Statelessness (5 February 2020). Available at: <https://www.statelessness.eu/updates/blog/birthright-citizenship-and-children-born-conflict-zone> accessed 3 February 2023. This amendment seems to be at odds with international children's rights, including the obligation not to punish and discriminate children on the basis of their parents' actions.

110 The Foreign Terrorist Fighters Knowledge Hub (n. 83).

111 Translation by the author.

112 Staatscourant, Besluit van 13 oktober 2020, nr. 3003480, tot wijziging van het Besluit van de Minister van Veiligheid en Justitie van 2 maart 2017, nr. 2050307, tot vaststelling van de lijst met organisaties die een bedreiging vormen voor de nationale veiligheid (26 Oktober 2020) Nr. 52922. Available at: <https://open.overheid.nl/documenten/ronl-2fb8da11-34e3-4c21-bd57-b8d98a6e1b1a/pdf> accessed 27 March 2023.

nates from persons who have joined a terrorist organization abroad".[113] The explanatory memorandum to the legislative proposal explains further that it is "objectionable to wait to revoke Dutch citizenship until the person has returned to the Netherlands and been prosecuted and convicted under criminal law, precisely because of the immediate threat to national security".[114]

Thus, in contrast to the ground contained in Article 14(2), this second ground does not require a criminal conviction before nationality may be stripped. Both grounds are implemented as administrative measures as they are decided upon by the Minister of Justice and Security. In addition, Article 14(8) provides that nationality may not be withdrawn if it would result in statelessness. Therefore, like Australia, Belgium and Denmark, the Netherlands may, in line with its international obligation to avoid statelessness, only use this measure when it concerns a multiple national. And like Australia and Denmark, these measures do not make a distinction between naturalized nationals and nationals by birth. The Netherlands has deprived 14 non-returned and two returned FTFs or family members of their nationality on either of these grounds.[115]

The United Kingdom's relevant provisions and amendments with regard to citizenship stripping were already discussed in the previous section because the UK has not only been active in depriving its FTFs and associated family members of their nationality, but used this measure to counter terrorism, more generally. The UK implemented its nationality deprivation power as an administrative measure as it is ordered by the Secretary of State, and when the order has been given, it takes immediate effect.[116] When comparing the UK's relevant provisions with those of other states discussed in this section, one aspect that stands out is the UK's exception to the clause protecting against statelessness when it comes to naturalized British nationals. With regard to nationals by birth, the Secretary of State may not order the withdrawal of their citizenship "if he is satisfied that the order would make a person stateless" and

113 Explanatory memorandum to the amendment of the Dutch Nationality Act in Connection with the Withdrawal of Dutch Nationality in the Interest of National Security, 4. Available at: <https://www.internetconsultatie.nl/rwn/details> accessed 27 March 2023. (Translation by the author).

114 *Ibid.* 6 (translation by the author).

115 The Foreign Terrorist Fighters Knowledge Hub (n. 83); see also, Minister of Justice and Security, Zesde rapportage uitreizigers, 5 4 52958 (17 June 2024) 4. Available at: <https://www.rijksoverheid.nl/documenten/kamerstukken/2024/06/17/tk-zesde-rapportage-uitreizigers> accessed 6 December 2024.

116 M. Bolhuis and J. van Wijk 2020 (n. 20) 358, 359; S. Krähenmann, 'Academy Briefing No. 7: Foreign Fighters under International Law' Geneva Academy of International Humanitarian Law and Human Rights (2014) 57.

hence,[117] may only deprive nationality when the person concerned holds multiple nationality. In contrast, with regard to naturalized British nationals, the Secretary of State may still strip nationality if the person does not actually hold another nationality but is merely *able* to obtain another nationality.[118] This provision may lead to *de facto* statelessness, which has, for example, happened in the Shamima Begum case that will be discussed later. On the basis of Section 40 of the British Nationality Act 1981, the UK is believed to have denationalized at least 19 non-returned FTFs or associated family members.[119]

As mentioned, Saudi Arabia is also among the states active in depriving their FTFs and associated family members of their nationality. It is suggested that Saudi Arabia deprived 13 non-returned FTFs or family members of their nationality.[120] Due to language restraints, it is difficult to obtain information on relevant Saudi Arabian legislation and practice. However, a country report from July 2022 of the Global Citizenship Observatory does provide some clarity.[121] According to this report, the Saudi Arabian Citizenship System 1954 (which is the title of the Saudi Arabian citizenship law) makes a distinction between nationals by birth and naturalized nationals when it comes to citizenship stripping. According to Article 13, Saudi nationals, both by birth and naturalized, can have their citizenship withdrawn on a number of grounds, including by obtaining another nationality and foreign military service without permission.[122] This provision does not include a terrorism-related ground. Nevertheless, Article 29 adds that "the King also has the authority to revoke the citizenship of individuals even if article 13 is not applicable to them".[123] For example, Saudi Arabia deprived Osama bin Laden of his nationality in 1994 and that of his son in 2018.[124] According to the country report, these instan-

---

117 British Nationality Act 1981, Section 40(4).

118 *Ibid.* Section 40(4A)(c).

119 The Foreign Terrorist Fighters Knowledge Hub (n. 83). The Institute on Statelessness and Inclusion and the Global Citizenship Observatory mention a number which is much higher. They mention that between 2000 and 2022, 212 persons were stripped of their British nationality on national security grounds. However, this number does not only include FTFs and their associated family members. Institute on Statelessness and Inclusion and Global Citizenship Observatory 2022 (n. 48) 29.

120 The Foreign Terrorist Fighters Knowledge Hub (n. 83).

121 Z. Alsabeehg, Report on Citizenship Law: Saudi Arabia (Global Citizenship Observatory, July 2022) RSC/GLOBALCIT-CR 2022/03. Available at: <https://cadmus.eui.eu/handle/1814/74632> accessed 28 March 2023.

122 *Ibid.* 13; Saudi Arabian Citizenship System 1954, Article 13(a) and (b).

123 *Ibid.* 13; Saudi Arabian Citizenship System 1954, Article 29.

124 'Saudi Arabia strips Osama bin Laden's son of citizenship' (*Reuters*, 1 March 2019). Available at: <https://www.reuters.com/article/world/saudi-arabia-strips-osama-bin-ladens-son-of-citizenship-idUSKCN1QI4PG/#:~:text=BEIRUT%20(Reuters)%20%2D%20Sa

ces show that "engaging in acts of terrorism can lead to the revocation of Saudi citizenship".[125] In addition to Articles 13 and 29, Article 21 provides that nationality of naturalized nationals may be revoked "if they are sentenced or imprisoned for more than one year for a criminal act connected to security or honour" or "if a court ruling proves that they committed or were involved in any act that disturbed the public security of the Kingdom or that renders their presence in the country unwanted".[126] These two grounds only apply to naturalized citizens, and such denaturalization is only allowed within 10 years of their naturalization.[127]

At first glance, the number of nationality deprivation cases in the six states that were discussed seems quite low. However, compared to other states, it can be said that these six states were 'active' in depriving their FTFs and associated family members of their nationality, as well as in promoting the policy. There are other states that, despite some of them having the necessary legislation in place, did not deprive their FTFs and associated family members of their nationality. For example, Tunisia, from which the largest number of FTFs traveled to Syria and Iraq per capita,[128] did not use nationality deprivation as a response to these individuals.[129] A number of states in Central Asia, like Azerbaijan, Kyrgyzstan, Uzbekistan and Kazakhstan, from which a considerable number of FTFs traveled,[130] and despite all having introduced nationality deprivation provisions between 2015 and 2017,[131] "transitioned from taking a peremptory position of no return and citizenship deprivation for those who travelled to the war zones to providing an active assistance in bringing them back".[132] Other examples of states that did not resort to this measure include

---

udi%20Arabia,published%20by%20the%20official%20gazette> accessed 9 December 2024.

125 Z. Alsabeehg 2022 (n. 121) 13.

126 *Ibid.* 14; Saudi Arabian Citizenship System 1954, Article 21.

127 *Ibid.*

128 B. Dodwell, D. Milton and D. Rassler, 'The Caliphate's Global Workforce: An Inside Look at the Islamic State's Foreign Fighter Paper Trail' Combating Terrorism Center at West Point (April 2016) Table 1 and 2. Available at: <https://ctc.westpoint.edu/the-caliphates-global-workforce-an-inside-look-at-the-islamic-states-foreign-fighter-paper-trail/> accessed 29 March 2023.

129 Institute on Statelessness and Inclusion and Global Citizenship Observatory 2022 (n. 48) 26.

130 B. Dodwell, D. Milton and D. Rassler 2016 (n. 128) Table 1 and 2.

131 Institute on Statelessness and Inclusion and Global Citizenship Observatory 2022 (n. 48) 29.

132 E. Zhirukhina, 'Foreign Fighters from Central Asia: Between Renunciation and Repatriation' The Italian Institute for International Political Studies (2 October 2019). Available

the United States,[133] which is otherwise known to adopt far-reaching counter-terrorism measures, Malaysia,[134] Algeria,[135] Sweden and the Czech Republic.[136] Yet other states, such as France, did use the measure but less frequently.[137] These numbers of nationality deprivation cases in the six states identified as being 'active', raise the question, why these states use such a severe measure, when it concerns such a low number of individuals. It appears that depriving FTFs and associated family members of their nationality is mainly a response by Western states, and in particular, Western (European) states. Five out of the six states are Western and four of them are European. Although this section is mainly built on data from the FTF Knowledge Hub, which only contains data from member states of the GCTF, other sources may reinforce this assumption.[138]

---

at: <https://www.ispionline.it/en/publication/foreign-fighters-central-asia-between-renunciation-and-repatriation-24072> accessed 29 March 2023.

133 According to the FTF Knowledge Hub, the United States deprived just one non-returned FTF or associated family member of her or his nationality. This is the case of Hoda Muthana. However, she was not stripped of her nationality on grounds of terrorism or national security. The United States determined she was not a citizen because of the diplomatic status of her father. Her father was a Yemeni diplomat and children of diplomats born in the United States are not automatically granted citizenship. 'Hoda Muthana: Alabama IS bride loses appeal for return to US' (*BBC News*, 12 January 2022). Available at: <https://www.bbc.co.uk/news/world-us-canada-59974939> accessed 9 December 2024.

134 A. El-Muhammady, 'Managing the Returning Foreign Terrorist Fighters and Their Families: Malaysian Experience' ICCT Policy Brief (January 2023) 5. Available at: < https://www.icct.nl/publication/managing-returning-foreign-terrorist-fighters-and-their-families-malaysian-experience> accessed 29 March 2023.

135 According to the FTF Knowledge Hub, Algeria does have the necessary legislations in place to deprive nationality based on national security but has not applied this measure in relation to terrorism.

136 Institute on Statelessness and Inclusion and Global Citizenship Observatory 2022 (n. 48) 26.

137 The Foreign Terrorist Fighters Knowledge Hub (n. 83). France only deprived three returned FTFs or associated family members of their nationality.

138 See, for example, T. Laine, "'Passing the Buck': Western States Race to Denationalize Foreign Terrorist Fighters" 12 Journal of Peacebuilding & Development (2017) 2; M. Bolhuis and J. van Wijk 2020 (n. 20); 'Open Letter from National Security Professionals to Western Governments: Unless We Act Now, the Islamic State Will Rise Again' (11 September 2019) Available at: <https://thesoufancenter.org/wp-content/uploads/2019/09/FTF-Open-Letter.pdf> accessed 30 March 2023.

any appeal, and was based on the belief that Begum was entitled to the nationality of Bangladesh, a state she never even visited.[148] It should be made clear, however, that at the time the decision was made, Begum did not actually hold Bangladeshi citizenship, and there was merely the *belief* that she would be *entitled* to it. Bangladesh, however, contested this claim and Bangladesh's Foreign Minister, Abdul Momen, made clear that she is "not our problem" and "[w]e have nothing to do with" her.[149] When the UK Secretary of State Javid was asked whether it was "morally right to export the problem" to Bangladesh instead of dealing with Begum in UK courts, he responded by arguing that his priority was the protection of the UK.[150]

Another example, which sparked a diplomatic dispute between Australia and New Zealand, is the case of Suhayra Aden. Suhayra Aden was a dual Australian and New Zealand national who traveled to Syria in 2014 and became affiliated with IS. In Syria, Aden married two Swedish FTFs, who both died, and had three children, of whom one passed away. Like Shamima Begum, it is not easy to determine whether Suhayra Aden should be labeled an FTF or instead be classified as an associated family member, as it is "unclear what role, if any, Aden may have had in IS".[151] In 2020, Australia stripped Aden of her Australian nationality while detained in Türkiye, based on one of the grounds for automatic loss of citizenship in the Australian Citizenship Act 2007, which were introduced in 2015 and repealed later in 2020. The Austra-

27/sajid-javid-difficult-to-strip-shamima-begum-of-uk-citizenship> accessed 9 December 2024.

148 On 26 February 2021, it was decided by the British Supreme Court that Begum was not entitled to return to the UK to challenge the decision to deprive her of her British nationality, *R (on the application of Begum) (Appellant) v Special Immigration Appeals Commission (Respondent) R (on the application of Begum) (Respondent) v Secretary of State for the Home Department (Appellant) Begum (Respondent) v Secretary of State for the Home Department (Appellant)* [2021] UKSC 7 (26 February 2021). Subsequently, she lost her appeal to regain her British citizenship. See, *Shamima Begum v. The Secretary of State for the Home Department* [2024] (Judgement) EWCA, CA-2023–000900 (32 February 2024).

149 'Bangladesh's Foreign Minister tells ITV News Shamima Begum is 'not our problem" (*ITV News*, 2 May 2019). Available at: <https://www.itv.com/news/2019-05-02/bangladeshs-foreign-minister-tells-itv-news-islamic-state-bride-shamima-begum-is-not-their-problem> accessed 9 December 2024.

150 P. Walker 2019 (n. 147).

151 J. Diaz, 'No Country Will Take Them: Alleged ISIS Widow with Kids the Latest of Many in Limbo' (*NPR News*, 26 March 2021). Available at: <https://www.npr.org/2021/03/26/975149256/no-country-will-take-them-alleged-isis-widow-with-kids-the-latest-of-many-in-lim#:~:text=Trump's%20Terms-,Australia%2C%20New%20Zealand%20Argue%20Over%20Who%20Takes%20In%20Alleged%20ISIS,between%20Australia%20and%20New%20Zealand> accessed 9 December 2024.

lian Prime Minister Morrison explained that it was his job "to put Australia's national security interests first" and that "Australia's interest here is that we do not want to see terrorists who fought with terrorism organisations enjoying privileges of citizenship".[152] However, compared to New Zealand, Aden had strong ties to Australia. She had left New Zealand at the age of six for Australia, where she lived since, traveled to Syria to join IS from Australia, while using her Australian passport. New Zealand Prime Minister, Ardern, responded to the deprivation of nationality by stating that Australia had "abdicated responsibility" for Aden, and New Zealand was "tired of having Australia exporting its problems" as Australia had effectively dumped the issue on New Zealand's doorstep.[153] Ardern also stated that Aden and her two young children, detained by the Turkish authorities, "are not Turkey's responsibility", and "with Australia refusing to accept the family, that makes them ours".[154] Eventually, New Zealand repatriated Aden and her children.[155]

As reiterated by the case of Suhayra Aden, Türkiye captured many alleged FTFs from other states, including some of those who escaped from detention facilities in Syria and later showed up on the Turkish side of the border. Some states of nationality, like Australia, have refused to take them back from Türkiye and have revoked their nationality. Türkiye expressed its disapproval by stating that "[c]ountries can't just revoke the citizenship of such ex-terrorists and expect Turkey to take care of them; this is unacceptable to us and it's also irresponsible", and that "Turkey is not a hotel for foreign terrorists."[156]

Then there is the case of FTF Jack Letts, involving the UK and Canada. Jack Letts is a dual British and Canadian national. Although he held Canadian nationality through his father, he was born and raised in the UK, went to

---

152 D. Welch, S. Dredge and S. Dziedzic, 'New Zealand Prime Minister Jacinda Ardern Criticises Australia for Stripping Dual National Terror Suspect's Citizenship' (*ABC News*, 16 February 2021). Available at: <https://www.abc.net.au/news/2021-02-16/jacinda-ardern-australia-stripping-dual-national-turkey-terror/13159300> accessed 9 December 2024.

153 *Ibid*; 'New Zealand Lashes at Australia in Citizenship Row over Terror Suspect' (*BBC News*, 16 February 2021). Available at: <https://www.bbc.co.uk/news/world-asia-56080282> accessed 9 December 2024.

154 R. Pannett, 'New Zealand to Resettle Suspected Islamic State Militant and her Children after Australia REVOKED Citizenship' (*The Washington Post*, 26 July 2021). Available at: <https://www.washingtonpost.com/world/2021/07/26/zealand-islamic-state-australia/> accessed 6 December 2024.

155 *Ibid.*

156 B. Mckernan, 'Turkey Threatens to Send Foreign Isis Suspects Home from Next Week' (*The Guardian*, 8 November 2019) Available at: <https://www.theguardian.com/world/2019/nov/08/turkey-isis-suspects-repatriation-islamic-state> accessed 6 December 2024; See also C. Orozobekova, *Foreign Fighters and International Peace: Joining Global Jihad and Marching Back Home* (Rowman & Littlefield 2023) 151–152.

school in the UK and in 2014 traveled from the UK to Syria at 19 years old. Allegedly, he married an Iraqi woman with whom he had a child. In 2019, the UK deprived Letts of his British nationality, based on Section 40 of the British Nationality Act 1981, while he was detained in an SDF prison in Syria. This unilateral act by the UK sparked a diplomatic dispute between the UK and Canada, with Canada accusing the UK Government of "offloading its responsibilities".[157] Canadian Member of Parliament John Mckay commented that the UK's response was like "[l]et's go out the door and leave Canada with a problem".[158]

In addition to Canada criticizing this unilateral move by the UK, the SDF also criticized states of nationality like the UK which refuse to take responsibility over their nationals. Like Jack Letts, who has been stuck in an SDF prison ever since he was arrested in 2017, a considerable number of third country nationals are still in legal limbo in the SDF-operated camps and prisons.[159] In a press release from March 2021, the SDF indicated that they "suffer from huge difficulties to accommodate ISIS fighters and their families" and that "the foreigners constitute a burden" to them, and they "need the cooperation of their countries and the international community".[160] With regard to Jack Letts, Canada appealed a court judgement which ordered the Government to repatriate him and three other Canadian male FTFs from Syria.[161] Eventually, the Federal Court of Appeal found that Canada has no obligation to repatriate them.[162]

157 D. Sabbagh, 'Jack Letts Stripped of British Citizenship' (*The Guardian*, 18 August 2019). Available at: <https://www.theguardian.com/world/2019/aug/18/jack-letts-stripped-british-citizenship-isis-canada> accessed 6 December 2024.

158 A. Coletta, 'An alleged ISIS Fighter Wants to Face Justice in Canada. Canada doesn't Want Him' (*The Washington Post*, 23 August 2019). Available at: <https://www.washingtonpost.com/world/the_americas/an-alleged-isis-fighter-wants-to-face-justice-in-canada-canada-doesnt-want-him/2019/08/22/01622dde-c4e5-11e9-8bf7-cde2d9e09055_story.html> accessed 6 December 2024.

159 J. Becker and L. Tayler, 'Revictimizing the Victims: Children Unlawfully Detained in Northeast Syria' Human Rights Watch (27 January 2023).

160 AANES, Press Release (18 March 2021). Available at: <http://kinderenteruguitkalifaat.nl/wp-content/uploads/2021/03/20210318-AANES-press-release.pdf > accessed 2 November 2021.

161 N. Yousif, 'Canada Appeals Ruling to Repatriate Citizens in Syria' (*BBC News*, 10 February 2023). Available at: <https://www.bbc.co.uk/news/world-us-canada-64605783> accessed 6 December 20024; Canadian Federal Court, *BOLOH 1(A), BOLOH 2(A) adult male only, BOLOH 12, and BOLOH 13 v. His Majesty the King and the Minister of Foreign Affairs and International Trade*, 2023 FC 98 (20 January 2023).

162 D. Major, 'Appeal Court Overturns Ruling Directing Ottawa to Repatriate 4 Men Detained in Syria' (*CBC News*, 31 May 2023). Available at: <https://www.cbc.ca/news/

A final example is the case of Neil Prakash, which led to a disagreement between Australia and Fiji. Neil Prakash was an Australian national by birth who has a Fijian father. Prakash had traveled to the conflict zone in Syria and Iraq in 2013 to fight for IS. After an Australian extradition request was denied by Türkiye in July 2018, as Türkiye decided to prosecute him itself, Australia stripped Prakash of his Australian citizenship in December 2018. Australia did so based on the in 2015-introduced and now repealed Section 35 of the Australian Citizenship Act, while he was detained in Türkiye.[163] The Australian Home Affairs Minister Dutton commented by saying, "Prakash is rotting in a jail at the moment and I hope he's there for a long period of time to come".[164] Australia held that it could strip Prakash of his Australian nationality, which he acquired by birth, because he also held or was entitled to, the Fijian nationality through his father. However, Prakash lived in Australia his entire life and departed to the conflict zone from Australia. Fiji's Head of Immigration Vuniwaqa contested Prakash being a Fijian national by saying: "[there are] no records of Mr Prakash being a Fiji citizen".[165] He also noted that Australia had not cooperated with Fiji on the matter and "[t]here was no formal communication with regards to the plans by the Australian Government".[166] Fiji's Prime Minister Bainimarama added that "[a]t any rate, he is a terrorist and a member of ISIS. We don't entertain them nor do we accommodate them."[167] In Türkiye, Prakash was convicted in March 2019 and sentenced

---

politics/court-overturns-ruling-to-repatriate-four-men-detained-syria-1.6860734> accessed 6 December 2024; Canadian Federal Court of Appeal, *His Majesty the King and the Minister of Foreign Affairs and International Trade v. BOLOH 1(a), BOLOH 2(a) male only, BOLOH 12, and BOLOH 13,* 2023 FCA 120 (31 May 2023).

163 Parliament of Australia, Neil Prakash stripped of Australian citizenship, Media Release (29 December 2018) Available at: <https://parlinfo.aph.gov.au/parlInfo/search/display/display.w3p;query=Id%3A%22media%2Fpressrel%2F6418327%22> accessed 3 April 2023.

164 D. Conifer, 'Peter Dutton Defends Process which Saw Jailed Islamic State Extremist Neil Prakash Stripped of Citizenship' (*ABC News*, 2 January 2019). Available at: <https://www.abc.net.au/news/2019-01-02/neil-prakash-lost-citizenship-automatically-says-peter-dutton/10679908> accessed 6 December 2024.

165 M. Doran, J. Macmillan and L. Movono, 'Fiji Casts Fresh Doubt on Decision to Strip Terrorist Neil Prakash of Australian citizenship' (*ABC News*, 8 January 2019). Available at: <https://www.abc.net.au/news/2019-01-08/neil-prakash-definitely-not-fijian-argue-officials/10698462> accessed December 2024.

166 *Ibid.*

167 H. Davidson, 'Dutton Insists Neil Prakash is Fijian citizen, but Fiji PM Says He 'Cannot Come Here' (*The Guardian*, 3 January 2019). Available at: <https://www.theguardian.com/australia-news/2019/jan/03/dutton-insists-neil-prakash-is-fijian-citizen-but-fiji-pm-says-he-cannot-come-here> accessed 6 December 2024.

An important question is to which state the alien may be expelled. Draft Article 22(1) of the ILC Draft Articles on the Expulsion of Aliens, first of all, mentions that an alien shall be expelled to his or her state of nationality, as it is undisputed that states of nationality are under the international legal obligation to receive their nationals (back) on their territories, which will further be elaborated upon in the next sub-section. This obligation has been described "as a necessary corollary of the right of a State to expel aliens in order to ensure the effectiveness of this right".[175] Thus, in general, only states of nationality are under an obligation to admit nationals who have been expelled from other states. It does, therefore, come as no surprise that states of nationality seem to be the most common states to which aliens are expelled.[176]

However, Article 22(1) further notes that there might be other states obliged to receive the alien. Paragraph 2 of the Commentary to Draft Article 22(1) notes that this "is intended to cover situations where a State other than the State of nationality of the expelled alien would be required to receive that person under a rule of international law, whether a treaty rule binding on that State or a rule of customary international law". The ILC Draft Articles, therefore, follow the well-established principle of international law that it lies within the sovereignty of each individual state to decide whether it admits aliens on its territory and, hence, states are not required to accept aliens on their territory, unless they are obliged to do so by a rule of international law.[177] As an example of such a rule, Jennings and Watts refer to specific treaty obligations pursuant to two conventions. First, the Convention between the Kingdom of Belgium, the Grand Duchy of Luxembourg and the Kingdom of the Netherlands on the transfer of controls of persons to the external frontiers of

---

Sadio Diallo, the ICJ ruled that the grounds on which an alien is expelled need to be clearly formulated. The Court determined that the ground on which Mr. Diallo was expelled as formulated in the expulsion decree was so vague that it was "impossible to know on the basis of which activities the presence of Mr. Diallo was deemed to be a threat to public order". Therefore, the Court deemed the expulsion of Mr. Diallo to be in violation of Article 13 of the ICCPR and Article 12(4) of the African Charter African Charter on Human and Peoples' Rights (ACHPR) (signed 1 June 1981, entered into force 21 October 1986) 1520 UNTS 217. See, *Case concerning Ahmadou Sadio Diallo (Republic of Guinea v. Democratic Republic of the Congo)* (Merits) [2010] ICJ Rep. 639, paras. 72, 73.

175 ILC, Expulsion of aliens, Memorandum by the Secretariat (10 July 2006) UN Doc. A/CN.4/565, para. 508.

176 *Ibid.* para. 507. The UN Special Rapporteur on the expulsion of aliens Kamto also noted, "a person is normally expelled to his or her State of nationality". See, ILC, 'Sixth report on the expulsion of aliens, by Mr. Maurice Kamto, Special Rapporteur' (18 March, 28 May and 9 July 2010) UN Doc. A/CN.4/625 and Add.1–2, para. 479.

177 ILC Draft Articles on the Expulsion of Aliens (n. 172) Commentary to Article 22, para. 1.

Benelux territory. Second, the Convention between Denmark, Finland, Norway and Sweden concerning the waiver of passport control at the intra-Nordic frontiers.[178] In practice, and especially when the person concerned is an (suspected) FTF or associated family member, the duty upon those states to admit the alien may be limited, as most of such treaties contain a restriction when public security, order or the vital interest of the state would be endangered.[179]

Treaties may also indirectly impose an obligation upon a state to allow entry of an alien, which is especially the case with human rights treaties. For example, a state may indirectly be obliged to admit an alien on its territory because denying entry would constitute a breach of that state's obligation to respect family life.[180] However, the right to family life, as well as other human rights which could potentially impose an indirect obligation on a particular state to accept an alien on its territory, may under certain circumstances be interfered with in the interest of national security.[181] In case of an FTF or family member, and in light of the fact that states' responses to them seem to be influenced by the potential national security threat they pose, the interest of the state in protecting its national security or preventing disorder and crime may be deemed to outweigh the individual's interest in, for example, enjoying family life.

Draft Article 22(1) of the ILC Draft Articles further mentions that an alien may be expelled to another state willing to accept him or her. However, when the person concerned poses a potential terrorist threat, it is unlikely that a state not obliged to admit the person would voluntarily accept him or her on its territory. Subsequently, Draft Article 22(2) notes that when no state of

178 R. Jennings and A. Watts (eds.), *Oppenheim's international Law, Vol 1: Peace* (9th edition, Longman Group UK Limited 1992) 898, 899; Convention between the Kingdom of Belgium, the Grand Duchy of Luxembourg and the Kingdom of the Netherlands on the transfer of controls of persons to the external frontiers of Benelux territory (signed 11 April 1960, entered into force 1 January 1974) 374 UNTS 3; Convention between Denmark, Finland, Norway and Sweden concerning the waiver of passport control at the intra-Nordic frontiers (signed 12 July 1957, entered into force 1 May 1958) 322 UNTS 245.

179 K. Doehring, "Aliens, Admission" in R. Bernhardt (ed.), *Encyclopedia of Public International Law Vol. 1* (Elsevier Science Publishers 1992) p. 108.

180 R. Jennings and A. Watts (eds.) 1992 (n. 178) 898, 899. In the *Case of Solomon v. the Netherlands*, the ECtHR held that, "while Article 8 of the Convention does not in itself guarantee a right to enter or remain in a particular country, issues may arise where a person is excluded, or removed from a country where his close relatives reside or have the right to reside. However, the State's obligation to admit to its territory aliens who are relatives of persons resident there will vary according to the circumstances of the case". *Case of Solomon v. the Netherlands* [2000] (Decision as to the admissibility) ECtHR App. No. 44328/98 (5 September 2000).

181 See, for example ECHR, Article 8(2).

nationality or any other state obliged to receive the alien has been identified and no state is willing to accept the alien, "the alien may be expelled to any State where he or she has a right of entry or stay or, where applicable, to the State from where he or she has entered the expelling State". The provision, therefore, creates a hierarchy for determining to which state an alien may be expelled. Expelling the alien to his/her state of nationality or any other state obliged or willing to accept the alien is thus preferred. Other factors that may influence the choice of destination of an alien who is to be expelled include, the prohibition of *refoulement*,[182] other restrictions based on human rights law,[183] the individual's own choice of destination,[184] his/her right to return to his or her own country,[185] the principle of non-discrimination and the admissibility of the alien to a particular state.[186] Nevertheless, territorial states have a broad discretion in determining to which state the alien is expelled. Different views have been expressed regarding the question whether it constitutes an internationally wrongful act to expel an alien to a state which is under no obligation to admit the person and has not otherwise agreed to do so.[187]

It can be concluded that within the context of the FTFs phenomenon, territorial states have a right to expel FTFs and their family members because they may pose a threat to national security and public order. Türkiye made this clear by, *inter alia*, stating that it "is not a hotel for foreign terrorists".[188] Nevertheless, the right of a state to expel an alien on the one hand, and the right of another state to refuse to admit the expellee in the absence of an obligation to do so, may create a conflict. This may especially be the case if the person concerned potentially poses a threat to the national security of the state to which he or she is to be expelled. However, states of nationality have a clear obligation to (re)admit their nationals to their territory and hence, the

182 ILC Draft Articles on the Expulsion of Aliens (n. 172), Articles 23, 24.

183 See, for example Human Rights Committee, 'General Comment no. 31, The nature of the general legal obligation imposed on States Parties to the Covenant' (26 May 2004) UN Doc. CCPR/C/21/Rev.1/Add. 13, para. 12.

184 ILC Draft Articles on the Expulsion of Aliens (n. 172) commentary to Article 22, para. 1; Human Rights Committee, 'General Comment No. 15: The Position of Aliens Under the Covenant' (11 April 1986) UN Doc. HRI/GEN/1/Rev.9 (Vol. I) para. 9.

185 The Human Rights Committee has expressly stated that a state may not arbitrarily prevent an alien's return to his own country by deporting him or her to a third country. *Ibid.* para. 8.

186 International Convention on the Elimination of All Forms of Racial Discrimination (signed 7 March 1966, entered into force 4 January 1969) 660 UNTS 195, Article 5(d)(ii).

187 ILC, Expulsion of aliens, Memorandum by the Secretariat (n. 175) para. 595.

188 B. Mckernan 2019 (n. 156); C. Orozobekova 2023 (n. 156) 151–152.

alien is generally expelled to that state. When the state of nationality deprives the person of his or her nationality and is, therefore, no longer obliged to admit the person, it can be argued that the territorial state is affected in the effective exercise of its sovereign right to expel the alien. In those instances, the territorial state is forced to deal with the potentially dangerous person stuck on its territory, with potentially no state willing to accept the alien. The next sub-section will further elaborate upon states of nationality's obligation to (re)admit their nationals.

4.2 States of Nationality's Obligation to (Re)Admit Nationals vis-à-vis Other States

A derivative of the right of the territorial state to expel aliens is that states of nationality are under an obligation to admit their nationals (back) on their territory. The obligation to admit nationals is "generally accepted as an inherent duty of States resulting from the conception of nationality" and "based on the territorial supremacy of States".[189] In addition, this obligation is a consequence of the earlier discussed human right to leave and return to "one's own country" as contained in the ICCPR, the right to enter "the State of which he is a national" as contained in the ECHR, or similar formulations of this right contained in other human rights instruments.[190] The obligation of states of nationality to re-admit their nationals into their territory is a derivative of the right to expel aliens and owed to the territorial state. The reason behind this is that this state generally admits nationals of another state on its territory on the assumption that their state of nationality will admit them back because they are obliged to do so under international law.[191]

With regard to the question, which states are obliged to receive an alien other than his or her state of nationality, the Commentary to the ILC Draft Articles on the Expulsion of Aliens also refers to the determination of the Human Rights Committee in General Comment No. 27, regarding the meaning of "his own country" in Article 12(4) of the ICCPR.[192] In this General Comment, the Human Rights Committee determined the right to return to "his

---

189 P. Weis, *Nationality and Statelessness in International Law* (Sijthof & Noordhoff 1979) 47.

190 See, for example, ACHR Article 22(5) which states that "[n]o one can be expelled from the territory of the state of which he is a national or be deprived of the right to enter it".

191 S. Krähenmann, 'The Obligations under International Law of the Foreign Fighter's State of Nationality or Habitual Residence, State of Transit and State of Destination' in A. de Guttry, F. Capone and C. Paulussen (eds.) 2016 (n. 11) 249.

192 Human Rights Committee, General Comment No. 27: Freedom of Movement Article 12 (1 November 1999) UN Doc. CCPR/C/21/Rev.1/Add.9, para. 20.

own country" to encompass more than just the right to return to his or her state of nationality. The term "his own country" also encompasses states to which the person has special ties, which could, for example, include a person's state of former nationality if he or she was stripped of that nationality, the person's state of long-term residence or the state to which the person has close family or financial ties. Other factors, which "may in certain circumstances result in the establishment of close and enduring connections between a person and a country", can also be taken into account, including the absence of such ties elsewhere.[193] Thus, by referring to this determination by the Human Rights Committee, the ILC seems to suggest that a state to which an alien has such close, special ties that it can be considered as "his own country", despite not being its state of nationality, may also be obliged to admit the person.

This reasoning may also explain why some authors are of the opinion that the obligation to re-admit nationals is not terminated upon deprivation of nationality while the individual is abroad. For example, Boll is of the opinion that "denationalization of individuals while they are abroad, unrelated to the acquisition of another nationality, cannot terminate a duty of admission".[194] He notes that "[n]ationality may be lost, but states' obligations vis-à-vis each other can persist".[195] Weis, however, is of the opinion that customary international law does not dictate a general duty to re-admit former nationals but rather notes that there is an exception where a state denationalizes its nationals while abroad "solely for the purpose of denying them readmission or to prevent their return".[196]

Notably, the ECHR does not go as far as granting a broader right to return to "his own country". The ECHR only grants a right in Protocol No. 4 Article 3(2) to return to his/her state of nationality. Although the issue was raised, the Committee of Experts, which was given the task to draft the Protocol, did not make a decision on whether Article 3 "excluded the possibility for a State to deprive one of its nationals of his or her nationality in order to expel him or her as an alien, or to prevent him or her from returning".[197] The Com-

193 *Ibid.* See also, Human Rights Committee, *Warsame v. Canada* (1 September 2011) UN Doc. CCPR/C/102/D/1959/2010, paras. 8.4–8.6; Human Rights Committee, *Nystrom v. Australia* (1 September 2011) UN Doc. CCPR/C/102/D/1557/2007 paras. 7.4–7.6.

194 A. Boll, *Multiple Nationality and International Law* (Martinus Nijhoff Publishers 2007) 289.

195 *Ibid.*

196 P. Weis 1979 (n. 189) 57.

197 *H.F. and Others v. France* [2022] (Judgement) ECtHR App. Nos. 24384/19 and 44234/20 (14 September 2022) para. 249; Guide on Article 3 of Protocol No. 4 of the ECHR (updated

mittee did not want to incorporate a provision prohibiting such conduct as it was found inadvisable "to touch on the delicate question of the legitimacy of measures depriving individuals of nationality".[198] However, the Court has explicitly "not ruled out the possibility that deprivation of nationality could be problematic under this provision".[199]

However, states are not only under the obligation to (re)admit their nationals, they are also under the obligation not to expel their own nationals. States of nationality are under such an obligation because expelling their nationals would force other states to admit aliens, and as previously mentioned, it is accepted under international law that states have a sovereign right to regulate the entry of aliens into their territory. In other words, the admission of aliens lies within the sovereignty of each state. Thus, a state of nationality may only expel a national with the consent of the state to whose territory the individual is to be expelled and the state of nationality is under an obligation to receive its nationals back.[200] These two obligations are also reflected in Security Council Resolution 2178 (2014), addressing the FTFs phenomenon in Syria and Iraq, which notes that although states are obligated to prevent FTFs from entry into and transit through their territories, this shall not "oblige any State to deny entry or require the departure from its territories of its own nationals or permanent residents".[201] It should, however, be noted that states of nationality may impose requirements on the admission of their nationals, for example, by requiring proof of nationality through a passport or other documentation.

As a response to the FTFs phenomenon in Syria and Iraq, some states of nationality have prevented the return of those individuals by depriving them of their nationality while they were abroad. In this regard, "the UK government is even known *to wait* for individuals to be abroad before it revokes their British nationality".[202] Such conduct by states of nationality can arguably be said to circumvent their obligation under international law to re-admit

---

30 November 2022), para. 19. Available at: <https://www.echr.coe.int/Documents/Guide_Art_3_Protocol_4_ENG.pdf> accessed 9 May 2023; Explanatory Report to Protocol No. 4 to the Convention for the Protection of Human Rights and Fundamental Freedoms, securing certain rights and freedoms other than those already included in the Convention and in the first Protocol thereto, para. 23. Available at: <https://rm.coe.int/16800c92c0> accessed 9 May 2023.

198 Explanatory Report to Protocol No. 4 to the ECHR (n. 197) para. 23.

199 *H.F. and Others v. France* (n. 197) 249.

200 *Ibid.* 46.

201 UNSC Resolution 2178 (2014) (n. 6) para. 8.

202 M. Bolhuis and J. van Wijk 2020 (n. 20) 358.

their nationals.[203] This is because, when a state of nationality deprives an FTF or a family member of his/her nationality after his/her departure, it is in principle no longer obliged to admit that person back to its territory, since he or she is no longer a national of that state. Moreover, if we acknowledge that those states of former nationality are still obliged to re-admit their former nationals, or at least if they have deprived them of their nationality while abroad to throw off their obligation to re-admit them, those states would, even after denationalization, act in violation of their obligation to re-admit FTFs and associated family members who held their nationality.

5 The Role of the Notion of Predominant Nationality

The examples of Suhayra Aden and Jack Letts clearly illustrate that the state depriving the FTF or associated family member of his or her nationality first, is occasionally the state with which the individual concerned had the closest ties, as compared to his or her other state(s) of nationality. In the case of Suharyra Aden, she moved away from New Zealand when she was 6 years old and ever since lived in Australia, had her family in Australia, traveled to Syria from Australia and used her Australian passport. Yet, Australia stripped her of her nationality. In the case of Jack Letts, he was born and raised in the UK, went to school in the UK and traveled from the UK to Syria. Nevertheless, the UK revoked his nationality. In both instances, the person had the closest links to the state which eventually deprived his/her nationality. This practice raises the question whether there is a role in this context for the notion of predominant nationality, which was initially developed within the framework of diplomatic protection. And if this notion can be applied, it should be considered whether any legal implications or a special responsibility upon the state of predominant nationality can be attached to it. These issues will respectively be dealt with in this section, starting with a brief discussion of how the notion of predominant nationality was first developed in the field of diplomatic protection.

5.1 Predominant Nationality and Diplomatic Protection

Diplomatic protection involves "the invocation by a State, through diplomatic action or other means of peaceful settlement, of the responsibility of another State for an injury caused by an internationally wrongful act of that State to a

203 See also A. Sánchez Frías 2020 (n. 12) 121; S. Krähenmann 2016 (n. 191) 249.

natural or legal person that is a national of the former State".[204] Diplomatic protection is connected to nationality because a state may only exercise such protection if the individual concerned has that state's nationality at the time of the violation and at the time responsibility is invoked.[205] Therefore, cases of multiple nationality pose the question whether a state of nationality may exercise diplomatic protection against a state whose nationality the person concerned also possesses. There are, believed to be, two doctrines in this regard: the doctrine of equal nationality and the doctrine of predominant nationality.

The first doctrine is that of equality, previously also referred to as the doctrine of non-responsibility of states in claims of multiple nationals.[206] This doctrine dictates that both or all the individual's nationalities are equal and a state of nationality may, therefore, not exercise diplomatic protection against another state of nationality. This is reflected in Article 4 of the 1930 Hague Convention on Certain Questions Relating to the Conflict of Nationality Law, which provides that "[a] State may not afford diplomatic protection to one of its nationals against a State whose nationality such person also possesses". The doctrine of equality does not take into account the quality of the connection between an individual and his or her state of nationality. Therefore, according to Boll, this doctrine "reflect[s] the general rule that it is up to each state to determine who possesses its nationality, and the overriding principle of the sovereign equality of states vis-à-vis one another".[207] In the past, there was strong support for this doctrine.[208] In its 1949 *Reparations for Injuries* Advisory Opinion, the ICJ described the practice of states not to exercise diplomatic protection against the state whose nationality the individual also possess as "[t]he ordinary practice".[209] This doctrine may, however, lead to unsatisfactory results for multiple nationals, as it leaves them without the possibility of diplomatic protection where wrong has been done by one of their states of nationality.

---

204 ILC, 'Draft Articles on Diplomatic Protection with commentaries' in the Report of the International Law Commission on the work of its fifty-eight session (2006) UN Doc. A/61/10, Article 1.

205 *Ibid.* Article 5(1).

206 Z. Rode, 'Dual Nationals and the Doctrine of Dominant Nationality' 53 The American Journal of International Law (1959) 1: 140, 141.

207 A. Boll 2007 (n. 194) 119.

208 ILC Draft Articles on Diplomatic Protection (n. 204) commentary to Article 7, para. 2; Z. Rode 1959 (n. 206) 141.

209 *Reparation for injuries suffered in the service of the United Nations* (Advisory Opinion) [1949] ICJ Rep. 174, p. 186.

The second doctrine is that of predominant nationality. This doctrine dictates that a person who holds multiple nationalities should be treated as only possessing one nationality if he or she is more closely connected to one of those nationalities. The doctrine of predominant nationality is reflected in Article 7 of the ILC Draft Articles on Diplomatic Protection, which provides that

> [a] State of nationality may not exercise diplomatic protection in respect of a person against a State of which that person is also a national unless the nationality of the former State is predominant, both at the date of injury and at the date of the official presentation of the claim.

This rule departs from the previous rule contained in the 1930 Hague Convention. The ILC essentially held that when diplomatic protection is exercised by a state of nationality against another state of nationality, the equality doctrine should be adhered to, unless it could be rebutted by proof of a predominant nationality. In the 1930 Hague Convention, the predominant nationality doctrine only seems to be applied vis-à-vis third states, i.e., not between states of nationality, since its Article 5 states that

> [w]ithin a third State, a person having more than one nationality shall be treated as if he had only one. [...] [E]ither the nationality of the country in which he is habitually and principally resident, or the nationality of the country with which in the circumstances he appears to be in fact most closely connected.

This leads to the conclusion that if a person has insufficient connection to one of his/her states of nationality, this can constitute a ground for non-recognition of that nationality by other states. The effective link or genuine connection doctrine as adopted by the ICJ in the *Nottebohm Case* has arguably helped develop the predominant nationality principle in the context of diplomatic protection of multiple nationals.[210] However, the 1955 *Mergé* claim of the Italian–United States Conciliation Commission, which also refers to the *Nottebohm Case*, has been indicated to constitute a starting point for the development of the doctrine of predominant nationality.[211] The Commission

210 A. Boll 2007 (n. 194) 118. As Spiro explains, "[a]lthough *Nottebohm* did not itself involve dual nationality [...], the test translated to the cases involving dual nationals". See, P. Spiro, 'Multiple Nationality' MPEPIL (last updated April 2008) para. 10.

211 ILC Draft Articles on Diplomatic Protection with commentaries (n. 204) commentary to Article 7, para. 4.

noted the existence of two complementary principles in cases of diplomatic protection of dual nationals. According to the Commission,

> [t]he principle, based on the sovereign equality of States, which excludes diplomatic protection in the case of dual nationality, must yield before the principle of effective nationality whenever such nationality is that of the claiming State. But it must not yield when such predominance is not proved because the first of these two principles is generally recognised and may constitute a criterion of practical application for the elimination of any possible uncertainty.[212]

According to the ILC, the predominant nationality doctrine presently prevails, i.e., the principle of equality unless there is proof of a predominant nationality, and is a rule of customary international law.[213] Already in 1959, Rode mentioned that the doctrine of equality "might gradually fall into disuse".[214]

Factors influencing the determination of predominant nationality include

> [h]abitual residence, the amount of time spent in each country of nationality, date of naturalization (i.e. the length of the period spent as a national of the protecting State before the claim arose); place, curricula and language of education; employment and financial interests; place of family life; family ties in each country; participation in social and public life; use of language; taxation, bank account, social security insurance; visits to the other State of nationality; possession and use of passport of the other State; and military service.[215]

As stated in the commentary to the ILC Draft Articles on Diplomatic Protection, none of those factors are exhaustive and the weight accorded to each factor will vary depending on the circumstances of each case.[216] Nevertheless, some authors imply that most weight should be accorded to the residence of the individual. For example, Rode explained that "[t]he essence of the doc-

212 *Mergé case* [1955] Italian–United States Conciliation Commission Decision No. 55, UNRIAA Vol. XIV, p. 247; see also *Iran v. United States* (Decision) [6 April 1984] IUSCT Case No. A/18 37, para. 50.

213 ILC Draft Articles on Diplomatic Protection with commentaries (n. 204) commentary to Article 7, para. 4.

214 Z. Rode 1959 (n. 206) 143; see also C. Forcese, "The Capacity to Protect: Diplomatic Protection of Dual Nationals in the 'War on Terror'" 17 European Journal of International Law (2006) 2: 386–389.

215 ILC Draft Articles on Diplomatic Protection with commentaries (n. 204) commentary to Article 7, para. 5.

216 *Ibid.*

that is where their links reside."[226] Similarly, in the Shamima Begum case, Bangladesh pointed to the fact that Begum had a British mother, was born in Britain and that "[s]he has no relation with Bangladesh".[227] Bangladesh's Foreign Minister Abdul Momen seems to point towards the lack of any link between Bangladesh and Begum while simultaneously pointing out the existence of strong connection between Begum and the UK.[228] In the case of Jack Letts, the Canadian Government did not want to go into much detail on the specific case, but Canada's Member of Parliament John Mckay stated that there is not much sympathy for Letts in Canada because his ties to Canada are "remote" and his Canadian citizenship is merely "a citizenship of convenience".[229] And although Fiji contested that Neil Prakash was a Fijian national altogether, Fiji also pointed, *inter alia*, towards the fact that he was born in Australia, acquired Australian citizenship by birth, lived in Australia all his life and that he "never set foot in Fiji".[230] Thus, Fiji seemingly pointed to Prakash's close ties to Australia as compared to his very weak connection to Fiji. On the basis of these examples, it can be argued that responses by states of residual nationality can be read as an implicit reference towards the notion of predominant nationality.

5.2.2 Relevance of the Notion

If the notion of predominant nationality can indeed be applied in the context of nationality deprivation, the question remains what the relevance is of the notion and whether there are legal implications attached to a determination of predominance of nationality. A possible answer to this question can be found in the fact that some states active in depriving FTFs and their associated family members of their nationality seem to take into account the person's connection to his or her other state(s) of nationality, as compared to his or her connection to the depriving state, when taking a nationality deprivation

226 *Ibid.*

227 S. Najmus Sakib, 'Bangladesh Will Not Accept ISIS Girl Shamima Begum' (*Anadolu Agency News*, 16 February 2020). Available at: <https://www.aa.com.tr/en/asia-pacific/bangladesh-will-not-accept-isis-girl-shamima-begum/1735373> accessed 9 December 2024.

228 *Ibid.*

229 A. Coletta 2019 (n. 158).

230 S. Molloy, 'Neil Prakash Case Explained: Aussie-Born Terrorist Causing Diplomatic War of Words with Fiji' (*news.com.au*, 9 January 2019). Available at: <https://www.news.com.au/national/crime/neil-prakash-case-explained-aussieborn-terrorist-causing-diplomatic-war-of-words-with-fiji/news-story/c68cd0dae42e4e953e62d5e06346199e> accessed 9 December 2024.

decision. Evidence for this can be found in those states' nationality laws or the legislative history of those laws.

Australia's nationality deprivation law provides a clear example. As mentioned before, the newly introduced Sections 36C and 36D of the Australian Citizenship Act 2007 allow a court, including through an application by the Minister, to strip a convicted person of his or her Australian nationality. In deciding whether to withdraw nationality, Section 36C explicitly requires the court to have regard to "the person's connection to the other country of which the person is a national or citizen and the availability of the rights of citizenship of that country to the person".[231] The Explanatory Memorandum to the Australian Citizenship Amendment (Citizenship Repudiation) Act 2023 also mentioned that "[t]he court's decision to make the order must be informed further by its consideration of the person's connection to their other country of citizenship (and by extension, any residual connection to Australia)".[232] It stipulates that "[i]n certain circumstances, cessation of a person's Australian citizenship may not be the preferred outcome, having regard to Australia's bilateral relationships [and] international relations more broadly".[233]

Another example is Denmark's preparatory work to the current Article 8B (1) of the Act on Danish Nationality. The preparatory work to this Article clearly states that

> a decision to deprive citizenship requires a proportionality test to be conducted, weighing the seriousness of the crime against the impact on the person of his or her loss of Danish citizenship. Such a determination involves evaluating the person's ties to Denmark as compared with his or her ties to another country of which he or she is a citizen, including family ties in both countries. However, even very serious crimes should not result in loss of citizenship *if the person has no connection or very little connection to the other country*.[234]

---

231 Australian Citizenship Act 2007, Section 36C(6)(c).

232 Explanatory Memorandum to the Australian Citizenship Amendment (Citizenship Repudiation) Act 2023, p. 4. Available at: <https://www.aph.gov.au/Parliamentary_Business/Bills_Legislation/Bills_Search_Results/Result?bId=r7129> accessed 9 December 2024.

233 *Ibid*. pp. 13, 18.

234 Translation retrieved from the case of *Johansen v. Denmark* (n. 219) para. 22 (emphasis added). The preparatory work to Section 8B of the Act on Danish Nationality can be found here: <https://www.folketingstidende.dk/ebog/20031A1?s=4896> accessed 26 April 2023.

The preparatory work further adds that "[i]n these cases, Denmark ought to take responsibility for the individual Danish citizen".[235] The legislative proposal with regard to Section 8B(3), which was added in 2019, also mentions that

> [t]he significance which deprivation of Danish nationality has on a person must be considered individually based on the circumstances of the person concerned. In this assessment, *particular importance should be attached to the person's ties to Denmark and other countries, including the country or countries of which the person concerned is also a national.* In this connection, the duration and nature of a person's stay in Denmark and abroad may also be taken into account. Special importance should thus be attached to the question of where the person concerned grew up, just as less importance may be attached to a stay abroad if the stay abroad is due to work for Danish interests, or if, during their stay abroad, the person concerned kept close ties to Denmark through repeat holiday visits, participation in Danish associations abroad, etc. Importance may also be attached to a person's current family relations in Denmark and abroad as well as the person's roots, including whether the family has had long-term ties to Denmark. Language skills may also be important, especially the extent to which the person concerned masters Danish and the language of the country or countries of which the person concerned is also a national.[236]

The factors, which must be taken into account when determining the strength of someone's ties to Denmark, seem to correspond with some of the factors relevant for the determination of a person's predominant nationality according to the ILC, for the purpose of diplomatic protection. For example, a person's language skills, family relations, the amount of time spent in each country of nationality and the person's visits to the other state of nationality.

These factors were also taken into account in a decision by the Danish Supreme Court from 22 March 2023. This case concerned a woman with both Iranian and Danish nationality. She obtained her Danish nationality by birth and held the Iranian nationality through her parents. In April 2015, she

235 Translation retrieved from C. Prener, 'The ECtHR on citizenship revocation: Solving or compounding the confusion?' Global Citizenship Observatory (29 March 2022). Available at: <https://globalcit.eu/the-ecthr-on-citizenship-revocation-solving-or-compounding-the-confusion/> accessed 25 April 2023.

236 Translation retrieved from Ministry of Foreign Affairs of Denmark 2019 (n. 107) p. 4. (emphasis added).

traveled to Syria when she was 20 years old to join IS. In March 2019, she was captured and detained in an SDF-controlled camp in Syria together with her two children. Through an administrative decision on 17 June 2020, based on Article 8B(3) of the Act on Danish Nationality, Denmark deprived her of her nationality. However, the Danish Supreme Court eventually ruled that this decision was invalid. In its judgement, the Supreme Court confirmed that the legislative history of Article 8B of the Act on Danish Nationality shows that nationality may not be withdrawn when the person concerned has no or only a very weak connection to his or her other state(s) of nationality and that in such instances, Denmark should take responsibility for the actions of its national.[237] The Court highlighted that the woman in question had "very little" connections with Iran as she never lived nor otherwise resided for a considerable period of time in that state, has no contact with any family in Iran and does not speak Farsi.[238] At the same time, she had "a strong connection" to Denmark, *inter alia*, because she was born, raised and schooled in the country, her parents and sister lived there and she spoke Danish.[239] Because of her very weak links to Iran, compared to her close connections to Denmark, the Danish Supreme Court ruled that the nationality deprivation decision was not in accordance with the proportionality requirement according to Article 8B(3) of the Act on Danish Nationality.[240]

On the basis of this judgement, it seems that when Denmark wishes to deprive nationality but is clearly the person's state of predominant nationality, this should be taken into account when considering the proportionality of such a decision. Predominance of nationality seems to be a factor which must be given considerable weight. However, in the earlier mentioned case of Adam Johansen, the Danish Supreme Court seems to have come to a different conclusion on proportionality and the weight that should be given to predominance of nationality. The Court ruled that Johansen's ties to Tunisia, although weak, were not insignificant and the deprivation of his Danish nationality was, therefore, not disproportionate. Eventually, Johansen filed a case against Denmark before the ECtHR in which he submitted that this decision constituted a

237 *A v Ministry of Immigration and Integration,* Danish Supreme Court, Case BS-23360/2022-HJR (22 March 2023) p. 7. Available at: <https://www.domstol.dk/hoejesteret/aktuelt/2023/3/afgoerelse-om-fratagelse-af-dansk-statsborgerskab-var-ugyldig/> accessed 1 May 2023.

238 *Ibid.* 8. Translation by the author.

239 *Ibid.* 7. Translation by the author.

240 *Ibid.* 8.

violation of his rights contained in Article 8 of the ECHR. In its judgement of 1 February 2022, the ECtHR started by saying that an arbitrary revocation of citizenship "might in certain circumstances raise an issue under Article 8 of the Convention".[241] However, the ECtHR ruled that the decision concerning

241 *Johansen v. Denmark* (n. 219) paras. 44, 45. According to the ECtHR the notion of 'private life' "is a broad term not susceptible to exhaustive definition. It covers the physical and psychological integrity of a person" and may "embrace multiple aspects of the person's physical and social identity". See, *Case of Genovese v. Malta* [2011] (Judgement) ECtHR App. No. 53124/09 (11 October 2011) para. 30. Accordingly, the right to private life also encompasses the right to an identity and the right to personal development. See, *Case of Bărbulescu v. Romania* [2017] (Judgement) ECtHR App. No. 61496/08 (5 September 2017) para. 70.

The notion of 'family life' is also very broad and refers to the actual existence of close personal ties between the persons concerned. See, *Case of K. and T. v. Finland* [2001] (Judgement) ECtHR App. No. 25702/94 (12 July 2001) para. 150. The ECtHR clarified that this notion is not solely confined to relationships based on marriage, i.e., married couples and their children, but may also extent to other *de facto* relationships. See, *Case of Genovese v. Malta* para. 29 and *Case of X. Y. and Z. v. The United Kingdom* [1997] (Judgement) ECtHR App. No. 21830/93 (22 April 1997) para. 36. Multiple factors can be taken into account in determining whether a relationship amounts to 'family life', "including whether the couple live together, the length of their relationship and whether they have demonstrated their commitment to each other by having children together or by any other means". See, *Case of X. Y. and Z. v. The United Kingdom* para. 36. Furthermore, the term also includes near relatives such as grandparents and grandchildren, as well as siblings. Situations in which there is not yet an established relationship but there is a real interest in establishing future family ties could also fall within the notion of 'family ties'. See, *Case of Anayo v. Germany* [2010] (Judgement) ECtHR App. No. 20578/07 (21 December 2010) para. 57. However, relationships between adults and their parents do not necessarily fall within this notion unless "additional factors of dependence, other than normal emotional ties, are shown to exist". *Case of Senchishak v. Finland* [2014] (judgement) ECtHR App. No. 5049/12 (18 November 2014) para. 55. For a further explanation of the notion of 'family life', see A. Büchler, 'the Right to Respect for Private and Family Life: the Case Law of the European Court of Human Rights on Parenthood and Family Forms' in A. Büchler and H. Keller (eds.), *Family forms and parenthood: theory and practice of Article 8 ECHR in Europe* (Intersentia 2016) 30–32.

A person who is deprived of his/her nationality may, first of all, have strong family ties to his/her state of former nationality. When a person has to leave that state or is unable to return as a result of nationality deprivation, the right to family life, which guarantees the right to live together as a family, may potentially be infringed upon because the person is separated from his or her family. Secondly, the right to private life may also be infringed upon through such practices, because of the impact on the individual's identity, of which nationality is a part, and the person's personal, social and economic relations to the depriving state that make up his or her private life. *Case of Slivenko v. Latvia* (Judgement) [2003] ECtHR App. no. 48321/199 (9 October 2003) para. 96; *Case of Genovese v. Malta* para. 33; *Case of Ghoumid and Others v. France* [2020] (Judgement) ECtHR App. No. 52273/16 (25 June 2020) para. 43.

the deprivation of Adam Johansen's nationality was not arbitrary, *inter alia*, because it was "to a large extent a result of the applicant's own choices and actions" and because the Court considered "it legitimate for Contracting States to take a firm stand against those who contribute to terrorist acts, which it cannot condone in any circumstances".[242] Besides a role in the proportionality test for factors which determine predominance of nationality, this case shows that in assessing whether a decision to withdraw nationality is proportionate, the ECtHR attaches great importance to national security and states' assessment of national security issues.

Despite the importance attached to national security considerations, the examples given in this sub-section imply that an FTF or family member's predominant nationality must be taken into account when determining whether deprivation of nationality is proportionate. This proportionality requirement is part of human rights law and also, *inter alia*, required by the prohibition of arbitrary deprivation of nationality.[243] The analysis of these two states' nationality laws and legislative history shows that these states seem to be of the opinion that predominance of nationality should be taken into account when taking a decision on the deprivation of nationality. They may even believe that states of predominant nationality have a special responsibility not to deprive nationality in such circumstances, as it may otherwise disproportionately affect the individual concerned. Based on these two examples, the role of the notion of predominant nationality remains within the vertical dimension of nationality deprivation, meaning that it is of relevance for determining the proportionality of a state's decision towards the individual concerned, not towards other states involved. A progressive interpretation of the notion of predominant nationality would, however, also stress its relevance within the horizontal dimension to this practice. Nationality deprivation seems particularly unfair when the buck is passed to a state to which the individual only has loose ties, in which the individual may never have resided, or which the individual may never even have visited. A role for the notion of predominant nationality in the regulation of responsibility shunning and risk exportation through nationality revocation would mean that states of predominant nationality do not only have a special responsibility not to deprive nationality because it may be disproportionate towards the individual con-

242 *Johansen v. Denmark* (n. 219) paras. 50, 51.

243 See, for example, UDHR, Article 15(2); Arab Charter on Human Rights, Article 29; ACHR, Article 20(3); ECN, Article 4(c); ASEAN Human Rights Declaration (19 November 2012) Article 18. Available at: <https://asean.org/asean-human-rights-declaration/> accessed 11 May August 2023.

cerned but also because of the undesirable consequences towards other states involved.

5.2.3 Security Perspective

A role for this notion within the horizontal perspective to nationality deprivation is even more important when looking at it from a security perspective. Deprivation of predominant nationality hampers reintegration and rehabilitation efforts. How can someone properly (re)integrate into a society to which he or she does not have any or only a very weak connection? For example, in a state in which she or he does not have a social safety net, does not have any family, has never resided and/or does not speak the language? A study from the Radicalisation Awareness Network shows that "[t]he family members of the returnee can play a crucial role in the challenging period of resocialization and reintegration into society" and that "[f]amily members can provide a getaway back to society".[244] Furthermore, "a resilient family environment" may help "to prevent future involvement with extremist and terrorist groups".[245] The study also identified isolation as one of the issues which may complicate the reintegration of returnees.[246] In general, the state of predominant nationality, to which an FTF or associated family member has the closest connection and in which his or her family lives, seems to be in the best position to reintegrate and rehabilitate him or her. Hence, depriving an FTF or accompanying family member of his or her predominant nationality is not only questionable in terms of the proportionality of the measures, it is likely ineffective from a security perspective. Individuals who "are and feel part of society are less likely to fall back and become attracted to terrorist or violent extremist groups (again)".[247] Finally, while nationality deprivation may make the territory of the depriving state safer in the short term, it does not prevent the person from disappearing under the radar and illegally traveling back to the depriving state, which might be more likely when the depriving state was the person's state of predominant nationality. This discussion as to whether the deprivation of nationality actually makes the territory of the depriving state safer, is

244 Radicalisation Awareness Network, RAN Manual Responses to Returnees: Foreign Terrorist Fighters and their Family Members (2nd edition, 2022). 77 Available at: <https://home-affairs.ec.europa.eu/system/files/2022-12/ran_manual_responses_returning_foreign_terrorists_and_their_families_en.pdf> accessed 22 June 2023.

245 *Ibid.* 11.

246 *Ibid.* 13, 77.

247 *Ibid.* 74.

also relevant in light of the obligation to prevent terrorism, to which we will turn in the next section.

6 Nationality Deprivation as a Violation of an Obligation to Prevent and Cooperate in Combatting Terrorism and Other General Principles of Inter-state Behavior

After having discussed a number of concrete norms, this section will consider general obligations and principles of inter-state behavior. First, this section will zero in on the obligation to prevent terrorism and a possible obligation to cooperate in combating terrorism. Second, this section will examine other general principles of inter-state behavior. A focus will be placed on the general principle of good faith as referring to a standard of behavior.

6.1 An Obligation to Prevent and Cooperate

In a statement in response to the UK depriving Jack Letts of his British nationality, the Canadian Public Safety Minister Goodale said that "[t]errorism knows no borders, so countries need to work together to keep each other safe", instead of acting unilaterally.[248] This statement raises the question whether cooperation in response to terrorist threats should currently be seen as merely a tool to prevent terrorism, or whether cooperation to respond to terrorist threats should rather be seen as a legally binding obligation requiring states, *inter alia*, not to adopt certain measures which may negatively affect other states. A legal basis for an independent obligation to cooperate in combating terrorism can potentially be found in a number of Security Council resolutions, such as Resolutions 1373 (2001), 1566 (2004), 2178 (2014) and 2322 (2016).[249] In Resolution 1373 (2001), while acting under Chapter VII, the Security Council called upon states to "cooperate on administrative and judicial matters to prevent the commission of terrorist acts" and to "[c]ooperate, particularly through bilateral and multilateral arrangements and agreements, to prevent and suppress terrorist attacks".[250] Acting under Chapter VII again,

248 " Canada slams UK decision to 'off-load' Islamist fighter" (*Reuters,* 18 August 2019). Available at: <https://www.reuters.com/article/world/canada-slams-uk-decision-to-off-load-islamist-fighter-idUSKCN1V907K/> accessed 9 December 2024.

249 UNSC Resolution 1373 (28 September 2001) UN Doc. S/RES/1373 (2001); UNSC Resolution 1566 (2004) UN Doc. S/RES/1566 (2004); UNSC Res. 2178 (2014) (n. 6); UNSC Resolution 2322 (12 December 2016) UN Doc. S/RES/2322 (2016).

250 UNSC Res. 1373 (2001) (n. 249) paras. 3(b) and (c).

the Security Council likewise called upon "States to cooperate fully in the fight against terrorism" in Resolution 1566 (2004).[251] In Resolution 2178 (2014), the Security Council specifically addressed states' responses to the FTFs phenomenon. Acting under Chapter VII, the Council called upon all states, "in accordance with their obligations under international law, to cooperate in efforts to address the threat posed by foreign terrorist fighters".[252] As a final example, in Resolution 2322 (2016) the Security Council called upon states to "cooperate on administrative, police and judicial matters to prevent the commission of terrorist acts and to counter the FTF threat, including returnees".[253]

When one analyzes these provisions carefully and in comparison with other provisions, it stands out that the Security Council uses less strong wording in the provisions referring to cooperation. In these provisions, the Council repeatedly *calls upon* states to cooperate. For some other obligations, the Council seems to use stronger wording, by *deciding* that states *shall* do something or refrain from doing something. For example, in Resolution 2178 (2014), the Security Council *calls upon* states "to cooperate in efforts to address the threat posed by" FTFs, but *decides* that states *shall* "prevent and suppress the recruiting, organizing, transporting or equipping of" FTFs.[254] While the term 'decides' is commonly understood to indicate that the Council is imposing a legally binding obligation,[255] the term 'calls upon' is more ambiguous and "[i]n its practice, the [Security Council] has generally used the [term] for non-binding suggestions of different intensity".[256] However, the term 'calls upon' is equivocal as in some, albeit exceptional, instances it has been used to refer to legally binding obligations. For example, in the *Namibia* Advisory Opinion, the ICJ determined that when the Security Council *called upon* South Africa to immediately withdraw from Namibia, the Council imposed a legally binding obligation upon South Africa.[257] It should also be mentioned that even when the Council is acting under Chapter VII, which it did in Resolutions 1373 (2001), 1566 (2004) and 2178 (2014), it "may make recommendations which, while they may be of great significance [...] and impose political obligations, are

251 UNSC Res. 1566 (2004) (n. 249) para. 2.

252 UNSC Res. 2178 (2014) (n. 6) para. 4.

253 UNSC Res. 2322 (2016) (n. 249) para. 9(a).

254 UNSC Res. 2178 (2014) (n. 6) paras. 4 and 5.

255 B. Simma, D. Khan, G. Nolte et al. (eds.), *The Charter of the United Nations: A Commentary Vol II* (3rd edition, Oxford University Press, 2012) 1265; United Nations Charter (signed 26 June 1945, entered into force 24 October 1945) 1 UNTS 16, Article 25.

256 *Ibid.*

257 *Legal Consequences for States of the Continued Presence of South Africa in Namibia (South West Africa) notwithstanding Security Council Resolution 276 (1970)* (Advisory Opinion) [1971] ICJ Rep. 16, p. 115.

not legally binding as such."[258] Thus, even though the Security Council acted under Chapter VII, the language used by the Council in Resolutions 1373 (2001) , 1566 (2004) and 2178 (2014) when referring to cooperation in combating terrorism, may create doubt as to whether the obligation to cooperate can be viewed in itself as a legally binding obligation. Nevertheless, "even nonbinding resolutions of the Council may have considerable political weight. They are not always without legal significance, particularly if repeated,"[259] like the obligation to cooperate in question. Lauterpacht went even further by saying,

> [a] Resolution recommending to an Administering State a specific course of action creates *some* legal obligation which, however rudimentary, elastic and imperfect, is nevertheless a legal obligation and constitutes a measure of supervision. The State in question, while not bound to accept the recommendation, is bound to give it due consideration in good faith.[260]

In sum, the language of the Security Council resolutions that refer to cooperation in combating terrorism suggests that it is not a legally binding obligation in and of itself. However, it may still carry much political weight and states may not just set it aside. It could be argued that states must at least consider the cooperation with other states, all the more because the Security Council called upon states to cooperate in their efforts to fight terrorism multiple times. It should also briefly be mentioned that, although not referring to terrorism explicitly, in contrast to the Security Council, the General Assembly used more firm language in the 1970 Friendly Relations Declaration when indicating that states "have the duty to" and "shall co-operate with other States in the maintenance of international peace and security".[261]

Besides the above mentioned Security Council resolutions, obligations to cooperate can also be found in several specialized counter-terrorism conventions. The relevant provisions mention that "States Parties shall cooperate in the prevention of" the specialized offences which constitute the object of conventions.[262] However, as these treaties are only applicable to specific terrorist

---

258 M. Wood and E. Sthoeger, *The UN Security Council and International Law* (Cambridge University Press 2022) 32.

259 *Ibid.* 33.

260 *Voting Procedure on Questions relating to Reports and Petitions concerning the Territory of South West Africa* (Advisory Opinion) [1955] ICJ Rep. 67, Separate Opinion of Judge Lauterpacht p. 118, 119.

261 UNGA Resolution 2625 (XXV) (24 October 1970) UN Doc. A/Res/2625(XXV) para. 1.

262 See, for example, Article 18 of the International Convention for the Suppression of the Financing of Terrorism (adopted 9 December 1999, entered into force 10 April 2002) 2178

offences and only valid for states party to them, it is doubtful whether a general obligation to cooperate in combating terrorism can be deduced from these treaties.

It can be argued that a more general obligation to cooperate in combating terrorism stems from, and is part of, the obligation to prevent terrorism.[263] The reason behind this is that terrorism constitutes an international threat, which can pre-eminently be evidenced by the FTFs phenomenon in Syria and Iraq, which requires an international response and can only be prevented through the cooperation of states. The obligation to prevent terrorism, in turn, stems from a state's positive obligations to protect the fundamental rights of its population, including the right to life and security,[264] and is, as discussed in the previous chapter, a well-established obligation under international law.[265] The obligation to prevent terrorism is also reflected in the above mentioned Security Council Resolutions, such as Resolution 1373 (2001) in which the Council *decided* that all states *shall* "[t]ake the necessary steps to prevent the commission of terrorist acts".[266] Contrary to the provision on cooperation in the same Resolution, this provision is unequivocally formulated as a legally binding obligation.

This line of thought would suggest that the obligation to cooperate in combating terrorism should be viewed as a means to realize the prevention of terrorism, instead of "an obligation in itself, which commits [states], legally, to working with other States".[267] This reasoning also seems to be reflected in some Security Council Resolutions. For example, Resolution 1373 (2001) calls upon states to "[c]ooperate [...] *to prevent* and suppress terrorist attacks",[268]

UNTS 197; Article 4 of the International Convention against the taking of hostages (adopted 17 December 1979, entered into force 3 June 1983) 1316 UNTS 205; and Article 15 of the International Convention for the Suppression of Terrorist Bombings (adopted 15 December 1997, entered into force 23 May 2001) 2149 UNTS 256.

263 M. Feinberg, 'Terrorism Inside Out: Legislating For Humanity To Cooperate Against Terrorism' 42 North Carolina Journal of International Law (2017) 2: 508.

264 ICCPR Articles 2, 6 and 9; The Office of the United Nations High Commissioner for Human Rights (OHCHR) mentioned that "[i]n order to fulfil their obligations under human rights law to protect the life and security of individuals under their jurisdiction, States have a right and a duty to take effective counter-terrorism measures, to prevent and deter future terrorist attacks". See, OHCHR, Human Rights, Terrorism and Counter-terrorism, Fact Sheet No. 32 (1 July 2008) 8, 9. Available at: <https://www.ohchr.org/en/publications/fact-sheets/fact-sheet-no-32-terrorism-and-counter-terrorism> accessed 12 April 2023.

265 *Ibid.* 510.

266 UNSC Res. 1373 (2001) (n. 249) para. 2(b).

267 M. Feinberg 2017 (n. 263) 515.

268 UNSC Res. 1373 (2001) (n. 249) para. 3(c) (emphasis added).

and Resolution 2178 (2014) calls upon states "to cooperate *in efforts to address* the threat posed by foreign terrorist fighters".[269] In addition, in the preamble of Resolution 2322 (2016), the Security Council stressed "that terrorism can only be defeated by a sustained and comprehensive approach involving the active participation and collaboration of all States and international and regional organizations to impede, impair, isolate, and incapacitate the terrorist threat".[270] In the preamble of Resolution 2396 (2017) the Council reaffirmed "that terrorism poses a threat to international peace and security and that countering this threat requires collective efforts on national, regional and international levels".[271]

Even if the obligation to cooperate in combating terrorism is not generally seen as a legally binding obligation in itself but rather as a necessary means to adhere to the well established obligation to prevent terrorism, it may entail that states must work together in their efforts to prevent terrorism. In doing so, states must take the interests of other states into account and avoid adopting measures which have a clear negative impact on other states. Such contents of an obligation to cooperate would at least prevent practices like the shunning and shifting of responsibilities in response to terrorist threats. If cooperation, as a means to adhere to the obligation to prevent terrorism, is understood in this way, and states are to comply with it, an assessment of a state's own national security alone is arguably not sufficient when depriving an FTF or accompanying family member of his/her nationality.

Therefore, Feinberg proposes the introduction of an impact assessment for counter-terrorism measures, which would oblige states to conduct such an assessment with regard to new counter-terrorism measures, not only for the impact they would have on their own territory, but also for the impact these measures would have on other states.[272] Only if states have regard to the possible negative impact of their counter-terrorism measures extraterritorially, weigh the interests of other involved states and act accordingly, would they act in full compliance with their obligation to prevent terrorism of which the obligation to cooperate in combating terrorism may be part.

In conclusion, although cooperation in combating terrorism as referred to in multiple Security Council resolutions may currently not be seen as an independent, legally binding obligation, it does find some legal basis in the

269 UNSC Res. 2178 (2014) (n. 6) para. 4 (emphasis added).
270 UNSC Res. 2322 (2016) (n. 249) pre-ambular para. 12.
271 UNSC Resolution 2396 (21 December 2017) UN Doc. S/RES/2396 (2017) pre-ambular para. 3.
272 M. Feinberg 2017 (n. 263) 542.

Security Council's repeated call upon states to cooperate and in the well-established obligation to prevent terrorism of which an obligation to cooperate may be part. In other words, the legal basis of an obligation to cooperate in combatting terrorism is sufficient to argue that states should not put aside completely the interests of, and effects of their actions on, other states in order to protect their own interests through unilateral action. The shunning of responsibilities and the shifting of security threats through nationality deprivation as a response to FTFs and their associated family members who traveled to Syria and Iraq, goes against the very spirit of the Security Council's call "to cooperate in efforts to address the threat posed by foreign terrorist fighters" as contained in Resolution 2178 (2014) and the Council's repeating efforts in calling upon states to cooperate in combating terrorism, more generally. In addition, nationality deprivation arguably does not contribute to the furtherance of states' obligation to prevent terrorism as "the risk is not addressed, but *exported* somewhere else" and "in the long term, the person deprived of nationality could become a risk for the security of the depriving country and of the people under its jurisdiction, in case such a person disappears off the radar and manages to get back to the country that turned its back against him or her".[273] In sum, it can be asserted that the practice of passing the buck to other states through the deprivation of nationality may be incompatible with both the Security Council's call to cooperate as well as with the obligation to prevent terrorism.[274]

6.2 An Act of Bad Faith?

In response to Suhayra Aden being stripped of her Australian citizenship, Jacinda Ardern, Prime Minister of New Zealand at the time, said "I never believed that the right response was simply a race to revoke citizenship, that is not the right thing to do. Australia did not act in good faith."[275] Through this statement, the Prime Minister seems to refer to Australia's action as being

---

273 C. Paulussen, 'Towards a Right to Sustainable Security of Person in Times of Terrorism? Assessing Possibilities and Limitations through a Critical Evaluation of Citizenship Stripping and Non-repatriation Policies' 26 Journal of Conflict and Security Law (2021) 1: 10, 11.

274 In Resolution 2263 (2019) the Parliamentary Assembly to the Council of Europe also reaffirmed that the "exporting of risks" through deprivation of nationality goes against, what the Assembly referred to as, "the principle of international co-operation in combating terrorism". See, Parliamentary Assembly of the Council of Europe Resolution 2263 (2019) (n. 143) para. 8.

275 D. Welch, S. Dredge and S. Dziedzic 2021 (n. 152).

contrary to the general principle of good faith under international law. To determine whether the revocation of nationality resulting in the shunning of responsibilities and the shifting of security threats can really be seen as an act of bad faith, it should, first of all, be set out what good faith as a general principle actually entails.

The concept of good faith in international law is used in different ways. Kolb notes that good faith has three distinct meanings in international law.[276] First, good faith refers to an erroneous belief regarding a legally relevant fact. In that sense, good faith designates a subjective legal fact to which the law attaches consequences.[277] Second, good faith refers to a standard of behavior, requiring states to act reasonably and fairly.[278] Finally, good faith is used to refer to legitimate expectations generated through deliberate acts. The second meaning of the principle of good faith may, in particular, be relevant for the issue of responsibility shunning and risk exportation as a result of nationality revocation. A question which it raises is, however, what the meaning is of notions like 'reasonable' and 'fair', which determine the standard of behavior that is expected of states if they are to act in good faith.

As Kolb notes, "[o]n such notions, there cannot exist a once-and-for-all answer valid everywhere and at all times. The legal norm must be referred back to the feelings and conceptions predominant in a given society, ie of the 'reasonable man'."[279] Thus, the standard of conduct required by good faith depends on multiple factors and may vary in time and place. As Kolb concludes, good faith requires a legal standard of normal or expected social behavior.[280] Furthermore, as Sourgens notes, good faith requires conduct that is communicative, cooperative, solidary and contains a duty of taking account of the other's interests and concerns.[281] Good faith as a standard of conduct has, for example, been referred to by the Arbitral Tribunal in the *Rainbow Warrior* Case between France and New Zealand. The Tribunal ruled that "the French Republic did not make efforts in good faith to obtain New Zea-

276 R. Kolb, *Good Faith in International Law* (Hart Publishing 2017) 15.

277 *Ibid.*15–17. Good faith referring to a subjective legal fact features less prominently in the international legal order than in national legal orders as it is more suitable to natural persons.

278 *Ibid.* 22, 23.

279 Kolb 2017 (n. 276) 22.

280 *Ibid.*

281 F. Sourgens, *Good Faith in Transnational Law: A Pluralist Account* (Brill Nijhoff 2022) pp. 117–131.

land's consent" when making a unilateral decision to repatriate a French officer.[282]

Good faith, especially when it is used to refer to a particular standard of behavior, tempers what Kolb calls "insolent unilateralism".[283] This way, good faith may limit the unilateral exercise of sovereign rights by requiring that they must be exercised in a reasonable and fair manner. The deprivation of nationality by a state constitutes the unilateral exercise of such a sovereign right, the right of states to determine who are its nationals and who are not, to which this reasoning applies. Consequently, good faith tempers the unilateral act of depriving a national of his or her nationality because states may, in accordance with this standard of behavior, only do so in a fair and reasonable manner towards other states.

Within the context of an international phenomenon involving multiple states like the FTFs phenomenon in Syria and Iraq, the standard of fair and reasonable behavior must include acting communicative, cooperative and with due regard towards the interests of other states.[284] Shunning responsibilities and passing the buck to other states by denationalizing an FTF or associated family member cannot be considered as 'fair' or 'reasonable' towards those other states. This may, in particular, be the case in two situations. First, when the state of predominant nationality deprives nationality and thereby passes the problem to a state of residual nationality which does not have a meaningful connection to the individual. As was set out in the previous chapter, states of predominant nationality are generally in a much better position to reintegrate and rehabilitate the person, as opposed to the state of residual nationality where the individual concerned may have never lived, has no family or economic ties and may not even speak the language.

Second, it is particularly questionable whether the practice of nationality deprivation meets the required standard of fair and reasonable behavior when the buck is passed to a state or actor which may not have the evidence, capacity, resources or desire "to do something about the problem, that is: prosecute, rehabilitate, reintegrate and monitor" the individual if necessary.[285] For example, as mentioned above, the SDF itself warned the international community that they "suffer from huge difficulties to accommodate ISIS fighters and their families" and that it "constitutes a great burden to" them "which [they] cannot

282 *Rainbow Warrior* (*New Zealand v France*) (Arbitration Tribunal) (1990) XX RIAA 260, para. 94.

283 Kolb 2017 (n. 276) 22.

284 B. Cheng, General Principles of Law as Applied by International Courts and Tribunals (Stevens & Sons Limited 1953) 133–134.

285 C. Paulussen 2021 (n. 273) 22.

bear on [their] own".[286] Walker asked the question whether it is "appropriate or even lawful to 'export' terrorism risks to other countries, especially as they probably have less information and capability to deal with the risk".[287] While four out of the six states active in depriving their FTFs and accompanying family members of their nationality were European, it is "European governments [that] have the resources to handle these people through prosecution, surveillance, or reintegration, as appropriate".[288] And as put by Renard and Coolsaet, "[w]hile many people beware of radicalisation in Europe's prisons, it is hard to imagine a worse environment than prisons in Syria and Iraq, where some of the most dangerous terrorists in the world are packed together".[289] Western (European) states, which are the states most active in the practice of nationality deprivation, are generally, well equipped to deal with the potential terrorism risk posed by FTFs and family members. The practice of nationality deprivation shows that those well-equipped states discharge their responsibilities over these individuals and the potential terrorist threat they embody, and in some cases, shift it to states or actors such as the SDF. These are the actors which are less equipped to address this possible threat by prosecuting, rehabilitating, reintegrating, monitoring or surveilling them, if deemed to be appropriate. Moreover, this horizontal dimension to the deprivation of nationality illustrates all the more that it is not in line with the previously discussed obligation to prevent terrorism. Citizenship revocation leading to the shunning of responsibilities and the shifting of risks may thus create "an unfair and unmanageable burden for weaker States" or the SDF and does, therefore, not address the threat posed by FTFs but merely exports it to other states or actors.[290]

Although it is difficult to determine categorically that depriving states did act in bad faith, as this is subject to a weighing exercise of different interests, factors and circumstances, it can be concluded that nationality deprivation within the FTFs phenomenon in Syria and Iraq constitutes what Kolb calls

286 AANES, Press Release 2021 (n. 160).

287 C. Walker, Counter terrorism and Security Bill 2014–15 Submission to Joint Committee on Human Rights (5 December 2014) 6. Available at: <https://www.parliament.uk/globalassets/documents/joint-committees/human-rights/Submission_from_Prof_Clive_Walker_091214.pdf> accessed 4 April 2023.

288 European Council on Foreign Relations, Open letter: Call for a managed return of ISIS foreign fighter (26 November 2019). Available at: <https://ecfr.eu/article/commentary_open_letter_a_managed_return_of_isis_foreign_fighters/> accessed 4 April 2023.

289 T. Renard and R. Coolsaet, 'From bad to worse: The fate of European foreign fighters and families detained in Syria, one year after the Turkish offensive' Security Policy Brief, Egmont Royal Institute for International Relations (28 October 2020) 7.

290 C. Walker 2020 (n. 67) 50.

"insolent unilateralism" which is regulated by the general principle of good faith as a standard of behavior.

7 Conclusions

In the previous chapter, Security Council Resolution 2178 (2014) was discussed in detail and it was explained that this Resolution, *inter alia*, aims to prevent the movement of and address the threat posed by FTFs and their accompanying family members. The present chapter has shown that the response of nationality deprivation does not prevent the movement of FTFs and their family members nor does it address the potential threat they embody. Rather, the response of nationality deprivation passes those individuals, together with a burden to counter terrorism and the responsibility to somehow deal with them, to other states or actors "like a hot potato".[291] Leaving aside the vertical, human rights perspective to the issue of nationality deprivation, this chapter examined the shunning of responsibilities and the shifting of risks through the deprivation of nationality in light of public international law. This examination took the form of a mapping exercise of different obligations, rights, concepts, principles and prohibitions under public international law, some of which are very much inter-connected. In passing the buck through deprivation of nationality, states not only act against the very spirit and fundamentals of the international legal order more generally, but may also act in violation of the specific norms of international law discussed in this chapter. States should be aware that in exporting responsibilities, potential terrorist threats and a burden to counter such threats, they may act beyond the edge of what is permitted by those norms. While international judicial bodies such as the ECtHR generally seem to avoid restricting states' discretion in nationality deprivation matters, it can be concluded from this chapter that by this kind of unilateral behavior, international legal norms may eventually be watered down. For example, what is an obligation to re-admit nationals worth if states can simply shun this legal responsibility by stripping nationality? And what is the right to expel aliens worth if states are affected in the effective exercise of such a right by the revocation of nationality? If these individuals indeed pose such a terrorist threat as depriving states emphasize, it should not be excluded that this practice may eventually lead to the responsibility, under international law, of

291 C. Paulussen 2021 (n. 273) 12.

depriving states for exporting risks of terrorism and increasing such risks on the territory of other states. Notably, those states that are active in this practice and try to evade their responsibilities are precisely those Western states advocating certain common values such as the rule of law, respect for international law and the promotion of the international legal order. Yet, when it comes to FTFs and their associated family members, they seem to put their own short-term interests first, to the detriment of other states and against the norms of international law discussed in this chapter as well as the underlying message of international law more broadly.

CHAPTER 4

(Non-)Repatriation

1 Introduction

This chapter will focus on another response to FTFs and their family members in Syria and Iraq. It will zero in on the issue of repatriation, or rather, certain states' reluctance or refusal to do so. As will be argued in this chapter, like the response of nationality deprivation, non-repatriation can also be seen as a way to shun responsibilities and to shift or externalize risks of terrorism. As van Waas and Brekoo describe it, while nationality deprivation "is a formal act of foreigner-making", denial of readmission through non-repatriation "is the *de facto* treatment of the individual as a foreigner".[1] Although constituting very different measures, one comprising action and the other omission, they "indirectly achieve a comparable effect: exclusion from the country of nationality and thereby externalisation of terrorist risk".[2]

In particular, states such as the Netherlands, France, the United Kingdom, Belgium, Denmark, Germany, Australia and Canada have been reluctant to repatriate their nationals from Syria and Iraq for a long time. For example, the Danish Minister of Foreign Affairs, Jeppe Kofod, noted that "[i]t would have been better if they had died in battle, but unfortunately, not all of them did" and that Denmark "owe[d] absolutely nothing to foreign fighters who have travelled to Syria and Iraq to fight for ISIS".[3] Those states reluctant to take active measures only repatriated small numbers of orphaned children on a case-by-case basis and very occasionally women and their children. Only recently, the majority of states previously reluctant to repatriate broke with this case-by-case approach and have repatriated substantial groups of

1 L. van Waas and A. Brekoo, 'Putting the "Foreign" in "Foreign Fighter": Nationality Deprivation and the Denial of Readmission' in F. Capone, C. Paulussen and R. Mignot-Mahdavi (eds.), *Returning Foreign Fighters: Responses, Legal Challenges and Ways Forward* (T.M.C. Asser Press 2023) 204.

2 *Ibid.* 210.

3 'It would be better if they had died in battle': Danish justice minister on returning Syria fighters (*The Local*, 27 March 2019). Available at: <https://www.thelocal.dk/20190327/it-would-be-better-if-they-had-died-in-battle-danish-justice-minister-on-returning-syria-fighters> accessed 18 December 2024. C. Lund Kristiansen, M. Skaerbaek and J. Blem Larsen, 'Regeringen: Fremmedkrigere skal nægtes hjælp i udlandet' (*Politiken*, 16 November 2019). Available at: <https://politiken.dk/danmark/politik/art7495750/Fremmedkrigere-skal-n%C3%A6gtes-hj%C3%A6lp-i-udlandet> accessed 18 December 2024.

 | HTTPS://DOI.ORG/10.1163/9789004773806-005

women and children from the SDF-controlled camps. For example, in November 2022, the Netherlands repatriated 12 women and 28 children from Northeast Syria. This was done after a district court determined the Government must repatriate the women or make concrete commitments to do so, otherwise their criminal case would be terminated.[4] In October 2022, France repatriated 15 women and 40 children.[5] Around the same time, as part of its plan to repatriate more than 60 Australian women and children,[6] Australia repatriated 4 women and 13 children from camps in Syria.[7] As a final example, on 5 October 2022, Germany announced that it had repatriated 26 women and 76 children over the course of six repatriation missions.[8] Nevertheless, as far as is publicly known, none of those states repatriated male FTFs detained in SDF-controlled prisons.

Some states that were or are reluctant to repatriate their FTFs and associated family members, such as the Netherlands, Australia, Belgium and the United Kingdom, were also active in depriving those individuals of their nationality. A relationship between the two responses can potentially be observed, as those states may have deprived those individuals of their nationality in order to evade potential responsibilities in the context of repatriation.

Notably, not all states adopted such a passive approach of non-repatriation during the first years after the fall of the IS caliphate. Some states, including

4 District Court of Rotterdam, ECLI:NL:RBROT:2022:3993 (11 May 2022).

5 See, for example, H. Sallon, 'With new mass repatriation of women and children from Syria, France breaks from "case-by-case" approach' (*Le Monde*, 20 October 2022). Available at: <https://www.lemonde.fr/en/international/article/2022/10/20/with-new-mass-repatriation-of-women-and-children-from-syria-france-breaks-away-from-case-by-case-approach_6001172_4.html> accessed 18 December 2024.

6 P. Mercer, 'Australia Plans to Rescue Citizens Stranded in Syrian Camps' (*VAO News*, 5 October 2022). Available at: <https://www.voanews.com/a/australia-plans-to-rescue-citizens-stranded-in-syrian-camps/6776646.html> accessed 18 December 2024.

7 Australian Government, The Hon Clare O'Neil MP Minister for Home Affairs, Media Release, 'Australian women and children repatriated from Syrian camps' (29 October 2022). Available at: <https://minister.homeaffairs.gov.au/ClareONeil/Pages/australian-women-repatriated-syrian-camps.aspx> accessed 18 December 2024.

8 German Federal Foreign Office, Press Release, 'Statement by Foreign Minister Baerbock on the repatriation of seven children, four women and one adolescent from north-eastern Syria' (5 October 2022). Available at: <https://www.auswaertiges-amt.de/en/newsroom/news/repatriation-syria/2556528#:~:text=A%20total%20of%2026%20women,no%20fault%20of%20their%20own> accessed 16 June 2023.

the United States,[9] Kazakhstan,[10] Uzbekistan,[11] Kyrgyzstan,[12] Kosovo[13] and Bosnia & Herzegovina,[14] actively repatriated their nationals. Not only have they repatriated women and children, but some of them have also repatriated male FTFs. For example, the President of Kazakhstan, Kassym-Jomart Tokayev, explicitly stated that "[n]o one from our people will be left behind".[15] Kazakhstan repatriated an estimated total of 719 FTFs and family members,[16] including 37 men who were all prosecuted on terrorist charges upon arrival.[17] Likewise, Kosovo's Minister of Justice, Abelard Tahiri, noted that "[w]e will not stop before bringing every citizen [...] back to their country and anyone that has committed any crime or was part of these terrorist organisations will face justice".[18] The United States' Assistant Attorney General for National Security, John Demers, noted that repatriation of American FTFs and family members was the United States' "moral responsibility to the American people and to the people of the countries to which these terrorists traveled".[19]

9 S. Kajjo, 'US Pushing Countries to Repatriate IS Foreign Fighters Held in NE Syria' (*VOA News*, 20 April 2023). Available at: <https://www.voanews.com/a/us-pushing-countries-to-repatriate-is-foreign-fighters-held-in-northeast-syria-/7059270.html> acces sed 18 December 2024.

10 S. Wolfe and C. Orozobekova, 'Lessons Learned from Kazakhstan's Repatriation and Rehabilitation of "Foreign Fighters"' Bulan Institute for Peace Innovations (20 June 2020).

11 Italian Institute for International Political Studies, 'Foreign Fighters from Central Asia: Between Renunciation and Repatriation' (2 October 2019).

12 *Ibid.*

13 T. Avdimetaj and J. Coleman, 'What EU Member States can learn from Kosovo's experience in repatriating former foreign fighters and their families' Clingendael Netherlands Institute of International Relations (May 2020).

14 A. Shtuni, 'The Western Balkans: Repatriated Foreign Terrorist Fighters, Sentencing Trends, and Security Considerations' Program on Extremism at George Washington University (September 2022).

15 Italian Institute for International Political Studies 2019 (n. 11).

16 Rights & Security International, Global Repatriations Tracker (last updated on 22 July 2024). Available at: <https://www.rightsandsecurity.org/action/resources/global-repatriations-tracker> accessed 14 March 2024.

17 Bulan Institute for Peace Innovations, 'The Compendium of Promising Practices in the Rehabilitation and Reintegration of ISIS-linked Women and Children' (November 2022).

18 'Syria war: Kosovo brings back 110 citizens including jihadists' (*BBC News*, 20 April 2019). Available at: <https://www.bbc.co.uk/news/world-europe-47998456> accessed 18 December 2024.

19 US Department of Justice, Office of Public Affairs, 'The United States Has Repatriated 27 Americans from Syria and Iraq including Ten Charged with Terrorism-Related Offenses for Their Support to ISIS' Press Release (1 October 2020). Available at: <https://www.justice.gov/opa/pr/united-states-has-repatriated-27-americans-syria-and-iraq-including-ten-charged-terrorism> accessed 4 July 2023.

Furthermore, the SDF itself called for the repatriation of FTFs and their family members to their states of origin.[20] Similar calls have been issued by powerful states like the United States and several international and regional organizations, including the UN, as well as international,[21] regional[22] and national[23] human rights organizations. For example, the UN has urged member states to repatriate their FTFs and associated family members from Syria and Iraq and has provided support to that end. In 2021, the UN launched the Global Framework for UN Support on Syria/Iraq Third Country National Returnees, led by the Office of Counter-Terrorism and the United Nations Children's Fund. The purpose of this Framework was

> to provide coordinated, 'all-of-United Nations' support to requesting member states on the protection, voluntary repatriation, prosecution, rehabilitation and reintegration of individuals with suspected links to United Nations-designated terrorist groups returning from Iraq and the Syrian Arab Republic.[24]

---

20 AANES, Press Release (18 March 2021) <http://kinderenteruguitkalifaat.nl/wp-content/uploads/2021/03/20210318-AANES-press-release.pdf> accessed 18 August 2023.

21 See, for example, Human Rights Watch, 'Syria: Dire Conditions for ISIS Suspects' Families' (23 July 2019). Available at: <https://www.hrw.org/news/2019/07/23/syria-dire-conditions-isis-suspects-families> accessed 18 December 2024.

22 See, for example, Council of Europe Commissioner for Human Rights, 'Council of Europe member states should urgently repatriate their under-age nationals stranded in Northern Syria' (28 May 2019). Available at: <https://www.coe.int/fi/web/commissioner/-/council-of-europe-member-states-should-urgently-repatriate-their-under-age-nationals-stranded-in-northern-syria> accessed 30 June 2023.

23 Défenseur des droits, Décision du Défenseur des droits n°2019–129 (22 May 2019). Available at: <https://juridique.defenseurdesdroits.fr/doc_num.php?explnum_id=18912> accessed 30 June 2023; Kinderombudsman, 'Kinderombudsman herhaalt: Nederland moet kinderen in Syrische kampen terughalen' (14 December 2021). Available at: <https://www.kinderombudsman.nl/nieuws/kinderombudsman-herhaalt-nederland-moet-kinderen-in-syrische-kampen-terughalen> accessed 30 June 2023.

24 UNSC, 'Thirteenth report of the Secretary-General on the threat posed by ISIL (Da'esh) to international peace and security and the range of United Nations efforts in support of Member States in countering the threat' UN Doc. S/2021/682 (27 July 2021) para. 46.

In addition, several UN experts,[25] the UN Committee on the Rights of the Child (CRC Committee),[26] the UN Human Rights Committee,[27] the UN Committee against Torture[28] and other UN entities have called upon states to repatriate their nationals or condemned them for failing to do so. The former UN Special Rapporteur on the promotion and protection of human rights and fundamental freedoms while countering terrorism, Fionnuala Ní Aoláin, and the former UN Special Rapporteur on arbitrary, summary and extra-judicial executions, Agnès Callamard, stated that

> the urgent return and repatriation of foreign fighters and their families from conflict zones is the only international law-compliant response to the increasingly complex and precarious human rights, humanitarian and security situation faced by those women, men and children who are detained in inhumane conditions in overcrowded camps, prisons, or elsewhere in the northern Syrian Arab Republic and Iraq.[29]

In July 2024, the UN Secretary General noted that

> [b]etween January and July 2024, 11 Member States repatriated 1,080 children, including nationals of Azerbaijan, Canada, Finland, Kyrgyzstan, Maldives, the Kingdom of the Netherlands, the Russian Federation, Spain, Tajikistan, the

25 OHCHR, 'Children in Northeast Syria must be urgently repatriated: UN experts' (31 March 2023). Available at: <https://www.ohchr.org/en/statements/2023/03/children-northeast-syria-must-be-urgently-repatriated-un-experts> accessed 30 June 2023; OHCHR, 'Syria: UN experts urge 57 States to repatriate women and children from squalid camps' (8 February 2021). Available at: <https://www.ohchr.org/en/press-releases/2021/02/syria-un-experts-urge-57-states-repatriate-women-and-children-squalid-camps> accessed 30 June 2023.

26 CRC Committee, *F.B. et al. and D.A. et al. v. France* (9 March 2022) UN Doc. CRC/C/89/D/77/2019; CRC/C/89/D/79/2019; CRC/C/89/D/109/2019; CRC Committee, *P.N et al. v. Finland* (20 October 2022) UN Doc. CRC/C/91/D/100/2019.

27 UN Human Rights Committee, Concluding observations on the sixth periodic report of Belgium (6 December 2019) UN Doc. CCPR/C/BEL/CO/6, paras. 13 and 14.

28 UN Committee against Torture, *C.P. et al. v. France* (2 March 2023) UN Doc. CAT/C/75/D/922/2019; UN Committee against Torture, *P.D. v. France* (15 February 2024) UN Doc. CAT/C/78/D/1045/2020.

29 UN Human Rights Special Procedures, Submission by the UN Special Rapporteur on the promotion and protection of human rights and fundamental freedoms while countering terrorism and the UN Special Rapporteur on arbitrary, summary and extra-judicial executions in the case of *H.F. and M.F. v. France* (Application No. 24384/19) before the European Court of Human Rights (28 September 2020). Available at: <https://www.ohchr.org/sites/default/files/Documents/Issues/Terrorism/SR/Final-Amicus_Brief_SRCT_SRSsummex.pdf> accessed 30 June 2023.

United Kingdom of Great Britain and Northern Ireland and the United States of America, from Northeast Syria.[30]

Nevertheless, as a result of certain states' long-time hesitance to repatriate, thousands of third-country women and children, as well as a considerable number of male FTFs, have spent years in camps and prisons in deplorable conditions in Syria and Iraq, and some of them in Turkish prisons after they were arrested on the Turkish side of the border.[31] Despite recent repatriation efforts, there are still believed to be a large number of third-country nationals detained in camps and prisons in the region. Research by Human Rights Watch indicates that as of 23 January 2023, nearly 10,000 third-country nationals from about 60 states still remained in the al-Hol and al-Roj camps in Northeast Syria. This number does not include those third-country nationals detained in other centers and prisons in (Northeast) Syria, Iraq or other states like Türkiye.[32]

Some of those individuals, or their family members back home, have tried to enforce repatriation by national court decisions, including in France,[33] Belgium,[34] Germany[35] and the Netherlands.[36] In spite of their efforts, most cases were without success.[37] For example, ruling on an application by 23 Dutch

30 UNSC, Nineteenth report of the Secretary-General on the threat posed by ISIL (Da'esh) to international peace and security and the range of United Nations efforts in support of Member States in countering the threat (31 July 2024) UN Doc. S/2024/583, para. 16.

31 Human Rights Watch, 'Thousands of Foreigners Unlawfully Held in NE Syria' (23 March 2021). Available at: <https://www.hrw.org/news/2021/03/23/thousands-foreigners-unlawfully-held-ne-syria> accessed 18 December 2024.

32 J. Becker and L. Tayler, 'Revictimizing the Victims: Children Unlawfully Detained in Northeast Syria' Human Rights Watch (27 January 2023). Available at: <https://www.hrw.org/news/2023/01/27/revictimizing-victims-children-unlawfully-detained-northeast-syria> accessed 18 December 2024.

33 See, for example, Tribunal Judiciaire de Paris, No. RG 20/51405 – No. Portalis 352J-W-B7D-CRH WO (12 March 2020).

34 See, for example, Rechtbank van eerste aanleg Brussel, nr. 18/28/C (19 juli 2018); Hof van Beroep Brussel, nr. 2018/KR/45 (12 September 2018). See also T. Van Poecke and E. Wauters, 'The Repatriation of European Nationals from Syria as Contested before Domestic Courts in Belgium and Beyond' Working Paper No. 229 (January 2021) 5–15. Available at: <https://ghum.kuleuven.be/ggs/documents/wp229-van-poecke-wauters-tvp-2.pdf> accessed 3 July 2023.

35 See, for example, Verwaltungsgericht Berlin, ECLI:DE:VGBE:2020:0127.34L334.19.00 (27 January 2019).

36 Court of Appeal of The Hague, ECLI:NL:GHDHA:2019:3208 (22 November 2019); Dutch Supreme Court, ECLI:NL:HR:2020:1148 (26 June 2020).

37 However, not all cases were unsuccessful. For example, a German court ordered the German state to repatriate a German national with her two children, which was upheld

women who requested to be repatriated together with their 55 children, the Court of Appeal in The Hague and ultimately the Dutch Supreme Court ruled that given the interests of the state and the circumstance that the women traveled to the conflict zone on their own initiative, and despite the compelling interests of the women and children, the state reasonably came to a decision not to repatriate them.[38] According to both courts, the state had not exceeded its wide margin of appreciation and did not act unlawfully by not repatriating the women and children.[39]

Besides national court decisions, some individuals have also tried to enforce their rights before international or regional courts and bodies, such as the CRC Committee and the ECtHR. In 2019, proceedings were initiated by four French nationals before the ECtHR.[40] The applicants alleged that France's refusal to repatriate their daughters and grandchildren from SDF-controlled camps in Northeast Syria violated their family members' rights under the ECHR, including their right to return to their country of nationality. On the question whether there exists a right to repatriation, the Court decided that "there is no obligation under international treaty law or customary international law for States to repatriate their nationals" and that "French citizens being held in the camps in north-eastern Syria cannot claim a general right to repatriation on the basis of the right to enter national territory".[41] Nonetheless, the ECtHR did find a violation of Article 3, para. 2 of Protocol No. 4 to the ECHR, as "the examination of the requests for repatriation made by the applicants on behalf of their family members was not surrounded by appropriate safeguards against arbitrariness".[42]

Academic debates on the issue of repatriation have also, to a large extent, focused on the question of whether there exists an obligation to repatriate or a right to be repatriated under international (human rights) law.[43] Like the

---

on appeal. See, Verwaltungsgericht Berlin, ECLI:DE:VGBE:2019:0710.34L245.19.00 (10 July 2019); Oberverwaltungsgericht Berlin-Brandenburg, ECLI:DE:OVGBEBB:2019:1106.OVG10S43.19.00 (6 November 2019).

38 Court of Appeal of The Hague, ECLI:NL:GHDHA:2019:3208 (22 November 2019) paras. 7.5–7.14; Dutch Supreme Court, ECLI:NL:HR:2020:1148 (26 June 2020) para. 3 and especially para. 3.21.2.

39 *Ibid.*

40 *Case of H.F. and Others v. France* [2022] (Judgement) ECtHR App. Nos. 24384/19 and 44234/20 (14 September 2022).

41 *Ibid.* para. 259.

42 *Ibid.* paras. 283–284.

43 See, for example, F. Capone, 'The children (and wives) of foreign ISIS fighters: Which obligations upon the States of nationality?' 60 Questions of International Law, Zoom-in (23 September 2019); C. Sandelowsky-Bosman and T. Liefaard, 'Children Trapped in

ECtHR, authors like McKeever, Capone, Bagheri and Bisset came to the conclusion that although international human rights law provides a strong legal basis for taking positive action, especially in the case of children, a strict legal obligation to actively repatriate as such cannot be deduced from international law.[44]

The present chapter is, however, not so much addressing this vertical, human rights perspective to the issue of repatriation. Rather, and like the previous chapters of this research, this chapter aims to approach the response of (non)repatriation from the perspective of inter-state relations. It is important to look at this response from the said perspective because, as will be argued in this chapter, a state's refusal to repatriate may lead to the externalization of potential threats of terrorism and the shunning of responsibilities. Such responsibilities include those that would come with repatriation, i.e., the obligation to investigate and prosecute suspects of terrorist offences and war crimes, the responsibility to detain such FTFs and family members, the responsibility to rehabilitate, reintegrate and monitor them, if appropriate, or to otherwise deal with the burden of potentially dangerous nationals and the responsibility to protect the population from threats of terrorism. Instead of looking at an individual right and a connected obligation to repatriate the individuals concerned, this chapter will shed more light on (non)repatriation policies by examining the extent to which public international law imposes limits on states' refusal to repatriate FTFs and their family members when such a response results in the shunning of responsibilities and the shifting of security risks.

In order to address this matter, this chapter will start with a more general introduction to the topic of repatriation under international law. A number of legal bases for repatriation under public international law will be touched upon. These legal bases, which can potentially and in part be found in con-

---

Camps in Syria, Iraq and Turkey: Reflections on Jurisdiction and State Obligations under the United Nations Convention on the Rights of the Child' 38 Nordic Journal of Human Rights (2020) 2; A. Spadaro, 'Repatriation of Family Members of Foreign Fighters: Individual Right or State Prerogative?' 70 International and Comparative Law Quarterly (2021) 1; D. McKeever, 'Repatriating Foreign Terrorist Fighters and Their Family Members: What International Law Requires, and What National Courts Will Do' 28 Journal of Conflict & Security Law (2022) 1; S. Bagheri and A. Bisset, 'International Legal Issues Arising from Repatriation of the Children of Islamic State' 27 Journal of Conflict & Security Law (2022) 3; C. Forcese, 'Homeward Bound? International Law and a State's Obligation to Repatriate Nationals Affiliated with Da'esh' 51 Israel Yearbook on Human Rights (2021).

44 D. McKeever 2022 (n. 43) 90; F. Capone 2019 (n. 43) 95, 96; S. Bagheri and A. Bisset 2022 (n. 43) 384.

sular law, human rights law and IHL, will be brought in connection to the FTFs phenomenon in Syria and Iraq. Because this introductory part brings multiple legal bases and issues concerning repatriation together, not all discussions contain an in-depth analysis. Besides these legal bases for repatriation, this introductory part will also set out which states were active in the repatriation of their nationals from the conflict zone in Syria and Iraq, or other states where they may have ended up in and which states can be considered as inactive in repatriation efforts. Thereafter, the horizontal dimension to the response of non-repatriation will be set out in more detail, together with the effects of non-repatriation policies on the international relations between states or between states and other actors. After this introductory part, this chapter will discuss and analyze those norms that determine the way public international law governs the shunning of responsibilities and the shifting of risks through the practice of non-repatriation. Although this chapter could have discussed public international law's stance towards this practice by discussing broader, more overarching principles and obligations (such as the obligation to prevent and cooperate in combatting terrorism), it will primarily focus on more specific parts of international law as well as secondary norms of state responsibility. This chapter will, first, examine states' refusal to repatriate FTFs and their family members from Syria and Iraq as a situation of *de facto* banishment. In that respect, the research will analyze why the ancient punishment of banishment eventually ceased to exist and the extent to which those reasons can likewise be applied to non-repatriation in the FTFs context. Second, the chapter will discuss states' reluctance or refusal to repatriate in light of their obligation to ensure respect for IHL. In this regard, the research will not only discuss states' obligation to ensure respect for IHL by other states, but will also address their potential obligation to ensure respect for IHL by non-state actors like the SDF. Third, this chapter will delve into the question of state responsibility for the inhumane circumstances in which FTFs and family members are being detained in Northeast Syria and will explore whether there is a suitable construction for such responsibility under international law. This is a particularly complex question as, at least from a moral point of view, there might be a shared responsibility between states refusing to repatriate and the SDF, who have repeatedly asked for help and called upon states of origin to repatriate. Finally, this chapter will analyze repatriation as a possible means to give effect to the obligation to make reparations for internationally wrongful acts, and in particular, in situations where it can be established that states knowingly tolerated, or acquiesced in, FTFs departing their territories.

2 Repatriation under Public International Law

As a way of introducing the topic of repatriation more broadly, this section will discuss a number of legal bases for repatriation under public international law. One legal basis of repatriation is provided by consular law, which will be discussed first. As will be shown, it falls within the sovereignty of states to decide on the provision of consular assistance, including in the form of repatriation. Besides consular law, this section will also briefly explain that there may be other branches of public international law that may require repatriation under certain circumstances, such as international human rights law and IHL. In the previous chapter, concerning the response of nationality deprivation, a state's obligation to (re)admit nationals and an individual's right to enter the state of which he or she is a national were elaborately discussed. Some have suggested that this obligation and right may also provide for an obligation to repatriate under international law. This would at least explain the overlap between states active in nationality deprivation and states reluctant to repatriate. Those states may have deprived nationality in order to avoid potential responsibilities to repatriate. While recognizing this relationship between nationality deprivation and non-repatriation policies, this section will explain the distinction between repatriation and the said obligation and right from a legal point of view.

2.1 Repatriation under the International Law of Consular Relations

International diplomatic and consular law has given states the legal tools for the maintenance of international relations with other states. Where diplomatic law, codified in the Vienna Convention on Diplomatic Relations (VCDR),[45] governs the exchange of diplomatic missions between states, consular law, codified in the Vienna Convention on Consular Relations (VCCR),[46] governs the exchange of consular posts.[47] Although "protecting in the receiv-

45 VCDR (adopted 18 April 1961, entered into force 24 April 1964) 500 UNTS 95.

46 VCCR (adopted 24 April 1963, entered into force 19 March 1967) 596 UNTS 261.

47 There are other important differences between diplomatic and consular law and relations. While diplomatic relations are mainly concerned with the relations between the sending and the receiving state, consular relations focus on the relations between the nationals of the sending state and the receiving state. Another difference is that establishing diplomatic relations with a particular state pertains to the recognition of that state as a subject of international law, this is not necessarily the case with establishing consular relations. See, A. Paulus and A. Dienelt, 'Vienna Convention on Consular Relations (1963)' MPEPIL (2011) paras. 4–6.

ing State the interests of the sending State and of its nationals" is both a diplomatic and a consular function, and listed as such both in the VCDR Article 3(b) and the VCCR Article 5(a), Article 5(e) of the VCCR also explicitly lists "helping and assisting nationals [...] of the sending State" as a consular function. The ILC explained in the commentary to its Draft Articles on Consular Relations,[48] which formed the basis for the adoption of the Convention, that while the consular function described in Article 5(a), "relates to the function which the consular official exercises vis-a-vis the authorities of the receiving State",[49] the consular function contained in Article 5(e), "covers any kind of help and assistance which the consul may extend to nationals of his State", including "assistance in case of distress [...], repatriation and the like".[50] Thus, repatriation is a form of consular assistance and part of the functions of a state's consular post. Therefore, consular assistance, including in the form of repatriation, is also to a large extent connected to nationality. Again, a reason for the connection between nationality deprivation practices and states' refusal or reluctance to repatriate. An exception to this proposition can, however, be found in Article 23 of the Treaty on the Functioning of the European Union and Directive 2015/637. This exception entails that a national of an EU member state, who finds himself or herself on the territory of a third state in which his or her state of nationality is not represented, is entitled to the protection by diplomatic or consular authorities of any EU member state.

Consular assistance should also be distinguished from diplomatic protection. As Spadaro explains, the latter "has a remedial character and is employed by the State of nationality of a person who has suffered an injury due to an internationally wrongful act of another State", while the former "is preventive and takes place before the commission of an internationally wrongful act".[51] However, like diplomatic protection, providing consular assistance, including in the form of repatriation, is commonly understood to be a state prerogative under consular law. Therefore, states are not required to provide such assistance.[52] Nevertheless, in the *LaGrand* Case, the ICJ determined that Article 36 (1) VCCR creates an individual right to consular assistance in the form of con-

48 ILC, 'Draft Articles on Consular Relations, with commentaries' in the Report of the International Law Commission on the work of its thirteenth session (1961) UN Doc. A/16/9.

49 *Ibid.* Commentary to Article 5, para. 10.

50 *Ibid;* A. Paulus and A. Dienelt 2011 (n. 47) para. 25.

51 A. Spadaro 2021 (n. 43) 256.

52 *Ibid.* 257; A. Paulus and A. Dienelt 2011 (n. 47) para. 8.; L. Lee and J. Quigley, *Consular Law and Practice* (3rd edn., Oxford University Press 2008) 135; J. Quigley, W. Aceves and S. Shank, *The Law of Consular Access: A Documentary Guide* (Routledge 2010) 97.

sular communication.[53] However, nationals of the sending state have such a right only vis-à-vis the receiving state, but not vis-à-vis their own state of nationality, i.e., the sending state.[54] In addition, a violation of the individual's right to consular communication also entails a violation of the right of the sending state, as the sending state has a right vis-à-vis the receiving state, but no obligation, to provide consular assistance, including in the form of consular communication.[55] In other words, "[u]nder consular law, both the sending State and its nationals are holders of certain rights vis-à-vis the [receiving] State, but consular law does not create rights which can be claimed by an individual against their State of nationality".[56]

Some argue that the issue of repatriation from Northeast Syria, unlike the issue of repatriation from Iraq, is not regulated by consular law at all because this body of law does not apply to relations between states and non-state actors.[57] On the other hand, there are those who counter such arguments by pointing to the fact that the AANES is an actor with state-like powers, that non-state actors in control over persons and/or territory, absent of state governmental control, have certain responsibilities to, among others, exercise consular relations and the fact that the inter-state dimension to consular law is less prominent in national consular law.[58] In any case, the Security Council has urged member states, in Resolution 2396 (2017), to ensure consular access to their detained nationals, including their FTFs.[59]

Despite there being no obligation upon states of nationality to provide consular assistance under international consular law, some states have gone further than what international law requires here and did incorporate an obligation to provide consular assistance in their national laws. For example, the German Consular Law provides that "consular officers shall help Germans [...] requiring assistance" and "shall care for Germans remanded in custody

---

53 *LaGrand* (*Germany v. United States of America*) (Judgement) [2001] ICJ Rep. 466, para. 77. The Inter-American Court of Human Rights (IACtHR) even determined this right to constitute a human right. See, The Right to Information on Consular Assistance in the Framework of the Guarantees of the Due Process of Law (Advisory Opinion) [1999] OC-16/99, paras. 84, 141.

54 This was also confirmed by the ICJ in the *Avena* Case. *Avena and Other Mexican Nationals* (*Mexico v. United States of America*) (Judgement) [2004] ICJ Rep. 12, para. 40.

55 *Ibid.*

56 A. Spadaro 2021 (n. 43) 257, 258; See, also, J. Quigley, W. Aceves and S. Shank 2010 (n. 52) 97.

57 See, for example, A. Spadaro 2021 (n. 43) 262.

58 T. Van Poecke and E. Wauters 2021 (n. 34) 28, 29.

59 UNSC Resolution 2396 (21 December 2017) UN Doc. S/RES/2396 (2017) para. 6.

pending trial or serving a prison sentence".[60] Although this language can be considered as imposing an obligation upon the state to provide consular assistance, considerable latitude is given regarding the kind of consular assistance that is required.

Likewise, Article 75 of the Belgian Consular Code provides that consular assistance is rendered to Belgian nationals.[61] This was interpreted by the Brussels Court of First Instance as entailing a duty to provide consular assistance to Belgian nationals.[62] According to Article 78, consular assistance is, among other situations, rendered to Belgians who are: (1) victims of a serious crime; (2) arrested or detained; or (3) in a state of extreme emergency. Although repatriation is not explicitly mentioned in the Code, preparatory works mention repatriation as a possible form of consular assistance in situations of extreme emergency.[63] Notably, the aforementioned interpretation of Article 75 was given in a case concerning two women who had traveled to Syria to join their husbands and who were convicted *in absentia* for participation in the activities of IS.[64] The two women requested the repatriation of their six children. The Court ruled that the children could indeed claim consular assistance, as they found themselves in a state of extreme emergency, detained and were victims of serious crimes.[65] However, the two women could not, given the fact that they deliberately traveled to an area where an armed conflict was going on, a circumstance which precludes a claim to consular assis-

60 German Law on Consular Officers, Their Functions and Powers of 11 September 1974, Articles 5(1) and 7. Translation retrieved from: <https://www.auswaertiges-amt.de/blob/232092/835fd523b3d0de7a3e13bd6a851da1b7/konsulargesetz-data.pdf> accessed 6 July 2023.

61 Article 75 of the Belgian Consular Code of 21 December 2013 states: "Consular assistance is reserved exclusively for Belgians, for persons with a status as refugee or stateless person granted by Belgium and for citizens of the European Union who are not represented in third countries and who are treated as Belgian citizens with regard to assistance." (Translation by the author).

62 Dutch Speaking Court of First Instance Brussels, No. 2018/XX/C (26 December 2018) p. 16; See, also, French Speaking Court of First Instance of Brussels, No. 19/129/C (30 October 2019) pp. 22–24 and French Speaking Court of First Instance Brussels, No. 19/87/C (2 December 2019) pp. 23–26. In these two decisions, the Court also ruled that Article 75 of the Belgian Consular Code creates a subjective right to consular assistance in the situations listed in Article 78.

63 Belgische Kamer van Volksvertegenwoordigers, Wetsontwerp tot wijziging van het consulair Wetboek (14 March 2018) 3, 4 and 16–18. Available at: <https://www.lachambre.be/FLWB/PDF/54/2989/54K2989001.pdf> accessed 6 July 2023.

64 Dutch Speaking Court of First Instance Brussels (n. 62) 4 and 5.

65 *Ibid.* 16.

tance as per Article 83 of the Consular Code.[66] Belgium argued, among others, that consular services were not possible because the Belgian embassy and consulate in Syria were no longer operational.[67] The Court ruled, however, that this does not exclude other options for action.[68] For example, consular assistance could be rendered by consulates or embassies from other EU countries or by Belgian consulates or embassies in a neighboring country, such as Türkiye, Lebanon, Jordan or Israel.[69] Furthermore, Belgium could cooperate with the Kurdish authorities, who are in control of the region where the children are located and who actively support repatriation.[70] Belgium also argued that cooperation with the Kurdish authorities may not lead to the desired result, as the authorities refuse to separate mothers and children, and repatriating the former would go against Belgium's policy to only repatriate children.[71] The Court decided that this policy may not be invoked to refuse repatriation of the children and deemed the policy to be unlawful, i.e., because it violates the children's right to contact with their parents,[72] their right to family life[73] and the prohibition of inhuman or degrading treatment or punishment.[74] Moreover, the Court noted that "Belgium has the legislation and institutions that have the potential to realize punishment and rehabilitation with the greatest possible limitation of risks" and "[t]hat potential is much smaller in Syria".[75] The Court ruled that if repatriating the mothers would be a *de facto* requirement to repatriate the children, the state would have to bring back the mothers as well.[76] However, the Court did not impose a general obligation to repatriate the children, i.e., due to external and changing circumstances that may make it difficult to realize such an obligation. Rather, the Court required the state to enable their travel by: (1) providing the necessary documents; (2) reaching an agreement with the local authorities, in particular those in control of the camp; and (3) securing their travel.

As this case illustrates, although international consular law does not require states to provide consular assistance, and does not impose an obliga-

66 *Ibid.* 16, 17.
67 *Ibid.* 17.
68 *Ibid.*
69 *Ibid.* 17, 18.
70 *Ibid.* 18.
71 *Ibid.* 19.
72 CRC (signed 20 November 1989, entered into force 2 September 1990) 1577 UNTS 3, Articles 5 and 9.
73 ECHR (signed 4 November 1950, entered into force 3 September 1953) ETS 5, Article 8.
74 ECHR, Article 3; Dutch Speaking Court of First Instance Brussels (n. 62) 19, 20.
75 Dutch Speaking Court of First Instance Brussels (n. 62) 19 (translation by the author).
76 *Ibid.* 20.

tion upon states to repatriate their FTFs or family members from Syria, Iraq or other states, national consular law may provide for such an obligation. At least in the case of children. Nevertheless, in the Belgian case at hand, the Brussels Court of Appeal eventually overturned the decision by declaring the women's claim inadmissible, without ruling on the merits of the case.[77]

2.2 Other Legal Bases for Repatriation

Besides consular law, an obligation to repatriate may, under certain circumstances, be found in other branches of public international law. As mentioned in the introduction to this chapter, the issue of repatriation in the context of FTFs and their families in Syria and Iraq has often been scrutinized from a human rights perspective. In specific cases, an obligation to repatriate may be found in international human rights law. If States of nationality exercise extraterritorial jurisdiction over their nationals abroad, those States are indeed obliged to prevent, or respond to violations of their human rights, arguably including by ensuring their repatriation. However, it must thus first be established whether the state in question actually exercised extraterritorial jurisdiction. Multiple nationals abandoned in Syria and Iraq, or their family members back home, have tried to enforce repatriation by national court decisions, including in France,[78] Belgium,[79] Germany[80] and the Netherlands.[81] Most of those national courts found that the State was under no obligation to repatriate those nationals abroad because of a lack of extraterritorial jurisdiction. For example, the French-speaking Court of First Instance Brussels concluded with regard to human rights law that Belgium does not exercise control or authority over the applicant or the al-Roj camp in Northeast Syria, in which she is detained. Hence, the Court concluded that Belgium neither directly nor indirectly exercised jurisdiction.[82] Similarly, the Dutch Court of First Instance in The Hague ruled that, as the children are abroad, the Netherlands has no jurisdiction and, insofar as the interests of the chil-

77 Brussels Court of Appeal, No. 2019/KR/4 (27 February 2019).

78 See, for example, Tribunal Judiciaire de Paris, No. RG 20/51405 – No. Portalis 352J-W-B7D-CRH WO (12 March 2020).

79 See, for example, Rechtbank van eerste aanleg Brussel, nr. 18/28/C (19 juli 2018); Hof van Beroep Brussel, nr. 2018/KR/45 (12 September 2018). See also T. Van Poecke and E. Wauters 2021 (n. 34) 5–15.

80 See, for example, Verwaltungsgericht Berlin, ECLI:DE:VGBE:2020:0127.34L334.19.00 (27 January 2019).

81 See, for example, Court of Appeal of The Hague, ECLI:NL:GHDHA:2019:3208 (22 November 2019); Dutch Supreme Court, ECLI:NL:HR:2020:1148 (26 June 2020).

82 French-speaking Court of First Instance Brussels, No. 19/30/C (7 June 2019) p. 20.

dren are harmed, cannot be held accountable for violations of the CRC or the ECHR.[83]

The same request was brought before the ECtHR in the case of *H.F. and others v. France.* More specifically, the applicants alleged that France's refusal to repatriate their daughters and grandchildren, held in camps in Northeast Syria, violated their rights under the ECHR, including the prohibition of torture or inhuman or degrading treatment or punishment under Article 3 and their right to return under Article 3(2) of Protocol No. 4 to the ECHR.[84] With regard to Article 3, the Court ruled that France did not exercise jurisdiction, by stating

> that the applicants cannot validly argue that the mere decision of the French authorities not to repatriate their family members has the effect of bringing them within the scope of France's jurisdiction as regards the ill-treatment to which they are subjected in Syrian camps under Kurdish control.[85]

However, with regard to Article 3(2) of Protocol No. 4, France did exercise jurisdiction according to the Court, because "there are special features which enable France's jurisdiction".[86]

In contrast with these domestic court decisions and the ECtHR, the CRC Committee adopted a more expansive approach. In its admissibility decision in the case of *L.H. et al. v. France*, the Committee found that France exercised jurisdiction over French children detained in the camps in Northeast Syria because France, "as the State of the children's nationality, has the capability and the power to protect the rights of the children in question by taking action

---

83 Court of First Instance The Hague, ECLI:NL:RBDHA:2019:11909 (11 November 2019) para. 4.5.

84 *H.F. and Others v. France* (n. 40) para. 3.

85 *Ibid.* para. 203.

86 *Ibid.* para. 214. The Court distinguishes five special features. First of all, the French nationality of the individuals concerned. Secondly, the fact that the applicant officially requested the French authorities to repatriate and assist their daughters and grandchildren multiple times. Thirdly, the fact that their family members were facing a real and imminent threat to their lives and physical well-being, as well as the extreme vulnerability of the children. The living conditions in the camps were regarded as incompatible with the fundamental value of respect for human dignity. Fourthly, the fact that the individuals were not able to leave the camps or reach French territory, or the territory of any other state from which they could reach the French authorities, without the help of those authorities. Finally, the fact that the Kurdish authorities have indicated that they are willing to hand over the French women and children to the French authorities. See para. 203.

to repatriate them or provide other consular responses".[87] This approach to extraterritorial jurisdiction is referred to as a 'functional approach', i.e., one which does not focus on control over territory or persons but rather on control over rights and states' ability to protect those rights. One remarkable element about this decision is that the nationality of the children was clearly an important factor in determining whether France exercised extraterritorial jurisdiction over them. This is controversial because states' obligations under international human rights law do not depend on nationality. International human rights law applies irrespective of a person's nationality.[88] Besides the issue of nationality, the CRC Committee's decision was criticized for several reasons. Among others, for creating uncertainty and potential for arbitrariness by failing to create a clear standard or legal test for jurisdiction, for taking into account France's previous repatriation efforts as a factor for establishing jurisdiction, which would potentially discourage states from taking future action, and for its lack of a threshold criterion, which could lead to burdensome protective obligations upon states.[89] Nevertheless, as was expected, the CRC Committee decided on the merits of the case that France should "[t]ake urgent positive measures to repatriate the child victims".[90]

Another legal basis for repatriation in public international law can potentially be found in IHL. IHL makes reference to repatriation with regard to two categories of protected persons, prisoners of war and civilian internees. The treatment of prisoners of war is regulated by Articles 109 and 118 of the Third Geneva Convention (GCIII).[91] However, those Articles only apply to IAC. In armed conflicts not of an international character, regulated by Common Arti-

87 CRC Committee, *L.H. et al. v. France* (2 November 2020) UN Doc. CRC/C/85/D/79/2019; CRC/C/85/D/109/2019, para. 9.7. A similar approach to extraterritorial jurisdiction over children detained in camps in Northeast Syria was taken by the Committee in the following cases: CRC Committee, *F.B. et al v France* (4 February 2021) CRC/C/86/D/R.77/2019; *P.N et al. v. Finland* (n. 26).

88 See for example, CRC Art. 2(1). See also H. Duffy, 'International human rights law and terrorism: an overview' in B. Saul (ed.), *Research Handbook on International Law and Terrorism* (2nd edition, Edward Elgar Publishing 2020) 319, 320.

89 See, for example, M. Milanovic, 'Repatriating the Children of Foreign Terrorist Fighters and the Extraterritorial Application of Human Rights' EJIL:Talk! (10 November 2020); A. Spadaro 2021 (n. 43) 262, 263; S. Bagheri and A. Bisset 2022 (n. 43) 10, 11. See, also, M. Emberland, 'The Committee on the Rights of the Child's Admissibility Decisions in the 'Syrian Camps Cases' against France: a Critique from the Viewpoint of Treaty Interpretation' 23 Human Rights Law Review (2023) 2.

90 *F.B. et al. and D.A. et al. v. France* (n. 26) para. 8(c).

91 Geneva Convention Relative to the Treatment of Prisoners of War (adopted 12 August 1949, entered into force 21 October 1950) 75 UNTS 135. Prisoners of war are members of the armed forces or other militias or volunteer corps belonging to a party to the conflict

cle 3 to the Geneva Conventions and Additional Protocol II, prisoner of war status does not exist. The protection of civilians during IACs is regulated by Articles 132 to 134 of the Fourth Geneva Convention (GCIV).[92] As with the repatriation of prisoners of war, these Articles in the GCIV only apply during IACs. Common Article 3 and Additional Protocol II do not provide for equivalent provisions. As the International Committee of the Red Cross (ICRC) noted, there is a "substantial disparity between the robust and detailed provisions" regarding the conditions in which prisoners of war and civilians may

---

who have fallen into the power of the enemy, as well as others listed in Article 4 to the GCIII. Article 109 provides for the repatriation of prisoners of war during hostilities. The first paragraph of the Article states that "[p]arties to the conflict are bound to send back to their own country, regardless of number or rank, seriously wounded and seriously sick prisoners of war, after having cared for them until they are fit to travel". Article 110 of the GCIII specifies in detail which wounded and sick prisoners of war are eligible for repatriation to their own country or to a neutral country. Thus, wounded or injured prisoners of war may be repatriated during the armed conflict. It should be emphasised that the repatriation of prisoners of war during hostilities only applies to a limited group, i.e., those who are wounded or injured. Because the group of prisoners of war eligible for repatriation during hostilities is narrow, most prisoners of war are repatriated after the end of hostilities. After the armed conflict, repatriation of prisoners of war is regulated by Article 118 of the GCIII. This provision provides that "[p]risoners of war shall be released and repatriated without delay after the cessation of active hostilities".

92 Convention relative to the Protection of Civilian Persons in Time of War (adopted 12 August 1949, entered into force 21 October 1950) 75 UNTS 1950. Article 42 of GCIV provides for the internment of civilians "only if the security of the Detaining Power makes it absolutely necessary". Article 132 provides that during hostilities, civilian internees must be released when their internment is no longer necessary and parties to an IAC conflict must actively pursue agreements for the repatriation of certain groups of those civilian internees, e.g., children, pregnant women and mothers with young children or infants. The group of civilian internees that is eligible for repatriation remains, therefore, small. After hostilities have ended, on the other hand, all internees should be released and repatriated to their state of origin. To that end, Articles 133 and 134 provide that "[i]nternment shall cease as soon as possible" and the parties to the Convention "shall endeavour, upon the close of hostilities or occupation, to ensure the return of all internees to their last place of residence, or to facilitate their repatriation". This more cautious formulation may show that "there is no straightforward obligation under IHL to repatriate civilians in the same way as [prisoners of war]: belligerent parties are, rather, asked to consider this possibility in good faith". See, P. Kilibarda and G. Gaggioli, 'Detention of Suspected Terrorists in Connection with Armed Conflict: A Focus on Release and Repatriation' in M. Schmitt and C. Koschnitzky (eds.), *Prisoners of War in Contemporary Conflict* (Oxford University Press 2023) 266. Nevertheless, Article 85(4)(b) of Additional Protocol I regards "unjustifiable delay in the repatriation of prisoners of war or civilians" as a grave breach of that Protocol. Despite the more cautious formulation in Article 134 of the GCIV, listing delay to repatriate civilians as a grave breach of Protocol I does speak in favor of a more unequivocal obligation to repatriate civilian internees. See, P. Kilibarda and G. Gaggioli 2023 (n. 92) 266.

be detained, released and repatriated in IACs, and the "very basic rules" in NIACs.[93]

As Mckeever notes, "the rules pertaining to NIACs are plainly of greater relevance to persons who are held in camps controlled by a non-State party to the armed conflict" in Syria.[94] The same can be said about FTFs as members of, and their family members affiliated with, non-state armed groups like IS detained in Iraqi prisons.[95] As Syria and Iraq are both not a party to the Additional Protocol II, the IHL regime that is applicable is Common Article 3 together with customary rules of IHL.

Although Common Article 3 does provide for a minimum level of treatment of detainees, it does not mention repatriation. The ICRC's study on customary IHL lists the following rule as constituting custom:

> "A. Prisoners of war must be released and repatriated without delay after the cessation of active hostilities.
> B. Civilian internees must be released as soon as the reasons which necessitated internment no longer exist, but at the latest as soon as possible after the close of active hostilities.
> C. Persons deprived of their liberty in relation to a non-international armed conflict must be released as soon as the reasons for the deprivation of their liberty cease to exist.
> The persons referred to may continue to be deprived of their liberty if penal proceedings are pending against them or if they are serving a sentence lawfully imposed".[96]

With regard to detained persons in NIAC, this rule only mentions their release but does not say anything about repatriation. A lack of reference to repatriation in Common Article 3 and in the ICRC's study on customary IHL can be

93 ICRC, Strengthening Legal Protection for Persons deprived of their Liberty in relation to Non-international Armed Conflict, Regional Consultations 2012–13, Background paper. Available at: <https://www.icrc.org/en/doc/assets/files/2013/strengthening-legal-protection-detention-consultations-2012-2013-icrc.pdf> accessed 17 July 2023.

94 D. McKeever 2022 (n. 43) 92; Rulac Geneva Academy, 'Non-international armed conflicts in Syria' (last updated 3 June 2023) available at: <https://www.rulac.org/browse/conflicts/non-international-armed-conflicts-in-syria> accessed 17 July 2023.

95 Rulac Geneva Academy, 'Non-international armed conflicts in Iraq' (last updated 18 May 2023) available at: <https://www.rulac.org/browse/conflicts/non-international-armed-conflicts-in-iraq> accessed 17 July 2022.

96 ICRC, Customary IHL Database, Rule 128 Release and Return of Persons Deprived or their Liberty. Available at: <https://ihl-databases.icrc.org/en/customary-ihl/v1/rule128> accessed 17 July 2023.

explained by the fact that NIACs occur within the territory of a single state and "it makes no sense to 'repatriate' [detained persons] abroad, to a country whose nationals they are not, perhaps by their own State of nationality".[97] In NIACs, persons detained will, in most instances, already be detained on the territory of their state of nationality and/or origin, which makes repatriation "a moot point".[98] However, when detained persons in NIAC are foreign nationals, like FTFs and their family members detained in Syria and Iraq, the question of repatriation does come into play, even though the conflict occurs on the territory of a single state. On the one hand, there are authors who, therefore, argue that an obligation to repatriate does exist in such circumstances. For example, in the context of FTFs and their family members detained in SDF-controlled camps and prisons, Stigall notes that "in both international and non-international armed conflict, persons detained must be repatriated unless they are pending criminal proceedings by the detaining authority",[99] and that "the general idea in international law is that, no matter the type of conflict in question, and barring an issue of *non-refoulement*, detained individuals are to be repatriated [...] when their detention is no longer necessary".[100] On the other hand, there are authors who are more cautious and who argue that the rules applicable to NIACs, including customary IHL, do not go as far as imposing an obligation to repatriate foreign detainees. For example, within the context of detained FTFs and family members, Mckeever notes that "it is difficult to argue that [Common Article 3 and customary IHL] are sufficiently prescriptive as to create an obligation on States of origin to repatriate their nationals from northern Syria".[101] In addition, Kilibarda and Gaggioli indicate that such an obligation to repatriate FTFs and their family members from SDF-controlled camps and prisons "would have to be sought in [international human rights law] or domestic legislation".[102] There thus appears to be a difference of opinion regarding the issue of repatriation of foreign detainees, like FTFs and their associated family members, in NIACs such as those in Syria and Iraq.

97 P. Kilibarda and G. Gaggioli 2023 (n. 92) 262. See, also, S. Sivakumaran, 'Armed Conflict-Related Detention of Particularly Vulnerable Persons: Challenges and Possibilities' 94 International Law Studies (2018) 63, 64.

98 P. Kilibarda and G. Gaggioli 2023 (n. 92) 262.

99 D. Stigall, 'The Syrian Detention Conundrum: International and Comparative Legal Complexities' 11 Harvard National Security Journal (2020) 75.

100 *Ibid.* 76.

101 D. McKeever 2022 (n. 43) 100.

102 P. Kilibarda and G. Gaggioli 2023 (n. 92) 293.

A final legal basis for repatriation in public international law could potentially be found in a number of Security Council Resolutions, including Resolutions 1373 (2001),[103] 2178 (2014)[104] and 2396 (2017).[105] For example, in Resolution 2396 (2017), the Security Council called upon member states

> to develop and implement comprehensive and tailored prosecution, rehabilitation, and reintegration strategies and protocols, in accordance with their obligations under international law, including with respect to foreign terrorist fighters and spouses and children accompanying returning and relocating foreign terrorist fighters.[106]

Such calls by the Security Council may provide a legal basis for repatriation. At the least, repatriation amounts to a positive implementation of these Resolutions and refusal to do so might run counter to these calls. Furthermore, all three Resolutions call upon member states to "ensure that any person who participates in the financing, planning, preparation or perpetration of terrorist acts or in supporting terrorist acts is brought to justice".[107] Although the obligation to prosecute terrorist offences will be elaborated upon in the next chapter, within the context of repatriation, it is important to already mention that the only viable option to bring those individuals to justice, in a way which upholds international (human rights) law standards, is to prosecute them at home. This would, however, require states to repatriate their FTFs and family members first. In addition to the call to prosecute suspects of terrorist offences, Resolution 2178 (2014) also calls upon member states to prevent the radicalization of individuals to terrorism.[108] Likewise, states' obligation to prevent radicalization to terrorism might also require states to return their FTFs and family members, as it has been said that the camps and prisons in Northeast Syria in which they are detained constitute breeding grounds for radicalization. In sum, the only way for states to give effect to these calls from the Security Council would, in these circumstances, be to repatriate their FTFs and family members.

---

103 UNSC Resolution 1373 (29 September 2001) UN Doc. S/RES/1373 (2001).
104 UNSC Resolution 2178 (24 September 2014) UN Doc. S/RES/2178 (2014).
105 UNSC Res. 2396 (2017) (n. 59).
106 *Ibid.* para. 30.
107 UNSC Res. 1373 (2001) (n. 103) para. 2(e); UNSC Res. 2178 (2014) (n. 104) para. 6; UNSC Res. 2396 (2017) (n. 59) paras. 29, 30.
108 UNSC Res. 2178 (2014) (n.104) para. 4.

2.3 Repatriation, the Right to Return and the Obligation to Re-admit Nationals

In the context of state responses to the FTFs phenomenon, there is certainly a relationship between the response of nationality deprivation and states' refusal to repatriate. In light of the individual's right to enter the territory of the state of which he or she is a national, as laid down in Article 3(2) Additional Protocol No. 4 to the ECHR,[109] or the right to enter one's own country, as laid down in Article 12(4) ICCPR,[110] states may have deprived nationality in order to avoid repatriation responsibilities. Some authors, like Kilibarda and Gaggioli, have indeed expressed the view that, according to them, an obligation to repatriate "may exist under the right to enter one's own country".[111] However, legally speaking, a distinction can be made between the right to return, the obligation to (re)admit and the measure of repatriation. The previous chapter of this research elaborately discussed states' obligation to re-admit nationals and those nationals' right to enter or return to, in the case of the ECHR, the state of which he or she is a national or, in the case of the ICCPR, his or her own country. Although, at first glance, one might think the opposite, states' obligation to (re)admit nationals is not the same as an obligation to repatriate those nationals from abroad. Likewise, the right to enter one's state of nationality is not the same as the right to be repatriated to that state. In order to show the difference, two scenarios should be distinguished.[112]

First, the scenario where an individual travels, or is deported, to his or her state of nationality and shows up at the border. For example, Türkiye has on multiple occasions deported FTFs or their associated family members back to their states of origin.[113] This is what happened with the Dutch Xaviera S.[114] She traveled to Syria in 2014 to join IS and was arrested in Türkiye in 2018. Later, Türkiye deported her to the Netherlands. In such a situation, the law is clear. Xaviera S. had a right to enter the Netherlands, her state of nationality, and the

---

109 Additional Protocol No. 4 to the ECHR (signed 16 September 1996, entered into force 2 May 1968) ETS 46.

110 ICCPR (adopted 16 December 1966, entered into force 23 March 1976) 999 UNTS 171.

111 P. Kilibarda and G. Gaggioli 2023 (n. 92) 293.

112 L. van Waas and A. Brekoo 2023 (n. 1) 213.

113 I. Sariyuce and E. Mackintosh, 'Turkey begins deporting suspected ISIS fighters to US, UK, Germany' (*CNN*, 14 November 2019). Available at: <https://edition.cnn.com/2019/11/14/europe/turkey-deports-isis-fighters-us-uk-germany-gbr-intl/index.html> accessed 18 December 2024.

114 'Turkije stuurt twee IS-vrouwen terug naar Nederland' (*NOS*, 19 November 2019). Available at: <https://nos.nl/artikel/2311186-turkije-stuurt-twee-is-vrouwen-terug-naar-nederland> accessed 18 December 2024.

Netherlands was under an obligation to readmit her to its territory. In light of the broader human right to return to his or her own country as contained in the ICCPR, the same might be true for states of habitual residence.

A comparable situation is when a national does not show up at the border but reaches the embassy or consulate of his or her state of nationality or habitual residence abroad and requests assistance. Van Waas and Brekoo note in this regard that it is "commonly accepted practice of states to honour the request for assistance by their nationals when they approach a diplomatic representation in a third country".[115] For example, the Netherlands indicated that their FTFs and associated family members in Syria and Iraq have a right to return but that they will have to reach a diplomatic or consular representation in the region themselves. Only then the Netherlands would facilitate their return.[116] A spokesperson from the German Ministry of Interior also explained that "[i]n principle, all German citizens and those suspected of having fought for so-called IS have the right to return", but this is only possible if the person concerned has consular access, which "the German government cannot guarantee [...] due to the armed conflict" in Syria.[117] A similar position was, among others, taken by Norway.[118] Mehra and Paulussen have compared such policies with regard to detained FTFs and family members in Syria and Iraq to "showing a detainee the key to his or her cell [...] and then telling the person he or she is entitled to this key, but keeping it out of grasp".[119] These two situations, forming the first scenario, are summarized by van Waas and Brekoo as "where nationals are found 'knocking at the doors'".[120] In such situations, states are obliged to allow re-entry on their territory based on the individual's right to return.

---

115 L. van Waas and A. Brekoo 2023 (n. 1) 213, 214.

116 Letter from the Ministers of Justice and Security and Foreign Affairs to the House of Representatives, 'Reactie op het verzoek van het lid Buitenweg, gedaan tijdens de Regeling van Werkzaamheden van 5 februari 2019, over het bericht 'Nederland onderzoekt terughalen vrouwelijke Syriëgangers en kinderen' 21 February 2019. Available at: <https://www.tweedekamer.nl/kamerstukken/brieven_regering/detail?id=2019Z03634&did=2019D07750> accessed 20 July 2023.

117 'Germany cool on Trump appeal to take back IS fighters from Syria' (*Reuters*, 17 February 2019). Available at: <https://www.reuters.com/article/idUSKCN1Q60JE/> accessed 18 December 2024.

118 P. Lote, D. Krekling and H. Carlsen, 'Solberg: – Norske IS-krigere har rett til å komme hjem' (*NRK*, 16 February 2019). Available at: <https://www.nrk.no/urix/solberg_-_-norske-is-krigere-har-rett-til-a-komme-hjem-1.14434249> accessed 18 December 2024.

119 T. Mehra and C. Paulussen, 'The Repatriation of Foreign Fighters and Their Families: Options, Obligations, Morality and Long-Term Thinking' ICCT Perspective (6 March 2019).

120 L. van Waas and A. Brekoo 2023 (n. 1) 214.

In the second scenario, the individual is abroad and finds himself or herself far removed from the territory of his/her state of nationality or habitual residence and unable to reach a diplomatic or consular mission.[121] This is exactly the scenario in which detained FTFs and associated family members find themselves in Syria and Iraq, far away from their state of nationality or, in the broader terms of the ICCPR, their own country. Furthermore, they are generally unable to reach a diplomatic or consular representation, not only because many states have closed their embassies and consulates in Syria but also because these individuals are not allowed to leave the camps and prisons in which they are detained. Unlike in the first scenario, the right to enter and the obligation to re-admit offer no solution in this second scenario. The obligation to (re)admit nationals does not entail a positive obligation upon states to actively facilitate such (re)admission through repatriation. Similarly, the right to enter or return may entail a duty upon states to allow entry into their territory, when the individual travels to his or her state of nationality or habitual residence independently, and issue travel documents to make the person's return possible, but it does not constitute a right to active facilitation of such (re)entry through repatriation from abroad.[122] Such a reading of the right to return to his or her state of nationality was also confirmed by the ECtHR in the case of *H.F. and Others v. France*. The Court ruled that "French citizens being held in the camps in north-eastern Syria cannot claim a general right to repatriation on the basis of the right to enter national territory".[123] Nevertheless, this right "may impose on a State certain positive obligations *vis-à-vis* its nationals in order to ensure that their right to enter national territory is practical and effective", such as "the obligation to issue them with travel documents to enable them to cross a border".[124]

From the discussion above, it can be concluded that the right to enter or return to one's state of nationality or his or her own country, as well as the obligation to (re)admit nationals, do not entail an obligation to repatriate from abroad.

---

121 *Ibid.* 213.

122 *Ibid.* 214.

123 *H.F. and Others v. France* (n. 40) para. 259.

124 *Ibid.* para. 260.

3 (Non-)Repatriation of Foreign Terrorist Fighters and Their Families from Syria and Iraq

This section will zero in on the reluctance or refusal of certain states to repatriate their FTFs and associated family members from Syria and Iraq. However, it will first be outlined which states were particularly active in repatriating their nationals. As will be shown, there have been a number of states, among others from Central Asia, that have led the way in repatriating their nationals. Thereafter, this section will try to set out which states were particularly inactive in repatriating their nationals and what their policies and considerations were for such a passive approach. Despite recent repatriation efforts, there are several European states that have been unwilling to repatriate their nationals for a very long time. After these issues have been addressed, it will be set out to what extent there are elements of responsibility shunning and risk externalization visible in this passive response to the FTFs phenomenon.

3.1 States Active in Repatriation

Accurate figures on the number of repatriations from Syria and Iraq are difficult to obtain. However, Rights & Security International, a non-governmental organization dedicated to, *inter alia*, documenting human rights abuses committed in the name of national security, has developed a 'Global Repatriations Tracker'.[125] Through this database, Rights & Security International documents numbers of repatriations from camps, prisons and other facilities in Northeast Syria. Repatriations from other parts of Syria or from Iraq are therefore not included. In addition to various other sources, this section will draw from the figures in this database, as it provides a comprehensive overview of repatriations, at least from Northeast Syria. However, when looking at these figures, it should be kept in mind that they are estimates only and that they need to be placed in perspective. Some states have or had many more FTFs and family members of their nationality detained in the region than other states and high numbers of repatriations do, therefore, not necessarily mean a high proportion of nationals repatriated.

From the figures provided by the Global Repatriations Tracker, it seems that there are a number of states that can be considered as 'active' in repatriating their nationals from Northeast Syria. These states not only repatriated relatively high numbers of nationals, but they also started their repatriation

125 Rights & Security International, Global Repatriations Tracker (n. 16).

efforts right after the fall of the IS caliphate and not only repatriated children but also women and sometimes even male FTFs. These states include, in particular, Kazakhstan, Kosovo, Uzbekistan and Tajikistan.[126]

Kazakhstan repatriated the highest count of FTFs and family members from Northeast Syria, an estimated 719.[127] This is a relatively high number as compared to the number of Kazakh nationals that traveled to the conflict zone. Although estimates vary, Cook and Vale indicate that between April 2013 and June 2018, around 500 to 600 Kazakh nationals became affiliated with IS. This number does not yet include those nationals who became affiliated with other non-state armed groups.[128] Other sources mention a higher number, some mention around 800 and others more than 1,000 Kazakh nationals.[129] Kazakhstan not only repatriated an estimated 494 children and 188 women, but also around 37 male FTFs from Northeast Syria, which is the highest number of the very few states that have repatriated men.[130] In addition, Kazakhstan also repatriated children from Iraqi prisons where they were detained together with their mothers.[131] Where other states were reluctant to repatriate for a very long time, Kazakhstan already started repatriating its nationals in January 2019, even three months before IS lost its last stronghold of Baghouz.[132] In a press statement regarding the country's first repatriation operations, President Kassym-Jomart Tokayev reaffirmed Kazakhstan's "commitments to combat terrorism and to provide comprehensive assistance to citizens in difficult situations". He noted that "[t]he humanitarian action will continue" and that

126 *Ibid.*

127 *Ibid.*

128 J. Cook and G. Vale, 'From Daesh to "Diaspora": Tracing the Women and Minors of Islamic State' ICSR Report (2018), Figure 5.

129 See, for example, F. Najibullah, 'The Women Who Came Home: Kazakhstan Tries To Rehabilitate Islamic State Returnees' (*Radio Free Europe/Radio Liberty*, 23 June 2019). Available at: <https://www.ecoi.net/en/document/2011740.html> accessed 18 December 2024; A. Gussarova, 'Repatriating Foreign Fighters: The Case of Kazakhstan' (*European Eye on Radicalization*, 17 April 2020). Available at: <https://eeradicalization.com/repatriating-foreign-fighters-the-case-of-kazakhstan/> accessed 18 December 2024.

130 Rights & Security International, Global Repatriations Tracker (n. 16).

131 UNICEF, Repatriation and reintegration of children affected by conflict in Syria and Iraq to Central Asia: A Compendium of Promising Practices from Kazakhstan, Kyrgyzstan, Tajikistan and Uzbekistan (June 2023) p. 14. Available at: <https://www.unicef.org/eca/reports/repatriation-and-reintegration-children-affected-conflict-syria-and-iraq-central-asia> accessed 24 July 2023.

132 Rights & Security International, Global Repatriations Tracker (n. 16); F. Najibullah 2019 (n. 129).

"[n]o one from our people will be left behind".[133] Notably, the repatriation operations were referred to as humanitarian action. In addition, Wolfe and Orozobekova note that throughout Kazakhstan's repatriation policy children were defined as victims and in its press statement, President Tokayev also noted that Kazakh "children should not suffer in a foreign land and be responsible for the mistakes of their parents".[134] Those repatriated Kazakh nationals who were not arrested and charged with terrorism or other offences, including children, were subjected to comprehensive rehabilitation and reintegration programs.[135]

Another state that was particularly active in repatriating its nationals is Kosovo. According to the Global Repatriations Tracker, Kosovo repatriated at least 242 nationals from Northeast Syria.[136] This number does not only include women and children but also male FTFs. This can be said to be a relatively high number, not only because Kosovo saw an estimated 359 nationals who became affiliated with IS travel to the conflict zone, but also given the small size of Kosovo's population (1.9 million).[137] Kosovo's first repatriation mission, in which it, with assistance from the United States, repatriated 74 children, 32 women and 4 men, was already back in April 2019.[138] All four male FTFs were immediately arrested and three of those men were eventually prosecuted and sentenced for terrorism-related offences.[139] All women were investigated and 10 of them were placed under house arrest.[140] Eventually, 16 of those women were prosecuted and sentenced for terrorism-related offences.[141] According to Avdimetaj and Coleman, most notable about Kosovo's approach is that,

133 Statement from the President of Kazakhstan Kassym-Jomart Tokayev (10 May 2019). Available at: <https://www.akorda.kz/en/speeches/internal_political_affairs/in_speeches_and_addresses/statement-from-the-president-of-kazakhstan-kassym-jomart-tokayev> accessed 24 July 2024. Translation by the author.

134 S. Wolfe and C. Orozobekova 2020 (n. 10); Statement from the President of Kazakhstan Kassym-Jomart Tokayev (10 May 2019) (n. 133) Translation by the author.

135 S. Wolfe and C. Orozobekova 2020 (n. 10).

136 Rights & Security International, Global Repatriations Tracker (n. 16).

137 J. Cook and G. Vale 2018 (n. 128) figure 5.

138 T. Avdimetaj and J. Coleman 2020 (n. 13) 2.

139 United Nations Interim Administration Mission in Kosovo, Report of the Secretary-General (31 March 2020) UN Doc. S/2020/255, para. 13. T. Avdimetaj and J. Coleman 2020 (n. 13) 3.

140 T. Avdimetaj and J. Coleman 2020 (n. 13) 3.

141 United Nations Interim Administration Mission in Kosovo, Report of the Secretary-General 2020 (n. 139) para. 13; T. Avdimetaj and J. Coleman 2020 (n. 13) 3.

> in combination with the focus on prosecution where warranted (and where sufficient evidence exists), actors across the government have emphasised the obligation to repatriate citizens, including the need for rehabilitation and focus on the eventual reintegration of the returnees back into society.[142]

The Kosovan Government, including the Kosovan security services, was in favor of repatriation because it "was considered to be a more sustainable approach than leaving their citizens in Syria, where circumstances shifted rapidly from day to day".[143]

Uzbekistan can also be mentioned as a state active in repatriating its nationals. It repatriated an estimated total of 339 women and children from Northeast Syria.[144] It started its first repatriation mission to Northeast Syria in May 2019, with which it repatriated 148 women and children.[145] In addition to these repatriations from Syria, Uzbekistan repatriated 64 children from Iraq whose mothers were serving prison sentences.[146] However, Uzbekistan did not repatriate any male FTFs. Although 339 nationals is a high number when compared to other states, it should be kept in mind that Uzbekistan also had a relatively high number of nationals who traveled to the conflict zone. It is estimated that between 1,500 and 2,500 Uzbek nationals traveled to Syria and Iraq and became affiliated with IS.[147] Nevertheless, many of those may have died in the conflict, have already returned or are located in other places than in Northeast Syria.

The same can be said for Tajikistan. Tajikistan repatriated an estimated total of 384 nationals from camps and other facilities in Northeast Syria, of which at least 210 children, 90 women and an unknown number of male

142 T. Avdimetaj and J. Coleman 2020 (n. 13) 2.

143 Radicalisation Awareness Network, Ex Post Paper, 'Study Visit: Returned Women and Children – Studying an Ongoing Experience on the Ground' 10–11 December 2019, Pristina, Kosovo, Available at: <https://home-affairs.ec.europa.eu/system/files/2020-01/ran_study_visit_kosovo_11_10122019_en.pdf> accessed 24 July 2023. See, also, S. Keller, 'An Effective Form of Judicial Treatment of Foreign Terrorist Fighters in Kosovo?' EJIL: Talk! (20 July 2023).

144 Rights & Security International, Global Repatriations Tracker (n. 16).

145 'Uzbekistan repatriates 148 women and children linked to ISIS from Syria' (*The Defense Post*, 30 May 2019). Available at: <https://thedefensepost.com/2019/05/30/uzbekistan-repatriate-isis-women-children-syria/> accessed 18 December 2024.

146 UNICEF, Repatriation and reintegration of children from Uzbekistan affected by conflict in Syria and Iraq (June 2023). Available at: <https://www.unicef.org/eca/reports/repatriation-and-reintegration-children-uzbekistan-affected-conflict-syria-and-iraq> accessed 24 July 2023.

147 J. Cook and G. Vale 2018 (n. 128) figure 5.

FTFs.[148] In 2019, Tajikistan also repatriated 84 children from prisons or other detention facilities in Iraq.[149] At an early stage, Tajikistan made its commitment clear to repatriate all its citizens from Syria and Iraq, in order to counter future threats to national security.[150] In its repatriation efforts, the country prioritized minors.[151] Tajikistan's President Emomali Rahmon proclaimed that "not a single Tajik child will be left in a foreign country".[152]

Besides the above-mentioned states, there are a number of other states that should be mentioned here. First, Russia repatriated a high number of children from Northeast Syria, an estimated 294, in multiple repatriation missions starting from March 2019.[153] Besides those detained in Northeast Syria, Russia also repatriated children from Iraq.[154] However, there is no public information available on whether Russia also repatriated adult FTFs or associated family members. Another state that should be mentioned here is the United States. The United States saw an estimated total of 272 nationals travel to Syria and Iraq who became affiliated with IS, which is a relatively small number.155 According to the Global Repatriations Tracker, it has repatriated an estimated 38 nationals from camps, prisons and other facilities in Northeast Syria, of which at least 17 children, 5 women and 3 men.[156] Except for children, the United States only repatriates those "against whom criminal charges have been lodged for offenses relating to their support for ISIS".[157] The United States should be mentioned here as a state 'active' in repatriating its nationals, not only because it has actively repatriated its own nationals, but also because it is active in promoting repatriation policies. It has continuously

148 Rights & Security International, Global Repatriaions Tracker (n. 16).

149 UNICEF 2023 (n. 131) 11.

150 F. Najibullah and M. Ahmadi, 'No IS Kids Left Behind: Tajikistan To Repatriate Dozens Of Islamic State Children from Iraq' (*Radio Free Europe/Radio Liberty*, 12 March 2019). Available at: <https://www.rferl.org/a/no-is-kids-left-behind-tajikistan-to-repatriate-dozens-of-islamic-state-children-from-iraq/29817362.html> accessed 18 December 2024.

151 Italian Institute for International Political Studies 2019 (n. 11).

152 *Ibid.*

153 Rights & Security International, Global Repatriations Tracker (n. 16).

154 'Russia says 27 children of ISIL members arrive from Iraq' (*Al Jazeera*, 10 February 2019). Available at: <https://www.aljazeera.com/news/2019/2/10/russia-says-27-children-of-isil-members-arrive-from-iraq> accessed 23 May 2025.

155 J. Cook and G. Vale 2018 (n. 128) figure 5.

156 Rights & Security International, Global Repatriations Tracker (n. 16).

157 US Department of Justice, Office of Public Affairs, Press Release: The United States Has Repatriated 27 Americans from Syria and Iraq Including Ten Charged with Terrorism-Related Offenses for Their Support to ISIS (1 October 2020). Available at: <https://www.justice.gov/opa/pr/united-states-has-repatriated-27-americans-syria-and-iraq-including-ten-charged-terrorism> accessed 25 April 2023.

called upon "other nations, particularly in Western Europe, to take responsibility for their citizens" and repatriate them from Syria and Iraq.[158] In addition, the United States has offered other states its assistance "with repatriation, providing diplomatic and logistical assistance, as well as aiding with rehabilitation, reintegration, and, where applicable, investigation and efforts to ensure accountability through prosecution".[159] In 2020, the United States used its veto with regard to a draft Security Council resolution submitted by Indonesia on the prosecution, rehabilitation and reintegration of terrorists, and in particular, FTFs and their family members.[160] Explaining its veto, the US representative said:

> The Indonesian draft resolution before us (S/2020/852), supposedly designed to reinforce international action on counterterrorism, was worse than no resolution at all. This draft resolution was meant to address the prosecution, rehabilitation and reintegration of terrorists, including foreign terrorist fighters and their accompanying family members. And yet it fails to even include reference to the crucial first step – repatriation to countries of origin or nationality. The United States provides the example here, bringing back our citizens and prosecuting them where appropriate. All nations need to take responsibility for their citizens who engage in terror. [...] Terrorist fighters and their families are easily ignored if they are someone else's problem. But I tell the Council now, and I say this with absolute conviction: failing to address head-on the importance of repatriation will inevitably perpetuate the problem of terrorism.[161]

Thus, the United States used its veto because the resolution failed to mention repatriation, let alone call upon member states to repatriate their FTFs and associated family members. This sharply contrasts with the stance of the EU members of the Security Council at the time, which appeared to have "made

---

158 *Ibid.* See, also, S. Kajjo 2023 (n. 9).

159 US Department of Justice, Secretary Antony J. Blinken and Saudi Foreign Minister Prince Faisal bin Farhan Al Saud at the Global Coalition to Defeat ISIS Ministerial Opening Session (8 June 2023). Available at: <https://www.state.gov/secretary-antony-j-blinken-at-the-global-coalition-to-defeat-isis-ministerial-opening-session/> accessed 25 July 2023.

160 UNSC, Indonesia: draft resolution (31 August 2020) UN Doc. S/2020/852; UNSC, Letter dated 31 August 2020 from the President of the Security Council addressed to the Secretary-General and the Permanent Representatives of the members of the Security Council (1 September 2020) UN Doc. S/2020/870, annex 1.

161 *Ibid.* annex 21; UNSC, Letter dated 31 August 2020 from the President of the Security Council addressed to the Secretary-General and the Permanent Representatives of the members of the Security Council (31 August 2020) UN Doc. S/2020/865.

clear that including the word 'repatriation' in the draft resolution was a red line".[162] Two other states that should, finally, briefly be mentioned here are Bosnia and Herzegovina and North Macedonia, primarily because they both, besides women and children, also repatriated male FTFs.[163]

3.2 States Inactive in Repatriation

In stark contrast with the active repatriation policies of those states mentioned in the previous sub-section, stand the passive approaches of other states that have refused or been reluctant to repatriate their nationals from Syria and Iraq for a long time. Based on, *inter alia*, figures from the Global Repatriations Tracker, those states are mainly European states, including France, the United Kingdom, the Netherlands, Belgium, Germany, Sweden, Spain, Austria and Denmark. Although these European states have all adopted a passive approach to the issue of repatriation, there is no consistency in their policies. Therefore, this sub-section will set out a number of those states' policies and practices with regard to the issue of repatriation, starting with France.

When looking at the total number of repatriations by France, it seems at first sight as if the French Government has been quite active in repatriating its nationals. According to the Global Repatriations Tracker, France repatriated 167 children and 56 women from camps, prisons and other detention facilities in Northeast Syria.[164] However, as mentioned earlier, these numbers need to be placed in perspective. They should, first, be viewed in light of the fact that France saw by far the highest number of nationals travel to the conflict zone out of all European states. An estimated 1,910 French nationals traveled to Syria and/or Iraq and became affiliated with IS.[165] Because of this high number, it can be assumed that there were, or still are, more French nationals detained in Northeast Syria than other European nationals. A study from October 2019 estimated that there were still around 130 adults and 270–320 French children detained in Syria and Iraq, which was indeed the highest number among European nationals.[166] Second, when looking at France's repa-

162 Security Council Report, Arria-Formula Meeting on Repatriation and Reintegration of Children Affected by Armed Conflict (28 January 2021). Available at: <https://www.securitycouncilreport.org/whatsinblue/2021/01/arria-formula-meeting-on-repatriation-and-reintegration-of-children-affected-by-armed-conflict.php> accessed 9 November 2023.

163 Rights & Security International, Global Repatriations Tracker (n. 16).

164 *Ibid.*

165 J. Cook and G. Vale 2018 (n. 128) figure 5.

166 T. Renard and R. Coolsaet, 'New figures on European nationals detained in Syria and Iraq' Egmont Royal Institute for International Relations (15 October 2019).

triation missions from Northeast Syria, the first one taking place in March 2019, one can see that it only repatriated small numbers of unaccompanied, orphaned and/or seriously vulnerable children for the first years after the fall of the caliphate.[167] This practice aligns with France's policy as of 2018, to only repatriate French children on a case-by-case basis, but not their mothers.[168] In accordance with this policy, France only repatriated 35 children from March 2019 until July 2022.[169] France has categorically refused to repatriate adults from Syria and Iraq for a long time. French Foreign Minister Jean-Yves Le Drian referred to these adult FTFs and associated family members as 'enemies' of the state who should face justice in Syria or Iraq.[170]

As a result, multiple cases entailing requests for repatriation were initiated before French national courts. French courts have, however, on multiple occasions rejected those cases. For example, the *Tribunal Administratif de Paris* declared in at least two cases brought by two women detained in Northeast Syria, acting also on behalf of their children, that it lacked jurisdiction to adjudicate the matter, *inter alia*, because the requests related to the conduct of foreign affairs over which the court did not have competence.[171] The *Conseil d'État* also dismissed the appeal in these two cases as well as in two other cases based on the same reasoning.[172] In yet a different case, the *Tribunal Judiciare de Paris* declared itself incompetent to adjudicate on the repatriation of a woman and her four children from the al-Roj camp in Northeast Syria

167 See, for example, J. McAuley, 'France repatriates five children of French militants who joined the Islamic State' (*The Washington Post*, 16 March 2019). Available at: <https://www.washingtonpost.com/world/europe/france-repatriates-five-children-of-french-militants-who-joined-the-islamic-state/2019/03/16/ecc3ae99-5050-4d8c-964e-c5232d85fc7e_story.html> accessed 18 December 2024; 'Syrian Kurds transfer 12 orphans from jihadist families to France for repatriation' (*France 24*, 10 June 2019). Available at: <https://www.france24.com/en/20190610-france-orphans-jihadist-families-syria-kurds-transfer> accessed 18 December 2024; Human Rights Watch, 'France Repatriates More Children from Northeast Syria' (24 June 2020). Available at: <https://www.hrw.org/news/2020/06/24/france-repatriates-more-children-northeast-syria> accessed 1 August 2023.

168 M. Semo and E. Vincent 'Vers une exfiltration des enfants de djihadistes français retenus en Syrie'(*Le Monde*, 24 October 2018). Available at: <https://www.lemonde.fr/syrie/article/2018/10/24/vers-une-exfiltration-des-enfants-de-djihadistes-retenus-en-syrie_5373635_1618247.html> accessed 18 December 2024.

169 Rights & Security International, Global Repatriations Tracker (n. 16) Core data.

170 'France snubs Trump's appeal to repatriate IS fighters en masse, for now' (*Reuters*, 18 February 2019). Available at: <https://www.reuters.com/article/world/france-snubs-trumps-appeal-to-repatriate-islamic-state-fighters-en-masse-for-n-idUSKCN1Q70LJ/> accessed 18 December 2024.

171 Tribunal Administratif de Paris, No. 1906076/9 (9 April 2019) paras. 7 and 8; Tribunal Administratif de Paris, No. 1906077/9 (9 April 2019) paras. 7 and 8.

172 Conseil d'État, Nos. 429668, 429669, 429674 and 429701 (23 April 2019).

because the requests for repatriation necessarily involved an examination of France's foreign relations, which falls within the power of the administration and outside the jurisdiction of the judiciary.[173] In the case of *H.F. and others v. France*, the ECtHR examined the way in which France had dealt with the repatriation requests of the applicants' daughters and grandchildren detained in camps in Northeast Syria. The ECtHR ruled that because responses by the French executive authorities to repatriation requests of the applicants' daughters and grandchildren fell short of an individual decision, and because the national court proceedings in which the courts declared themselves incompetent lacked an individual and independent review of the repatriation requests, the examination of the requests "was not surrounded by appropriate safeguards against arbitrariness".[174] As the requests for repatriation concerned the implementation of the applicant's daughters and grandchildren's right to enter national territory, France had violated Article 3(2) of Protocol No. 4 to the ECHR by failing to ensure such safeguards.

Shortly before this judgement by the ECtHR was rendered, France started to repatriate larger groups of French nationals from Northeast Syria, not only children but also adult women.[175] France's first larger repatriation mission was on 5 July 2022, in which it repatriated 35 children and 16 women. Despite these efforts in repatriating women and children, France still refuses to repatriate any male FTFs. In April 2023, it was estimated that more than 100 French children and around 50 French women were still detained in Northeast Syria.[176] One possible explanation for the shift in France's approach to repatriation is decisions by the CRC Committee and the Committee against Torture in response to complaints brought by French nationals.[177] The CRC Committee

---

173 Tribunal Judiciaire de Paris (n. 33) 5–6.

174 *H.F. and Others v. France* (n. 40) paras. 272–284, and in particular para. 283.

175 'France repatriates 51 children, mothers from Syrian camps' (*Al Jazeera*, 5 July 2022). Available at: <https://www.aljazeera.com/news/2022/7/5/france-repatriates-children-mothers-from-syrian-refugee-camps> accessed 18 December 2024; 'France repatriates 40 children, 15 women from camps in Syria' (*Al Jazeera*, 20 October 2022). Available at: <https://www.aljazeera.com/news/2022/10/20/france-repatriates-40-children-15-women-from-camps-in-syria> accessed 18 December 2024; 'France repatriates 47 nationals from northeastern Syria camps' (*Al Jazeera*, 24 January 2023). Available at: <https://www.aljazeera.com/news/2023/1/24/france-repatriates-47-nationals-from-north-east-syria#:~:text=In%20October%2C%2040%20children%20and,also%20live%20in%20the%20camps> accessed 18 December 2024.

176 Human Rights Watch, France: Submission to the UN Committee on the Rights of the Child (26 April 2023). Available at: <https://www.hrw.org/news/2023/04/26/france-submission-un-committee-rights-child> accessed 31 July 2023.

177 CRC Committee, *F.B. et al. and D.A. et al. v. France* (n. 26); Committee against Torture, *C. P. et al. v. France* (n. 28); Committee against Torture, *P.D. v. France* (n. 28).

rendered a decision in February 2022 and the Committee against Torture in November 2022 and November 2023, respectively. Both treaty bodies ordered France to, in the wording of the CRC Committee, "take urgent positive measures to repatriate" and in the wording of the Committee against Torture, "to take all reasonable measures, including the repatriation of", and "to continue its efforts to ensure repatriation".[178] In addition to these decisions by UN treaty bodies, in September 2022, France was ordered by the ECtHR to re-examine the repatriation requests and to ensure appropriate safeguards against arbitrariness in doing so.[179] These successive reprimands could have been a reason for France to change its approach from July 2022 onwards.[180]

As of December 2017, Belgium took the position that Belgian children until the age of 10 should be treated as victims and should, therefore, be allowed to return to Belgium.[181] The Belgian Minister of Justice, Koen Geens, even stated that it was the Government's 'obligation' to return Belgian children.[182] As children between 10 and 18 could present a security threat, the question regarding their return would be approached on a 'case-by-case' basis.[183] Despite this cautiously lenient approach towards children, up until July 2021, Belgium only repatriated seven, all but one of them orphaned, children from Northeast Syria.[184] Before the first repatriation mission in June 2019, Koen Geens emphasised that no practical steps were taken because bringing back the children, especially those detained with their mothers, was "a complicated

178 CRC Committee, *F.B. et al. and D.A. et al. v. France* (n. 26) para. 8(c); Committee against Torture, *C.P. et al. v. France* (n. 28) para. 9; Committee against Torture, *P.D. v. France* (n. 28) para. 9.

179 *H.F. and Others v. France* (n. 40) para. 6(a).

180 S. Koller, 'Prosecution of Returnees from Syria and Iraq in France: Insights and Recommendations for Policymakers and Security Agencies' CEP Policy Paper (March 2023) 7.

181 T. Renard and R. Coolsaet, 'Children in the Levant: Insights from Belgium on the dilemmas of repatriation and the challenges of reintegration' Egmont Royal Institute for International Relations, Security Policy Brief No. 98 (July 2018) p. 6.

182 'Geens: 'Als dit Belgische kinderen zijn, dan is het onze plicht ze terug te halen'' (*De Standaard*, 29 May 2018). Available at: <https://www.standaard.be/cnt/dmf20180529_03534762> accessed 18 December 2024.

183 T. Renard and R. Coolsaet 2018 (n. 181) 6.

184 'Belgium takes back six children of Isis fighters from Syrian camps' (*The Guardian*, 15 June 2019). Available at: <https://www.theguardian.com/world/2019/jun/15/belgium-takes-back-six-children-of-isis-fighters-from-syrian-camps> accessed 18 December 2024; A. Vanrenterghem and E. Maerevoet, 'Belgische jongen van 9, die door moeder ontvoerd was naar IS-gebied in Syrië, is terug in ons land' (*VRT News*, 25 December 2022). Available at: <https://www.vrt.be/vrtnws/nl/2020/12/25/belgische-jongen-van-9-die-door-moeder-ontvoerd-was-naar-is-geb/> accessed 18 December 2024.

legal tangle".[185] Contrary to children, Belgium has refused to take back any adult FTFs or family members for a long time, as this was "not in the interest of the country".[186] Only as of July 2021, Belgium seems to have broken with its previous approach and started to repatriate larger groups of children from Northeast Syria together with their mothers.[187] This shift in Belgium's approach towards the issue of repatriation can, at least partly, be explained by the installment of a new Government in October 2020, with Alexander De Croo as Prime Minister. De Croo has advocated in favor of repatriating children and, if necessary, women. In response to the repatriation of 16 children and 6 women on 21 June 2022, he explained that the Government decided to repatriate those women and children because they were detained "in very bad conditions with a very high risk of being exposed to extremism and brainwashing over which we have no control".[188] He further explained that "an analysis by our security services shows that it is better for our safety to bring back those children – and if necessary, those women – because then we will be safer as a country".[189] Such an explanation shows that states' approaches to the issue of repatriation are highly dependent upon the political situation in those states. The responses by some opposition parties in Belgium to the two repatriation missions as of June 2021 also show that the repatriation of FTFs and associated family members remains a sensitive and politically controversial topic.[190]

185 De Standaard 2018 (n. 182).

186 'Le retour des jihadistes belges n'est 'pas dans l'intérêt du pays' (*Le Vif*, 1 March 2018). Available at: <https://www.levif.be/belgique/le-retour-des-jihadistes-belges-nest-pas-dans-linteret-du-pays/> accessed 18 December 2024.

187 Rights & Security International, Global Repatriations Tracker (n. 16) Core data; J. Stroobants, 'La Belgique va rapatrier les enfants de djihadistes détenus en Syrie' (*Le Monde*, 5 March 2021). Available at: <https://www.lemonde.fr/international/article/2021/03/05/la-belgique-va-rapatrier-les-enfants-de-djihadistes-detenus-en-syrie_6072068_3210.html> accessed 18 December 2024.

188 I. Vrancken, 'Tweede groep Belgische vrouwen en kinderen van IS-strijders gerepatrieerd naar ons land' (*VRT News*, 21 June 2022) (Translation by the author). Available at: <https://www.vrt.be/vrtnws/nl/2022/06/20/tweede-groep-belgische-vrouwen-en-kinderen-van-is-strijders-gere/> accessed 19 March 2024.

189 *Ibid.* (translation by the author).

190 See for example, S. Sanen, '"Regering speelt met onze veiligheid": N-VA en Vlaams Belang vinden repatriëring IS-vrouwen onbegrijpelijk' (*VRT News*, 21 June 2022). Available at: <https://www.vrt.be/vrtnws/nl/2022/06/21/reacties-op-repatriering/> accessed 19 March 2024.

It is estimated that Belgium has repatriated a total of 32 children and 13 women from Northeast Syria.[191] In October 2019, Renard and Coolsaet estimated that there were around 69 Belgian children and 57 adults detained in Northeast Syria.[192] Therefore, there are likely still a considerable number of Belgian nationals waiting to be repatriated.

As mentioned earlier, the Netherlands adopted a passive approach as well and "does not actively focus on repatriation".[193] Although recognizing Dutch nationals' right to return and, in principle, wanting to cooperate in their controlled return, the Dutch Government has refused to actively engage in repatriation efforts. The Netherlands required its nationals to reach a Dutch diplomatic or consular representation in the region themselves, despite those nationals not being able to leave the camps in which they are detained and the Netherlands having closed its representation in Syria. The Dutch Government has given multiple reasons for this passive approach, including that the return of Dutch FTFs and/or their family members would jeopardize Dutch national security,[194] a repatriation mission would put the lives of Dutch civil servants at risk due to the unsafe situation in Northeast Syria,[195] and because a repatriation mission would force the Netherlands to enter into relations with an unrecognized non-state entity as well as with the Assad regime and might, therefore, have serious repercussions for its international relations and foreign policy.[196] These reasons were also advanced against repatriation in the earlier-mentioned case concerning the repatriation requests of 23 Dutch women, together with their 55 children, in which the Hague Court of Appeal and ultimately the Dutch Supreme Court ruled that the state had not exceeded its wide margin of appreciation and did not act unlawfully by not repatriating the women and children.[197]

191 Rights & Security International, Global Repatriations Tracker (n. 16) Core data.

192 T. Renard and R. Coolsaet 2019 (n. 166).

193 CRC Committee, Combined fifth and sixth periodic reports submitted by the Netherlands under Article 44 of the Convention pursuant to the simplified reporting procedure, due in 2019 (7 May 2021) UN Doc. CRC/C/NLD/5–6, para. 209.

194 Court of Appeal of The Hague 2019 (n. 36) para. 7.11.

195 *Ibid.* para. 7.12.

196 *Ibid.* para. 7.13. See, also, Letter by the Dutch Minister of Justice to the Speaker of the Dutch House of Representatives (6 December 2018). Available at: <https://www.tweedekamer.nl/kamerstukken/brieven_regering/detail?id=2018Z23191&did=2018D58508> accessed 18 December 2024.

197 Court of Appeal of The Hague 2019 (n. 36) paras. 7.5–7.14; Dutch Supreme Court 2020 (n. 36) para. 3 and especially paras. 3.14 and 3.21.2.

In accordance with this passive approach, up until February 2022, the Netherlands only repatriated five children and one woman.[198] From February 2022 onwards, the Netherlands seems to have more actively repatriated larger groups of not only Dutch children but also adult women from North-east Syria. In a mission on 3 February 2022, it repatriated 11 children and 5 women, and on 2 November 2022, 28 children and 12 women were returned to the Netherlands.[199] However, the Dutch Government did not change its approach to repatriation on its own initiative, but because the District Court of Rotterdam ruled in multiple criminal cases that the prosecution against the women would be terminated if the Government did not repatriate them, or make concrete commitments to that end, within a certain period of time.[200] Therefore, the Netherlands seems to have repatriated the women out of fear for impunity. If the Netherlands had not repatriated them, and they would have otherwise returned to the Netherlands somehow, the Netherlands would no longer be able to prosecute them. The Dutch Minister of Justice, Dilan Yesilgöz, declared at the time that this was not a risk she was willing to take.[201] After the two substantive repatriation missions in 2022, the Government explained that they only repatriated those women and children because of the judicial interference and to prevent them from remaining unpunished, but that their priority remains to have Dutch FTFs and family members prosecuted in the region.[202] The Dutch General Intelligence and Security Service

198 'French, Dutch Islamic State orphans repatriated from Syria-Kurdish-led authority' (*Reuters*, 10 June 2019). Available at: <https://www.reuters.com/article/business/french-dutch-islamic-state-orphans-repatriated-from-syria-kurdish-led-authority-idUSL8N23H1SI/> accessed 18 December 2024; 'Dutch woman and three children repatriated from Syrian ISIL camp' (*Al Jazeera*, 5 June 2021). Available at: <https://www.aljazeera.com/news/2021/6/5/dutch-woman-and-three-children-repatriated-from-syria-isil-camp> accessed 18 December 2024; See also Rights & Security International, Global Repatriations Tracker (n. 16) Core data.

199 'Nederland haalt vijf IS-vrouwen en hun elf kinderen terug uit Syrië' (*NOS*, 3 February 2022). Available at: <https://nos.nl/artikel/2415535-nederland-haalt-vijf-is-vrouwen-en-hun-elf-kinderen-terug-uit-syrie> accessed 18 December 2024; 'Twaalf Nederlandse IS-vrouwen en hun 28 kinderen opgehaald uit Syrië' (*NOS*, 1 November 2022). Available at: <https://nos.nl/artikel/2450620-twaalf-nederlandse-is-vrouwen-en-hun-28-kinderen-opgehaald-uit-syrie> accessed 18 December 2024; See also Rights & Security International, Global Repatriations Tracker (n. 16) Core data.

200 District Court Rotterdam, ECLI:NL:RBROT:2020:1445 (17 February 2020); District Court Rotterdam, ECLI:NL:RBROT:2020:5273 (16 June 2020); District Court Rotterdam, ECLI:NL:RBROT:2021:10090 (11 October 2021); District Court Rotterdam, ECLI:NL:RBROT:2022:3993 (11 May 2022).

201 NOS 2022 (n. 199).

202 'Terrorismebestrijding: Verslag van een schriftelijk overleg' Tweede Kamer, vergaderjaar 2022–2023, 29754 Nr. 656 (22 November 2022) paras. 14–16. Available at: <https://www.

(AIVD) stated that, as of July 2023, there are still 25 adult FTFs or family members and 30 children in camps or detention centers in Northeast Syria.[203]

When looking at Germany, their policy with regard to the repatriation of their nationals seems to be quite inconsistent.[204] Germany appears to have so far repatriated an estimated 80 children, 27 women and 1 man from Northeast Syria on a case-by-case basis. The adolescent man was taken to Syria when he was 11 years old.[205] From the start, Germany has adopted the position that it is, in principle, willing to repatriate children from Syria and Iraq, but due to security concerns and concerns regarding German foreign policy, it is not willing to actively repatriate adult FTFs or family members.[206] Like the Netherlands, the German Ministry of Interior also stated that although "all German citizens and those suspected of having fought for so-called IS have the right to return", a necessary condition for their return is consular access.[207] Thus, requiring their detained FTFs and family members to reach a diplomatic representation in the region, while those in Syria are closed. In addition, the German Minister of Foreign Affairs, Heiko Maas, noted that the return of adults would only be possible if "we can guarantee that these people can be immediately sent here to appear in court and that they will be detained".[208] This insinuates that Germany would only repatriate those nationals against whom sufficient evidence is available to prosecute them at home.

All in all, like the other European states discussed so far in this sub-section, Germany adopted a passive approach towards the issue of repatriation. Like in France, the Netherlands and Belgium, there have also been cases filed before German courts containing requests for repatriation. Notably, the *Oberverwaltungsgericht Berlin-Brandenburg* has been the only national court of last

---

tweedekamer.nl/kamerstukken/detail?id=2022D48646&did=2022D48646> accessed 20 March 2024.

203 AIVD, Uitreizigers en terugkeerders: Hoeveel Nederlanders zijn uitgereisd en bevinden zich nog in de regio? Available at: <https://www.aivd.nl/onderwerpen/terrorisme/uitreizigers-en-terugkeerders> accessed 3 August 2023.

204 See, on Germany's repatriation policy, K. Roithmaier, 'Germany and its Returning Foreign Terrorist Fighters: New Loss of Citizenship Law and the Broader German Repatriation Landscape' ICCT Perspective (18 April 2019).

205 German Federal Foreign Office, Statement by Foreign Minister Baerbock on the repatriation of seven children, four women and one adolescent from north-eastern Syria (5 October 2022). Available at: <https://www.auswaertiges-amt.de/en/newsroom/news/repatriation-syria/2556528> accessed 11 December 2024.

206 T. Van Poecke and E. Wauters 2021 (n. 34) 38.

207 Reuters 2019 (n. 117).

208 'Germany says repatriation of Syria jihadists 'extremely difficult'' (*The Local*, 18 February 2019). Available at: <https://www.thelocal.de/20190218/germany-says-repatriation-of-syria-jihadists-extremely-difficult> accessed 18 December 20224.

instance ruling that the Government was under a constitutional obligation to repatriate a woman together with her three children from the al-Hol camp in Northeast Syria.[209]

Until 20 December 2020, Germany only repatriated seven children and one woman from Northeast Syria in two repatriation missions.[210] From December 2020 onwards, there seems to be a change in Germany's passive approach, as it started to repatriate larger groups of women and children.[211] After the first substantive repatriation mission in December 2020, in which 23 children and 8 women were repatriated, Heiko Maas noted that the mission was based on "humanitarian grounds" and that its successful completion was "good news and an encouraging sign that we will be able to make repatriations happen in other cases, too".[212] After Germany's final repatriation mission on 6 October 2022, Heiko Maas his successor, Annalena Baerbock, declared that, "thanks to this operation, almost all known cases have now been closed".[213]

The United Kingdom has so far only repatriated 21, mostly orphaned or unaccompanied, children and 3 women from Northeast Syria in six separate repatriation missions.[214] Although exact numbers are unknown, Reprieve, a UK-based non-governmental organization, estimated in 2021 that "[o]f the

209 Oberverwaltungsgericht Berlin-Brandenburg, ECLI:DE:OVGBEBB:2019:1106.OVG10S43.19.00 (6 November 2019). An obligation to repatriate from the al-Roj camp was denied in a subsequent case. See, Oberverwaltungsgericht Berlin-Brandenburg, ECLI:DE:OVG-BEBB:2020:0610.OVG10S64.19.00 (10 June 2020).

210 'Germany takes back 'Islamic State' mother from Syria' (*Deutsche Welle*, 23 November 2019). Available at: <https://www.dw.com/en/germany-takes-back-islamic-state-mother-and-her-three-children-from-syria/a-51378413> accessed 18 December 2024; 'Syrian Kurds hand over IS children to Germany' (*Deutsche Welle*, 19 August 2019). Available at: <https://www.dw.com/en/syrian-kurds-hand-over-four-islamic-state-children-to-germany/a-50078700> accessed 18 December 2024.

211 See, for example, 'Germany and Denmark repatriate women, children from Syria camp' (*Al Jazeera*, 7 October 2021). Available at: <https://www.aljazeera.com/news/2021/10/7/germany-denmark-repatriates-women-children-from-syria-camp> accessed 18 December 2024; 'Germany repatriates female IS members and their children' (*Deutsche Welle*, 31 March 2022). Available at: <https://www.dw.com/en/germany-repatriates-female-is-members-and-their-children/a-61315115> accessed 18 December 2024.

212 S. Kajjo, 'Germany Repatriates Three IS Women, 12 Children from Syria' (*VOA News*, 20 December 2020). Available at: <https://www.voanews.com/a/extremism-watch_germany-repatriates-three-women-12-children-syria/6199789.html> accessed 21 March 2024.

213 Federal Foreign Office, 'Statement by Foreign Minister Baerbock on the repatriation of seven children, four women and one adolescent from north-eastern Syria', Press Release (5 October 2022). Available at: <https://www.auswaertiges-amt.de/en/newsroom/news/repatriation-syria/2556528> accessed 4 August 2023.

214 Rights & Security International, Global Repatriations Tracker (n. 16) Core data.

estimated 800 British nationals who travelled to ISIS territories in Syria and Iraq, [...] no more than 25 British adults and 34 British children remain in the region", as well as a number of former British nationals whose citizenship has been deprived.[215] In their report from 2018, Cook and Vale estimate that around 425 British nationals had already returned to the UK.[216] Those individuals were not actively repatriated by the UK Government, as they only repatriated an estimated total of 21 UK nationals from November 2019 onwards. The FTFs Knowledge Hub specifies that around 40 returned FTFs or family members have been prosecuted in the UK.[217] In addition, the head of MI5, the British Security Service, has said that more than 130 British nationals who traveled to Syria and Iraq to fight with IS have died in the region.[218] It can thus be said that relatively few British nationals are left in Northeast Syria and detained in SDF-run camps and prisons.

Despite the low numbers of British nationals left in the region, the UK has upheld a passive approach to the issue of repatriation. According to the UK Special Representative for Syria, Jonathan Hargreaves, it has been the UK's "longstanding policy" to consider each case "on a case by case basis, taking into account all relevant considerations, including national security".[219] In addition, the UK is willing to repatriate unaccompanied or orphaned children "where feasible, and subject to national security concerns".[220] Notably, the UK's ongoing reluctance to repatriate seems to contrast with the other European states discussed in this sub-section, which eventually, after several years, and albeit for different underlying reasons, started to repatriate their nationals more actively. However, the UK seems to stick with its passive approach to only repatriate unaccompanied or orphaned children on a case-by-case basis.

---

215 Reprieve, 'Trafficked to ISIS: British families detained in Syria after being trafficked to Islamic State' (2021) 19. Available at: <https://reprieve.org/uk/2021/04/30/trafficked-to-syria/> accessed 4 August 2023.

216 J. Cook and G. Vale 2018 (n. 128) figure 5.

217 The Foreign Terrorist Fighters Knowledge Hub is available at: <https://www.foreignterroristfighters.info/> accessed 20 March 2024.

218 G. Corera, 'MI5 boss Andrew Parker warns of 'intense' terror threat' (*BBC News*, 17 October 2017). Available at: <https://www.bbc.com/news/uk-41655488> accessed 20 March 2024.

219 S. Hooper, 'Two British nationals repatriated from northeast Syria camps' (*Middle East Eye*, 13 October 2022). Available at: <https://www.middleeasteye.net/news/two-british-nationals-repatriated-northeast-syria-camps> accessed 18 December 2024.

220 L. Fisher, 'UK under fresh pressure to bring home nationals held in Syria' (*Financial Times*, 27 July 2023). Available at: <https://www.ft.com/content/39adea5e-5fe9-4042-8b27-fc0789c22d8d> accessed 18 December 2024.

A submission by some Members of Parliament from multiple parties, forming the All-Party Parliamentary Group on Trafficked Britons in Syria, to the British Parliament's Foreign Affairs Committee, shows that the issue of repatriation is also a controversial and politically sensitive topic in the UK. The Parliamentary Group noticed that "[t]he UK Government's refusal to repatriate has made Britain an outlier while our closest allies, including the United States, Australia, Canada, France, and Germany, accept the necessity of repatriations".[221] They also submitted that "the UK's stance has damaged long-standing security relationships with its closest allies" and that the UK is "abandoning Kurdish allies who fought against ISIS, by refusing to take accountability for Britons in the region and leaving Kurdish authorities to take responsibility for their continued detention".[222] As in the other states discussed in this sub-section, the issue of repatriation has been the subject of parliamentary debate, but so far, the UK has not yet changed its passive approach towards the issue.

After analyzing the policies of these states, it has been shown that, as opposed to states like Kazakhstan, Kosovo, Uzbekistan and Tajikistan, the European states discussed all initially adopted a passive approach towards the issue of repatriation. It can be said that in almost all of these European states, the issue of repatriation was subject to political debate and can be said to have constituted, or still constitutes, a politically controversial topic. Notably, none of the European governments took a proactive stance towards the issue of repatriation from the beginning. What can also be observed is that the states inactive in their repatriation efforts made a difference in their policies between men, women and children. This difference may have been caused by the wording of Security Council Resolution 2396 (2017), which asked states to make a distinction between FTFs and their family members "who may not have been engaged in foreign terrorist fighter-related offenses".[223] Most European states, including Germany and Belgium, did show a willingness to repatriate children from the start and later onwards also adult women, irrespective of whether those women could be classified as FTFs instead of family members. Conversely, none of those European states repatriated male FTFs. Therefore, on 1 February 2022, several UN experts called in separate letters upon,

221 All-Party Parliamentary Group (APPG) on Trafficked Britons in Syria, Written evidence submitted by the All-Party Parliamentary Group on Trafficked Britons in Syria (MEN A0030) (October 2023) para. 9. Available at: < https://committees.parliament.uk/writtenevidence/125323/html/#_edn21> accessed 20 March 2023.

222 *Ibid.* paras. 11, 12.

223 UNSC Res. 2396 (2017) (n. 59).

inter alia, France, Germany and the United Kingdom to repatriate the boys and men detained in Northeast Syria holding their citizenship.[224]

Finally, it can be observed that at a certain point in time, respectively in 2020, 2021 and 2022, Germany, Belgium, France and the Netherlands increased the pace in which they repatriated women and children. Although in the case of the Netherlands, only after a district court ordered the Government to do so, and in the case of France, because it was ordered to do so by a number of international courts and bodies. This change in approach can, however, not yet be observed in the UK's policy. The UK still only repatriates children on a case-by-case basis and subject to national security concerns.

3.3 The Horizontal Dimension

As already briefly mentioned in the introduction to this chapter, although denationalization and non-repatriation are two different responses to the phenomenon, they achieve a comparable result. Both responses lead to the exclusion of a person whose state of origin has come to be seen as unwanted, and therewith to the externalization of a risk of terrorism. However, while nationality deprivation formally terminates the legal bond of nationality, non-repatriation does not officially break that bond but does lead to the "erosion of the core content of nationality",[225] that is, the right to enter and remain in one's country of nationality.[226] When states revoke nationality, they take some action to actually deprive the individual of their nationality. But when states refuse to repatriate, they take no action at all. Non-repatriation can take the form of actively refusing readmission through repatriation or passively obstructing such readmission by, for example, requiring detained FTFs or family members to reach a diplomatic representation in the region themselves or otherwise withholding consular assistance.[227] Although in the case of both passive and active refusal of repatriation, citizenship status is left intact, it generates "a new iteration of what is in effect the same policy".[228] Hence, Tripkovic qualifies the resistance to repatriate FTFs and their associated family

224 Letter by UN experts, Information received concerning the situation of a number of boys and men holding your Excellency's citizenship currently detained in North-East Syria (1 February 2022) Refs. AL FRA 1/2022; AL DEU 1/2022; AL AUT 1/2022; AL GBR 1/2022; AL SWE 1/2022. Available at: <https://spcommreports.ohchr.org/TmSearch/Results> accessed 16 August 2023.

225 L. van Waas and A. Brekoo 2023 (n. 1) 220, 221.

226 *Ibid.*

227 *Ibid.* 210–212.

228 *Ibid.* 212.

members by European states as "*de facto* denationalization".[229] In this subsection, it will be argued that there are elements of responsibility shunning and risk externalization visible in the response of non-repatriation. Because the responses of nationality deprivation and non-repatriation create a similar result, the analysis below will be kept relatively short, as there is considerable overlap with the horizontal dimension to nationality deprivation analyzed in the previous chapter.

It can be argued that through states' refusal or reluctance to repatriate FTFs and their family members from Syria, Iraq or other states like Türkiye, those states essentially evade the responsibilities that would come with repatriation. Those responsibilities include to investigate, prosecute, detain, reintegrate, rehabilitate and surveil those individuals, if appropriate, and to protect the population from potential threats of terrorism. In addition, through such inaction, states essentially export not only the responsibility to somehow deal with those potentially dangerous nationals to territorial states or non-state actors in control, but also externalize a potential security threat that those FTFs and family members potentially pose, as well as a burden to counter such a threat. Like the response of nationality deprivation, the policy of non-repatriation externalizes terrorism threats and increases such threats on the territory of other states. In other words, those states reluctant to repatriate have tried to "externalise the threat of the 'fighter' through the (re)branding of the problem as 'foreign'".[230]

Such a strategy of externalizing risks of terrorism might indeed keep the territories of those states of origin more safe in the short term, but several security experts, as well as some European states' own security services, have pointed to the more long-term security challenges that would arise when governments keep the issue of repatriation in limbo and continue their passive approach.[231] It has become increasingly clear that such policies not only increase risks of terrorism in the region where FTFs and their family members

229 M. Tripkovic, 'No country for "bad" men: Volatile citizenship and the emerging features of global neocolonial Penality' XX The British Journal of Criminology (2023) XX: 2.

230 L. van Waas and A. Brekoo 2023 (n. 1) 204.

231 T. Renard and R. Coolsaet 2018 (n. 181) 3, 4; NCTV, 'Veiligheidsimplicaties wel of niet terughalen van uitreizigers en minderjarige kinderen uit kampen in Syrië: Analyse NCTV' 3, 4. Available at: <https://open.overheid.nl/documenten/ronl-71c3ebab-a957-441d-8759-9b2e7086e85c/pdf> accessed 15 August 2023; S. Alonso, 'OM, AIVD en NCTV: 'Haal IS-gangers op voor berechting' (*NRC*, 16 June 2021). Available at: <https://www.nrc.nl/nieuws/2021/06/16/om-aivd-en-nctv-haal-is-gangers-op-voor-berechting-a4047599> accessed 18 December 2024.

are detained, but may also prove to be harmful for European security in the long-term.

As with the shunning of responsibilities and the shifting of security threats as a result of nationality deprivation, as a consequence of states' reluctance or refusal to repatriate, the buck is passed to other states or actors like the AANES and the SDF which may not have the willingness, the capacity or the legal framework to deal with the responsibility over other states' FTFs and associated family members, including the burden to counter the risk of terrorism those foreign nationals potentially pose. Hence, those territorial states, along with the AANES and the SDF, to which the problem is shifted, have called upon European states to repatriate their nationals on multiple occasions. However, for many years, without avail. For example, as was already mentioned in the previous chapter, the AANES declared various times that it is not willing nor able to prosecute FTFs and that it does not have the capacity to manage the camps and detention facilities in which they are detained.[232] They consistently appealed upon states to repatriate their nationals and affirmed that they constitute "a great burden on [them], which [they] cannot bear on [their] own".[233] Although relying on its sovereign right to prosecute adult fighters, the Iraqi Government has asked "all diplomatic missions in Iraq, resident and nonresident, to take back their nationals who have served their sentences and children who are not convicted".[234] Likewise, Iraq urged states to repatriate their nationals from camps and other detention facilities in Northeast Syria as this

232 AANES, Press Release 2021 (n. 20); See, also, 'SDF calls for international tribunal for ISIL detainees' (*Al Jazeera*, 25 March 2019). Available at: <https://www.aljazeera.com/news/2019/3/25/sdf-calls-for-international-tribunal-for-isil-detainees> accessed 18 December 2024. However, in June 2023 the AANES announced that they would start prosecuting foreign nationals. See, J. Seldin, 'Syrian Kurds Launch New Attempt to Prosecute Captured IS Foreign Fighters' (*VOA News*, 15 June 2023). Available at: <https://www.voanews.com/a/syrian-kurds-launch-new-attempt-to-prosecute-captured-is-foreign-fighters/7139770.html> accessed 11 December 2024.

233 AANES, Press Release 2021 (n. 20).

234 'Iraq calls for repatriation of children of foreign militants' (*Arab News*, 3 July 2018). Available at: <https://www.arabnews.com/node/1332791/middle-east> accessed 8 April 2025. See, also, Bulan Institute for Peace Innovations, 'Detention and Prosecution of Former ISIS Fighters in Iraq: Lessons Learned and an Assessment of the Deficits of the Judicial System' Policy Paper (August 2020).

became a "source of terrorism" in the region.[235] Other states in the region, like Türkiye, have issued similar calls.[236]

In sum, like nationality deprivation, states' long-time reluctance to repatriate has externalized risks of terrorism and has passed the problem of somehow dealing with potentially dangerous and radicalized individuals to territorial states as well as the AANES and the SDF. Therefore, there are certainly elements of responsibility shunning and risk externalization visible in the response of non-repatriation. The next part of this chapter will zero in on a number of primary and secondary norms of public international law that are relevant in relation to this practice of burden shifting through states' reluctance or refusal to repatriate those individuals from Syria, Iraq and other states where they may reside.

4 Non-repatriation as *de facto* Banishment

In the previous chapter, it was mentioned that a comparison can be made between the measure of nationality deprivation and the ancient punishment of banishment or exile. Several scholars have made this comparison and argued that banishment is re-appearing as a punishment through the practice of citizenship withdrawal.[237] Macklin contended that "after decades in exile, banishment is back".[238] In this section, it will be argued that non-repatriation policies in the context of FTFs in Syria and Iraq can likewise be seen as *de facto* banishment. Besides zeroing in on the ways in which banishment was used as a punishment, it will be examined why banishment eventually disappeared. Furthermore, this section will argue that one of the reasons for its disappearance, its incompatibility with the interests and sovereign rights of the receiv-

235 'Iraq Urges Countries to Repatriate Their Citizens from Camp Linked to Extremist IS Group' (*VOA News*, 12 June 2023). Available at: <https://www.voanews.com/a/iraq-urges-countries-to-repatriate-their-citizens-from-camp-linked-to-extremist-is-group-/7133812.html> accessed 18 December 2024.

236 C. Winter, 'Turkey: Germany must take back IS members' (*Deutsche Welle*, 11 April 2019). Available at: <https://www.dw.com/en/turkey-demands-germany-take-back-20-captured-islamic-state-members/a-51100753> accessed 21 March 2023.

237 See, for example, A. Macklin, 'The Return of Banishment: Do the New Denationalisation Policies Weaken Citizenship?' in R. Bauböck (ed.), *Debating Transformations of National Citizenship* (Springer 2018); S. Pillai and G. Williams, 'Twenty-First Century Banishment: Citizenship Stripping in Common Law Nations' 66 International & Comparative Law Quarterly (2017) 3; R. Kingston, 'The Unmaking of Citizens: Banishment and the Modern Citizenship Regime in France' 9 Citizenship Studies (2005) 1.

238 A. Macklin 2018 (n. 237) 163.

ing state, can equally be applied to non-repatriation policies in the FTFs context in Syria and Iraq.

4.1 The Ancient Punishment of Banishment

Although banishment is difficult to define as it appeared in a range of different forms all across Europe until around the 19th century, it involves "the formal punishment of expulsion of an individual from the territorial boundaries of a political community leading to the loss of rights and privileges associated with membership".[239] In other words, "banishment was a symbolic and legal act of communal *disownment*".[240] Banishment could be permanent or for a specific period of time. Furthermore, it could be applied to an individual outside the territory by preventing his or her return, and it could be applied to an individual inside the territory by deporting him or her and subsequently preventing return. As briefly touched upon in the previous chapter, banishment was already used as a punishment in ancient Greece, *inter alia*, through the practice of *ostracism*, and in the Roman Empire, *inter alia*, through the practice of *deportatio*.

In the Middle Ages, the punishment was also widely used. For example, in 1491, the German city of Ulm started a campaign to cleanse the town of the "many strangers and useless people [that] linger here [...], who should be outside the city rather than inside".[241] This campaign led to the banishment of more than a thousand convicts. In Cracow, in the second half of the 14th century, banishment was imposed as a penalty on a broad range of offences, which led to the banishment of "a dozen killers and two or three times as many assaulters" every year in the 1360s.[242] In the French city of Dijon "it was applied to all sorts of crimes, from insults to the authorities and forgery, to sodomy, rape and prostitution".[243] Dean explains that, when strictly enforced, banishment was generally a fearful punishment in the Middle Ages, "pushing exiles into destitution and banditry, cutting their contacts with family and friends, and exposing them to the unpunishable violence of bandit-catchers".[244]

---

239 M. Gibney, 'Banishment and the pre-history of legitimate expulsion power' 24 Citizenship Studies (2020) 3: 279.

240 *Ibid.*

241 J. Coy, *Strangers and Misfits: Banishment, Social Control, and Authority in Early Modern Germany* (Brill 2008) 1.

242 T. Dean, *Crime in Medieval Europe 1200–1550* (Routledge 2014) 129.

243 *Ibid.*

244 *Ibid.* 129, 130.

Later, in early modern Europe, banishment offered "a way of ridding communities of unwanted itinerants, like vagrants and beggars, who were costly and annoying to host because of their dependence upon the community for support".[245] The punishment thus offered a way of controlling borders. However, when traveling became easier and more efficient in the early 17th century, countries began "to use expulsion *to* a particular place overseas" instead of "*from* the town, city, or kingdom".[246] From around the 17th century onwards, a number of European states, including France, Germany, Austria and Britain, began to banish convicted criminals to overseas colonies, sometimes also subjecting them to enforced labor. Besides being used as a punishment, this practice also served the purpose of colonial expansion. It was most widely used in Britain. From 1718 to 1776, when the United States became independent, Britain banished and transported between 30,000 and 50,000 convicts across the Atlantic Ocean, most of them to Maryland and Virginia.[247] Similarly, Britain also banished convicted criminals to Australia until the 1860s.[248]

As compared to other forms of punishment, banishment offered particular benefits. First, banishment was less expensive and less demanding on facilities and human resources than, for example, imprisonment. Second, banishment was a fairly simple punishment "since the authorities had no ongoing responsibility".[249] One of the key features of banishment was "the community's washing its hands of the offender" and "ending any relationship of responsibility between the society and the malefactor".[250] In other words, banishment was an act of disowning the unwanted individual and abdicating responsibility for that person. Imprisonment, on the other hand, involves the state taking on full responsibility for the person concerned, putting the individual in "a situation of unique dependence on the state".[251] Therefore, banishment was a favorable punishment. Another factor that was seen as a unique benefit of banishment was that it literally removed persons from society who were seen as unwanted. The punishment tried to protect the community by placing potentially dan-

245 M. Gibney 2020 (n. 239) 287.

246 *Ibid.* 288; J. Bleichmar, 'Deportation as Punishment: A Historical Analysis of the British Practice of Banishment and Its Impact on Modern Constitutional Law' 14 Georgetown Immigration Law Journal (1999) 1: 129.

247 M. Gibney 2020 (n. 239) 288; J. Bleichmar 1999 (n. 246) 116, 117.

248 See, in general, A. Shaw, *Convicts and the Colonies: A Study of Penal Transportation from Great Britain and Ireland to Australia and other Parts of the British Empire* (Faber and Faber 1966).

249 J. Bleichmar 1999 (n. 246) 122.

250 M. Gibney 2020 (n. 239) 295.

251 *Ibid.*

gerous persons outside the boundaries of that community. As Gibney puts it, "the punishment promises to purify the community. By purging society of failed members, banishment demonstrates the worth of membership and affirms the symbolic boundaries of community."[252] Banishment, therefore, achieved the same result as the death penalty but was more merciful and could also be imposed for just a certain period of time. Finally, banishment created the perception of security within the community and "was an important tool for the state to develop popular perceptions of the ability of the justice system to provide for" that security.[253] Using banishment as a punishment provided the state with an easy way to express its power.

4.2 Why Banishment Ceased to Exist: The Interests and Sovereignty of Other States

Shaw noted that until a certain point in time, the overseas societies to which convicted criminals were banished and transported "could usually be ignored".[254] However, already in early times, the penalty of banishment was critiqued by some for imposing a burden upon other societies. Spierenburg notes that already in the 1600s, "the Leiden magistrates stated, that we 'banish [undesirable individuals] upon each other's necks'".[255] Because public order concerns transcended the local level, "the magistrates of Amsterdam and Leiden, and their colleagues in some other towns, wanted to cooperate, instead of diverting their problems to each other" by banishing unwanted individuals.[256] Similarly, Voltaire criticized the punishment as akin to "throwing into our neighbour's field the stones that incommode us in our own".[257] And in the early 1700s, the Dutch jurist Van Bynkershoek wrote that

> it is wholly unreasonable that while I expel criminals from my territory to prevent them from committing offences there, I nevertheless permit them to commit crimes in another's territory. I banish a criminal from my domain, who accordingly goes to the jurisdiction of a neighbouring prince or judge […]; and in turn the neighbouring prince or judge drives some criminal out of his realm who, accordingly, comes to dwell in mine. So both expel their criminals and

252 *Ibid.* 279.
253 R. Kingston 2005 (n. 237) 27.
254 A. Shaw 1966 (n. 248) 21.
255 P. Spierenburg, 'Close to the Edge: Criminals and Marginals in Dutch Cities' 31 Eighteenth-Century Studies (1998) 3: 355.
256 *Ibid.*
257 Voltaire, *A Philosophical Dictionary: Vol. 2* (William Dugdale 1843) 192.

> receive as many in return. And perhaps when I banish one I receive three from the neighbouring territory, which is larger than mine. The practice then is useless and contrary to the dictates of kinship.[258]

However, throughout the 17th and 18th centuries, these criticisms, on the back of the then well-established punishment of banishment, remained exceptional.[259]

Only in the 19th century did these critiques become more widespread. One of the reasons for this being that "the effect of nationalism and popular sovereignty in destination colonies meant that it was harder for European states to treat these countries simply as dumping grounds for its offenders".[260] For example, in the 1840s, anti-transportation campaigns unfolded in Australia, claiming that banishment to their territory was "incompatible with [their] existence as a free colony, desiring self-government to be the receptacle of another country's felons".[261] Kingston observes that in France at the end of the 18th century, a

> general wish emerged that banishment be abolished as a penalty and replaced by imprisonment and forced labour. The rationale, it would seem, had nothing to do with concerns for moderation, but rather was phrased as a means to greater efficiency in punishment as it was thought that the present practice of banishment was a senseless exchange of undesirables among villages, provinces and states.[262]

In his search for the reasons why banishment eventually disappeared as a punishment in the 19th century, Gibney suggests, like Kingston did,

> that the punishment of 'disowning' citizens through expulsion receded not because banishment came to be considered cruel or antiquated, but because it was increasingly at odds with the sovereign rights of other states […] and with changes in the way membership in the state was conceptualised.[263]

---

258 C. van Bynkershoek, *Quaestionum Juris Publici Libri Duo*. Vol. II translated by T. Frank (Clarendon Press 1930) Book II, Chapter 17.
259 M. Gibney 2020 (n. 239) 290.
260 *Ibid.* 292.
261 *Ibid.*; R. Hughes, *The Fatal Shore* (Alfred A. Knopf 1987) 555.
262 R. Kingston 2005 (n. 237) 28.
263 M. Gibney 2020 (n. 239) 296.

Thus, banishment did not necessarily disappear because it was seen as having disproportionate consequences for the individual concerned or because of other human rights concerns, the first human rights instrument prohibiting arbitrary exile, the Universal Declaration of Human Rights, was indeed only adopted in 1948.[264] One of the reasons why banishment ceased to be applied as a punishment was because, with the emergence of modern territorial states consisting of particular national communities of peoples, it became to be seen as infringing upon the sovereignty of other states, including their sovereign rights to admit and expel aliens. The decolonization of states that were previously used as 'dumping grounds' for other states' unwanted citizens and the development of contemporary human rights law only reinforced those changes, which led to the disappearance of banishment as a punishment.

Another reason for the disappearance of banishment, which can be deduced from the foregoing, is a more practical one, related to the efficiency of the punishment. States may have also stopped the practice of banishment because it gave them undesired individuals back from other states, possibly even more than they had banished themselves in the first place. This can, for example, be seen in Kingston's observation that banishment came to be seen as a "senseless exchange of undesirables" and that of van Bynkershoek saying that the practice of banishment was useless because states "expel their criminals and receive as many in return".[265] States may therefore have ended the practice of banishment because, with other state's undesired nationals knocking on their doors in return, the punishment was no longer an efficient way to get rid of undesirables.

What can be concluded is that banishment ceased to exist as a punishment, first, because states could no longer just ignore the interests and sovereignty of other states and second, because it was no longer efficient and to their own benefit.

4.3 Non-repatriation as *de facto* Banishment

Technically, non-repatriation policies in the FTFs context in Syria and Iraq are, of course, not the same as the ancient punishment of banishment. Although non-repatriation could be perceived as a form of punishment, its purpose is not to punish the individual concerned. In addition, most FTFs and associated family members traveled to the conflict zone on their own initiative, instead of being banished and deported to another state's territory. However, non-repa-

264 UDHR (adopted 10 December 1948) UNGA Res. 217 A(III), Article 9.
265 R. Kingston 2005 (n. 237) 28.

triation policies in this context may practically be seen as a form of banishment.

First, because those policies lead to a similar result and have the same (short-term) benefits. Like banishment, refusal to repatriate FTFs and associated family members is a rather easy, cost-efficient and prompt way for states to keep those individuals who they have come to see as unwanted away from their societies to which they may pose a threat. By adopting such policies of non-repatriation, states exclude FTFs and their family members from their societies and try to make sure those persons stay far away from their territories. Moreover, by refusing to repatriate, states shun the responsibilities that would come with repatriation. Actively bringing them back, on the other hand, would mean taking full responsibility over those individuals, as this would mean that the state has to investigate, prosecute, detain, rehabilitate, reintegrate and surveil those individuals, if deemed to be necessary, and protect the population from the terrorist threat that they potentially pose. Non-repatriation is, therefore, a rather simple way of abdicating responsibilities and in that way responding to the potential threat that FTFs and their family members may pose.

Second, like banishing individuals from states' territories, policies of non-repatriation in the FTFs context might be a symbolic way of the state to come across as taking a firm stance against potential national security threats. However, such policies may only create a perception of security, as, like banishment, they do not prevent the unwanted individual from coming back under the radar on their own initiative in the future. Banishment and non-repatriation, therefore, have the same (short-term) benefit of excluding the person from society, but without providing for a long-term solution.

Finally, and most importantly for this research, non-repatriation policies in the FTFs context in Syria and Iraq can be, and have been, critiqued for some of the same reasons why banishment as a punishment eventually disappeared. Among other reasons of efficiency, banishment ceased to exist as a punishment because it came to be seen as incompatible with the interests and sovereignty of other states. Preventing the return of FTFs and their family members through the adoption of non-repatriation policies likewise infringes upon the interests and sovereign rights of territorial states, in particular their sovereign rights to expel those aliens from their territories. Without their states of origin wanting them back, those unwanted FTFs and family members are basically stuck on the territories of the states where they reside, most likely without there being another state to which they can be expelled, as was explained in the previous chapter. This not only infringes upon the interest of those territorial states to stay free from another state's unwanted and potentially dangerous nationals, but may also be incompatible with their sovereignty and, in particular, the effective exercise of their sovereign right to expel those aliens. Without the repatriation of those FTFs and family members by their states of origin, they are practically banished to stay in Iraqi prisons or SDF-controlled camps and detention facilities, for an unlimited period of time. Like the punishment of banishment, through such non-repatriation policies, the problem of what to do with those unwanted nationals, as well as a burden to counter-terrorism, is diverted to other states, against all those states' interests.

In sum, with those non-repatriation policies, states disregard the interests and sovereignty of the state on whose territory they leave their FTFs or family members who potentially pose a risk of terrorism. What eventually led to the disappearance of banishment as a punishment was, among other reasons, the sentiment that "[a] national whose presence is wholly undesirable in his own state cannot with reason or comity be wished upon another state",[266] a sentiment which can, and should, equally apply to states passing the buck of dealing with their FTFs and family members through their refusal to repatriate.

5 States' Reluctance or Refusal to Repatriate and Their Obligation to Ensure Respect for IHL

This section will examine states' refusal or reluctance to repatriate in light of their obligation to ensure respect for IHL. Common Article 1 to the Geneva Conventions imposes an obligation upon the "High Contracting Parties" to "respect and to ensure respect" for the Geneva Conventions. This obligation is important to consider because it requires states to take the horizontal implications of their actions and omissions into account, and obliges them to consider the impact of their policies and practices on other states or territories under the control of a non-state actor like the SDF. But before we turn to the substantive analysis of this obligation, it is necessary to briefly examine the detention of FTFs and family members in light of IHL.

5.1 Detention in Northeast Syria in Light of IHL

As set out before, there is still a large group of third-country nationals detained in SDF-controlled camps and prisons in Northeast Syria. Several reports indi-

266 R. Higgins, 'The Right in International Law of an Individual to Enter, Stay in and Leave a Country' 49 International Affairs (1973) 3: 350.

cate extreme overcrowding, shortages of food, clean water, medicine, adequate shelter, security and rising levels of violence.[267] Reportedly, in July 2020, already 700 people had died in the al-Hol and al-Roj camps.[268] In addition, those third-country nationals have never been brought before a court to challenge their continued detention, making their confinement indefinite and arbitrary. These circumstances are not in compliance with the minimum standards of detention and potentially amount to inhumane treatment of detainees in violation of IHL.[269] In addition, the Committee against Torture also confirmed that these circumstances amount to inhumane and degrading treatment as prohibited by the Convention against Torture and Other Cruel, Inhuman or Degrading Treatment or Punishment.[270] Common Article 3 to the Geneva Conventions, applicable in NIACs, provides that as a minimum "[p]ersons taking no active part in the hostilities, including members of armed forces who have laid down their arms and those placed 'hors de combat' by sickness, wounds, detention, or any other cause, shall in all circumstances be treated humanely". Furthermore, Rule 99 of the ICRC's study on customary IHL specifies that the prohibition on arbitrary deprivation of liberty reflects a rule of customary international law.[271] They also make clear that arbitrary deprivation of liberty is not compatible with the minimum standards of treatment in Common Article 3.[272] Rule 118 of the ICRC's customary IHL study also specifies that "persons deprived of their liberty must be provided

---

267 Human Rights Watch 2021 (n. 31); UNICEF, 'Nearly 850 children at immediate risk as violence continues in northeast Syria' (23 January 2022). Available at: <https://www.unicef.org/mena/press-releases/nearly-850-children-immediate-risk-violence-continues-northeast-syria> accessed 14 September 2023; OHCHR, 'Syria: UN expert calls for an end to mass arbitrary and indefinite detentions and urges protection for children in Northeast Syria' (21 July 2023). Available at: <https://www.ohchr.org/en/press-releases/2023/07/syria-un-expert-calls-end-mass-arbitrary-and-indefinite-detentions-and-urges> accessed 14 September 2023.

268 E. Lederer, 'UN official: 700 people died in Syrian camps for IS families' (*AP News*, 10 July 2020). Available at: <https://apnews.com/article/9732632ffe89f1acf64ff91cd60dd76a> accessed 18 December 2024.

269 Common Article 3(1) to the Geneva Conventions; ICRC, Customary IHL Database, Rule 87 Humane Treatment. Available at: <https://ihl-databases.icrc.org/en/customary-ihl/v1/rule87> accessed 14 September 2023; ICCPR, Article 7; ECtHR, Article 3.

270 *C.P. et al. v. France* (n. 28) para. 7.5.

271 ICRC, Customary IHL Database, Rule 99 Deprivation of Liberty. Available at: <https://ihl-databases.icrc.org/en/customary-ihl/v1/rule99> accessed 22 March 2024.

272 *Ibid.*

with adequate food, water, clothing, shelter and medical attention".[273] A lack of such necessities may also amount to inhumane treatment in violation of Common Article 3.[274]

Based on the before mentioned reports on the circumstances in which FTFs and family members are detained in Northeast Syria and the rules of IHL mentioned, it can and has been argued that the detention of FTFs and family members in Northeast Syria is not only in violation of IHL because the treatment of detainees may amount to inhumane treatment in violation of Common Article 3 to the Geneva Conventions, but also because their detention amounts to arbitrary deprivation of liberty, in violation of customary IHL applicable in NIACs.

5.2 The Obligation to Ensure Respect by Other States and Non-state Actors

The obligation to 'respect' IHL is straightforward and means that states must comply in good faith with the provisions of the Geneva Conventions. However, the scope of the obligation to 'ensure respect' is debated. The controversy largely surrounds the question whether states do not only have an obligation "to ensure the compliance of their own armed forces, and individuals and groups under their jurisdiction", but "also have to ensure that *other* states respect their obligations under the Conventions".[275] In other words, the question is whether the obligation to ensure respect provides for what has been referred to as an "external element".[276]

Much of this debate was initially sparked in response to the ICJ's judgement of 1986 in the *Nicaragua* Case.[277] In this judgement, the ICJ found that

> there is an obligation on the United States Government, in the terms of Article 1 of the Geneva Conventions, to "respect" the Conventions and even "to ensure respect" for them "in all circumstances", since such an obligation does not

---

273 ICRC, Customary IHL Database, Rule 118: Provision of Basic Necessities to Persons Deprived of Their Liberty. Available at: <https://ihl-databases.icrc.org/en/customary-ihl/v1/rule118> accessed 22 March 2024.

274 *Ibid.*

275 C. Wiesener and A. Kjeldgaard-Pedersen, 'Ensuring Respect by Partners: Revisiting the Debate on Common Article 1' 27 Journal of Conflict & Security Law (2022) 2: 136.

276 M. Zwanenburg, 'The "External Element" of the Obligation to Ensure Respect for the Geneva Conventions: A Matter of Treaty Interpretation' 97 International Law Studies (2021) 621.

277 *Military and Paramilitary Activities in and against Nicaragua* (*Nicaragua v. United States of America*) (Merits) [1986] ICJ Rep. 14.

> derive only from the Conventions themselves, but from the general principles of humanitarian law to which the Conventions merely give specific expression. The United States is thus under an obligation not to encourage persons or groups engaged in the conflict in Nicaragua to act in violation of the provisions of Article 3 common to the four 1949 Geneva Conventions.[278]

The Court seemed to recognize that the obligation to ensure respect contains an external element and obliges states not only to make sure they comply with the Conventions themselves, but also not to encourage other states or non-state actors involved in an armed conflict to violate IHL. It should also be noted that in the ICJ's view, states are not only under an obligation to ensure respect by other states but also by non-state actors, and that the ICJ is, therefore, of the opinion that this obligation does not only apply to armed conflicts of an international character but also to those of a non-international character.[279] In 2004, the Court reiterated this external dimension in its *Wall* Advisory Opinion, by stating that "every State party to that Convention, whether or not it is a party to a specific conflict, is under an obligation to ensure that the requirements of the instruments in question are complied with".[280] Therefore, the Court found that

> all the States parties to the Geneva Convention relative to the Protection of Civilian Persons in Time of War of 12 August 1949 are under an obligation, while respecting the United Nations Charter and international law, to ensure compliance by Israel with international humanitarian law as embodied in that Convention.[281]

In 2016, the controversy regarding the meaning and scope of the obligation to ensure respect was triggered again, this time by the ICRC's Commentary to the Geneva Conventions. While recognizing that "the expression 'ensure respect', has raised a variety of questions over the last decades", the ICRC finds that

278 *Ibid.* para. 220.

279 R. Geiß, 'Common Article 1 of the Geneva Conventions: Scope and content of the obligation to 'ensure respect' – 'narrow but deep' or 'wide and shallow'?' in H. Krieger, *Inducing Compliance with International Humanitarian Law: Lessons from the African Great Lakes Region* (Cambridge University Press 2015) 420; ICRC, *Commentary on the First Geneva Convention: Convention (I) for the Amelioration of the Condition of the Wounded and Sick in Armed Forces in the Field* (Cambridge University Press 2016) para. 125.

280 *Legal Consequences of the Construction of a Wall in the Occupied Palestinian Territory* (Advisory Opinion) [2004] ICJ Rep. 136, para. 158.

281 *Ibid.* para. 159.

"States, whether neutral, allied or enemy, must do everything reasonably in their power to ensure respect for the Conventions by others that are Party to a conflict",[282] and explained that "the proper functioning of the system of protection provided by the Conventions demands that States Parties not only apply the provisions themselves, but also do everything reasonably in their power to ensure that the provisions are respected universally".[283] The ICRC thus recognized the external element of Common Article 1 and, furthermore, by mentioning states' obligation to ensure respect by 'others' who are party to an armed conflict, instead of by states or High Contracting Parties, it seems to have recognized that the obligation also applies to non-state actors involved in an armed conflict and hence, to NIACs. The ICRC also endorsed this reading of Common Article 1 in its study on customary rules of IHL, Rule 144 of which provides that "States may not encourage violations of international humanitarian law by parties to an armed conflict. They must exert their influence, to the degree possible, to stop violations of international humanitarian law."[284]

Nevertheless, some commentators are of the opinion that the obligation to ensure respect in Common Article 1 does not contain an external element, which would mean that states are only under an obligation to ensure that their own armed forces, as well as groups or individuals under their instructions, direction or control, comply with IHL.[285] However, like the ICRC and the ICJ, most commentators are of the opinion that Common Article 1 does

---

282 ICRC 2016 (n. 279) para. 153.

283 *Ibid.* para. 119.

284 ICRC, Customary IHL Database, Rule 144 Ensuring Respect for International Humanitarian Law Erga Omnes. Available at: <https://ihl-databases.icrc.org/en/customary-ihl/v1/rule144> accessed 16 October 2023.

285 See, for example, V. Robson, 'The Common Approach to Article 1: The Scope of Each State's Obligation to Ensure Respect for the Geneva Conventions' 25 Journal of Conflict & Security Law (2020) 1; M. Schmitt and S. Watts, 'Common Article 1 and the Duty to "Ensure Respect"' 96 International Law Studies (2020) 674. According to this reading of the obligation, third states bear no positive or negative obligations under Common Article 1 to ensure that other states or non-state actors that are party to an armed conflict respect IHL. For example, after examining the scope of Common Article 1 by applying the established principles of treaty interpretation, Robson concludes that "[t]here is no general duty to prevent or bring to an end breaches by other parties to conflict. Responsibility for compliance lies with the parties themselves, and other States may choose, as a matter of policy, to take such steps as are appropriate in each conflict to encourage universal respect". V. Robson 2020 (n. 285) 115. Arguments against an external dimension to Common Article 1, *inter alia*, rest on statements of states like the United States, the UK and Canada, who have opposed or have taken a critical stance towards this reading of the obligation to ensure respect, the selectiveness of reactions to breaches of IHL by other states or non-state actors, and the *travaux préparatoires* of the Geneva Conventions. C. Wiesener and A. Kjeldgaard-Pedersen 2022 (n. 275) 137–139; V. Robson 2020 (n.

contain an external dimension and, therefore, imposes an obligation upon third states not involved in an armed conflict.[286] Arguing in favor of an external dimension to Common Article 1, Zwanenburg points to state practice and, as an example, cites part of a 'User's Guide to Common Positions' developed by the Council of the European Union, which defines "common rules governing the control of exports of military technology and equipment".[287] This guide interprets Common Article 1

> as conferring a responsibility on third party states not involved in an armed conflict to not encourage a party to an armed conflict to violate international humanitarian law, nor to take action that would assist in such violations, and to take appropriate steps to cause such violations to cease. They have a particular responsibility to intervene with states or armed groups over which they might have some influence.[288]

Kessler also points towards the fact that other international organizations have openly adopted the ICRC's interpretation of the obligation to ensure respect.[289] For example, in a report on the situation in the Palestinian and other Arab territories occupied by Israel since 1967, the UN Secretary-General recommended

> that the Security Council should consider making a solemn appeal to all the High Contracting Parties to the Fourth Geneva Convention that have diplomatic relations with Israel, drawing their attention to their obligation under article 1 of the Convention to ".. ensure respect for the present Convention in all circumstances" and urging them to use all the means at their disposal to

285) 109; A. Breslin, 'A Reflection on the Legal Obligation for Third States to Ensure Respect for IHL' 22 Journal of Conflict & Security Law (2017) 1: 10.

286 See, for example, M. Zwanenburg 2021 (n. 276); C. Wiesener and A. Kjeldgaard-Pedersen 2022 (n. 275); A. Breslin 2017 (n. 285); U. Palwankar, 'Measures available to States for fulfilling their obligation to ensure respect for international humanitarian law' International Review of the Red Cross (1994) 298; B. Kessler, 'The Duty to 'Ensure Respect' under Common Article 1 of the Geneva Conventions: Its Implications on International and Non-international Armed Conflicts' 44 German Yearbook of International Law (2001).

287 Council of the European Union, User's Guide to Council Common Position 2008/944/CFSP defining common rules governing the control of exports of military technology and equipment (20 July 2015) 10858/15, COARM 172, CFSP/PESC 393. Available at: <https://data.consilium.europa.eu/doc/document/ST-10858-2015-INIT/en/pdf> accessed 16 October 2023.

288 *Ibid.* 55.

289 B. Kessler 2001(n. 286) 504.

> persuade the Government of Israel to change its position as regards the applicability of the Convention.[290]

Thus, both regional and international organizations have endorsed the ICRC's interpretation of the obligation to ensure respect for the Geneva Conventions.

From the analysis above, it can be concluded that there is extensive support for an external dimension to the obligation to ensure respect contained in Common Article 1 and that such an obligation also applies in NIAC.

5.3 Negative and Positive Obligations to Ensure Respect

In line with the ICRC's commentary,[291] the external dimension to this rule has been interpreted as encompassing both a negative and a positive obligation upon third states. On the one hand, it imposes a negative external obligation upon states not to encourage, aid or assist IHL violations by parties to an armed conflict. This obligation, which essentially means that states may not contribute to IHL violations by other states or non-state actors, is less contentious in international law. This negative obligation is similar to Article 16 of the ARSIWA in the sense that they both regulate states' aid or assistance to other states or non-state actors. However, Common Article 1 distinguishes itself from Article 16 of the ARSIWA because it does not entail a specific knowledge or intent requirement. According to the ICRC, rendering aid or assistance violates the obligation to ensure respect when there is an "expectation" which is "based on facts or knowledge of past patterns" that it would violate IHL.[292] In addition, the ICJ found that encouragement of certain acts violates the obligation to ensure respect when it is offered to persons and in circumstances in which it is "likely or foreseeable" that such acts will violate IHL.[293] Moynihan explains the difference between the negative obligation to ensure respect and Article 16 of the ARSIWA clearly by the following example:

> if an assisting state knows that the receiving state systematically commits violations of IHL with certain weapons, under the duty to 'ensure respect' for IHL the assisting state has to deny further transfers of those weapons, even if those weapons could also be used lawfully. In that case, the track record of the recipi-

290 UNSC, Report Submitted to the Security Council by the Secretary-General in Accordance with Resolution 605 (1987) (21 January 1988) UN Doc. 8/19443, para. 27.

291 ICRC 2016 (n. 279) paras. 153–173.

292 *Ibid.* para. 161.

293 *Military and Paramilitary Activities in and against Nicaragua* (*Nicaragua v. United States of America*) (n. 277) para. 256.

> ent state suggests a clear and foreseeable risk that the weapons could be used to violate IHL, so the assisting state must refrain from transferring them. By comparison, for responsibility to arise under Article 16 it would be necessary to meet all four of its conditions, including that the assisting state knows or is virtually certain that the particular weapons transferred will be used in breach of IHL, and that those weapons will contribute significantly to the wrongful act.[294]

Hence, Article 16 of the ARSIWA requires more than only an "expectation", "likeliness" or "foreseeability".

On the other hand, the obligation to ensure respect also imposes a positive external obligation upon states to "do everything reasonably in their power to prevent and bring such violations to an end".[295] This positive obligation can already be read in the Council of the European Union's User's Guide to Common Positions and the UN Secretary-General's report on the situation in the Palestinian and other Arab territories as cited above. This obligation requires third states to "take proactive steps to bring violations of the Conventions to an end, and to bring an erring Party to a conflict back to an attitude of respect for the Conventions, in particular by using their influence on that Party".[296] This positive obligation does not only contain an obligation to stop ongoing violations but also to prevent foreseeable future violations and, in case they have already occurred, to prevent further violations.[297] The obligation is one of due diligence, i.e., an obligation of means not of result.[298] States must thus make "reasonable efforts" within their capacity to ensure respect,[299] but what those efforts entail and, therefore, what the obligation encompasses exactly will depend on the specific circumstances of each case.

Those circumstances include the severity of the violation, the means that are reasonably available to the state, and the degree of influence the state has over the state or non-state actor responsible for the breach.[300] Although the ICJ was ruling on the obligation to prevent genocide, which is also subject to

---

294 H. Moynihan, 'Aiding and Assisting: Challenges in Armed Conflict and Counterterrorism' Chatham House Royal Institute of International Affairs, Research Paper (November 2016) para. 89 (footnotes omitted). Available at: <https://www.chathamhouse.org/sites/default/files/publications/research/2016-11-11-aiding-assisting-challenges-armed-conflict-moynihan.pdf> accessed 13 September 2023.

295 ICRC 2016 (n. 279) para. 154.

296 *Ibid.* para. 164.

297 *Ibid.*

298 *Ibid.* para. 165.

299 A. Breslin 2017 (n. 285) 6.

300 ICRC 2016 (n. 279) para. 165.

a due diligence standard, and not specifically on the obligation to ensure respect for IHL, in the *Genocide* Case, the Court found that

> [v]arious parameters operate when assessing whether a State has duly discharged the obligation concerned. The first, which varies greatly from one State to another, is clearly the capacity to influence effectively the action of persons likely to commit, or already committing, genocide. This capacity itself depends, among other things, on the geographical distance of the State concerned from the scene of the events, and on the strength of the political links, as well as links of all other kinds, between the authorities of that State and the main actors in the events.[301]

These parameters given by the ICJ with regard to the obligation to diligently prevent genocide are also of relevance for the obligation to ensure respect for IHL. Like the ICJ in the *Genocide* Case, others, including the ICRC, have also concluded that "[t]he duty to ensure respect for the Geneva Conventions is particularly strong in the case of a partner in a joint operation" or where the state is otherwise in a unique position to influence the behavior of the state or non-state actor because it, for example, "participates in the financing, equipping, arming or training of the armed forces" of a state or a non-state actor.[302] It can be said that the stronger the relationship, influence or leverage is between the third state and the responsible state or non-state actor engaged in an armed conflict, the greater the steps are that the third state needs to take in order to fulfill its obligation to ensure respect. Thynne further notes that in the case of states partnered with or assisting other states or non-state actors in detention operations, the due diligence obligation to ensure respect for IHL "involves taking reasonable steps to make oneself aware; to investigate the circumstances; to question the perceived facts surrounding detention facilities; to delve further into what is happening in those places to the detainees; and to take active steps to stop any violations or stop engagement".[303]

---

301 *Case Concerning Application of the Convention on the Prevention and Punishment of the Crime of Genocide* (*Bosnia and Herzegovina v. Serbia and Montenegro*) (*Genocide Case*) (Judgement) [2007] ICJ Rep. 43, para. 430.

302 ICRC 2016 (n. 279) para. 167; See, also, A. Breslin 2017 (n. 285) 22; C. Wiesener and A. Kjeldgaard-Pedersen 2022 (n. 275)153; J. Maddocks, 'State Responsibility for International Law Violations Involving Non-state Actors in Armed Conflict' (PhD in Law, University of Reading 2021) 309–311.

303 K. Thynne, 'The obligation to ensure respect in relation to detention in armed conflict' in E. Massingham and A. McConnachie (eds), *Ensuring Respect for International Humanitarian Law* (Routledge 2020) 164.

5.4 Repatriation as a Possible Measure to Ensure Respect for IHL

The question that arises is what those "active steps" may entail to stop violations of IHL. In other words, what measures are states such as France, Belgium, the Netherlands, Germany and the United Kingdom required to take in order to ensure respect for IHL and stop the arbitrary deprivation of liberty and ill-treatment of detainees, including, but not limited to, their own nationals. One of the measures states of nationality can take in order to comply with their obligation to ensure respect for IHL is to actively repatriate their nationals. Repatriation, instead of externalizing the risk of terrorism and shifting the burden of detention to the SDF, might be the only way to end the ill-treatment of detainees, in any case of those holding their nationality, and stop the arbitrary deprivation of their liberty. Furthermore, repatriation and prosecution in their countries of origin is most likely the only way these FTFs and family members will be brought to any genuine form of justice. Thus, actively returning those individuals is the most effective way to ensure respect for the obligation to investigate and prosecute war crimes under IHL.

Palwankar has non-exhaustively set out multiple measures that could be taken under the obligation to ensure respect for IHL by other states or non-state actors and classified them into four categories: measures to exert diplomatic pressure, coercive measures, measures in cooperation with international organizations and measures contributing to humanitarian efforts.[304] With regard to the last category, he explicitly mentions repatriation as a possible measure to fulfill the obligation to ensure respect.[305] Mckeever concludes that, although "rules of IHL are not sufficiently prescriptive to create an obligation on States of origin to repatriate their nationals from northern Syria", active repatriation may be one of the measures with which states can fulfill their obligation to ensure respect for IHL in these circumstances.[306] However, he notes that "common article 1 does not oblige States to take this step ahead of others".[307] Thus, active repatriation by states of origin could be among the possible measures to fulfill their obligation to ensure respect for IHL, but the obligation does not specifically require such a line of action.

Nevertheless, it was previously mentioned that the stronger the relationship, influence or leverage between the third state and the, in this case, non-state actor is, the more active steps are required from the third state in order to

304 U. Palwankar 1994 (n. 286).

305 *Ibid.* 23–24.

306 Mckeever 2022 (n. 43) 25, 31–34.

307 *Ibid.* 34.

fulfill its obligation to ensure respect. States such as France, Belgium, the Netherlands, Germany and the United Kingdom, who have been reluctant or refused to repatriate their nationals and thereby shunned the responsibilities that would come with repatriation, can be said to have a level of influence and leverage over the SDF. This is not only because the SDF is left with those states' potentially dangerous nationals in its custody, but also because some of those states have, among others, as part of the US-led coalition against IS, contributed to the detention facilities in which FTFs and family members are detained in Northeast Syria.[308] For example, the UK seems to have "invested 20 million dollars in expanding Hasaka's Al-Sina'a prison",[309] which is one of the SDF-controlled prisons in Northeast Syria in which IS fighters, including FTFs, are detained. Therefore, it could be argued that those states must take greater measures to stop the ongoing ill-treatment and arbitrary detention of detainees by the SDF. In other words, in order to fulfill their obligation to ensure respect for IHL, these states must take more active measures than other states that may not have such a degree of influence over the SDF. Although the obligation to ensure respect for IHL is not only directed towards third states' own nationals, repatriation of their nationals would be a suitable and effective step justified by their degree of influence and reasonably within those states' powers.

In sum, the obligation to ensure respect for IHL is important to consider because it requires states to take the horizontal implications of their refusal or reluctance to repatriate into account, and requires them to consider the effects of their policies on the territories of other states or those under the control of a non-state actor like the SDF. Those states reluctant or refuse to repatriate must take active measures in order to ensure respect for IHL by the SDF in the treatment of detainees. One of those measures could be to actively repatriate their FTFs and family members detained in SDF-controlled camps and detention facilities.

308 Letter by UN experts, Ref. AL AUT 1/2022; AL DEU 1/2022; AL FRA 1/2022; AL SWE 1/2022 (n. 224) 2.

309 Letter by UN experts, Ref. AL GBR 1/2022 (n. 224) 2. See, also, 'UK funding renovation, expansion of ISIS prison in Rojava: defence ministry' (*Rudaw*, 2 August 2021). Available at: <https://www.rudaw.net/english/middleeast/syria/02082021> accessed 18 December 2021.

6 States' Reluctance or Refusal to Repatriate and Potential Constructions for Their Responsibility under Public International Law

In the previous section, the conditions in which FTFs and family members have been detained for many years were briefly addressed. It was said that these conditions likely amount to inhumane treatment and arbitrary, prolonged detention in violation of IHL. Besides assessing their detention under IHL, this section will also address the detention of FTFs and family members under international human rights law, and will raise the question of to whom these breaches of international law can actually be attributed. Is it the SDF that has control over the camps and prisons in which these individuals are detained? And what about the fact that they have continuously asked states of origin for help? Or should those breaches of IHL and international human rights law be attributed to those states of origin that have refused or been reluctant to repatriate their FTFs and family members for many years? And what about the fact that some states have (financially) contributed to detention facilities in Northeast Syria? Perhaps they did so only to make the detention circumstances better, but can this nonetheless entail a certain degree of responsibility for the deplorable circumstances within the detention centers? This section will engage with the question of who can be held responsible for the way in which these individuals are detained in Northeast Syria. Morally speaking, one could make an argument of shared responsibility between the SDF and states of origin. Can such moral responsibility be translated to state responsibility under the rules of public international law? This section will problematize and explore whether there is a potential legal construction for state responsibility under public international law.

6.1 The Responsibility Question

In the previous section, it was mentioned that FTFs and family members' detention potentially amounts to inhumane treatment and arbitrary deprivation of liberty in violation of the applicable norms of IHL in NIAC. Besides IHL, their detention situation should also be discussed under international human rights law. International human rights law does not cease to apply in situations of armed conflict, but applies alongside IHL.[310] It thus remains relevant to also look at possible violations of international human rights law.

Those detainees in SDF-controlled camps and prisons in Northeast Syria have been detained for years without the prospect of a trial, without the prospect of release and in otherwise very poor and over-crowded conditions. Besides violating IHL, these conditions may also amount to a violation of international human rights law. For example, a violation of the right to life,[311] the prohibition of torture or other cruel, inhuman or degrading treatment or punishment,[312] the right to adequate food, clothing,[313] the highest attainable standard of physical and mental health[314] and the right to liberty and security of person, which includes the prohibition of arbitrary detention.[315] For example, in its *F.B. et al. and D.A. et al. v. France* decision, the CRC Committee noted with regard to the children's right to life that "there is sufficient information to establish that the conditions of detention pose an imminent and foreseeable threat to the lives of the child victims".[316] In addition, with regard to the prohibition of torture or other cruel, inhuman or degrading treatment or punishment, the Committee considered that

> there is sufficient evidence to establish that the prolonged detention of the child victims in the conditions described, including in particular the lack of health care, food, water, sanitation facilities and education, has an impact on their development and constitutes cruel, inhuman or degrading treatment or punishment.[317]

Likewise, the Committee against Torture considered in its *C.P. et al. v. France* decision that

> there is sufficient information to establish that the conditions in which the complainants' relatives are being detained in the camps in the north-east of

310 *Legality of the Threat or Use of Nuclear Weapons* (Advisory Opinion) [1996] ICJ Rep. 226, para. 25; *Legal Consequences of the Construction of a Wall in the Occupied Palestinian Territory* (n. 280) para. 106.

311 ICCPR, Article 6; CRC, Article 6.

312 ICCPR, Article 7; CRC, Article 37(a); CAT, Article 2, 16.

313 ICESCR, Article 11.

314 *Ibid.* Article 12; CRC, Article 24.

315 ICCPR, Article 9; CRC, Article 37(b). See for a discussion of the detention circumstances in Northeast Syria under a number of those human rights: Human Rights Watch 2021 (n. 31).

316 *F.B. et al. and D.A. et al. v. France* (n. 26) para. 6.7.

317 *Ibid.* para. 6.8.

> the Syrian Arab Republic, including in particular the lack of health care, food, water and sanitation facilities, amount to inhuman and degrading treatment.[318]

Finally, with regard to the al-Hol and al-Roj camps in Northeast Syria, the former UN Special Rapporteur on the promotion and protection of human rights and fundamental freedoms while countering terrorism, Fionnuala Ní Aoláin, endorsed that "the conditions of confinement in both camps constitute arbitrary and indefinite mass detention without legal or judicial process".[319] Thus, there seems to be sufficient support to say that the detention of FTFs and family members in Northeast Syria, in SDF-administered camps and other detention facilities, violates IHL as well as international human rights law.

The question remains to which state or actor these breaches of public international law can or should be attributed. In other words, who should be held responsible for these breaches? On the one hand, the SDF is in control of the detention facilities in which these breaches occur, so the easiest way to resolve the responsibility question might be to hold the SDF responsible for those breaches of international law. On the other hand, the SDF is a non-state actor lacking state-like capabilities to effectively deal with those third-country nationals. In other words, the SDF may not have the capacity to carry out detention in compliance with IHL and international human rights law without the assistance of other states or international organizations. Those individual's states of origin have ignored calls for help by the SDF and have refused to repatriate them, leaving the SDF with the problem. In that way, it could even be argued that the SDF was, at least to some extent, forced to commit these breaches of international law. Schiciano accurately catches this tension within the question of responsibility by stating:

> [w]hile it may seem most straightforward to lay the blame for these violations at the feet of the AANES, there is an intuitive sense of injustice in concluding that the weakest entity, with the fewest resources and no formal recognition as a State, should be liable for management of a problem from which other, wealthier States have benefited – and which, they have openly admitted, they do not want to handle themselves.[320]

318 *C.P. et al. v. France* (n. 28) para. 7.5.

319 OHCHR 2023 (n. 267).

320 E. Schiciano, 'See No Evil: Assessing U.S. State Responsibility for Violations at al-Hol' 61 Columbia Journal of Transnational Law (2023) 1: 219.

Accordingly, the question has been raised whether FTFs and family member's states of origin can be held responsible in these circumstances. For example, Sandelowsky-Bosman and Liefaard pose the question "whether the Dutch Government through its policy of not reaching out to children with ties to the Netherlands or accepting the help of others (the Kurds, the United States and the Red Cross) does not in fact support or facilitate the direct violations by local State and non-State actors".[321] Human Rights Watch expressed its concern that "[g]overnments that actively contribute to this abusive confinement may be complicit in the unlawful detention and collective punishment of thousands of people, most of them women and young children".[322] Similarly, a number of UN experts pointed out that the way in which FTFs and their family members are detained, "raise[s] serious questions of State responsibility and of complicity in the facilitation, sustainment and continuation of the serious human rights violations that are taking place in the prisons and detention centers in North-East Syria".[323] Furthermore, Ní Aoláin pointed out that "States of nationality enabling the mass arbitrary detention of boys may also have legal responsibility for human rights violations under international law".[324] These authorities thus seem to point to some kind of responsibility of states of origin for having facilitated the arbitrary detention and other breaches of international law through their policies of non-repatriation. The question is, however, whether this is a moral, political or legal argument. And if it is a legal argument, this raises the question of what the relevant legal framework is in this respect. In other words, there may be a shared responsibility between states of origin and the SDF from a moral or political standpoint, but is there also a suitable construction for responsibility from a legal point of view?

The remaining part of this section will explore whether this tension between states' refusal to repatriation and the arbitrary detention of FTFs and their family members in Northeast Syria can be tied to the ILC's Draft Articles on the Responsibility of States for Internationally Wrongful Acts

---

321 C. Sandelowsky-Bosman and T. Liefaard (n. 43)153.

322 Human Rights Watch 2021 (n. 31).

323 Letter by UN experts, Information received concerning the alleged arbitrary detention and inadequate detention conditions of Mr. Jack Letts, a Canadian citizen, currently detained in a detention center in the North-East region of the Syrian Arab Republic at least since 2017 (8 June 2022) ref. UA CAN 3/2022, 4. Available at: <https://spcommreports.ohchr.org/TmSearch/Results> accessed 21 August 2023; See also Letter by UN experts, Refs. AL FRA 1/2022; AL DEU 1/2022; AL AUT 1/2022; AL GBR 1/2022; AL SWE 1/2022 (n. 224).

324 OHCHR 2023 (n. 267).

(ARSIWA).[325] Put differently, instead of determining who can be held responsible under public international law, the next sub-section will examine whether there is a possible legal construction for responsibility in the ARSIWA, and if so, what the necessary constellation of facts would have to be for such responsibility under public international law.

6.2 A (Principal) Wrongful Act by the SDF?

A first question that arises when thinking about a possible construction for responsibility is whether the SDF can be said to have committed an (principal) internationally wrongful act. It was said before that it is now generally accepted that non-state actors are bound by an increasing number of obligations under international law, including obligations under customary international law, IHL and international human rights law. In fact, it is undisputed that non-state actors have obligations under IHL. In particular, non-state actors have obligations under Common Article 3 to the Geneva Conventions, to which both states and non-state actors must equally adhere. The question of whether non-state actors, including non-state armed groups, bear obligations under international human rights law is less settled. However, it is often argued that "[t]he further a [non-state armed group] displaces the power and authority of the state whose territory it is operating within, the more likely it becomes that it will bear greater [international human rights law] obligations".[326] Therefore, a non-state armed group exercising governmental functions and *de facto* control over territory and persons may arguably be subject to obligations under international human rights law, at least, to a greater extent than non-state armed groups that do not exercise such control. In this regard, the SDF can be said to exercise state-like functions and has *de facto* control over Northeast Syria and its population. This particular non-state actor can thus, in accordance with the above line of argumentation, be

325 ILC, 'Draft Articles on Responsibility of States for Internationally Wrongful Acts, with commentaries' in the Report of the International Law Commission on the work of its fifty-third session (2001) UN Doc. A/56/10.

326 See, also, R. Mackenzie-Gray Scott, 'State Responsibility for Complicity in the Internationally Wrongful Acts of Non-state Armed Groups' 24 Journal of Conflict & Security Law (2019) 2: 404, 405; see, also, J. Maddocks 2021 (n. 302) 298; K. Fortin, *The Accountability of Armed Groups under Human Rights Law* (Oxford University Press 2017) 152–173; D. Amoroso, 'Armed Opposition Groups' (and Foreign Fighters') Abidance by International Human Rights Law: The Issue of Compliance in Syria and Iraq' in A. de Guttry, F. Capone and C. Paulussen, *Foreign Fighters under International Law and Beyond* (T.M.C. Asser Press 2016) 209, 210; L. Zegveld, *Accountability of Armed Opposition Groups in International Law* (Cambridge University Press 2002) 148–151.

said to bear obligations under international human rights law, including not to treat individuals inhumanely.[327]

In sum, it can be said that the relevant international legal norms and corresponding obligations regarding arbitrary detention and inhumane treatment apply to the SDF. However, the question is whether in these circumstances the SDF can be said to have committed an international wrongful act, and if it has committed such an act, what does it consist of?

The SDF has continuously declared that it does not have the capacity to manage the camps and detention facilities in which third-country nationals are detained.[328] They have called upon states of origin as well as the international community to cooperate for years, and clearly indicated that these foreign nationals constitute a burden to them that they are unable to bear on their own.[329] Therefore, it is questionable whether the prolonged, arbitrary detention and the circumstances in which those FTFs and family members are detained can be attributed to the SDF. Especially in light of the fact that the SDF has been calling for help in detaining those FTFs and family members for many years, and the fact that they are a non-state actor without the necessary capacity to detain those individuals in compliance with international law. At least from a moral point of view, attribution to the SDF would create a sense of injustice, but could this be translated into a legal argument?

This would lead us to exploring the possible invocation of a circumstance precluding wrongfulness. If non-state actors can at all invoke such circumstances precluding wrongfulness, the most suitable one that comes to mind is *force majeure*, i.e., material impossibility of performance.[330] However, *force majeure* may not be applicable because it would be difficult to uphold that the SDF had absolutely no element of free choice. This can, for example, be shown by the fact that they have also threatened to release IS fighters and affiliates, including FTFs and their family members.[331] Without touching upon what scenario would be more desirable from a national, regional or international security point of view, for the purpose of a plea of *force majeure*, it would be difficult to uphold that there was no element of choice but to arbitrarily detain those FTFs and family members in circumstances which amount to inhuman treatment.

---

327 ICCPR, Article 7.

328 AANES, Press Release 2021 (n. 20); See, also, *Al Jazeera* 2019 (n. 232).

329 AANES, Press Release 2021 (n. 20).

330 ARSIWA, Article 23.

331 P. Taneja and J. Abdi, 'Islamic State: Kurdish forces threaten to stop guarding camps' (*BBC*, 25 November 2022). Available at: <https://www.bbc.com/news/world-middle-east-63745833> accessed 8 April 2024.

Although the ARSIWA may not provide for a suitable circumstance precluding wrongfulness which could be invoked by the SDF, concluding that they have therefore committed an internationally wrongful act by arbitrarily detaining FTFs and their family members, in circumstances which amount to inhumane treatment, may still seem too simplistic. The fact remains that the SDF is not a state and although it exercises governmental functions and *de facto* control over territory and persons, as a non-state actor, it still lacks state-like capabilities and it has indeed repeatedly made clear that it does not have the ability to address the burden these third-country nationals pose.[332] Despite their calls for help, states of origin have refused to repatriate their nationals for a long time or still refuse to do so. Essentially, leaving the SDF, a non-state armed group, to deal with the problem.

6.3 Complicity as a Possible Construction for Responsibility

When considering the question whether, by failing to repatriate their FTFs and family members, states like the United Kingdom, the Netherlands and France have facilitated the arbitrary detention and inhuman treatment of their FTFs and family members in Northeast Syria, the mode of legal responsibility that at first sight seems most suitable is that of complicity, i.e., aiding or assisting in the commission of an internationally wrongful act. A construction for responsibility whereby the inhumane treatment and arbitrary detention on the territory of another state would directly be attributable to states of origin, who do not have effective control over the SDF, does in any case not seem suitable under these circumstances. Therefore, responsibility for complicity, together with the facts necessary for establishing such responsibility, will be further examined.

Under public international law, states can be held responsible for complicity in the commission of an internationally wrongful act committed by another state. Although the concept of complicity originates in national criminal law,[333] within the international law of state responsibility, it "is a form of participation in the wrongful act of another State" and,[334] according to Lanovoy, can be defined as the "responsibility of a State [...] for its action

332 AANES, Press Release 2021 (n. 20).

333 V. Coli, 'Complicity In The Commission Of Internationally Wrongful Acts: A New Perspective In The Law Of State Responsibility (2021) Working Paper Serie n. 3/2019–2020 LUISS Academy 4. Available at: <https://luissuniversitypress.it/wp-content/uploads/2021/11/03_Coli.pdf> accessed 11 September 2023.

334 V. Lanovoy, *Complicity and its Limits in the Law of International Responsibility* (Hart Publishing 2016) 4.

or omission, knowingly facilitating the commission of an internationally wrongful act by another actor".[335] Although not using the term complicity itself, the subject was codified by the ILC in its ARSIWA. Expressing complicity by prohibiting 'aid and assistance', Article 16 of those Draft Articles reads as follows:

> "A State which aids or assists another State in the commission of an internationally wrongful act by the latter is internationally responsible for doing so if:
> (a) that State does so with knowledge of the circumstances of the internationally wrongful act; and
> (b) the act would be internationally wrongful if committed by that State".

Responsibility for complicity is also part of customary international law, which was first recognized by the majority of states during the drafting process of the ARSIWA,[336] and subsequently acknowledged by the ICJ in the *Genocide* Case.[337] There are, nevertheless, persistent uncertainties regarding the constituent elements of complicity which can be found in Article 16. The first constituent element is the material or objective element, which requires actual aid or assistance and a nexus with the principal wrongful act. The second element is the knowledge or subjective element, which requires a degree of knowledge of the circumstances of the wrongful act. The last constituent element that must be met in order to hold a state responsible for complicity is the opposability element, meaning that the assisting state must be bound by the same obligation as was breached by the actor that received the aid or assistance.

Now that it is clear what complicity actually entails, there are a number of issues that already arise when looking at it as a possible construction for responsibility in the context of FTFs and their family members detained in Syria and Iraq. The first issue is whether the SDF can be said to have committed an internationally wrongful act at all. This matter was already discussed in the previous sub-section, in which it was concluded that this remains highly questionable due to their lack of capacity to detain those foreign nationals in compliance with international law and their continued calls for help. The second issue that arises, before having looked at the constituent elements

---

335 *Ibid.*

336 V. Coli 2021 (n. 333) 8; V. Lanovoy 2016 (n. 334) 163, 164. Lanovoy also notes that "today there is overwhelming support from States and international organisations for the existence of the rule on responsibility for complicity".

337 *Genocide Case* (n. 301) para. 420.

for complicity as a possible construction for responsibility, is the fact that Article 16 only speaks of aid or assistance to "another State". The SDF is clearly not a state and it should thus first be determined whether states can be complicit in an internationally wrongful act by a non-state actor.

Several arguments have been put forward by other scholars in favor of applying Article 16 to aid or assistance provided to non-state actors. First of all, at the time the ARSIWA was drafted, the question whether, or to what degree, non-state actors could bear obligations under international law was still unsettled and controversial.[338] In Jackson's words, "the historical failure of international law to regulate the conduct of non-state actors directly limited the possibility of state responsibility for complicity in these situations".[339] There was "simply no international wrong for the state to be complicit in".[340] Today, however, it is generally accepted that non-state actors are bound by an increasing number of obligations under international law, including obligations under customary international law, IHL and international human rights law. As Jackson logically concludes from this development, "[w]herever international law imposes obligations on non-state actors, so state complicity in violations thereof would give rise to international responsibility".[341]

Secondly, and although the issue was still unsettled and controversial at the time the ARSIWA was drafted, there are references to a complicity rule with regard to non-state actors in the preparatory work of Article 16. For example, the work includes the following statement:

> We shall take into consideration only the case of complicity of a State in an international offence committed by another State, even though it may well be presumed that the same principles would apply if one of the protagonists were a subject of international law other than a State.[342]

Special Rapporteur Ago, therefore, seems to show support for a complicity rule with regard to non-state actors. In addition, Special Rapporteur Riphagen directs attention to an example of state aid or assistance to a non-state actor.

338 R. Goodman and V. Lanovoy, 'State Responsibility for Assisting Armed Groups: A Legal Risk Analysis' Just Security (22 December 2016).

339 M. Jackson, *Complicity in International Law* (Oxford University Press 2015) 176.

340 *Ibid.*

341 *Ibid.* 202.

342 Seventh report on State Responsibility by Mr. Roberto Ago, Special Rapporteur – the internationally wrongful act of the State, source of international responsibility (continued) UN Doc. A/CN.4/307 and Add.1 & 2 and Corr.1 & 2, Yearbook of the ILC (1789) vol. I (1), p. 60.

More specifically, he pointed towards aid or assistance "to a people which is the victim of the maintenance by force of colonial domination".[343] Different from what the text and commentary of Article 16 would suggest, aid or assistance to non-state actors was thus, to some extent, considered in the ILC's preparatory works.[344]

A third argument that has been given in favor of applying the principle of Article 16 to non-state actors is that the ARSIWA was not meant to be exhaustive.[345] This can be evidenced by the fact that in 2011, the ILC adopted the Draft Articles on the Responsibility of International Organizations (DARIO),[346] and international organizations are, like non-state armed groups, non-state actors. If states incur responsibility for circumventing an obligation by causing an international organization to act in violation of that obligation, why would states not also incur responsibility for circumventing an obligation by causing another non-state actor, like a non-state armed group, to act in breach of that obligation? As explained by Maddocks,

> [n]one of the states within the US-led Coalition could lawfully detain those fighters in the poor conditions, without any fair trial guarantees, in which they are held by the SDF. Had a member of the anti-ISIS coalition caused an [international organization], rather than [a] [non-state actor], to detain individuals in a manner that breached the state's international legal obligations, [DARIO] provides for that state's international responsibility to be engaged.[347]

Moreover, in the *Genocide* Case, the ICJ seems to have applied Article 16 by analogy to aid or assistance rendered by the Federal Republic of Yugoslavia to the Republika Srpska, a non-state actor.[348] In the *Genocide* Case, the ICJ determined that states were under an obligation not to be complicit in genocide, based on the Genocide Convention.[349] In determining whether the Federal

343 Fourth report on the content, forms and degrees of international responsibility (part 2 of the draft articles), by Mr. Willem Riphagen, Special Rapporteur UN Doc A/CN.4/366 and Add. l, Yearbook of the ILC (1983) Vol. II(1), p. 13.

344 See, also, R. Mackenzie-Gray Scott 2019 (n. 326) 374–376.

345 See, for example, R. Goodman and V. Lanovoy 2016 (n. 338).

346 ILC, Draft articles on the responsibility of international organizations, in the Report of the International Law Commission on the work of its sixty-third session (2011) UN Doc. A/66/10.

347 J. Maddocks 2021 (n. 302) 303 (footnote omitted).

348 *Genocide Case* (n. 301).

349 *Ibid.* para. 167; Convention on the Prevention and Punishment of the Crime of Genocide (adopted 9 December 1948, entry into force 12 January 1951) 78 UNTS 277.

Republic of Yugoslavia breached this obligation, the Court applied Article 16 of the ARSIWA by analogy and stated:

> The Court sees no reason to make any distinction of substance between "complicity in genocide", within the meaning of Article III, paragraph (e), of the Convention, and the "aid or assistance" of a State in the commission of a wrongful act by another State within the meaning of the aforementioned Article 16 [...]. In other words, to ascertain whether the Respondent is responsible for "complicity in genocide" within the meaning of Article III, paragraph (e), [...] it must examine whether organs of the respondent State, or persons acting on its instructions or under its direction or effective control, furnished "aid or assistance" in the commission of the genocide in Srebrenica, in a sense not significantly different from that of those concepts in the general law of international responsibility.[350]

Scholars have referred to this judgement as a basis for the extension of the law of state responsibility for complicity to include aid or assistance rendered to non-state actors.[351]

Finally, states have also pointed towards Article 16 of the ARSIWA with regard to aid or assistance rendered to non-state actors. For example, in its position on a proposal to lift an EU arms embargo against Syria, Austria referred to Article 16 of the ARSIWA in relation to the envisaged provision of arms to the Syrian opposition, and stated that:

> When applying these principles to the envisaged supply of arms to the Syrian opposition, it is to be considered that war crimes, including murder, extrajudicial killings and torture, are perpetrated by anti-Government armed groups in Syria, as reported by the UN Commission of Inquiry, as well as suicide bombings and attacks against and hostage-taking of UNDOF peacekeepers, as is known from the daily news. Should supplied arms be used by armed opposition groups in Syria in the commission of internationally wrongful acts, the States who had supplied these arms and had knowledge of these acts would incur State responsibility for their aid and assistance in the commission of such acts.[352]

---

350 *Genocide Case* (n. 301) para. 420.

351 See, for example, V. Lanovoy 2016 (n. 334) 319–329 and M. Jackson 2015 (n. 339) 201–216.

352 J. Borger, The Austrian position on arms embargo in Syria – official document (*The Guardian*, 15 May 2013) section 4. Available at: <https://www.theguardian.com/world/julian-borger-global-security-blog/interactive/2013/may/15/austria-eu-syria-arms-embargo-pdf> accessed 22 September 2023.

However, the Netherlands formulated a different position. Between 2015 and 2018, the Netherlands provided non-lethal assistance to a number of non-state armed opposition groups operating in Syria. As opposed to aid or assistance rendered to another state, the Dutch Government noted that it was not convinced that a complicity rule exists which could lead to state responsibility for aid or assistance rendered to such non-state armed groups.[353]

Although the position of states towards this question is thus different, because of the above-described arguments, a valid claim could be made that the complicity rule enshrined in Article 16 of the ARSIWA extends to internationally wrongful acts committed by non-state actors, including non-state armed groups like the SDF.

Besides these preliminary issues that arise with regard to complicity as a possible framework for responsibility, there are three constituent elements that would also need to be fulfilled. The opposability element is certainly met, as both the SDF and states of origin are under the same IHL and human rights obligations to treat detainees humanely and not to submit them to arbitrary detention without the prospect of a trial or release. However, it may not be possible to make the claim that responsibility through complicity provides for an appropriate framework of legal responsibility in these circumstances because of the material and knowledge elements.

First, because the material element requires actual aid or assistance, for example, in the form of providing weapons, personnel, training, intelligence, or providing financial, logistical or technical support.[354] It is unlikely that those states that have been reluctant or have refused to repatriate their FTFs and family members could be held responsible for complicity merely as a consequence of their inaction. In other words, it is questionable whether states' inaction with regard to repatriation can qualify as aid or assistance. Besides actual aid or assistance, the material element also requires a sufficient nexus between the aid or assistance and the principal wrongful conduct. Although there is uncertainty about the required level of contribution to the commission of the wrongful act, it remains questionable whether states' inaction can be said to have directly contributed to the arbitrary detention of their nationals in circumstances which amount to inhumane treatment. In addition, it was mentioned that some states of origin have (financially) contributed to, among others, the expansion of prisons in Northeast Syria. However,

---

353 'Actuele situatie in Noord-Afrika en het Midden-Oosten: Brief van de Minister van Buitenlandse Zaken', Tweede Kamer, Vergaderjaar 2019–2020, 32623 Nr. 299 (31 august 2020) 4.

354 R. Mackenzie-Gray Scott 2019 (n. 326) 385; H. Moynihan 2016 (n. 294) para. 19.

the question remains whether states have done so in order to improve the situation in those detention facilities or whether they have done so in order to avoid having to repatriate their FTFs and family members detained in those facilities.

The second reason why it may be difficult to make the claim that complicity provides for a suitable framework of legal responsibility in these circumstances has to do with the knowledge element. There is considerable debate about the degree of knowledge or state of mind necessary in order to hold a state responsible for aiding or assisting another actor in the commission of an internationally wrongful act, i.e., whether that is actual knowledge or intent. Because of, *inter alia*, extensive media reporting,[355] reports by the United Nations,[356] other international and regional (human rights) organizations,[357] as well as statements by the SDF themselves,[358] it may not be credible to uphold that states of origin did not have knowledge about the circumstances in which detainees, including their own nationals, were held in Northeast Syria. But is such knowledge sufficient to fulfill this constituent element of complicity? The more difficult question seems to be whether it can also be said that those states intended to facilitate the indefinite and arbitrary

355 See, for example, 'Inside a prison full of alleged ISIS fighters' (*CBS News*, 18 October 2019). Available at: <https://www.cbsnews.com/pictures/inside-a-syrian-prison-for-isis-suspects/> accessed 27 September 2019; N. Cumming-Bruce, 'Horrid Conditions in Syria Camp Where ISIS Families Fled Risk Fostering Extremism' (*The New York Times*, 11 September 2019). Available at: <https://www.nytimes.com/2019/09/11/world/middleeast/syria-camp-isis-families-islamic-state-extremism.html> accessed 27 September 2019; 'Aid agencies warn of 'dire conditions' at Syria camp for those fleeing Islamic State' (*Middle East Eye*, 6 March 2019). Available at: < https://www.middleeasteye.net/news/aid-agencies-warn-dire-conditions-syria-camp-those-fleeing-islamic-state> accessed 28 September 2023.

356 See, for example, 'UN report on Syria conflict highlights inhumane detention of women and children' (*UN News*, 11 September 2019). Available at: <https://news.un.org/en/story/2019/09/1046102> accessed 17 September 2023; OHCHR 2021 (n. 25); OHCHR 2023 (n. 267); UNICEF 2022 (n. 267).

357 See, for example, Human Rights Watch, Northeast Syria: Boys, Men Held in Inhumane Conditions (8 October 2019). Available at: <https://www.hrw.org/news/2019/10/08/northeast-syria-boys-men-held-inhumane-conditions> accessed 27 September 2023; Amnesty International, 'Syria: Repatriate at least 27,000 children held in dire conditions in North-East Syria' (30 November 2021). Available at: < https://www.amnesty.org/en/latest/news/2021/11/syria-repatriate-at-least-27000-children-held-in-dire-conditions-in-north-east-syria/> accessed 27 September 2023; Rights & Security International, 'Europe's Guantanamo: The indefinite detention of European women and children in North East Syria' (17 February 2021). Available at: <https://www.rightsandsecurity.org/assets/downloads/Europes-guantanamo-THE_REPORT.pdf> accessed 28 September 2023.

358 See, for example, AANES, Press Release 2021 (n. 20).

detention, amounting to inhuman treatment. Perhaps we should accept that imputing intent would go too far in these circumstances. Maybe the continuance of FTFs and family members' arbitrary and indefinite detention should only be seen as a (at some point in time foreseeable) consequence of states' non-repatriation policies, adopted to make sure that their FTFs and family members stay away from their territories.

The discussion of complicity as a possible construction for responsibility under public international law has brought many questions and issues with regard to such a construction to the forefront. It can be concluded that applying complicity as a framework for state responsibility to the complex relationship between states' non-repatriation policies on the one hand, and the SDF-controlled detention of FTFs and family members on the other hand, might raise more questions than it solves. Therefore, the next sub-sections will explore whether there are other possible constructions for responsibility or whether we should conclude that there perhaps exists a legal responsibility vacuum in these circumstances.

6.4 Other Possible Constructions for Responsibility

Besides responsibility for complicity, there are two other potential frameworks for legal responsibility that can be discussed. First, aggravated responsibility for complicity as contained in Article 41 of the ARSIWA. Second, coercion as contained in Article 18 of the ARSIWA.

6.4.1 Aggravated Responsibility for Complicity

Some commentators have voiced their concern that the circumstances in the SDF-controlled camps and prisons could cumulatively, and especially in the case of children, amount to torture.[359] The prohibition of torture constitutes a peremptory norm of international law, i.e., a norm of *jus cogens*. The Commission of Inquiry on the Syrian Arab Republic "also found that the form, severity, duration and intensity of the physical and mental suffering inflicted may amount to the war crime of committing outrages upon personal dignity, in

---

359 J. Becker and L. Tayler 2023 (n. 32); See, also, Rights & Security International 2021 (n. 357); OHCHR, 'Position of the United Nations Special Rapporteur on the promotion and protection of human rights and fundamental freedoms while countering terrorism on the human rights of adolescents/juveniles being detained in North-East Syria' (May 2021) 2, 3. Available at: <https://www.ohchr.org/sites/default/files/Documents/Issues/Terrorism/SR/UNSRCT_Position_human-rights-of-boys-adolescents-2021_final.pdf> accessed 29 September 2023.

particular humiliating and degrading treatment, in relation to each interned individual".[360] War crimes are, like torture, serious breaches of international law. In the previously discussed letters by a number of UN experts, it was noted that "where serious breaches of international law are committed, States must not render aid or assistance in maintaining the situation created by the serious breach and must cooperate to bring it to an end".[361] Both the Commission of Inquiry on the Syrian Arab Republic and the UN experts seem to refer to another provision in the ARSIWA which, like the previously discussed Article 16, regulates aid or assistance of one state to another.

Article 41(2) stipulates that "[n]o State shall recognize as lawful a situation created by a serious breach within the meaning of article 40, nor render aid or assistance in maintaining that situation".[362] This provision has been referred to as the regime of aggravated responsibility for complicity, as it deals not with any breach of international law but only with serious breaches of international law. As Lanovoy notes, this provision "can be said to operate as a *lex specialis* in relation to Article 16 ARSIWA".[363] Instead of dealing with aid or assistance in the commission of the principal wrongful act, Article 41(2) deals with aid or assistance after the internationally wrongful act was committed, but which assists the responsible state in maintaining the situation created by that act.[364] In other words, as explained by the ILC in its commentary to the Article, "[i]t extends beyond the commission of the serious breach itself to the maintenance of the situation created by that breach, and it applies whether or not the breach itself is a continuing one".[365] However, it is uncertain whether Article 41 is part of customary international law, an uncertainty which the ILC seems to have recognized by stating that "the legal regime of serious breaches is itself in a state of development".[366]

On the one hand, the Article is more restrictive than Article 16 of the ARSIWA as it only applies to aid or assistance rendered in maintaining a situation created by a serious breach of international law. Article 40 clarifies that a serious breach is a "gross or systematic failure by the responsible State to fulfil"

360 Human Rights Council, '"No End in Sight": Torture and ill-treatment in the Syrian Arab Republic 2020–2023: Independent International Commission of Inquiry on the Syrian Arab Republic' (10 July 2023) UN Doc. A/HRC/53/CRP.5, para. 115.

361 Letters by UN experts 2022 (n. 224).

362 See also ILC, Draft conclusions on identification and legal consequences of peremptory norms of general international law (*jus cogens*) (2022) UN Doc. A/77/10, conclusion 19.

363 V. Lanovoy 2016 (n. 334) 106; H. Aust, *Complicity and the Law of State Responsibility* (Cambridge University Press 2011) 336.

364 ARSIWA, commentary to Article 41, para. 11.

365 *Ibid.*

366 *Ibid.* para. 14.

an obligation "arising under a peremptory norm of general international law". In other words, two elements need to be satisfied: there does not only have to be a breach of a peremptory norm of international law, i.e., a norm of *jus cogens*, but that breach must also be gross or systematic. The prohibition against torture, including in the context of the treatment of detainees, is generally recognized as a peremptory norm and also mentioned as an example of such a norm in the ILC's commentary to Article 40.[367] Nevertheless, there still exists uncertainty as to which norms exactly qualify as *jus cogens*. For example, in its Advisory Opinion on the *Legality of the Threat or Use of Nuclear Weapons*, the ICJ found that the basic rules of IHL "are to be observed by all States whether or not they have ratified the conventions that contain them, because they constitute intransgressible principles of international customary law".[368] The ILC concludes from this passage in the ICJ's Advisory Opinion that it would, therefore, "also seem justified to treat these as peremptory".[369] However, this still leaves us with uncertainty regarding which rules of IHL can be regarded as fundamental and which, therefore, fall within the category of *jus cogens*. It has been said that the prohibition of humiliating, degrading or inhuman treatment under Common Article 3 to the Geneva Conventions, applicable in NIAC and part of customary international law, is so fundamental that it falls within this category.[370] And although the ILC did not categorize it as such, certain UN bodies and domestic courts considered arbitrary depriva-

---

367 *Ibid.* para. 5.

368 *Legality of the Threat or Use of Nuclear Weapons* (n. 310) para. 79. With regard to this Advisory Opinion, President Bedjaoui submitted a Declaration in which he stated: "I have no doubt that most of the principles and rules of humanitarian law and, in any event, the two principles, one of which prohibits the use of weapons with indiscriminate effects and the other the use of arms causing unnecessary suffering, form part of *jus cogens*". See, p. 273. In addition, Judge Weeramantry submitted a Dissenting Opinion in which he stated that "[t]he rules of the humanitarian law of war have clearly acquired the status of *jus cogens*, for they are fundamental rules of a humanitarian character, from which no derogation is possible without negating the basic considerations of humanity which they are intended to protect". See, p. 496.

369 ARSIWA, commentary to Article 40, para. 5.

370 ICRC, Basic rules of international humanitarian law in armed conflicts (31 December 1988). Available at: <https://www.icrc.org/en/doc/resources/documents/misc/basic-rules-ihl-311288.htm> accessed 6 October 2023. See, also, V. Chetail, 'The contribution of the International Court of Justice to international humanitarian law' 85 International Review of the Red Cross (2003) 850: 247–267 and R. Nieto-Navia, 'International Peremptory Norms (*Jus Cogens*) and International Humanitarian Law' in L. Vohrah, F. Pocar, Y. Featherstone et al. (eds.), *Man's Inhumanity to Man: Essays on International Law in Honour of Antonio Cassese* (Brill Nijhoff 2003) 632–640.

tion of liberty to constitute a norm of *jus cogens* as well.[371] If these norms can indeed be said to fall within that category, we can further explore whether Article 41(2) could provide for a suitable framework for responsibility under public international, applicable to the situation of states' non-repatriation policies and FTFs and their family members' detention in Northeast Syria.

Although Article 41(2) is more restrictive due to its focus on serious breaches of international, it can, on the other hand, be said to be broader in scope than Article 16 because there is no knowledge requirement. This is because, as the ILC explained in its commentary, "it is hardly conceivable that a State would not have notice of the commission of a serious breach by another State".[372] The issues and uncertainties that arose when applying the knowledge element in our discussion of Article 16 would, therefore, not arise with aggravated responsibility for complicity as a possible construction for responsibility under public international law. An additional factor why aggravated responsibility for complicity could potentially be a more suitable framework for responsibility in the circumstances at hand, would be that there is less focus on an initial wrongful act. One of the reasons why it would be difficult to hold states of origin responsible for complicity in the *commission* of an internationally wrongful act was that it was uncertain what exactly the principal wrongful act was, and more specifically, whether a principal wrongful act could be attributed to the SDF at all. Instead of dealing with the aid or assistance in the commission of the principal wrongful act, Article 41(2) deals with aid or assistance *after* the internationally wrongful act was committed but which assists in maintaining the situation that was created by that act.[373] There thus seems to be less emphasis on the initial wrongful act here and hence, the question of to whom that initial wrongful act can be attributed.

Nevertheless, in order to establish a state's responsibility under Article 41 (2), there still needs to be actual aid or assistance, and a connection between the aid or assistance rendered and the maintenance of the situation caused by the serious breach. Thus, similar issues that arose with regard to complicity emerge with regard to aggravated responsibility for complicity. The most difficult issue is whether a state's continued inaction to repatriate amounts to 'aid or assistance'. Other questions would be whether states of origin can be held responsible for facilitating the maintenance of a situation, created by a

---

371 UNGA, Report of the Working Group on Arbitrary Detention (24 December 2012) UN Doc. A/HRC/22/44, paras. 37–75; *Belhaj and another v Straw and others, Rahmatullah (No 1) v Ministry of Defence and another* [2017] UKSC 3, para. 271.

372 ARSIWA, commentary to Article 41, para. 11.

373 *Ibid.*

wrongful act, if it is unclear to whom that wrongful act can be attributed: to the SDF, those states themselves or perhaps both? Can states of origin be held responsible for aiding and assisting in maintaining the indefinite and arbitrary detention, amounting to inhumane treatment and possibly torture, if by refusing to repatriate for years these states themselves have, at least in part, contributed to the creation of that situation? Additional questions can also be raised with regard to the more narrow scope of aggravated responsibility for complicity. For example, can the breach of international law in question meet the threshold of gross or systematic?

6.4.2 Cooperation to Bring any Serious Breach to an End

Like responsibility for complicity, it is questionable whether aggravated responsibility for complicity would provide a suitable framework in this context. However, Article 41 also requires that "States shall cooperate to bring to an end through lawful means any serious breach". Therefore, if the prohibition of torture and the prohibition of inhuman treatment, including arbitrary detention amounting to such treatment, can indeed be said to constitute norms of *jus cogens*, and their breach would indeed reach the threshold of a "serious breach", then states would at least be under an obligation to "cooperate to bring to an end" such serious breaches, whether attributable to the SDF or not.[374] It hardly needs any explanation that the most effective way to "bring to an end" the indefinite detention and inhuman treatment of FTFs and their family members in Northeast Syria seems to be for states origin to repatriate them.

6.4.3 Coercion

One final construction for responsibility that can be explored is that of coercion. Article 18 of the ARSIWA reads as follows: "[a] State which coerces another State to commit an act is internationally responsible for that act if: (a) the act would, but for the coercion, be an internationally wrongful act of the coerced State; and (b) the coercing State does so with knowledge of the circumstances of the act". From the outset, it should be noted that it is questionable whether this construction for derived state responsibility constitutes customary international law, mainly because the provision lacks support in

374 ARSIWA, Article 41(1).

state practice.[375] Nevertheless, if, besides the coercion of another state, this framework can also be applied to the coercion of a non-state actor, this form of responsibility under public international law may, at first sight, seem suitable to address the complicated relationship between states of origin, the SDF and the circumstances in which FTFs and their family members are detained. It seems plausible to argue that by refusing to repatriate and by failing to respond to the repeated calls for help by the SDF, states of origin have, to some extent, forced the SDF to commit the wrongful acts of arbitrary and indefinite detention, amounting to inhuman treatment. Let us then explore what the more specific requirements are that would have to be met, and what the necessary constellation of facts would be for such a state responsibility construction.

One essential element in Article 18 of the ARSIWA is the necessary degree of coercion. The ILC explains in its commentary to the provision that the coercive conduct must give the coerced state "no effective choice but to comply with the wishes of the coercing State".[376] The ILC clarified that "[i]t is not sufficient that compliance with the obligation is made more difficult or onerous, or that the acting State is assisted or directed in its conduct".[377] Coercion can thus be equated with *force majeure*, which is why "in most cases where Article 18 is applicable, the responsibility of the coerced State will be precluded".[378] It can thus be concluded that coercion may consist of different types of conduct, not necessarily involving the threat or use of force, but a necessary requirement is that the coercing conduct leaves the coerced state without any possibility of complying with the obligation breached. In other words, similar to *force majeure* as a circumstance precluding wrongfulness, there may not be an element of choice on behalf of the coerced state.

States of origin have indeed refused to repatriate their FTFs and family members and have failed to act on the continued calls for repatriation by the SDF. However, it might go too far to say that states of origin exercised such pressure on the SDF that they denied the SDF any effective choice in the matter but to breach the prohibitions of inhuman treatment and arbitrary deprivation of liberty. And then we have not yet discussed whether the willful *inaction* of a state, without there being a direct obligation to act, could meet the necessary degree of coercion at all, in order to apply this framework for

---

375 J. Fry, 'Coercion, Causation, and the Fictional Elements of Indirect State Responsibility' 40 Vanderbilt Journal of Transnational Law (2007) 3:613, 619–629.

376 ARSIWA, commentary to Article 18, para. 2.

377 *Ibid.* para. 1.

378 *Ibid.* para. 4.

responsibility. Article 18 follows a binary approach in the sense that coercion either leads to the full responsibility of the coercing state or it does not. Put differently, it is not possible to allocate varying degrees of responsibility, depending on the intensity of the coercion in a given case. This lack of flexibility in Article 18 also seems to be the reason why coercion does not constitute a suitable legal framework for responsibility under the present circumstances. Neither allocating full responsibility to states of origin, nor allocating full responsibility to the SDF, seems to be just in these circumstances.

6.5 A Legal Responsibility Vacuum

After exploring different ways in which the circumstances at hand can potentially be tied to the ILC's ARSIWA, we may need to conclude that there is a legal vacuum here. On the one hand, it would go too far to hold states of origin directly and legally responsible for the circumstances in which their FTFs and family members are detained in Northeast Syria, in camps and detention facilities over which they have no effective control. On the other hand, it would not be right to hold the SDF directly responsible for the breaches of international law by the way in which those individuals are detained. They constitute a non-state armed group lacking the necessary capacity to take care of those third-country nationals in compliance with international law, and they have continuously called upon states of origin as well as the international community for help, without avail. As the discussion in this section has shown, none of the frameworks for derived responsibility that, at first instance, may seem suitable actually seem to fit to the unique situation at hand. This leaves us with the conclusion that there seems to be a legal responsibility vacuum in this context. Although moral or political arguments for the responsibility of states of origin that have refused to repatriate for a long time may surely be made, it does not seem easy to transform this into a legal argument.

7 Repatriation as a Means to Give Effect to the Obligation to Make Reparations for Internationally Wrongful Acts

In the second chapter of this research, it was concluded that states are under an obligation to prevent FTF travel, an obligation which is owed to states of destination, i.e., Syria and Iraq, and states through which FTFs and their family members transit on their way to the conflict zone, such as Türkiye. It was also concluded that this obligation is subject to a standard of due diligence and, although it would admittedly be difficult to prove, if a state knowingly allows or acquiesces to FTFs and their accompanying family members departing its territory, its responsibility for violating the obligation to prevent the travel of such individuals could potentially be invoked. It is well known that if a state commits an intentionally wrongful act, the obligation to make reparations in favor of the injured state(s) automatically arises. This section will explore whether, in such circumstances, the repatriation of FTFs and their family members from states like Syria, Iraq and Türkiye can be seen as a form of restitution and hence, as a means to fulfill states' obligation to make reparations for failing to diligently prevent the departure of such individuals.

7.1 The Obligation to Make Reparations

There are two principles that form the foundation of the international law on reparations. First, the principle that an internationally wrongful act automatically generates an obligation to make reparations.[379] The obligation to make reparations is, therefore, "the immediate corollary of a State's responsibility" and does not depend upon a demand or protest by an injured party.[380] Second, the principle that reparation must, as far as possible, eradicate all the consequences of the internationally wrongful act. In other words, reparation must re-establish the situation that is affected by the breach.[381] This has also been referred to as the principle of 'full reparations'. These two general principles are also mentioned by the PCIJ in the *Factory at Chorzów* Case. In the jurisdictional phase of the Case, the Court found:

> It is a principle of international law that the breach of an engagement involves an obligation to make reparation in an adequate form. Reparation therefore is the indispensable complement of a failure to apply a convention and there is no necessity for this to be stated in the convention itself.[382]

---

379 D. Shelton, 'Righting Wrongs: Reparations in the Articles on State Responsibility' 96 The American Journal of International Law (2002) 4: 835; ILC, ARSIWA, commentary to Article 31, para. 4.

380 ILC, ARSIWA 2001, commentary to Article 31, para. 4.

381 D. Shelton 2002 (n. 379) 835; ARSIWA, commentary to Article 31, para. 2, 3.

382 *Case Concerning the Factory at Chorzów (Germany v. Poland)* (Jurisdiction) [1927] PCIJ Rep Series A No. 9, p. 21.

On the merits, the Court found that it is "even a general conception of law, that any breach of an engagement involves an obligation to make reparation".[383] The obligation to make reparations, which is part of customary international law, is a new and separate obligation arising from the breach of a primary obligation, but existing independently thereof.[384] With regard to the second principle, that of full reparations, the PCIJ stated that "[t]he essential principle contained in the actual notion of an illegal act [...] is that reparation must, as far as possible, wipe out all the consequences of the illegal act and reestablish the situation which would, in all probability, have existed if that act had not been committed".[385] The obligation to make reparations thus entails a duty to place the injured party in a position as if no illegal act was committed.

These foundational principles of the obligation to make reparations are also reflected in the ILC's ARSIWA. Article 31 of which reads as follows: "1. The responsible State is under an obligation to make full reparation for the injury caused by the internationally wrongful act. 2. Injury includes any damage, whether material or moral, caused by the internationally wrongful act of a State." As explicitly stated in paragraph 1 of the Article, the ILC adopted the principle of full reparations. In addition to this provision, Article 34 makes clear that, in some cases, full reparations will only be achieved through the combination of different forms of reparations, that is restitution, compensation and/or satisfaction. In its commentary to Article 34, the ILC clarified that "[w]iping out all the consequences of the wrongful act may [...] require some or all forms of reparation to be provided, depending on the type and extent of the injury that has been caused".[386] Moreover, the obligation to make full reparations is also formulated by the ILC in Article 31 as a direct corollary to a state's responsibility, "i.e. as an obligation of the responsible State resulting from the breach, rather than as a right of an injured State or States".[387] Both principles, which form the foundation of the international law on reparations, are thus reflected in the ARSIWA. Although traditionally these two principles also form the basis for reparations towards non-state actors, including individuals, the ILC Articles only apply to reparations in favor of states. Gillard notes that while between states the obligation to make reparations is well established, "with regard to individual victims of violations of human rights law and international humanitarian law the position remains more uncer-

383 *Case Concerning the Factory at Chorzów* (*Germany v. Poland*) (Merits) [1928] PCIJ Rep Series A No. 17, p. 29.
384 D. Shelton, 'Reparations' MPEPIL (2015) para. 7.
385 *Case Concerning the Factory at Chorzów* (*Germany v. Poland*) (Merits) (n. 383) p. 47.
386 ARSIWA, commentary to Article 34, para. 2.
387 *Ibid.* commentary to Article 31, para. 4.

tain".[388] That being said, this section is only concerned with the obligation to make reparations in inter-state relations, as the obligation to prevent FTF travel is owed by states of origin to states of destination or transit.

The obligation to make full reparations is limited by two elements. First, the responsible state is only under an obligation to make reparation for the "injury" caused by its wrongful act. A state is therefore not obliged to make reparations for "merely abstract concerns or general interests of a State which is individually unaffected by the breach".[389] Nevertheless, "injury" is defined by the ILC in a flexible way as "any damage, whether material or moral, caused by the internationally wrongful act of a State". In its commentary, the ILC explains that "material" damage includes "damage to property or other interests of the State and its nationals which is assessable in financial terms", while "moral" damage includes "such items as individual pain and suffering, loss of loved ones or personal affront associated with an intrusion on one's home or private life".[390] However, actual harm is not always required, just like actual harm is not an essential element of an internationally wrongful act. Whether actual harm to another state is required depends upon the primary obligation involved. With regard to some obligations, such as the obligation to refrain from the use of force in international relations, the essence of a violation is causing actual harm to another state, while with regard to other obligations, such as the due diligence obligation to prevent the departure of FTFs, "what matters is the failure to take necessary precautions to prevent harm even if in the event no harm occurs".[391] Thus, although the existence of actual harm is very much relevant for the form and quantity of reparations, there is no general requirement that a state should have suffered actual harm or damage before an obligation to make reparations arises. Although it is possible that the presence of FTFs on the territory of Syria and Iraq has posed harm to such states, *inter alia*, through the commission of terrorist attacks, this is not a requirement for those states to be able to seek reparations.

Second, the element of a causal link between the wrongful act and the injury has to be examined. Article 31 of the ILC Articles specifies that it is only the injury "caused by the internationally wrongful act" for which the responsible state must make full reparations. The obligation to make reparations does, therefore, not involve reparations for "any and all consequences

388 E. Gillard, 'Reparation for violations of international humanitarian law' 85 International Review of the Red Cross (2003) 851: 530.

389 ARSIWA, commentary to Article 34, para. 5.

390 *Ibid.*

391 *Ibid.* commentary to Article 31, para. 6.

flowing from an internationally wrongful act" but, rather, only "the injury resulting from and ascribable to the wrongful act".[392] In its commentary, the ILC explains that, although the element of a causal link is not the same for every wrongful act, as much will depend upon the primary obligation breached, the element of a causal link excludes "injury that is too 'remote' or 'consequential' to be the subject of reparation".[393]

Reparation can occur in multiple forms, that is, in the form of restitution, compensation and/or satisfaction. Compensation consists of a monetary payment covering "any financially assessable damage including loss of profits".[394] Satisfaction covers immaterial injury and may consist of "an acknowledgement of the breach, an expression of regret, a formal apology or another appropriate modality".[395] This section is most concerned with restitution as a form of reparation.

7.2 Restitution as a Form of Reparation

There is no one uniform definition of restitution. Broadly speaking, two definitions can be distinguished: a broader definition, which defines restitution as (re)establishing the situation that would have existed if the internationally wrongful act had not been committed, and a more narrow definition according to which restitution is defined as re-establishing the *status quo ante*, i.e., the situation that existed prior to the commission of the internationally wrongful act.[396] The first definition is broader because it encompasses all the measures that a responsible state must take in order to "wipe out all the consequences of the illegal act and reestablish the situation which would, in all probability, have existed if that act had not been committed".[397] This way, restitution can be taken as a synonym for reparation. The narrow definition of restitution is also referred to as "restitution in kind", and "has the advantage of focusing on the assessment of a factual situation and of not requiring a hypothetical inquiry into what the situation would have been if

392 *Ibid.* commentary to Article 31, para. 9.
393 *Ibid.* para. 10.
394 *Ibid.* Article 36(2).
395 *Ibid.* Article 37(2).
396 *Ibid.* commentary to Article 35, para. 2; D. Shelton 2002 (n. 379) 850; C. Gray, 'The Different Forms of Reparation: Restitution' in J. Crawford, A. Pellet, and S. Olleson (eds.), *The Law of International Responsibility* (Oxford University Press 2010) 590.
397 *Case Concerning the Factory at Chorzów* (*Germany v. Poland*) (Merits) (n. 383) p. 47; A. Tanzi, 'Restitution' MPEPIL (2021) para. 1.

the wrongful act had not been committed".[398] This definition excludes subsequent consequences after the breach, such as loss of the use of goods which a responsible state failed to deliver. The ILC adopted the more narrow definition of restitution in Article 35 of the ARSIWA, which reads as follows:

> "A State responsible for an internationally wrongful act is under an obligation to make restitution, that is, to re-establish the situation which existed before the wrongful act was committed, provided and to the extent that restitution:
> (a) is not materially impossible;
> (b) does not involve a burden out of all proportion to the benefit deriving from restitution instead of compensation".

Because restitution conforms most closely to the foundational principle that reparations must "wipe out all the consequences", restitution has been said to be the primary form of reparation.[399] This primacy of restitution was also upheld by the PCIJ in the *Factory at Chorzów* Case, in which the Court found that the responsible state was under "the obligation to restore the undertaking and, if this be not possible, to pay its value at the time of the indemnification, which value is designed to take the place of restitution which has become impossible".[400] The primacy of restitution can also be seen in the ILC Articles. Besides restitution coming first in the list of forms of reparation contained in Article 34, the primacy of restitution is also confirmed by Article 36(1), which provides for compensation "insofar as such damage is not made good by restitution". Notably, Gray calls attention to the "significant gap between the theoretical primacy of restitution and the relative rarity of its occurrence in practice".[401] Restitution is in practice often replaced by monetary compensation, *inter alia*, because tribunals often only have the competence to order compensation, for example, the Iran–US Claims Tribunal. In addition, because injured states may still choose another form of reparation instead of restitution. This option for the injured state to choose its preferred form of reparation is also reflected in the ILC Articles. Article 43(2) affirms that "[t]he injured State may specify [...] what form reparation should take". This right of election is, however, not absolute, *inter alia*, because the injured state may not claim compensation instead of restitution when the obligation breached concerns a norm of

398 ARSIWA, commentary to Article 35, para. 2; see, also, C. Gray 2010 (n. 396) 590.
399 ARSIWA, commentary to Article 35, para. 3; D. Shelton 2015 (n. 384) para. 8; A. Tanzi 2021 (n. 397) para. 5; C. Gray 2010 (n. 396) 589.
400 *Case Concerning the Factory at Chorzów* (*Germany v. Poland*) (Merits) (n. 383) p. 48.
401 C. Gray 2010 (n. 396) 589.

jus cogens and/or one with an *erga omnes* character.[402] As an example of a situation in which an injured state may not claim compensation or satisfaction instead of restitution, the ILC explicitly mentions "one involving the life or liberty of individuals".[403] Although the obligation to prevent FTF travel does not involve a peremptory norm of international law and is neither owed to the international community as a whole, the situation does involve "the life or liberty of individuals", i.e., those of FTFs and family members whose travel was not prevented and who are now arbitrarily and indefinitely detained in camps and detention facilities in Northeast Syria.

Besides the right of election of injured states, restitution is limited by two other elements contained in Article 35 of the ARSIWA. First, Article 35(a) specifies that a responsible state is under an obligation to make restitution "provided and to the extent that restitution [...] is not materially impossible". In its commentary, the ILC explained that "restitution is not impossible merely on grounds of legal or practical difficulties, even though the responsible State may have to make special efforts to overcome these" and that "the mere fact of political or administrative obstacles to restitution does not amount to impossibility".[404] Rather, restitution may be "materially impossible", for example, when property whose return is requested has disappeared or is fundamentally altered.[405] Second, restitution does not have to be made when it involves "a burden out of all proportion to the benefit deriving from restitution instead of compensation".[406] This limitation, however, only applies when there is "a grave disproportionality".[407] When, as a result of the balancing exercise, there is no clear preference for compensation, the position of the injured state should be preferred.[408]

Finally, restitution can come in multiple forms. Material restitution can be distinguished from legal restitution. Legal restitution can, for example, entail "the revocation, annulment, or amendment of a piece of internal legislation enacted in breach of a rule of international law, or of the rescinding or reconsideration of an administrative or judicial act".[409] Material restitution, on the other hand, can, *inter alia*, involve the return of unlawfully seized objects or

402 ARSIWA, commentary to Article 43, para. 6.
403 *Ibid.*
404 *Ibid.* commentary to Article 35, para. 8.
405 C. Gray 2010 (n. 396) 596.
406 ARSIWA, Article 35(b).
407 *Ibid.* commentary to Article 35, para. 11.
408 *Ibid.*
409 A. Tanzi 2021(n. 397) para. 2; see, also, *Jurisdictional Immunities of the State* (*Germany v. Italy: Greece intervening*) (Judgement) [2012] ICJ Rep. 99, para. 137.

occupied territory, as well as the return of unlawfully detained or arrested persons.[410] For example, in the merits stage of the *Armed Activities on the Territory of the Congo* Case, the Democratic Republic of the Congo requested the ICJ to adjudge and declare that Uganda shall withdraw its nationals from Congolese territory,[411] which is a clear request for material restitution. Restitution in the form of the return of persons is, evidently, also most relevant for the question of repatriation, to which we will turn now.

7.3 Repatriation of FTFs and Their Family Members as a Way to Make Restitution

As was mentioned before, when a state knowingly tolerates or acquiesces to the departure of FTFs from its territory, that states' responsibility could be invoked for failing to take appropriate measures to prevent FTF travel. Before going further into the analysis, it should be mentioned, as was also set out in the second chapter on the prevention of FTF travel, that the obligation to prevent such travel was only imposed upon states by the Security Council with the adoption of Resolution 2178 in 2014. Although it was also explained that this obligation has a broader legal basis in international law than this Security Council Resolution, e.g., in the no-harm and non-intervention principles, it could be argued that before 2014, during the first wave of foreign nationals traveling to Syria to join the uprising against president Assad, states were not yet under such a clear, explicit obligation to prevent the travel of their nationals or habitual residents. Nevertheless, after IS pronounced its caliphate in June 2014 and the Security Council adopted its Resolution 2178 in September 2014, states were certainly under a due diligence obligation to prevent the travel of the second wave of FTFs and accompanying family members. Toleration of, or acquiescence to, their departure would be in violation of their obligation to diligently prevent such travel.

As can be concluded from the analysis in the previous sub-sections, in such a scenario, the responsible state would be under an obligation to make reparations. As Farley rightfully points out,

---

410 ARSIWA, commentary to Article 35, para. 5. See, also, *Case concerning the Temple of Preah Vihear* (*Cambodia v. Thailand*) (Merits) [1962] ICJ Rep. 6, p. 36, 37; *United States Diplomatic and Consular Staff in Tehran* (*United States of America v Iran*) (Judgement) [1980] ICJ Rep. 3, pp. 44, 45.

411 *Armed Activities on the Territory of the Congo* (*Democratic Republic of the Congo v. Uganda*) (Judgement [2005] ICJ Rep. 168, p. 181.

> [k]nowing failure to restrain the travel of nationals or habitual residents to foreign conflict zones, or knowing failure to impede the recruitment of nationals or habitual residents to become foreign fighters, should be clearly defined as internationally wrongful conduct, compensable at international law.[412]

In other words, states of origin that have knowingly allowed their nationals to travel to Syria or Iraq to join IS may have breached their obligation to diligently prevent FTF travel vis-à-vis Syria and Iraq and hence, an obligation towards those states to make reparations automatically arises. Although there are multiple forms of reparation that could be made in order to fulfill this obligation to make reparations under international law, it was shown above that restitution holds primacy over other forms of reparation. Restitution as a way of reparation entails that a responsible state has to re-establish the situation as it was before the internationally wrongful act was committed. As Farley also points out, establishing the situation before a state of origin breached its due diligence obligation to prevent FTF travel logically entails the withdrawal, i.e., repatriation, of such individuals back to the state from which they traveled. [413] Only if those FTFs and their family members are repatriated, possibly in combination with other forms of reparation, will the situation be re-established as it was before the responsible state failed to take adequate and appropriate measures to prevent their travel.

States that have refused or have been reluctant to return their nationals have tried to justify non-repatriation policies by, *inter alia*, referring to repatriation potentially jeopardizing their national security, complicated legal hurdles, insufficient evidence to prosecute them at home, and to repercussions for international relations and foreign policy. Those states may also raise such concerns with regard to the question of whether restitution in the form of repatriation is not "materially impossible". However, the ILC clearly explained that "restitution is not impossible merely on grounds of legal or practical difficulties, even though the responsible State may have to make special efforts to overcome these" and that "the mere fact of political or administrative obstacles to restitution does not amount to impossibility".[414] Such concerns that have been raised by states against repatriation may, therefore, not form an obstacle to repatriation as a means to give effect to the obligation to make reparations vis-à-vis Syria, Iraq, and potentially transit states like Türkiye.

---

412 B. Farley, 'Regulating the Foreign-Fighter Phenomenon' 64 Virginia Journal of International Law (2023) 1: 115, 116.

413 *Ibid.* 101.

414 ARSIWA, commentary to Article 35, para. 8.

8 Conclusions

Certain states' long-time refusal or reluctance to repatriate their own FTFs and associated family members, who traveled to Syria and Iraq to join IS, stands in sharp contrast with other states that have, from the beginning, actively repatriated their nationals and promoted such active repatriation policies on the international level. This chapter aimed to look at the issue of repatriation from a horizontal perspective and answer the question of the extent to which public international law limits non-repatriation policies when such a response leads to the shunning of responsibilities and the shifting of security risks to other actors. It should be noted that this inquiry could have entailed analyzing states' passive behavior towards repatriation in light of more general, overarching obligations under international law, such as the obligation to cooperate in combatting terrorism and the obligation to prevent terrorism. In this regard, it can well be argued that the shunning of responsibilities and the externalization of risks through non-repatriation policies go against these obligations. However, these more general obligations to prevent and cooperate have already been extensively addressed in the previous chapter on the response of nationality deprivation, a response which achieves a comparable result to that of non-repatriation.

In general, an FTF or family member's state of origin is in the best position to investigate, prosecute, and in particular, reintegrate and rehabilitate the FTF or family member, if necessary. That is the state to whom he or she has the closest ties, on whose territory he or she radicalized and from whose territory he or she departed to the conflict zone. Nevertheless, by their refusal to repatriate, states of origin have shunned those responsibilities that would come with repatriation. In addition, through their inaction and passive behavior, they have shifted such responsibilities to other states, and to a non-state actor without the necessary capacity to take on such responsibilities and to deal with the risk of terrorism that those individuals may pose.

Multiple norms of public international law that were discussed clearly speak in favor of states taking active action to repatriate their FTFs and family members and require those states to take the effects of their inactions and passive approaches on the territories of other states into account. Although non-repatriation might constitute a rather easy, cost-efficient and prompt way for states to keep those individuals away from their territory, an analysis of the ancient punishment of banishment and the reasons for its disappearance showed that other states may no longer be used as 'dumping grounds' for other states' unwanted nationals. Unfortunately, the rules of state responsibility do not seem to allow for the necessary flexibility in order to respond to the complex detention situation that was at least in part created by states' non-repatriation policies. Nevertheless, in the exceptional circumstance that a lack of action in preventing the travel of FTFs can be proven, territorial and transit states may have a legal ground to stand on in requesting repatriation from states of origin as a form of restitution, to correct the wrongs that might have been done to them by the presence and actions of FTFs on their territory. Although public international law does not impose a direct obligation upon states to repatriate, the analysis in this chapter still shows that, even when only looking at the horizontal dimension to the issue of repatriation, the most international law-compliant way to act is still for states to refrain from avoiding the responsibilities that would come with repatriation.

CHAPTER 5

Prosecution

1 Introduction

This final chapter will zero in on states' approaches towards the prosecution of FTFs. Security Council Resolution 2178 (2014) clearly obliges states to criminalize certain FTF activity, to ensure that they are brought to justice, and to implement prosecution strategies to that end.[1] This international call for the prosecution of FTFs has resonated at the regional level and has led states to implement a wide range of FTF-related offences.[2] States of nationality seem to face political pressure and a call from the population to react strongly.[3]

This pressure may have led some state officials to appeal for an even stronger reaction than prosecution. For example, in 2017, the British Minister of State, Rory Stewart, said: "I'm afraid we have to be serious about the fact these people are a serious danger to us, and unfortunately the only way of dealing with them will be, in almost every case, to kill them."[4] In the same year, French

---

1 UNSC Resolution 2178 (24 September 2014) UN Doc. S/RES/2178 (2014) paras. 4 and 6.

2 See on the EU level, Additional Protocol to the Council of Europe Convention on the Prevention of Terrorism (adopted 19 May 2015, entered into force 1 July 2017) CETS 217. The preamble to the Additional Protocol explicitly mentions that it has regard to Security Council Resolution 2178 (2014) and, in particular, paragraphs 4 to 6 thereof. See also Directive (EU) 2017/541 of the European Parliament and of the Council of 15 March 2017 on combating terrorism and replacing Council Framework Decision 2002/475/JHA and amending Council Decision 2005/671/JHA, Official Journal of the European Union (31 March 2017) L88/6. Pre-ambular paragraph 5 of the Directive explicitly mentions Security Council Resolution 2178 (2014) and its requirement to ensure that offences related to the FTFs phenomenon are punishable on the national level.

3 In 2017, Sky News conducted a data poll and asked British people, first, whether there are any cases where British nationals who joined IS should be allowed to return without prosecution. Seventy percent of those questioned, answered that all returning jihadists should automatically be prosecuted. Second, they asked what they thought of the maximum penalty for being a member of IS (10 years in prison), without committing any other crime. Fifty-one percent of those questioned were of the opinion that 10 years in prison was not long enough. A. Joshi, 'Sky Data poll: Britons back prosecuting returning jihadists' (*Sky News*, 2 November 2017). Available at: <https://news.sky.com/story/sky-data-poll-britons-back-prosecuting-returning-jihadists-11109878> accessed 24 March 2024. See also C. Paulussen and K. Pitcher, 'Prosecuting (Potential) Foreign Fighters: Legislative and Practical Challenges' ICCT Research Paper (January 2018) 33.

4 K. McCann, '"The only way" of dealing with British Islamic State fighters is to kill them in almost every case, minister says' (*The Telegraph*, 22 October 2017). Available at: <https://

 | HTTPS://DOI.ORG/10.1163/9789004773806-006

Defense Minister Florence Parly said that if French jihadists died in Syria and Iraq, "it's for the best".[5] Likewise, Dutch Prime Minister Mark Rutte expressed his opinion that "Dutch nationals traveling to Syria or Iraq as jihadists are better off dying there than returning to the Netherlands."[6] Finally, the US special presidential envoy for the US-led coalition against IS, Brett McGurk, mentioned that their mission was to make sure that any FTF "will die here in Syria".[7]

Nevertheless, varying numbers of FTFs have returned and have been prosecuted by their states of nationality. For example, out of the estimated 360 to 400 returned British FTFs and family members, 40 were prosecuted in the United Kingdom.[8] Of the estimated 460 returned German FTFs and family members, 140 were prosecuted in Germany.[9] And out of the estimated 377 returned French FTFs and family members, 305 were prosecuted in France.[10] Despite the pressure faced to prosecute, in some states, including in the United Kingdom, a discrepancy can be noticed between the relatively low number of prosecutions and the number of FTFs and adult family members who have returned to their state of nationality. Although there may be a plurality of reasons for this, one of the reasons for this discrepancy may be the myriad of challenges faced by prosecutors when prosecuting FTFs. A significant challenge in this regard is the difficulty of obtaining the necessary evidence from the conflict zone. Authorities fear that, due to a lack of evidence, they will not be able to successfully prosecute FTFs and family members upon

---

www.telegraph.co.uk/news/2017/10/22/way-dealing-british-islamic-state-fighters-kill-almost-every/> accessed 25 April 2024.

5 T. Liabot, 'Florence Parly : "S'il y a des djihadistes qui périssent à Raqqa, c'est tant mieux"' (*Le Journal du Dimanche*, 15 October 2017) (translation by the author). Available at: <https://www.lejdd.fr/Politique/florence-parly-sil-y-a-des-djihadistes-qui-perissent-a-raqqa-cest-tant-mieux-3464891> accessed 25 April 2024.

6 'Rutte: uitgereisde jihadisten kunnen beter sneuvelen' (*NOS*, 5 March 2015) (translation by the author). Available at: <https://nos.nl/artikel/2022943-rutte-uitgereisde-jihadisten-kunnen-beter-sneuvelen> accessed 9 April 2025.

7 'U.S. vows foreign ISIS fighters in Raqqa will "die in Raqqa"' (*CBS News*, 30 June 2017). Available at: <https://www.cbsnews.com/news/us-brett-mcgurk-foreign-isis-fighters-raqqa-will-die-in-raqqa/> accessed 25 April 2024.

8 These estimates are drawn from the Foreign Terrorist Fighters Knowledge Hub, developed by the T.M.C. Asser Institute and the ICCT. The Foreign Terrorist Fighters Knowledge Hub is available at: <https://www.foreignterroristfighters.info/> accessed 24 March 2024.

9 *Ibid.*

10 *Ibid.* It should be noted that these numbers of returned and prosecuted FTFs and family members do not include children.

return or “merely for the ‘safety-net’ charge of membership of a terrorist organisation, usually leading to a relatively low sentence”.[11] Another challenge to the prosecution of FTFs and associated family members in their states of nationality seems to be that states need to have the right laws and criminal offences in place. Although many states enacted FTF-related offences in their criminal laws in accordance with Security Council Resolution 2178 (2014), such as travel for terrorist purposes or entering and remaining in a designated area, those laws criminalizing FTF activity were enacted only after many FTFs departed and “do not seem to have been used by national prosecutors, who prefer relying on well-established and pre-existing offences”.[12] The offence that seems to have been used mainly is participation in a terrorist organization, which is easier to prove but leads to relatively low sentences.[13] These challenges faced by national authorities in the prosecution of FTFs and their family members, and the fear that they would go free unpunished, may have also been a reason for some states of nationality to refuse to repatriate them and to strip them of their nationality.

Potentially for the same reasons as mentioned above, certain states, including France, Belgium, the United Kingdom and the Netherlands, have actively advocated for the prosecution of their FTFs in the region, i.e., in Syria and Iraq. According to the Netherlands, those individuals need to be prosecuted where the crimes are committed because that is where the victims are and where the evidence is located, which increases the chance of successful convictions.[14] Likewise, France’s position seems to be that French FTFs “must be tried wherever they committed their crimes”,[15] and the United Kingdom’s priority “will

11 C. Paulussen and T. Mehra, ‘Evidentiary and Charging Matters in the Context of Prosecuting Returning Foreign Fighters Before National Courts’ in F. Capone, C. Paulussen and R. Mignot-Mahdavi (eds.), *Returning Foreign Fighters: Responses, Legal Challenges and Ways Forward* (T.M.C. Asser Press 2023) 123 (footnote omitted).

12 T. Renard, ‘Europe and Its Returning Foreign Fighters: Overview of the Policy Response’ in F. Capone, C. Paulussen and R. Mignot-Mahdavi (eds.) 2023 (n. 11) 20.

13 *Ibid.*

14 ‘Bestrijding internationaal terrorisme: Brief van de Minister van Buitenlandse Zaken’ Tweede Kamer, Vergaderjaar 2019 – 2020, 27 925, Nr. 688 (16 December 2019). Available at: <https://www.tweedekamer.nl/kamerstukken/brieven_regering/detail?id=2019D52034&did=2019D52034> accessed 24 March 2024.

15 ‘Iraq says it will prosecute French ISIL fighters’ (*Al Jazeera*, 25 February 2019). Available at: <https://www.aljazeera.com/news/2019/2/25/iraq-says-it-will-prosecute-french-isil-fighters> accessed 25 April 2024; see also J. Dettmer, ‘France Insists French Jihadists Should Face Justice Wherever They Are’ (*VOA News*, 16 February 2018). Available at: <https://www.voanews.com/a/france-insists-french-jihadists-should-face-justice-/4257463.html> accessed 25 April 2024.

always be to see whether justice can be done in the region".[16] Similar calls for prosecution in the region came from Belgium.[17]

In Syria, such proposals would mean that FTFs would have to be prosecuted by the AANES, a non-state actor in control of Northeast Syria, where many FTFs and family members are still detained. In fact, the AANES relatively recently announced that they will launch a new attempt to prosecute FTFs.[18] As will be discussed in this chapter, despite the fact that it raises serious challenges, among others concerning fair trial standards, impartiality, independence and the recognition of judgements, the prosecution of their nationals in the region by a non-state actor, is an option that certain states, including France and the Netherlands, seriously look into.

In Iraq, such proposals for prosecution in the region would mean that FTFs would have to be indicted by a state that imposes the death penalty and is known for a lack of fair trial standards.[19] In fact, FTFs from France, Germany and Belgium have already been prosecuted by Iraqi courts and sentenced to death.[20] Despite the fair trial concerns that prosecution in Iraqi courts would bring, and states' abolishment of and opposition towards the death penalty, certain states, including France, actively advocate for the prosecution of their nationals in Iraq.

16 UK Parliament, Hansard, 'UK Nationals returning from Syria, Volume 654: debated on Monday 18 February 2019'. Available at: <https://hansard.parliament.uk/commons/2019-02-18/debates/69E286BB-03A2-4467-AB65-B3059436CD53/UKNationalsReturningFromSyria> accessed 25 April 2024.

17 'Premier Michel wil Syriëstrijders bij voorkeur ter plaatse laten berechten' (*De Morgen*, 18 February 2019). Available at: <https://www.demorgen.be/nieuws/premier-michel-wil-syriestrijders-bij-voorkeur-ter-plaatse-laten-berechten~baae5ee5/?referrer=https://www.google.com/> accessed 29 April 2024.

18 J. Seldin, 'Syrian Kurds Launch New Attempt to Prosecute Captured IS Foreign Fighters' (*VOA News*, 15 June 2023). Available at: <https://www.voanews.com/a/syrian-kurds-launch-new-attempt-to-prosecute-captured-is-foreign-fighters/7139770.html> accessed 19 November 2024.

19 See, for example, Human Rights Watch, Flawed Justice: Accountability for ISIS Crimes in Iraq (2017) 10. Available at: <https://www.hrw.org/report/2017/12/05/flawed-justice/accountability-isis-crimes-iraq> accessed 25 September 2024.

20 'French Islamic State members sentenced to death in Iraq' (*BBC News*, 27 May 2019). Available at: <https://www.bbc.com/news/world-middle-east-48414670> accessed 25 April 2024; 'Iraq sentences German woman to death over IS involvement' (*BBC News*, 21 January 2018). Available at: <https://www.bbc.com/news/world-middle-east-42765106> accessed 25 April 2024. 'Belgium takes back six children of Isis fighters from Syrian camps' (*The Guardian*, 15 June 2019). Available at: <https://www.theguardian.com/world/2019/jun/15/belgium-takes-back-six-children-of-isis-fighters-from-syrian-camps> accessed 25 April 2024.

While it indeed makes sense to prosecute FTFs and family members where the crimes have been committed, not only because it is easier to access evidence but also because it might create a greater sense of justice for victims who are located in the region, it will be argued that there are elements of responsibility shunning and burden shifting visible in this approach to prosecution. This chapter will again approach this issue from an inter-state perspective. It will examine to what extent public international law limits the shunning of the responsibility to prosecute by refusing to return their FTFs and family members, and the shifting of the burden to prosecute those individuals to Iraq and the AANES. Is such an approach permitted under international law, and if so, under what conditions? Or are there important limits that public international law imposes upon states adopting such policies towards the prosecution of their FTFs and family members?

In order to address these questions, this chapter will first elaborate upon the prosecution of FTFs and their family members, who may not be considered FTFs but may still have committed crimes, in several states of nationality. Although prosecutors certainly face a number of difficulties, it will be shown that, in certain states of nationality, FTFs and family members have been successfully prosecuted. Second, this chapter will set out some legal challenges faced by prosecutors at the national level. Because multiple issues surrounding the prosecution of FTFs will be brought together, not all discussions in this introductory part will contain an in-depth analysis. Moreover, it will be argued that this push towards prosecution in Syria and Iraq can be seen as containing elements of responsibility-shunning and risk or burden-shifting. After this first introductory part, this chapter will zero in on a number of norms that may play a role in the way public international law governs this practice. First, this chapter will examine states' approaches towards prosecution in the region under their obligation to prosecute war crimes and terrorist offences. Second, this chapter will analyze the priority that certain states of nationality attach to prosecution in the region in light of the subsidiarity principle. Finally, states of nationality's support for prosecution by the AANES and Iraq will be assessed under their *non-refoulement* obligation. Although *non-refoulement* is a human rights principle dictating that states may not return persons to a country in which they may face violations of certain fundamental human rights, there is also an essential inter-state perspective to this norm, as it regulates the return or expulsion of a person from one state to another.

2 The Prosecution of Foreign Terrorist Fighters and Their Family Members in States of Nationality

Returnees from the first influx of individuals who had traveled to Syria and Iraq, i.e., those who traveled to the conflict zone before 2014, were not always prosecuted by their states of nationality, "either for lack of evidence against them, or because they were not considered a security threat".[21] In addition, in the first years of the phenomenon, women were often seen as "naïve lovers lured to the caliphate through romantic scams" and were labeled as "jihadi brides".[22] However, with the security threat posed by returnees becoming clearer and with more women returning from the conflict zone who were no longer merely perceived as victims, due to the increasing knowledge about the variety of roles they had played in the caliphate, states of nationality started to prosecute returnees more systematically since 2014/2015.[23] This change in approach by states of nationality may also have to do with the fact that IS had established its caliphate in June 2014, and it thus became more difficult for returnees to uphold that they had merely traveled for humanitarian reasons. The present section will discuss the prosecution of FTFs and family members in certain states of nationality and several legal challenges that prosecutors have faced on the national level. In this regard, this section will particularly focus upon Germany, because Germany has not only prosecuted returnees for terrorist offences, but has also been a pioneer in (cumulatively) prosecuting returnees for core international crimes. France will also be focused on because, as indicated in the introduction, France prosecuted a relatively high number of returnees. This section will also try to briefly touch upon prosecution in other European states, in particular states that have expressed their preference for prosecution in the region, including the Netherlands, the United Kingdom and Belgium.

2.1 Germany

Germany saw approximately 1,150 FTFs and family members travel to the conflict zone in Syria and Iraq.[24] The German Government indicated that up until

21 T. Renard 2023 (n. 12) 19.

22 T. Renard, T. Mehra and M. Herbach, 'Introduction' in T. Mehra, T. Renard and M. Herbach (eds.), *Female Jihadis Facing Justice: Comparing Approaches in Europe* (ICCT, 2024) 1.

23 *Ibid.* 2; T. Renard 2023 (n. 12) 19.

24 Deutscher Bundestag, 'IS-Anhänger und deren Kinder im In- und Ausland – Stand: 31. Dezember 2022' Drucksache 20/5589 (7 February 2023). Available at: <https://dip.bundestag.de/vorgang/is-anh%C3%A4nger-und-deren-kinder-im-in-und-ausland-stand

31 December 2022, around 40 percent of German FTFs and family members returned to Germany, whether on their own initiative, through repatriation or by way of expulsion from third states such as Türkiye.[25] The Government also indicated that up until that time, 107 returnees had been prosecuted and 133 preliminary proceedings were still pending.[26] Based on the most recently available information, the FTFs Knowledge Hub indicates that out of the estimated 460 returned German FTFs and adult family members, 140 were prosecuted upon return in Germany.[27]

Germany implemented a number of criminal offences pursuant to Security Council Resolution 2178 (2014). In response to this Resolution, Germany first amended its counter-terrorism legislation in 2015 to expand the provision in Germany's Criminal Code (Section 89a) dealing with preparatory acts of terrorism, to include preparing to "leave Germany for the purpose of committing a serious offence endangering the state", which includes receiving or providing terrorist training.[28] This amendment also criminalized the collecting, accepting or providing financial means with knowledge or intention that these will be used for, *inter alia*, committing terrorist offences. In addition to these amendments, the German Criminal Code (Section 89c) also criminalizes establishing or maintaining relations with a terrorist organization. Forming a terrorist organization, participating as a member, supporting and recruiting for a terrorist organization is also criminalized in the German Criminal Code (Sections 129a and 129b). The most common criminal offence for which both male and female FTFs and family members are prosecuted in Germany is the crime of membership of a terrorist organization. For example, Koller notes that out of the 26 convicted female returnees in Germany as of August 2022,

/295751?f.wahlperiode=20&rows=25&pos=7> accessed 30 April 2024; Cook and Vale estimate that 960 German FTFs and family members traveled to Syria and Iraq between April 2013 and June 2018 and became affiliated with IS. See J. Cook and G. Vale, 'From Daesh to 'Diaspora': Tracing the Women and Minors of Islamic State' ICSR Report (2018) p. 17, Figure 5.

25 Deutscher Bundestag 2023 (n. 24) 3.

26 *Ibid.*

27 FTF Knowledge Hub (n. 8).

28 See for a translated version of the German Criminal Code (*Strafgesetzbuch – StGB*): <https://www.gesetze-im-internet.de/englisch_stgb/englisch_stgb.html#p0965> accessed 8 May 2024.

25 were convicted for membership of a terrorist organization, among other crimes.[29]

Before 2014, returnees were not systematically prosecuted in Germany. Although FTFs and their family members did depart and return to Germany before that time, "it appears prosecutions were uncommon".[30] A reason for the fact that Germany started to prosecute returnees only in mid-2014, could be that the number of FTFs and family members who departed Germany was at its peak during that time.[31] The scale of the problem and the potential security threat posed by these individuals may have become clearer to German prosecutors.

Like in other European states, there is a clear distinction between the prosecution of male and female returnees. Up until 2018, no female returnees were prosecuted. As possible reasons for this delay in the prosecution of female FTFs and family members, Koller mentions "gender-based stereotypes that assume that women do not play an important role in terrorist organizations", "a lack of clarity of which criminal offenses can concretely be used against female IS members", the fact that female returnees were usually involved in less serious crimes than men, as well as the fact that "fewer details were known due to ISIS policy confining women to the domestic sphere".[32] Only from 2018 onwards did German prosecutors begin to shift their attention towards female returnees. The case of Sibel H. has been pointed out as a trigger for this development.[33] Sibel H. traveled to Syria twice, the first time in October 2013, returning to Germany in January 2014, and the second time in March 2016. She finally returned to Germany in April 2018. The German Federal Public Prosecutor General requested an arrest warrant for her, which was declined by the *Bundesgerichtshof,* because merely staying in IS territory was not enough to be

---

29 S. Koller, 'Prosecution of German Women Returning from Syria and Iraq: Insights and Recommendations for Policymakers and Security Agencies' (Counter Extremism Project Policy Paper, August 2022) 9; See also T. Mehra, 'Doubling Down on Accountability in Europe: Prosecuting "Terrorists" for Core International Crimes and Terrorist Offences Committed in the Context of the Conflict in Syria and Iraq' XVII Perspectives on Terrorism (2023) 4: 80. Although this research is not based on German cases only, the majority of cases included in the research were from Germany.

30 K. Braun, '"Home, Sweet Home": Managing Returning Foreign Terrorist Fighters in Germany, The United Kingdom and Australia' 20 International Community Law Review (2018) 3–4: 323.

31 S. Koller, 'The German Approach to Female Violent Extremist Offenders' in T. Mehra, T. Renard and M. Herbach (eds.) 2024 (n. 22) 64.

32 S. Koller 2022 (n. 29) 8; S. Koller 2024 (n. 31) 65.

33 S. Koller 2022 (n. 29) 8; S. Koller 2024 (n. 31) 66.

charged with membership of a terrorist organization.[34] Because women often did not fulfill combat functions or other violent roles in the caliphate, which could be used as a basis for the charge of membership of a terrorist organization, other types of evidence were needed in order to charge women for this offence.[35] Therefore, after the case of Sibel H., German prosecutors have argued that other types of activities, including marrying an IS fighter, running a household in the IS caliphate, having children and thereby contributing to the next generation of IS supporters, the possession of weapons and living in pillaged houses provided for by IS, formed the basis for membership of a terrorist organization.[36] After new evidence became available, Sibel H. was eventually prosecuted and convicted for, among other crimes, membership of a terrorist organization, as it was, *inter alia*, proven that she not only lived in IS territory but also supported her husband's activities by running the household.[37]

One key aspect of the prosecution of returnees in Germany is the cumulative prosecution of core international crimes. Put differently, Germany has become a pioneer in prosecuting FTFs and their family members not only for terrorist offenses, such as membership of a terrorist organization, or other (regular) criminal offences, but also for core international crimes in accordance with the Code of Crimes against International Law (CCAIL). Such an approach "ensures the full criminal responsibility of perpetrators, delivers more justice for victims, and results in higher sentences".[38] Although the German CCAIL already entered into force in 2002, only from 2011 onwards prosecutions of core international crimes started to occur more regularly.[39] This was, among others, triggered by the start of the Syrian Civil War and the opening of so-called 'structural investigations' by the German Federal

34 S. Koller 2022 (n. 29) 8; S. Koller 2024 (n. 31) 66; T. Mehra 2023 (n. 29) 4: 81.

35 S. Koller 2022 (n. 29) 8; S. Koller 2024 (n. 31) 66.

36 S. Koller 2022 (n. 29) 8, 9; S. Koller, 'Gendered Differences in the Prosecution of Daesh Returnees in Germany' in NATO Centre of Excellence Defence Against Terrorism, Gender in Terrorism and Counterterrorism: Gendered Dynamics in Military Effectiveness, Prosecution and Radicalization, Workshop Report (13–15 September 2022) 28. Available at: <https://www.coedat.nato.int/publication/workshop_reports/13-GENDER_AND_COUNTERTERRORISM_REPORT(2022).pdf> accessed 14 May 2024.

37 Oberlandesgericht München, *Sibel H.*, Case 7 St 9/19 (4) (29 April 2022).

38 Eurojust, the Genocide Network, 'Cumulative Prosecution of Foreign Terrorist Fighters for Core International Crimes and Terrorism-Related Offences' (May 2020) 5. Available at: <https://www.eurojust.europa.eu/sites/default/files/Partners/Genocide/2020-05_Report-on-cumulative-prosecution-of-FTFs_EN.PDF> accessed 16 May 2024.

39 J. Geneuss, 'On the Relationship between German International Criminal Law and Counterterrorism Criminal Law' 21 Journal of International Criminal Justice (2023) 4: 841.

Prosecutor General, i.e., broader investigations into a conflict situation in order to gather evidence instead of an investigation into one person and one or more specific crimes.[40,41] A structural investigation into crimes committed by the Syrian Government was opened on 15 September 2011, and an investigation into crimes committed by non-state actors, including IS, in Syria and Iraq was opened on 1 August 2014.[42] German FTFs and family members have, upon return, indeed been (cumulatively) prosecuted for core international crimes. For example, Germany has prosecuted returnees for the war crimes of pillaging, outrage upon personal dignity, inhumane and degrading treatment, killing protected persons under IHL, and child recruitment into an armed group.[43] Returnees have also been prosecuted in Germany for crimes against humanity, including perpetrating or aiding and abetting slavery and rape.[44] Germany is also the first European country to prosecute a returnee for genocide. Besides war crimes, crimes against humanity and membership of a terrorist organization, the German woman Jalda A. was convicted of aiding and abetting genocide for the enslavement and abuse of a Yazidi woman.[45] Koller notes that, in total, twelve female returnees have been convicted for core international crimes.[46]

The fact that Germany has prosecuted relatively many returnees may be due to several factors related to Germany's prosecutorial strategy. First, Germany's structural investigation into crimes committed by IS in Syria and Iraq. Such structural investigations allow for the gathering and securing of evidence for future cases. The active collection of evidence at an early stage through such proactive investigations, for example, helps to successfully identify potential suspects, prove core international crimes' contextual elements or uncover certain patterns of criminality and command structures. As Mehra explains, through structural investigations, "prosecutors can build a solid case and obtain necessary evidence before the perpetrator is identified

40 *Ibid.*

41 W. Kaleck and P. Kroker, 'Syrian Torture Investigations in Germany and Beyond: Breathing New Life into Universal Jurisdiction in Europe?' 16 Journal of International Criminal Justice (2018) 1: 180.

42 *Ibid.*

43 Eurojust 2020 (n. 38), 16–20.

44 S. Koller 2022 (n. 36) 10, 11; S. Koller, 'ISIS Women in Court: Jennifer W. – Taking Responsibility' The CounterPoint Blog (30 August 2023).

45 S. Koller 2022 (n. 29) 12–14; TRIAL International, 'Universal Jurisdiction Annual Review 2023' (2023) 63.

46 S. Koller 2024 (n. 31) 66.

and charged".[47] A different factor that may have influenced the relatively high number of prosecutions of FTFs and family members in German courts is the many Syrian refugees present on German territory, among them victims who may act as witnesses. For example, Yazidi women acted as witnesses in a few German court cases against FTFs or family members, including in the earlier-mentioned case of Jalda A.[48] Moreover, as shown in the previous chapter, from December 2020 onwards, Germany has started to repatriate larger numbers of women and children from Syria and Iraq. This could, of course, have influenced the number of prosecutions of female returnees in Germany. Conversely, Germany still refuses to repatriate male FTFs, which could explain why, together with the fact that many male FTFs may have died in battle, as of 2019, most charged returnees in Germany are female.[49]

2.2 France

Out of all European states, France saw the highest absolute number of FTFs, as well as family members traveling to Syria and Iraq. An estimated 1,910 French nationals traveled to the conflict zone and became affiliated with IS.[50] In May 2018, it was estimated that, in the case of France, there was a return rate of 12%.[51] Based on the most recently available information about individuals who joined terrorist groups in Syria and Iraq, the FTF Knowledge Hub indicates that, out of the estimated 367 FTFs and adult family members that returned to France, 305 were prosecuted upon return.[52] This can thus be

47 T. Mehra 2023 (n. 29) 82.

48 Doughty Street Chambers, Press Release, 'German court hands down second genocide conviction against ISIS member following enslavement and abuse of Yazidi woman in Syria' (28 July 2022). Available at: <https://www.doughtystreet.co.uk/news/german-court-hands-down-second-genocide-conviction-against-isis-member-following-enslavement> accessed 16 May 2024.

49 S. Koller 2022 (n. 36) 28.

50 J. Cook and G. Vale 2018 (n. 24), p. 17, Figure 5; other sources mention a lower estimate. For example, Koller mentions an estimate of at least 1,490 individuals who left France and traveled to Syria and Iraq to join IS. S. Koller, 'Prosecution of Returnees from Syria and Iraq in France Insights and Recommendations for Policymakers and Security Agencies' CEP Policy Paper (March 2023) 6.

51 A. Scherrer, 'The return of foreign fighters to EU soil: Ex-post evaluation' European Parliamentary Research Service, PE 621.811 (May 2018) 32.

52 FTF Knowledge Hub (n. 8). It should be noted that the figures provided for by Cook and Vale in their study from 2018 as well as in Koller's study from 2023 only focus on those individuals who became affiliated the IS, while the FTF Knowledge Hub focuses on "individuals who have left their country of residence or nationality to join terrorist groups in Syria and Iraq".

said to be a relatively high number of prosecutions. Notably, and contrary to Germany,[53] France also conducted 42 trials *in absentia*.[54]

The French Penal Code contains several terrorism offences. Although most of the provisions in the Code were already introduced in the late 1980s and 1990s, a number of those provisions were amended or incorporated in the Penal Code in 2012, 2014 and 2016, in response to French nationals traveling to Syria and Iraq as well as the occurrence of various terrorist attacks on French soil. These offences include direct provocation or public glorification of terrorist acts,[55] apology for terrorism,[56] encouragement to be recruited by a terrorist organization,[57] and preparation to commit a terrorist act.[58] Another provision in the Penal Code that should be mentioned here is Article 421-2-1, which was already incorporated in the Penal Code in 1996. This provision criminalizes the "participation in any group formed or association established with a view to the preparation, marked by one or more material actions, of any of the acts of terrorism provided for under the previous articles".[59] This terrorism offence is also referred to as "association of wrongdoing in relation to a terrorist enterprise" (*association de malfaiteurs en relation avec une entreprise terroriste,* which will be abbreviated as AMT).[60] Multiple studies point out that most French returnees, both men and women, were charged with AMT.[61] AMT consists of three key elements: (1) there must be a group or association with a terrorist purpose; (2) a material act of participation; and (3) the intention to participate while being conscious of the group or association's terrorist aim. A distinction has to be made between AMT as an offence (*délit*)

53 In Germany, trials *in absentia* are not allowed in accordance with Section 285(1) of the German Code of Criminal Procedure.

54 FTF Knowledge Hub (n. 8).

55 French Penal Code, Article 421-2-5.

56 *Ibid.* Article 421-2-5-1.

57 *Ibid.* Article 421-2-4.

58 *Ibid.* Article 421-2-6.

59 *Ibid.* Article 421-2-1. Translation retrieved from: F. Galli, 'Case Studies of National Counter-Terrorism Policies: Case Study of France' in E. Shor and S. Hoadley, *International Human Rights and Counter-Terrorism* (Springer 2019) 375.

60 S. Weill, 'French foreign fighters: The engagement of administrative and criminal justice in France' 100 International Review of the Red Cross No. 907/908/909 (2018) 223.

61 *Ibid.* 10, 11; M. Hecker, 'The French Approach to Female Violent Extremist Offenders' in T. Mehra, T. Renard and M. Herbach (eds.) 2024 (n. 22) 44; R. Mignot-Mahdavi, 'The Lack of Individualisation of Sentences and Their Enforcement at the Expense of Reintegration in France' in F. Capone, C. Paulussen and R. Mignot-Mahdavi (eds.) 2023 (n. 11) 183; S. Weill 2018 (n. 60) 223; H. Decœur, 'The Criminalisation of Armed Jihad under French Law: Guilt by Association in the Age of Enemy Criminal Law' 25 European Journal of Crime, Criminal Law and Criminal Justice (2017) 306.

and AMT as a felony (*crime*). AMT as an offence is punishable by up to 10 years in prison. AMT as a felony is punishable by up to 30 years in prison for participation and life imprisonment for leadership roles in the group. Until 2016, returnees from Syria and Iraq were prosecuted for AMT as an offence.[62] However, from April 2016 onwards, all returnees are systematically prosecuted for AMT as a felony.[63] Although not committed by returnees from Syria or Iraq, the Charlie Hebdo attack on 7 January 2015 is pointed out as a reason for this policy change.[64] This shift in France's prosecution policy means that returnees face much higher prison sentences.

It seems that the number of prosecutions of French FTFs and family members exponentially increased as more of them returned to France and more information became available on the scale of the phenomenon and the threat those individuals potentially posed. Another reason that has most likely influenced France's turn to more systematically prosecuting returnees is the heightened security threat level in the country after a number of large-scale terrorist attacks. Those include the Charlie Hebdo attack, the series of attacks in Paris at, among other locations, the Bataclan theater on 13 November 2015, and the 14 July 2016 attack on the Promenades des Anglais in Nice. IS took responsibility for most of these attacks, and a number of those who carried out the attacks in Paris on 13 November 2015 were returnees from the conflict zone in Syria and Iraq. The amount of cases involving Islamist terrorism under investigation in France went up from 26 in 2013 to 136 in 2015, and 324 in September 2016.[65]

However, as was the case in Germany, female returnees were not systematically investigated and prosecuted upon their return to France until around 2016/2017. Although approximately a third of those French nationals who traveled to Syria and Iraq were women, they were seen "as naïve or ignorant, lured by their (male) partners to travel to Syria and, once in ISIS territory, as only

62 S. Weill 2018 (n. 60) 231.

63 *Ibid.* 231, 232; S. Koller 2023 (n. 50) 3.

64 'Le procureur de Paris François Molins: « Le risque d'attentat est renforcé »' (*Le Monde*, 2 September 2016). Available at: <https://www.lemonde.fr/police-justice/article/2016/09/02/francois-molins-l-affaiblissement-de-l-ei-renforce-le-risque-d-attentat_4991439_1653578.html> accessed 26 June 2024; S. Weill, 'Transnational Jihadism and the Role of Criminal Judges: An Ethnography of French Courts' 47 Journal of Law and Society (2020) 1: 38; S. Koller 2023 (n. 50) 10.

65 'François Molins annonce un « durcissement considérable » de la politique pénale en matière de terrorisme' (*Le Monde*, 2 September 2016). Available at : <https://www.lemonde.fr/police-justice/article/2016/09/02/francois-molins-annonce-un-durcissement-considerable-de-la-politique-penale-en-matiere-de-terrorisme_4991487_1653578.html> accessed 20 June 2024.

fulfilling their role of housewives and mothers".[66] As in other European states, including Germany, women were, at the beginning of the FTF flow into Syria and Iraq, not considered as a potential security threat.[67] However, this policy of not systematically investigating and prosecuting women upon return may have started to change after the aforementioned terrorist attacks on French soil from 2015 onwards, in some of which women played an indirect role.[68] In addition, different studies point to the failed terrorist attack by two French women on 4 September 2016 as a turning point in the public perception of female FTFs and family members in France.[69] Inès Madani and Ornella Gilligmann tried to detonate a car bomb in front of a crowded terrace near the Notre-Dame Cathedral in Paris. Although the two were not returnees from Syria or Iraq, this incident clearly demonstrated that, like men, women may also pose a security threat and are capable of plotting and carrying out terrorist attacks. Koller mentions that, as of January 2023, 305 returnees were prosecuted in France, of which 107 women and 198 men.[70] Of those prosecuted, 192 returnees were convicted, which includes 36 women and 156 men.[71]

One final aspect of the prosecution of returnees that should be touched upon is the prosecution for core international crimes in French courts. Like Germany, France started a structural investigation in 2016 in order to collect evidence on genocide and crimes against humanity committed by IS against religious and ethnic minorities in Syria and Iraq, including the Yazidi community.[72] Although the prosecution of core international crimes is possible in France, prosecutions have focused on the terrorist crime of AMT, as it is, among other reasons, much easier to prove.[73] Nevertheless, according to Koller, core international crimes receive increasingly more attention in French courts.[74] The first French FTF who is being prosecuted, *in absentia*, for crimes against humanity and genocide is Sabri Essid.[75] However, his case is still under investigation at the time of writing. Other returnees are also being investigated or charged with core international crimes.[76]

66 S. Koller 2023 (n. 50) 18.
67 *Ibid.*
68 M. Hecker (n. 61) 55.
69 S. Koller 2023 (n. 50) 18; M. Hecker 2024 (n. 61) 44, 45.
70 S. Koller 2023 (n. 50) 13.
71 *Ibid.*
72 Eurojust 2020 (n. 38) 21, 22.
73 M. Hecker 2024 (n. 61) 46; S. Weill 2018 (n. 60) 234, 235.
74 S. Koller 2023 (n. 50) 3.
75 TRIAL International 2023 (n. 45) 48.
76 See, for example, 'France charges ex-wife of top IS group official with crimes against humanity' (*France 24*, 28 April 2024). Available at: <https://www.france24.com/en/

2.3 Other (European) States

Belgium saw an estimated number of 498 nationals travel to the conflict zone to join IS.[77] Including those who joined other terrorist organizations, approximately 140 adult FTFs and family members returned to Belgium in various ways.[78] During the first wave of FTFs and family members traveling to Syria and Iraq, Belgian authorities were more lenient and did not systematically investigate and prosecute returnees, both male and female. Although this more lenient approach already started to change progressively in 2013, Renard notes that the May 2014 terrorist attack on the Jewish Museum in Brussels fundamentally changed this policy, at least with regard to male returnees.[79] Only from 2015 onwards, female FTFs and family members started to be systematically investigated and prosecuted upon return to Belgium.[80] Although it is not clear how many of them concern returned FTFs and family members, Renard and Coolsaet note that "[t]errorism investigations have indeed increased considerably, from 60 in 2012 to 313 in 2015, before decreasing to 280 in 2016 and 250 in 2017".[81] Because court judgements are not publicly available in Belgium, it is not clear how many Belgian returnees have exactly been prosecuted. However, Renard estimates that "about 70 percent of the Belgian returnees were prosecuted".[82] Notably, it is said that out of those European states that have conducted trials *in absentia*, Belgium has

europe/20240428-france-charges-ex-wife-of-top-is-group-official-with-crimes-against-humanity> accessed 26 June 2024.

77 J. Cook and G. Vale 2018 (n. 24), p. 17, Figure 5.

78 FTF Knowledge Hub (n. 8). It should again be noted that the figures provided for by Cook and Vale in their study from 2018 only focus on those individuals who became affiliated the IS, while the FTF Knowledge Hub focusses on "individuals who have left their country of residence or nationality to join terrorist groups in Syria and Iraq". Among those 140 adult FTFs and family members who have returned to Belgium are thus individuals who have joined other groups than IS.

79 T. Renard, 'The Belgian Approach to Female Violent Extremist Offenders' in T. Mehra, T. Renard and M. Herbach (eds.) 2024 (n. 22) 20; see also T. Renard and R. Coolsaet, 'From the Kingdom to the Caliphate and Back: Returnees in Belgium' in T. Renard and R. Coolsaet, 'Returnees: who are they, why are they (not) coming back and how should we deal with them?' Egmont Paper 101 (February 2018) 24. Available at: <https://www.egmontinstitute.be/app/uploads/2018/02/egmont.papers.101_online_v1-3.pdf> accessed 1 July 2024.

80 T. Renard 2024 (n. 79) 20; T. Renard and R. Coolsaet 2018 (n. 79) 25.

81 T. Renard and R. Coolsaet 2018 (n. 79) 30.

82 T. Renard 2023 (n. 12) 19.

prosecuted the most FTFs in their absence.[83] Belgium incorporated a number of new offences in its Criminal Code in 2013, 2015, 2016, and 2017, including incitement to terrorism,[84] travel for terrorist purposes,[85] and preparation of terrorist acts.[86] However, the most common offence for which these Belgian returnees are prosecuted seems to be that of participation in a terrorist organization.[87] Regarding the prosecution of core international crimes, so far, no Belgian FTFs or family members have been reported to be (cumulatively) charged with such crimes.

By contrast, the Netherlands did prosecute returnees for core international crimes. The Netherlands saw approximately 300 FTFs and family members travel to the conflict zone, who became affiliated with IS.[88] An estimated total of 90 Dutch adults have returned so far.[89] Although no exact numbers are mentioned, the Dutch Minister of Justice and Security clarified in a report from June 2024 that most returnees have been sentenced to time in prison or are still being prosecuted.[90] Mentioning a more exact number concerning women, Mehra notes that as of 15 July 2023, 28 female violent extremist offenders have been prosecuted in the Netherlands, 19 of whom traveled to the conflict zone in Syria and Iraq.[91] In addition, a "significant number of women are still being investigated and are awaiting trial".[92] Like in Germany, France and Belgium, female returnees were not systematically prosecuted during the first wave of FTFs and family members returning from the conflict zone. With regard to women, Mehra notes that only from 2015/2016 onwards

83 Z. Heij, 'Trials in absentia of foreign terrorist fighters in the Netherlands and Belgium' 4 Crimmigratie & Recht (2020) 1: 59.

84 Belgian Criminal Code, Article 140bis.

85 *Ibid.* Article 140sexies.

86 *Ibid.* Article 140septies.

87 *Ibid.* Article 140; T. Renard 2024 (n. 79) Figure 2.3, p. 23. S. Wittendorp and E. Bakker, 'Inventarisatie Rechtszaken tegen Jihadistische Buitenlandse Strijders: een Vergelijking tussen Nederland, België, Denemarken, Duitsland, Frankrijk, het VK en de VS' Institute of Security and Global Affairs (ISGA) Report (December 2017) 40. Available at: <https://scholarlypublications.universiteitleiden.nl/handle/1887/62015> accessed 1 July 2024.

88 J. Cook and G. Vale 2018 (n. 24), p. 17, Figure 5.

89 FTF Knowledge Hub (n. 8). Again, this number of returnees also includes individuals who joined other groups than IS.

90 Ministry of Justice and Security, Zesde rapportage uitreizigers, No. 5 4 52958 (17 June 2024). Available at: <https://www.rijksoverheid.nl/documenten/kamerstukken/2024/06/17/tk-zesde-rapportage-uitreizigers> accessed 3 July 2024.

91 T. Mehra, 'The Dutch Approach to Female Violent Extremist Offenders' in T. Mehra, T. Renard and M. Herbach (eds.) 2024 (n. 22) 95, 96 and Figure 5.2.

92 *Ibid.* 97.

an active policy was adopted by the Prosecutor's Office of investigating and, if possible, prosecuting female returnees.[93] For the first few years, like in the other states discussed, there thus seems to be a discrepancy between the treatment of male and female FTFs and family members upon return in the Netherlands. In addition to possible other offences, such as child neglect and core international crimes, the Public Prosecutor charges all Dutch FTFs and family members with both participation in a terrorist organization and preparation of terrorist offences.[94] Like Germany, the Netherlands has charged returnees with core international crimes.[95] In December 2024, a Dutch court sentenced a female returnee to ten years in prison for the slavery of a Yazidi woman as a crime against humanity.[96] Other returnees have, besides terrorist offences, been prosecuted for the war crime of outrage upon personal dignity.[97]

A final state that will briefly be touched upon is the United Kingdom. The UK saw approximately 850 FTFs and family members travel to Syria and Iraq to join IS.[98] So far, an estimated total of 360 to 400 have returned.[99] Although the Government has repeatedly said that "it would seek to prosecute anyone who has travelled abroad to engage in terrorism related activity",[100] only around 40 returnees have been "successfully prosecuted so far".[101] Thus, only approximately 10% of British returnees have been prosecuted at home.[102] This can be said to be a relatively low number of returnees facing trial, especially

93 *Ibid.* 98; B. van Ginkel and S. Minks, 'Addressing the Challenges of Returnees: Threat Perception, Policies and Practices in the Netherlands' in T. Renard and R. Coolsaet 2018 (n. 79) 65.

94 T. Mehra 2024 (n. 91) 98; B. van Gestel, 'Bestraffing van Syriëgangers' 69 Ars Aequi (November 2020) 1007; Dutch Criminal Code, Articles 96 and 140a.

95 T. Mehra 2023 (n. 29) 88.

96 District Court of The Hague, ECLI:NL:RBDHA:2024:20594 (11 December 2024).

97 Eurojust 2020 (n. 38) 20.

98 J. Cook and G. Vale 2018 (n. 24) p. 17, Figure 5.

99 FTF Knowledge Hub (n. 8); Again, this number of returnees also includes individuals who joined other groups than IS.

100 J. Dawson, 'Shamima Begum: What powers exist to deal with returning foreign fighters?' House of Commons Library (20 February 2019). Available at: <https://commonslibrary.parliament.uk/shamima-begum-what-powers-exist-to-deal-with-returning-foreign-fighters/> accessed 4 July 2024.

101 L. Dearden, 'Only one in 10 jihadis returning from Syria prosecuted, figures reveal' (*The Independent*, 21 February 2019). Available at: < https://www.independent.co.uk/news/uk/home-news/shamima-begum-isis-return-uk-syria-jihadis-terror-threat-prosecute-nationality-a8790991.html> accessed 4 July 2024; see also T. Renard 2023 (n. 12) 19; A. Efrat, *Intolerant Justice: Conflict and Cooperation on Transnational Litigation* (Oxford University Press 2023) 106.

102 A research conducted by the BBC reveals an even lower number of three percent in July 2021. D. De Simone, 'Man admits sharing Islamic State beheading videos' (*BBC*

given the relatively higher numbers of prosecutions in other states. Among the main reasons mentioned for this low prosecution rate is the difficulty in gathering evidence from a conflict zone.[103] However, it should be said that such evidentiary challenges are faced by most states of nationality, to which we will turn in the next sub-section.[104] The most commonly used crime for which British returnees have been prosecuted is preparation of a terrorist act, contained in Section 5 of the UK Terrorism Act 2006.[105] So far, the UK has not yet prosecuted returnees for core international crimes.

2.4 Legal Challenges

As was seen in the previous sub-sections, the prosecution of FTFs and their family members at the national level differs. Nevertheless, national prosecutors have faced similar challenges in building their cases against returnees. Before we delve into the horizontal dimension, we will discuss a number of legal challenges that prosecutors have faced at the national level. However, given the range of legal issues addressed in this section, not all can be analyzed in equal depth.

2.4.1 Evidentiary Challenges

One of the most significant challenges faced by prosecutors in the investigation and prosecution of FTFs and family members in the national courts of their home states is obtaining the necessary evidence. Several factors contribute to the difficulty of collecting relevant, reliable and admissible evidence in this context. First, although such evidence may not be necessary for all types of charges, it may not be possible to physically travel to conflict-ridden, chaotic or insecure areas to collect evidence. Such missions would at least involve

---

News, 29 July 2021). Available at: <https://www.bbc.com/news/uk-58012430> accessed 4 July 2024.

103 C. Walker, 'Foreign Terrorist Fighters and UK Counter Terrorism Laws' in J. Rehman and A. Shahid (eds.), *The Asian Yearbook of Human Rights and Humanitarian Law Vol. 2* (Brill Nijhoff 2018) 187.

104 See also J. Hall KC, 'Returning from Islamic State: Risk and Response' Independent Reviewer of Terrorism Legislation, Speech at King's College London (27 February 2023) para. 32. Available at: <https://terrorismlegislationreviewer.independent.gov.uk/wp-content/uploads/2023/02/KCL-Speech-final1.pdf> accessed 4 July 2024; K. Braun 2018 (n. 30) 325.

105 See, T. Gherbaoui, *Europe's Foreign Fighter Conundrum: Legal Responses, the Rule of Law, and Human Rights* (T.M.C. Asser Press 2025) 134–136; C. Walker 2018 (n. 103) 186, 188.

significant security risks.[106] This makes it not only challenging to obtain physical evidence, but also to collect witness statements or identify victims in areas where the crimes have been committed. Second, many states do not have diplomatic relations with Syria and do not recognize the Assad government as the legitimate authority in Syria. This makes it impossible for states that want to prosecute their FTFs and family members at home to enter into judicial cooperation agreements with Syria.[107] The same goes for evidence located in other areas not under the control of any legitimate government, such as Northeast Syria. For example, judicial cooperation with the AANES is a complex matter as it is not a recognized state. Furthermore, some states fear that cooperation with the AANES would sever diplomatic relations with Türkiye.[108] Third, instead of relying on evidence located in volatile areas abroad, prosecutors might want to rely on information found on the internet, such as photos, videos and posts on social media.[109] However, using information found on the internet as evidence comes with its own challenges. Those challenges include the difficulty of proving the authenticity and reliability of a photo or social media post. It is a difficult exercise to precisely determine the time, date and location of the internet-based evidence and to prove that it has not been manipulated.[110] In addition, "open source evidence is not only easily manipulated, but it can also be readily removed on the basis of algorithms and machine learning technology from the servers of social media companies like Facebook, YouTube and Twitter, thus possibly removing evidence" based on which FTFs and their family members can be successfully prosecuted in their home states.[111] Finally, prosecutors might want to build their case based on

106 T. Mehra, 'Bringing (Foreign) Terrorist Fighters to Justice in a Post-ISIS Landscape Part III: Collecting Evidence from Conflict Situations' ICCT Perspective (12 June 2018); B. van Ginkel, 'Prosecuting Foreign Terrorist Fighters: What Role for the Military?' ICCT Policy Brief (9 May 2016) 7.

107 B. van Ginkel, C. Paulussen and T. Mehra, 'Diversifying the Sources of Evidence in Terrorism Cases before Criminal Courts in (Post-)Conflict and High-Risk Situations: The Role of the Military' in J. Ohlin, C. Finkelstein, C. Fuller (et al.), *Between Crime and War: Hybrid Legal Frameworks for Asymmetric Conflict* (Oxford University Press 2022) 498; B. van Ginkel 2016 (n. 106) 7.

108 B. van Ginkel, C. Paulussen and T. Mehra 2022 (n. 107) 498.

109 K. Aksamitowska, 'Digital Evidence in Domestic Core International Crimes Prosecutions: Lessons Learned from Germany, Sweden, Finland and the Netherlands' 19 Journal of International Criminal Justice (2021) 1: 191.

110 K. Aksamitowska 2021 (n. 109) 198, 199; C. Paulussen and T. Mehra 2023 (n. 11) 130.

111 C. Paulussen and T. Mehra 2023 (n. 11) 130, 131. See also Human Rights Watch, '"Video Unavailable" Social Media Platforms Remove Evidence of War Crimes' (10 September 2020). Available at: <https://www.hrw.org/report/2020/09/10/video-unavailable/social-media-platforms-remove-evidence-war-crimes> accessed 10 July 2024.

intelligence. This brings additional challenges because, by the principle of equality of arms, the defendant should also have access to the intelligence information in order to be able to challenge it.[112] In addition, intelligence information may not be used as evidence if it will be made public in an open court.[113] These four, are among the main factors why national prosecutors face evidentiary challenges when investigating and prosecuting FTFs and their family members.

As can also be observed in the previous sub-sections, the most common crime for which FTFs and family members are prosecuted in the (European) states that were addressed is that of membership of a terrorist organization. Such a crime is generally easier to prove than, for example, murder with a terrorist intent, let alone core international crimes.[114] The result of these evidentiary obstacles is thus that returnees are often prosecuted for what van Ginkel, Paulussen and Mehra call "lesser" crimes, such as membership of a terrorist organization, preparation of terrorist offences or incitement to terrorism, instead of the actual crimes that they may have committed in the conflict zone.[115] These, so to speak, 'safety-net charges' often lead to relatively low sentences.[116] According to a Europol report from 2017, the average sentence for jihadists across EU Members states was five years in prison.[117]

2.4.2 Trials in Absentia

Besides evidentiary challenges, another difficulty is the question of what to do with those who are still (believed to be) in the region and the possibility of trials *in absentia*. Prosecuting FTFs and family members *in absentia*, instead of repatriating them and prosecuting them at home in their presence, could circumvent the difficulty of, and responsibilities coming with repatriation. In the FTFs in Syria and Iraq context, trials *in absentia* have been conducted by a

---

112 B. van Ginkel 2016 (n. 106) 8; K. Braun, 'Prospects and challenges of prosecuting foreign fighters in Australia' Australian Strategic Policy Institute, Counterterrorism Yearbook (2020) 41.

113 K. Hardy, 'Why is it so difficult to prosecute returning fighters?' (*SBS News*, 11 August 2017). Available at: <https://www.sbs.com.au/news/article/why-is-it-so-difficult-to-prosecute-returning-fighters/vx3wfakjb> accessed 10 July 2024.

114 B. van Ginkel, C. Paulussen and T. Mehra 2022 (n. 107) 499.

115 *Ibid.* 516.

116 C. Paulussen and T. Mehra 2023 (n. 11) 123.

117 Europol, 'European Union Terrorism Situation and Trend Report' (2017) 52. Available at: <https://www.europol.europa.eu/sites/default/files/documents/tesat2017.pdf> accessed 11 July 2024.

number of states, including France, the Netherlands and Belgium.[118] Other states, including Germany, do not allow for trials to take place in the absence of the accused.

Although international law provides a suspect with a clear right to be present at trial, proceedings *in absentia* are not necessarily in violation of that right, as long as specific limits or conditions are guaranteed. Article 14(3)(d) of the ICCPR stipulates that everyone shall be entitled to "be tried in his presence".[119] Although not mentioned explicitly, the right to a fair trial contained in Article 6 of the ECHR has been interpreted to provide for a similar right as "the object and purpose of the Article taken as a whole show that the person charged with a criminal offence is entitled to take part in the hearing".[120] Despite being controversial in light of the human right to a fair trial, trials *in absentia* are not prohibited per se. The Human Rights Committee determined that trials *in absentia* are permitted "in the interest of the proper administration of justice", when suspects "decline to exercise their right to be present".[121] However, such proceedings are only in compliance with Article 14(3)(d) if "the necessary steps are taken to summon accused persons in a timely manner and to inform them beforehand about the date and place of their trial and to request their attendance".[122] Likewise, the ECtHR held that "neither the letter nor the spirit of Article 6 of the Convention prevents a person from waiving of his own free will, either expressly or tacitly, the entitlement to the guarantees

118 The biggest case in Europe in which suspects were prosecuted *in absentia* is the Belgian Sharia4Belgium case. In this case, 46 members of the Sharia4Belgium group, which was labeled by a Belgian judge as a terrorist organization, were prosecuted. Of those 46, 36 were prosecuted *in absentia*. 'Sharia4Belgium trial: Belgian court jails members' (*BBC News*, 11 February 2015). Available at: <https://www.bbc.com/news/world-europe-31378724> accessed 5 August 2024.

119 ICCPR (adopted 16 December 1966, entered into force 23 March 1976) 999 UNTS 171.

120 *Case of Colozza v. Italy* [1985] (judgement) ECtHR App. No. 9024/80 (12 February 1985) para. 27; ECHR (signed 4 November 1950, entered into force 3 September 1953) ETS 5.

121 Human Rights Committee, General Comment No. 32: Right to equality before courts and tribunals and to a fair trial Article 14 (23 August 2007) UN Doc. CCPR/C/GC/32, para. 36.

122 *Ibid.* Likewise, the ECtHR held that "neither the letter nor the spirit of Article 6 of the Convention prevents a person from waiving of his own free will, either expressly or tacitly, the entitlement to the guarantees of a fair trial", and that "where a person charged with a criminal offence had not been notified in person, it could not be inferred merely from his status as a 'fugitive' [...], that he had waived his right to appear at the trial and defend himself". See, *Case of Sobolewski v. Poland (No. 2)* [2009] (Judgement) ECtHR App. No. 19847/07 (9 June 2009) para. 36 and *Case of Sejdovic v. Italy* [2006] (Judgement) ECtHR App. No. 56581/00 (1 March 2006) para. 87.

of a fair trial",[123] and that "where a person charged with a criminal offence had not been notified in person, it could not be inferred merely from his status as a 'fugitive' [...], that he had waived his right to appear at the trial and defend himself". [124] In accordance with the accused's right to defend himself in person or through legal assistance of his own choosing, as part of the right to a fair trial and as contained in Article 14(3)(d) of the ICCPR and Article 6(3)(c) of the ECHR, the accused who is absent has the right to be represented by a lawyer.[125] In addition, the accused "should, once he becomes aware of the proceedings, be able to obtain, from a court which has heard him, a fresh determination of the merits of the charge".[126] Nevertheless, proceedings *in absentia* remain controversial under international human rights law as "trials where the suspect is not physically present and cannot effectively use his or her procedural rights to (cross-)examine witnesses and challenge inculpatory evidence are considerably less likely to be fair ones".[127]

In the debate of whether trials *in absentia* should be conducted or not, a balance must be struck between, on the one hand, the right to a fair trial of the accused and, on the other hand, the public interest and the interest of justice.[128] From the perspective of the latter, there may be good reasons to provide for the possibility of holding trials in the absence of the accused. For example, because victims should "receive prompt redress for the harm they have suffered".[129] Moreover, as the ECtHR stated: "the impossibility of holding a trial by default may paralyse the conduct of criminal proceedings, in that

123 *Case of Sobolewski v. Poland (No. 2)* [2009] (Judgement) ECtHR App. No. 19847/07 (9 June 2009) para. 36.

124 *Case of Sejdovic v. Italy* (n. 122) para. 87.

125 Human Rights Committee 2007 (n. 121) para. 38. The ECtHR has on numerous occasions found a violation of Article 6(1) of the ECHR in cases where the absent defendant was denied representation by a lawyer. See for example *Case of Poitrimol v. France* [1993] (Judgement) ECtHR App. No. 14032/88 (23 November 2993) paras. 32–38. In this case the Court explicitly said that "[a]lthough not absolute, the right of everyone charged with a criminal offence to be effectively defended by a lawyer, assigned officially if need be, is one of the fundamental features of a fair trial. A person charged with a criminal offence does not lose the benefit of this right merely on account of not being present at the trial." See, para. 34.

126 *Case of Colozza v. Italy* (n. 120) para. 29.

127 C. Paulussen and T. Gherbaoui, 'Trials in Absentia of Foreign Fighters and Their Families?' ICCT Perspective (1 August 2022). Available at: <https://www.icct.nl/publication/trials-absentia-foreign-fighters-and-their-families> accessed 8 August 2024.

128 B. Drevet, 'Report on France' in S. Quattrocolo and S. Ruggeri (eds.), *Personal Participation in Criminal Proceedings: A Comparative Study of Participatory Safeguards and In Absentia Trials in Europe* (Springer 2019) 100.

129 C. Paulussen and T. Gherbaoui 2022 (n. 127).

it may lead, for example, to dispersal of the evidence, expiry of the time-limit for prosecution or a miscarriage of justice".[130] There may thus be solid reasons prosecutors would want to prosecute FTFs and family members in their absence, especially if they are suspected of committing more serious crimes. From the perspective of the accused's right to a fair trial, there may be good reasons why the presence of the suspect is of utmost importance. Although the accused who is absent has the right to be represented by a lawyer,[131] without the accused's side of the story being (sufficiently) heard, it is difficult to verify the accuracy of his or her statements and compare them to those of the witness(es) and victim(s).[132] By being present during the trial, the accused is generally in a much better position to defend his or her case. Striking a balance between the accused's fundamental right to a fair trial and the interest of justice may thus be said to be a legally challenging exercise.[133]

Another legal challenge regarding trials *in absentia* is the difficulty in establishing that the accused knew of the proceedings against him or her. The situation of FTFs and family members in Syria and Iraq raises the question of how one summons a person in a conflict zone, especially if the whereabouts of the

130 *Case of Colozza v. Italy* (n. 120) para. 29.

131 Human Rights Committee 2007 (n. 121) para. 38. The ECtHR has on numerous occasions found a violation of Article 6(1) of the ECHR in cases where the absent defendant was denied representation by a lawyer. See for example *Case of Poitrimol v. France* (n. 125) paras. 32–38. In this case the Court explicitly said that "[a]lthough not absolute, the right of everyone charged with a criminal offence to be effectively defended by a lawyer, assigned officially if need be, is one of the fundamental features of a fair trial. A person charged with a criminal offence does not lose the benefit of this right merely on account of not being present at the trial." See, para. 34.

132 *Case of Marcello Viola v. Italy* [2006] (Judgement) ECtHR App. No. 45106/04 (5 October 2006) para. 50.

133 C. Paulussen and T. Gherbaoui 2022 (n. 127). Paulussen and Gherbaoui note that it might also be in the public interest to hold a trial in the accused's presence, especially when it concerns a person accused of a serious crime like terrorism. Such trials "constitute a unique occasion to expose the perverse criminal minds of alleged terrorists and the fundamental flaws in their ideologies. Debunking their ideas in their very presence and in full view of the public would showcase the strength of the rule of law." In this view, repatriating FTFs and family members to prosecute them in their presence would not only preserve their right to a fair trial but would also serve the public interest. With regard to the interest of justice, one could also argue that a trial with the accused being present more adequately meet the needs of victims. As Wheeler argues, trials *in absentia* do not meet all the needs of victims as the accused "often possesses information that is fundamental to establishing the full and complete truth about a situation", an absent accused "cannot apologize for his or her behaviour", and "cannot be punished, thus thwarting the sense of justice sought by the victims". See, C. Wheeler, 'Justice in the Absence of the Accused: Can the Rights of Victims be Fully Vindicated without the Participation of the Accused?' 17 Journal of International Criminal Justice (2019) 2: 429.

individual are unknown. In the Netherlands, the Public Prosecution Service has tried to approach FTFs and family members in Syria and Iraq in three ways. First, by posting advertisements regarding the prosecution of Dutch FTFs and family members on Facebook. Second, by contacting them directly through social media platforms like WhatsApp and Telegram. And third, by requesting family members to forward the summons.[134] It may still be challenging to establish with certainty that those FTFs and family members in the conflict zone had knowledge of the summons.

2.4.3 Relationship between IHL and Counter-terrorism Legislation

Another legal challenge to the prosecution of FTFs and their family members in states of nationality is the relationship between IHL and counter-terrorism legislation. We have seen so far that the prosecution of (returned) FTFs and family members in the national courts of their home states has predominantly focused on counter-terrorism legislation. However, IHL is also applicable to those individuals who traveled to Syria and Iraq to join groups like IS engaged in an armed conflict. These groups are non-state armed groups engaged in a NIAC, and those members who directly participate in hostilities have been referred to as unprivileged or unlawful combatants under IHL.[135] The activities of family members, or those who did not directly participate in hostili-

134 Z. Heij 2020 (n. 83) 56.

135 In IAC, combatants are "[m]embers of the armed forces of a Party to a conflict". See, Article 43(2) of Protocol additional to the Geneva Conventions of 12 August 1949, and relating to the protection of victims of international armed conflicts (Protocol I) (signed 8 June 1977, entered into force 7 December 1978) 1125 UNTS 3. In such conflicts, civilians are those who do not qualify as a combatant. See, Article 50 of Additional Protocol I. Only combatants have the right to participate in hostilities. See, Article 43(2) of the Protocol Additional to the Geneva Conventions of 12 August 1949, and relating to the Protection of Victims of Non-International Armed Conflicts (Protocol II) (signed 8 June 1977, entered into force 7 December 1978). Those persons who directly participate in hostilities but who are not entitled to do so are referred to as unlawful or unprivileged combatants. In NIAC, combatant status does not exist at all. However, members of non-state armed groups who directly participate in hostilities have similarly been referred in literature as unprivileged or unlawful combatants. See for example, H. Cuyckens and C. Paulussen, 'The Prosecution of Foreign Fighters in Western Europe: The Difficult Relationship Between Counter-Terrorism and International Humanitarian Law' 24 Journal of Conflict & Security Law (2019) 3: 541, 542; see also B. Saul, 'Terrorism and International Humanitarian Law' in B. Saul (ed.), *Research Handbook on International Law and Terrorism* (2nd edition Edward Elgar 2020) 201–202. When such persons are captured and/or detained in NIAC, they fall under the protection of Common Article 3 to the Geneva Conventions, Additional Protocol II as well as customary IHL.

ties but are merely associated with the group, can also be assessed under IHL, if their activities are sufficiently connected to the armed conflict.[136] The activities of those FTFs and their family members who joined groups like IS may thus not only be assessed under counter-terrorism legislation but also under IHL.

States' focus on counter-terrorism legislation in prosecuting (returned) FTFs and family members may cause a number of legal challenges. There is an inherent tension between IHL and counter-terrorism legislation. Some acts of terrorism are also prohibited under IHL. For example, IHL prohibits the execution of civilians and persons *hors de combat*, deliberate, indiscriminate or disproportionate attacks against civilians or civilian objects, attacks on cultural property, the use of certain types of weapons, as well as hostage-taking. Besides these general prohibitions, IHL also specifically prohibits "acts or threats of violence the primary purpose of which is to spread terror among the civilian population".[137] Thus, some acts that would, in peacetime, be considered as terrorist find comparable prohibitions during armed conflict in IHL. When violated, the aforementioned prohibitions under IHL are all considered to be grave breaches and thus punishable as war crimes.[138] However, some activities are lawful acts of war under IHL but are prohibited and labeled as terrorist under states' national criminal laws governing acts of terrorism, including attacks on military objectives. Counter-terrorism legislation may thus criminalize the activity of an FTF who is a member of a non-state armed group, like an attack on a member of the armed forces of a state with which the group is engaged in an armed conflict, that is lawful under IHL.[139] The same FTF activity may thus be qualified differently depending on

136 H. Cuyckens, 'Foreign fighters and the tension between counterterrorism and international humanitarian law: A case for cumulative prosecution where possible' 103 International Review of the Red Cross (2021) 916–917: 583; For example, there are women who were prosecuted for the war crime of pillaging as they lived in houses seized by IS after the lawful owners fled the area during the armed conflict. Eurojust 2020 (n. 38) 17–18.

137 Additional Protocol I, Article 51(2); ICRC, Customary IHL Database, Rule 2. Violence Aimed at Spreading Terror among the Civilian Population. Available at: <https://ihl-databases.icrc.org/en/customary-ihl/v1/rule2> accessed 14 August 2024. See also B. Saul 2020 (n. 134) 205–208.

138 H. Cuyckens and C. Paulussen 2019 (n. 135) 545. See also H-P Gasser, 'Acts of terror, "terrorism" and international humanitarian law' 84 International Review of the Red Cross (2002) 847.

139 T. Van Poecke and H. Cuyckens, 'The Qualification of the Activities of (Returned) Foreign Fighters Under National Criminal Law' in F. Capone, C. Paulussen and R. Mignot-Mahdavi (eds.) 2023 (n. 11) 149.

the lens of the applicable regime through which it is looked at.[140] This is problematic because prosecuting members of non-state armed groups for acts of terrorism, regardless of whether they acted in compliance with IHL, risks undermining the incentive to respect IHL.[141] Because members of non-state armed groups engaged in a NIAC do not enjoy combatant immunity, IHL does not prohibit states from prosecuting such persons for their participation in hostilities, including for acts which are lawful under IHL.[142] However, because of these compliance considerations, IHL does discourage the prosecution of members of a non-state armed group for lawful acts of war.[143]

In order to prevent acts which are permitted under IHL from being prosecuted as terrorist offences, most experts stress that "activities governed by IHL should not be assessed under criminal law instruments on terrorism".[144] This does not mean that FTFs and their family members may not be prosecuted for terrorist offences at all, as long as those acts fall outside the conduct of hostilities. For example, membership of a terrorist organization, certain preparatory acts or training for a terrorist attack upon return to their home state may fall outside the conduct of hostilities, and can thus still be prosecuted as a terrorist offence.[145]

A final question is, then, why has the focus been on the counter-terrorism paradigm instead of IHL when it comes to the prosecution of FTFs and their family members? Literature on this topic indicates that there are three rea-

140 S. Krähenmann, 'The interplay between international humanitarian law, terrorism and the "foreign terrorist fighter" regime' 112 Proceedings of the ASIL Annual Meeting (2018) 307, 308.

141 H. Cuyckens and C. Paulussen 2019 (n. 135) 542–543; B. Saul, 'From conflict to complementarity: Reconciling international counterterrorism law and international humanitarian law' 103 International Review of the Red Cross (2021) 916–917: 166–172; See also B. Saul 2020 (n. 135) 207, 208.

142 H. Cuyckens and C. Paulussen 2019 (n. 135) 542–543.

143 This discouragement to prosecute members of a non-state armed group at the end of hostilities is articulated in Article 6(5) of Additional Protocol II, which is applicable in NIAC and says: "At the end of hostilities, the authorities in power shall endeavour to grant the broadest possible amnesty to persons who have participated in the armed conflict, or those deprived of their liberty for reasons related to the armed conflict, whether they are interned or detained." See also H. Cuyckens and C. Paulussen 2019 (n. 135) 543.

144 T. Van Poecke, F. Verbruggen and W. Yperman, 'Terrorist offences and international humanitarian law: The armed conflict exclusion clause' 103 International Review of the Red Cross (2021) 916–917: 321; see also B. Saul 2021 (n. 141) 200, 201; H. Cuyckens and C. Paulussen 2019 (n. 135) 562, 563; T. Van Poecke and H. Cuyckens 2023 (n. 139) 149–151.

145 H. Cuyckens and C. Paulussen 2019 (n. 135) 562.

sons why IHL has not commonly been relied upon in this context.[146] First, there is the evidentiary issue that plays a role here. As explained above, terrorist offences like membership of a terrorist organization are often much easier to prove than war crimes. Second, domestic judges seem to be less acquainted with IHL. Finally, there seems to be a misunderstanding that IHL leads to impunity. This is incorrect as FTFs who are members of a non-state armed group do not enjoy combatant immunity. However, because of the above-mentioned compliance considerations, FTFs should only be prosecuted for unlawful acts of war. In addition, when it comes to their activities in armed conflict, as well as activities of their family members with a sufficient connection to the armed conflict, they should preferably be prosecuted for war crimes instead of terrorist offences.

2.4.4 Prosecution of Children

Another legal challenge, or rather a dilemma, that national prosecutors may have faced is what to do with those child returnees who were born in the conflict zone or traveled as children, either on their own or brought to the conflict zone by their parents. Children may have been recruited by IS, forced to take part in hostilities or forced to commit crimes. The CRC Committee indeed declared, in its concluding observations on the fifth periodic report of Syria, that it has credible and corroborated information about "[t]he recruitment and use of children in hostilities, including children under the age of 15, some as young as 4 years old, and children of foreign origin, by armed groups and, on some occasions, by the armed forces of the State and affiliated militias".[147] Other sources also confirm that boys have been recruited by IS in Syria and Iraq on a large scale, and girls have possibly been taught how to use weapons.[148] Because of their exposure to IS ideology and violence, as well as their potential radicalization, it appears that Western states have predominantly regarded those children "as young terrorists likely to pose danger

146 *Ibid.* 563, 564; H. Cuyckens 2021 (n. 136) 600–602; T. Van Poecke, F. Verbruggen and W. Yperman, 2021 (n. 144) 916–917: 322, 323; C. Paulussen, H. Cuyckens and K. Fortin, 'The Prosecution of Foreign Fighters under International Humanitarian Law: Misconceptions and Opportunities' ICCT Perspective (13 December 2019).

147 CRC Committee, Concluding observations on the fifth periodic report of the Syrian Arab Republic (6 March 2019) UN Doc. CRC/C/SYR/CO/5, para. 49.

148 National Coordinator for Security and Counterterrorism (NCTV) and the General Intelligence and Security Service (AIVD), 'The Children of ISIS: The indoctrination of minors in ISIS-held territory' (26 April 2017) 13–15. Available at: <https://english.aivd.nl/publications/publications/2017/04/26/the-children-of-isis.-the-indoctrination-of-minors-in-isis-held-territory> accessed 21 August 2024.

to Western societies".[149] This can, among others, be evidenced by states' reluctance or refusal to repatriate children from Syria and Iraq, as was seen in the previous chapter.[150]

This focus on seeing children as perpetrators contrasts with calls from international actors "to treat children associated with armed groups primarily as victims".[151] In Resolution 2427 (2018), the Security Council also emphasized that "children who have been recruited in violation of applicable international law by armed forces and armed groups and are accused of having committed crimes during armed conflicts should be treated primarily as victims of violations of international law".[152] With regard to returning children, including those child travelers who return from the conflict zone as adults, there is a call to treat those IS-associated children as 'child soldiers'.[153] Child soldiers are regarded as victims and not as perpetrators and should therefore not bear criminal responsibility.[154] Instead, in such cases, liability lies with the

149 C. Nyamutata, 'Young Terrorists or Child Soldiers? ISIS Children, International Law and Victimhood' 25 Journal of Conflict & Security Law (2020) 2: 241.

150 H. Duffy, '"Foreign Terrorist Fighters": A Human Rights Approach?' 29 Security and Human Rights (2018) 168, 169; United Nations Interregional Crime and Justice Research Institute, 'Children and Counter-Terrorism' (2016) 77. Available at: <https://unicri.it/report-children-and-counter-terrorism> accessed 21 August 2024; J. Becker, 'Some Child Soldiers Get Rehabilitation, Others Get Prison' Human Rights Watch (4 March 2019). Available at: <https://www.hrw.org/news/2019/03/04/some-child-soldiers-get-rehabilitation-others-get-prison> accessed 21 August 2024; F. Capone, 'The Status of Foreign Fighters' Family Members Under Counter-Terrorism Law and International Humanitarian Law: Overcoming the Victims/Perpetrators Dichotomy?' in F. Capone, C. Paulussen and R. Mignot-Mahdavi (eds.) (2023) (n. 11) 55, 56.

151 Human Rights Council, 'Annual report of the Special Representative of the Secretary-General for Children and Armed Conflict' (28 December 2015) UN Doc. A/HRC/31/19, para. 65; see also, UNICEF, 'The Paris Principles: Principles and Guidelines on Children Associated with Armed Forced or Armed Groups' (February 2007) para. 3.6. Available at: <https://www.unicef.org/mali/media/1561/file/ParisPrinciples.pdf> accessed 21 August 2024.

152 UNSC Resolution 2427 (9 July 2018) UN Doc. S/RES/2427 (2018) para. 20. See also R. van Ark, D. Prabhat and F. Gordon, *Children's Rights, 'Foreign Fighters' and Counter-Terrorism: Children of Nowhere* (Edward Elgar 2024).

153 C. Nyamutata 2020 (n. 149) 245–251; C. Rigotti and J. Zomignani Barboza, 'Unfolding the case of returnees: How the European Union and its member States are addressing the return of foreign fighters and their families' 103 International Review of the Red Cross (2021) 916–917: 697–699; F. Capone, 'Child Soldiers: The Expanding Practice of Minors Recruited to Become Foreign Fighters' in A. de Guttry, F. Capone and C. Paulussen (eds.), *Foreign Fighters under International Law and Beyond* (T.M.C. Asser Press 2016) 187–204.

154 The Paris Principles (n. 151) para. 3.6; Optional Protocol to the Convention on the Rights of the Child on the involvement of children in armed conflict (adopted 25 May 2000, entered into force 12 February 2002) 2173 UNTS 222; CRC, Article 39.

recruiter, as conscripting and enlisting child soldiers is a war crime under international law.[155]

In each case involving a child, prosecutors thus face a complex dilemma between victimization and perpetration. Paulussen and Pitcher note that in cases involving children, "it may be necessary to seriously consider the value of prosecution".[156] As Capone notes, "[e]specially in the case of children, [...] the focus should be on prevention, reintegration and disengagement, not on punishment and deterrence".[157] Nevertheless, there are examples of returnees who have been prosecuted for particularly grave crimes committed when they were still a child. For instance, in 2021, Germany prosecuted Sarah O. Together with her husband, she held seven Yazidi women, one of whom died in captivity. Upon her return to Germany, Sarah O. was convicted for "membership in a foreign terrorist organisation, assault, deprivation of liberty, aiding and abetting rape, enslavement and religious and gender-based persecution as crimes against humanity".[158] Although she was 23 years old when she was convicted, at the time of these offences, Sarah O. was still a child, and she was, therefore, prosecuted under juvenile law.

3 The Horizontal Dimension

These challenges faced by national authorities in the prosecution of FTFs and their family members, and most likely the evidentiary challenge in particular, as well as the fear that those individuals would go free upon return, may have played a role in certain states' refusal to repatriate and their support for the prosecution of their nationals in the region. As explained in the introduction to this chapter, certain states, including France, Belgium, the United Kingdom and the Netherlands, have actively advocated for prosecuting their FTFs where the crimes have been committed; in other words, in Syria and Iraq.

155 Rome Statute of the International Criminal Court (adopted 17 July 1998, entered into force 1 July 2002) 2187 UNTS 3, Article 8(2)(b)(xxvi) and Article 8(2)(e)(vii). It should be noted that the definition of child soldiers under the Rome Statute adopts a lower age threshold of fifteen years old.

156 C. Paulussen and K. Pitcher 2018 (n. 3) 23.

157 F. Capone 2016 (n. 153) 202.

158 Doughty Street Chambers, 'German court convicts a third ISIS member of crimes against humanity committed against Yazidis' (18 June 2021). Available at: <https://www.doughtystreet.co.uk/news/german-court-convicts-third-isis-member-crimes-against-humanity-committed-against-yazidis> accessed 22 August 2024.

The option to create an international tribunal for the prosecution of crimes committed by IS was, and still is, being explored as well. Sweden was the first state to propose the creation of a tribunal to prosecute FTFs, which would be "one effective way of keeping the most dangerous fighters out of Europe".[159] Other European states, including the Netherlands, Norway, Finland, Denmark, Austria, Germany, Belgium, France, Switzerland and the United Kingdom, seem to have shown interest in this proposal.[160] Such a tribunal would "transfer the jurisdiction they each have over members of [IS] to the tribunal".[161] In 2024, the Dutch Government also expressed its intention to take the initiative to establish an international tribunal to prosecute crimes committed by IS, including genocide.[162] However, there seem to be many complications involved in setting up such an international tribunal. Such complications, among others, concern the scope of the initiative, as it would not cover crimes committed by other actors such as the Assad regime, its geographical location, expenses and the way to establish such a tribunal, as the initiative would likely face a veto in the Security Council or would need consent from the territorial state(s).[163] In addition, "[t]he concept ran into opposition because it seemed

---

159 H. Warrell, 'Sweden proposes international tribunal to try Isis fighters' (*Financial Times*, 19 May 2019). Available at: <https://www.ft.com/content/9086250e-7802-11e9-bbad-7c18c0ea0201> accessed 26 August 2024.

160 Those states, together with delegations from the EU and UNITAD, attended an expert meeting on the establishment of an international tribunal to prosecute IS fighters hosted by Sweden. Bulan Institute for peace innovations, 'Establishing an Ad Hoc Tribunal to Bring ISIS Fighters into Justice: Prospects, Limits and National Alternatives' Policy Paper (April 2021) 10. Available at: <https://bulaninstitute.org/582-2/> accessed 26 August 2024.

161 P.A. Nollkaemper, 'Advies Internationaal Tribunaal ISIS' (22 July 2019) 7. Available at: <https://zoek.officielebekendmakingen.nl/blg-894850.pdf> accessed 26 August 2024. Translation retrieved from: S. Rapp, 'SCSL Symposium: A Legal Legacy that Opens the Way to Justice in Challenging Places and Times–Part II' Opinio Juris (15 March 2021). Available at: <https://opiniojuris.org/2021/03/15/scsl-symposium-a-legal-legacy-that-opens-the-way-to-justice-in-challenging-places-and-times-part-ii/> accessed 26 August 2024.

162 'Hoofdlijnenakkoord tussen de fracties van PVV, VVD, NSC en BBB' (16 May 2024) 25. Available at: <https://www.kabinetsformatie2023.nl/documenten/publicaties/2024/05/16/hoofdlijnenakkoord-tussen-de-fracties-van-pvv-vvd-nsc-en-bbb> accessed 14 April 2024.

163 A. Dworkin, 'A tribunal for ISIS fighters?' European Council on Foreign Relations (31 May 2019). Available at: <https://ecfr.eu/article/commentary_a_tribunal_for_isis_fighters/> accessed 26 August 2024; R. Lu Phillips, 'A Tribunal for ISIS Fighters – A National Security and Human Rights Emergency' Just Security (30 March 2021). Available at: <https://www.justsecurity.org/75544/a-tribunal-for-isis-fighters-a-national-security-and-human-rights-emergency/> accessed 26 August 2024.

designed to avoid the states' responsibility to take back their own citizens".[164] As noted by Impunity Watch, PAX and the Syrian Center for Media and Freedom of Expression, "the proposal for an ISIS-only tribunal represents an effort by European states to outsource their responsibility for dangerous or highly vulnerable individuals to a region recovering from decades of conflict with plenty of its own challenges to address".[165]

These obstacles in establishing an international tribunal to prosecute FTFs may have also turned states' attention to domestic prosecution in the region. As set out in the introduction to this chapter, states' continuous calls for prosecution where the crimes have been committed essentially mean that their nationals would have to be prosecuted by the AANES in Northeast Syria or Iraqi courts. With regard to prosecution in Syria by the AANES, the Netherlands is one of the states that actively explored this opportunity, as this could "meet the desire to try ISIS fighters in the region where the crimes were committed, the vast majority of victims were made and the evidence is located".[166] At the same time, it was also recognized that political, logistical and legal problems still hindered prosecution by the AANES. Such issues include, according to the Netherlands, whether the terrorism laws on the basis of which the AANES has tried Syrian IS fighters are in compliance with international legal standards, the AANES's request for financial assistance and expertise to deal with its lack of well-trained prosecutors, judges and lawyers, and the fact that cooperation with the AANES in the prosecution of FTFs might raise objections in light of the principle of non-intervention and Syria's sovereignty.[167] Other objections that the Netherlands also noted included the compliance with human rights standards and the sustainability of the AANES's authority in Northeast Syria.[168] Nevertheless, the former Dutch Minister of Foreign Affairs, Stef Blok, noted that the proposal by the AANES to prosecute FTFs "deserves our serious attention".[169] The Dutch Government

164 S. Rapp 2021 (n. 161).

165 Impunity Watch, PAX and Syrian Center for Media and Freedom of Expression, 'ISIS-only tribunal: selective, politicised justice will do more harm than good' Policy Brief (31 October 2019). Available at: <https://www.impunitywatch.org/publications/isis-only-tribunal-selective-politicised-justice-will-do-more-harm-than-good/> accessed 28 August 2024.

166 'Bestrijding internationaal terrorisme: Brief van de Minister van Buitenlandse Zaken' Tweede Kamer, Vergaderjaar 2019–2020, 27 925, nr. 708 (31 March 2020) p. 2 (translation by the author). Available at: <https://www.tweedekamer.nl/kamerstukken/brieven_regering/detail?id=2020D12276&did=2020D12276> accessed 24 March 2024.

167 *Ibid.*

168 *Ibid.*

169 *Ibid.* (translation by the author).

was clearly "serious about collaboration with the […] SDF and the Autonomous Administration", and the option of prosecution by the AANES "was considered a viable one".[170] France also seems to have reacted positively to the idea of their FTFs being prosecuted in Northeast Syria by the AANES. In response to a repatriation request by a number of French women and children held in SDF-controlled camps in Northeast Syria, the French authorities said that "[i]t is up to the local authorities to decide on any liability of these French adults for offences committed in this territory on account of their membership of a terrorist organization".[171] France's former Minister of Justice, Nicole Belloubet, also said that if French nationals were given access to a lawyer, the AANES could "eventually proceed to trials". Likewise, the UK Government responded to a parliamentary question regarding British citizens detained in Northeast Syria by saying that "[a]ny decision in relation to the […] prosecution of detainees is ultimately a matter for authorities under whose jurisdiction the individuals are detained or located".[172] Although the AANES has so far only prosecuted Syrian nationals, they have relatively recently announced that they will indeed launch a new attempt to prosecute FTFs. Reportedly, they have asked the international community to "provide coaching and support to help them maintain standards of due process such as provision of defence lawyers".[173] Why prosecution by the AANES may be problematic from an international legal perspective and whether there are reasons why prosecution of FTFs by AANES courts should be supported will be elaborated on later in this chapter.

Some states also actively explore the option of prosecution in Iraq. In 2019, a number of French FTFs were transferred from SDF custody to Iraq, after which eleven of them were sentenced to death by an Iraqi court during a trial that reportedly lasted only two hours each.[174] Multiple sources discuss

170 J. Jongerden, 'The Netherlands and the prosecution and trial of Islamic State suspects in Rojava/The Autonomous Administration in North and East Syria' 3 The Commentaries (2021) 1: 148–154, in particular pp. 151 and 153.

171 *Case of H.F. and Others v. France* [2022] (Judgement) ECtHR App. Nos. 24384/19 and 44234/20 (14 September 2022), para. 46.

172 UK Parliament, Written questions, answers and statements, Islamic State: British Nationals Abroad, Question for Home Office, UIN 12905 (5 February 2020). Available at: <https://questions-statements.parliament.uk/written-questions/detail/2020-02-05/12905> accessed 26 August 2024.

173 T. Mehra and M. Wentworth, 'New Kid on the Block: Prosecution of ISIS Fighters by the Autonomous Administration of North and East Syria' ICCT Perspective (16 March 2021).

174 A. Rubin, 'France Hands ISIS Suspects to Iraq, Which Sentences Them to Hang' (*The New York Times*, 29 May 2019). Available at: <https://www.nytimes.com/2019/05/29/world/middleeast/france-iraq-isis-trials.html?searchResultPosition=1> accessed

the key role that France has played in these death sentences by Iraq.[175] Although France "took great care to deny responsibility and avoid publicly discussing that role", "at the very least, France worked to secure the approval of the Kurdish militias and/or of the Iraqi authorities to bring its nationals to Iraq".[176] In addition, France's Junior Interior Minister, Laurent Nuñez, responded by saying that Iraq "is a sovereign state that dispenses justice," and that France has "no reason to oppose having these individuals judged there".[177] In October 2019, French Foreign Minister Jean-Yves Le Drian traveled to Baghdad to persuade the Iraqi Government to transfer FTFs detained in prisons in Northeast Syria, including those holding French nationality, to Iraq to face trial there and be detained in Iraqi prisons.[178] In cooperation with Iraq, the Netherlands also explored whether its FTFs could be prosecuted by Iraqi courts because "trial in Iraq meets the importance that the Netherlands attaches to trial in the region where the crimes were committed and the victims and evidence are located".[179] However, the Netherlands also expressed

---

27 August 2024; Commission nationale consultative des droits de l'homme, 'Avis sur les ressortissants français condamnés à mort ou encourant la peine de mort en Irak' Journal Officiel de la République Française (2 February 2020) 28. Available at: <https://www.legifrance.gouv.fr/download/pdf?id=X_ITR5qVFUPm_4P-l2WtunL207VjIwKzqav-IgcPbmc=> accessed 27 August 2024.

175 W. Fache, 'Jihadistes français jugés en Irak: "Nous ne voulions pas de leur transfert vers un pays qui condamne à mort"' (*France Info*, 12 August 2019). Available at: <https://www.francetvinfo.fr/france/jihadistes-francais/jihadistes-francais-juges-en-irak-nous-ne-voulions-pas-de-leur-transfert-vers-un-pays-qui-condamne-a-mort_3574439.html> accessed 27 August 2024; 'UN expert urges efforts from France for the return of 7 nationals awaiting execution in Iraq' Press Release (12 August 2019). Available at: <https://www.ohchr.org/en/press-releases/2019/08/un-expert-urges-efforts-france-return-7-nationals-awaiting-execution-iraq> accessed 27 August 2024.

176 A. Efrat and D. Richemond-Barak, 'How Alive Is the Anti-Death Penalty Norm? Evidence from the British and French Treatment of ISIS Foreign Fighters' 8 Journal of Global Security Studies (2023) 1: 11.

177 A. Rubin, 'French ISIS Supporters on Death Row in Iraq Ask for Mercy' (*The New York Times*, 3 June 2019). Available at: <https://www.nytimes.com/2019/06/03/world/middleeast/iraq-islamic-state-syria-france.html?searchResultPosition=1> accessed 27 August 2024.

178 J. Irish, 'France's Le Drian to go to Iraq to discuss trials for jihadists from Syria' (*Reuters*, 16 October 2019). Available at: <https://www.reuters.com/article/us-mideast-iran-france/frances-le-drian-to-go-to-iraq-to-discuss-trials-for-jihadists-from-syria-idUSKBN1WV0RG/> accessed 27 August 2024.

179 Tweede Kamer, 'Bestrijding internationaal terrorisme: Brief van de Minister van Buitenlandse Zaken', vergaderjaar 2019–2020, 27925, nr. 672 (11 November 2019). Available at: <https://www.tweedekamer.nl/kamerstukken/brieven_regering/detail?id=2019D45279&did=2019D45279> accessed 26 April 2024. See also, M. Kerres, 'Minister Blok wil IS-strijders in Irak berechten' (*NRC*, 25 September 2019). Available at: <https://www.nrc.nl/

its concern that such trials in Iraq can only take place when the death penalty is not imposed and a fair trial is guaranteed.[180] As shown above, such concerns have already proved to be valid. Not only have FTFs from France, but also from Germany and Belgium, been prosecuted by Iraqi courts and sentenced to death.[181] The option favored by the UK, France and the Netherlands, which have only repatriated small numbers of individuals and which have refused to repatriate all of their nationals and prosecute them at home, seems to be to transfer them to Iraq to face trial there.[182] In exchange, the Iraqi Government has reportedly asked those states to cover the cost of trials and detention.[183] Later on, this chapter will delve more substantially into the Iraqi judicial system and the proceedings by which FTFs have been prosecuted.

It can undoubtedly be argued that there is an element of responsibility-shunning and burden-shifting visible in those states' push towards prosecution in Iraq or by the AANES in Northeast Syria. By refusing to bring back their nationals to prosecute them at home, states essentially shun their responsibility to prosecute war crimes and terrorist offences. In other words, and as will be explained further in the next section, by refusing to return their FTFs and family members, states abdicate the legal responsibility to prosecute those individuals. At the same time, by pushing for prosecution in the region and

nieuws/2019/09/25/nederland-isers-in-irak-berechten-a3974688> accessed 25 April 2024.

180 Tweede Kamer, 'Bestrijding internationaal terrorisme: Brief van de Minister van Buitenlandse Zaken' 2019 (n. 178).

181 'Iraq sentences German woman to death over IS involvement' (*BBC News*, 21 January 2018). Available at: <https://www.bbc.com/news/world-middle-east-42765106> accessed 25 April 2024. 'Belgium takes back six children of Isis fighters from Syrian camps' (*The Guardian*, 15 June 2019). Available at: <https://www.theguardian.com/world/2019/jun/15/belgium-takes-back-six-children-of-isis-fighters-from-syrian-camps> accessed 25 April 2024.

182 A. Dworkin, 'Beyond good and evil: Why Europe should bring ISIS foreign fighters home' European Council on Foreign Relations (25 October 2019); All-Party Parliamentary Group on Trafficked Britons in Syria, 'Report of the Inquiry by the All-Party Parliamentary Group on Trafficked Britons in Syria' (21 September 2022) 32. Available at: <https://appgtraffickedbritons.org/inquiry-into-trafficked-people-to-isis/> accessed 27 August 2024.

183 'L'Irak propose de juger les djihadistes étrangers contre 1,8 milliard d'euros' (*Le Parisien*, 10 April 2019). Available at: <https://www.leparisien.fr/international/l-irak-propose-de-juger-les-djihadistes-etrangers-contre-1-8-milliard-d-euros-10-04-2019-8050656.php> accessed 27 August 2024; J. Stork, 'Iraq proposes 'pay-to-prosecute' for Islamic State foreign fighters' (*The New Arab*, 30 April 2019). Available at: <https://www.newarab.com/opinion/iraq-proposes-pay-prosecute-islamic-state-foreign-fighters> accessed 27 August 2024.

pointing to the primacy of territorial jurisdiction in Iraq and Northeast Syria, states of nationality essentially shift the burden of prosecution to Iraq and the AANES. Others have directed attention to this practice of burden-shifting by using the term 'outsourcing'. For example, in the New York Times, it was noted that "France, a country that prides itself as a champion of human rights and opponent of the death penalty, essentially outsourced the judicial process to Iraq."[184] Stigall notes that European states "outsource the responsibility of prosecution" to the Kurdish authorities.[185] Likewise, Fakih, Middle East Director at Human Rights Watch, argued that "France and other countries should not be outsourcing management of their terrorism suspects to abusive justice systems."[186] Finally, Pugliese called European states' practice of pushing for prosecution by Iraq and the AANES in order to "keep them away from Europe", a "clear-cut unofficial policy of outsourcing".[187]

Now that the horizontal dimension to the issue of prosecution has been set out, the remaining part of this chapter will examine the shunning of the responsibility to prosecute and states' support for the trial of their FTFs and family members in Syria and Iraq, from a public international law perspective. In other words, looking at the inter-state perspective on the issue of prosecution, the second part of this chapter will examine to what extent such responsibility shunning and burden-shifting to another state, or non-state actors such as the AANES, is limited by public international law. We will start delving into this question by examining the international legal obligation to prosecute terrorist offences and war crimes.

4 Shunning the Obligation to Prosecute Terrorist Offences and War Crimes

This section will delve into the question of the extent to which public international law imposes an obligation upon states of nationality to prosecute FTFs and their family members who may have committed crimes. In doing so, this part of the research will, first, look at whether an obligation to prosecute ter-

184 A. Rubin 2019 (n. 177).

185 D. Stigall, 'The Syrian Detention Conundrum: International and Comparative Legal Complexities' 11 Harvard National Security Journal (2020) 66.

186 Human Rights Watch, 'Iraq: French Citizens Allege Torture, Coercion' (31 May 2019). Available at: <https://www.hrw.org/news/2019/05/31/iraq-french-citizens-allege-torture-coercion> accessed 28 August 2024.

187 M. Pugliese, 'France and Foreign Fighters: The Controversial Outsourcing of Prosecution' Italian Institute for International Political Studies (19 December 2019).

rorist offences can be said to exist based on a number of Security Council resolutions and specialized counter-terrorism conventions. Second, this section will likewise examine whether an obligation to prosecute war crimes can be deduced from IHL. Importantly, it will be addressed when an obligation to prosecute is triggered and what such an obligation actually entails. Finally, states of nationality's support for prosecution in the region and their inaction to ensure the trial of their FTFs at home will be viewed in light of such an obligation to prosecute terrorist offences and war crimes.

4.1 Obligation to Prosecute Terrorist Offences

An obligation to prosecute terrorist offences may find its legal basis in multiple Security Council resolutions, including Resolutions 1373 (2001),[188] 1456 (2003),[189] 1566 (2004),[190] 2170 (2014),[191] 2178 (2014)[192] and 2396 (2017).[193] In Resolution 1373 (2001), the Security Council *decided* that states *shall* "[d]eny safe haven to those who finance, plan, support, or commit terrorist acts, or provide safe havens" and "[e]nsure that any person who participates in the financing, planning, preparation or perpetration of terrorist acts or in supporting terrorist acts is brought to justice".[194] As explained earlier in this research, the terms 'decides' and 'shall' are commonly understood to indicate that the Council is imposing a legally binding obligation upon states. Although using less authoritative terms, the Security Council has reiterated this obligation to bring terrorists to justice and deny safe haven in later resolutions. For example, in Resolution 1566 (2004), the Security Council called upon states to "cooperate fully in the fight against terrorism [...] in order to find, deny safe haven and bring to justice [...] any person who supports, facilitates, participates or attempts to participate in the financing, planning, preparation or commission of terrorist acts or provides safe havens".[195] Specifically in relation to FTFs, in Resolution 2170 (2014) the Security Council likewise called upon states "to take national measures to [...] bring to justice, in accordance with applicable international law, foreign terrorist fighters of, ISIL, [Al Nusrah

188 UNSC Res. 1373 (28 September 2001) UN Doc. S/RES/1373 (2001) para. 2(e).
189 UNSC Res. 1456 (20 January 2003) UN Doc. S/RES/1456 (2003) para. 3.
190 UNSC Res. 1566 (8 October 2004) UN Doc. S/RES/1566 (2004) para. 2.
191 UNSC Res. 2170 (15 August 2014) UN Doc. S/RES/2170 (2014) paras. 5, 8.
192 UNSC Res. 2178 (2014) (n. 1) para. 6.
193 UNSC Res. 2396 (21 December 2017) UN Doc. S/RES/2396 (2017) para. 17, 23, 30.
194 UNSC Res. 1373 (2001) (n. 188) para. 2(c) and (e).
195 UNSC Res. 1566 (2004) (n. 190) para. 2.

Front] and all other individuals, groups, undertakings and entities associated with Al-Qaida" and to cooperate in this effort.[196] In Resolutions 2178 (2014) and 2396 (2017), the Security Council repeated the obligation to bring terrorists to justice by explicitly referring to Resolution 1373 (2001).[197] In addition, both Resolutions require states "to develop and implement appropriate investigative and prosecutorial strategies, regarding those suspected of the foreign terrorist fighter-related offenses".[198] It should be highlighted that in these resolutions, the Security Council called upon states to prosecute 'terrorists' and 'terrorist acts' without giving any clarity on what those concepts mean. The definitional deficits surrounding the concept of a FTF are likewise problematic in light of the Security Council's call to prosecute such individuals. Because of the vague and broad definition of a FTF provided by the Security Council, it may not be clear who exactly states should prosecute and, equally as important, who they should not prosecute.

Notably, the Security Council uses less authoritative terms in these later resolutions, as the Council *calls upon* states to bring terrorists to justice. As explained in Chapter 3, although acting under Chapter VII, such wording may create doubt as to whether the Council is imposing a legally binding obligation. Nevertheless, in light of the authoritative terms used in Resolution 1373 (2001), where the Security Council, acting under Chapter VII, clearly imposed a legally binding obligation, it would be difficult to argue that the obligation to bring terrorists to justice is not binding upon member states. As Feinberg concludes, "as a result of Resolution 1373, all 193 states are now legally bound by international law to" bring suspected terrorists to justice.[199]

Besides these Security Council resolutions, another legal basis for such an obligation to prosecute terrorist offences, albeit specific types of such offences, can be found in most specialized counter-terrorism conventions. First, the majority of these treaties require states to establish jurisdiction over specific offences, *inter alia*, when the offence is committed by a national of that state or when the offence is committed on its territory. For example, Article 4 of the Convention for the Suppression of Unlawful Seizure of Aircraft requires states to "take such measures as may be necessary to establish its jurisdiction over the offence [...]".[200] Second, most counter-terrorism conventions also require

---

196 UNSC Res. 2170 (2014) (n. 191) para. 8.

197 UNSC Res. 2178 (2014) (n. 1) para. 6; UNSC Res. 2396 (2017) (n. 193) para. 17.

198 UNSC Res. 2396 (2017) (n. 193) para. 18; UNSC Res. 2178 (2014) (n. 1) para. 4.

199 M. Feinberg, *Sovereignty in the Age of Global Terrorism: The Role of International Organisations* (Brill Nijhoff 2016) 39.

200 See also, for example, International Convention against the taking of hostages (adopted 17 December 1979, entered into force 3 June 1983) 1316 UNTS 205, Article 5; International

states parties to cooperate in investigating and prosecuting or extraditing terrorist suspects.[201] For example, Article 7 of the same Convention imposes the following obligation:

> The State Party in the territory of which the alleged offender is found shall, if it does not extradite him, be obliged, without exception whatsoever and whether or not the offence was committed in its territory, to submit the case to its competent authorities for the purpose of prosecution [...].[202]

This obligation has also been referred to by the expression *aut dedere aut judicare.* It essentially requires "a state which has hold of someone who has committed a crime of international concern either to extradite the offender to another state which is prepared to try him or else to take steps to have him prosecuted before its own courts".[203] Security Council Resolutions 1456 (2003) and 1566 (2004) connect the obligation to bring terrorists to justice to the obligation to "extradite or prosecute", by requiring states to fulfill the former obligation "in accordance with international law, in particular on the basis of the principle to extradite or prosecute".[204] Nevertheless, as was mentioned above, and as opposed to Resolution 1373 (2001), the Security Council did not impose a legally binding obligation upon states in these two resolutions.

Now that the legal basis of the obligation to prosecute terrorist offences has been set out, we should briefly mention its underlying rationale. The primary purpose of the obligation to prosecute terrorist offences and bring terrorists to justice is to make sure terrorists do not enjoy impunity for the crimes they have committed and do not find a 'safe haven' where they remain unpunished. With regard to the obligation to extradite or prosecute contained in the specialized counter-terrorism conventions, it is noted that the main reason why

---

Convention for the Suppression of the Financing of Terrorism (adopted 9 December 1999, entered into force 10 April 2002) 2178 UNTS 197, Article 7.

201 See, for example, the International Convention for the Suppression of the Financing of Terrorism, Article 10; International Convention for the Suppression of Terrorist Bombings (adopted 15 December 1997, entered into force 23 May 2001) 2149 UNTS 256, Article 8; International Convention against the taking of hostages, Article 8.

202 See also, for example, the International Convention for the Suppression of the Financing of Terrorism, Article 10; International Convention for the Suppression of Terrorist Bombings, Article 8; International Convention against the taking of hostages, Article 8.

203 C. Bassiouni and E. Wise, *Aut Dedere Aut Judicare: The Duty to Extradite or Prosecute in International Law* (Kluwer Academic Publishers 1995) 3.

204 UNSC Resolution 1456 (2003) (n. 189) para. 3; UNSC Res. 1566 (2004) (n. 190) para. 2; C. Paulussen, 'Impunity for international terrorists? Key legal questions and practical considerations' ICCT Research Paper (April 2012) 15.

this obligation exists is because we "should not allow criminals to find their own 'safe haven' and avoid prosecution for committed crimes".[205] The underlying rationale of the obligation to prosecute is thus the fight against impunity for terrorist offences.

Considering the above, the question that should still be addressed is what this obligation to bring terrorists to justice or prosecute terrorist acts actually entails. In 2004, the UN Counter Terrorism Committee interpreted the obligation to bring terrorists to justice contained in Security Council Resolution 1373 (2001) as an obligation which "obliges States to prosecute and try all those responsible for acts of terrorism, wherever they are committed."[206] The Committee further went on to say that "[t]his measure is designed to ensure that terrorists have no place of refuge, since each State will be competent to try them or extradite them."[207] However, requiring states to be *competent* to try terrorist suspects, i.e., requiring states to establish jurisdiction, is something different from requiring states to *actually* exercise that jurisdiction unconditionally by prosecuting and trying terrorist suspects. An obligation to necessarily prosecute and try all terrorist suspects would impair prosecutorial discretion in deciding whether to bring a person to trial and may constitute an undesirable strict approach. In addition, such a strict obligation to prosecute and try terrorist suspects is not what is required by the previously mentioned specialized counter-terrorism conventions. For example, Article 10(1) of the International Convention for the Suppression of the Financing of Terrorism states the following:

> The State Party in the territory of which the alleged offender is present shall, in cases to which article 7 applies, if it does not extradite that person, be obliged, without exception whatsoever and whether or not the offence was committed in its territory, to submit the case without undue delay to its competent authorities for the purpose of prosecution, through proceedings in accordance with the laws of that State. Those authorities shall take their decision in the same

205 V. Stefanovska, 'Modern Application of the Principle Aut Dedere Aut Judicare in Acts of Terrorism and Torture' 56 Journal of Criminology and Criminal Law (2018) 44. See also, K. Kittichaisaree, *The Obligation to Extradite or Prosecute* (Oxford University Press 2018) 99–168. R. van Steenberghe, 'The Obligation to Extradite or Prosecute Clarifying its Nature' 9 Journal of international criminal justice (2011) 5: 3.

206 UNSC, Note by the President of the Security Council (26 January 2004), UN Doc. S/2004/70, Annex: Report by the Chair of the Counter-Terrorism Committee on the problems encountered in the implementation of Security Council Resolution 1373 (2001) p. 6.

207 *Ibid.*

manner as in the case of any other offence of a grave nature under the law of that State.

This provision requires states to establish (extraterritorial) jurisdiction over the specific offence,[208] and requires prosecutorial authorities, after receiving a file, to decide in accordance with their own national laws and practices whether to prosecute and try the person.[209] The ILC also noted that "[t]he obligation to prosecute is actually an obligation to submit the case to the prosecuting authorities; it does not involve an obligation to initiate a prosecution. Indeed, in light of the evidence, fulfilment of the obligation may or may not result in the institution of proceedings".[210] Likewise, instead of requiring states to exercise their jurisdiction and bring terrorists to trial, the General Assembly called upon states to ensure that "the jurisdiction of their courts *enables* them to bring to trial the perpetrators of terrorist acts".[211]

The obligation to bring terrorists to justice thus seems to require states to, first, have the necessary national laws and procedures in place to ensure the competence of their courts to prosecute terrorist offences and, second, when a suspect is found on its territory it obliges states to submit the case to their competent authorities for the purpose of prosecution, without "automatic punishment, judgement or prosecution".[212] With regard to the latter obligation, absolute as it is, it "does not necessarily guarantee that a terrorist offender will be brought to justice".[213] Although this obligation does not entail a duty to secure the presence of the suspect on their territory, as such a duty would be excessively onerous upon states, it has been argued that the obligation to bring terrorists to justice does entail an obligation "to make investigations into the whereabouts of alleged offenders".[214]

---

208 International Convention for the Suppression of the Financing of Terrorism, Article 7.

209 S. Betti, 'The Duty to Bring Terrorists to Justice and Discretionary Prosecution' 4 Journal of International Criminal Justice (November 2006) 5: 1110–1111.

210 ILC, 'The obligation to extradite or prosecute (*aut dedere aut judicare*) Final Report of the International Law Commission' in the Report of the ILC on the work of its sixty-sixth session (2014) UN Doc. A/69/10, para. 21.

211 S. Betti 2006 (n. 209) 1111–1112; see, for example, UNGA Resolution 56/88 (24 January 2002) UN Doc. A/RES/56/88, para. 7; UNGA Resolution 57/27 (15 January 2003) UN Doc. A/RES/57/27, para. 7; UNGA Resolution 59/46 (16 December 2004) UN Doc. A/RES/59/46, para. 9 (emphasis added).

212 R. van Steenberghe 2011 (n. 205) 1091.

213 K. Trapp, *State Responsibility for International Terrorism* (Oxford University Press 2011) 128.

214 R. Kolb, 'The Exercise of Criminal Jurisdiction over International Terrorists' in A. Bianchi (ed.), *Enforcing International Law Norms Against Terrorism* (Hart Publishing 2004) 269.

4.2 Obligation to Prosecute War Crimes

The Geneva Conventions and their Additional Protocols impose a number of obligations upon states to suppress violations of IHL. Regarding IACs, IHL dictates that states are obliged to "undertake to enact any legislation necessary to provide effective penal sanctions for persons committing, or ordering to be committed, any of the grave breaches of the present Convention".[215] States must thus, first of all, have the necessary laws in place so that they are *able* to exercise jurisdiction over alleged perpetrators of war crimes. In addition, IHL stipulates that states

> shall be under the obligation to search for persons alleged to have committed, or to have ordered to be committed, such grave breaches, and shall bring such persons, regardless of their nationality, before its own courts. It may also, if it prefers, and in accordance with the provisions of its own legislation, hand such persons over for trial to another High Contracting Party concerned, provided such High Contracting Party has made out a "prima facie" case.[216]

This provision clearly imposes an obligation upon all states, not only those party to an armed conflict, to prosecute grave breaches of IHL. It is also an application of the obligation to extradite or prosecute, which was discussed in the previous sub-section, as it requires states to either bring suspects before their own courts or extradite them to another state. It is made clear that the obligation to prosecute applies to "grave breaches" of the Geneva Conventions and of Additional Protocol I.[217] In this regard, it can be observed that, according to the ICTY, acts of terror, i.e., "[a]cts or threats of violence the primary purpose of which is to spread terror among the civilian population",[218] also qualify as a "grave breach" of IHL.[219] Besides prosecuting grave breaches, Article 49, paragraph three of Geneva Convention I also specifies that states "shall take measures necessary for the suppression of all acts contrary to the provi-

215 Geneva Convention I Article 49, Geneva Convention II Article 50, Geneva Convention III Article 129, Geneva Convention IV Article 146, see also Additional Protocol I Article 85(1).

216 Geneva Convention I Article 49, Geneva Convention II Article 50, Geneva Convention III Article 129, Geneva Convention IV Article 146, see also Additional Protocol I Article 85(1).

217 Violations that qualify as "grave breaches" are specified in Geneva Convention I, Article 50; Geneva Convention II, Article 51; Geneva Convention III, Article 130; Geneva Convention IV, Article 147; and Additional Protocol I Articles 11(4) and 85(2)-(4).

218 Additional Protocol I, Article 51(2) and Additional Protocol II, Article 13(2).

219 ICTY Trial Chamber I, *Prosecutor v. Stanislav Galić* No. IT-98–29-T (5 December 2003) paras. 106–112.

sions of the present Convention other than the grave breaches".[220] Based on this paragraph's text, it remains unclear whether this entails an obligation to prosecute violations other than "grave breaches". The 2016 ICRC Commentary explains that "States Parties will determine the best way to fulfil these obligations" and that they may take "a wide range of measures".[221] It thus appears that states may themselves decide what measures they take in order to suppress breaches of IHL which do not qualify as "grave breaches". In the same Commentary, the ICRC also makes clear that the obligation to prosecute war crimes implies

> that each State Party must provide in its national legislation for the mechanisms and procedures to ensure that it can actively search for alleged offenders, make a preliminary inquiry into the facts and, when so warranted, submit any such cases to the appropriate authorities for prosecution.[222]

The obligation does thus "not imply an absolute duty to prosecute or to punish".[223] Rather, the decision whether or not to prosecute is up to the competent authorities of a state, in accordance with the requirements under national law. As to when this obligation is triggered, the ICRC clarifies that the obligation does not mean that states "must search for and prosecute any alleged perpetrators the world over".[224] Like the obligation to prosecute terrorist offences, the obligation to investigate and, if appropriate, prosecute war crimes is directed towards custodial states and, therefore, triggered when a particular state realizes that a suspect is present on its territory or under its jurisdiction.

Regarding armed conflicts not of an international character, an obligation to prosecute war crimes is neither mentioned in Common Article 3 nor in Additional Protocol II. Still, the ICRC recognized, as a rule of customary international law, an obligation upon states to "investigate war crimes allegedly committed by their nationals or armed forces, or on their territory, and, if appropriate, prosecute the suspects".[225] In addition, states "must also investi-

---

220 See also Geneva Convention II Article 50(3), Geneva Convention III Article 129(3), Geneva Convention IV Article 146(3), see also Additional Protocol I Article 85(1).

221 ICRC, *Commentary on the First Geneva Convention: Convention (I) for the Amelioration of the Condition of the Wounded and Sick in Armed Forces in the Field* (Cambridge University Press, 2016) para. 2896.

222 *Ibid.* 2860.

223 *Ibid.* 2861.

224 *Ibid.* 2866.

225 ICRC, Customary IHL Database, Rule 158 Prosecution of War Crimes. Available at: <https://ihl-databases.icrc.org/en/customary-ihl/v1/rule158> accessed 21 October 2024.

gate other war crimes over which they have jurisdiction and, if appropriate, prosecute the suspects".[226] States are thus not only under an obligation to investigate and, if appropriate, prosecute war crimes in relation to IACs but also those in relation to NIACs, as per customary international law. Furthermore, this obligation does not only extend to war crimes committed on their territory or by their nationals, but to all such crimes. According to the ICRC, customary IHL also dictates that "States must make every effort to cooperate, to the extent possible, with each other in order to facilitate the investigation of war crimes and the prosecution of the suspects".[227] Such cooperation could, *inter alia*, take the form of extradition, exchange of documents and assistance with arrest or investigation. Although it does not seem to be an absolute obligation to cooperate, it is mentioned that there is an expectation in customary IHL "that States should make efforts in good faith to do so, to the extent possible".[228]

Finally, the rationale behind the obligation to investigate and, if appropriate, prosecute war crimes should be briefly mentioned. In its Commentary to Article 49 of Geneva Convention I, paragraph two of which encompasses the obligation in question, the ICRC stated that "[t]he object and purpose of this paragraph is clearly to give all States Parties the means to prevent impunity and to deny safe haven to alleged perpetrators of grave breaches".[229] In this regard, the preamble of the Rome Statute also mentions this aim of preventing impunity by affirming that "the most serious crimes of concern to the international community as a whole must not go unpunished" and that "it is the duty of every State to exercise its criminal jurisdiction over those responsible for international crimes".[230] Besides the fight against impunity, another purpose of the obligation to investigate and, if appropriate, prosecute war crimes that should be mentioned here is that effective penalties for those who violate IHL are an essential way of ensuring respect for this field of law.[231] Therefore, it could be said that the obligation is reinforced by the obligation to ensure respect for IHL, which was discussed in the previous chapter of this research.

226 *Ibid.*

227 ICRC, Customary IHL Database, Rule 161 International Cooperation in Criminal Proceedings. Available at: <https://ihl-databases.icrc.org/en/customary-ihl/v1/rule161> accessed 21 October 2024.

228 *Ibid.*

229 ICRC Commentary 2016 (n. 221) paras. 2864, 2868.

230 Rome Statute, pre-ambular paras. 4 and 6.

231 ICRC Commentary 2016 (n. 221), paras. 2823, 2830.

4.3 Defeating the Object and Purpose of the Obligation to Prosecute

What can be concluded from the previous two sub-sections is that all states are under an obligation to investigate and, if appropriate, prosecute terrorist offences and war crimes. FTFs and family members' states of nationality are thus equally under such an obligation with regard to their nationals, even if the offences were committed abroad. From the analysis above, it can, however, also be concluded that this obligation does not require states of nationality to enforce their jurisdiction outside of their own territory by arresting their FTFs and bringing them back home for the purpose of prosecution.[232] Instead, the obligation to investigate and, if appropriate, prosecute is only triggered when a suspect is allegedly present on that state's territory or under its jurisdiction, which is currently not the case in the context of FTFs and their associated family members, who remain stuck in Syria and Iraq. Nevertheless, it can be argued that by refusing to bring their nationals back in order to prosecute them at home, states of nationality are essentially evading the obligation to investigate and, when appropriate, prosecute war crimes and terrorist offences. In other words, by making sure those individuals stay away from their territory, states do not directly violate the obligation, which is only triggered when the suspect is present on the state's territory, but they do make sure to avoid the obligation to investigate and, if appropriate, prosecute those FTFs and family members. Yurechko likewise concludes that states of nationality, by refusing to bring them home for the purpose of prosecution, are "skirting their obligations" which require them to prosecute all those responsible for terrorist offences and war crimes wherever they are committed.[233]

In addition, it can be argued that by refusing to return their nationals and by pushing for prosecution in the region, by a state which imposes the death penalty and is known for a lack of fair trial standards or a non-state actor without the necessary resources and capacity to prosecute in compliance with international law standards, as will further be elaborated upon in the next section, states of nationality are directly acting against the object and purpose of this obligation. The underlying rationale of both obligations is to ensure that perpetrators of terrorist offences and war crimes do not remain unpunished and do not enjoy safe haven. States of nationality pushing for prosecution in the region by the AANES defeats this object and purpose of

232 See also D. Mckeever, 'Repatriating Foreign Terrorist Fighters and Their Family Members: What International Law Requires, and What National Courts Will Do' 28 Journal of Conflict & Security Law (2023) 1: 97.

233 C. Yurechko, 'Outsourced: The European Union's reliance on external actors in the fight against jihadi terrorism' 24 The Columbia Journal of European Law (2018) 3: 777.

fighting impunity. As a result of this practice, their nationals have remained unpunished in Northeast Syria for years. States of nationality's inaction in bringing their FTFs and family members home for the purpose of investigation and, if appropriate, prosecution and their active push for prosecution elsewhere has provided those suspects with a safe haven in camps and prisons in Northeast Syria, where they do not face justice for the crimes they may have committed. Moreover, even if the AANES were to eventually start the prosecution of foreign nationals, without international cooperation or assistance, they most likely would not have the capacity to do so in accordance with international law, which will be explained further in the next section. In this regard, Cuyckens raises the question whether "having them trialled [*sic*] by a non-State actor would actually discharge States from their obligation to do so".[234]

Pushing for prosecution in the region by Iraq may likewise be said to thwart the object and purpose of states of nationality's obligation to prosecute terrorist offences and war crimes. Someone who is prosecuted by a state that, as will also be further elaborated on in the next section, seriously lacks fair trial standards cannot be said to have been brought to any form of 'justice'. Considering the object and purpose of the obligation to investigate and, if appropriate, prosecute war crimes and terrorist offences, it could be argued that states of nationality should repatriate their nationals to prosecute them at home because that is most likely the only way in which they will properly be brought to justice, in accordance with international (human rights) law standards. In other words, although not legally required by the obligation in question, considering the underlying rationale of the obligation and the importance to make sure that suspects of grave crimes do not go unpunished, it can indeed be said that states of nationality should investigate and, when appropriate, prosecute their FTFs even if that means they have to be brought home for that purpose.

Instead of active repatriation to investigate and potentially prosecute them at home, it could also be argued that states of nationality would act in furtherance of the underlying rationale of their obligation to prosecute, by merely rendering assistance to Iraq and the AANES to ensure that their nationals can be brought to justice there, in full compliance with international (human rights) law. Nevertheless, especially in the case of the AANES, it is questionable whether states of nationality would be willing to render such assistance, including in light of their diplomatic relations with Türkiye, the issue of recognition of judgements and perhaps risks of responsibility for com-

234 H. Cuyckens 2021 (n. 136) 596.

plicity under public international law. As long as the death penalty is imposed, such assistance is equally questionable with regard to Iraq. In sum, considering their obligation to investigate and, if appropriate, prosecute war crimes and terrorist offences as well as the underlying rationale of this obligation, the most international law-compliant way to act seems to be for states of nationality to bring back their nationals and prosecute them at home.

5 Limits to the Primacy of Territorial States' Jurisdiction

This section will examine whether public international law imposes limits on states of nationality pushing for prosecution by territorial states. In other words, it will be analyzed whether there are, or should be, limits to the extent that states of nationality may defer the exercise of jurisdiction to Iraq and Syria. In order to do so, states of nationality's approach to prosecution in the region will be analyzed in light of the subsidiarity principle. The principle of subsidiarity entails that "responsibility for public action, where necessary, lies with the competent body closest to those directly affected by that action".[235] Within the international law of jurisdiction, this principle means that states should refrain from exercising jurisdiction *unless* the state with the strongest link to the situation is unable or unwilling to take adequate measures.[236] In light of a progressive interpretation of this principle, it will be argued that, to fight impunity, states of nationality should not defer the exercise of jurisdiction to territorial states if such states are unable or unwilling to genuinely prosecute. Arguably, in such circumstances, states of nationality should exercise their own jurisdiction over FTFs and family members based on the active nationality principle. Before we zoom in on the definitions of 'unable' and 'unwilling' in international law and to what extent Syria and Iraq may satisfy those definitions, it will be examined in more detail what the principle of subsidiarity entails and how it is applied within the international law of jurisdiction.

235 C. Maia and E. Gardounis, 'Subsidiary Jurisdiction' MPEPIL (December 2021) para. 1; see also I. Feichtner, 'Subsidiarity' MPEPIL (October 2007).

236 C. Maia and E. Gardounis 2021 (n. 235) para. 4.

5.1 The Principle of Subsidiarity as Limiting the Primacy of Territorial Jurisdiction

International law sets out the circumstances under which states can exercise jurisdiction by offering a number of permissive principles that states can rely upon when applying their laws to persons, property and circumstances, even outside of their own territory.[237] These jurisdictional principles are the territoriality principle, the nationality principle, the protective principle and the universality principle. Although there is no hierarchy between those principles, the territoriality principle is generally considered to have primacy, as territorial jurisdiction is viewed as "the fundamental rule" or the "cornerstone" of the international jurisdictional order.[238] This view is based on the principles of sovereign equality and non-intervention.[239] Every state has the sovereign right to prosecute crimes that have been committed on their territory. As mentioned, this "presumption in favour of jurisdiction for the territorial sovereign" does not mean those jurisdictional principles are hierarchically structured.[240] It does mean that the exercise of extraterritorial jurisdiction based on one of the other principles needs specific justification.[241] Put differently, "States are free to assert jurisdiction in their own territory unless a prohibitory rule of international law prevents them from doing so; whereas outside their territory their jurisdictional claim must be supported by an international legal rule that allows them to exercise jurisdiction."[242]

It should be noted that it has not always been the case that the territoriality principle was viewed as having primacy over the nationality principle for the exercise of extraterritorial jurisdiction. As Chehtman notes, "the original conception of law was personal, and [...] only the appearance of the territorial

237 C. Ryngaert, *Jurisdiction in International Law* (Oxford University Press 2015) 29, 30.

238 *Ibid.* 36, 37; see also F. Jessberger, W. Kaleck and A. Schueller, 'Concurring Criminal Jurisdictions under International Law' in M. Bergsmo (ed.), *Complementarity and the Exercise of Universal Jurisdiction for Core International Crimes* (Torkel Opsahl Academic EPublisher and Peace Research Institute Oslo 2010) 238, 239.

239 C. Ryngaert 2015 (n. 237) 36.

240 A. Bianchi, 'Jurisdictional Rules in Customary International Law' in K. Meessen (ed.), *Extraterritorial Jurisdiction in Theory and Practice* (Kluwer Law International 1996) 87.

241 C. Ryngaert, 'Universal Jurisdiction over International Crimes and Gross Human Rights Violations: the Role of the Principle of Subsidiarity' in G. Ziccardi Capaldo (ed.), *The Global Community Yearbook of International Law and Jurisprudence 2015* (Oxford University Press 2016) 276.

242 A. Bianchi 1996 (n. 240) 83.

state gave rise to the right to subject aliens to the *lex loci*".[243] Similarly, Gallant explains that "law has not been based on territoriality always and everywhere" and that "[d]uring the classical period of modern international law, nationality jurisdiction needed no justification – or at least no more justification than territoriality".[244] A concrete example is the exercise of extraterritorial jurisdiction by Western states over their nationals residing abroad in Asia and the Middle East in the nineteenth century. In the Ottoman Empire, China, Japan and other states in the Middle East and Asia, foreign nationals were not subject to those states' territorial jurisdiction.[245] Rather, due to so-called unequal treaties,[246] foreign nationals were subject to the jurisdiction of their state of origin. In other words, "Western powers arrogated to themselves the monopoly of jurisdiction over their own, not, as one might suspect, to lighten the load of dominated nations but, rather, to bypass, in effect, their jurisdiction."[247] That way, it can thus be said that with regard to those foreign nationals, the nationality principle for the exercise of extraterritorial jurisdiction had primacy over the territorial jurisdiction of the state in which they resided. When it comes to the exercise of (extraterritorial) jurisdiction, it thus fluctuates over time whether territorial jurisdiction holds primacy over the jurisdiction of the state of nationality.

Nevertheless, besides sovereignty of the territorial state, in the case of mass atrocities like those committed by IS, there may be other reasons why territorial criminal jurisdiction should be given a special place, and such states should be able to prosecute crimes committed on their territory. Prosecution of crimes in the state on whose territory they have been committed not only makes it easier to access evidence and to locate witnesses and capture suspects who are most likely already present on that state's territory, but it might also create a greater sense of justice for victims of those crimes. In addition,

243 A. Chehtman, *The Philosophical Foundations of Extraterritorial Punishment* (Oxford University Press 2010) 59, 60.

244 K. Gallant, *International Criminal Jurisdiction: Whose Law Must We Obey?* (Oxford University Press 2022) 347, 352.

245 M. Tait Slys, *Exporting Legality: The Rise and Fall of Extraterritorial Jurisdiction in the Ottoman Empire and China* (Graduate Institute Publications 2014); Y. Sumiyoshi, 'State Practices and Interpretation of International Law in Early Japan (1865–): Capitulations in Japan and its Abolishment' 5 Meiji Law Journal (1997) 15.

246 An unequal treaty has been defined as "an agreement, which favours the interests of one of the parties or of one group of parties". See, I. Detter, 'The Problem of Unequal Treaties' 15 International and Comparative Law Quarterly (1966) 4: 1078.

247 F. Mégret, '"Do Not Do Abroad What You Would Not Do at Home?": An Exploration of the Rationales for Extraterritorial Criminal Jurisdiction over a State's Nationals' 57 Canadian Yearbook of international Law/Annuaire canadien de droit international (2020) 9.

prosecution where the crimes have been committed contributes to "effective historytelling, societal reconciliation and rule of law entrenchment", which is especially important in post-conflict societies.[248] Local prosecutions may contribute to "achieving stability, developing and entrenching democratic institutions and attitudes, and recovering from the implications of past mass atrocity, reconciliation, and rehabilitation".[249] It can thus be said that territorial states, i.e., Syria and Iraq, have the primary jurisdiction to prosecute crimes that have been committed on their territories. In fact, as set out in the previous section, territorial states even have an obligation to investigate and, if appropriate, prosecute war crimes and terrorist offences committed on their territory. Although there is no hierarchy among the permissive principles for the exercise of jurisdiction, territorial states should be given the opportunity to prosecute atrocity crimes, like those committed by IS, that occurred on their territory. However, a territorial state's "first right of way to prosecute cases of mass atrocities does not as a matter of course mean that the [territorial] state has the final say as to an eventual prosecution".[250] This is where the principle of subsidiarity comes into play.

As mentioned in the short introduction to this section, within the international law of jurisdiction, the principle of subsidiarity means that states should refrain from exercising jurisdiction *unless* the state with the strongest link to the situation is unable or unwilling to prosecute. Put differently, other states can and should, to fight impunity, exercise subsidiary jurisdiction when the state with the strongest nexus to the situation is unable or unwilling to prosecute.[251] Although in a different form, this principle can be found in Article 17 of the Rome Statute. This Article dictates that the ICC may not exercise its jurisdiction if the case "is being investigated or prosecuted by a State which has jurisdiction over it, unless the State is unwilling or unable genuinely to carry out the investigation or prosecution", or if the case "has been investigated by a State which has jurisdiction over it and the State has decided not to prosecute the person concerned, unless the decision resulted from the unwillingness

248 C. Ryngaert, 'Horizontal complementarity' in C. Stahn and M. El Zeidy (eds.), *The International Criminal Court and Complementarity: From Theory to Practice* (Cambridge University Press 2011) 886.

249 H. Moodrick-Even Khen, 'Revisiting Universal Jurisdiction: The Application of the Complementarity Principle by National Courts and Implications for Ex-Post Justice in the Syrian Civil War' 30 Emory International Law Review (2015) 2: 270 (footnote omitted).

250 C. Ryngaert, 'Complementarity in Universality Cases: Legal-Systemic and Legal Policy Considerations' in M. Bergsmo (ed.) 2010 (n. 237) 198.

251 C. Ryngaert, 'The concept of jurisdiction in international law' in A. Orakhelashvili (ed.), *Research Handbook on Jurisdiction and Immunities in International Law* (Edward Elgar Publishing Limited 2015) 67.

or inability of the State genuinely to prosecute". The ICC thus exercises complementary jurisdiction if a state is unable or unwilling to prosecute. Complementarity is also what distinguishes the ICC from the ad hoc tribunals, the International Criminal Tribunal for the former Yugoslavia (ICTY) and the International Criminal Tribunal for Rwanda (ICTR), which were both not complementary to national jurisdiction but had primacy over it. The ICC's complementarity is a form of vertical subsidiarity, which means that it governs the jurisdictional relationship between a state and an international institution. Another example of such vertical subsidiarity, although in a different form, can be found in the ECtHR. The principle of subsidiarity is reflected in the Court's admissibility criteria. Article 35(1) of the ECHR dictates that "[t]he Court may only deal with the matter after all domestic remedies have been exhausted". The Court's jurisdiction is thus subsidiary to the protection of human rights by national courts.[252] Similar forms of vertical subsidiarity can be found in other international and regional human rights protection mechanisms, such as Article 46(1)(a) of the ACHR, Article 56(5) of the ACHPR, Article 41(1)(c) of the ICCPR and Article 3(1) of the Optional Protocol to the ICESCR.[253] These instruments have also recognized some exceptions to the rule that domestic remedies must have been exhausted. For example, when the domestic remedy is unreasonably prolonged,[254] when the domestic remedy is "unlikely to bring effective relief to the person",[255] and when the "domestic legislation of the state concerned does not afford due process of law for the protection of the right or rights that have allegedly been violated".[256]

After having discussed two forms of vertical subsidiarity in international law, it is time to zero in on subsidiarity in its horizontal form. That is, subsidiarity as governing the jurisdictional relationship between two or more states. Such horizontal subsidiarity has gained most traction within the field of universal jurisdiction over core international crimes. Per the universality principle, states may exercise jurisdiction based solely on the particularly grave

252 See also *Case of Kudla v. Poland* [2000] (Judgement) ECtHR App No. 30210/96 (26 October 2000) para. 152.

253 ACHR (signed 22 November 1969, entered into force 18 July 1978) 1144 UNTS 123; ACHPR (signed 27 June 1981, entered into force 21 October 1986) 1520 UNTS 217; Optional Protocol to the ICESCR (adopted 10 December 2008, entered into force 5 May 2013) 2922 UNTS 29.

254 See for example, Optional Protocol to the ICCPR, Article 5(2)(b); ACHPR, Article 56(5).

255 Convention against Torture and Other Cruel, Inhuman or Degrading Treatment or Punishment (signed 10 December 1984, entered into force 26 June 1987) 1465 UNTS 85 (CAT), Article 22(5)(b).

256 ACHR, Article 46(2)(a).

nature of the crime, "without regard to where the crime was committed, the nationality of the alleged or convicted perpetrator, the nationality of the victim, or any other connection to the state exercising such jurisdiction".[257] Under the universality principle, the particularly grave nature of the crime may thus confer jurisdiction on any state, even those without a nexus to the crime. Within this field, the subsidiarity principle has been relied upon "as a principle of jurisdictional restraint".[258] It was first mentioned in a separate opinion by judges Higgins, Kooijmans and Buergenthal in the *Arrest Warrant* Case.[259] They noted that "[a] State contemplating bringing criminal charges based on universal jurisdiction must first offer to the national State of the prospective accused person the opportunity itself to act upon the charges concerned".[260] The *Institut de Droit International* incorporated subsidiarity in their Resolution on universal criminal jurisdiction with regard to the crime of genocide, crimes against humanity and war crimes. The following restriction on the exercise of universal jurisdiction was adopted:

> Any State having custody over an alleged offender should, before commencing a trial on the basis of universal jurisdiction, ask the State where the crime was committed or the State of nationality of the person concerned whether it is prepared to prosecute that person, unless these States are manifestly unwilling or unable to do so.[261]

This paragraph embodies the principle of subsidiarity as it restrains the exercise of universal jurisdiction when there are other states with a closer nexus to the situation, which are prepared to bring the suspect to justice, unless these states are unwilling or unable to prosecute. The principle of subsidiarity, as limiting the exercise of universal jurisdiction, can also be found in a number of states' national laws. Ryngaert notes that prosecutorial application of subsidiarity is required by law in Belgium, Spain and Switzerland, applied as a prudential doctrine in Austria, and used to guide the exercise of prosecutorial

257 S. Macedo, *Universal Jurisdiction: National Courts and the Prosecution of Serious Crimes under International Law* (University of Pennsylvania Press 2004) 21.

258 C. Ryngaert 2015 (n. 237) 223.

259 *Case Concerning the Arrest Warrant of 11 April 2000* (Judgement) [2002] ICJ Rep. 3.

260 *Ibid.* Joint separate opinion of Judges Higgins, Kooijmans and Buergenthal, para. 81.

261 *Institut de Droit International*, Seventeenth Commission, Krakow Session, Resolution on Universal Criminal Jurisdiction with regard to the Crime of Genocide, Crimes against Humanity and War Crimes (2005). Available at: <https://www.idi-iil.org/en/sessions/krakow-2005/?post_type=publication> accessed 17 September 2024.

discretion in Germany, the UK, Denmark, Norway and Sweden.[262] For example, Section 153f of the German Code of Criminal Procedure stipulates that the German public prosecution office may dispense the prosecution of a suspect if the offence is being prosecuted by an international court or by a state on whose territory the crime was committed, whose national is suspected of having committed the crime or whose national was harmed by the crime.[263] Outside Europe, there are also states that incorporate some form of subsidiarity in their national laws. For example, in its Crimes Against Humanity and War Crimes Act, Canada incorporated that double jeopardy protection applies to someone who has previously been prosecuted and convicted or acquitted outside Canada, unless

> "the proceedings in that court
> (a) were for the purpose of shielding the person from criminal responsibility; or
> (b) were not otherwise conducted independently or impartially in accordance with the norms of due process recognized by international law, and were conducted in a manner that, in the circumstances, was inconsistent with an intent to bring the person to justice".[264]

Although different forms of subsidiarity can be found in states' national laws, it can be said that there seems to be substantial support for the principle of subsidiarity in its horizontal form, at least within the context of universal jurisdiction.[265]

When progressively interpreted, this principle may also apply more broadly in its horizontal form, outside the context of the universality principle. As Mégret argues, "[a]lthough the principle of complementarity is most often thought of in the vertical context of international criminal tribunal to domestic court, it may have a role to play in the horizontal context of domestic court to domestic court" and be of broader scope "whenever a conflict of criminal jurisdiction arises".[266] Although the crimes have not been committed on their territory, states of nationality may prosecute their nationals based on the nationality principle for the exercise of extraterritorial jurisdiction. However, for the reasons mentioned above, it is in theory true that, especially in the case of mass atrocities, perpetrators may be most appropriately prosecuted based

262 C. Ryngaert 2016 (n. 241) 280, 281.
263 German Code of Criminal Procedure 1987, Section 153f.
264 Crimes Against Humanity and War Crimes Act (S.C. 2000, c 24), Section 12(2).
265 C. Ryngaert 2016 (n. 241) 280.
266 F. Mégret 2020 (n. 247) 39 and footnote 117.

on the territoriality principle in the states where they have committed their crimes. Therefore, under the principle of subsidiarity, states of nationality should in such circumstances indeed defer the exercise of jurisdiction to such territorial states. However, in accordance with the subsidiarity principle in its horizontal form, such deference by states of nationality may not be unconditional. In light of the subsidiarity principle, those states of nationality should defer the exercise of jurisdiction to states which entertain the strongest nexus to the situation, *unless* those states are unable or unwilling to investigate or prosecute. To ensure that grave crimes do not remain unpunished, states of nationality should thus not invoke the priority of territorial jurisdiction without making an assessment of whether those states are actually willing and able to investigate and prosecute.

In the following sub-sections, this progressive interpretation of the subsidiarity principle will be applied in the context of FTFs in Syria and Iraq. Starting with the necessary assessment of whether the territorial states in question, i.e., Syria and Iraq, are willing and able to prosecute those FTFs and family members.

5.2 Prosecution in Iraq: Willing to Prosecute?

The terms 'unwilling' and 'unable' have more than one meaning in international law. The terms have, for example, been used within the law on the use of force,[267] international criminal law, as well as in other fields of international law.[268] Because this study concerns the prosecution of grave crimes, the meaning of the terms 'unwilling' and 'unable' will be deduced from international criminal law and, more specifically, from Article 17 of the Rome Statute. Although the vertical relationship between a state and the ICC is very different from the horizontal relationship between two or more states, and the complementarity principle as enshrined in the Rome Statute does, therefore, not apply as such in inter-state relations, "the standard established by the complementarity principle can be taken into consideration and may be, as a guiding principle, transferred to inter-state relations".[269]

---

267 L. Jordan, '"Unwilling or Unable"' 103 International Law Studies (2024) 151.

268 See for example, within the field of international refugee law, M. Janmyr, *Protecting Civilians in Refugee Camps: Unable and Unwilling States, UNHCR and International Responsibility* (Brill Nijhoff, 2013).

269 F. Jessberger, W. Kaleck and A. Schueller 2010 (n. 238) 242.

5.2.1 Meaning of the Term 'Unwilling'

Article 17(2) of the Rome Statute contains the meaning of the term 'unwilling' and specifies that:

> In order to determine unwillingness in a particular case, the Court shall consider, having regard to the principles of due process recognized by international law, whether one or more of the following exist, as applicable: (a) The proceedings were or are being undertaken or the national decision was made for the purpose of shielding the person concerned from criminal responsibility for crimes within the jurisdiction of the Court referred to in article 5; (b) There has been an unjustified delay in the proceedings which in the circumstances is inconsistent with an intent to bring the person concerned to justice; (c) The proceedings were not or are not being conducted independently or impartially, and they were or are being conducted in a manner which, in the circumstances, is inconsistent with an intent to bring the person concerned to justice.

Importantly, in determining a state's willingness or unwillingness to prosecute, regard must be given to "the principles of due process recognized by international law".[270] In *Al-Senussi*, the ICC Appeals Chamber clarified that Article 17(2)(c) cannot be interpreted to mean that violations of the suspects' due process rights *per se* amount to unwillingness.[271] The Appeals Chamber noted that the primary intention of the provision is not "to protect the domestic due process rights of a suspect" but to ensure "that an accused does not evade justice".[272] However, this does not mean that "the Court must turn a blind eye to clear and conclusive evidence demonstrating that the national proceedings completely lack fairness".[273] Hence, the threshold of unwillingness may be met in extreme cases of due process violations such as "proceedings that are, in reality, little more than a predetermined prelude to an execution, and which are therefore contrary to even the most basic understanding of justice", or less extreme cases "when the violations of the rights of the suspect are so egregious that it is clear that the international community would not accept that the accused was being brought to any genuine form of jus-

---

270 *Ibid.* Article 17(2).

271 ICC Appeals Chamber, Judgment on the appeal of Mr Abdullah Al-Senussi against the decision of Pre-Trial Chamber I of 11 October 2013 entitled "Decision on the admissibility of the case against Abdullah Al-Senussi". In the Case of *the Prosecutor v. Saif Al-Islam Gaddafi and Abdullah Al-Senussi*, No. ICC-01/II-01/IIOA6 (24 July 2014), para. 220.

272 *Ibid.* para. 228.

273 *Ibid.* para. 229.

tice".[274] In light of this, Mégret and Samson also pose the question, "what degree or type of rights violations should warrant a finding that a state is" unwilling to prosecute.[275] They argue that the test "is not whether the right to a fair trial has been violated in itself, but whether the degree to which it has been violated is such that one cannot realistically say that there has been a trial at all".[276] Similarly, El Zeidy notes that Article 17, including paragraph 2 (c), is "in effect a test of the good faith of national authorities".[277] Of influence to such a test might be the absence of an adversarial debate, the complete inability for the suspect to present his or her case, or other evidence that the outcome of the trial is predetermined, no access to legal representation, severe intimidation of witnesses, clear partiality of judges, the use of evidence obtained by resort to torture and the issuance of grossly inadequate sentences.[278] A combination of such due process violations might indeed "deprive a trial of its character as a trial" and hence, may warrant the determination that a state is indeed unwilling to prosecute.[279]

5.2.2 Proceedings in Iraqi Courts

Now that the meaning of the term 'unwilling' as defined in international criminal law has been set out in some more detail, we will look more closely into the proceedings in Iraqi courts in order to determine whether or to what extent those proceedings, by which FTFs and family members have been prosecuted, fulfill this definition. This analysis will, for the most part, be based on a number of NGO and UN reports. First of all, a Human Rights Watch report from 2017 which is, among others, based on visits to Iraqi prisons and courts in Baghdad and Erbil, interviews with judges handling cases of IS suspects, meetings with Iraqi Federal Government officials as well as officials from the Kurdistan Regional Government, consultations with local lawyers and other

274 *Ibid.* para. 230.

275 F. Mégret and M. Samson, 'Holding the Line on Complementarity in Libya: The Case for Tolerating Flawed Domestic Trials' 11 Journal of International Criminal Justice (2013) 3: 384.

276 *Ibid.* 385.

277 M. El Zeidy, 'The Principle of Complementarity: A New Machinery to Implement International Criminal Law' 23 Michigan Journal of International Law (2002) 4: 900.

278 F. Mégret and M. Samson 2013 (n. 275) 585, 386; ICC Office of the Prosecutor, 'Informal expert paper: The principle of complementarity in practice' (2003) Annex 4. Available at: <https://www.icc-cpi.int/sites/default/files/RelatedRecords/CR2009_02250.PDF> accessed 16 September 2024.

279 F. Mégret and M. Samson 2013 (n. 275) 387.

legal experts, and interviews with families of IS suspects.[280] Secondly, information will be drawn from another Human Rights Watch report from 2019, in which not only a number of concerns are raised but also a number of improvements are being observed since its previous report from 2017.[281] Thirdly, the analysis in this section will be based on a 2020 report by the United Nations Assistance Mission for Iraq (UNAMI) and the OHCHR.[282] This report is based on the monitoring of 794 hearings in Iraqi criminal courts in several governorates; 619 of these court hearings concerned defendants being prosecuted under anti-terrorism laws; and 28 cases concerned foreign defendants from 11 different states.[283] Findings in these reports will be supplemented by other, more recent sources.[284] In these reports, a number of common concerns have been raised. These concerns relate, among others, to the broad definitions in, and interpretations of, the anti-terrorism laws, a lack of strategy in prosecuting IS suspects, disproportionate sentences and the death penalty, fairness of hearings, as well as torture and ill-treatment. Before we delve into

280 Human Rights Watch 2017 (n. 19) 10.

281 Human Rights Watch, Iraq: Key Courts Improve ISIS Trial Procedures: But Changes Needed in Laws, Response to Torture, Other Courts (13 March 2019). Available at: <https://www.hrw.org/news/2019/03/13/iraq-key-courts-improve-isis-trial-procedures> accessed 25 September 2024.

282 United Nations Assistance Mission for Iraq and the Office of the United Nations High Commissioner for Human Rights, Human Rights in the Administration of Justice in Iraq: Trials under the anti-terrorism laws and implications for justice, accountability and social cohesion in the aftermath of ISIL (January 2020). Available at: <https://www.ohchr.org/en/documents/country-reports/human-rights-administration-justice-iraq-trials-under-anti-terrorism-laws> accessed 25 September 2024.

283 *Ibid.* 1.

284 See, for example, The International Bar Association's Human Rights Institute, Justice and Accountability for the Atrocities of Daesh: Progress Made and the Way Forward, Working Draft (March 2023) 13. Available at: <https://www.ibanet.org/Daesh-Justice-and-accountability-report-2023> accessed 25 September 2024. Commission Nationale Consultative des Droits de L'Homme, Opinion on French nationals sentenced to death or facing the death penalty in Iraq (28 January 2020). Available at: <https://www.cncdh.fr/sites/default/files/2021-04/A%20-%202020%20-%201%20-%20VA%20-%20Opinion%20French%20death%20penalty%20Iraq%2C%20jan%202020.pdf> accessed 27 September 2024; V. Mironova, 'Iraq's Broken Justice System for Islamic State Fighters' Lawfare (24 July 2020). Available at: <https://www.lawfaremedia.org/article/iraqs-broken-justice-system-islamic-state-fighters> accessed 27 September 2024; Human Rights Watch, Iraq: Unlawful Mass Executions Resume: Adopt Death Penalty Moratorium, Judicial System Reforms (24 January 2024). Available at: <https://www.hrw.org/news/2024/01/24/iraq-unlawful-mass-executions-resume> accessed 2 October 2024; Amnesty International, 'Amnesty International report 2022/23: the state of the world's human rights' (2023). Available at: <https://www.amnesty.org/en/documents/pol10/5670/2023/en/> accessed 16 April 2025.

these specific concerns, it should be noted that the reports on which this analysis is primarily based date back to between 2017 and 2020, and it could well be that some of the concerns they raise have, over the years, been improved. For example, in their report from 2019, Human Rights Watch already notes improvements in evidentiary standards. While reading the following analysis, this should be kept in mind.

5.2.2.1 Broad Anti-terrorism Laws and Absence of a Strategy

The Iraqi judiciary has dealt with an enormous amount of terrorism-related cases in the past couple of years, and most likely, many cases are yet to come. To give an indication, from January 2018 to October 2019, the Iraqi judiciary processed more than 20,000 cases against IS suspects, with thousands still pending as of January 2020.[285] Almost all IS suspects are prosecuted under the Federal Anti-terrorism Law or the Kurdistan Regional Government's Anti-terror Law. Both laws are based on broad definitions of terrorism. Individual acts of terrorism under the federal law as well as the Kurdistan regional law "range from 'use of violence to spread fear' to 'any act with terrorist motives that threatens the national unity of the State' to 'damage to public property'".[286] Article 4 of the Federal Anti-terrorism Law prescribes the mandatory application of the death penalty for "anyone who committed, incited, planned, financed, or assisted in a terrorist act".[287] Life imprisonment is prescribed for "anyone who covers up such an act or harbors those who participated".[288] The Kurdistan Regional Government's Anti-terror Law also imposes the death penalty for a range of terrorist acts, and for others, life imprisonment or a sentence not exceeding 15 years in prison. Almost all IS suspects are prosecuted for 'membership' of, or 'association' with, a terrorist group.[289] While the Kurdistan Regional Government's Anti-terror Law explicitly criminalizes membership in a terrorist organization, punishable with life in prison, under the Federal Anti-terrorism Law membership is not explicitly criminalized but interpreted very broadly as a contribution to, or participation in, activities of the group, and therefore falling under Article 4 and incurring the death penalty.[290] UNAMI has expressed its concern about the wide use and interpretation of membership or association with a terrorist organization as a basis for the conviction

285 UNAMI and OHCHR 2020 (n. 282) iv.
286 *Ibid.* 4.
287 Human Rights Watch 2017 (n. 19) 29.
288 *Ibid.* 29, 30.
289 *Ibid.* 27; UNAMI and OHCHR 2020 (n. 282) 10.
290 UNAMI and OHCHR 2020 (n. 282) 9, 10; The International Bar Association's Human Rights Institute 2023 (n. 284) 20.

of IS suspects in Iraqi courts.[291] In the hearings UNAMI attended, those individuals were "almost exclusively" sentenced under Article 4 of the Federal Anti-terrorism Law.[292] This broad interpretation of membership and association allowed Iraqi courts to systematically convict a wide variety of suspects under this provision. For instance, cases ranged from individuals who had provided "basic support to ISIL members, such as cooking or selling vegetables and family members of ISIL members, including women and children",[293] as well as "those who may have supported the group against their will, or in a civilian or civil service capacity",[294] to those who actually participated in hostilities. As Human Rights Watch described it, Iraqi federal courts "appear to be prosecuting a random assortment of ISIS suspects for affiliation with ISIS, with no prioritization of those responsible for the most serious crimes".[295] Likewise, Human Rights Watch noted that courts in Iraqi Kurdistan exclusively charge IS suspects for "membership in ISIS, including those who are not alleged to have committed any other crime" and that they "are carrying out prosecutions without any apparent strategy on how to prioritize cases".[296] In addition, Iraq does not have jurisdiction to prosecute core international crimes committed on its territory, as they are not codified in Iraqi law.[297] The absence of a strategy for the prosecution of suspected members of IS and the demand for a strong reaction by the judiciary have thus led to the conviction of thousands of IS suspects with little or no distinction as to the severity of the offences that they may have committed.[298]

5.2.2.2 Evidentiary Concerns

In terms of the evidence used to sustain these convictions, the reports examined address a number of concerns. First, Iraqi courts seem to have used evidence obtained through torture. For example, Human Rights Watch notes that the torture of IS suspects was allegedly widespread and often used to obtain confessions.[299] According to Amnesty International, long prison sentences as well as the death penalty have been imposed on IS suspects in Iraqi

291 UNAMI and OHCHR 2020 (n. 282) 9, 10; Human Rights Watch also identified the vague counter-terrorism law as a "major concern". Human Rights Watch 2019 (n. 281).

292 UNAMI and OHCHR 2020 (n. 282) 10.

293 *Ibid.*

294 Human Rights Watch 2017 (n. 19) 30.

295 *Ibid.* 27.

296 *Ibid.* 36.

297 UNAMI and OHCHR 2020 (n. 282) 6; Human Rights Watch 2017 (n. 19) 27.

298 A. Ferlin, 'Criminal Liability and Prosecution of Islamic State Fighters in Iraq' Journal of Criminal Justice and Security 23 (2021) 4: 371, 372.

299 Human Rights Watch 2017 (n. 19) 49–52; Human Rights Watch 2024 (n. 284).

courts "following convictions based primarily on torture-tainted 'confessions'".[300] UNAMI also notes that it has received credible reports about torture and ill-treatment by Iraqi authorities, "in particular for the purpose of forced confessions".[301] In addition, they observe that in 260 out of 619 terrorism-related hearings that they attended, the defense raised allegations of torture or ill-treatment which occurred during interrogations.[302] Even when the defense claimed that confessions were extracted through torture, the confessions were admitted as evidence and were not questioned.[303] In some terrorism-related cases, forced or coerced confessions were even "the primary or sole source of evidence" on which the conviction was based.[304] Besides the heavy reliance on confessions by the defendant, including those obtained through torture, Iraqi courts seem to rely on anonymous witnesses and secret informants, without the possibility for the defense to challenge such evidence by, for example, cross-examining witnesses.[305] UNAMI found that in at least 428 out of the 619 terrorism-related hearings that they observed in Iraqi courts, in addition to confessions, the primary evidence relied upon included statements by anonymous witnesses and information retrieved from security or intelligence reports.[306] In none of those instances was the defense able to rebut or challenge such evidence, nor was any other measure adopted to compensate for the disadvantage.[307] Worth mentioning is also that there is little or no protection or assistance provided to witnesses or those who wish to act as one. And indeed, it has been reported that "those testifying have been subjected to various pressures and threats".[308] A final concern with regard to the evidence used by Iraqi courts in terrorism-related trials is the use of other unreliable evidence. It has been observed that judges sometimes base the defendants' guilt on their "geographic proximity to ISIS activities, or on a spousal or familial relationship to" other defendants,[309] on their "identification as ISIS members by community members without further investiga-

300 Amnesty International 2023 (n. 284) 201.

301 UNAMI and OHCHR 2020 (n. 282) 9.

302 *Ibid.* 8, 9.

303 *Ibid.* 9; The International Bar Association's Human Rights Institute 2023 (n. 284) 19.

304 US Department of State, 2023 Country Reports on Human Rights Practices: Iraq. Available at: <https://www.state.gov/reports/2023-country-reports-on-human-rights-practices/iraq/> accessed 30 September 2024; V. Mironova 2020 (n. 284); Human Rights Watch 2017 (n. 19) 31.

305 UNAMI and OHCHR 2020 (n. 282) 8; Human Rights Watch 2017 (n. 19) 29.

306 UNAMI and OHCHR 2020 (n. 282) 8.

307 *Ibid.*

308 The International Bar Association's Human Rights Institute 2023 (n. 284) 20.

309 US Department of State 2023 (n. 304).

tion",[310] or on wanted lists.[311] It should be noted that in its 2019 report, Human Rights Watch did notice a number of improvements regarding the use of evidence compared to its 2017 report. In its 2019 report, it is observed that some Iraqi courts "are requiring a higher evidentiary standard to detain and prosecute suspects, minimizing the court's reliance on confessions alone, erroneous wanted lists, and unsubstantiated allegations".[312] However, in other courts, "judges continue to process cases solely based on a defendant's confession, with the defendant frequently alleging torture to extract the statement".[313]

5.2.2.3 Other Fair Trial Issues

The reliance on confessions alone, including those incurred through torture, as well as the reliance on anonymous witnesses, security or intelligence reports, and other unreliable evidence, combined with a lack of opportunity for the defense to challenge incriminating evidence, highly affects the fairness of trials in Iraqi courts. Other fair trial issues that have been reported include, first of all, the effectiveness of legal representation. Although Iraqi courts generally appointed a lawyer when the defendant had no lawyer of his/her own choosing, reports suggest that defendants were consistently denied a lawyer during interrogations.[314] In addition, defense lawyers, particularly those who were court-appointed, only played a passive role during both the investigative and trial stages.[315] UNAMI notes that the role of a lawyer at the trial stage "appeared to be limited to requesting the court to exercise leniency towards the defendant, without posing any questions or carrying out other interventions".[316] Human Rights Watch observed hearings during which the court-appointed lawyers "did not speak once [...], with the judge and the court reporter directly questioning the defendant".[317] With regard to lawyers chosen by the IS suspect themselves, Mironova mentions that they "are likely to be arrested themselves and charged with supporting the terrorist group".[318] Private lawyers previously arrested in any case had a "chilling effect" on such

310 Human Rights Watch 2017 (n. 19) 21.
311 Human Rights Watch 2019 (n. 281).
312 *Ibid.*
313 *Ibid.*
314 UNAMI and OHCHR 2020 (n. 282) 7; Human Rights Watch 2017 (n. 19) 41.
315 UNAMI and OHCHR 2020 (n. 282) 7, 8.
316 *Ibid.* 7.
317 Human Rights Watch 2017 (n. 19) 41.
318 V. Mironova 2020 (n. 284).

private representation.[319] Moreover, the defense counsels appointed by Iraqi courts were generally only appointed on the day of the trial and, therefore, had no adequate time to prepare the case.[320] In this regard, UNAMI concluded that of the 475 terrorism-related hearings during which the defendant had a court-appointed lawyer, the "defence lawyers were almost exclusively assigned at the beginning of the trial session only, and therefore had little or no opportunity to familiarize themselves with the case file or prepare their defence".[321] Consequently, those lawyers had no prior knowledge of the case or the evidence against the suspects they were supposed to defend. With regard to private lawyers, it is likewise mentioned that they were often refused access to court files.[322] Another fair trial issue mentioned is that of public access to hearings. Although trials were generally not entirely closed to the public, instances have been reported where public access was dependent upon authorization by courts, in particular, in cases related to terrorism.[323] Furthermore, the dates of hearings as well as the names of the defendants were not made public in advance, which made it difficult to attend those hearings, including for victims.[324]

5.2.2.4 Lack of Victim Participation and Prosecution of Children

Two other concerns that should briefly be touched upon are the lack of victim participation in terrorism-related trials in Iraqi courts and the prosecution of children. Because of the issues regarding public access to hearings, as mentioned above, the attendance of victims in trials regarding IS suspects was limited.[325] Agnès Callamard, former UN Special Rapporteur on extrajudicial, summary or arbitrary executions, noted that during a trial in which four men were sentenced to death for membership in IS, "no victims participated in the trial, or presented their testimony as witnesses".[326] Human Rights Watch also noted that "the ongoing trials grant victims no meaningful opportunities to

319 Human Rights Watch, 'Iraq: Lawyers Arrested for Work in ISIS Courts: Chilling Effect on Private Legal Representation' (10 August 2017). Available at: <https://www.hrw.org/news/2017/08/10/iraq-lawyers-arrested-work-isis-courts> accessed 30 September 2024.

320 Commission Nationale Consultative des Droits de L'Homme 2020 (n. 284) 6; A. Ferlin 2021 (n. 298) 371; UNAMI and OHCHR 2020 (n. 282) 6, 7.

321 UNAMI and OHCHR 2020 (n. 282) 6.

322 *Ibid.* 7; Human Rights Watch 2024 (n. 284).

323 UNAMI and OHCHR 2020 (n. 282) 12.

324 *Ibid.* 13.

325 *Ibid.* 5.

326 OHCHR, Iraq: UN expert says prosecution of ISIL leadership must be fair and thorough (4 April 2019). Available at: <https://www.ohchr.org/en/news/2019/04/iraq-un-expert-says-prosecution-isil-leadership-must-be-fair-and-thorough> accessed 1 October 2024.

participate, including to attend, testify, or submit questions to suspects".[327] Besides the lack of victim participation in these trials, it should be reiterated here that the heavy reliance of Iraqi courts on membership of, or association with IS, instead of the actual crimes that they have committed, fails to do justice to victims. With regard to the prosecution of children, it is noted with concern that the minimum age for criminal prosecution in Iraq is set at the very low age of nine years old, and Iraq has indeed tried hundreds of children for their alleged affiliation with IS.[328]

5.2.2.5 The Death Penalty

Finally, the issue of the often disproportionate sentences handed down in Iraqi courts, including the death penalty. Although Article 4 of the Federal Anti-terrorism Law provides for two penalties only, either the death penalty or life imprisonment, with membership in a terrorist organization incurring the death penalty, judges reportedly have some judicial discretion in deciding which penalties to impose.[329] Although the Kurdistan Regional Government's Anti-terror Law imposes the death penalty for a range of terrorist activities, it has been noted that a "de facto moratorium" has been placed on the death penalty.[330] UNAMI observes that "[o]f the 317 terrorism-related trial hearings in Federal courts attended which involved the pronouncement of sentences, judges applied the death penalty in 100 instances, involving 105 defendants".[331] By contrast, out of the 105 other trial hearings attended, those not related to terrorism, the death penalty was only imposed 3 times.[332] In addition, in at least 19 terrorism-related trial hearings, "observations indicate that the defendants were sentenced to death even though the accusation only referred to mere 'membership of a terrorist organization' without reference to any acts of violence".[333] International human rights law determines that in countries where the death penalty has not yet been abolished, it may only be imposed "for the most serious crimes".[334] Imposing the death penalty for membership

327 Human Rights Watch 2017 (n. 19) 22, 23.

328 UNAMI and OHCHR 2020 (n. 282) 4; Human Rights watch, Iraq: Step Toward Justice for ISIS Child Suspects: Improved Trials Should Be Replicated (13 December 2020). Available at: <https://www.hrw.org/news/2020/12/13/iraq-step-toward-justice-isis-child-suspects#:~:text=For%20years%2C%20Iraqi%20and%20Kurdistan,of%20ISIS%20involvement%2C%20if%20any> accessed 1 October 2024.

329 UNAMI and OHCHR 2020 (n. 282) 10; Human Rights Watch 2017 (n. 19) 29, 30.

330 UNAMI and OHCHR 2020 (n. 282) 12; Human Rights Watch 2017 (n. 19) 52.

331 UNAMI and OHCHR 2020 (n. 282) 12.

332 *Ibid.*

333 *Ibid.*; Human Rights Watch 2024 (n. 284).

334 ICCPR, Article 6(2).

of a terrorist organization, without any conclusive evidence or even reference to an act of violence, surely does not meet the threshold of "most serious crime".[335] In general, many of the crimes for which the death penalty is prescribed in both the Federal Anti-terrorism Law as well as the Kurdistan Regional Government's Anti-terror Law would not meet this threshold.[336] Moreover, the violations of fair trial guarantees as outlined above, including the use of evidence obtained through torture, the lack of effective legal representation, as well as adequate time to prepare for the suspect's defense, may render the death sentence arbitrary, and execution of such a sentence may, as a result, constitute a violation of the right to life.[337]

5.2.3 Unwilling to Prosecute?

The question then remains whether, or to what extent, Iraq can be said to satisfy the international criminal law definition of being 'unwilling' to prosecute. At the beginning of this sub-section, it was said that violations of fair trial guarantees per se do not amount to a state being 'unwilling' to prosecute. However, it was also observed that the threshold of unwillingness may still be met in extreme cases of fair trial violations where the proceedings are "little more than a predetermined prelude to an execution" and, therefore, "contrary to the most basic understanding of justice".[338] Or in other cases where due process violations are so flagrant that the accused was not "being brought to any genuine form of justice".[339] It was also mentioned at the beginning of this sub-section that factors which can be taken into account when trying to answer the question of whether the threshold of 'unwillingness' is met, include the absence of an adversarial debate, the complete inability for the suspect to present his or her case or other evidence that the outcome of the trial is predetermined, no access to legal representation, severe intimidation of witnesses, clear partiality of judges, the use of evidence obtained by

335 UNAMI and OHCHR 2020 (n. 282) 12.

336 *Ibid.* 5.

337 *Ibid.* 11; see also Human Rights Committee, 'General comment No. 36 Article 6: right to life' (3 September 2019) UN Doc. CCPR/C/GC/36, para. 35. In this General Comment the Human Rights Committee noted that "[t]he term 'the most serious crimes' must be read restrictively and appertain only to crimes of extreme gravity involving intentional killing. Crimes not resulting directly and intentionally in death, such as attempted murder, corruption and other economic and political crimes, armed robbery, piracy, abduction, drug and sexual offences, although serious in nature, can never serve as the basis, within the framework of article 6, for the imposition of the death penalty." (footnotes omitted).

338 ICC Appeals Chamber 2014 (n. 271) para. 230.

339 *Ibid.*

resort to torture and the issuance of grossly inadequate sentences. After the analysis of trials against IS suspects in Iraqi courts, it has become clear that a number of those elements can be said to be present. The analysis above showed a clear lack of adequate legal representation and, due to lawyers only being appointed at the beginning of the trial hearing, no time to adequately prepare a defense. Also, due to the fact that lawyers generally played only a passive role during trial and, in some cases, did not even speak once, suspects were, in the majority of cases, unable to present, let alone effectively defend, their cases. These circumstances also bring into question whether a true adversarial debate can be said to have taken place during those trials. If it can be said that an adversarial debate did take place, it was not one based on the principle of equality of arms. Another factor that could point to Iraq's unwillingness to prosecute is the widespread practice of torture to obtain confessions and the subsequent, sometimes exclusive, reliance on such confessions to come to a conviction. Other factors that could point to the outcome of trials being predetermined include the widespread use of evidence obtained through anonymous witnesses, secret informants, and information based on security and intelligence reports, without an opportunity for the defense to challenge such evidence. The same can be said about the use of other unreliable evidence discussed, such as geographical proximity to IS activities or the identification as a member of IS by another person without further investigation. A final factor that could indeed point towards unwillingness is the disproportionate sentences handed down by Iraqi courts in terrorism-related cases. Death sentences have been imposed for mere membership of a terrorist organization without any evidence or reference to acts of violence. Human Rights Watch has even reported that the death sentence was imposed on a man who had served as a cook for IS.[340]

These various factors have been the reason why some authors have concluded that "Iraq is likely to qualify as an 'extreme' case satisfying the Rome Statute's definition of a State 'unwilling' to prosecute."[341] There is no set answer for the question where the threshold of unwillingness lies exactly and how egregious fair trial violations have to be in order to find a trial "inconsistent with an intent to bring the person concerned to justice".[342] What can be concluded here is that, because of the severe due process violations in the reports and other sources examined, there are clear indications that Iraqi tri-

340 Human Rights Watch 2017 (n. 19) 30.

341 M. Seet, "Cosmopolitan Citizenship', Territorial Borders, and Bringing Denationalized Terrorists to Justice' 19 Journal of International Criminal Justice (2021) 2: 270.

342 Rome Statute, Article 17(2)(c).

als by which IS suspects have been prosecuted may indeed not be considered as a "genuine form of justice".[343] Such circumstances could warrant a finding that these trials indeed fulfill the international criminal law definition of 'unwilling' to genuinely prosecute IS suspects, including FTFs and their family members.

5.3 Prosecution in (Northeast) Syria: Able to Prosecute?

5.3.1 Meaning of the Term 'Unable'

Like the meaning of the term 'unwilling', the meaning of the term 'unable' can be deduced from international criminal law. More specifically, this term is elaborated upon in Article 17(3) of the Rome Statute, which says:

> In order to determine inability in a particular case, the Court shall consider whether, due to a total or substantial collapse or unavailability of its national judicial system, the State is unable to obtain the accused or the necessary evidence and testimony or otherwise unable to carry out its proceedings.

From the outset, it can be observed that the notion of 'unable' is more objective and descriptive than that of 'unwilling'. There must be either a collapse of the state's national judicial system or that judicial system must be unavailable, and this must have undermined the state's ability to obtain the accused, necessary evidence and testimony, or otherwise carry out its proceedings. Moreover, the Article addresses two types of collapses: a 'total collapse' or a 'substantial collapse'. A 'total collapse' has been said to be assumed when "the state authorities have lost control over its territory to an extent that the administration of justice has broken down completely, or where the authorities, while exercising effective (military or police) control over the territory, do not perform such administration".[344] A 'substantial collapse' is said to be the case "where the state authorities, even though not completely dysfunctional, are not generally capable of ensuring the investigation of the case and the prosecution of the responsible individuals".[345] Kleffner argues that a clear example of a situation in which a state's national judicial system can be said

343 ICC Appeals Chamber 2014 (n. 271) para. 230.

344 M. Benzing, 'The Complementarity Regime of the International Criminal Court: International Criminal Justice between State Sovereignty and the Fight against Impunity' 7 Max Planck Yearbook of United Nations Law (2003) 614.

345 *Ibid.* (footnote omitted).

to have substantially collapsed, is when "the relevant authorities initiate an investigation against members of an armed opposition group during an internal armed conflict, but the State's national judicial system has collapsed in areas under effective control of that group".[346] During the drafting of the Rome Statute, the term 'substantial collapse' was purposefully chosen instead of 'partial collapse' in order to

> preclude the Court from assuming jurisdiction merely because an armed conflict exists in a State and the judicial system is partially affected. Even in such instances, the State may be able, through shifting resources or transferring the trial to other venues, to effect a genuine prosecution.[347]

The ICC Pre-Trial Chamber I discussed the notion of 'unavailability' in the *Gaddafi* Case. In this Case, the Chamber held that Libya's national judicial system was 'unavailable' in the sense of Article 17(3) because of the Libyan Government's "substantial difficulties in exercising its judicial powers fully across the entire territory".[348] Due to this lack of control, Libya was, among others, "unable to obtain the accused" who was in detention under the control of the Zintan militia.[349] Interesting to note is thus that with regard to both notions, 'total or substantial collapse' as well as 'unavailability', a determination of a state's lack of effective control over its territory is relevant. Therefore, Seet concludes that "[f]ragile states with lack of effective control over their territories are hence 'unable' to prosecute".[350]

5.3.2 The Syrian Governmental Authorities

With regard to FTFs and associated family members detained in Northeast Syria, at least before the fall of the Assad regime in December 2024, the Syrian Governmental authorities were likely to satisfy the international criminal law definition of 'unable' to genuinely prosecute those individuals. It goes too far to say that there was a total collapse of the Syrian Government's national

346 J. Kleffner, *Complementarity in the Rome Statute and National Criminal Jurisdictions* (Oxford University Press 2008) 155.

347 J. Holmes, 'Complementarity: National Courts versus the ICC' in A. Cassese, P. Gaeta and J. Jones (eds.), *The Rome Statute of the International Criminal Court: A Commentary* (Oxford University Press, 2002) 677.

348 ICC Pre-Trial Chamber I, *Decision on the admissibility of the case against Saif Al-Islam Gaddafi*, No. ICC-01/11–01/11 (31 May 2013) para. 205.

349 *Ibid.* paras. 206–208.

350 M. Seet 2021 (n. 341) 265.

judicial system. Although Assad's Government authorities were unlikely to abide by international human rights standards,[351] and the conflict "had an extensive impact on the justice system",[352] there was a national judicial system existing and functioning in Government-held areas. As in the *Gaddafi* case, in which the ICC Pre-Trial Chamber clarified that although there are difficulties in exercising judicial powers over its entire territory, "the administration of justice may exist and function in Libya",[353] it cannot be said that the Syrian Government's national judicial system had completely broken down and that the administration of justice was not performed at all.

In that case, we need to look at whether it can be said that there was a 'substantial collapse' or 'unavailability' of Syria's national judicial system when Assad was still in power, and particularly in relation to the prosecution of FTFs and their family members held in Northeast Syria.[354] As was mentioned earlier, a state's lack of effective control over certain parts of its territory is relevant for both notions. It could well be argued that there was a 'substantial collapse' of Syria's justice system. Substantial parts of Syria's territory were not under the effective control of the Assad Government. For example, Northwest Syria was predominantly controlled by Hay'et Tahrir al-Sham and other anti-Government armed groups, parts of Northern Syria were occupied by Türkiye and Turkish-backed rebels, such as the National Syrian Army, and the Northeastern part of Syria was controlled by the AANES and the

351 See, for example, the following report on widespread and systematic use of torture and cruel, inhuman or degrading treatment including by the Syrian Government: Human Rights Council, Independent International Commission of Inquiry on the Syrian Arab Republic, "No End in Sight": Torture and ill-treatment in the Syrian Arab Republic 2020–202, UN Doc. A/HRC/53/CRP.5 (10 July 2023); See also Human Rights Council, Report of the Independent International Commission of Inquiry on the Syrian Arab Republic, UN Doc. A/HRC/57/86 (12 August 2024) paras.15–28; Human Rights Council, Report of the Office of the United Nations High Commissioner for Human Rights: Compilation on the Syrian Arab Republic, UN Doc. A/HRC/WG.6/40/SYR/2 (17 November 2021), paras. 30–35; Human Rights Council, Report of the Independent International Commission of Inquiry on the Syrian Arab Republic, UN Doc. A/HRC/46/55 (11 March 2021) paras. 16–27.

352 United Nations Syria Country Team, Report prepared in accordance with paragraph 15 (B) of resolution 5/1 of the HR Council for the Third Universal Periodic Review of the Syrian Arab Republic, 3. Available at: <file:///C:/Users/asscherid/Downloads/Syria 20U NCT_UPR40_SYR_E_Main%20(2).pdf> accessed 4 October 2024; Human Rights Council 17 November 2021 (n. 350) para 30.

353 ICC Pre-Trial Chamber I 2013 (n. 348) para. 215.

354 Rome Statute, Article 17(3).

SDF.[355] It is estimated that in March 2023, only 70 percent of Syria's territory was under the control of the Syrian Government and its allies, which include Russian and Iranian forces as well as pro-Government militias.[356] It can thus be said that the Syrian Government's lack of effective control over certain parts of its territory was of such an extent that it did not have the necessary judicial power over considerable parts of its territory, including the area where most FTFs and associated family members are still detained. Such a lack of effective control over Northeast Syria paralyzed the Syrian Government's national judicial system in fulfilling its functions with regard to the investigation and prosecution of FTFs and their family members. It can well be argued that this amounted to a 'substantial collapse' of Syria's judicial infrastructure in specific relation to the investigation and prosecution of those individuals.

In the *Gaddafi* case, the ICC Pre-Trial Chamber I did not address whether there was a 'substantial collapse' but only considered the 'unavailability' of Libya's national justice system. Following the reasoning of the Pre-Trial Chamber I, it could also be argued that the Assad Government's administration of justice was 'unavailable' in relation to FTFs and their family members who were detained in Northeast Syria under the control of the SDF. The Chamber noted that "substantial difficulties in exercising its judicial powers fully across the entire territory" led to Libya not being able to apply its national judicial system in full in areas or aspects relevant to Gaddafi's case.[357] Hence, its national system was considered to be 'unavailable'. Clearly, due to its lack of effective control over Northeast Syria, as well as other large parts of its territory, the Syrian Government was indeed not able to apply its national judicial system to those individuals. Although such a determination is, of course, highly case-specific, these circumstances were most likely to create significant problems in carrying out proceedings against those FTFs and family members detained by the SDF. Hence, at least before the fall of the Assad regime in December 2024 and the new Syrian Government taking over con-

355 The Carter Center, 'Syria Map: Exploring Historical Control in Syria' (last updated 1 October 2024). Available at: <https://www.cartercenter.org/news/multimedia/map/exploring-historical-control-in-syria.html> accessed 4 October 2024; Council of Foreign Relations, 'Global Conflict Tracker: Conflict in Syria' (last updated 13 February 2024). Available at: <https://www.cfr.org/global-conflict-tracker/conflict/conflict-syria> accessed 4 October 2024; F. Balanche, 'The Assad Regime Has Failed to Restore Full Sovereignty Over Syria' The Washington Institute for Near East Policy, Policy Watch 3433 (10 February 2021). Available at: <https://www.washingtoninstitute.org/policy-analysis/assad-regime-has-failed-restore-full-sovereignty-over-syria> accessed 4 October 2024.

356 M. Yacoubian, 'Syria's Stalemate Has Only Benefitted Assad and His Backers' United States Institute of Peace (14 March 2023).

357 ICC Pre-Trial Chamber I (n. 348), 205.

trol of Northeast Syria in January 2026, Syria could be 'unable' to genuinely prosecute FTFs and their associated family members detained by the SDF. Other scholars have come to similar conclusions. For example, Seet also concludes that Syria "likely constitutes a state 'unable' to prosecute" those individuals detained in Northeast Syria, which Seet refers to as a 'black spot', i.e., a space "outside the state's effective control".[358]

5.3.3 The Autonomous Administration of North and East Syria

While it is true that FTFs and associated family members have been detained without facing trial for years, before the new Syrian Government took over control of Northeast Syria in January 2026, the AANES announced that, besides prosecuting Syrian nationals, it would also start prosecuting foreign nationals. On 15 June 2023, it was announced that the AANES would start judicial proceedings against about 2,000 FTFs detained in Northeast Syria.[359] This raises the question of to what extent the AANES can, from a legal point of view, fill the void of judicial power left by the Syrian Government.

5.3.3.1 Can the AANES Lawfully Administer Justice?

The starting point for analyzing the question of whether non-state armed groups can lawfully establish courts and administer justice in areas under their control is found in IHL, and, as we are dealing with a NIAC, in Common Article 3 of the Geneva Conventions. Common Article 3(1)(d) prohibits "the passing of sentences and the carrying out of executions without previous judgment pronounced by a regularly constituted court, affording all the judicial guarantees which are recognized as indispensable by civilized peoples".[360] Two criteria can be deduced from this provision. First, a court must be "regularly constituted" and, second, such a court must "afford all the judicial guarantees which are recognized as indispensable by civilized peoples". With

358 M. Seet 2021 (n. 341) 263–266, 269; A. Jomaa, 'Addressing Jurisdictional Challenges in Prosecuting ISIL Fighters' 11 Berkeley Journal of Middle Eastern & Islamic Law (2020) 1: 39.

359 J. Seldin, 'Syrian Kurds Launch New Attempt to Prosecute Captured IS Foreign Fighters' (*VOA News*, 15 June 2023). Available at: <https://www.voanews.com/a/syrian-kurds-launch-new-attempt-to-prosecute-captured-is-foreign-fighters/7139770.html> accessed 4 October 2024.

360 Similarly, as for international armed conflicts, Article 75(4) of Additional Protocol I stipulates that "[n]o sentence may be passed and no penalty may be executed on a person found guilty of a penal offence related to the armed conflict except pursuant to a conviction pronounced by an impartial and regularly constituted court respecting the generally recognized principles of regular judicial procedure".

regard to the first criterion, Common Article 3 does not specify what is meant by a "regularly constituted court". Could this include a court established by a non-state armed group? If the term "regularly constituted" is understood to mean a court which is established in accordance with the national laws of the state in force at the time,[361] Common Article 3 would indeed prohibit the creation of courts and the administration of justice by non-state armed groups.[362] This is because it is unlikely that the national laws of a state would authorize the establishment of courts by non-state armed (opposition) groups. There seems to be a "consensus that the reference to a 'regularly constituted' court in Common Article 3 was indeed originally to be understood in the sense of a court established pursuant the national law of the state, thus implying the illegality of" courts established by non-state armed groups.[363] However, other provisions of IHL may give more clarity on the interpretation of this notion, as "the legality of justice practices of armed groups cannot be assessed purely on the basis of a few words in Common Article 3".[364] Article 66 of the Fourth Geneva Convention, which applies in IAC, mentions that courts need to be "properly constituted". The ICRC's Commentary of 1958 to this provision makes clear that this term has the same meaning as "regularly constituted" in Common Article 3, and adds that such courts must be "set up in accordance with the recognized principles governing the administration of justice".[365] By contrast, Article 6(2) of Additional Protocol II, applicable in NIAC but to which Syria is not a state party, omits the notion "regularly" or "properly constituted court" entirely. Instead, the provision stipulates that "[n]o sentence shall be passed and no penalty shall be executed on a person found guilty of an offence except pursuant to a conviction pronounced by a court offering the essential guarantees of independence and impartiality". The Article goes on to list a

361 This is indeed what the position of the ICRC seems to be in its study on customary IHL. In its commentary to Rule 100 on fair trial guarantees, the ICRC notes that "[a] court is regularly constituted if it has been established and organized in accordance with the laws and procedures already in force in a country". ICRC, Customary IHL Database, Rule 100 Fair Trial Guarantees. Available at: <https://ihl-databases.icrc.org/en/customary-ihl/v1/rule100> accessed 10 October 2024.

362 R. Provost, *Rebel Courts: The Administration of Justice by Armed Insurgents* (Oxford University Press 2021) 152.

363 *Ibid.* 152.

364 *Ibid.* 215; H. Duffy, 'De facto justice: Prosecution by non-state actors in armed conflict' in K. Fortin and E. Heffes, *Armed Groups and International Law: In the Shadowland of Legality and Illegality* (Edward Elgar Publishing 2023) 247.

365 J. Pictet (ed.), *The Geneva Conventions of 12 August 1949: Commentary, Vol IV: Geneva Convention Relative to the Protection of Civilian Persons in Time of War* (ICRC 1958) Article 66, p. 340.

number of such "essential guarantees of independence and impartiality", including non-retroactivity, presumption of innocence and the right to be present.[366] In its Commentary from 1987, the ICRC makes clear that the term "regularly constituted court" in Common Article 3 was deliberately replaced by "a court offering the essential guarantees of independence and impartiality" as the former term may be understood to prevent Article 6(2) of Additional Protocol II from applying to courts established by non-state armed groups.[367] Therefore, in drafting the Additional Protocols, the ICRC seems to have taken into account that requiring courts to be "regularly constituted" in the sense that they need to be established in accordance with the national laws of the state already in force, does not reflect the reality of NIACs in which non-state armed groups do establish courts and administer justice. Article 6(2) of Additional Protocol II thus kept the door open for non-state armed groups to lawfully establish courts and administer justice, as long as such courts adhere to essential fair trial guarantees. In its subsequent Commentary from 2016, the ICRC indeed makes clear that this focus "on the capacity of the court to conduct a fair trial" instead of "on how it is established", takes better into account "the reality of non-international armed conflict".[368] This provision in Additional Protocol II does raise the question of whether the lawfulness of courts established by non-state armed groups should still depend on two distinct criteria, which dictate that a court must not only offer essential fair trial guarantees but must also be regularly constituted. The ICRC seems to clarify this by explicitly stating in the same Commentary that "courts are regularly constituted as long as they are constituted in accordance with the 'laws' of the armed group",[369] thus signaling that the two notions should not be conflated. Provost is also of the opinion that "[t]he requirement of independence and impartiality, touching on the decision-making process, is distinct from the requirement of regularly constitution [*sic*], reflecting the establishment of the court".[370] What can, in any case, be said is that the position of the ICRC in interpreting the notion of "regularly constituted court" seems to have evolved along with the reality of armed conflicts and non-state actors establishing and operating courts in practice.

Sources outside the field of IHL may also be relevant for the interpretation of this notion. As it remains applicable during armed conflict, interna-

366 Additional Protocol II to the Geneva Conventions, Article 6(2)(c)(d) and (e).

367 Y. Sandoz, C. Swinarski and B. Zimmermann (eds.), *Commentary on the Additional Protocols of 8 June 1977 to the Geneva Conventions of 12 August 1949* (ICRC 1987) para. 4600.

368 ICRC Commentary 2016 (n. 221) para. 678.

369 *Ibid.* para. 692.

370 R. Provost 2021 (n. 362) 216.

tional human rights law may, in particular, be of relevance here. International human rights law generally refers to a court "established by law". For example, Article 14(1) of the ICCPR refers to a "competent, independent and impartial tribunal established by law" and Article 6 of the ECHR likewise refers to an "independent and impartial tribunal established by law". In the *Case of Ilaşcu and Others v. Moldova and Russia*, the ECtHR interpreted this notion in light of a tribunal established by a non-state actor. It found that

> [i]n certain circumstances, a court belonging to the judicial system of an entity not recognised under international law may be regarded as a tribunal "established by law" provided that it forms part of a judicial system operating on a "constitutional and legal basis" reflecting a judicial tradition compatible with the Convention, in order to enable individuals to enjoy the Convention guarantees.[371]

The notion of "established by law" is thus interpreted by the ECtHR in line with the ICRC's interpretation of the notion of "regularly constituted court" in its 2016 Commentary, as a court which is based on 'law' broadly defined, and not necessarily referring to the pre-existing national laws of the state. What can, in any case, be concluded from the analysis above is that international law does not prohibit non-state actors from establishing and operating courts. In theory, the AANES lawfully established their own justice system in Northeast Syria. By early 2021, an estimated 8,000 Syrian IS fighters and Turkish-backed militias had already been prosecuted in Northeast Syria by the AANES.[372] Because their calls for repatriation were without avail, they asked support from the international community to also try third-country FTFs and associated family members in AANES courts.[373]

5.3.3.2 Desirability of Having FTFs Prosecuted by the AANES

Without going into detail about the procedures through which that justice system in Northeast Syria has been established and thereby determining whether it consist of courts which were regularly constituted, the following analysis will address the question of to what extent it would be desirable, from an international legal perspective, to have FTFs and associated family members prosecuted in those AANES courts. Through this analysis, the question of whether

---

371 *Case of Ilaşcu and Others v. Moldova and Russia* [2004] (Judgement) ECtHR App No. 48787/99 (8 July 2004) para. 460.

372 R. Provost 2021 (n. 362) 370.

373 T. Mehra and M. Wentworth, 2021 (n. 173).

such trials adhere to fundamental fair trial guarantees will, to some extent, be touched upon.

First, it should, in that regard, be noted that the AANES' constitution, which is called the 'Social Contract',[374] provides for several articles which dictate fundamental rights and freedoms that echo the UDHR, the ICCPR and other international human rights instruments. For example, the constitution abolishes the death penalty and prohibits civilians from standing trial before military courts. In addition, the constitution contains fundamental rule of law principles such as the independence of the judiciary and the separation of powers between the legislature, executive and the judiciary. Notably, the constitution also requires all judicial institutions to be composed of at least 40 percent female members. Commentators note that, especially, human rights standards in the AANES constitution are "significantly more progressive than that of the Syrian state", and "the protection given to fundamental rights and freedoms in Rojava compares favourably to that in many states, and in particular Syria".[375] It has also been noted that the prosecution of FTFs and their associated family members may be a way for the AANES and the SDF to "maintain 'law and order' and to ensure respect for humanitarian law".[376] For example, Duffy argues that trials by non-state actors or non-state armed groups such as the AANES and the SDF may be "imperative to a semblance of rule of law in the large swathes of the globe that are, in fact, under the exclusive control of [non-state armed groups]".[377] Finally, an argument mentioned in favor of prosecuting FTFs and family members by the AANES is that this may "fill the familiar impunity gap" left by the territorial state, i.e., Syria, and states of nationality.[378]

Conversely, it has also been mentioned that although in theory the AANES' constitution protects human rights, fundamental freedoms, and essential rule of law principles, fundamental human rights flaws have also been reported, especially with regard to terrorism trials. For example, Nadim Houry, former Director of Human Rights Watch's Terrorism and Counter-Terrorism Program, noted that "proceedings are deeply flawed. There are no defense lawyers

374 See, for an English translation of the AANES' constitution, <https://civiroglu.net/the-constitution-of-the-rojava-cantons/> accessed 10 October 2024.

375 R. Provost 2021 (n. 362) 365, 366, 368; G. Sary, 'Kurdish Self-governance in Syria: Survival and Ambition' Chatham House (15 September 2016) 11. Rojava is a name for the region in Northeast Syria under control of the AANES and the SDF.

376 ICRC Commentary 2016 (n. 221) para. 689; H. Duffy, 2023 (n. 364) 269.

377 H. Duffy 2023 (n. 364) 269.

378 *Ibid.* 268.

to represent suspects and no appeals process."[379] Furthermore, "a frail level of rule of law" has been documented in Northeast Syria, which "commonly consist of arbitrary arrest and detention practices, investigations and trials on the basis of political opposition, and mistreatment in detention".[380] Amnesty International also reports a number of fair trial issues, including the reliance on evidence obtained through torture or other ill-treatment,[381] a lack of access to legal counsel,[382] and an ineffective right to appeal.[383] In addition to a lack of defense counsels, there is reportedly also a lack of qualified judges, prosecutors and witness protection.[384] For these reasons, it has been questioned whether the AANES has the resources and the capacity to effectively administer justice, address the human rights and rule of law issues mentioned above, and adhere to guarantees of independence and impartiality.[385] Likewise, the former UN Special Rapporteur on the promotion and protection of human rights and fundamental freedoms while countering terrorism, Fionnuala Ní Aoláin, concluded that

> given the complexity of the military situation on the ground, and the lack of resources including judicial, technical and legal capacity in the territory concerned, also considering the practical deficiencies in legal processes conducted against Syrian nationals, the fundamental guarantees of fair trial cannot be currently delivered by the detaining authority in Northeast Syria.[386]

---

379 N. Houry, 'Bringing ISIS to Justice: Running Out of Time?' Just Security (5 February 2019). Available at: <https://www.justsecurity.org/62483/bringing-isis-justice-running-time/> accessed 10 October 2024.

380 R. Provost 2021 (n. 362) 372.

381 Amnesty International, Aftermath: Injustice, Torture and Death in Detention in Northeast Syria (2024). 182–184. Available at: <https://www.amnesty.org/en/documents/mde24/7752/2024/en/> accessed 24 October 2025.

382 *Ibid.* 185–187.

383 *Ibid.* 187–188.

384 *Ibid.* 181.

385 E. Heffes, 'Administration of justice by armed groups: Some legal and practical concerns' Humanitarian Law & Policy (22November 2018). Available at: <https://blogs.icrc.org/law-and-policy/2018/11/22/administration-of-justice-armed-groups-some-legal-practical-concerns/> accessed 10 October 2024.

386 UNHCHR, Position Paper of the United Nations Special Rapporteur on the promotion and protection of human rights and fundamental freedoms while countering terrorism, 'The prosecution of individuals with alleged links to designated non-State armed groups for crimes committed in the Northeast of Syria as a key aspect of the rights of victims of terrorism' (September 2023) 13–16. Available at: <https://www.ohchr.org/en/special-procedures/sr-terrorism/detention-and-repatriations-north-east-syria> accessed 24 October 2025.

States of nationality have so far refused any form of involvement in those trials. The AANES requested the international community to play a role in the prosecution of FTFs and third-country family members to overcome the aforementioned difficulties. One proposal from the AANES was to have international judges on the bench, which would enhance "independence and impartiality, and the legitimacy, competence and capacity of the bench, particularly to try international crimes".[387] However, such efforts to obtain international support were not successful. As a result of states' refusal to play a role in the prosecution of their nationals, "the approach of the AANES has changed from asking for the international community to play a role in the trials to asking them to provide coaching and support to help them maintain standards of due process such as provision of defence lawyers", which has likewise been without avail.[388] Among other possible reasons, states of nationality have likely been hesitant to provide such assistance because of the risk of being held responsible for complicity in violations of international law. However, without states' cooperation, it will not only be very unlikely that those rule of law, human rights, as well as practical difficulties such as the lack of judges, prosecutors and defense counsels, can be resolved, it will also be very unlikely that judgements rendered by AANES courts will eventually be recognized abroad, including by states of nationality.

Concerning the various difficulties that have been highlighted, without cooperation and oversight from states to ensure that trials of third-country FTFs and family members are in compliance with IHL, due process, and other human rights guarantees, prosecution by the AANES may not be a desirable solution. Although prosecution by AANES courts could indeed fill the impunity gap existing in Northeast Syria, such prosecution of FTFs and family members by the AANES may be undesirable when there is no assistance, support, coaching or other form of cooperation by states that can oversee and influence such proceedings.

5.3.3.3 What If a Non-state Actor Would Be 'Willing' and 'Able' to Prosecute?

The final question is, what is the consequence of all of this for the subsidiarity principle in inter-state relations? Even if it may not be a desirable solution in practice, the remaining question is thus what the consequence would be if an entity other than a state would be 'able' and 'willing' to prosecute? In other words, could the prosecution by a non-state actor in control of part of the territorial state's territory count as a national prosecution for the purpose of

387 H. Duffy 2023 (n. 364) 256.

388 T. Mehra and M. Wentworth 2021 (n. 173).

the subsidiarity principle? In the context of the subsidiarity principle in its vertical form, this issue has already arisen before the ICC. First, with regard to a request for an investigation into the situation in Georgia. The *de facto* separated region of South Ossetia administered justice in the territory it controlled. The admissibility issue that came up was whether it could be said that there was a national investigation or prosecution "by a State which has jurisdiction over it" in the sense of Article 17 of the Rome Statute. In its Decision of January 2016, the ICC Pre-Trial Chamber I found that "any proceedings undertaken by the *de facto* authorities of South Ossetia are not capable of meeting the requirements of article 17 of the Statute, due to South Ossetia not being a recognized State".[389] Second, the issue rose in the *Al-Werfalli* case as part of the Libya situation. Mahmoud Al-Werfalli was a commander within the 'Libyan National Army', a non-state armed group engaged in a NIAC against the Libyan Government and led by General Haftar. General Haftar had ordered the arrest of Al-Werfalli for a series of killings twice, but he was eventually released both times. Accordingly, the question arose whether "the case against Mr. Al-Werfalli is being or has been investigated in Libya within the meaning of article 17(1)(a)-(b) of the Statute".[390] The Pre-Trial Chamber I avoided answering the question regarding investigation and prosecution by non-state armed groups and noted that,

> irrespective of whether the entity exercising authority in the territory controlled by the [Libyan National Army] can be considered a State for the purposes of article 17 of the Statute, there remains a situation of inactivity. The Chamber recalls that for a case to be considered as "being investigated" within the meaning of article 17(1)(a) of the Statute, tangible, concrete and progressive investigative steps must have been taken.[391]

Besides these two instances before the ICC, the issue has also been discussed in the literature. For example, Kleffner notes that "the phenomenon of proceedings carried out by [organized armed groups] is conspicuously absent

389 ICC Pre-Trial Chamber I, Decision on the Prosecutor's request for authorization of an investigation of the situation in Georgia, No. ICC-01/15 (27 January 2016), para. 40.

390 ICC Pre-Trial Chamber I, In the Case of *the Prosecutor v. Mahmoud Mustafe Busayf Al-Werfalli*, No. ICC-01/11–01/17 (4 July 2018), para. 29.

391 *Ibid.* para. 27.

from the wording of the provisions of the Rome Statute relating to complementarity and their drafting history".[392] He eventually concludes that

> investigations and prosecutions or decisions not to prosecute have to be those of 'a State'. There is thus no obstacle to the admissibility of such cases if an investigation, prosecution or decision not to prosecute were that of an [organized armed group]. This is so regardless of whether or not such proceedings meet the requirements of willingness and ability that flow from a converse reading of Article 17(2) and (3).[393]

Schabas and El Zeidy note that an overly narrow interpretation of the term 'state' in Article 17 "could lead to an increase in the impunity gap" and that in the case of entities "whose status is contested but which enjoy an undisputed control of the territory and have the capacity to exercise jurisdiction", the Court might "nonetheless be willing to consider arguments as to the entity's standing for the purpose of article 17".[394] As an example, they give entities which are "unable to become a State Party in accordance with article 125 of the Statute because of the controversy surrounding [their] status at the United Nations", such as Taiwan.[395] They subsequently note that "entities which exhibit less State-like competencies" are more problematic.[396] Provost notes that there are circumstances under which entities like the AANES in North-east Syria "might properly be characterised as a state pursuant to Article 17 of the Rome Statute even if they are not recognised as states under public international law more generally",[397] i.e., when a state exercises effective control over such an entity, when a state authorizes the exercise of public authority, or when it acts as a *de facto* organ of that state.[398] Nevertheless, he also observes

392 J. Kleffner, 'The law and policy of complementarity in relation to 'criminal proceedings' carried out by non-state organized armed groups' in C. Stahn and M. El Zeidy (eds.) 2011 (n. 248) 708.

393 *Ibid.* 717; see also, J. Kleffner 2008 (n. 346) 109, 110. He notes that "regardless of the question of whether such authorities can be considered 'competent' – given that they regularly meet serious objections from a standpoint of impartiality and independence – the availability of such measures do not qualify as investigations, prosecutions and decisions not to prosecute by a 'State'" (footnote omitted).

394 W. Schabas and M. El Zeidy, 'Article 17 Issue of Admissibility' in O. Triffterer and K. Ambos, *Rome Statute of the International Criminal Court: A Commentary* (Verlag C. H. Beck, 3rd edition 2016) 795.

395 *Ibid.*

396 *Ibid.*

397 R. Provost 2021 (n. 362) 399.

398 *Ibid.* 399–402.

that this is most likely not the case with AANES courts as "Syria denies that a provincial authority has validly been established in Rojava".[399]

To sum up, some are of the opinion that there is room for arguing that prosecution by a non-state actor in control of part of a state's territory counts as a national prosecution for the purpose of Article 17 of the Rome Statute. However, even following this argumentation, the prosecution of FTFs by AANES courts would likely not qualify as a national prosecution "by a State which has jurisdiction". This is the case even if such a court would be 'able' and 'willing' to prosecute and could fill the void of judicial power left by the Syrian Government, which is deemed to be 'unable' to prosecute itself. Translated to the subsidiarity principle in inter-state relations, this would mean that states may not refer to the primacy of territorial jurisdiction and accordingly defer the exercise of jurisdiction to territorial states, if that would mean prosecution by a non-state actor in control over part of a state's territory, which is itself unable to exercise such jurisdiction.

5.4 Limits to the Primacy of Syria and Iraq's Jurisdiction

The analysis above focused on the international criminal law definitions of 'unable' and 'unwilling' as part of the complementarity principle in the Rome Statute, which is a form of vertical subsidiarity between a state and an international institution. However, as previously discussed, when interpreted progressively, the subsidiarity principle may also operate in the horizontal context of state to state jurisdiction, even beyond the universality principle alone. In this horizontal context, the subsidiarity principle dictates that the state with the strongest nexus to a given situation should be afforded the first opportunity to exercise criminal jurisdiction, *unless* that state is unable or unwilling to investigate or prosecute. In other words, before another state may actively support the exercise of jurisdiction by the state with the strongest nexus, a determination must be made as to whether that state is both 'able' and 'willing' to prosecute.

In the context of FTFs and their family members in Syria and Iraq, certain states of nationality have, rather than repatriating their nationals for domestic prosecution, supported the prosecution of such individuals in the region. By advocating for local prosecution, these states have effectively transferred the burden to prosecute onto states that are likely 'unwilling' or 'unable' to do so. In accordance with the progressive interpretation of the subsidiarity principle, states of nationality should, however, not support prosecutions in Syria and

---

399 *Ibid.* 403.

Iraq without first ensuring that these territorial states are genuinely able and willing to investigate and prosecute FTFs and their family members. Since it has been established that Syria and Iraq likely meet the international criminal law definitions of 'unable' and 'unwilling', the consequence is clear: in accordance with the subsidiarity principle and in pursuit of combating impunity, states of nationality should not defer jurisdiction to these territorial states.

In order to avoid impunity, states of nationality should not support the prosecution of their nationals in territorial states if it is clear that local prosecution is not possible. In such circumstances, states of nationality should take responsibility for the acts of their nationals abroad and prosecute them based on the active nationality principle. As Mégret observes "[t]he inability or unwillingness of the territorial state to prosecute certain crimes, depending on the character or gravity of the crime, might be understood as [...] needing to be overcome by the nationality state's intervention".[400] The nexus between states of nationality and the crimes committed abroad by their nationals, coupled with their interest in accountability for those crimes and the interest of the international community in preventing impunity for serious crimes such as war crimes and terrorist offences, strongly supports the exercise of jurisdiction based on the active nationality principle.

6 Pushing towards Prosecution by the AANES and Iraq: An Assessment under the Rules of *Non-refoulement*

This final section will assess states' push for prosecution by the AANES and Iraq in light of the rules of *non-refoulement*. The principle of *non-refoulement* can, among other legal bases, be found in international human rights law. Besides this vertical human rights dimension, there is also a clear inter-state dimension to this principle, which justifies it being discussed here. This horizontal dimension lies in the fact that the principle of *non-refoulement* regulates the transfer of a person from one state or territory to another state or territory. To begin with, this section will explain the principle of *non-refoulement* in more detail and will discuss its legal basis in refugee law, as well as human rights law and IHL. Thereafter, it will be argued that shunning the responsibility to prosecute and shifting the burden of prosecution to Iraq and the AANES directly goes against the object and purpose of *non-refoulement*. This is especially the case with states' push towards prosecution in Iraq, a

400 F. Mégret 2020 (n. 247) 39.

state which adopts the death penalty after trials which have been said to lack fair trial standards.

6.1 *Non-refoulement*

At its core, the principle of *non-refoulement* entails that states are prohibited from transferring, sending, expelling, deporting, extraditing or otherwise returning a person to a state, territory, authority or control where he or she faces a real risk of being subjected to violations of particular fundamental rights.[401] In addition, the principle also extends to what is referred to as 'chain' or 'indirect' *refoulement*, which means that states are likewise prohibited from transferring a person to another state where he or she would be at risk of subsequently being removed to yet another state, territory, authority or control in violation of the principle of *non-refoulement*.[402] *Non-refoulement* is a cornerstone of international refugee law. Article 33(1) of the 1951 Convention Relating to the Status of Refugees incorporated the principle and stipulates that states may not "expel or return ('refouler') a refugee in any manner whatsoever to the frontiers of territories where his life or freedom would be threatened on account of his race, religion, nationality, membership of a particular social group or political opinion".[403] Although this provision is non-derogable and not subject to reservations, there are a number of exceptions to it. First, Article 33(2) makes clear that the *non-refoulement* obligation does not apply to refugees who pose "a danger to the security of the country in which he is" and those refugees who, "having been convicted by a final judgment of a particularly serious crime", constitute "a danger to the community of that country". The Refugee Convention, therefore, does allow *refoulement* if a danger to the national security or community of the state of refuge can be proven. However, the threshold for these exceptions is high.[404] Second, those who do not fulfill the definition of a refugee as laid down in Article 1 of the Convention are mandatorily excluded from the protection of *non-refoulement* in international refugee law.[405]

---

401 C. Ferstman, 'Torture and non-refoulement' in M. Evans and J. Modvig (eds.), *Research Handbook on Torture* (Edgar Elgar 2020) 336.

402 *Ibid.*

403 Convention Relating to the Status of Refugees (adopted 28 July 1951, entered into force 22 April 1954) 189 UNTS 137.

404 R. Bruin and K. Wouters, 'Terrorism and the non-derogability of non-refoulement' 15 International Journal of Refugee Law (2003) 1: 16, 17.

405 Article 1(A)(2) of the 1951 Refugee Convention defines a refugee as a person who "owing to well-founded fear of being persecuted for reasons of race, religion, nationality, mem-

Besides being a central norm of refugee law, the principle can also be found in international human rights law. *Non-refoulement* can, among others, be found in the Convention against Torture and Other Cruel, Inhuman or Degrading Treatment or Punishment (CAT), the ICCPR and the ECHR. Article 3 of the CAT explicitly says that states shall not "expel, return ('refouler') or extradite a person to another state where there are substantial grounds for believing that he would be in danger of being subjected to torture". Notably, this provision frames the danger narrowly by referring to torture only. In its General Comment on the implementation of Article 3, the UN Committee against Torture underlined this limitation but also encouraged states to "consider whether the nature of the other forms of ill-treatment that a person facing deportation is at risk of experiencing could likely change so as to constitute torture, before making an assessment on each case relating to the principle of 'non-refoulement'".[406] Article 7 of the ICCPR provides that "[n]o one shall be subjected to torture or to cruel, inhuman or degrading treatment or punishment". In interpreting this Article, the Human Rights Committee accepted it to encompass a *non-refoulement* obligation and noted that states may "not expose individuals to the danger of torture or cruel, inhuman or degrading treatment or punishment upon return to another country by way of their extradition, expulsion or refoulement".[407] The protection against *refoulement* under the ICCPR is thus broader than under the CAT, as it frames the danger to encompass not only torture but also cruel, inhuman or degrading treatment. Like the ICCPR, Article 3 of the ECHR stipulates that "[n]o one shall be subjected to torture or to inhuman or degrading treatment or punish-

bership of a particular social group or political opinion, is outside the country of his nationality and is unable or, owing to such fear, is unwilling to avail himself of the protection of that country; or who, not having a nationality and being outside the country of his former habitual residence as a result of such events, is unable or, owing to such fear, is unwilling to return to it". In addition, Article 1(F) excludes persons from refugee status "with respect to whom there are serious reasons for considering that: (a) he has committed a crime against peace, a war crime, or a crime against humanity, as defined in the international instruments drawn up to make provision in respect of such crimes; (b) he has committed a serious non-political crime outside the country of refuge prior to his admission to that country as a refugee; (c) he has been guilty of acts contrary to the purposes and principles of the United Nations".

406 UN Committee against Torture, General Comment No. 4 (2017) on the implementation of article 3 of the Convention in the context of article 22 (4 September 2018) UN Doc. CAT/C/GC/4, para. 16.

407 Human Rights Committee, General Comment No. 20: Prohibition of Torture, or Other Cruel, Inhuman or Degrading Treatment or Punishment Article 7 (10 March 1992) UN Doc. A/44/40, para. 9.

ment".[408] The ECtHR has interpreted this provision as encompassing an obligation of *non-refoulement*. In the case of *Soering v. the United Kingdom*, the Court held that transferring a person to a state where he or she risks experiencing torture, inhuman or degrading treatment or punishment would be in violation of Article 3 and would "plainly be contrary to the spirit and intendment of the Article".[409] The inclusion of cruel, inhuman or degrading treatment or punishment into the obligation of *non-refoulement* by these treaty regimes is significant, as it allows risks of ill-treatment upon return to be captured by the *non-refoulement* obligation, including exceptional risks posed by harmful detention and living conditions.[410]

Within international human rights law, there is thus a clear *non-refoulement* obligation when it comes to torture and cruel, inhuman or degrading treatment or punishment. Unlike the *non-refoulement* obligation in the 1951 Refugee Convention, the aforementioned human rights protections are not subject to exceptions. Even when there is a risk of terrorism, the ECtHR has upheld the absolute nature of the prohibition of torture and the guarantee against *refoulement*.[411] The *non-refoulement* principle in human rights law is applicable to all individuals, not only those who satisfy the definition of a refugee. Moreover, while refugee law requires a causal nexus between the ill-treatment feared and particular grounds or causes for that treatment, such as race, religion or nationality, in human rights law, the rights of *non-refoulement* are unrelated to any such grounds or causes. It can thus be said that human rights law allows for a broader protection against *refoulement* than the 1951 Refugee Convention.

Besides the prohibition of torture and other forms of ill-treatment, the principle of *non-refoulement* has also been read into Article 6 of the ICCPR and Article 2 of the ECHR, which contain the right to life. Put differently, these human rights treaties have been interpreted as recognizing an obligation of

408 See also, Articles 5(2) and 22(8) of the ACHR; Article 13(4) of the Inter-American Convention to Prevent and Punish Torture (adopted 9 December 1985, entered into force 28 February 1987) OAS Treaty Series, No. 67; Article 5 of the ACHPR; and Article 19(2) of the Charter of Fundamental Rights of the European Union (adopted 12 December 2007, entered into force 1 December 2009) Official Journal of the European Union C 326/391.

409 *Case of Soering v. the United Kingdom* [1989] (Judgement) ECtHR App. No. 14038/88 (7 July 1989) para. 88.

410 See, for example, *Case of Aswat v. the United Kingdom* [2013] (Judgement) ECtHR App. No. 17299/12 (16 April 2013) paras. 49,50; and *Case of M.S.S. v. Belgium and Greece* [2011] (Judgement) ECtHR App. No. (21 January 2011) paras. 366–367; See also C. Ferstman 2020 (n. 401) 344, 345.

411 *Case of Saadi v. Italy* [2008] (Judgement) ECtHR App. No. 37201/06 (28 February 2008) paras. 127, 137–139. See also para. 80.

non-refoulement when there is a real risk of arbitrary deprivation of life. For example, the Human Right Committee noted that a state, "which has itself abolished the death penalty, would violate an individual's right to life under article 6, paragraph 1, if it were to remove a person to a country where they are under a sentence of death".[412] In addition, the Committee recalled that "the imposition of a death sentence on a person after an unfair trial is to subject that person wrongfully to the fear that he/she will be executed" which would violate the prohibition of inhuman treatment contained in Article 7 of the ICCPR.[413] Similarly, the ECtHR ruled that states should not transfer individuals "to stand trial on capital charges or in any other way subjecting individuals within its jurisdiction to a real risk of being sentenced to the death penalty".[414] Like the Human Rights Committee, the ECtHR also ruled that a well-founded fear of being executed may give rise to a significant degree of mental suffering which constitutes inhuman treatment in violation of Article 3 of the ECHR.[415] In addition to the prohibition of torture and other forms of ill-treatment and the right to life, the prohibition of *refoulement* has also been extended to other grounds, including a risk of being tried by a special or *ad hoc* court,[416] enforced disappearance,[417] a flagrant breach of the right to liberty and security,[418] and a risk of a flagrant denial of justice.[419]

Apart from refugee law and human rights law, the principle of *non-refoulement* can also be found in IHL. With regard to IAC, the Geneva Conventions III and IV contain a number of clear norms on the transfer of detainees. In more or less the same terms, these Conventions determine that prisoners of war and protected persons who are deprived of their liberty "may only be transferred by the Detaining Power to a Power which is a party to the

412 Human Rights Committee, *Kwok Yin Fong v. Australia* (23 November 2009), UN Doc. CCPR/C/97/D/1442/2005, paras. 9.4, 9.7.

413 *Ibid.*

414 *Case of Al-Saadoon and Mufdhi v. The United Kingdom* [2010] (Judgement) ECtHR App. No. 61498/08 (4 October 2010) para. 137.

415 *Ibid.*; *Case of Öcalan v. Turkey* [2005] (Judgement) ECtHR App. No. 46221/99 (12 May 2005) para. 169.

416 Article 13(4) of the Inter-American Convention to Prevent and Punish Torture.

417 The International Convention for the Protection of All Persons from Enforced Disappearance (adopted 20 December 2006, entered into force 23 December 2010) 2716 UNTS 3, Article 16.

418 *Case of Othman (Abu Qatada) v. The United Kingdom* [2012] (Judgement) ECtHR App. No. 8139/09 (9 May 2012) para. 233; *Case of Al Nashiri v Romania* [2018] (Judgement) ECtHR App. No. 33234/12 (8 October 2018) para. 596.

419 *Case of Soering v. the United Kingdom* (n. 408) para. 113; *Case of Othman (Abu Qatada) v. The United Kingdom* (n. 418) para. 258.

Convention and after the Detaining Power has satisfied itself of the willingness and ability of such transferee Power to apply the Convention".[420] Important to note is thus that the Geneva Conventions do not only prohibit transfer when there is a risk of torture, ill-treatment or a risk of arbitrary deprivation of life, but instead, when the receiving power is not willing or able to apply the respective Conventions as a whole. Put differently, all potential violations of the Conventions are relevant under these *non-refoulement* provisions. Although these provisions only apply to certain categories of persons, i.e., prisoners of war and civilians who are "in the hands of a Party to the conflict or Occupying Power of which they are not nationals",[421] it can be said that the rules on *non-refoulement* in IHL applicable in international armed conflict are much broader than those that can be found in refugee law and human rights law.[422] In addition, Article 45 of the Fourth Geneva Convention stipulates that "[i]n no circumstances shall a protected person be transferred to a country where he or she may have reason to fear persecution for his or her political opinions or religious beliefs", which resembles the prohibition of *refoulement* in the 1951 Refugee Convention. Also interesting is that both Geneva Conventions provide for post-transfer obligations, something that cannot be found either in refugee law or human rights law. They provide that if the receiving power "fails to carry out the provisions of the Convention in any important respect", the transferring power shall "take effective measures to correct the situation or shall request the return" of the transferred person.[423]

IHL applicable in NIAC, i.e., Common Article 3, Additional Protocol II to the Geneva Conventions, and customary IHL, does not contain an explicit *non-refoulement* obligation. Although this has been subject to debate, Common Article 3 has been interpreted to implicitly contain such an obligation.[424] In the ICRC's view,

420 Article 12 of Geneva Convention III and Article 45 Geneva Convention IV.

421 Article 4 Geneva Convention IV.

422 T. Rodenhäuser, 'Partnering in detention and detainee transfer operations' in R. Kolb, G. Gaggioli and P. Kilibarda, *Research Handbook on Human Rights and Humanitarian Law* (Edgar Elgar 2022) 397.

423 Article 12 of Geneva Convention III and Article 45 Geneva Convention IV.

424 T. Rodenhäuser 2022 (n. 422) 397, 398; B. Farley, 'Detainee Transfers and the Principle of Non-refoulement in Relation to "Non-belligerent Supporting States" in Non-international Armed Conflicts' 27 Journal of Conflict & Security Law (2022) 2: 199; OHCHR, Non-Refoulement and the Obligations of States to Persons Arbitrarily Detained in North-East Syria: Position Paper of the United Nations Special Rapporteur on the Promotion and Protection of Human Rights and Fundamental Freedoms while Countering Terrorism (October 2023) 5, 6. Available at: <https://www.ohchr.org/en/special-procedures/sr-terrorism/detention-and-repatriations-north-east-syria> accessed 14 November 2024.

> [b]ecause of the fundamental rights it protects, common Article 3 should be understood as also prohibiting Parties to the conflict from transferring persons in their power to another authority when those persons would be in danger of suffering a violation of those fundamental rights upon transfer.[425]

The reasoning it provides for this contention is similar to that provided by the Human Rights Committee and the ECtHR when arguing that a prohibition of *refoulement* can be read into the absolute prohibitions of torture, cruel, inhuman or degrading treatment or punishment. The ICRC explains that "humanitarian law applicable in non-international armed conflict should not be circumvented by transferring persons" and

> if the absolute prohibitions in human rights law mean that authorities must not only refrain from subjecting persons to such treatment but also from transferring them to places where they will be subjected to such treatment, there is no reason why it should not be the same under humanitarian law.[426]

An additional argument that has been advanced is built upon the obligation to ensure respect for the Geneva Conventions contained in Common Article 1. If a party to the armed conflict transfers a detainee to another authority, in whose custody there is reason to believe that the detainee would be subjected to torture, inhumane treatment or other violations of fundamental rights laid down in Common Article 3, the transferring power surely has not done everything in its power to ensure respect for that Common Article.[427]

What can be concluded from the foregoing is that the principle of *non-refoulement* has a firm legal basis in public international law. It is now widely accepted that a *non-refoulement* obligation, at least with regard to the prohibition of torture, is part of customary international law.[428] Some have even

---

425 ICRC Commentary 2016 (n. 221) para. 708.

426 *Ibid.* paras. 710 and 712. See also M. Sanderson, 'The Syrian Crisis and the Principle of *Non-Refoulement*' 89 International Law Studies (2013) 799.

427 *Ibid.* 711; B. Farley 2022 (n. 424) 199; T. Rodenhäuser 2022 (n. 422) 398.

428 C. Moran, 'Strengthening the principle of non-refoulement' 25 The International Journal of Human Rights (2021) 6: 1040; E. Lauterpacht and D. Bethlehem, 'The scope and content of the principle of non-refoulement: Opinion' in E. Feller, V. Türk and F. Nicholson (eds.), *Refugee Protection in International Law: UNHCR's Global Consultations on International Protection* (Cambridge University Press 2003) 87–177; C. Costello and M. Foster, 'Non-refoulement as Custom and *Jus Cogens*? Putting the Prohibition to the Test' in M. den Heijer and H. van der Wilt (eds.), *Netherlands Yearbook of International Law 2015* (T.M.C. Asser Press 2016) 273–327.

argued that it has attained the status of a *jus cogens* norm.[429] One final thing to mention here is that there is a widespread view that a state's *non-refoulement* obligations are not restricted to its own territory but apply "in any territory under its jurisdiction or any area under its control or authority".[430] This extra-territorial reach of the *non-refoulement* obligation becomes increasingly important to stress now that states have adopted practices "to actively impede individuals who may wish to seek protection from accessing their territories".[431] For example, through pushbacks at sea and physical barriers at their borders, as well as certain states' plans to process asylum seekers offshore, including the UK's plan to process asylum seekers in Rwanda and the Netherland's plan to send asylum seekers to Uganda for that purpose. States' *non-refoulement* obligations continue to apply extraterritorially to individuals under their jurisdiction. Actions taken exclusively outside a state's own territory may, therefore, still breach the principle of *non-refoulement*. With regard to pushbacks at sea, the ECtHR held that such practices can indeed breach the principle of *non-refoulement*, even if they occurred on the high seas.[432]

6.2 The Practice of Responsibility Shunning and Burden Shifting in Light of *Non-refoulement*

First of all, it should be noted that in the FTFs context in Syria and Iraq, the principle of *non-refoulement*, as discussed above, means that an FTF or family member may not be returned to his or her state of origin if he or she faces a real risk of being subjected to, *inter alia*, torture, cruel, inhumane or degrading treatment or punishment, or an arbitrary deprivation of life. However, as discussed at the beginning of this chapter, certain states of nationality have not tried to get their FTFs and family members back to prosecute them at home but instead have actively advocated for their prosecution in Iraq or by AANES courts in Northeast Syria. Those states' active encouragement of, possible engagement in, and support for prosecution by Iraq and the AANES is in direct conflict with the whole idea of *non-refoulement* as set out in the previous subsection. In light of the fact that Iraq uses the death penalty and the many fair trial concerns with regard to both Iraqi and AANES courts, including practices

429 C. Costello and M. Foster 2016 (n. 428); J. Allain, 'The *jus cogens* Nature of *non-refoulement*' 13 International Journal of Refugee Law (2001) 4.

430 UN Committee against Torture 2018 (n. 406) para. 10.

431 C. Ferstman 2020 (n. 401), 348.

432 *Case of Hirsi Jamaa and Others v. Italy* [2012] (Judgement) ECtHR App. No. 27765/09 (23 February 2012).

of torture, states of nationality's practice of shifting the burden to prosecute to Iraq and the AANES, ignores the very spirit and objective of the principle of *non-refoulement*. This is especially the case with regard to their push for the transfer of their nationals from Northeast Syria to Iraq to be prosecuted there. For example, France has allegedly been engaged in, or at least actively encouraged, the transfer of French detainees from Northeast Syria to Iraq, where they were sentenced to death following trials which only lasted two hours with a court-appointed lawyer who reportedly only met his client a few minutes before the start of the trial.[433] Even if those states are not actively involved in the removal of a person to any other territory, and there may thus not be a direct violation of their *non-refoulement* obligation, their active encouragement for those individuals to be transferred to, and prosecuted in, especially Iraq, results in serious violations of human rights in another jurisdiction. Furthermore, a state that has itself abolished the death penalty should not encourage the prosecution of its nationals in another state where the death penalty could be imposed. Instead, states should uphold the non-derogability of the principle of *non-refoulement* as well as fundamental human rights such as the right to life and the prohibition of torture and, for that reason, take steps to return their nationals for the purpose of prosecution at home.

7 Conclusions

This chapter has stressed important reasons why territorial states should be given the chance to prosecute atrocity crimes committed on their territory, like those committed by IS. However, this chapter has also tried to show that other states may not just blindly advocate for prosecution in such territorial states. Although, in theory, territorial states like Syria and Iraq may indeed be in the best position to prosecute, FTFs and family members' states of nationality should not invoke the primacy of territorial jurisdiction when it is clear that local prosecution is not possible because those states are unwilling or unable to actually and genuinely prosecute. Public international law does not seem to provide for a straightforward obligation dictating that states of nationality must exercise their criminal jurisdiction in case the state with the closest connection to the crimes is unable or unwilling to prosecute. However,

433 A. Rubin 2019 (n. 177); Commission Nationale Consultative des Droits de L'Homme 2020 (n. 284); S. Foltyn, 'Inside the Iraqi courts sentencing foreign Isis fighters to death' (*The Guardian*, 2 June 2019). Available at: <https://www.theguardian.com/world/2019/jun/02/inside-the-iraqi-courts-sentencing-foreign-isis-fighters-to-death> accessed 18 November 2024.

by continuing to point towards prosecution by a state which adopts the death penalty and which does not uphold fair trial standards as well as a non-state actor which does not have the capacity to prosecute in a manner which would guarantee standards of due process, independence and impartiality, and by refusing to return their nationals home for the purpose of prosecution, states of nationality directly go against the important goals towards which international law is directed. These include the prevention of impunity and ensuring that terrorists and war criminals do not enjoy safe haven; the non-derogable prohibition of torture; cruel, inhumane and degrading treatment or punishment; the right to life; and the right to a fair trial. These are all fundamental norms of public international law.

Furthermore, the active support of states of nationality for the prosecution of their FTFs and family members, especially in Iraq where they are at risk of being sentenced to death, raises serious questions about the robustness of the anti-death penalty norm in those states, their willingness to uphold the most fundamental human rights norms and to do so in good faith. States which have all for a long time advocated for the abolishment of the death penalty, seem far less insistent on upholding the anti-death penalty norm, as well as the prohibition of torture and fair trial standards, and may even seem willing to sacrifice such fundamental norms when it concerns individuals who joined a terrorist organization and potentially committed grave crimes.

This chapter aimed to answer the question to what extent international law limits the shunning of the responsibility to prosecute and the shifting of the burden to prosecute to a non-state actor like the AANES and a state like Iraq, which adopts the death penalty and practices of torture. What can be said is that by doing so, states of nationality push the law's boundaries and directly go against the underlying objects and purposes of the norms of public international law that are relevant to such practices. States' practice of responsibility shunning and burden shifting to Iraq and the AANES goes against the central ideals of public international law and signals a lack of good faith and double standards in upholding non-derogable norms of paramount importance to this field of law.

CHAPTER 6

Conclusion

1 States' Responses to the Foreign Terrorist Fighters Phenomenon in Syria and Iraq

Foreigners have participated in many conflicts in the past, with romanticized views of such individuals and multiple literary works being written about their experiences.[1] Although so-called 'foreign fighters' have been around for long, the phenomenon of individuals traveling to Syria and Iraq to join terrorist organizations following the outbreak of the Syrian Civil War in 2011 was unprecedented in several aspects. Notably, it prompted extraordinary, far-reaching responses by these individuals' states of origin. Through the adoption of Resolution 2178 in September 2014, the Security Council obliged states to take extensive measures to address the threat posed by so-called 'foreign terrorist fighters'.[2] Measures imposed by the Security Council included those to prevent, suppress, criminalize and punish, *inter alia*, the (attempt to) travel, and the financing, recruiting, organizing, transporting and equipping of such FTFs.[3] In addition, the Security Council ordered states to prevent the movement of such individuals through border controls and controls on the issuance of identity papers and travel documents,[4] as well as to employ traveler risk assessments and screening procedures.[5] Furthermore, the Security Council urged states to exchange information on such individuals,[6] and called upon them to require airlines to provide advance passenger information.[7] In sum, the Security Council required states to adopt measures with signifi-

1 See, for example, the novel *Homage to Catalonia* written by George Orwell, the novel *For Whom the Bell Tolls* written by Ernest Hemingway, as well as the novel *L'Espoir*, written by the French writer and politician André Malraux, who, like Orwell and Hemingway, fought for the Republicans during the civil war in Spain in the 1930s.
2 UNSC Res. 2178 (24 September 2014) UN Doc. S/RES/2178 (2014).
3 *Ibid.* paras. 4, 5, 6, 8.
4 *Ibid.* para. 2.
5 *Ibid.*
6 *Ibid.* para. 3.
7 *Ibid.* para. 9.

cant human rights implications,[8] without providing the necessary clarity on multiple aspects of the term 'foreign terrorist fighter' and its definition.[9]

In implementing this legally binding resolution, and with the threat that such FTFs and their accompanying family members potentially pose becoming more apparent, states of origin started adopting a wide range of measures. These include criminal and administrative measures to prevent travel, depriving individuals of their nationality, refusing repatriation and extending possibilities to prosecute. Overall, states of origin's responses to FTFs and their family members in Syria and Iraq, and especially those by European states, were and still are characterized by a wish to prevent their return and by an approach of trying to take their hands off the problem. This study argued that, through their responses of nationality deprivation, non-repatriation and their support for prosecution in the region, states of origin have largely shunned their responsibilities and shifted burdens and risks to other actors. These include states of destination, states of transit and states of residual nationality as well as the AANES in Northeast Syria. Furthermore, this study argued that inadequate efforts to prevent the travel of FTFs can likewise result in the shifting of a security threat and a corresponding burden to counter such a threat to other states.

In light of these horizontal, inter-state implications of states of origin's responses to the FTFs phenomenon in Syria and Iraq, this research engaged with questions such as: to what extent are states required to take the interests and potential impact on the security of other states and their population into account in their approach to the FTFs phenomenon? Are states, legally speaking, free to refrain from taking action and look the other way? And when a state's nationals or habitual residents travel, to what extent do responsibilities of their states of origin travel with them? More specifically, this research aimed to answer the following question: to what extent does public international law limit the shunning of responsibilities and the shifting of security

8 See, for example H. Duffy, '"Foreign Terrorist Fighters": A Human Rights Approach?' 29 Security and Human Rights (2018); F. Capone, 'Countering "Foreign Terrorist Fighters": A Critical Appraisal of the Framework Established by the UN Security Council Resolutions' 25 Italian Yearbook of International Law (2016) 1; L. Tayler, 'Foreign Terrorist Fighter Laws: Human Rights Rollbacks under UN Security Council Resolution 2178' 18 International Community Law Review (2016); L. Ginsborg, 'One step forward, two steps back: The Security Council, 'foreign terrorist fighters', and human rights' in M. Nowak and A. Charbord (eds.), *Using Human Rights to Counter Terrorism* (Edward Elgar 2018).

9 H. Duffy, 'International human rights law and terrorism: an overview' in B. Saul (ed.), *Research Handbook on International Law and Terrorism* (2nd edition, Edward Elgar Publishing 2020) 326, 327.

risks, as visible in states' responses to the phenomenon of foreign terrorist fighters and their family members in Syria and Iraq?

This study has focused upon four different responses by states of origin: (1) prevention of travel; (2) nationality deprivation; (3) refusal or reluctance to repatriate; and (4) prosecution or, rather, states' support for prosecution by Iraq and the AANES in Northeast Syria. Throughout four chapters, each addressing one of these different responses, the research has tried to answer the central research question. In this Conclusion, a few lessons learned, challenges, reflections and takeaways from these four chapters will be elaborated upon.

1.1 Prevention of Travel

Chapter 2 demonstrated that the obligation to prevent FTFs from traveling derives not only from several Security Council resolutions, in particular Resolutions 1373 (2001) and 2178 (2014),[10] but also from broader principles of public international law. These foundational norms, including the obligation to prevent transboundary harm to other states and the obligation not to interfere in the internal affairs of other states, provide a more comprehensive legal basis for state action. The chapter argued that greater emphasis should be placed on these underlying principles, both by states in deciding which measures to take as well as in assessing state compliance. Because these principles are first and foremost concerned with harm posed to other states, such a focus may encourage states to look beyond their own national interests and may bring their responsibilities and their actions and omissions in relation to other states more to the foreground. Although this conclusion was developed within the specific context of the FTFs phenomenon in Syria and Iraq, broader lessons can be drawn from it; lessons that can assist international cooperation efforts in tackling other transnational problems.

States frequently prioritize their own national interests without due regard for the implications of their actions and omissions on the interests of other states or on the interests of the international community more broadly. This tendency towards unilateralism is evident not only in the field of counter-terrorism but also across other areas, including migration, climate change and global health, and is very much a sign of the times. In the climate change context, major greenhouse gas-emitting states have often failed to adopt or comply with adequate mitigation measures, *inter alia*, due to economic con-

10 UNSC Res. 1373 (28 September 2001) UN Doc. S/RES/1373, para. 2(g); UNSC Res. 2178 (2014) (n. 2) paras. 2, 4, 5, 6(a).

cerns or a lack of political will. Such failure has, however, disproportionately affected other states, in particular low-lying and climate-vulnerable states.[11] Similarly, in the global health context, 'vaccine nationalism' and export bans during the COVID-19 pandemic undermined equitable access to essential health resources in other, less wealthy states.[12] In such contexts, where states' actions or inactions pose extraterritorial burdens or risks to other states, there is merit in re-emphasizing foundational principles of international law to help states to come up with more sustainable and long-term solutions. These foundational principles not only include the obligation to prevent transboundary harm and the obligation not to interfere in the internal affairs of other states, but also obligations of prevention, cooperation, and good faith as a standard of behavior. Strengthening and emphasizing such core principles of inter-state relations may encourage states to act as 'responsible neighbors', and may underline that states' own interests and other states' interests are very often intertwined. This remains the case even in a world of renewed nationalism and deglobalization.

1.2 Nationality Deprivation

While states have frequently rewarded supporters by bestowing nationality, e.g., Russia offering citizenship to foreign fighters in its war against Ukraine,[13] states have also stripped nationality of those they deem unwanted. In Chapter 3, it was explained that the measure of nationality deprivation has been used to prevent FTFs and their family members from returning or to otherwise exclude unwanted nationals from society. The practice of getting rid of disobedient or undesired nationals is a practice originally associated with authoritarian regimes. For example, Saudi Arabia and Russia have tried to get rid of

11 See, for example, B. Mayer, *International Law Obligations on Climate Change Mitigation* (Oxford University Press 2022); See for an analysis of states' failure to adopt climate change mitigation measures under international human rights law, B. Mayer, 'Climate Change Mitigation as an Obligation under Human Rights Treaties?' 115 The American Journal of International Law (2021) 3.

12 See, for example, T. Adekola and F. Majekolagbe, 'Human rights law, intellectual property and vaccine nationalism: lessons for the post-COVID-19 world' 29 Australian Journal of Human Rights (2023) 2; J. Pauwelyn, 'Export Restrictions in Times of Pandemic: Options and Limits under International Trade Agreements' 54 Journal of World Trade (2020) 5.

13 I. Nechepurenko, 'To Bolster Russia's Army, Putin Eases Citizenship Path for Foreign Fighters' (*The New York Times*, 5 January 2024). Available at: <https://www.nytimes.com/2024/01/05/world/europe/putin-russia-army-foreigners-citizenship.html> accessed 19 June 2025.

dissidents abroad through targeted killings, including the cases of Jamal Khashoggi and Alexander Litvinenko.[14] Another method of exclusion employed by authoritarian states is the politically motivated revocation or denial of passports to exiled dissidents. For instance, both China and Belarus have reportedly refused to renew or revoke the passports of exiled opposition figures, dissidents or ethnic activists abroad.[15] Furthermore, Bahrain has used the measure of nationality deprivation as a tool of oppression, targeting not only those convicted for terrorist offences but also human rights defenders, political dissidents, academics and journalists.[16]

Chapter 3 demonstrated that, beginning in the early 2000s, several European states started to expand the power to deprive nationality as part of their counter-terrorism efforts. Especially in their response to FTFs and their family members in Syria and Iraq, the measure of nationality deprivation became more widely used by European states. The expansion of this practice in Europe raises the critical concern whether those European states are fully aware that such measures mirror those employed by authoritarian regimes to silence and exclude unwanted nationals. Do European states really want to be associated with such practices? The normalization of this approach risks setting a dangerous precedent, especially when European states start to use these practices in different contexts. In fact, its application already seems to be expanding beyond the counter-terrorism context as it is increasingly being suggested as an appropriate measure in other situations. For example, politicians in the Netherlands suggested the expansion of nationality deprivation powers as a possible response to anti-Semitism following riots in the context of a football match between Ajax and Maccabi Tel Aviv in Amsterdam on

---

14 See, for example M. Milanovic, 'The Murder of Jamal Khashoggi: Immunities, Inviolability and the Human Right to Life' 20 Human Rights Law Review (2020) 1; see also the Case of *Carter v. Russia*, in which the ECtHR ruled that Russia was responsible for violating the right to life of Alexander Litvinenko. *Case of Carter v. Russia* [2021] (Judgement) ECtHR App. No. 20914/07 (21 September 2021).

15 F. Vincent, 'Belarus' exiled opposition figures are threatened with losing their citizenship' (*Le Monde*, 8 September 2023). Available at: <https://www.lemonde.fr/en/international/article/2023/09/08/belarus-exiled-opponents-are-threatened-with-losing-their-citizenship_6128543_4.html> accessed 19 June 2025; H. Szadziewski, 'Weaponized Passports: the Crisis of Uyghur Statelessness' Uyghur Human Rights Project (1 April 2020).

16 Salam for Democracy and Human Rights, Institute on Statelessness and Inclusion and the Hawiati MENA Statelessness Network, Arbitrary Revocation of Nationality in Bahrain: a Tool of Oppression (2021). Available at: <https://salam-dhr.org/arbitrary-revocation-of-nationality-in-bahrain-a-tool-of-oppression/> accessed 19 June 2025.

7 November 2024.[17] This development reflects a dangerous trend towards stigmatizing and excluding nationals from society, simplifying societal problems through xenophobic approaches, labeling certain individuals in society as unwanted and hence instrumentalizing the insiders-outsiders dichotomy for political gain.[18]

Within the FTF context, this chapter illustrated that in several cases, the first state to strip nationality was the state of predominant nationality, i.e., the state to which the individual concerned had the closest ties. Leaving the responsibility to re-admit such individuals and to subsequently prosecute, reintegrate and rehabilitate them, if appropriate, with a state of residual nationality, to which the individual concerned may not have a meaningful connection, in which he/she may not have any family members and in which he/she may never have resided. Because of its close ties to the individual concerned, states of predominant nationality are generally best equipped to reintegrate FTFs and their family members in their society and provide for the most suitable environment to minimize the risk of renewed involvement with terrorism. Therefore, this study advocated a role for the notion of predominant nationality and a special responsibility upon states of predominant nationality. This is not only important from an international (human rights) law point

---

17 COT Instituut voor Veiligheids- en Crisismanagement, 'Onder druk: Evaluatie van de gebeurtenissen in Amsterdam rond de wedstrijd Ajax – Maccabi Tel Aviv op 7 November 2024' (June 2025). Available at: <https://www.amsterdam.nl/bestuur-organisatie/college/burgemeester/persberichten/onderzoeksrapport-ajax-macabbi/> accessed 7 July 2025.

18 However, there is also an increasingly visible opposition towards this practice. In a recent decision, the District Court of Amsterdam ruled that the Dutch Government could not strip a Dutch–Moroccan dual national of his Dutch nationality, because doing so would constitute direct racial discrimination. The Court found that the distinction between a person with only the Dutch nationality, who cannot be deprived of that nationality, and a person with dual nationality, who can be deprived of his or her Dutch nationality, was based on descent or national or ethnic origin, thereby violating the International Convention on the Elimination of All Forms of Racial Discrimination. This judgement can be read as a counterbalance to the increasing tendency among Dutch politicians to consider, or threaten with, nationality deprivation as a response to societal challenges. District Court of Amsterdam, ECLI:NL:RBAMS:2025:1849 (24 March 2025); International Convention on the Elimination of All Forms of Racial Discrimination (signed 7 March 1966, entered into force 4 January 1969) 660 UNTS 195 (ICERD), Article 2(1) (a). See also OHCHR, Amicus brief, Presented by the UN Special Rapporteur on Contemporary Forms of Racism, Racial Discrimination, Xenophobia and Related Intolerance, before the Dutch Immigration and Naturalization Service (23 October 2018). Available at: <https://www.ohchr.org/sites/default/files/Documents/Issues/Racism/SR/Amicus/DutchImmigration_Amicus.pdf> accessed 20 June 2025.

of view but also from a long-term national and international security perspective.

1.3 (Non-)Repatriation

Chapter 4 examined states' refusal or long-time hesitance to repatriate their FTFs and family members in Syria and Iraq. It challenged the assumption that because their nationals are located abroad, outside their control, states of origin are free to look the other way and shift the problem those individuals potentially pose to regional actors. Two reflections emerging from this discussion should be mentioned here.

First, in a relatively recent decision, the CRC Committee found that France exercised extraterritorial jurisdiction over French children detained in camps in Northeast Syria.[19] Among the relevant factors, the nationality of the children played an important role in the Committee's finding that France exercised extraterritorial jurisdiction over them. This decision by the CRC Committee thus implies a special responsibility upon states of nationality in relation to their nationals abroad. While this study supports the idea of such a responsibility upon states of nationality, irrespective of any alleged criminal conduct of their nationals abroad, tying extraterritorial jurisdiction under international human rights law to nationality may not be the right way to establish such a special responsibility. In particular, for the important reason that states' obligations under international human rights law do, and indeed should, not depend on a person's nationality.[20]

Second, in this chapter, it was demonstrated that the law of state responsibility lacks the necessary flexibility to respond to the complex detention situation that was, at least in part, caused by states of origin's non-repatriation policies. However, it is important to emphasize that the value of international law extends beyond invoking state responsibility and obtaining a decision by an international court.[21] International law is of much greater significance. It

19 CRC Committee, *L.H. et al. v. France* (2 November 2020) UN Doc. CRC/C/85/D/79/2019; CRC/C/85/D/109/2019. See also CRC Committee, *F.B. et al v France* (4 February 2021) CRC/C/86/D/R.77/2019.

20 See for example, CRC Art. 2(1).

21 Because of jurisdictional barriers, it will be unlikely that an international claim can be brought before a court handling inter-state disputes, in particular the ICJ. However, it is more likely that individuals will bring claims on the national and on the international level. For example, before human rights treaty bodies and before regional human rights courts such as the ECtHR. In fact, some individuals have already brought such claims on the national and international level. Some of these cases have been discussed throughout this research. See, for example, CRC Committee, *F.B. et al. and D.A. et al. v. France*

gives us the legal language and arguments to hold states accountable for their behavior. Even though there exists a legal vacuum in the international law of state responsibility when it comes to the situation in Northeast Syria, international law does impose limits on states' inaction and passive behavior. In that regard, this study provides the arguments and the language of public international law for condemning states' policies and practices of shunning responsibilities and shifting risks, including their refusal to repatriate.

1.4 Prosecution

The final chapter of this study examined the issue of prosecution and focused on the states of origin's support or push for prosecution in the region by Iraq and the AANES in Northeast Syria. This study underscored that there are important reasons why territorial states should be able to exercise their jurisdiction over crimes committed on their territory, especially in the case of mass atrocities. This also reflects the primacy that is generally given in international law to the territoriality principle for the exercise of jurisdiction. However, this study argued that states of nationality should not invoke such territorial jurisdiction if it is clear that local prosecution is not possible, either because the territorial state does not have the capacity to prosecute, is not willing, or otherwise does not have the ability to prosecute in accordance with international (human rights) law standards. In such circumstances, states of nationality should take responsibility for the acts of their nationals abroad and prosecute them based on the active nationality principle.

Chapter 5 showed that international law imposes important constraints on the extent to which states can shift the burden to prosecute onto regional actors. At the same time, it is also important to acknowledge the substantial challenges faced by national prosecutors in pursuing cases against FTFs and their family members and, in particular, the difficulty of securing the necessary admissible evidence for successful prosecutions.

In light of these obstacles, the reluctance of states of origin to actively repatriate such individuals is, to some extent, understandable, especially where there is a risk that they would go free and remain unpunished upon return. However, these challenges cannot be used to justify violations of international

---

(9 March 2022) UN Doc. CRC/C/89/D/77/2019; CRC/C/89/D/79/2019; CRC/C/89/D/109/2019; CRC Committee, *P.N et al. v. Finland* (20 October 2022) UN Doc. CRC/C/91/D/100/2019; UN Committee against Torture, *C.P. et al. v. France* (2 March 2023) UN Doc. CAT/C/75/D/922/2019; UN Committee against Torture, *P.D. v. France* (15 February 2024) UN Doc. CAT/C/78/D/1045/2020; *Case of H.F. and Others v. France* [2022] (Judgement) ECtHR App. Nos. 24384/19 and 44234/20 (14 September 2022).

legal obligations or serve as a basis to systematically undermine their object and purpose. States of origin remain bound by international legal obligations such as those requiring states to prosecute war crimes and terrorist offences. Therefore, instead of finding ways to shift the burden to prosecute away to Iraq and the AANES, states should prioritize ways to build strong cases against FTFs at home, and if necessary, against their family members.

Such efforts may include enhancing cooperation with international bodies that have collected evidence, such as the United Nations Investigative Team to Promote Accountability for Crimes Committed by Daesh (UNITAD),[22] and the International, Impartial and Independent Mechanism to assist in the investigation and prosecution of persons responsible for the most serious crimes under International Law committed in the Syrian Arab Republic since March 2011 (IIIM).[23] In this regard, states should work together to strengthen international efforts aimed at securing evidence, and should perhaps consider establishing a permanent body to assist national authorities in prosecuting suspected perpetrators of grave crimes. States could also focus more on inter-state cooperation through mutual legal assistance, including seeking support from institutions such as the European Union Agency for Criminal Justice Cooperation (Eurojust).[24] This is especially relevant in cases involving FTFs, where the alleged criminal conduct often spans multiple countries. In such cases, coordinated efforts to collect and share admissible evidence can significantly strengthen cases against FTFs within the state of origin's jurisdiction.

In sum, instead of pushing the burden to prosecute away to a state that adopts the death penalty or to a non-state actor without the necessary capacity, states of origin should prioritize strengthening their ability to bring cases against FTFs and, where appropriate, their family members within their own jurisdiction, in accordance with international law.

---

22 UNITAD was established pursuant to Security Council Resolution 2379 (2017), based on a request from the Government of Iraq. See Security Council Resolution 2379 (21 September 2017) UN Doc. S/RES/2379. UNITAD concluded its mandate on 17 September 2024 pursuant to Security Council Resolution 2697 (15 September 2023) UN Doc. S/RES/2697.

23 The IIIM was established by the UN General Assembly, pursuant to General Assembly Resolution 71/248 (11 January 2017) UN Doc. A/RES/71/248.

24 Eurojust was created in 2002 and operates on the basis of Article 85 of the Treaty of Lisbon and the Eurojust Regulation. See, Treaty of Lisbon amending the Treaty on European Union and the Treaty establishing the European Community (signed 13 December 2007, entered into force 1 December 2009) 2702 UNTS 47938; Regulation (EU) 2018/1727 of 14 November 2018 on the European Union Agency for Criminal Justice Cooperation (Eurojust).

2 Shunning Responsibilities and Shifting Risks: The Limits of Public International Law

This study made clear that, in the context of states' responses to the FTFs phenomenon in Syria and Iraq, public international law imposes constraints on the shunning of responsibilities and the exportation of security risks in a number of ways. These constraints arise not only from core principles and general obligations of prevention, cooperation and standards of good faith, but also from more specific legal norms and their underlying rationales. In addition to analyzing these limitations, this research also made proposals for legal change through alternative interpretations of the law.

Although this research is a case study of FTFs and their family members in Syria and Iraq, its central argument has broader relevance. First, it contributes to both academic and practical debates on the broader topic of foreign (terrorist) fighters and the way that states should respond to them. As multiple experts have pointed out, current or future armed conflicts, including in the Middle East, will inevitably attract new flows of such individuals.[25] In other words, "where there is war, there will be a willing cohort".[26] This can, for example, be evidenced by the foreign fighter flow that emerged after the full-scale invasion by Russia of Ukraine in February 2022,[27] FTFs traveling to Somalia, Mali and other African countries to join terrorist organizations there,[28] and concerns that, after the US withdrew from Afghanistan in August 2021, Afghanistan would become "a home for foreign fighters to train and

25 P. Gurski, *Western Foreign Fighters: The Threat to Homeland and International Security* (Rowman & Littlefield 2017) 136; D. Byman, *Road Warriors: Foreign Fighters in the Armies of Jihad* (Oxford University Press 2019) 240; T. Hegghammer, 'The Rise of Muslim Foreign Fighters: Islam and the Globalization of Jihad' 35 International Security 3: 91; D. Malet, *Foreign Fighters: Transnational Identity in Civil Conflicts* (Oxford University Press 2013) 213, 214.

26 P. Gurski 2017 (n. 25) 136.

27 B. McKernan, 'Ukraine appeals for foreign volunteers to join fight against Russia' (*The Guardian*, 27 February 2022). Available at: <https://www.theguardian.com/world/2022/feb/27/ukraine-appeals-for-foreign-volunteers-to-join-fight-against-russia> accessed 9 May 2025; H. Sokolova-Stekh, 'How Russia is recruiting foreigners to fight in Ukraine' (*Deutsche Welle*, 22 August 2024). Available at: <https://www.dw.com/en/how-russia-is-recruiting-foreigners-to-fight-in-ukraine/a-70019040> accessed 9 May 2025.

28 J. Seldin, 'Foreign fighters flocking to Islamic State in Somalia' (*VOA News*, 20 November 2024). Available at: <https://www.voanews.com/a/foreign-fighters-flocking-to-islamic-state-in-somalia/7871573.html> accessed 9 May 2025; A. Zelin, 'The Islamic State on the March in Africa' The Washington Institute for Near East Policy (1 March 2024). Available at: <https://www.washingtoninstitute.org/policy-analysis/islamic-state-march-africa> accessed 9 May 2025.

plot".[29] The core message of this research is that states should not dodge their responsibilities and displace burdens and risks on other states, especially those lacking the capacity to manage them effectively. Although focusing on the context of FTFs in Syria and Iraq, the legal analysis and argumentation presented in this study also aim to inform the way that states respond to such future foreign (terrorist) fighter flows. It aims to discourage states of origin from resorting to measures like nationality deprivation, refusal to repatriate or otherwise taking their hands off the potential problem in ways that undermine international law.

Second, this case study reflects a broader and increasingly worrying trend that extends beyond the context of states' responses to current and future flows of foreign (terrorist) fighters. The way that states have responded to the FTFs phenomenon in Syria and Iraq risks setting an alarming precedent. More specifically, the outsourcing of responsibilities and far-reaching measures that result in the shifting of burdens and security threats onto other states, are becoming common in other contexts as well. For example, it appears increasingly acceptable for states to invoke the measure of nationality deprivation. As noted earlier, the Netherlands has debated employing this measure in response to alleged anti-Semitic behavior, demonstrating that states are not only using nationality deprivation as a counter-terrorism measure but now also considering using this measure to exclude nationals in other contexts. This tendency to shift responsibilities and export burdens and risks to other states is also evident in the migration context. Several European states, including the United Kingdom,[30] Italy[31] and the Netherlands,[32] have concluded or consider concluding agreements to transport asylum seekers to third states, such as Rwanda, Albania and Uganda. Likewise, the European Union has entered into arrangements with southern Mediterranean states, including Libya and Tunisia, aimed at externalizing border controls and man-

---

29 D. Byman, 'Counterterrorism Successes against Foreign Fighters' Lawfare (10 November 2021). Available at: <https://www.lawfaremedia.org/article/counterterrorism-successes-against-foreign-fighters> accessed 9 May 2025.

30 'What is the UK's plan to send asylum seekers to Rwanda?' (*BBC News*, 13 June 2024). Available at <https://www.bbc.com/news/explainers-61782866> accessed 23 June 2025.

31 R. Shehu, 'Italy sends migrants to Albania in third try to start scheme' (*Deutsche Welle*, 31 January 2025). Available at: <https://www.dw.com/en/italy-sends-migrants-to-albania-in-third-try-to-start-scheme/a-71464347#:~:text=According%20to%20the%202023%20agreement,seekers%20were%20returned%20to%20Italy> accessed 23 June 2025.

32 S. Pronk, 'Kabinet wil mogelijkheid verkennen asielzoekers uit te zetten naar Oeganda' (*NRC*, 16 October 2024). Available at: <https://www.nrc.nl/nieuws/2024/10/16/kabinet-wil-mogelijkheid-asielzoekers-uit-te-zetten-naar-oeganda-verkennen-a4869608> accessed 23 June 2025.

aging migration flows extraterritorially.[33] A similar dynamic can be observed in Australia's offshore detention regime, under which migrants arriving by boat are sent to offshore detention facilities in Nauru and Papua New Guinea, where they are indefinitely detained under inhumane conditions.[34] These practices effectively transfer the burden and responsibility to protect such vulnerable individuals to third states that often have less economic strength and fewer organizational capabilities to ensure due process and adequate protection.

Within this broader trend of states outsourcing responsibilities and exporting burdens and security threats, three further observations emerge and warrant brief attention. First, it has become clear that states favor short-term responses over sustainable long-term solutions. As this study has demonstrated, this tendency is particularly visible in the context of FTFs and their family members in Syria and Iraq. Responses such as nationality deprivation, refusal to repatriate and supporting the prosecution of their nationals by a non-state actor instead of prosecuting them domestically, all point towards a preference for immediate political and security gains over long-term sustainable solutions. Second, it has become apparent that states increasingly resort to old ways of treating nationals. As examined in this study, practices of nationality deprivation and states' actions to otherwise exclude or disown nationals whom they have come to see as unwanted closely resemble the antiquated punishment of banishment. In a way, this shows that states are moving backwards in how they treat some of their nationals. Third, in the terrorism context, far-reaching measures are becoming available to authorities once the terrorism label is applied, including the measure of nationality deprivation. However, vague and legally ambiguous notions of terrorism have allowed states to resort to such far-reaching, often preventative and coercive, counter-terrorism measures with regard to an ever-broader group of people. It has become increasingly easy to expand the terrorism label to, for example,

---

33 L. Martini and T. Megerisi, 'Road to nowhere: Why Europe's border externalisation is a dead end' European Council on Foreign Relations (14 December 2023).

34 See for example, J. Barnes, 'Suffering to Save Lives: Torture, Cruelty, and Moral Disengagement in Australia's Offshore Detention Centres' 35 Journal of Refugee Studies (2022) 4; A. Pronk, 'The price of deterrence Australia's path to maintaining sovereign borders' Clingendael Report (February 2024). The Human Rights Committee ruled that Australia remained responsible for the arbitrary detention of migrants in these offshore detention facilities. See, Human Rights Committee, *M. I. et al. v. Australia* (23 January 2025) UN Doc. CCPR/C/142/D/2749/2016; Human Rights Committee, *M. Nabhari v. Australia* (22 January 2025) UN Doc. CCPR/C/142/D/3663/2019.

progressive dissidents, such as climate activists.[35] This raises the question of where the expansion of the notion of terrorism and the use of these far-reaching measures will stop. As reflected in this study, applying the terrorism label increasingly serves as a way for states to draw the line between nationals worthy of protection and nationals unworthy of such protection,[36] between insiders and outsiders.

In sum, although this research is a case study, it reflects a broader tendency with significant implications. These types of far-reaching measures and states' passive behavior, whereby they shift their problems to other states and shed people whom they perceive as unwanted, risks becoming the norm of how states respond to a range of societal challenges. This pattern of pushing away burdens, responsibilities, threats and undesired people is deeply concerning for at least two reasons. First, because it leaves vulnerable individuals caught in a web of states unwilling to provide protection, raising significant human rights concerns. Second, because it not only undermines and weakens international law, but also the core principles on which international law and the international legal order are based, as well as international law's essential character of reciprocity.

Reciprocity implies that states mutually owe each other equivalent rights and obligations.[37] The observance and effectiveness of international law are to a large extent dependent upon this character of reciprocity. Compliance by one state incentivizes other states to do the same. This dynamic is particularly

35 C. Gearty, *Homeland Insecurity: The Rise and Rise of Global anti-Terrorism Law* (Polity Press 2024) 202, 203.

36 For example, the guarantees and protection of criminal law that often do not apply to counter-terrorism measures, including fair trial guarantees, opportunities to challenge, judicial review, high standards of proof etc. Other forms of protection include consular assistance, including in the form of repatriation, and protection from extradition. In addition, with regard to the measure of nationality deprivation, the protection offered by, and rights associated with, the nationality of a particular state.

37 Whelan defines reciprocity as referring to the "legal interdependence of the corresponding rights and obligations States mutually owe each other" A. Whelan, *Reciprocity in Public International Law* (Cambridge University Press 2023) 6. Kałduński explains reciprocity as "returning like behaviour with the like" and envisioning "tit-for-tat (an exchange of things that may be different, but equal in value) or tat-for-tat (an exchange that is identical in both form and value) treatment that balances rights and obligations". See, M. Kałduński, 'Introduction: Framework of the Book' in M. Kałduński (ed.), *Reciprocity in International Law* (Palgrave Macmillan 2024) 9. In Simma's words, reciprocity refers to "a relationship between two or more States under which a certain conduct by one party is in one way or another juridically dependent upon that of the other party". See, B. Simma, 'Reciprocity' Max Planck Encyclopedias of International Law (April 2008) para 2.

important because the international legal order lacks a central enforcement mechanism similar to national legal systems. This study, however, highlighted a growing tendency in which the relationship between states is no longer grounded in reciprocity, i.e., one characterized by an equivalent exchange of rights and obligations, but rather, in the exporting, offloading and dumping of problems onto other states. In this context, states must realize that international law's reciprocal character serves their own long-term self-interest. Observing international legal obligations and respecting the rights of other states strengthens the very international legal framework that protects them in return. Conversely, disregarding the rights of other states and violating international legal obligations undermines the very system that protects all participants. It is thus to states' own benefit to observe rules of international law and in their own benefit that such rules continue to exist and do not lose their power. This self-interest in preserving international law's character of reciprocity is especially relevant for European states, which are unlikely to benefit from a world order in which powerful states such as the United States and China operate entirely unconstrained by international law.

In recent years, states have progressively undermined international law. They have abandoned international institutions, withdrawn from international conventions, challenged the authority of international courts and tribunals and invoked international law to justify violations. Examples include withdrawals from the ICC,[38] sanctions against the institution and its staff members,[39] political initiatives to curtail the power of the ECtHR,[40] rejections of decisions by international courts[41] and withdrawals from humanitarian dis-

---

38 Burundi and the Philippines have both withdrawn from the Rome Statute. See for an analysis of the implications of such withdrawals Y. Tan, 'Withdrawal from the Rome Statute Its Impact on the Continuity of ICC Proceedings' 22 Journal of International Criminal Justice (2024) 3–4. In addition, Hungary has recently announced that it will be withdrawing from the Rome Statute. See, 'Hungarian lawmakers approve bill to quit International Criminal Court' (*Reuters*, 20 May 2025). Available at: <https://www.reuters.com/world/hungarian-lawmakers-approve-bill-quit-international-criminal-court-2025-05-20/> accessed 26 June 2025.

39 J. Galbraith, 'U.S. Sanctions on the International Criminal Court: The Details and The Pattern' Verfassungsblog (7 June 2025).

40 K. Dzehtsiarou, 'The United Kingdom and the European Convention on Human Rights: Together Until the End?' 5 European Convention on Human Rights Law Review (2024).

41 P. Ngendakumana, Swiss parliament spurns European climate ruling: Both chambers accused the ECHR of "judicial activism." (*Politico*, 12 June 2024). Available at: <https://www.politico.eu/article/swiss-parliament-european-court-human-rights-votes-reject-european-climate-ruling/?ref=climateinthecourts.com> accessed 18 June 2024.

armament treaties.[42] Notably, the United States withdrew from the Paris Agreement, the World Health Organization and the UN Human Rights Council, the UK withdrew from the European Union and the Security Council has been paralyzed because of its permanent members' veto power. In addition, the United States threatening to occupy Greenland and Canada, and Russia's full-scale invasion of Ukraine in February 2022, are all examples of developments eroding and undermining international law. These developments exemplify a broader 'backlash' against international law, which is fueled by, *inter alia*, nationalism, populism and a resurgence of unilateralism.[43] This 'backlash' occurs against the backdrop of heightened geopolitical tensions, in which the role played by international law has become less central. States appear increasingly reluctant to engage in the development of international law and less willing to commit themselves to new rules of international law. The question is how international law should respond to such a turn against it. As reflected in this study, in such times we must return to international law's core. Rather than seeking to establish new norms of international law and making states commit to them, this study underscored the renewed importance of the fundamentals of public international law. In these times, marked by a growing disengagement from the rules-based international legal order, reaffirming the fundamentals of international law may prove more effective in reinforcing the international legal system. A return to the core of international law, to fundamental principles, could not only strengthen international law itself but also foster a deeper commitment for states to take each other's interests into account, thereby serving their own interests in the long run.

However, this study is not solely concerned with how states undermine international law; it is also concerned with how their conduct erodes their own credibility. European states consistently promote certain values such as the rule of law, equality, human dignity and human rights.[44] Furthermore, the Treaty of Lisbon explicitly mentions that the EU shall contribute to "the strict observance and the development of international law".[45] Yet, these same states are now offloading responsibilities and externalizing burdens and risks in ways that fundamentally contradict the values they claim to uphold. European states are now using far-reaching measures like nationality deprivation, which is a tool associated with authoritarian regimes seeking to suppress

42 L. Wu, 'Breaking the Window: Withdrawals from Humanitarian Disarmament Treaties' EJIL:Talk! (17 June 2025).

43 J. Nijman and W. Werner (eds.), *Netherlands Yearbook of International Law 2018: Populism and International Law* (Springer 2019).

44 These core values are laid down in the Lisbon Treaty, Articles 2 and 3.

45 Lisbon Treaty, Article 3(5).

nationals deemed to be unwanted. Isn't this a clear case of double standards? On the one hand, those states promote human rights and the rule of law as core societal values, but on the other hand, treat their nationals in a similar way as authoritarian states that do not embrace human rights and the rule of law as core values for dealing with their nationals. In doing so, European states risk undermining their own credibility and reputation, together with the values they purport to defend.

Throughout its four chapters, this study has offered the legal tools and legal language for condemning states' inaction and passive behavior. Although this research is a case study, focusing on the FTFs phenomenon in Syria and Iraq, it stands for a much bigger and problematic development on the national and international level. A development in which states increasingly shun responsibilities and shift risks away from their territory, instead of pursuing sustainable long-term solutions. In the context of FTFs and their family members in Syria and Iraq, such responses by states of origin have resulted in the indefinite detention of thousands of third-country nationals in camps and other detention facilities in Northeast Syria and in Iraqi prisons. Likewise, in other settings, such practices have resulted in societal challenges being exported to other states and individuals being pushed into the hands of states unable to provide them with the necessary protection. If this disturbing development continues to spread, it will have far-reaching consequences, not only for the international legal order, but also for individuals who are affected by these practices, and perhaps most of all for the character of our societies. This study, therefore, should also be read as a compelling invitation, based on public international law, for states to act differently, primarily – but by no means exclusively – in the case of FTFs and their family members in Syria and Iraq.

Treaties and National Legislation

International Treaties

1907 Hague Convention Respecting the Rights and Duties of Neutral Powers and Persons in Case of War on Land (adopted 18 October 1907, entered into force 26 January 1910) 205 CTS 299

1907 Hague Convention of Neutral Powers in Naval War (adopted 18 October 1907, entered into force 26 January 1910) 205 CTS 395

1930 Convention on Certain Questions Relating to the Conflict of Nationality Law (signed 13 April 1930, entered into force 1 July 1937) 179 UNTS 89 (1930 Hague Convention)

1945 United Nations Charter (signed 26 June 1945, entered into force 24 October 1945) 1 UNTS 16 (UN Charter)

1948 Convention on the Prevention and Punishment of the Crime of Genocide (adopted 9 December 1948, entry into force 12 January 1951) 78 UNTS 277

1949 Geneva Convention for the Amelioration of the Condition of the Wounded and Sick in Armed Forces in the Field (signed 12 August 1949, entered into force 21 October 1950) 75 UNTS 31 (GCI)

1949 Geneva Convention for the Amelioration of the Condition of the Wounded, Sick and Shipwrecked Members of the Armed Forces at Sea (signed 12 August 1949, entered into force 21 October 1950) 75 UNTS 85 (GCII)

1949 Geneva Convention Relative to the Treatment of Prisoners of War (signed 12 August 1949, entered into force 21 October 1950) 75 UNTS 135 (GCIII)

1949 Convention relative to the Protection of Civilian Persons in Time of War (signed 12 August 1949, entered into force 21 October 1950) 75 UNTS 1950 (GCIV)

1950 Convention for the Protection of Human Rights and Fundamental Freedoms (signed 4 November 1950, entered into force 3 September 1953) ETS 5 (ECHR)

1951 Convention Relating to the Status of Refugees (adopted 28 July 1951, entered into force 22 April 1954) 189 UNTS 137

1957 Convention between Denmark, Finland, Norway and Sweden Concerning the Waiver of Passport Control at the Intra-Nordic Frontiers (signed 12 July 1957, entered into force 1 May 1958) 322 UNTS 245

1960 Convention between the Kingdom of Belgium, the Grand Duchy of Luxembourg and the Kingdom of the Netherlands on the Transfer of Controls of Persons to the External Frontiers of Benelux Territory (signed 11 April 1960, entered into force 1 January 1974) 374 UNTS 3

1961 Vienna Convention on Diplomatic Relations (adopted 18 April 1961, entered into force 24 April 1964) 500 UNTS 95 (VCDR)

HTTPS://DOI.ORG/10.1163/9789004773806-008

1961 Convention on the Reduction of Statelessness (signed 30 August 1961, entered into force 13 December 1975) 989 UNTS 175 (1961 Statelessness Convention)

1963 Vienna Convention on Consular Relations (adopted 24 April 1963, entered into force 19 March 1967) 596 UNTS 261 (VCCR)

1966 International Convention on the Elimination of All Forms of Racial Discrimination (signed 7 March 1966, entered into force 4 January 1969) 660 UNTS 195 (ICERD)

1966 International Covenant on Civil and Political Rights (adopted 16 December 1966, entered into force 23 March 1976) 999 UNTS 171 (ICCPR)

1966 International Covenant on Economic, Social and Cultural Rights (signed 16 December 1966, entered into force 3 January 1976) 993 UNTS 3 (ICESCR)

1969 American Convention on Human rights (signed 22 November 1969, entered into force 18 July 1978) 1144 UNTS 123 (ACHR)

1970 Convention for the Suppression of Unlawful Seizure of Aircraft (adopted 16 December 1970, entered into force 14 October 1971) 806 UNTS 105

1977 Protocol Additional to the Geneva Conventions of 12 August 1949, and Relating to the Protection of Victims of International Armed Conflicts (Protocol I) (signed 8 June 1977, entered into force 7 December 1978) 1125 UNTS 3

1977 Protocol Additional to the Geneva Conventions of 12 August 1949, and Relating to the Protection of Victims of Non-international Armed Conflicts (Protocol II) (signed 8 June 1977, entered into force 7 December 1978)

1979 International Convention Against the Taking of Hostages (adopted 17 December 1979, entered into force 3 June 1983) 1316 UNTS 205

1981 African Charter on Human and Peoples' Rights (signed 1 June 1981, entered into force 21 October 1986) 1520 UNTS 217(ACHPR)

1984 Convention against Torture and Other Cruel, Inhuman or Degrading Treatment or Punishment (signed 10 December 1984, entered into force 26 June 1987) 1465 UNTS 85

1985 Inter-American Convention to Prevent and Punish Torture (adopted 9 December 1985, entered into force 28 February 1987) OAS Treaty Series, No. 67

1989 Convention on the Right of the Child (signed 20 November 1989, entered into force 2 September 1990) 1577 UNTS 3 (CRC)

1989 International Convention Against the Recruitment, Use, Financing and Training of Mercenaries (adopted 4 December 1989, entered into force 20 October 2001) 2163 UNTS 75

1996 Additional Protocol No. 4 to the ECHR (signed 16 September 1996, entered into force 2 May 1968) ETS 46

1997 European Convention on Nationality (adopted 6 November 1997, entered into force 1 March 2000) ETS No. 166 (ECN)

1997 International Convention for the Suppression of Terrorist Bombings (adopted 15 December 1997, entered into force 23 May 2001) 2149 UNTS 256

1998 Rome Statute of the International Criminal Court (adopted 17 July 1998, entered into force 1 July 2002) 2187 UNTS 3 (Rome Statute or ICC Statute)

1999 International Convention for the Suppression of the Financing of Terrorism (adopted 9 December 1999, entered into force 10 April 2002) 2178 UNTS 197

2000 Optional Protocol to the Convention on the Rights of the Child on the Involvement of Children in Armed Conflict (adopted 25 May 2000, entered into force 12 February 2002) 2173 UNTS 222

2004 League of Arab States, Arab Charter on Human Rights (signed 23 May 2004, entered into force 15 March 2008) 12 Int'l Hum. Rts. Rep. 893 (2005)

2006 The International Convention for the Protection of All Persons from Enforced Disappearance (adopted 20 December 2006, entered into force 23 December 2010) 2716 UNTS 3

2007 Charter of Fundamental Rights of the European Union (adopted 12 December 2007, entered into force 1 December 2009) Official Journal of the European Union C 326/391

2007 Treaty of Lisbon Amending the Treaty on European Union and the Treaty Establishing the European Community (signed 13 December 2007, entered into force 1 December 2009) 2702 UNTS 47938

2008 Optional Protocol to the International Covenant on Economic, Social and Cultural Rights (adopted 10 December 2008, entered into force 5 May 2013) 2922 UNTS 29

2015 Additional Protocol to the Council of Europe Convention on the Prevention of Terrorism (adopted 19 May 2015, entered into force 1 July 2017) CETS 217

2024 Protocol to the African Charter on Human and Peoples' Rights Relating to the Specific Aspects of the Right to a Nationality and the Eradication of Statelessness in Africa (signed 18 February 2024, not yet in force) adopted by Doc. Assembly/AU/Dec.885 (XXXVII)

National Legislation

Algeria, Code of Nationality 1970
Austria, Citizenship Act 1985
Australia, Customs Act 1901
Australia, Criminal Code Act 1995
Australia, Passports Act 2005
Australia, Citizenship Act 2007
Australia, Autonomous Sanctions Regulations 2011
Australia, Foreign Fighters Amendment Act 2014
Australia, Citizenship Amendment (Allegiance to Australia) Act 2015

Australia, Citizenship Amendment (Citizenship Cessation) Act 2020
Australia, Citizenship Amendment (Citizenship Repudiation) Act 2023
Australia, Counter-Terrorism Legislation Amendment (Declared Areas) Bill 2024
Bahrain, Nationality Act 1963
Belgium, Code of Belgian Nationality 1984
Belgium, Act of 4 December 2012 Amending the Code of Belgian Nationality in Order to Make the Acquisition of Belgian Nationality Migration-Neutral
Belgium, Consular Code of 21 December 2013
Belgium, Act of 20 July 2015 to Strengthen the Fight Against Terrorism
Belgium, Criminal Code 1867
Canada, Criminal Code (R.S.C. 1985 c. C-46)
Canada, Crimes Against Humanity and War Crimes Act (S.C. 2000, c. 24)
Canada, Strengthening Canadian Citizenship Act (S.C. 2014 c. 22)
Denmark, Act on Danish Nationality 1950
Denmark, Danish Penal Code 1930
France, Law No. 2014–1353 of 13 November 2014, strengthening the provisions relating to the fight against terrorism
France, French Penal Code 1994
Germany, Nationality Act of 22 July 1913
Germany, Law on Consular Officers, Their Functions and Powers of 11 September 1974
Germany, Criminal Code 1998
Germany, Code of Criminal Procedure 1987
Italy, Italian Citizenship Act 1992
Poland, Polish Citizenship Act 1920
Romania, Act No. 21/1991 on Romanian Citizenship
Saudi Arabia, Saudi Arabian Citizenship System 1954
The Netherlands, Dutch Criminal Code 1881
The Netherlands, Nationality Act 1984
The Netherlands, Civil Code 1838
The Netherlands, Citizenship and Residency Act 1892
United Kingdom, Foreign Enlistment Act of 1819
United Kingdom, Nationality Act 1981
United Kingdom, Nationality, Immigration and Asylum Act 2002
United Kingdom, Immigration, Asylum and Nationality Act 2006
United Kingdom, Immigration Act 2014
United Kingdom, UK Terrorism Act 2006
United States, US Neutrality Act of 1794
United States, Naturalization Act 1906
United States, McCarran Act of 1952

Cases

Permanent Court of International Justice and International Court of Justice

The Case of the S.S. Lotus (*France v. Turkey*) (Judgement) [1927] PCIJ Rep. Series A, No. 10

Case concerning the Factory at Chorzów (*Germany v. Poland*) (Jurisdiction) [1927] PCIJ Rep. Series A No. 9

Case concerning the Factory at Chorzów (*Germany v. Poland*) (Merits) [1928] PCIJ Rep. Series A No. 17

The Corfu Channel Case (Merits) [1949] ICJ Rep. 4

Reparation for injuries suffered in the service of the United Nations (Advisory Opinion) [1949] ICJ Rep. 174

Voting Procedure on Questions relating to Reports and Petitions concerning the Territory of South West Africa (Advisory Opinion) [1955] ICJ Rep. 67

Nottebohm Case (*Liechtenstein v. Guatemala*) (Second Phase) [1955] ICJ Rep. 4

Case concerning the Temple of Preah Vihear (*Cambodia v. Thailand*) (Merits) [1962] ICJ Rep. 6

Legal Consequences for States of the Continued Presence of South Africa in Namibia (*South West Africa*) *notwithstanding Security Council Resolution 276* (*1970*) (Advisory Opinion) [1971] ICJ Rep. 16

United States Diplomatic and Consular Staff in Tehran (*United States of America v. Iran*) (Judgement) [1980] ICJ Rep. 3

Case concerning Military and Paramilitary Activities In and against Nicaragua (*Nicaragua v. United States of America*) (Merits) [1986] ICJ Rep. 14

Legality of the Threat or Use of Nuclear Weapons (Advisory Opinion) [1996] ICJ Rep. 226

LaGrand (*Germany v. United States of America*) (Judgement) [2001] ICJ Rep. 466

Case concerning the Arrest Warrant of 11 April 2000 (Judgement) [2002] ICJ Rep. 3

Avena and Other Mexican Nationals (*Mexico v. United States of America*) (Judgement) [2004] ICJ Rep. 12

Legal Consequences of the Construction of a Wall in the Occupied Palestinian Territory (Advisory Opinion) [2004] ICJ Rep. 136

Armed Activities on the Territory of the Congo (*Democratic Republic of the Congo v. Uganda*) (Judgement) [2005] ICJ Rep. 168

Case concerning Application of the Convention on the Prevention and Punishment of the Crime of Genocide (*Bosnia and Herzegovina v. Serbia and Montenegro*) (Judgement) [2007] ICJ Rep. 43

Case concerning Ahmadou Sadio Diallo (*Republic of Guinea v. Democratic Republic of the Congo*) (Merits) [2010] ICJ Rep. 639

Jurisdictional Immunities of the State (*Germany v. Italy: Greece intervening*) (Judgement) [2012] ICJ Rep. 99

International Criminal Court

ICC Pre-Trial Chamber I, *Decision on the admissibility of the case against Saif Al-Islam Gaddafi*, No. ICC-01/11–01/11 (31 May 2013)

ICC Appeals Chamber, Judgment on the appeal of Mr Abdullah Al-Senussi against the decision of Pre-Trial Chamber I of 11 October 2013 entitled "Decision on the admissibility of the case against Abdullah Al-Senussi". In the Case of *the Prosecutor v. Saif Al-Islam Gaddafi and Abdullah Al-Senussi*, No. ICC-oI/II-oI/IIOA6 (24 July 2014)

ICC Pre-Trial Chamber I, Decision on the Prosecutor's request for authorization of an investigation of the situation in Georgia, No. ICC-01/15 (27 January 2016)

ICC Pre-Trial Chamber I, In the Case of *the Prosecutor v. Mahmoud Mustafe Busayf Al-Werfalli*, No. ICC-01/11–01/17 (4 July 2018)

International Criminal Tribunal for the Former Yugoslavia

ICTY Trial Chamber, *The Prosecutor v. Dusko Tadić* (Judgment) No. IT-94–1-T (7 May 1997)

ICTY Trial Chamber, *Prosecutor v. Stanislav Galić* (Judgement) No. IT-98–29-T (5 December 2003)

Committee on the Rights of the Child

CRC Committee, *L.H. et al. v. France* (2 November 2020) UN Doc. CRC/C/85/D/79/2019; CRC/C/85/D/109/2019

CRC Committee, *F.B. et al. and D.A. et al. v. France* (9 March 2022) UN Doc. CRC/C/89/D/77/2019; CRC/C/89/D/79/2019; CRC/C/89/D/109/2019

CRC Committee, *P.N et al. v. Finland* (20 October 2022) UN Doc. CRC/C/91/D/100/2019

Human Rights Committee

Human Rights Committee, *Nystrom v. Australia* (1 September 2011) UN Doc. CCPR/C/102/D/1557/2007

Human Rights Committee, *Kwok Yin Fong v. Australia* (23 November 2009) UN Doc. CCPR/C/97/D/1442/2005

Human Rights Committee, *Warsame v. Canada* (1 September 2011) UN Doc. CCPR/C/102/D/1959/2010

Human Rights Committee, *M. Nabhari v. Australia* (22 January 2025) UN Doc. CCPR/C/142/D/3663/2019

Human Rights Committee, *M. I. et al. v. Australia* (23 January 2025) UN Doc. CCPR/C/142/D/2749/2016

Committee against Torture

Committee against Torture, *C.P. et al. v. France* (2 March 2023) UN Doc. CAT/C/75/D/922/2019

Committee against Torture, *P.D. v. France* (15 February 2024) UN Doc. CAT/C/78/D/1045/2020

European Court of Human Rights

Case of Colozza v. Italy [1985] (Judgement) ECtHR App. No. 9024/80 (12 February 1985)

Case of Soering v. the United Kingdom [1989] (Judgement) ECtHR App. No. 14038/88 (7 July 1989)

Case of Poitrimol v. France [1993] (Judgement) ECtHR App. No. 14032/88 (23 November 1993)

Case of Chahal v. the United Kingdom [1996] (Judgement) ECtHR App. No. 22414/93 (15 November 1996)

Case of X. Y. and Z. v. The United Kingdom [1997] (Judgement) ECtHR App. No. 21830/93 (22 April 1997)

Case of Solomon v. the Netherlands [2000] (Decision as to the admissibility) ECtHR App. No. 44328/98 (5 September 2000)

Case of Kudla v. Poland [2000] (Judgement) ECtHR App No. 30210/96 (26 October 2000)

Case of K. and T. v. Finland [2001] (Judgement) ECtHR App. No. 25702/94 (12 July 2001)

Case of Slivenko v. Latvia [2003] (Judgement) ECtHR App. no. 48321/199 (9 October 2003)
Case of Ilaşcu and Others v. Moldova and Russia [2004] (Judgement) ECtHR App No. 48787/99 (8 July 2004)
Case of Öcalan v. Turkey [2005] (Judgement) ECtHR App. No. 46221/99 (12 May 2005)
Case of Sejdovic v. Italy [2006] (Judgement) ECtHR App. No. 56581/00 (1 March 2006)
Case of Marcello Viola v. Italy [2006] (Judgement) ECtHR App. No. 45106/04 (5 October 2006)
Case of Saadi v. Italy [2008] (Judgement) ECtHR App. No. 37201/06 (28 February 2008)
Case of Sobolewski v. Poland (No. 2) [2009] (Judgement) ECtHR App. No. 19847/07 (9 June 2009)
Case of Al-Saadoon and Mufdhi v. The United Kingdom [2010] (Judgement) ECtHR App. No. 61498/08 (4 October 2010)
Case of Anayo v. Germany [2010] (Judgement) ECtHR App. No. 20578/07 (21 December 2010)
Case of M.S.S. v. Belgium and Greece [2011] (Judgement) ECtHR App. No. (21 January 2011)
Case of Genovese v. Malta [2011] (Judgement) ECtHR App. No. 53124/09 (11 October 2011)
Case of Hirsi Jamaa and Others v. Italy [2012] (Judgement) ECtHR App. No. 27765/09 (23 February 2012)
Case of Othman (Abu Qatada) v. The United Kingdom [2012] (Judgement) ECtHR App. No. 8139/09 (9 May 2012)
Case of Aswat v. the United Kingdom [2013] (Judgement) ECtHR App. No. 17299/12 (16 April 2013)
Case of Senchishak v. Finland [2014] (Judgement) ECtHR App. No. 5049/12 (18 November 2014)
Case of Bărbulescu v. Romania [2017] (Judgement) ECtHR App. No. 61496/08 (5 September 2017)
Case of Al Nashiri v. Romania [2018] (Judgement) ECtHR App. No. 33234/12 (8 October 2018)
Case of Ghoumid and Others v. France [2020] (Judgement) ECtHR App. No. 52273/16 (25 June 2020)
Case of Carter v. Russia [2021] (Judgement) ECtHR App. No. 20914/07 (21 September 2021)
Case of H.F. and Others v. France [2022] (Judgement) ECtHR App. Nos. 24384/19 and 44234/20 (14 September 2022)
Case of Johansen v. Denmark [2022] (Decision) ECtHR App. No. 27801/19 (3 March 2022)

Case of Mørck Jensen v. Denmark [2023] (Judgement) ECtHR App. No. 60785/19 (18 January 2023)

Inter-American Court of Human Rights

The Right to Information on Consular Assistance in the Framework of the Guarantees of the Due Process of Law (Advisory Opinion) [1999] OC-16/99

Arbitration

Mergé case [1955] Italian-United States Conciliation Commission Decision No. 55, UNRIAA Vol. XIV
Iran v. United States (Decision) [6 April 1984] IUSCT Case No. A/18 37
Rainbow Warrior (*New Zealand v. France*) (Arbitration Tribunal) (1990) XX RIAA 260

National Cases

Australia

Alqudsi v. Commonwealth of Australia [2015] NSWSC 1222 (27 August 2015)
Alexander v. Minister for Home Affairs [2022] (Judgement) HCA 19 (8 June 2022)
Benbrika v. Minister for Home Affairs & Anor [2023] (Judgement) HCA 33 (1 November 2023).

Belgium

Dutch speaking Court of First Instance Brussels, No. 18/28/C (19 juli 2018)
Court of Appeal Brussels, No. 2018/KR/45 (12 September 2018)
Dutch speaking Court of First Instance Brussels, No. 2018/XX/C (26 December 2018)
Hof van Beroep Brussel, No. 2019/KR/4 (27 February 2019)
French speaking Court of First Instance Brussels, No. 19/30/C (7 June 2019)
French speaking Court of First Instance Brussels, No. 19/129/C (30 October 2019)
French speaking Court of First Instance Brussels, No. 19/87/C (2 December 2019)

Canada

Canadian Federal Court, *BOLOH 1(A), BOLOH 2(A) adult male only, BOLOH 12, and BOLOH 13 v. His Majesty the King and the Minister of Foreign Affairs and International Trade*, 2023 FC 98 (20 January 2023)

Canadian Federal Court of Appeal, *His Majesty the King and the Minister of Foreign Affairs and International Trade v. BOLOH 1(a), BOLOH 2(a) male only, BOLOH 12, and BOLOH 13*, 2023 FCA 120 (31 May 2023)

Denmark

A v. Ministry of Immigration and Integration, Danish Supreme Court, Case BS-23360/2022-HJR (22 March 2023)

France

Conseil d'État, Avis sur la constitutionnalité et la compatibilité avec les engagements internationaux de la France de certaines mesures de prévention du risque de terrorisme' No. 390867 (17 December 2015)

Tribunal Administratif de Paris, No. 1906076/9 (9 April 2019)

Tribunal Administratif de Paris, No. 1906077/9 (9 April 2019)

Conseil d'État, Nos. 429668, 429669, 429674 and 429701 (23 April 2019).

Tribunal Judiciaire de Paris, No. RG 20/51405 – No. Portalis 352J-W-B7D-CRH WO (12 March 2020)

Germany

Verwaltungsgericht Berlin, ECLI:DE:VGBE:2020:0127.34L334.19.00 (27 January 2019)

Verwaltungsgericht Berlin, ECLI:DE:VGBE:2019:0710.34L245.19.00 (10 July 2019)

Oberverwaltungsgericht Berlin-Brandenburg, ECLI:DE:OVGBEBB:2019:1106.OVG10S4 3.19.00 (6 November 2019)

Berlin-Brandenburg, ECLI:DE:OVGBEBB:2020:0610.OVG10S64.19.00 (10 June 2020)

Oberlandesgericht München, *Sibel H*, Case 7 St 9/19 (4) (29 April 2022)

The Netherlands

District Court of Rotterdam, ECLI:NL:RBROT:2013:8265 (23 October 2013)

District Court of Rotterdam, ECLI:NL:RBROT:2013:8266 (23 October 2013)

Court of First Instance The Hague, ECLI:NL:RBDHA:2019:11909 (11 November 2019)

Court of Appeal of The Hague, ECLI:NL:GHDHA:2019:3208 (22 November 2019)
District Court Rotterdam, ECLI:NL:RBROT:2020:1445 (17 February 2020)
Dutch Supreme Court, ECLI:NL:HR:2020:1148 (26 June 2020)
District Court Rotterdam, ECLI:NL:RBROT:2020:5273 (16 June 2020)
District Court Rotterdam, ECLI:NL:RBROT:2021:10090 (11 October 2021)
District Court of Rotterdam, ECLI:NL:RBROT:2022:3993 (11 May 2022)
District Court of The Hague, ECLI:NL:RBDHA:2024:20594 (11 December 2024)
District Court of Amsterdam, ECLI:NL:RBAMS:2025:1849 (24 March 2025)

United Kingdom

Secretary of State for the Home Department v. Al-Jedda (Judgement) [2013] UKSC 62 (9 October 2013)

Belhaj and another v. Straw and others, Rahmatullah (No 1) v. Ministry of Defence and another [2017] UKSC 3

R (on the application of Begum) (Appellant) v. Special Immigration Appeals Commission (Respondent) R (on the application of Begum) (Respondent) v. Secretary of State for the Home Department (Appellant) Begum (Respondent) v. Secretary of State for the Home Department (Appellant) [2021] UKSC 7 (26 February 2021)

Shamima Begum v. The Secretary of State for the Home Department [2023] (Judgement) SIAC, SC/163/2019 (22 February 2023)

R (on the application of AAA and others) (Respondents/Cross Appellants) v. Secretary of State for the Home Department (Appellant/Cross Respondent) [2023] (Judgement) UKSC 42 (15 November 2023)

Shamima Begum v. The Secretary of State for the Home Department [2024] (Judgement) EWCA, CA-2023–000900 (32 February 2024)

Documents

UN Documents

General Assembly

UNGA Res. 217 A(III) Universal Declaration of Human Rights (10 December 1948)
UNGA Res. 2625 (XXV) (24 October 1970) UN Doc. A/Res/2625(XXV)
UNGA Res. 36/103 (9 December 1981) UN Doc. A/RES/36/103
UNGA Res. 56/88 (24 January 2002) UN Doc. A/RES/56/88
UNGA Res. 57/27 (15 January 2003) UN Doc. A/RES/57/27
UNGA Res. 59/46 (16 December 2004) UN Doc. A/RES/59/46
UNGA, Report of the Working Group on arbitrary detention (24 December 2012) UN Doc. A/HRC/22/44
UNGA, Use of mercenaries as a means of violating human rights and impeding the exercise of the right of peoples to self-determination (19 August 2015) UN Doc. A/70/330
UNGA, Report of the Working Group on the use of mercenaries as a means of violating human rights and impeding the exercise of the right of peoples to self-determination on its mission to Belgium (8 July 2016) UN Doc. A/HRC/33/43/Add.2
UNGA Res. 71/248 (11 January 2017) UN Doc. A/RES/71/248
UNGA, Report of the Working Group on the use of mercenaries as a means of violating human rights and impeding the exercise of the right of peoples to self-determination (6 August 2018) UN Doc. A/73/303

Security Council

UNSC, Report Submitted to the Security Council by the Secretary-General in accordance with Resolution 605 (1987) (21 January 1988) UN Doc. 8/19443
UNSC Res. 1267 (15 October 1999) UN Doc. S/RES/1267 (1999)
UNSC Res. 1373 (28 September 2001) UN Doc. S/RES/1373 (2001)
UNSC Res. 1456 (20 January 2003) UN Doc. S/RES/1456 (2003)
UNSC, Note by the President of the Security Council (26 January 2004) UN Doc. UN Doc. S/2004/70, Annex: Report by the Chair of the Counter-Terrorism Committee on the problems encountered in the implementation of Security Council Resolution 1373 (2001)
UNSC Res. 1566 (8 October 2004) UN Doc. S/RES/1566 (2004)
UNSC Res. 1988 (17 June 2011) UN Doc. S/RES/1988 (2011)

UNSC Res. 1989 (17 June 2011) UN Doc. S/RES/1989 (2011)
UNSC Res. 2170 (15 August 2014) UN Doc. S/RES/2170 (2014)
UNSC Res. 2178 (24 September 2014) UN Doc. S/RES/2178 (2014)
UNSC Res. 2253 (17 December 2015) UN Doc. S/RES/2253 (2015)
UNSC, CTED, 'Implementation of Security Council Resolution 2178 (2014) by States Affected by Foreign Terrorist Fighters' UN Doc. S/2015/338 (31 August 2016)
UNSC Res. 2322 (12 December 2016) UN Doc. S/RES/2322 (2016)
UNSC Res. 2379 (21 September 2017) UN Doc. S/RES/2379 (2017)
UNSC Res. 2396 (21 December 2017) UN Doc. S/RES/2396 (2017)
UNSC Resolution 2427 (9 July 2018) UN Doc. S/RES/2427 (2018)
UNSC, Indonesia: draft resolution (31 August 2020) UN Doc. S/2020/852
UNSC, Letter dated 31 August 2020 from the President of the Security Council addressed to the Secretary-General and the Permanent Representatives of the members of the Security Council (31 August 2020) UN Doc. S/2020/865
UNSC, Letter dated 31 August 2020 from the President of the Security Council addressed to the Secretary-General and the Permanent Representatives of the members of the Security Council (1 September 2020) UN Doc. S/2020/870
UNSC, 'Thirteenth report of the Secretary-General on the threat posed by ISIL (Da'esh) to international peace and security and the range of United Nations efforts in support of Member States in countering the threat' UN Doc. S/2021/682 (27 July 2021)
UNSC Res. 2610 (17 December 2021) UN Doc. S/RES/2610 (2021)
UNSC Res. 2697 (15 September 2023) UN Doc. S/RES/2697 (2023)
UNSC, Nineteenth report of the Secretary-General on the threat posed by ISIL (Da'esh) to international peace and security and the range of United Nations efforts in support of Member States in countering the threat (31 July 2024) UN Doc. S/2024/583

Human Rights Committee

Human Rights Committee, 'General Comment No. 15: The Position of Aliens Under the Covenant' (11 April 1986) UN Doc. HRI/GEN/1/Rev.9 (Vol. I)
Human Rights Committee, General Comment No. 20: Prohibition of Torture, or Other Cruel, Inhuman or Degrading Treatment or Punishment Article 7 (10 March 1992) UN Doc. A/44/40
Human Rights Committee, General Comment No. 27: Freedom of Movement Article 12 (1 November 1999) UN Doc. CCPR/C/21/Rev.1/Add.9

Human Rights Committee, 'General Comment no. 31, The nature of the general legal obligation imposed on States Parties to the Covenant' (26 May 2004) UN Doc. CCPR/C/21/Rev.1/Add. 13

Human Rights Committee, General Comment No. 32: Right to equality before courts and tribunals and to a fair trial Article 14 (23 August 2007) UN Doc. CCPR/C/GC/32

Human Rights Committee, 'General comment No. 36 Article 6: right to life' (3 September 2019) UN Doc. CCPR/C/GC/36

Human Rights Committee, Concluding observations on the sixth periodic report of Belgium (6 December 2019) UN Doc. CCPR/C/BEL/CO/6

Committee on the Rights of the Child

CRC Committee, Concluding observations on the fifth periodic report of the Syrian Arab Republic (6 March 2019) UN Doc. CRC/C/SYR/CO/5

CRC Committee, Combined fifth and sixth periodic reports submitted by the Netherlands under Article 44 of the Convention pursuant to the simplified reporting procedure, due in 2019 (7 May 2021) UN Doc. CRC/C/NLD/5–6

Committee against Torture

Committee against Torture, General Comment No. 4 (2017) on the implementation of article 3 of the Convention in the context of article 22 (4 September 2018) UN Doc. CAT/C/GC/4

Human Rights Council

Human Rights Council, 'Annual report of the Special Representative of the Secretary-General for Children and Armed Conflict' (28 December 2015) UN Doc. A/HRC/31/19

Human Rights Council, Report of the Independent International Commission of Inquiry on the Syrian Arab Republic, UN Doc. A/HRC/46/55 (11 March 2021)

Human Rights Council, Report of the Office of the United Nations High Commissioner for Human Rights: Compilation on the Syrian Arab Republic, UN Doc. A/HRC/WG.6/40/SYR/2 (17 November 2021)

Human Rights Council, Independent International Commission of Inquiry on the Syrian Arab Republic, "No End in Sight": Torture and ill-treatment in the Syrian Arab Republic 2020–202, UN Doc. A/HRC/53/CRP.5 (10 July 2023)

Human Rights Council, Report of the Independent International Commission of Inquiry on the Syrian Arab Republic, UN Doc. A/HRC/57/86 (12 August 2024)

International Law Commission

ILC, 'Nationality, including Statelessness – National Legislation Concerning Grounds for Deprivation of Nationality – Memorandum Prepared by Mr. Ivan S. Kerno, Expert of the International Law Commission' (6 April 1953) UN Doc. A/CN.4/66

ILC, 'Draft Articles on Consular Relations, with commentaries' in the Report of the International Law Commission on the work of its thirteenth session (1961) UN Doc. A/16/9

ILC, Seventh report on State Responsibility by Mr. Roberto Ago, Special Rapporteur – the internationally wrongful act of the State, source of international responsibility (continued) UN Doc. A/CN.4/307 and Add.1 & 2 and Corr.1 & 2, Yearbook of the ILC (1789) vol. I(1)

ILC, Fourth report on the content, forms and degrees of international responsibility (part 2 of the draft articles), by Mr. Willem Riphagen, Special Rapporteur UN Doc. A/CN.4/366 and Add. l, Yearbook of the ILC (1983) Vol. II(1)

ILC, 'Draft Articles on Prevention of Transboundary Harm from Hazardous Activities, which indicates that States ' in the Report of the International Law Commission on the work of its 53rd session (2001) UN Doc. A/RES/56/82

ILC, 'Draft Articles on Responsibility of States for Internationally Wrongful Acts, with commentaries' in the Report of the International Law Commission on the work of its fifty-third session (2001) UN Doc. A/56/10

ILC, 'Preliminary report on the expulsion of aliens, by Mr. Maurice Kamto, Special Rapporteur' (2 June 2005) UN Doc. A/CN.4/554

ILC, Expulsion of aliens, Memorandum by the Secretariat (10 July 2006) UN Doc. A/CN.4/565

ILC, 'Draft Articles on Diplomatic Protection with commentaries' in the Report of the International Law Commission on the work of its fifty-eight session (2006) UN Doc. A/61/10

ILC, 'Sixth report on the expulsion of aliens, by Mr. Maurice Kamto, Special Rapporteur' (18 March, 28 May and 9 July 2010) UN Doc. A/CN.4/625 and Add.1–2

ILC, Draft articles on the responsibility of international organizations, in the Report of the International Law Commission on the work of its sixty-third session (2011) UN Doc. A/66/10

ILC, 'Draft articles on the expulsion of aliens' in the Report of the International Law Commission on the work of its sixty-sixth session (2014) UN Doc. A/69/10

ILC, 'The obligation to extradite or prosecute (*aut dedere aut judicare*) Final Report of the International Law Commission' in the Report of the ILC on the work of its sixty-sixth session (2014) UN Doc. A/69/10

ILC, Draft conclusions on identification and legal consequences of peremptory norms of general international law (*jus cogens*) (2022) UN Doc. A/77/10

Other UN Documents

Report of the United Nations Conference on the Human Environment (Stockholm, 5–16 June 1972) UN Doc. A/CONF. 48/14/Rev.1

Report of the United Nations Conference on Environment and Development (Rio de Janeiro, 3–14 June 1992) UN Doc. A/CONF.151/26 (Vol. I)

UNICEF, 'The Paris Principles: Principles and Guidelines on Children Associated with Armed Forced or Armed Groups' (February 2007)

Letter dated 18 June 2014 from the Permanent Representative of the Syrian Arab Republic to the United Nations addressed to the Secretary-General (20 June 2014) UN Doc. S/2014/42

Statement of the representative of the Syrian Arab Republic during the discussions on the Report of the Secretary-General on the implementation of Security Council Resolution 2139 (26 June 2014) UN Doc. S/PV.7212

Statement from the representative of the Syrian Arab Republic during a discussion on the situation in the Middle East (14 July 2014) Un Doc. S/PV.7216, 12–15

IS and Al-Qaida Sanctions Committee, Travel ban: explanation of terms (approved on 24 February 2015) <https://www.un.org/securitycouncil/sites/www.un.org.securitycouncil/files/eot_travel_ban_english.pdf> accessed 2 February 2022

United Nations Interim Administration Mission in Kosovo, Report of the Secretary-General (31 March 2020) UN Doc. S/2020/255

Letter by UN experts, Information received concerning the situation of a number of boys and men holding your Excellency's citizenship currently detained in North-East Syria (1 February 2022) Refs. AL FRA 1/2022; AL DEU 1/2022; AL AUT 1/2022; AL GBR 1/2022; AL SWE 1/2022 <https://spcommreports.ohchr.org/TmSearch/Results> accessed 16 August 2023

Letter by UN experts, Information received concerning the alleged arbitrary detention and inadequate detention conditions of Mr. Jack Letts, a Canadian citizen, currently detained in a detention center in the North-East region of the Syrian Arab Republic at least since 2017 (8 June 2022) ref. UA CAN 3/2022

United Nations Syria Country Team, Report prepared in accordance with paragraph 15(B) of resolution 5/1 of the HR Council For the Third Universal Periodic Review of the Syrian Arab Republic

Other Documents

Institut de Droit International

Institut de Droit International, Resolution on the Principle of Non-intervention and Civil Wars (1975)

Institut de Droit International, The Principle of Non-Intervention in Civil Wars, Session of Wiesbaden (14 August 1975)

Institut de Droit International, Seventeenth Commission, Krakow Session, Resolution on Universal Criminal Jurisdiction with regard to the Crime of Genocide, Crimes against Humanity and War Crimes (2005)

Council of Europe

Parliamentary Assembly of the Council of Europe, 'Withdrawing nationality as a measure to combat terrorism: a human-rights compatible approach?' Resolution 2263 (2019)

Council of Europe Commissioner for Human Rights, 'Council of Europe member states should urgently repatriate their under-age nationals stranded in Northern Syria' (28 May 2019) <https://www.coe.int/fi/web/commissioner/-/council-of-europe-member-states-should-urgently-repatriate-their-under-age-nationals-stranded-in-northern-syria> accessed 30 June 2023

Explanatory Report to Protocol No. 4 to the Convention for the Protection of Human Rights and Fundamental Freedoms, securing certain rights and freedoms other than those already included in the Convention and in the first Protocol thereto <https://rm.coe.int/16800c92c0> accessed 9 May 2023.

Guide on Article 3 of Protocol No. 4 of the ECHR (updated 30 November 2022) <https://www.echr.coe.int/Documents/Guide_Art_3_Protocol_4_ENG.pdf> accessed 9 May 2023

Miscellaneous

Association of Southeast Asian Nations, ASEAN Human Rights Declaration (19 November 2012)

Council of the European Union, User's Guide to Council Common Position 2008/944/CFSP defining common rules governing the control of exports of military technology and equipment (20 July 2015) 10858/15, COARM 172, CFSP/PESC 393

Directive (EU) 2017/541 of the European Parliament and of the Council of 15 March 2017 on combating terrorism and replacing Council Framework Decision 2002/

475/JHA and amending Council Decision 2005/671/JHA, Official Journal of the European Union (31 March 2017) L88/6

ICC Office of the Prosecutor, 'Informal expert paper: The principle of complementarity in practice' (2003)

Regulation (EU) 2018/1727 of 14 November 2018 on the European Union Agency for Criminal Justice Cooperation (Eurojust)

Bibliography

AANES, The Constitution of the Rojava Cantons <https://civiroglu.net/the-constitution-of-the-rojava-cantons/>; accessed 7 July 2025

Adekola T and Majekolagbe F, 'Human rights law, intellectual property and vaccine nationalism: lessons for the post-COVID-19 world' 29 Australian Journal of Human Rights (2023) 2

Aksamitowska K, 'Digital Evidence in Domestic Core International Crimes Prosecutions: Lessons Learned from Germany, Sweden, Finland and the Netherlands' 19 Journal of International Criminal Justice (2021) 1

Allsopp H and van Wilgenburg W, *The Kurds of Northern Syria: Governance, Diversity and Conflicts* (Iraq Institute for Strategic Studies/Bloomsbury Publishing Plc 2019)

Almutawa A and Walker C, 'Citizenship as a privilege and the Weakness of International Law: The Consequences for Citizenship Deprivation in Bahrain and the UK' 14 Journal of Human Rights Practice (2022) 3

Alsabeehg Z, 'Report on Citizenship Law: Bahrain' Global Citizenship Observatory (March 2021)

Alsabeehg Z, 'Report on Citizenship Law: Saudi Arabia' Global Citizenship Observatory, RSC/GLOBALCIT-CR 2022/03 (July 2022)

Amnesty International, 'Amnesty International report 2022/23: the state of the world's human rights' (2023) <https://www.amnesty.org/en/documents/pol10/5670/2023/en/> accessed 16 April 2025

Amnesty International, 'Syria: Repatriate at least 27,000 children held in dire conditions in north-east Syria' (30 November 2021) <https://www.amnesty.org/en/latest/news/2021/11/syria-repatriate-at-least-27000-children-held-in-dire-conditions-in-north-east-syria/> accessed 27 September 2023

Amnesty International, Aftermath: Injustice, Torture and Death in Detention in North-east Syria' (2024) <https://www.amnesty.org/en/documents/mde24/7752/2024/en/> accessed 24 October 2025

Amoroso D, 'Armed Opposition Groups' (and Foreign Fighters') Abidance by International Human Rights Law: The Issue of Compliance in Syria and Iraq' in de Guttry A, Capone F and Paulussen C, *Foreign Fighters under International Law and Beyond* (T.M.C. Asser Press 2016)

Ansong A, 'The Concept of Sovereign Equality of States in International Law' II The Ghana Institute of Management and Public Administration Law Review (2016) 1

Arielli N, Frei G and Van Hulle I, 'The Foreign Enlistment Act, International Law, and British Politics, 1819–2014' 38 The International History Review 4

Arielli N, *From Byron to bin Laden: A History of Foreign War Volunteers* (Harvard University Press 2018)

Ark, van R, Prabhat D and Gordon F, *Children's Rights, 'Foreign Fighters' and Counter-Terrorism: Children of Nowhere* (Edward Elgar 2024)

Ashraph S, Cheung Ka-man C and Cook J (eds.), *Holding ISIL Accountable: Prosecuting Crimes in Iraq and Syria* (ICCT Press 2024)

Asscher I, 'Shifting responsibilities and security threats by depriving foreign terrorist fighters of their nationality' 29 Journal of Conflict & Security Law (2024) 2

Aust H, *Complicity and the Law of State Responsibility* (Cambridge University Press 2011)

Avdimetaj T and Coleman J, 'What EU Member States can learn from Kosovo's experience in repatriating former foreign fighters and their families' Clingendael Netherlands Institute of International Relations (May 2020)

Bagheri S and A. Bisset A, 'International Legal Issues Arising from Repatriation of the Children of Islamic State' 27 Journal of Conflict & Security Law (2022) 3

Bakker E, Paulussen C and Entenmann E, 'Returning Jihadist Foreign Fighters: Challenges Pertaining to Threat Assessment and Governance of this Pan-European Problem' 25 Security and Human Rights (2014) 1

Balanche F, 'The Assad Regime Has Failed to Restore Full Sovereignty Over Syria' The Washington Institute for Near East Policy, Policy Watch 3433 (10 February 2021)

Barnes J, 'Suffering to Save Lives: Torture, Cruelty, and Moral Disengagement in Australia's Offshore Detention Centres' 35 Journal of Refugee Studies (2022) 4

Bassiouni C and Wise E, *Aut Dedere Aut Judicare: The Duty to Extradite or Prosecute in International Law* (Kluwer Academic Publishers 1995)

Bauböck R (ed.), *Debating Transformations of National Citizenship* (Springer 2018)

Bauböck R, Ersbøll E, Groenendijk K et al. (eds.), *Acquisition and Loss of Nationality Volume 1: Comparative Analyses: Policies and Trends in 15 European Countries* (Amsterdam University Press, IMISCOE Research Series 2006)

Becker J and Tayler L, 'Revictimizing the Victims: Children Unlawfully Detained in Northeast Syria' Human Rights Watch (27 January 2023) <https://www.hrw.org/news/2023/01/27/revictimizing-victims-children-unlawfully-detained-northeast-syria> accessed 18 December 2024

Becker J, 'Some Child Soldiers Get Rehabilitation, Others Get Prison' Human Rights Watch (4 March 2019)

Becker T, *Terrorism and the State: Rethinking the Rules of State Responsibility* (Hart Publishing 2006)

Belova-Dalton O, 'Foreign (Terrorist) Fighters and their Families in Finland, Sweden, Latvia, Lithuania, (Northwestern) Russia and their Impact on Estonia' Estonian Academy of Security Sciences (2022)

Benzing M, 'The Complementarity Regime of the International Criminal Court: International Criminal Justice between State Sovereignty and the Fight against Impunity' 7 Max Planck Yearbook of United Nations Law (2003)

Bergsmo M (ed.), *Complementarity and the Exercise of Universal Jurisdiction for Core International Crimes* (Torkel Opsahl Academic EPublisher and Peace Research Institute Oslo 2010)

Bernhardt R (ed.), *Encyclopedia of Public International Law Vol. 1* (Elsevier Science Publishers 1992)

Betti S, 'The Duty to Bring Terrorists to Justice and Discretionary Prosecution' 4 Journal of International Criminal Justice (November 2006) 5

Bianchi A (ed.), *Enforcing International Law Norms Against Terrorism* (Hart Publishing 2004)

Bianchi A, 'Jurisdictional Rules in Customary International Law' in Meessen K (ed.), *Extraterritorial Jurisdiction in Theory and Practice* (Kluwer Law International 1996)

Bleichmar J, 'Deportation as Punishment: A Historical Analysis of the British Practice of Banishment and Its Impact on Modern Constitutional Law' 14 Georgetown Immigration Law Journal (1999) 1

Boekestein T, 'Deprivation of Nationality as a Counter-Terrorism Tool: A Comparative Analysis of Canadian and Dutch Legislation' 5 Transnational Human Rights Review (2018)

Bolhuis M and van Wijk J, 'Citizenship Deprivation as a Counterterrorism Measure in Europe; Possible Follow-Up Scenarios, Human Rights Infringements and the Effect on Counterterrorism' 22 European Journal of Migration and Law (2020) 3

Boll A, *Multiple Nationality and International Law* (Martinus Nijhoff Publishers 2007)

Borgers M and van Sliedregt E, 'The Meaning of the Precautionary Principle for the Assessment of Criminal Measures in the Fight Against Terrorism' 2 Erasmus Law Review (2009) 2

Borgers M *De vlucht naar voren* (Boom Juridische uitgevers 2007)

Bothe M, 'Neutrality, Concept and General Rules' Max Planck Encyclopedia of Public International Law (October 2015)

Boutin B, 'Administrative Measures against Foreign Fighters: In Search of Limits and Safeguards' ICCT Research Paper (December 2016)

Braun K, "Home, Sweet Home': Managing Returning Foreign Terrorist Fighters in Germany, The United Kingdom and Australia' 20 International Community Law Review (2018) 3–4

Braun K, 'Prospects and challenges of prosecuting foreign fighters in Australia' Australian Strategic Policy Institute, Counterterrorism Yearbook (2020)

Breslin A, 'A Reflection on the Legal Obligation for Third States to Ensure Respect for IHL' 22 Journal of Conflict & Security Law (2017) 1

Brownlie I, 'Volunteers and the Law of War and Neutrality' 5 International & Comparative Law Quarterly (October 1956) 4

Bruin R and Wouters K, 'Terrorism and the non-derogability of non-refoulement' 15 International Journal of Refugee Law (2003) 1

Büchler A and Keller H (eds.), *Family forms and parenthood: theory and practice of Article 8 ECHR in Europe* (Intersentia 2016)

Büchler A, 'the Right to Respect for Private and Family Life: the Case Law of the European Court of Human Rights on Parenthood and Family Forms' in Büchler A and Keller H (eds.), *Family forms and parenthood: theory and practice of Article 8 ECHR in Europe* (Intersentia 2016)

Bulan Institute for Peace Innovations, 'Detention and Prosecution of Former ISIS Fighters in Iraq: Lessons Learned and an Assessment of the Deficits of the Judicial System' Policy Paper (August 2020)

Bulan Institute for Peace Innovations, 'Establishing an Ad Hoc Tribunal to Bring ISIS Fighters into Justice: Prospects, Limits and National Alternatives' Policy Paper (April 2021)

Bulan Institute for Peace Innovations, 'The Compendium of Promising Practices in the Rehabilitation and Reintegration of ISIS-linked Women and Children' (November 2022)

Burchardt D and Gulati R, 'International Counter-terrorism Regulation and Citizenship-stripping Laws: Reinforcing Legal Exceptionalism' 23 Journal of Conflict & Security Law (2018) 2

Byman D and Shapiro J, 'Be Afraid. Be a Little Afraid: The Threat of Terrorism from Western Foreign Fighters in Syria and Iraq' Foreign Policy at Brookings, Policy Paper No. 34 (November 2014)

Byman D, 'Counterterrorism Successes Against Foreign Fighters' Lawfare (10 November 2021)

Byman D, *Road Warriors: Foreign Fighters in the Armies of Jihad* (Oxford University Press 2019)

Bynkershoek, van C, *Quaestionum Juris Publici Libri Duo*. Vol. II translated by Frank T (Clarendon Press 1930)

Capone F, "Worse" than Child Soldiers? A Critical Analysis of Foreign Children in the Ranks of ISIL' 17 International Criminal Law Review (2017) 1

Capone F, 'Child Soldiers: The Expanding Practice of Minors Recruited to Become Foreign Fighters' in de Guttry A, Capone F and Paulussen C (eds.), *Foreign Fighters under International Law and Beyond* (T.M.C. Asser Press 2016)

Capone F, 'Countering "Foreign Terrorist Fighters": A Critical Appraisal of the Framework Established by the UN Security Council Resolutions' 25 Italian Yearbook of International Law (2016) 1

Capone F, 'The children (and wives) of foreign ISIS fighters: Which obligations upon the States of nationality?' 60 Questions of International Law, Zoom-in (23 September 2019)

Capone F, 'The Status of Foreign Fighters' Family Members Under Counter-Terrorism Law and International Humanitarian Law: Overcoming the Victims/Perpetrators

Dichotomy?' in Capone F, Paulussen C and Mignot-Mahdavi R (eds.), *Returning Foreign Fighters: Responses, Legal Challenges and Ways Forward* (T.M.C. Asser Press 2023)

Capone F, Paulussen C and Mignot-Mahdavi R (eds.), *Returning Foreign Fighters: Responses, Legal Challenges and Ways Forward* (T.M.C. Asser Press 2023)

Cassese A, Gaeta P and Jones J (eds.), *The Rome Statute of the International Criminal Court: A Commentary* (Oxford University Press 2002)

Chehtman A, *The philosophical foundations of extraterritorial punishment* (Oxford University Press 2010)

Cheng B, General Principles of Law as Applied by International Courts and Tribunals (Stevens & Sons Limited 1953)

Chetail V, 'The contribution of the International Court of Justice to international humanitarian law' 85 International Review of the Red Cross (2003) 850

Chu T and Braithwaite A, 'The impact of foreign fighters on civil conflict outcomes' 1 Research and Politics (2017) 7

Clapham A and Gaeta P, *The Oxford Handbook of International Law in Armed Conflict* (Oxford University Press 2014)

Coco A, de Souza Diaz T, 'Part I: Due Diligence and COVID-19: States' Duties to Prevent and Halt the Coronavirus Outbreak' EJIL:TALK! (24 March 2020)

Coli V, 'Complicity In The Commission Of Internationally Wrongful Acts: A New Perspective In The Law Of State Responsibility (2021) Working Paper Serie n. 3/ 2019–2020 LUISS Academy

Commission Nationale Consultative des Droits de L'Homme, 'Avis sur les ressortissants français condamnés à mort ou encourant la peine de mort en Irak' Journal Officiel de la République Française (2 February 2020) <https://www.legifrance.gouv.fr/download/pdf?id=X_ITR5qVFUPm_4P-l2WtunL207VJIwKzqav-IgcPbmc=> accessed 27 August 2024

Commission Nationale Consultative des Droits de L'Homme, Opinion on French nationals sentenced to death or facing the death penalty in Iraq (28 January 2020) <https://www.cncdh.fr/sites/default/files/2021-04/A%20-%202020%20-%201%20-%20VA%20-%20Opinion%20French%20death%20penalty%20Iraq%2C%20jan%202020.pdf> accessed 27 September 2024

Conte A, 'States' Prevention and Responses to the Phenomenon of Foreign Fighters against the Backdrop of International Human Rights Obligations' in de Guttry A, Capone F and Paulussen C (eds.), *Foreign Fighters under International Law and Beyond* (T.M.C. Asser Press 2016)

Cook J and Vale G, 'From Daesh to 'Diaspora' II: The Challenges Posed by Women and Minors After the Fall of the Caliphate' 12 CTC Sentinel (2019) 6

Cook J and Vale G, 'From Daesh to 'Diaspora': Tracing the Women and Minors of Islamic State' ICSR Report (2018)

Costello C and Foster M, 'Non-refoulement as Custom and *Jus Cogens*? Putting the Prohibition to the Test' in den Heijer M and van der Wilt H (eds.), *Netherlands Yearbook of International Law 2015* (T.M.C. Asser Press 2016)

COT Instituut voor Veiligheids- en Crisismanagement, 'Onder druk: Evaluatie van de gebeurtenissen in Amsterdam rond de wedstrijd Ajax – Maccabi Tel Aviv op 7 November 2024' (June 2025)

Coulombe C, *The Pope's Legion The Multinational Fighting Force that Defended the Vatican* (Palgrave Macmillan, 2008)

Council of Foreign Relations, 'Global Conflict Tracker: Conflict in Syria' (last updated 13 February 2024) <https://www.cfr.org/global-conflict-tracker/conflict/conflict-syria> accessed 4 October 2024

Coy J, *Strangers and Misfits: Banishment, Social Control, and Authority in Early Modern Germany* (Brill 2008)

Crawford J, Pellet A, and Olleson S (eds.), *The Law of International Responsibility* (Oxford University Press 2010)

Cuyckens H and Paulussen C, 'The Prosecution of Foreign Fighters in Western Europe: The Difficult Relationship Between Counter-Terrorism and International Humanitarian Law' 24 Journal of Conflict & Security Law (2019) 3

Cuyckens H, 'Foreign fighters and the tension between counterterrorism and international humanitarian law: A case for cumulative prosecution where possible' 103 International Review of the Red Cross (2021) 916–917

Dawson L, 'A Comparative Analysis of the Data on Western Foreign Fighters in Syria and Iraq: Who Went and Why?' ICCT Research Paper (February 2021)

Day A and Malone D, 'The Role of the United Nations in Shaping Global Security Law' in Geiß R and Melzer N (eds.), *The Oxford Handbook on the International Law of Global Security* (Oxford University Press, 2021)

Dean T, *Crime in Medieval Europe 1200–1550* (Routledge 2014)

Decœur H, 'The Criminalisation of Armed Jihad under French Law: Guilt by Association in the Age of Enemy Criminal Law' 25 European Journal of Crime, Criminal Law and Criminal Justice (2017)

Défenseur des droits, Décision du Défenseur des droits n°2019–129 (22 May 2019) <https://juridique.defenseurdesdroits.fr/doc_num.php?explnum_id=18912> accessed 30 June 2023

Denselow J, 'Iraq's Ho Chi Minh Trail: The Syrian-Iraqi Border Since 2003' 1 CTC Sentinel (May 2008) 6

Detter I, 'The Problem of Unequal Treaties' 15 International and Comparative Law Quarterly (1966) 4

Djordjević L, Constantin S and Kiss T (et al.) 15 European Yearbook of Minority Issues (2018) 2

Dodwell B, Milton D and Rassler D, 'The Caliphate's Global Workforce: An Inside Look at the Islamic State's Foreign Fighter Paper Trail' Combating Terrorism Center at West Point (April 2016)

Doehring K, "Aliens, Admission" in Bernhardt R (ed.), *Encyclopedia of Public International Law Vol. 1* (Elsevier Science Publishers 1992)

Doughty Street Chambers, 'German court convicts a third ISIS member of crimes against humanity committed against Yazidis' (18 June 2021) <https://www.doughtystreet.co.uk/news/german-court-convicts-third-isis-member-crimes-against-humanity-committed-against-yazidis> accessed 22 August 2024

Doughty Street Chambers, 'German court hands down second genocide conviction against ISIS member following enslavement and abuse of Yazidi woman in Syria' (28 July 2022) <https://www.doughtystreet.co.uk/news/german-court-hands-down-second-genocide-conviction-against-isis-member-following-enslavement> accessed 16 May 2024

Drevet B, 'Report on France' in S. Quattrocolo and S. Ruggeri (eds.), *Personal Participation in Criminal Proceedings: A Comparative Study of Participatory Safeguards and in absentia Trials in Europe* (Springer 2019)

Duffy H and van den Herik L, 'Terrorism and the Security Council' in Geiß R and Melzer N (eds.), *The Oxford Handbook on the International Law of Global Security* (Oxford University Press, 2021)

Duffy H, '"Foreign Terrorist Fighters": A Human Rights Approach?' 29 Security and Human Rights (2018)

Duffy H, 'De facto justice: Prosecution by non-state actors in armed conflict' in Fortin K and Heffes E (eds.), *Armed Groups and International Law: In the Shadowland of Legality and Illegality* (Edward Elgar Publishing 2023)

Duffy H, 'Foreign Fighters', Syrian Camps and the Jurisdictional Quagmire' in Capone F, Paulussen C and Mignot-Mahdavi R (eds.), *Returning Foreign Fighters: Responses, Legal Challenges and Ways Forward* (T.M.C. Asser Press 2023)

Duffy H, 'International human rights law and terrorism: an overview' in Saul B (ed.), *Research Handbook on International Law and Terrorism* (2nd edition, Edward Elgar Publishing 2020)

Duffy H, *The 'War on Terror' and the Framework of International Law* (Cambridge University Press 2015)

Dworkin A, 'A tribunal for ISIS fighters?' European Council on Foreign Relations (31 May 2019)

Dworkin A, 'Beyond good and evil: Why Europe should bring ISIS foreign fighters home' European Council on Foreign Relations (25 October 2019) <https://ecfr.eu/publication/beyond_good_and_evil_why_europe_should_bring_isis_foreign_fighters_home/> accessed 27 August 2024

Dzehtsiarou K, 'The United Kingdom and the European Convention on Human Rights: Together Until the End?' 5 European Convention on Human Rights Law Review (2024)

Efrat A and Richemond-Barak D, 'How Alive Is the Anti-Death Penalty Norm? Evidence from the British and French Treatment of ISIS Foreign Fighters' 8 Journal of Global Security Studies (2023) 1

Efrat A, *Intolerant Justice: Conflict and Cooperation on Transnational Litigation* (Oxford University Press 2023)

El-Muhammady A, 'Managing the Returning Foreign Terrorist Fighters and Their Families: Malaysian Experience' ICCT Policy Brief (January 2023)

Emberland M, 'The Committee on the Rights of the Child's Admissibility Decisions in the 'Syrian Camps Cases' against France: a Critique from the Viewpoint of Treaty Interpretation' 23 Human Rights Law Review (2023) 2

Encyclopaedia Britannica, 'Ostracism' (last updated 1 May 2025)

Ersbøll E, 'Birthright citizenship and children born in a conflict zone' European Network on Statelessness (5 February 2020)

Eurojust, the Genocide Network, 'Cumulative Prosecution of Foreign Terrorist Fighters for Core International Crimes and Terrorism-Related Offences' (May 2020) <https://www.eurojust.europa.eu/sites/default/files/Partners/Genocide/2020-05_Report-on-cumulative-prosecution-of-FTFs_EN.PDF> accessed 16 May 2024

European Council on Foreign Relations, Open letter: Call for a managed return of ISIS foreign fighter (26 November 2019). Available at: <https://ecfr.eu/article/commentary_open_letter_a_managed_return_of_isis_foreign_fighters/> accessed 4 April 2023

Europol, 'European Union Terrorism Situation and Trend Report' (2017) <https://www.europol.europa.eu/sites/default/files/documents/tesat2017.pdf> accessed 11 July 2024

Farley B, 'Detainee Transfers and the Principle of Non-refoulement in Relation to 'Non-belligerent Supporting States' in Non-international Armed Conflicts' 27 Journal of Conflict & Security Law (2022) 2

Farley B, 'Regulating the Foreign-Fighter Phenomenon' 64 Virginia Journal of International Law (2023) 1

Feichtner I, 'Subsidiarity' Max Planck Encyclopedia of Public International Law (October 2007)

Feinberg F, 'Terrorism inside out: Legislating for Humanity to Cooperate against Terrorism' 42 North Carolina Journal of International Law (2017) 2

Feinberg M, *Sovereignty in the Age of Global Terrorism: The Role of International Organisations* (Brill Nijhoff 2016)

Feller E, Türk V and Nicholson F (eds.), *Refugee Protection in International Law: UNHCR's Global Consultations on International Protection* (Cambridge University Press 2003)

Felter J and Fishman B, 'Becoming a Foreign Fighter: A Second Look at the Sinjar Records' in Bergen P et al. (eds.), *Bank Accounts, & Bleedout: Al-qa'ida's Road in and Out of Iraq* (Combatting Terrorism Center at West Point, Harmony Report 2006)

Ferlin A, 'Criminal Liability and Prosecution of Islamic State Fighters in Iraq' Journal of Criminal Justice and Security 23 (2021) 4

Ferro L and Verlinden N, 'Neutrality During Armed Conflicts: A Coherent Approach to Third-State Support for Warring Parties' 17 Chinese Journal of International Law (2018) 1

Ferstman C, 'Torture and non-refoulement' in M. Evans and J. Modvig (eds.), *Research Handbook on Torture* (Edgar Elgar 2020)

Fleck D, 'The Law of Neutrality' in Fleck D (ed.), *The Handbook of International Humanitarian Law* (4th edn., Oxford University Press 2021)

Flores M, 'Foreign Fighters Involvement in National and International Wars: A Historical Survey' in A de Guttry, F Capone and C Paulussen (eds.), *Foreign Fighters under International Law and Beyond* (T.M.C. Asser Press 2016)

Forcese C and Mamikon A, 'Neutrality Law, Anti-Terrorism, and Foreign Fighters: Legal Solutions to the Recruitment of Canadians to Foreign Insurgencies' 48 University of British Columbia law review (2015) 2

Forcese C, 'Homeward Bound? International Law and a State's Obligation to Repatriate Nationals Affiliated with Da'esh' 51 Israel Yearbook on Human Rights (2021)

Forcese C, 'The Capacity to Protect: Diplomatic Protection of Dual Nationals in the 'War on Terror'' 17 European Journal of International Law (2006) 2

Fortin K and Heffes E, *Armed Groups and International Law: In the Shadowland of Legality and Illegality* (Edward Elgar Publishing 2023)

Fortin K, *The Accountability of Armed Groups under Human Rights Law* (Oxford University Press 2017)

Fraser D and Caestecker F, 'Jews or Germans? Nationality Legislation and the Restoration of Liberal Democracy in Western Europe after the Holocaust' 31 Law and History Review (May 2013)

Fry J, 'Coercion, Causation, and the Fictional Elements of Indirect State Responsibility' 40 Vanderbilt Journal of Transnational Law (2007) 3

Galbraith J, 'U.S. Sanctions on the International Criminal Court: The Details and The Pattern' Verfassungsblog (7 June 2025)

Gallant K, *International Criminal Jurisdiction: Whose Law Must We Obey?* (Oxford University Press 2022)

Galli F, 'Case Studies of National Counter-Terrorism Policies: Case Study of France' in E. Shor and S. Hoadley, *International Human Rights and Counter-Terrorism* (Springer 2019)

Gasser H-P, 'Acts of terror, "terrorism" and international humanitarian law' 84 International Review of the Red Cross (2002)

Gearty C, *Homeland Insecurity: The Rise and Rise of Global anti-Terrorism Law* (Polity Press 2024)

Geiß R and Melzer N (eds.), *The Oxford Handbook on the International Law of Global Security* (Oxford University Press, 2021)

Geiß R, 'Common Article 1 of the Geneva Conventions: Scope and content of the obligation to 'ensure respect' – 'narrow but deep' or 'wide and shallow'?' in Krieger H, *Inducing Compliance with International Humanitarian Law: Lessons from the African Great Lakes Region* (Cambridge University Press 2015) 420

Geneuss J, 'On the Relationship Between German International Criminal Law and Counterterrorism Criminal Law' 21 Journal of International Criminal Justice (2023) 4

Gestel, van B, 'Bestraffing van Syriëgangers' 69 Ars Aequi (November 2020)

Gherbaoui T, *Europe's Foreign Fighter Conundrum: Legal Responses, the Rule of Law, and Human Rights* (T.M.C. Asser Press 2025)

Gibney M, 'Banishment and the Pre-history of Legitimate Expulsion Power' 24 Citizenship Studies (2020) 3

Gibney M, 'Deprivation of Citizenship Through a Political Lens: A political Scientist's Perspective' in Institute on Statelessness and Inclusion, The World's Stateless: Deprivation of Nationality (March 2020)

Gillard E, 'Reparation for violations of international humanitarian law' 85 International Review of the Red Cross (2003) 851

Ginkel, van B, 'The International Legal and Policy Framework on Returning Foreign Fighters: Focus on the United Nations and the Global Counterterrorism Forum' in Capone F, Paulussen C and Mignot-Mahdavi R (eds.), *Returning Foreign Fighters: Responses, Legal Challenges and Ways Forward* (T.M.C. Asser Press 2023)

Ginkel, van B and Entenmann E (eds.), 'The Foreign Fighters Phenomenon in the European Union: Profiles, Threats & Polies' ICCT Research Paper (April 2016) 14

Ginkel, van B and Minks S, 'Addressing the Challenges of Returnees: Threat Perception, Policies and Practices in the Netherlands' in Renard T and Coolsaet R (eds), 'Returnees: who are they, why are they (not) coming back and how should we deal with them?' Egmont Paper 101 (February 2018)

Ginkel, van B, 'Prosecuting Foreign Terrorist Fighters: What Role for the Military?' ICCT Policy Brief (9 May 2016)

Ginkel, van B, 'The Practice of the United Nations in Combatting Terrorism from 1946 to 2008: Questions of Legality and Legitimacy' (PhD thesis, Universiteit Utrecht 2010)

Ginkel, van B, Paulussen C and Mehra T, 'Diversifying the Sources of Evidence in Terrorism Cases before Criminal Courts in (Post-)Conflict and High-Risk Situations: The Role of the Military' in Ohlin J, Finkelstein C, Fuller C (et al.), *Between Crime and War: Hybrid Legal Frameworks for Asymmetric Conflict* (Oxford University Press 2022)

Ginsborg L, 'One step forward, two steps back: The Security Council, 'foreign terrorist fighters', and human rights' in M. Nowak and A. Charbord (eds.), *Using Human Rights to Counter Terrorism* (Edward Elgar 2018).

Global Center on Cooperative Security, Human Security Collective and the ICCT, 'Addressing the Foreign Terrorist Fighters Phenomenon from a European Union Perspective: UN Security Council Resolution 2178, Legal Issues, and Challenges and Opportunities for EU Foreign Security and Development Policy' Policy brief (December 2014)

Goodman R and Lanovoy V, 'State Responsibility for Assisting Armed Groups: A Legal Risk Analysis' Just Security (22 December 2016)

Gray C, 'The Different Forms of Reparation: Restitution' in Crawford J, Pellet A, and Olleson S (eds.), *The Law of International Responsibility* (Oxford University Press 2010)

Gurski P, *Western Foreign Fighters: The Threat to Homeland and International Security* (Rowman & Littlefield 2017)

Guttry, de A, 'The Role Played by the UN in Countering the Phenomenon of Foreign Terrorist Fighters' in de Guttry A, Capone F and Paulussen C (eds.), *Foreign Fighters under International Law and Beyond* (T.M.C. Asser Press 2016)

Guttry, de A, Capone F and Paulussen C (eds.), *Foreign Fighters under International Law and Beyond* (T.M.C. Asser Press 2016)

Hailbronner K, 'Nationality in public international law and European law' in Bauböck R, Ersbøll E, Groenendijk K et al. (eds.), *Acquisition and Loss of Nationality Volume 1: Comparative Analyses: Policies and Trends in 15 European Countries* (Amsterdam University Press, IMISCOE Research Series 2006)

Hall J KC, 'Returning from Islamic State: Risk and Response' Independent Reviewer of Terrorism Legislation, Speech at King's College London (27 February 2023) <https://terrorismlegislationreviewer.independent.gov.uk/wp-content/uploads/2023/02/KCL-Speech-final1.pdf> accessed 4 July 2024

Hamming T and Amarasingam A, 'Cubs of the Caliphate' in Ashraph S, Cheung Ka-man C and Cook J (eds.), *Holding ISIL Accountable: Prosecuting Crimes in Iraq and Syria* (ICCT Press 2024)

Harrison C, 'Gender, Catholic Spirituality, and French Responses to the Roman Question' 79 The Journal of Modern History (2007) 2

Hecker M, 'The French Approach to Female Violent Extremist Offenders' in Mehra T, Renard T and Herbach M (eds.), *Female Jihadis Facing Justice: Comparing Approaches in Europe* (ICCT, 2024)

Heffes E, 'Administration of justice by armed groups: Some legal and practical concerns' Humanitarian Law & Policy (22 November 2018)

Hegghammer T, 'The Rise of Muslim Foreign Fighters: Islam and the Globalization of Jihad' 35 International Security 3

Heij Z, 'Trials in absentia of foreign terrorist fighters in the Netherlands and Belgium' 4 Crimmigratie & Recht (2020) 1

Heijer, den M and van der Wilt H (eds.), *Netherlands Yearbook of International Law 2015* (T.M.C. Asser Press 2016)

Heller K, 'The Law of Neutrality Does Not Apply to the Conflict with Al-Qaeda, and It's a Good Thing Too: A Response to Chang' 47 Texas International Law Journal (2011) 115

Higgins R, 'The Right in International Law of an Individual to Enter, Stay in and Leave a Country' 49 International Affairs (1973) 3

Hoffman A and Furlan M, 'Challenges Posed by Returning Foreign Fighters' Program on Extremism (March 2020)

Holmes J, 'Complementarity: National Courts versus the ICC' in Cassese A, Gaeta P and Jones J (eds.), *The Rome Statute of the International Criminal Court: A Commentary* (Oxford University Press 2002)

Houry N, 'Bringing ISIS to Justice: Running Out of Time?' Just Security (5 February 2019)

Hughes R, *The Fatal Shore* (Alfred A. Knopf 1987)

Human Rights Watch, '"Video Unavailable" Social Media Platforms Remove Evidence of War Crimes' (10 September 2020) <https://www.hrw.org/report/2020/09/10/video-unavailable/social-media-platforms-remove-evidence-war-crimes> accessed 10 July 2024

Human Rights Watch, 'France Repatriates More Children from Northeast Syria' (24 June 2020) <https://www.hrw.org/news/2020/06/24/france-repatriates-more-children-northeast-syria> accessed 1 August 2023

Human Rights Watch, 'Iraq: French Citizens Allege Torture, Coercion' (31 May 2019) <https://www.hrw.org/news/2019/05/31/iraq-french-citizens-allege-torture-coercion> accessed 28 August 2024

Human Rights Watch, 'Iraq: Lawyers Arrested for Work in ISIS Courts: Chilling Effect on Private Legal Representation' (10 August 2017) <https://www.hrw.org/news/2017/08/10/iraq-lawyers-arrested-work-isis-courts> accessed 30 September 2024.

Human Rights Watch, 'Syria: Dire Conditions for ISIS Suspects' Families' (23 July 2019) <https://www.hrw.org/news/2019/07/23/syria-dire-conditions-isis-suspects-families> accessed 18 December 2024

Human Rights Watch, 'Thousands of Foreigners Unlawfully Held in NE Syria' (23 March 2021) <https://www.hrw.org/news/2021/03/23/thousands-foreigners-unlawfully-held-ne-syria> accessed 5 March 2025

Human Rights Watch, Bahrain: Citizenship Rights Stripped Away Authorities Take New Powers to Arbitrarily Revoke Nationality (21 August 2014) <https://www.hrw.org/news/2014/08/21/bahrain-citizenship-rights-stripped-away> accessed 20 March 2023

Human Rights Watch, Flawed Justice: Accountability for ISIS Crimes in Iraq (2017) <https://www.hrw.org/report/2017/12/05/flawed-justice/accountability-isis-crimes-iraq> accessed 25 September 2024

Human Rights Watch, France: Submission to the UN Committee on the Rights of the Child (26 April 2023) <https://www.hrw.org/news/2023/04/26/france-submission-un-committee-rights-child> accessed 31 July 2023

Human Rights Watch, Iraq: Key Courts Improve ISIS Trial Procedures: But Changes Needed in Laws, Response to Torture, Other Courts (13 March 2019) <https://www.hrw.org/news/2019/03/13/iraq-key-courts-improve-isis-trial-procedures> accessed 25 September 2024

Human Rights Watch, Iraq: Unlawful Mass Executions Resume: Adopt Death Penalty Moratorium, Judicial System Reforms (24 January 2024) <https://www.hrw.org/news/2024/01/24/iraq-unlawful-mass-executions-resume> accessed 2 October 2024

Human Rights Watch, Northeast Syria: Boys, Men Held in Inhumane Conditions (8 October 2019) <https://www.hrw.org/news/2019/10/08/northeast-syria-boys-men-held-inhumane-conditions> accessed 27 September 2023

ICRC, Basic rules of the Geneva Conventions and their Additional Protocols, ref. 0365 (31 December 1988)

ICRC, *Commentary on the First Geneva Convention: Convention (I) for the Amelioration of the Condition of the Wounded and Sick in Armed Forces in the Field* (Cambridge University Press 2016)

ICRC, Customary IHL Database <https://ihl-databases.icrc.org/en/customary-ihl/v1/rule128> accessed 17 July 2023

ICRC, Strengthening Legal Protection for Persons deprived of their Liberty in relation to Non-International Armed Conflict, Regional Consultations 2012–13, Background paper. <https://www.icrc.org/en/doc/assets/files/2013/strengthening-legal-protection-detention-consultations-2012-2013-icrc.pdf> accessed 17 July 2023

Impunity Watch, PAX and Syrian Center for Media and Freedom of Expression, 'ISIS-only tribunal: selective, politicised justice will do more harm than good' Policy Brief (31 October 2019)

Institute on Statelessness and Inclusion and Global Citizenship Observatory, 'Instrumentalizing Citizenship in the Fight Against Terrorism' (March 2022) <https://files.institutesi.org/Instrumentalising_Citizenship_Global_Trends_Report.pdf> accessed 20 March 2025.

Ip J, 'Reconceptualising the Legal Response to Foreign Fighters' International & Comparative Law Quarterly 69 (January 2020) 1

Italian Institute for International Political Studies, 'Foreign Fighters from Central Asia: Between Renunciation and Repatriation' (2 October 2019)

Jackson M, *Complicity in International Law* (Oxford University Press 2015)

Jaghai S and van Waas L, 'Stripped of Citizenship, Stripped of Dignity? A Critical Exploration of Nationality Deprivation as a Counter-Terrorism Measure' in Paulussen C and Scheinin M (eds.), *Human Dignity and Human Security in Times of Terrorism* (T.M.C. Asser Press 2020)

Jamnejad M and Wood M, 'The Principle of Non-intervention' 22 Leiden Journal of International Law (2009) 2

Janmyr M, *Protecting Civilians in Refugee Camps: Unable and Unwilling States, UNHCR and International Responsibility* (Brill Nijhoff, 2013)

Jennings R and Watts A (eds.), *Oppenheim's international Law, Vol 1: Peace* (9th edition, Longman Group UK Limited 1992)

Jessberger F, Kaleck W and Schueller A, 'Concurring Criminal Jurisdictions under International Law' in Bergsmo M (ed.), *Complementarity and the Exercise of Universal Jurisdiction for Core International Crimes* (Torkel Opsahl Academic EPublisher and Peace Research Institute Oslo 2010)

Jomaa A, 'Addressing Jurisdictional Challenges in Prosecuting ISIL Fighters' 11 Berkeley Journal of Middle Eastern & Islamic Law (2020) 1

Jones S, Dobbins J and Byman D et al., 'Rolling Back the Islamic State' RAND Corporation (2017)

Jongerden J, 'The Netherlands and the prosecution and trial of Islamic State suspects in Rojava/The Autonomous Administration in North and East Syria' 3 The Commentaries (2021) 1

Jordan L, '"Unwilling or Unable"' 103 International Law Studies (2024)

Kałduński M (ed.), *Reciprocity in International Law* (Palgrave Macmillan 2024)

Kałduński M, 'Introduction: Framework of the Book' in Kałduński M (ed.), *Reciprocity in International Law* (Palgrave Macmillan 2024)

Kaleck W and Kroker P, 'Syrian Torture Investigations in Germany and Beyond: Breathing New Life into Universal Jurisdiction in Europe?' 16 Journal of International Criminal Justice (2018) 1

Keller S, 'An Effective Form of Judicial Treatment of Foreign Terrorist Fighters in Kosovo?' EJIL:Talk! (20 July 2023)

Kessler B, 'The Duty to 'Ensure Respect' Under Common Article 1 of the Geneva Conventions: Its Implications on International and Non-International Armed Conflicts' 44 German Yearbook of International Law (2001)

Kilibarda P and Gaggioli G, 'Detention of Suspected Terrorists in Connection with Armed Conflict: A Focus on Release and Repatriation' in Schmitt M and Koschnitzky C (eds.), *Prisoners of War in Contemporary Conflict* (Oxford University Press 2023)

Kinderombudsman, 'Kinderombudsman herhaalt: Nederland moet kinderen in Syrische kampen terughalen' (14 December 2021) <https://www.kinderombudsman.nl/nieuws/kinderombudsman-herhaalt-nederland-moet-kinderen-in-syrische-kampen-terughalen> accessed 30 June 2023

Kingston R, 'The Unmaking of Citizens: Banishment and the Modern Citizenship Regime in France' 9 Citizenship Studies (2005) 1

Kittichaisaree K, *The Obligation to Extradite or Prosecute* (Oxford University Press 2018)

Kleffner J, 'The law and policy of complementarity in relation to 'criminal proceedings' carried out by non-state organized armed groups' in Stahn C and El Zeidy M (eds.), *The International Criminal Court and Complementarity: From Theory to Practice* (Cambridge University Press 2011)

Kleffner J, *Complementarity in the Rome Statute and National Criminal Jurisdictions* (Oxford University Press 2008)

Knights M and van Wilgenburg W, *Accidental Allies: The U.S.–Syrian Democratic Forces Partnership Against the Islamic State* (The Washington Institute for Near East Policy/Bloomsbury Publishing Plc 2021)

Kolb R, 'The Exercise of Criminal Jurisdiction over International Terrorists' in A. Bianchi (ed.), *Enforcing International Law Norms Against Terrorism* (Hart Publishing 2004)

Kolb R, Gaggioli G and Kilibarda P, *Research Handbook on Human Rights and Humanitarian Law* (Edgar Elgar 2022)

Kolb R, *Good Faith in International Law* (Hart Publishing 2017)

Koller S, 'Gendered Differences in the Prosecution of Daesh Returnees in Germany' in NATO Centre of Excellence Defence Against Terrorism, Gender in Terrorism and Counterterrorism: Gendered Dynamics in Military Effectiveness, Prosecution and Radicalization, Workshop Report (13–15 September 2022)

Koller S, 'ISIS Women in Court: Jennifer W. – Taking Responsibility' The CounterPoint Blog (30 August 2023)

Koller S, 'Prosecution of German Women Returning from Syria and Iraq: Insights and Recommendations for Policymakers and Security Agencies (Counter Extremism Project Policy Paper, August 2022)

Koller S, 'Prosecution of Returnees from Syria and Iraq in France: Insights and Recommendations for Policymakers and Security Agencies' CEP Policy Paper (March 2023)

Koller S, 'The German Approach to Female Violent Extremist Offenders' in Mehra T, Renard T and Herbach M (eds.), *Female Jihadis Facing Justice: Comparing Approaches in Europe* (ICCT, 2024)

Krähenmann S, 'Foreign Fighters under International Law and National Law' 108 Netherlands Military Law Review (2015) 6

Krähenmann S, 'Foreign Fighters under International Law' Geneva Academy of International Humanitarian Law and Human Rights, Academy Briefing No. 7 (October 2014) 6

Krähenmann S, 'Foreign-fighters, Terrorism and Counter-terrorism' in Saul B (ed.), *Research Handbook on International Law and Terrorism* (2nd edition, Edward Elgar Publishing 2020)

Krähenmann S, 'The interplay between international humanitarian law, terrorism and the "foreign terrorist fighter" regime' 112 Proceedings of the ASIL Annual Meeting (2018)

Krähenmann S, 'The Obligations under International Law of the Foreign Fighter's State of Nationality or Habitual Residence, State of Transit and State of Destination' in de Guttry A, Capone F and Paulussen C (eds.), *Foreign Fighters under International Law and Beyond* (T.M.C. Asser Press 2016)

Krieger H, *Inducing Compliance with International Humanitarian Law: Lessons from the African Great Lakes Region* (Cambridge University Press 2015) 420

Kruizinga S, 'The First Resisters: Tracing Three Dutchmen from the Spanish Trenches to the Second World War, 1936–1945' 27 War in History (2020) 3

Kulesza J, *Due Diligence in International Law* (BRILL 2016)

Kuning P, 'Prohibition of intervention' Max Planck Encyclopedia of Public International Law (2008)

Laine T, "Passing the Buck": Western States Race to Denationalize Foreign Terrorist Fighters' 12 Journal of Peacebuilding & Development (2017)

Lanovoy V, *Complicity and its Limits in the Law of International Responsibility* (Hart Publishing 2016)

Lauterpacht E (ed.), *International Law: Being the Collected Papers of Hersch Lauterpacht Vol. V* (Cambridge University Press 2004)

Lauterpacht E and Bethlehem D, 'The scope and content of the principle of non-refoulement: Opinion' in Feller E, Türk V and Nicholson F (eds.), *Refugee Protec-*

tion in International Law: UNHCR's Global Consultations on International Protection (Cambridge University Press 2003)

Lauterpacht H, 'The Future of Neutrality, December 1941' in Lauterpacht E (ed.), *International Law: Being the Collected Papers of Hersch Lauterpacht Vol. V* (Cambridge University Press 2004)

Layeb A, 'Mercenary Activity: United States Neutrality Laws and Enforcement' 10 New York Law School Journal of International and Comparative Law (1989) 3

Lee L and Quigley J, *Consular Law and Practice* (3rd edn., Oxford University Press 2008)

Lennon G, 'Precautionary tales: Suspicionless counterterrorism stop and search' 15 Criminology & Criminal Justice (2015) 1

Lepoutre J, 'Citizenship Loss and Deprivation in the European Union (27 + 1)' EUI Working Paper RSCAS 2020/29 (2020)

Lloydd M, 'Framing Foreign Fighting: Exploring the Scope of Prevention and the Categorisation of Fighters in International Law' in Paulussen C and Scheinin M (eds.), *Human Dignity and Human Security in Times of Terrorism* (T.M.C. Asser Press 2020)

Lloydd M, 'Retrieving Neutrality Law to Consider 'Other' Foreign Fighters under International Law' European Society of International Law Conference Paper Series, Conference Paper No. 8/2017 (ESIL Research Forum, Granada, 30–31 March 2017)

Lu Phillips R, 'A Tribunal for ISIS Fighters – A National Security and Human Rights Emergency' Just Security (30 March 2021)

Macedo S, *Universal Jurisdiction: National Courts and the Prosecution of Serious Crimes under International Law* (University of Pennsylvania Press 2004)

Mackenzie S, 'The Foreign Enlistment Act and the Spanish Civil War, 1936–1939' 10 Twentieth Century British History (1999) 1

Mackenzie-Gray Scott R, 'State Responsibility for Complicity in the Internationally Wrongful Acts of Non-State Armed Groups' 24 Journal of Conflict & Security Law (2019) 2

Macklin A, 'The Return of Banishment: Do the New Denationalisation Policies Weaken Citizenship?' in Bauböck R (ed.), *Debating Transformations of National Citizenship* (Springer 2018)

Maddocks J, 'State Responsibility for International Law Violations Involving Non-State Actors in Armed Conflict' (PhD in Law, University of Reading 2021)

Maia C and Gardounis E, 'Subsidiary Jurisdiction' Max Planck Encyclopedia of Public International Law (December 2021)

Malet D and Fritz J, 'Historical Responses to Foreign Fighters and Returnees' in Capone F, Paulussen C and Mignot-Mahdavi R (eds.), Returning Foreign Fighters: Responses, Legal Challenges and Ways Forward (T.M.C. Asser Press 2023)

Malet D and Hayes R, 'Foreign Fighter Returnees: An Indefinite Threat?' 32 Terrorism and Political Violence (2018) 8

Malet D, *Foreign Fighters: Transnational Identity in Civic Conflicts* (Oxford University Press 2013) 9

Maniszewska K, *Towards a New Definition of Terrorism: Challenges and Perspectives in a Shifting Paradigm* (Springer 2024)

Margolin D and Cook J, 'The Agency and Roles of Foreign Women in ISIL' in Ashraph S, Cheung Ka-man C and Cook J (eds.), *Holding ISIL Accountable: Prosecuting Crimes in Iraq and Syria* (ICCT Press 2024)

Martini L and Megerisi T, 'Road to nowhere: Why Europe's border externalisation Is a dead end' European Council on Foreign Relations (14 December 2023)

Massingham E and McConnachie A (eds), *Ensuring Respect for International Humanitarian Law* (Routledge 2020)

Mayer B, 'Climate Change Mitigation as an Obligation Under Human Rights Treaties?' 115 The American Journal of International Law (2021) 3

Mayer B, *International Law Obligations on Climate Change Mitigation* (Oxford University Press 2022)

McIntyre O and Mosedale T, 'The Precautionary Principle as a Norm of Customary International Law' 9 Journal of Environmental Law (1997) 2

McKeever D, 'Old Rules to Fix New Problems: Counterterrorism, Refugees and Withdrawal of Nationality' 29 Journal of Conflict & Security Law (2024) 1

McKeever D, 'Repatriating Foreign Terrorist Fighters and Their Family Members: What International Law Requires, and What National Courts Will Do' 28 Journal of Conflict & Security Law (2022) 1

Mckinney C, How many people have been stripped of their British citizenship? (10 January 2022) <https://freemovement.org.uk/how-many-people-have-been-stripped-of-their-british-citizenship-home-office-deprivation/> accessed 20 March 2023

Meessen K (ed.), *Extraterritorial Jurisdiction in Theory and Practice* (Kluwer Law International 1996)

Mégret F and Samson M, 'Holding the Line on Complementarity in Libya: The Case for Tolerating Flawed Domestic Trials' 11 Journal of International Criminal Justice (2013) 3

Mégret F, "Do Not Do Abroad What You Would Not Do at Home?": An Exploration of the Rationales for Extraterritorial Criminal Jurisdiction over a State's Nationals' 57 Canadian Yearbook of international Law/Annuaire canadien de droit international (2020)

Mehra T and Paulussen C, 'The Repatriation of Foreign Fighters and Their Families: Options, Obligations, Morality and Long-Term Thinking' ICCT Perspective (6 March 2019).

Mehra T and Wentworth M, 'New Kid on the Block: Prosecution of ISIS Fighters by the Autonomous Administration of North and East Syria' ICCT Perspective (16 March 2021)

Mehra T, 'Bringing (Foreign) Terrorist Fighters to Justice in a Post-ISIS Landscape Part III: Collecting Evidence from Conflict Situations' ICCT Perspective (12 June 2018)

Mehra T, 'Doubling Down on Accountability in Europe: Prosecuting 'Terrorists' for Core International Crimes and Terrorist Offences Committed in the Context of the Conflict in Syria and Iraq' XVII Perspectives on Terrorism (2023) 4

Mehra T, 'The Dutch Approach to Female Violent Extremist Offenders' in Mehra T, Renard T and Herbach M (eds.), *Female Jihadis Facing Justice: Comparing Approaches in Europe* (ICCT, 2024)

Mehra T, Renard T and Herbach M (eds.), *Female Jihadis Facing Justice: Comparing Approaches in Europe* (ICCT, 2024)

Mignot-Mahdavi R, 'The Lack of Individualisation of Sentences and Their Enforcement at the Expense of Reintegration in France' in Capone F, Paulussen C and Mignot-Mahdavi R (eds.), *Returning Foreign Fighters: Responses, Legal Challenges and Ways Forward* (T.M.C. Asser Press 2023)

Milanovic M, 'Repatriating the Children of Foreign Terrorist Fighters and the Extraterritorial Application of Human Rights' EJIL:Talk! (10 November 2020)

Milanovic M, 'Revisiting Coercion as an Element of Prohibited Intervention in International Law' 117 American Journal of International Law (2023) 4

Milanovic M, 'The Murder of Jamal Khashoggi: Immunities, Inviolability and the Human Right to Life' 20 Human Rights Law Review (2020) 1

Mironova V, 'Iraq's Broken Justice System for Islamic State Fighters' Lawfare (24 July 2020)

Moodrick-Even Khen H, 'Revisiting Universal Jurisdiction: The Application of the Complementarity Principle by National Courts and Implications for Ex-Post Justice in the Syrian Civil War' 30 Emory International Law Review (2015) 2

Moran C, 'Strengthening the principle of non-refoulement' 25 The International Journal of Human Rights (2021) 6

Morris J (ed.), *Rethinking Risk and the Precautionary Principle* (Butterworth Heinemann 2000)

Morris J, 'Defining the Precautionary Principle' in Morris J (ed.), *Rethinking Risk and the Precautionary Principle* (Butterworth Heinemann 2000)

Moynihan H, 'Aiding and Assisting: Challenges in Armed Conflict and Counterterrorism' Chatham House Royal Institute of International Affairs, Research Paper (November 2016)

Moynihan H, 'The Application of International Law to State Cyberattacks: Sovereignty and Non-intervention' Chatham House Research Paper (2 December 2019)

Mumford A, 'Buck-passing' in Brown G, McLean I and McMillan A (eds.), *A Concise Oxford Dictionary of Politics and International Relations* (4th edn., Oxford University Press 2018)

Nieto-Navia R, 'International Peremptory Norms (*Jus Cogens*) and International Humanitarian Law' in Vohrah L, Pocar F, Featherstone Y et al. (eds.), *Man's Inhumanity to Man: Essays on International Law in Honour of Antonio Cassese* (Brill Nijhoff 2003)

Nijman J and Werner W. (eds.), *Netherlands Yearbook of International Law 2018: Populism and International Law* (Springer 2019)

Nollkaemper P, 'Advies Internationaal Tribunaal ISIS' (22 July 2019) <https://zoek.officielebekendmakingen.nl/blg-894850.pdf> accessed 26 august 2024

Nonno, del E, Haquin Saenz L and Kaygusuz Akbay M, 'The Externalization of Asylum: A Process to Limit Asylum?' in Nikodinovska Krstevska A, Gavouneli M and Savić Bojanić M, *Outsourcing and Cooperation with Third Countries: Deconstructing the Formal and the Informal in Migration and Asylum Policies* (Editoriale Scientifica S.r.l. 2022)

Noorloos, van M, 'Legal Regulation of Subversive Expressions in Relation to Terrorist Travel: The Dutch Situation Against the Backdrop of International Human Rights Law' in F Capone, C Paulussen and R Mignot-Mahdavi (eds.), *Returning Foreign Fighters: Responses, Legal Challenges and Ways Forward* (T.M.C. Asser Press 2023)

Nowak N and Charbord A (eds.), *Using Human Rights to Counter Terrorism* (Edward Elgar 2018)

Nyamutata C, 'Young Terrorists or Child Soldiers? ISIS Children, International Law and Victimhood' 25 Journal of Conflict & Security Law (2020) 2

O'Driscoll F, 'Confounding the Garibaldian Liars: The Letters of Albert Delahoyde, Irish Soldier of the Papal Battalion of St Patrick and Papal Zouave in Italy, 1860–1870' 6 Studi irlandesi. A Journal of Irish Studies (2016) 6

OHCHR, 'Children in Northeast Syria must be urgently repatriated: UN experts' (31 March 2023) <https://www.ohchr.org/en/statements/2023/03/children-northeast-syria-must-be-urgently-repatriated-un-experts> accessed 30 June 2023

OHCHR, 'Position of the United Nations Special Rapporteur on the promotion and protection of human rights and fundamental freedoms while countering terrorism on the human rights of adolescents/juveniles being detained in North-East Syria' (May 2021) <https://www.ohchr.org/sites/default/files/Documents/Issues/Terrorism/SR/UNSRCT_Position_human-rights-of-boys-adolescents-2021_final.pdf> accessed 29 September 2023

OHCHR, 'Syria: UN expert calls for an end to mass arbitrary and indefinite detentions and urges protection for children in Northeast Syria' (21 July 2023) <https://www.ohchr.org/en/press-releases/2023/07/syria-un-expert-calls-end-mass-arbitrary-and-indefinite-detentions-and-urges> accessed 14 September 2023

OHCHR, 'Syria: UN experts urge 57 States to repatriate women and children from squalid camps' (8 February 2021) <https://www.ohchr.org/en/press-releases/2021/02/syria-un-experts-urge-57-states-repatriate-women-and-children-squalid-camps> accessed 30 June 2023

OHCHR, Amicus brief, Presented by the UN Special Rapporteur on Contemporary Forms of Racism, Racial Discrimination, Xenophobia and Related Intolerance, before the Dutch Immigration and Naturalization Service (23 October 2018)

OHCHR, Human Rights, Terrorism and Counter-terrorism, Fact Sheet No. 32 (1 July 2008) <https://www.ohchr.org/en/publications/fact-sheets/fact-sheet-no-32-terrorism-and-counter-terrorism> accessed 12 April 2023

OHCHR, Iraq: UN expert says prosecution of ISIL leadership must be fair and thorough (4 April 2019) <https://www.ohchr.org/en/news/2019/04/iraq-un-expert-says-prosecution-isil-leadership-must-be-fair-and-thorough> accessed 1 October 2024

OHCHR, Non-Refoulement and the Obligations of States to Persons Arbitrarily Detained in North-East Syria: Position Paper of the United Nations Special Rapporteur on the Promotion and Protection of Human Rights and Fundamental Freedoms while Countering Terrorism (October 2023) <https://www.ohchr.org/en/special-procedures/sr-terrorism/detention-and-repatriations-north-east-syria> accessed 14 November 2024

OHCHR, Position Paper of the United Nations Special Rapporteur on the promotion and protection of human rights and fundamental freedoms while countering terrorism, 'The prosecution of individuals with alleged links to designated non-State armed groups for crimes committed in the Northeast of Syria as a key aspect of the rights of victims of terrorism' (September 2023) <https://www.ohchr.org/en/special-procedures/sr-terrorism/detention-and-repatriations-north-east-syria> accessed 24 October 2025

OHCHR, UN Special Rapporteur on the promotion and protection of human rights while countering terrorism 'Extra-territorial jurisdiction of States over children and their guardians in camps, prisons, or elsewhere in the northern Syrian Arab Republic' (2020) <https://www.ohchr.org/sites/default/files/Documents/Issues/Terrorism/UNSRsPublicJurisdictionAnalysis2020.pdf> accessed 15 March 2024

Ohlin J, Finkelstein C, Fuller C (et al.), *Between Crime and War: Hybrid Legal Frameworks for Asymmetric Conflict* (Oxford University Press 2022)

Orakhelashvili A (ed.), *Research Handbook on Jurisdiction and Immunities in International Law* (Edward Elgar Publishing Limited 2015)

Orozobekova C, *Foreign Fighters and International Peace: Joining Global Jihad and Marching Back Home* (Rowman & Littlefield 2023)

OSCE Office for Democratic Institutions and Human Rights, 'Guidelines for Addressing the Threats and Challenges of "Foreign Terrorist Fighters" within a Human Rights Framework' (12 September 2018)

Palwankar U, 'Measures available to States for fulfilling their obligation to ensure respect for international humanitarian law' International Review of the Red Cross (1994) 298

Paulus A and Dienelt A, 'Vienna Convention on Consular Relations (1963)' Max Planck Encyclopedia of Public International Law (2011)

Paulussen C and Gherbaoui T, 'Trials in Absentia of Foreign Fighters and their Families?' ICCT Perspective (1 August 2022)

Paulussen C and Gillard E, 'Staying in an Area Controlled by a Terrorist Organisation: Crime or Operational Necessity?' ICCT Perspective (11 January 2021)

Paulussen C and Mehra T, 'Evidentiary and Charging Matters in the Context of Prosecuting Returning Foreign Fighters Before National Courts' in Capone F, Paulussen C and Mignot-Mahdavi R (eds.), *Returning Foreign Fighters: Responses, Legal Challenges and Ways Forward* (T.M.C. Asser Press 2023)

Paulussen C and Pitcher K, 'Prosecuting (Potential) Foreign Fighters: Legislative and Practical Challenges' ICCT Research Paper (January 2018)

Paulussen C and Scheinin M (eds.), *Human Dignity and Human Security in Times of Terrorism* (T.M.C. Asser Press 2020)

Paulussen C, 'Impunity for international terrorists? Key legal questions and practical considerations' ICCT Research Paper (April 2012)

Paulussen C, 'Stripping foreign fighters of their citizenship: International human rights and humanitarian law considerations' 103 International Review of the Red Cross (2021) 916–917

Paulussen C, 'Towards a Right to Sustainable Security of Person in Times of Terrorism? Assessing Possibilities and Limitations Through a Critical Evaluation of Citizenship Stripping and Non-Repatriation Policies' 26 Journal of Conflict and Security Law (2021) 1

Paulussen C, Cuyckens H and Fortin K, 'The Prosecution of Foreign Fighters under International Humanitarian Law: Misconceptions and Opportunities' ICCT Perspective (13 December 2019)

Pauwelyn J, 'Export Restrictions in Times of Pandemic: Options and Limits Under International Trade Agreements' 54 Journal of World Trade (2020) 5

Pejic J, 'Armed Conflict and Terrorism: There Is a (Big) Difference' in de Frías A, Samuel K and White N (eds.), *Counter-Terrorism: International Law and Practice* (Oxford University Press 2012)

Pictet J (ed.), *The Geneva Conventions of 12 August 1949: Commentary, Vol IV: Geneva Convention Relative to the Protection of Civilian Persons in Time of War* (ICRC 1958)

Pietrzak J, 'Poles in the Spanish Civil War (1936–1939): During the Conflict and After' Cuadernos de Historia Contemporánea 43 (2021)

Pillai S and Williams G, 'Twenty-First Century Banishment: Citizenship Stripping in Common Law Nations' 66 International & Comparative Law Quarterly (2017) 3

Pisillo-Mazzeschi R, 'The Due Diligence Rule and the Nature of the International Responsibility of States' 35 German Yearbook of International Law (1992) 9

Poecke, Van T and Cuyckens H, 'The Qualification of the Activities of (returned) Foreign Fighters under National Criminal Law' in Capone F, Paulussen C and Mignot-Mahdavi R (eds.), *Returning Foreign Fighters: Responses, Legal Challenges and Ways Forward* (T.M.C. Asser Press 2023)

Poecke, Van T and Wauters E, 'The Repatriation of European Nationals from Syria as Contested before Domestic Courts in Belgium and Beyond' Working Paper No. 229 (January 2021)

Poecke, Van T, Verbruggen F and Yperman W, 'Terrorist offences and international humanitarian law: The armed conflict exclusion clause' 103 International Review of the Red Cross (2021) 916–917

Pokalova E, *Returning Islamist Foreign Fighters: Threats and Challenges to the West* (Palgrave Macmillan 2020)

Prener C, 'The ECtHR on citizenship revocation: Solving or compounding the confusion?' Global Citizenship Observatory (29 March 2022)

Prener C, *Denationalisation and Its Discontents: Citizenship Revocation in the 21st Century: Legal, Political and Moral Implications* (Brill Nijhoff 2023)

Pronk A, 'The price of deterrence Australia's path to maintaining sovereign borders' Clingendael Report (February 2024)

Proulx V, 'Babysitting Terrorists: Should States Be Strictly Liable for Failing to Prevent Transborder Attacks?' 23 Berkeley Journal of International Law (2005) 3

Provost R, *Rebel Courts: The Administration of Justice by Armed Insurgents* (Oxford University Press 2021)

Pugliese M, 'France and Foreign Fighters: The Controversial Outsourcing of Prosecution' Italian Institute for International Political Studies (19 December 2019)

Quigley J, Aceves W and Shank S, *The Law of Consular Access: A Documentary Guide* (Routledge 2010)

Radicalisation Awareness Network, Ex Post Paper, 'Study Visit: Returned Women and Children – Studying an Ongoing Experience on the Ground' 10–11 December 2019, Pristina, Kosovo

Radicalisation Awareness Network, RAN Manual Responses to Returnees: Foreign Terrorist Fighters and their Family Members (2nd edition, 2022)

Rapp S, 'SCSL Symposium: A Legal Legacy that Opens the Way to Justice in Challenging Places and Times–Part II' Opinio Juris (15 March 2021)

Rehman J and Shahid A (eds.), *The Asian Yearbook of Human Rights and Humanitarian Law Vol. 2* (Brill Nijhoff 2018)

Renard T and Coolsaet R (eds), 'Returnees: who are they, why are they (not) coming back and how should we deal with them?' Egmont Paper 101 (February 2018)

Renard T and Coolsaet R, 'Children in the Levant: Insights from Belgium on the dilemmas of repatriation and the challenges of reintegration' Egmont Royal Institute for International Relations, Security Policy Brief No. 98 (July 2018)

Renard T and Coolsaet R, 'From bad to worse: The fate of European foreign fighters and families detained in Syria, one year after the Turkish offensive' Security Policy Brief, Egmont Royal Institute for International Relations (28 October 2020)

Renard T and Coolsaet R, 'From the Kingdom to the Caliphate and Back: Returnees in Belgium' in Renard T and Coolsaet R (eds), 'Returnees: who are they, why are they (not) coming back and how should we deal with them?' Egmont Paper 101 (February 2018)

Renard T and Coolsaet R, 'New figures on European nationals detained in Syria and Iraq' Egmont Royal Institute for International Relations (15 October 2019)

Renard T, 'Europe and Its Returning Foreign Fighters: Overview of the Policy Response' in Capone F, Paulussen C and Mignot-Mahdavi R (eds.), *Returning Foreign Fighters: Responses, Legal Challenges and Ways Forward* (T.M.C. Asser Press 2023)

Renard T, 'The Belgian Approach to Female Violent Extremist Offenders' in Mehra T, Renard T and Herbach M (eds.), *Female Jihadis Facing Justice: Comparing Approaches in Europe* (ICCT, 2024)

Renard T, Mehra T and Herbach M, 'Introduction' in Mehra T, Renard T and Herbach M (eds.), *Female Jihadis Facing Justice: Comparing Approaches in Europe* (ICCT, 2024)

Reprieve, 'Trafficked to ISIS: British families detained in Syria after being trafficked to Islamic State' (2021) <https://reprieve.org/uk/2021/04/30/trafficked-to-syria/> accessed 4 August 2023

Richards A, *Conceptualizing Terrorism* (Oxford University Press 2015)

Rights & Security International, 'Europe's Guantanamo: The indefinite detention of European women and children in North East Syria' (17 February 2021) <https://www.rightsandsecurity.org/assets/downloads/Europes-guantanamo-THE_REPORT.pdf> accessed 28 September 2023

Rights & Security International, Global Repatriations Tracker (last updated on 22 July 2024) <https://www.rightsandsecurity.org/action/resources/global-repatriations-tracker> accessed 20 March 2025.

Rigotti C and Zomignani Barboza J, 'Unfolding the case of returnees: How the European Union and its member States are addressing the return of foreign fighters and their families' 103 International Review of the Red Cross (2021) 916–917

Rinaldi A, *Ghosts of International Law: The Figure of the Foreign Fighter in a Cultural Perspective* (Cambridge University Press 2024)

Robson V, 'The Common Approach to Article 1: The Scope of Each State's Obligation to Ensure Respect for the Geneva Conventions' 25 Journal of Conflict & Security Law (2020) 1

Rode Z, 'Dual Nationals and the Doctrine of Dominant Nationality' 53 The American Journal of International Law (1959) 1

Rodenhäuser T, 'Partnering in detention and detainee transfer operations' in Kolb R, Gaggioli G and Kilibarda P, *Research Handbook on Human Rights and Humanitarian Law* (Edgar Elgar 2022)

Roithmaier K, 'Germany and its Returning Foreign Terrorist Fighters: New Loss of Citizenship Law and the Broader German Repatriation Landscape' ICCT Perspective (18 April 2019)

Rojava Information Center, 'Beyond the Frontlines: The Building of the Democratic System in North and East Syria' Rojava Information Center Report (2019) <https://rojavainformationcenter.org/2019/12/report-beyond-the-frontlines/> accessed 4 March 2025.

Roscini M, *International Law and the Principle of Non-Intervention: History, Theory, and Interactions with Other Principles* (Oxford University Press 2014)

Rulac Geneva Academy, 'International armed conflicts in Syria' (last updated 7 December 2023) <https://www.rulac.org/browse/conflicts/international-armed-conflict-in-syria> accessed 28 November 2024

Rulac Geneva Academy, 'Non-international armed conflicts in Iraq' (last updated 18 May 2023) <https://www.rulac.org/browse/conflicts/non-international-armed-conflicts-in-iraq> accessed 28 November 2024

Rulac Geneva Academy, 'Non-international armed conflicts in Syria' (last updated 10 August 2023) <https://www.rulac.org/browse/conflicts/non-international-armed-contlicts-in-syria> accessed 28 November 2024

Ruys T, 'Crossing the Thin Blue Line: An Inquiry into Israel's Recourse to Self-Defense against Hezbollah' 43 Stanford Journal of International Law (2007) 2

Ruys T, 'Of Arms, Funding and "Non-Lethal Assistance" – Issues Surrounding Third State Intervention in the Syrian Civil War' 13 Chinese Journal of International Law (2014) 1

Ryngaert C, 'Complementarity in Universality Cases: Legal-Systemic and Legal Policy Considerations' in Bergsmo M (ed.), *Complementarity and the Exercise of Universal Jurisdiction for Core International Crimes* (Torkel Opsahl Academic EPublisher and Peace Research Institute Oslo 2010)

Ryngaert C, 'Horizontal complementarity' in Stahn C and El Zeidy M (eds.), *The International Criminal Court and Complementarity: From Theory to Practice* (Cambridge University Press 2011)

Ryngaert C, 'The concept of jurisdiction in international law' in Orakhelashvili A (ed.), *Research Handbook on Jurisdiction and Immunities in International Law* (Edward Elgar Publishing Limited 2015)

Ryngaert C, 'Universal Jurisdiction over International Crimes and Gross Human Rights Violations: the Role of the Principle of Subsidiarity' in Ziccardi Capaldo G (ed.), *The Global Community Yearbook of International Law and Jurisprudence 2015* (Oxford University Press 2016)

Ryngaert C, *Jurisdiction in International Law* (Oxford University Press 2015)

Salam for Democracy and Human Rights, Institute on Statelessness and Inclusion and the Hawiati MENA Statelessness Network, Arbitrary Revocation of Nationality in Bahrain: a Tool of Oppression (2021)

Sánchez Frías A, 'From Dangerous Citizens to Foreign Criminals: Effects on Human Rights and State Sovereignty of Recent International and European Responses to the Terrorist Threat' Revista de Estudios Europeos (2020) 75

Sandelowsky-Bosman C and Liefaard T, 'Children Trapped in Camps in Syria, Iraq and Turkey: Reflections on Jurisdiction and State Obligations under the United Nations Convention on the Rights of the Child' 38 Nordic Journal of Human Rights (2020) 2

Sanderson M, 'The Syrian Crisis and the Principle of *Non-Refoulement*' 89 International Law Studies (2013)

Sandoz Y, Swinarski C and Zimmermann B (eds.), *Commentary on the Additional Protocols of 8 June 1977 to the Geneva Conventions of 12 August 1949* (ICRC 1987)

Sarlin S, 'Mercenaries or soldiers of the faith? The Pontifical Zouaves in the defense of the Roman Church (1860–1870)' 43 Millars: Espai i historia (2017) 2

Sary G, 'Kurdish Self-governance in Syria: Survival and Ambition' Chatham House (15 September 2016)

Saul B (ed.), *Research Handbook on International Law and Terrorism* (2nd edition, Edward Elgar Publishing 2020)

Saul B, 'Australia and International Counter-Terrorism Law and Practice' Sydney Law School Legal Studies Research Paper No. 16/41 (16 May 2016)

Saul B, 'From conflict to complementarity: Reconciling international counterterrorism law and international humanitarian law' 103 International Review of the Red Cross (2021) 916–917

Saul B, 'Preface' in Saul B (ed.), *Research Handbook on International Law and Terrorism* (2nd edition, Edward Elgar Publishing 2020)

Saul B, 'Terrorism and International Humanitarian Law' in Saul B (ed.), *Research Handbook on International Law and Terrorism* (2nd edition Edward Elgar 2020) 201–202.

Saul B, 'Terrorism in International and Transnational Criminal Law' Sydney Law School Legal Studies Research Paper No. 15/83 (September 2015)

Saul B, *Defining Terrorism in International Law* (Oxford University Press 2006)

Saul B, Submission to the PJCIS, Inquiry into the Counter-Terrorism Legislation Amendment (Foreign Fighters) Bill 2014 <https://www.aph.gov.au/Parliamentary_Business/Committees/Joint/Intelligence_and_Security/Counter-Terrorism_Legislation_Amendment_Foreign_Fighters_Bill_2014/Submissions> accessed 12 April 2022

Schabas W and El Zeidy M, 'Article 17 Issue of Admissibility' in Triffterer O and Ambos K, *Rome Statute of the International Criminal Court: A Commentary* (Verlag C. H. Beck, 3rd edition 2016)

Scheinin M, 'Back to post-9/11 panic? Security Council resolution on foreign terrorist fighters' Just Security (23 September 2014).

Scherrer A, 'The return of foreign fighters to EU soil: Ex-post evaluation' European Parliamentary Research Service, PE 621.811 (May 2018)

Schiciano E, 'See No Evil: Assessing U.S. State Responsibility for Violations at al-Hol' 61 Columbia Journal of Transnational Law (2023) 1

Schmitt M and Koschnitzky C (eds.), *Prisoners of War in Contemporary Conflict* (Oxford University Press 2023)

Schmitt M and Watts S, 'Common Article 1 and the Duty to "Ensure Respect"' 96 International Law Studies (2020) 674

Scott J, Proceedings of the Hague Peace Conferences: Translation of the Official Texts (William S. Hein & Co, 2000)

Security Council Report, Arria-Formula Meeting on Repatriation and Reintegration of Children Affected by Armed Conflict (28 January 2021) <https://www.securitycouncilreport.org/whatsinblue/2021/01/arria-formula-meeting-on-repatriation-and-reintegration-of-children-affected-by-armed-conflict.php> (accessed 9 November 2023)

Seet M, 'Cosmopolitan Citizenship', Territorial Borders, and Bringing Denationalized Terrorists to Justice' 19 Journal of International Criminal Justice (2021) 2

Seger P, 'The Law of Neutrality' in Clapham A and Gaeta P, *The Oxford Handbook of International Law in Armed Conflict* (Oxford University Press 2014)

Sexton M, 'What's in a Name? Proposing New Typologies for "Foreign Fighters"' 162 The RUSI Journal (2017) 5

Shaw A, *Convicts and the Colonies: A Study of Penal Transportation from Great Britain and Ireland to Australia and other Parts of the British Empire* (Faber and Faber 1966)

Shelton D, 'Reparations' Max Planck Encyclopedia of Public International Law (2015)

Shelton D, 'Righting Wrongs: Reparations in the Articles on State Responsibility' 96 The American Journal of International Law (2002) 4

Shor E and Hoadley S, *International Human Rights and Counter-Terrorism* (Springer 2019)

Shtuni A, 'The Western Balkans: Repatriated Foreign Terrorist Fighters, Sentencing Trends, and Security Considerations' Program on Extremism at George Washington University (September 2022)

Simma B, 'Reciprocity' Max Planck Encyclopedias of International Law (April 2008)

Simma B, Khan D, Nolte G et al. (eds.), *The Charter of the United Nations: A Commentary Vol II* (3rd edition, Oxford University Press, 2012)

Simpson M, 'Serving France in Rome: The *Zouaves Pontificaux* and the French Nation' 27 French History (2013) 1

Sivakumaran S, 'Armed Conflict-Related Detention of Particularly Vulnerable Persons: Challenges and Possibilities' 94 International Law Studies (2018)

Sommario E, 'The Status of Foreign Fighters under International Humanitarian Law' in de Guttry A, Capone F and Paulussen C (eds.), *Foreign Fighters under International Law and Beyond* (T.M.C. Asser Press 2016)

Sourgens F, *Good Faith in Transnational Law: A Pluralist Account* (Brill Nijhoff 2022)

Spadaro A, 'Repatriation of Family Members of Foreign Fighters: Individual Right or State Prerogative?' 70 International and Comparative Law Quarterly (2021) 1

Spierenburg P, 'Close to the Edge: Criminals and Marginals in Dutch Cities' 31 Eighteenth-Century Studies (1998) 3

Spiro P, 'A New International Law of Citizenship' 105 The American Journal of International Law (October 2011) 4

Spiro P, 'Multiple Nationality' Max Planck Encyclopedia of Public International Law (April 2008)

Stahn C and El Zeidy M (eds.), *The International Criminal Court and Complementarity: From Theory to Practice* (Cambridge University Press 2011)

Steenberghe, van R, 'The Obligation to Extradite or Prosecute Clarifying its Nature" 9 Journal of international criminal justice (2011) 5

Stefanovska V, 'Modern Application of the Principle Aut Dedere Aut Judicare in Acts of Terrorism and Torture' 56 Journal of Criminology and Criminal Law (2018)

Stern J and Wiener J, 'Precaution Against Terrorism' 9 Journal of Risk Research (2006) 4

Stigall D, 'The Syrian Detention Conundrum: International and Comparative Legal Complexities' 11 Harvard National Security Journal (2020)

Sumiyoshi Y, 'State Practices and Interpretation of International Law in Early Japan (1865—): Capitulations in Japan and its Abolishment' 5 Meiji Law Journal (1997)

Sunstein C, *Laws of Fear: Beyond the Precautionary Principle* (Cambridge University Press 2005)

Szadziewski H, 'Weaponized Passports: the Crisis of Uyghur Statelessness' Uyghur Human Rights Project (1 April 2020)

Szasz P, 'The Security Council Starts Legislating' (2002) 96 American Journal of International Law 4

T.M.C. Asser Institute and ICCT, The Foreign Terrorist Fighters Knowledge Hub <https://www.foreignterroristfighters.info/> accessed 20 March 2025

Tait Slys M, *Exporting Legality: The Rise and Fall of Extraterritorial Jurisdiction in the Ottoman Empire and China* (Graduate Institute Publications 2014)

Tanzi A, 'Restitution' Max Planck Encyclopedia of Public International Law (2021)

Tayler L, 'Foreign Terrorist Fighter Laws: Human Rights Rollbacks Under UN Security Council Resolution 2178' 18 International Community Law Review (2016);

Tennis K, *Outsourcing Control: The Politics of International Migration Cooperation* (McGill-Queen's University Press 2020)

The Carter Center, 'Syria Map: Exploring Historical Control in Syria' (last updated 1 October 2024) <https://www.cartercenter.org/news/multimedia/map/exploring-historical-control-in-syria.html> accessed 4 October 2024

The International Bar Association's Human Rights Institute, Justice and Accountability for the Atrocities of Daesh: Progress Made and the Way Forward, Working Draft (March 2023) <https://www.ibanet.org/Daesh-Justice-and-accountability-report-2023> accessed 25 September 2024

The Meir Amit Intelligence and Terrorism Information Center, 'The Phenomenon of Foreign Fighters from the Arab World in the Syrian Civil War, Most of Them Fighting in the Ranks of Organizations Affiliated with Al-Qaeda and the Global Jihad' (May 2014)

The Soufan Center, 'Open Letter from National Security Professionals to Western Governments: Unless We Act Now, the Islamic State Will Rise Again' (11 September 2019) <https://thesoufancenter.org/wp-content/uploads/2019/09/FTF-Open-Letter.pdf> accessed 30 March 2023

Thomson J, 'State Practices, International Norms, and the Decline of Mercenarism' 34 International Studies Quarterly (1990) 1

Thynne K, 'The obligation to ensure respect in relation to detention in armed conflict' in Massingham E and McConnachie A (eds), *Ensuring Respect for International Humanitarian Law* (Routledge 2020)

Trapp K, 'Back to Basics: Necessity, Proportionality, and the Right of Self-Defence Against Non-State Terrorist Actors' 56 International & Comparative Law Quarterly (2007) 1

Trapp K, *State Responsibility for International Terrorism* (Oxford University Press 2011)

TRIAL International, 'Universal Jurisdiction Annual Review 2023' (2023)

Triffterer O and Ambos K, *Rome Statute of the International Criminal Court: A Commentary* (Verlag C. H. Beck, 3rd edition 2016)

Tripkovic M, 'No country for 'bad' men: Volatile citizenship and the emerging features of global neocolonial Penality' XX The British Journal of Criminology (2023) XX

Trouwborst A, 'Prevention, Precaution, Logic and Law: The Relationship Between the Precautionary Principle and the Preventative Principle in International Law and Associated Questions' 2 Erasmus Law Review (2009) 2

Trouwborst A, *Evolution and Status of the Precautionary Principle in International Law* (Kluwer Law International 2002)

UN Human Rights Special Procedures, Submission by the UN Special Rapporteur on the promotion and protection of human rights and fundamental freedoms while countering terrorism and the UN Special Rapporteur on arbitrary, summary and extra-judicial executions in the case of *H.F. and M.F. v. France* (Application no. 24384/19) before the European Court of Human Rights (28 September 2020)

UNICEF, 'Nearly 850 children at immediate risk as violence continues in northeast Syria' (23 January 2022) <https://www.unicef.org/mena/press-releases/nearly-850-children-immediate-risk-violence-continues-northeast-syria> accessed 5 March 2025

UNICEF, Repatriation and reintegration of children affected by conflict in Syria and Iraq to Central Asia: A Compendium of Promising Practices from Kazakhstan, Kyrgyzstan, Tajikistan and Uzbekistan (June 2023)

UNICEF, Repatriation and reintegration of children from Uzbekistan affected by conflict in Syria and Iraq (June 2023) <https://www.unicef.org/eca/reports/repatriation-and-reintegration-children-uzbekistan-affected-conflict-syria-and-iraq> accessed 24 July 2023

United Nations Assistance Mission for Iraq and the OHCHR, Human Rights in the Administration of Justice in Iraq: Trials under the anti-terrorism laws and implications for justice, accountability and social cohesion in the aftermath of ISIL (January 2020) <https://www.ohchr.org/en/documents/country-reports/human-rights-administration-justice-iraq-trials-under-anti-terrorism-laws> accessed 25 September 2024.

United Nations Interregional Crime and Justice Research Institute, 'Children and Counter-Terrorism' (2016) <https://unicri.it/report-children-and-counter-terrorism> accessed 21 August 2024

United Nations, 'Greater Cooperation Needed to Tackle Danger Posed by Returning Foreign Fighters, Head of Counter-Terrorism Office Tells Security Council' SC/13097 (28 November 2017) <https://press.un.org/en/2017/sc13097.doc.htm> accessed 27 February 2025

United Nations, 'Security Council Unanimously Adopts Resolution Condemning Violent Extremism, Underscoring Need to Prevent Travel, Support for Foreign Terrorist Fighters' SC/11580 (24 September 2014) <https://press.un.org/en/2014/sc11580.doc.htm> accessed 3 March 2025

Upcher J, *Neutrality in Contemporary International Law* (Oxford University Press 2020)

Vohrah L, Pocar F, Featherstone Y et al. (eds.), *Man's Inhumanity to Man: Essays on International Law in Honour of Antonio Cassese* (Brill Nijhoff 2003)
Voltaire, *A Philosophical Dictionary: Vol. 2* (William Dugdale 1843)
Vonderhaar L, 'ISIS's Female Morality Police' Georgetown Security Studies Review (13 May 2021) <https://georgetownsecuritystudiesreview.org/2021/05/13/isiss-female-morality-police/> accessed 4 April 2023
Waas, van L and Brekoo A, 'Putting the 'Foreign' in 'Foreign Fighter': Nationality Deprivation and the Denial of Readmission' in Capone F, Paulussen C and Mignot-Mahdavi R (eds.), *Returning Foreign Fighters: Responses, Legal Challenges and Ways Forward* (T.M.C. Asser Press 2023)
Waas, van L and Jaghai S, 'All Citizens are Created Equal, but Some are More Equal Than Others' 65 Netherlands International Law Review (2018)
Waas, van L, 'Foreign Fighters and the Deprivation of Nationality: National Practices and International Law Implications' in A de Guttry, F Capone and C Paulussen (eds.), *Foreign Fighters under International Law and Beyond* (T.M.C. Asser Press 2016)
Walker C, 'Exporting Human Security in the Cause of Counter-Terrorism' in Paulussen C and Scheinin M (eds.), *Human Dignity and Human Security in Times of Terrorism* (T.M.C. Asser Press 2020)
Walker C, 'Foreign Terrorist Fighters and UK Counter Terrorism Laws' in Rehman J and Shahid A (eds.), *The Asian Yearbook of Human Rights and Humanitarian Law Vol. 2* (Brill Nijhoff 2018)
Walker C, Counter terrorism and Security Bill 2014–15 Submission to Joint Committee on Human Rights (5 December 2014) <https://www.parliament.uk/globalassets/documents/joint-committees/human-rights/Submission_from_Prof_Clive_Walker_091214.pdf> accessed 4 April 2023
Wautelet P, 'Deprivation of citizenship for 'jihadists' Analysis of Belgian and French practice and policy in light of the principle of equal treatment' (11 January 2016) <https://papers.ssrn.com/sol3/papers.cfm?abstract_id=2713742> accessed 24 March 2023
Weil P, *The Sovereign Citizen: Denaturalization and the Origins of the American Republic* (University of Pennsylvania Press 2013)
Weill S, 'French foreign fighters: The engagement of administrative and criminal justice in France' 100 International Review of the Red Cross No. 907/908/909 (2018)
Weill S, 'Transnational Jihadism and the Role of Criminal Judges: An Ethnography of French Courts' 47 Journal of Law and Society (2020) 1
Weis P, *Nationality and Statelessness in International Law* (Sijthof & Noordhoff 1979)
Wheeler C, 'Justice in the Absence of the Accused: Can the Rights of Victims be Fully Vindicated without the Participation of the Accused?' 17 Journal of International Criminal Justice (2019) 2

Whelan A, *Reciprocity in Public International Law* (Cambridge University Press 2023)
Wiesener C and Kjeldgaard-Pedersen A, 'Ensuring Respect by Partners: Revisiting the Debate on Common Article 1' 27 Journal of Conflict & Security Law (2022) 2
Wilgenburg, van W, 'Syrian Democratic Forces (Syria)' in 'Guns and Governance: How Europe should talk with non-state armed groups in the Middle East' European Council on Foreign Relations <https://ecfr.eu/special/mena-armed-groups/syrian-democratic-forces-syria/> accessed 4 March 2025.
Wittendorp S and Bakker E, 'Inventarisatie Rechtszaken tegen Jihadistische Buitenlandse Strijders: een Vergelijking tussen Nederland, België, Denemarken, Duitsland, Frankrijk, het VK en de VS' Institute of Security and Global Affairs (ISGA) Report (December 2017)
Wolfe S and Orozobekova C, 'Lessons Learned from Kazakhstan's Repatriation and Rehabilitation of "Foreign Fighters"' Bulan Institute for Peace Innovations (20 June 2020)
Wood M and Sthoeger E, *The UN Security Council and International Law* (Cambridge University Press 2022)
Wu L, 'Breaking the Window: Withdrawals from Humanitarian Disarmament Treaties' EJIL:Talk! (17 June 2025)
Yacoubian M, 'Syria's Stalemate Has Only Benefitted Assad and His Backers' United States Institute of Peace (14 March 2023)
Yurechko C, 'Outsourced: The European Union's reliance on external actors in the fight against jihadi terrorism' 24 The Columbia Journal of European Law (2018) 3
Zegveld L, *Accountability of Armed Opposition Groups in International Law* (Cambridge University Press 2002)
Zeidy, El M, 'The Principle of Complementarity: A New Machinery to Implement International Criminal Law' 23 Michigan Journal of International Law (2002) 4
Zelin A, 'Foreign Fighters Trickle into the Syrian Rebellion' The Washington Institute for Near East Policy (11 June 2012) Policy Watch No. 1950
Zelin A, 'The Islamic State on the March in Africa' The Washington Institute for Near East Policy (1 March 2024)
Zelin A, 'Up to 11,000 Foreign Fighters in Syria; Steep Rise Among Western Europeans' The Washington Institute for Near East Policy (17 December 2013)
Zhirukhina E, 'Foreign Fighters from Central Asia: Between Renunciation and Repatriation' The Italian Institute for International Political Studies (2 October 2019)
Ziccardi Capaldo G (ed.), *The Global Community Yearbook of International Law and Jurisprudence 2015* (Oxford University Press 2016)
Zwanenburg M, 'The "External Element" of the Obligation to Ensure Respect for the Geneva Conventions: A Matter of Treaty Interpretation' 97 International Law Studies (2021)

National Government Publications

The Netherlands

AIVD, 'Uitreizigers en terugkeerders: Hoeveel Nederlanders zijn uitgereisd en bevinden zich nog in de regio?' <https://www.aivd.nl/onderwerpen/terrorisme/uitreizigers-en-terugkeerders> accessed 5 March 2025

NCTV, 'Veiligheidsimplicaties wel of niet terughalen van uitreizigers en minderjarige kinderen uit kampen in Syrië: Analyse NCTV' <https://open.overheid.nl/documenten/ronl-71c3ebab-a957-441d-8759-9b2e7086e85c/pdf> accessed 15 August 2023

Explanatory memorandum to the amendment of the Dutch Nationality Act in Connection with the Withdrawal of Dutch Nationality in the Interest of National Security <https://www.internetconsultatie.nl/rwn/details> accessed 27 March 2023

Rijksoverheid, 'Toespraak van minister Koenders op het Global Counterterrorism Forum (GCTF) [Speech of Minister Koenders at the Global Counterterrorism Forum (GCTF)]' (11 January 2016) <https://rijksoverheid.sitearchief.nl/#archive> accessed 22 April 2025

NCTV and AIVD, 'The Children of ISIS: The indoctrination of minors in ISIS-held territory' (26 April 2017) <https://english.aivd.nl/publications/publications/2017/04/26/the-children-of-isis.-the-indoctrination-of-minors-in-isis-held-territory> accessed 21 August 2024

Letter by the Dutch Minister of Justice to the Speaker of the Dutch House of Representatives (6 December 2018) <https://www.tweedekamer.nl/kamerstukken/brieven_regering/detail?id=2018Z23191&did=2018D58508> accessed 18 December 2024

Letter from the Ministers of Justice and Security and Foreign Affairs to the House of Representatives, 'Reactie op het verzoek van het lid Buitenweg, gedaan tijdens de Regeling van Werkzaamheden van 5 februari 2019, over het bericht 'Nederland onderzoekt terughalen vrouwelijke Syriëgangers en kinderen' 21 February 2019 <https://www.tweedekamer.nl/kamerstukken/brieven_regering/detail?id=2019Z03634&did=2019D07750> accessed 20 July 2023

Tweede Kamer, 'Bestrijding internationaal terrorisme: Brief van de Minister van Buitenlandse Zaken', vergaderjaar 2019–2020, 27925, nr. 672 (11 November 2019) <https://www.tweedekamer.nl/kamerstukken/brieven_regering/detail?id=2019D45279&did=2019D45279> accessed 26 April 2024

Tweede Kamer, 'Bestrijding internationaal terrorisme: Brief van de Minister van Buitenlandse Zaken' Vergaderjaar 2019 – 2020, 27 925, Nr. 688 (16 December 2019)

<https://www.tweedekamer.nl/kamerstukken/brieven_regering/detail?id=2019D52034&did=2019D52034> accessed 24 March 2024

Tweede Kamer, 'Bestrijding internationaal terrorisme: Brief van de Minister van Buitenlandse Zaken' Tweede Kamer, Vergaderjaar 2019 -2020, 27 925, nr. 708 (31 March 2020) <https://www.tweedekamer.nl/kamerstukken/brieven_regering/detail?id=2020D12276&did=2020D12276> accessed 22 May 2025

Tweede Kamer, 'Actuele situatie in Noord-Afrika en het Midden-Oosten: Brief van de Minister van Buitenlandse Zaken' Vergaderjaar 2019–2020, 32623 Nr. 299 (31 August 2020) <https://www.tweedekamer.nl/kamerstukken/brieven_regering/detail?id=2020Z15280&did=2020D32986> accessed 23 May 2025

Staatscourant, Besluit van 13 oktober 2020, nr. 3003480, tot wijziging van het Besluit van de Minister van Veiligheid en Justitie van 2 maart 2017, nr. 2050307, tot vaststelling van de lijst met organisaties die een bedreiging vormen voor de nationale veiligheid (26 Oktober 2020) Nr. 52922 <https://open.overheid.nl/documenten/ronl-2fb8da11-34e3-4c21-bd57-b8d98a6e1b1a/pdf> accessed 27 March 2023

Letter from the Dutch Ministry of Justice to the Senate, 'Wetsvoorstel strafbaarstelling verblijf in een door een terroristische organisatie gecontroleerd gebied (35 125)' (12 May 2021) <https://www.rijksoverheid.nl/documenten/kamerstukken/2021/05/12/tk-wetsvoorstel-strafbaarstelling-verblijf-in-een-door-een-terroristische-organi satie-gecontroleerd-gebied-35-125> accessed 6 April 2022

Tweede Kamer, 'Terrorismebestrijding: Verslag van een schriftelijk overleg' Vergaderjaar 2022–2023, 29754 Nr. 656 (22 November 2022) <https://www.tweedekamer.nl/kamerstukken/detail?id=2022D48646&did=2022D48646> accessed 20 March 2024

'Hoofdlijnenakkoord tussen de fracties van PVV, VVD, NSC en BBB' (16 May 2024) <https://www.kabinetsformatie2023.nl/documenten/publicaties/2024/05/16/hoof dlijnenakkoord-tussen-de-fracties-van-pvv-vvd-nsc-en-bbb> accessed 14 April 2024

Minister of Justice and Security, Zesde rapportage uitreizigers, 5 4 52958 (17 June 2024) <https://www.rijksoverheid.nl/documenten/kamerstukken/2024/06/17/tk-zesde-rapportage-uitreizigers> accessed 6 December 2024

United Kingdom

UK Parliament, Hansard, 'Counter-Terrorism and Security Bill Volume 589: debated on Monday 15 December 2014' <https://hansard.parliament.uk/Commons/2014-12-15/debates/14121545000001/Counter-TerrorismAndSecurityBill> accessed 24 March 2025

UK Parliament, Hansard, 'UK Nationals returning from Syria Volume 654: debated on Monday 18 February 2019' <https://hansard.parliament.uk/commons/2019-02-18/

debates/69E286BB-03A2-4467-AB65-B3059436CD53/UKNationalsReturningFromSyria> accessed 25 April 2024

Dawson J, 'Shamima Begum: What powers exist to deal with returning foreign fighters?' House of Commons Library (20 February 2019) <https://commonslibrary.parliament.uk/shamima-begum-what-powers-exist-to-deal-with-returning-foreign-fighters/> accessed 4 July 2024

UK Parliament, Written questions, answers and statements, Islamic State: British Nationals Abroad, Question for Home Office, UIN 12905 (5 February 2020) <https://questions-statements.parliament.uk/written-questions/detail/2020-02-05/12905> accessed 26 August 2024

All-Party Parliamentary Group on Trafficked Britons in Syria, 'Report of the Inquiry by the All-Party Parliamentary Group on Trafficked Britons in Syria' (21 September 2022) <https://appgtraffickedbritons.org/inquiry-into-trafficked-people-to-isis/> accessed 27 August 2024

All-Party Parliamentary Group (APPG) on Trafficked Britons in Syria, Written evidence submitted by the All-Party Parliamentary Group on Trafficked Britons in Syria (MENA0030) (October 2023) <https://committees.parliament.uk/writtenevidence/125323/html/#_edn21> accessed 20 March 2023

Australia

Australian Federal Police, 'Fighting Terrorism Overseas' available at: <https://www.afp.gov.au/what-we-do/crime-types/fighting-terrorism/fighting-terrorism-overseas> accessed 5 April 2022

Australian Government, Australian National Security, 'Current declared areas' <https://www.nationalsecurity.gov.au/what-australia-is-doing/places-you-cant-go/current-declared-areas> accessed 30 March 2022

Australian Government, Australian National Security, 'Listed Terrorist Organizations' <https://www.nationalsecurity.gov.au/what-australia-is-doing/terrorist-organisations/listed-terrorist-organisations> accessed 30 March 2022

Australian Government, Department of Foreign Affairs and Trade, 'Syria sanctions regime' <https://www.dfat.gov.au/international-relations/security/sanctions/sanctions-regimes/syria-sanctions-regime> accessed 4 April 2022

The Parliament of the Commonwealth of Australia, Counter-Terrorism Legislation Amendment (Foreign Fighters) Bill 2014, Replacement Explanatory Memorandum <https://www.aph.gov.au/Parliamentary_Business/Bills_Legislation/Bills_Search_Results/Result?bId=s976> accessed 11 April 2022

Australian Government, Independent National Security Legislation Monitor, Annual Report 2014 (28 March 2014)

Senator Edwards, Senate Hansard, Counter-Terrorism Legislation Amendment (Foreign Fighters) Bill 2014 Second Reading Speech (28 October 2014) <https://www.aph.gov.au/Parliamentary_Business/Bills_Legislation/Bills_Search_Results/Result/Second_Reading_Speeches?BillId=s976&Page=2> accessed 15 May 2025

Australian minister for Foreign Affairs, 'Declaration of Al-Raqqa Province in Syria' (4 December 2014) <https://www.foreignminister.gov.au/minister/julie-bishop/media-release/declaration-al-raqqa-province-syria> accessed 30 March 2022

Australian Human Rights Commission, 'Independent National Security Legislation Monitor (INSLM) Statutory Deadline Review: Australian Human Rights Commission Submission to the Acting INSLM' (15 May 2017) <https://www.aph.gov.au/Parliamentary_Business/Committees/Joint/Intelligence_and_Security/DeclaredAreasProvisions/Submissions> accessed 6 April 2022

Australian Human Rights Commission, 'Review of the 'declared areas' provisions: Australian Human Rights Commission Supplementary Submission to the PJCIS' (3 November 2017) <https://www.aph.gov.au/Parliamentary_Business/Committees/Joint/Intelligence_and_Security/DeclaredAreasProvisions/Submissions> accessed 6 April 2022

Parliament of Australia, Neil Prakash stripped of Australian citizenship, Media Release (29 December 2018) <https://parlinfo.aph.gov.au/parlInfo/search/display/display.w3p;query=Id%3A%22media%2Fpressrel%2F6418327%22> accessed 3 April 2023

The Parliament of the Commonwealth of Australia, House of Representatives, the Australian Citizenship Amendment (Citizenship Cessation) Bill 2019, Explanatory Memorandum (2019) <https://www.aph.gov.au/Parliamentary_Business/Bills_Legislation/Bills_Search_Results/Result?bId=r6409> accessed 23 March 2023

Australian government, Independent National Security Legislation Monitor, Annual Report 2020–2021 (7 December 2021)

Australian Government, The Hon Clare O'Neil MP Minister for Home Affairs, Media Release, 'Australian women and children repatriated from Syrian camps' (29 October 2022) <https://minister.homeaffairs.gov.au/ClareONeil/Pages/australian-women-repatriated-syrian-camps.aspx> accessed 18 December 2024

Transcript of press conference, Parliament House (Canberra, 29 November 2022) Available at: <https://parlinfo.aph.gov.au/parlInfo/search/display/display.w3p;orderBy=date-eFirst;page=5;query=Neil%20Prakash;rec=8;resCount=Default> accessed 3 April 2023

Explanatory Memorandum to the Australian Citizenship Amendment (Citizenship Repudiation) Act 2023 <https://www.aph.gov.au/Parliamentary_Business/Bills_Legislation/Bills_Search_Results/Result?bId=r7129> accessed 9 December 2024

Belgium

Belgische Kamer van Volksvertegenwoordigers, Wetsontwerp tot wijziging van het consulair Wetboek (14 March 2018) <https://www.lachambre.be/FLWB/PDF/54/2989/54K2989001.pdf> accessed 6 July 2023

Denmark

Preparatory work of the Act on Danish Nationality <https://www.folketingstidende.dk/ebog/20031A1?s=4896> accessed 26 April 2023

Ministry of Foreign Affairs of Denmark, Response by the Government of the Kingdom of Denmark to communication of the Special Rapporteur on extrajudicial, summary or arbitrary executions, reference AL DNK 3/2019 (29 November 2019) <https://spcommreports.ohchr.org/TMResultsBase/DownLoadFile?gId=35114> accessed 27 March 2023

Danish Ministry of Immigration and Integration, International Migration – Denmark Report to the OECD (November 2022) <https://uim.dk/media/11385/international-migration-denmark-2022.pdf> accessed 24 March 2023

Germany

Deutscher Bundestag, Entwurf eines Dritten Gesetzes zur Änderung des Staatsangehörigkeitsgesetzes, Report No. 19/9736 (29 April 2019) <https://dserver.bundestag.de/btd/19/097/1909736.pdf> accessed 23 March 2023

Federal Foreign Office, 'Statement by Foreign Minister Baerbock on the repatriation of seven children, four women and one adolescent from north-eastern Syria', Press Release (5 October 2022) <https://www.auswaertiges-amt.de/en/newsroom/news/repatriation-syria/2556528> accessed 4 August 2023

Deutscher Bundestag, 'IS-Anhänger und deren Kinder im In- und Ausland – Stand: 31. Dezember 2022' Drucksache 20/5589 (7 February 2023) <https://dip.bundestag.de/vorgang/is-anh%C3%A4nger-und-deren-kinder-im-in-und-ausland-stand/295751?f.wahlperiode=20&rows=25&pos=7> accessed 30 April 2024

Canada

Government of Canada, Strengthening Canadian Citizenship Act: Protecting and promoting Canada's interests and values (6 February 2014) available at: <https://www.canada.ca/en/news/archive/2014/02/strengthening-canadian-citizenship-act-protecting-promoting-canada-interests-values.html> accessed 22 March 2023.

Kazakhstan

Statement from the President of Kazakhstan Kassym-Jomart Tokayev (10 May 2019) <https://www.akorda.kz/en/speeches/internal_political_affairs/in_speeches_and_addresses/statement-from-the-president-of-kazakhstan-kassym-jomart-tokayev> accessed 24 July 2024

Türkiye

Turkish Ministry of Foreign Affairs, 'Türkiye'nin DAEŞ ile mücadelesi ve Yabancı Terörist Savaşçılar (YTS) konusuna yaklaşımı [Turkey's fight against Daesh and its approach to Foreign Terrorist Fighters]' Available at: <https://www.mfa.gov.tr/turkiye_nin-yabanci-terorist-savascilarla-mucadelesi.tr.mfa> accessed 14 January 2025

Turkish Ministry of Interior, '2011 Yılından Günümüze, 102 Farklı Uyruktan 9 Bin Yabancı Terörist Savaşçı Sınır Dışı Edildi [Since 2011, 9,000 foreign terrorist fighters of 102 different nationalities have been deported]' (2 August 2022) <https://www.icisleri.gov.tr/2011-yilindan-gunumuze-102-farkli-uyruktan-9-bin-yabanci-terorist-savasci-sinir-disi-edildi> accessed 14 January 2025

United States

US Department of Justice, Office of Public Affairs, California Man Sentenced to 12 Years in Prison for Attempting to Join ISIL (7 June 2016) <https://www.justice.gov/opa/pr/california-man-sentenced-12-years-prison-attempting-join-isil> accessed 26 November 2024

US Department of Justice, Office of Public Affairs, 'The United States Has Repatriated 27 Americans from Syria and Iraq Including Ten Charged with Terrorism-Related Offenses for Their Support to ISIS' Press Release (1 October 2020) <https://www.justice.gov/opa/pr/united-states-has-repatriated-27-americans-syria-and-iraq-including-ten-charged-terrorism> accessed 4 July 2023

US Department of Justice, Secretary Antony J. Blinken and Saudi Foreign Minister Prince Faisal bin Farhan Al Saud at the Global Coalition to Defeat ISIS Ministerial Opening Session (8 June 2023) <https://www.state.gov/secretary-antony-j-blinken-at-the-global-coalition-to-defeat-isis-ministerial-opening-session/> accessed 25 July 2023

US Department of State, 2023 Country Reports on Human Rights Practices: Iraq <https://www.state.gov/reports/2023-country-reports-on-human-rights-practices/iraq/> accessed 30 September 2024

News Sources

Mcelroy D, 'William Hague warns of threat to Britain from Syria fighters' (*The Telegraph*, 24 April 2013)

Borger J, The Austrian position on arms embargo in Syria – official document (*The Guardian*, 15 May 2013)

Schmitt E, 'Worries Mount as Syria Lures West's Muslims' (*The New York Times*, 27 July 2013)

Sly L, 'Turkey confronts policy missteps on Syria with rise of al-Qaeda across the border' (*Washington Post*, 16 November 2013)

'Sharia4Belgium trial: Belgian court jails members' (*BBC News*, 11 February 2015)

'Rutte: uitgereisde jihadisten kunnen beter sneuvelen' (*NOS*, 5 March 2015)

Walker S, 'Russian media turn attention to Syria as Ukraine conflict dies down' (*The Guardian*, 1 October 2015)

Hille K, 'Russia and radicalisation: Homegrown problem' (*Financial Times*, 7 December 2015)

'Brussels attacks: Suspect Osama Krayem charged over Paris' (*BBC News*, 20 April 2016)

'Paris attacks: Who were the attackers?' (*BBC News*, 27 April 2016)

'Le procureur de Paris François Molins: « Le risque d'attentat est renforcé »' (*Le Monde*, 2 September 2016)

'François Molins annonce un « durcissement considérable » de la politique pénale en matière de terrorisme' (*Le Monde*, 2 September 2016)

European Council, 'Malta Declaration by the members of the European Council on the external aspects of migration: addressing the Central Mediterranean route' Press Release (3 February 2017)

Liabot T, 'Florence Parly: "S'il y a des djihadistes qui périssent à Raqqa, c'est tant mieux"' (*Le Journal du Dimanche*, 15 October 2017)

Corera G, 'MI5 boss Andrew Parker warns of "intense" terror threat' (*BBC News*, 17 October 2017)

McCann K, "The only way" of dealing with British Islamic State fighters is to kill them in almost every case, minister says' (*The Telegraph*, 22 October 2017)

Joshi A, 'Sky Data poll: Britons back prosecuting returning jihadists' (*Sky News*, 2 November 2017)

'U.S. vows foreign ISIS fighters in Raqqa will "die in Raqqa"' (*CBS News*, 30 June 2017)

Hardy K, 'Why is it so difficult to prosecute returning fighters?' (*SBS News*, 11 August 2017)

'Iraq sentences German woman to death over IS involvement' (*BBC News*, 21 January 2018)

Dettmer J, 'France Insists French Jihadists Should Face Justice Wherever They Are' (*VOA News*, 16 February 2018)

'Le retour des jihadistes belges n'est "pas dans l'intérêt du pays"' (*Le Vif*, 1 March 2018)

'Geens: 'Als dit Belgische kinderen zijn, dan is het onze plicht ze terug te halen" (*De Standaard*, 29 May 2018)

'Iraq calls for repatriation of children of foreign militants' (*Arab News*, 3 July 2018)

Semo M and Vincent E 'Vers une exfiltration des enfants de djihadistes français retenus en Syrie' (*Le Monde*, 24 October 2018)

Conifer D, 'Peter Dutton defends process which saw jailed Islamic State extremist Neil Prakash stripped of citizenship' (*ABC News*, 2 January 2019)

Wroe D, 'Prakash citizenship revocation could jeopardise extradition chances, says Law Council' (*The Sydney Morning Herald*, 3 January 2019)

Davidson H, 'Dutton insists Neil Prakash is Fijian citizen', but Fiji PM says he 'cannot come here' (*The Guardian*, 3 January 2019)

Doran M, Macmillan J and Movono L, 'Fiji casts fresh doubt on decision to strip terrorist Neil Prakash of Australian citizenship' (*ABC News*, 8 January 2019)

Molloy S, 'Neil Prakash case explained: Aussie-born terrorist causing diplomatic war of words with Fiji' (*news.com.au*, 9 January 2019)

'Russia says 27 children of ISIL members arrive from Iraq' (*Al Jazeera*, 10 February 2019)

Bannnerman L et al., 'Family of Isis bride Shamima Begum make plea for mercy' (*The Sunday Times*, 15 February 2019)

Lote P, Krekling D and Carlsen H, 'Solberg: – Norske IS-krigere har rett til å komme hjem' (*NRK*, 16 February 2019)

'Germany cool on Trump appeal to take back IS fighters from Syria' (*Reuters*, 17 February 2019)

'Germany says repatriation of Syria jihadists "extremely difficult"' (*The Local*, 18 February 2019)

'Premier Michel wil Syriëstrijders bij voorkeur ter plaatse laten berechten' (*De Morgen*, 18 February 2019)

'France snubs Trump's appeal to repatriate IS fighters en masse, for now' (*Reuters*, 18 February 2019)

Rawlinson K and Dodd V, 'Shamima Begum: Isis Briton faces move to revoke citizenship' (*The Guardian*, 19 February 2019)

Dearden L, 'Only one in 10 jihadis returning from Syria prosecuted, figures reveal' (*The Independent*, 21 February 2019)

'Iraq says it will prosecute French ISIL fighters' (*Al Jazeera*, 25 February 2019)

Walker P, 'Sajid Javid: difficult to strip Shamima Begum of UK citizenship (*The Guardian*, 27 February 2019)

'Saudi Arabia strips Osama bin Laden's son of citizenship' (*Reuters*, 1 March 2019)

'Aid agencies warn of "dire conditions" at Syria camp for those fleeing Islamic State' (*Middle East Eye*, 6 March 2019)

Rawlinson K, 'Brussels Jewish museum terror attack: French citizen convicted' (*The Guardian*, 7 March 2019)

Najibullah F and Ahmadi M, 'No IS Kids Left Behind: Tajikistan To Repatriate Dozens Of Islamic State Children From Iraq' (*Radio Free Europe/Radio Liberty*, 12 March 2019)

McAuley J, 'France repatriates five children of French militants who joined the Islamic State' (*The Washington Post*, 16 March 2019)

'SDF calls for international tribunal for ISIL detainees' (*Al Jazeera*, 25 March 2019)

"It would be better if they had died in battle': Danish justice minister on returning Syria fighters' (*The Local*, 27 March 2019)

'L'Irak propose de juger les djihadistes étrangers contre 1,8 milliard d'euros' (*Le Parisien*, 10 April 2019)

Winter C, 'Turkey: Germany must take back IS members' (*Deutsche Welle*, 11 April 2019)

Halla R and Dearden L, 'Shamima Begum 'was member of feared Isis morality police' in Syria' (*Independent*, 14 April 2019)

Syria war: Kosovo brings back 110 citizens including jihadists' (*BBC News*, 20 April 2019)

Stork J, 'Iraq proposes 'pay-to-prosecute' for Islamic State foreign fighters' (*The New Arab*, 30 April 2019)

Bangladesh's Foreign Minister tells ITV News Shamima Begum is 'not our problem" (*ITV News*, 2 May 2019)

Warrell H, 'Sweden proposes international tribunal to try Isis fighters' (*Financial Times*, 19 May 2019)

'French Islamic State members sentenced to death in Iraq' (*BBC News*, 27 May 2019)

Rubin A, 'France Hands ISIS Suspects to Iraq, Which Sentences Them to Hang' (*The New York Times*, 29 May 2019)

'Uzbekistan repatriates 148 women and children linked to ISIS from Syria' (*The Defense Post*, 30 May 2019)

Foltyn S, 'Inside the Iraqi courts sentencing foreign Isis fighters to death' (*The Guardian*, 2 June 2019)

Rubin A, 'French ISIS Supporters on Death Row in Iraq Ask for Mercy' (*The New York Times*, 3 June 2019)

'Syrian Kurds transfer 12 orphans from jihadist families to France for repatriation' (*France 24*, 10 June 2019)

'French, Dutch Islamic State orphans repatriated from Syria-Kurdish-led authority' (*Reuters*, 10 June 2019)

'Belgium takes back six children of Isis fighters from Syrian camps' (*The Guardian*, 15 June 2019)

Najibullah F, 'The Women Who Came Home: Kazakhstan Tries To Rehabilitate Islamic State Returnees' (*Radio Free Europe/Radio Liberty*, 23 June 2019)

Fache W, 'Jihadistes français jugés en Irak: "Nous ne voulions pas de leur transfert vers un pays qui condamne à mort"' (*France Info*, 12 August 2019)

'UN expert urges efforts from France for the return of 7 nationals awaiting execution in Iraq' Press Release (12 August 2019)

Sabbagh D, 'Jack Letts stripped of British citizenship' (*The Guardian*, 18 August 2019)

'Canada slams UK decision to 'off-load' Islamist fighter' (*Reuters*, 18 August 2019)

'Syrian Kurds hand over IS children to Germany' (*Deutsche Welle*, 19 August 2019)

Coletta A, 'An alleged ISIS fighter wants to face justice in Canada. Canada doesn't want him' (*The Washington Post*, 23 August 2019)

Cumming-Bruce N, 'Horrid Conditions in Syria Camp Where ISIS Families Fled Risk Fostering Extremism' (*The New York Times*, 11 September 2019)

'UN report on Syria conflict highlights inhumane detention of women and children' (*UN News*, 11 September 2019)

Kerres M, 'Minister Blok wil IS-strijders in Irak berechten' (*NRC*, 25 September 2019)

Irish J, 'France's Le Drian to go to Iraq to discuss trials for jihadists from Syria' (*Reuters*, 16 October 2019)

'Inside a prison full of alleged ISIS fighters' (*CBS News*, 18 October 2019)

'Denmark passes legislation to strip ISIL fighters of citizenship' (*Al Jazeera*, 24 October 2019)

Mckernan B, 'Turkey threatens to send foreign Isis suspects home from next week' (*The Guardian*, 8 November 2019)

Sariyuce I and Mackintosh E, 'Turkey begins deporting suspected ISIS fighters to US, UK, Germany' (*CNN*, 14 November 2019)

Lund Kristiansen C, Skaerbaek Mand and Blem Larsen J, 'Regeringen: Fremmedkrigere skal nægtes hjælp i udlandet' (*Politiken*, 16 November 2019)

'Turkije stuurt twee IS-vrouwen terug naar Nederland' (*NOS*, 19 November 2019)

'Germany takes back 'Islamic State' mother from Syria' (*Deutsche Welle*, 23 November 2019)

Najmus Sakib S, 'Bangladesh will not accept ISIS girl Shamima Begum' (*Anadolu Agency News*, 16 February 2020)

Gussarova A, 'Repatriating Foreign Fighters: The Case of Kazakhstan' (*European Eye on Radicalization*, 17 April 2020)

Lederer E, 'UN official: 700 people died in Syrian camps for IS families' (*AP News*, 10 July 2020)

Kajjo S, 'Germany Repatriates Three IS Women, 12 Children From Syria' (*VOA News*, 20 December 2020)

Whyte A, "'An enemy of our country' – Scott Morrison makes no apology after stripping citizenship of woman detained in Turkey' (*1 News*, 16 February 2021)

Welch D, Dredge S and Dziedzic S, 'New Zealand Prime Minister Jacinda Ardern criticises Australia for stripping dual national terror suspect's citizenship' (*ABC News*, 16 February 2021)

'New Zealand lashes at Australia in citizenship row over terror suspect' (*BBC News*, 16 February 2021)

Stroobants J, 'La Belgique va rapatrier les enfants de djihadistes détenus en Syrie' (*Le Monde*, 5 March 2021)

AANES, Press Release (18 March 2021) <http://kinderenteruguitkalifaat.nl/wp-content/uploads/2021/03/20210318-AANES-press-release.pdf> accessed 2 November 2021

Diaz J, 'No Country Will Take Them: Alleged ISIS Widow With Kids The Latest Of Many In Limbo' (*NPR News*, 26 March 2021)

'Dutch woman and three children repatriated from Syrian ISIL camp' (*Al Jazeera*, 5 June 2021)

Alonso S, 'OM, AIVD en NCTV: 'Haal IS-gangers op voor berechting' (*NRC*, 16 June 2021)

Vrancken I, 'Tweede groep Belgische vrouwen en kinderen van IS-strijders gerepatrieerd naar ons land' (*VRT News*, 21 June 2022)

Pannett R, 'New Zealand to resettle suspected Islamic State militant and her children after Australia revoked citizenship' (*The Washington Post*, 26 July 2021)

De Simone D, 'Man admits sharing Islamic State beheading videos' (*BBC News*, 29 July 2021)

'UK funding renovation, expansion of ISIS prison in Rojava: defence ministry' (*Rudaw*, 2 August 2021)

'Germany and Denmark repatriate women, children from Syria camp' (*Al Jazeera*, 7 October 2021)

'Hoda Muthana: Alabama IS bride loses appeal for return to US' (*BBC News*, 12 January 2022).

'Nederland haalt vijf IS-vrouwen en hun elf kinderen terug uit Syrië' (*NOS*, 3 February 2022)

Collins P, 'Australian ISIS terrorist is released from jail and thrown in immigration detention while Turkey figures out where to deport him to – but NO country will take him' (*Daily Mail Australia*, 27 February 2022)

McKernan B, 'Ukraine appeals for foreign volunteers to join fight against Russia' (*The Guardian*, 27 February 2022)

'Germany repatriates female IS members and their children' (*Deutsche Welle*, 31 March 2022)

De Simone D, 'Terror prosecutions of people back in UK from Syria not counted' (*BBC News*, 28 April 2022)

Registrar of the ECtHR, 'The European Court grants urgent interim measure in case concerning asylumseeker's imminent removal from the UK to Rwanda' Press Release (14 June 2022)

Sanen S, '"Regering speelt met onze veiligheid": N-VA en Vlaams Belang vinden repatriëring IS-vrouwen onbegrijpelijk' (*VRT News*, 21 June 2022)

'France repatriates 51 children, mothers from Syrian camps' (*Al Jazeera*, 5 July 2022)

Mercer P, 'Australia Plans to Rescue Citizens Stranded in Syrian Camps' (*VAO News*, 5 October 2022)

Hooper S, 'Two British nationals repatriated from northeast Syria camps' (*Middle East Eye*, 13 October 2022)

Sallon H, 'With new mass repatriation of women and children from Syria, France breaks from 'case-by-case' approach' (*Le Monde*, 20 October 2022)

'France repatriates 40 children, 15 women from camps in Syria' (*Al Jazeera*, 20 October 2022)

'Twaalf Nederlandse IS-vrouwen en hun 28 kinderen opgehaald uit Syrië' (*NOS*, 1 November 2022)

Taneja P and Abdi J, 'Islamic State: Kurdish forces threaten to stop guarding camps' (*BBC*, 25 November 2022)

McKenzie N and Pascual Juanola M, 'Alleged terrorist Neil Prakash headed to Melbourne for terror trial' (*The Sydney Morning Herald*, 2 December 2022)

Vanrenterghem A and Maerevoet E, 'Belgische jongen van 9, die door moeder ontvoerd was naar IS-gebied in Syrië, is terug in ons land' (*VRT News*, 25 December 2022)

'France repatriates 47 nationals from northeastern Syria camps' (*Al Jazeera*, 24 January 2023)

Yousif N, 'Canada appeals ruling to repatriate citizens in Syria' (*BBC News*, 10 February 2023)

Kajjo S, 'US Pushing Countries to Repatriate IS Foreign Fighters Held in NE Syria' (*VOA News*, 20 April 2023)

Major D, 'Appeal court overturns ruling directing Ottawa to repatriate 4 men detained in Syria' (*CBC News*, 31 May 2023)

'Iraq Urges Countries to Repatriate Their Citizens From Camp Linked to Extremist IS Group' (*VOA News*, 12 June 2023)

Seldin J, 'Syrian Kurds Launch New Attempt to Prosecute Captured IS Foreign Fighters' (*VOA News*, 15 June 2023)

Fisher L, 'UK under fresh pressure to bring home nationals held in Syria' (*Financial Times*, 27 July 2023)

Vincent F, 'Belarus' exiled opposition figures are threatened with losing their citizenship' (*Le Monde*, 8 September 2023)

Nechepurenko I, 'To Bolster Russia's Army, Putin Eases Citizenship Path for Foreign Fighters' (*The New York Times*, 5 January 2024).

'France charges ex-wife of top IS group official with crimes against humanity' (*France 24*, 28 April 2024)

Ngendakumana P, Swiss parliament spurns European climate ruling: Both chambers accused the ECHR of "judicial activism." (*Politico*, 12 June 2024)

'What is the UK's plan to send asylum seekers to Rwanda?' (*BBC News*, 13 June 2024)

Sokolova-Stekh H, 'How Russia is recruiting foreigners to fight in Ukraine' (*Deutsche Welle*, 22 August 2024)

S. Pronk, 'Kabinet wil mogelijkheid verkennen asielzoekers uit te zetten naar Oeganda' (*NRC*, 16 October 2024)

Al Ali W, 'Coalitie wil Nederlandse nationaliteit afnemen bij antisemitisme. Kan dat wel?' (*NRC*, 13 November 2024)

Seldin J, 'Foreign fighters flocking to Islamic State in Somalia' (*VOA News*, 20 November 2024)

Shehu R, 'Italy sends migrants to Albania in third try to start scheme' (*Deutsche Welle*, 31 January 2025)

'Hungarian lawmakers approve bill to quit International Criminal Court' (*Reuters*, 20 May 2025)

Index

HTTPS://DOI.ORG/10.1163/9789004773806-012